GOLF IN CANADA

GOLF IN CANADA

A History

James A. Barclay

M&S

CANADIAN CATALOGUING IN PUBLICATION DATA

Barclay, James A., 1923–
    Golf in Canada : a history

Includes bibliographical references and index.

ISBN 0-7710-1080-X

1. Golf – Canada – History. I. Title.

GV985.C3B36 1992   796.352'0971   C92-094655-0

The publisher wishes to thank the Royal Canadian Golf
Association for its cooperation and help with this project.

Every effort has been made to assign appropriate photo
credits. Any corrections will be made in subsequent editions.

DESIGN LAYOUT AND TYPESETTING BY ArtPlus Limited
MAPS BY James Loates

Printed and bound in Canada on acid-free paper

McClelland & Stewart Inc.
The Canadian Publishers
481 University Avenue
Toronto, Ontario
M5G 2E9

for Helen
and our favourite threesome

And many a year the Citadel's gray walls
Have seen the quiet golfers at their play:
Passing old ramparts, rusted cannon balls,
And sighting gunless ships the river way.

Thrilled with the peace of golf the players said:
"Those cruel wars can ne'er again have birth;
The living shall no longer mourn their dead
Untimely gathered to reluctant death."

– from "The Plains of Abraham," 1917, by Robert Stanley Wier
KC, the author of "O Canada!" and first president of the
Outremont Golf Club, Montreal, 1902.

CONTENTS

FOREWORD

by Marlene Stewart Streit

Jim Barclay told me a few years ago that he was researching and writing a history of golf in Canada; something much broader and more detailed than anything we have had in the past. I was very excited when he called to tell me that the book was soon to be published and requested I write a foreword. After reading some of the first chapters "hot off the press," I was even more excited. Needless to say, I am honoured and privileged to write a foreword for such a comprehensive history of golf in Canada.

This is a fascinating *story* of golf and golfers in Canada, most of it being told for the first time. Rather than being a boring history book full of information of who won what, where, when, Jim Barclay – a veritable walking encyclopedia when it comes to golf in Canada – tells our Canadian story in a flowing, easy-to-read style, with a great deal of humour. As I read selected chapters of the nearly completed book, I became so involved with its characters I could not put it down. It is obvious that Jim Barclay feels a great love for the game both as a player and as an author, and that the many years spent preparing this fine work were, in fact, a true labour of love. Fortunately for us, a Scot – although he tells me he has now lived in Canada longer than in Scotland! – has devoted eight years to researching and writing our story, and to seeking out the hundreds of photographs that grace its pages.

Other countries have books that record the history of their golf. Some authors – British and American – have written books about golf in general, and now and then Canada and some Canadians will be mentioned. However, these writers don't know very much about us up here – or over here – so what can they say? We Canadians are not very good about "tooting our own horn." We may achieve a great deal, but we don't celebrate enough. This is the book Canadian golf needs. While compiling the data and anecdotes, Jim Barclay has taken the story of golf in this country and made it more a *celebration* of Canadian golf.

I have always been aware of the names of golfers and administrators before my time. But to me, the history of golf in Canada really started with Ada Mackenzie and Sandy Somerville! I had seen names on trophies and in record books, but that is all they were - just names. Now, having read some early chapters, these names have become real people whose golfing past has been vividly brought to life.

The greatest joy golf has given me over the years is the people I have met along the way. I am thrilled to see the stories of so many of our outstanding golfers, many of whom I am privileged to call my friends, told in one magnificent book.

Golf in Canada is more than a history – it is a great celebration of Canadian golf, eloquently presented and beautifully illustrated. We Canadians *must* be proud of our heritage and our place in the golfing world. This book is a great gift not only for golfers but for all Canadians. Relax, read and enjoy it as much as I have. Thanks, Jim, for giving us so many happy memories.

FOREWORD

by

Ralph Costello, President of the
Royal Canadian Golf Association, 1981

One day in the fall of 1983, Jim Barclay, a retired oil company executive, showed up at Golf House, the headquarters of the Royal Canadian Golf Association at Glen Abbey. He had a unique proposition for the RCGA. He would like, he said, to make his services available, on a voluntary basis, as honorary curator of the golf association's museum.

Voluntary? Honorary? At no cost to the RCGA? The price was right, and, happily for the RCGA, Jim Barclay was soon acting not only as curator of the museum and as librarian, but as executive director of the fledging Canadian Golf Foundation. Using the management talents he had developed in the oil industry, he worked part-time in the museum and library, gave leadership to the Golf Foundation, and got to know the clubs and the golfers of Canada. In his spare time, he pursued his real objective: researching and writing the history of golf in Canada.

It was a monumental task that Barclay took on. A long road lay ahead, but he was not simply determined - he was bullheaded stubborn. And he was then turning sixty. The words of Churchill in a distillery come to mind: "So much to do, so little time to do it." Or something like that. Barclay would criss-cross the country several times, visiting provincial archives and golf clubs large and small. He would examine dust-laden minute-books and newspaper files. He would pore over old documents in libraries in a never-ending search for the most intimate details of the birth and growth of golf in Canada. He would spend hours, days, weeks, and eventually years in meticulously searching out and recording long-forgotten stories of the game and how it spread in Canada. He would trace the beginnings of the first clubs, the start of the first golf associations. Eventually he would have in his possession, in his files and in his mind, a treasure of information the likes of which no other researcher and no other writer had ever acquired in this country.

So, for Jim Barclay and the RCGA – for the golfers of Canada and indeed for history itself – this was to be a fortunate marriage. Now, some nine years later, with the publication of his book, golf in Canada is about to reap a substantial reward.

Barclay was not a writer by profession. He was an oil company executive, a man who graduated from Glasgow University with a degree in applied chemistry. He would spend his working life on the oil tour, moving from country to country and finally landing in Canada for his final spell of duty. It is obvious that somewhere along the way he acquired special skills as a researcher and writer. Perhaps the motivation was simply his love for the game of golf. What is clear is that he has produced a book of great historic value – and one that is also easy and pleasant to read. It is a book that could, just as easily, have plodded painfully and statistically through the pages of our golf history. But it does not. It comes to life in the most unusual and delightful of ways.

The book captures the challenges and controversies as the game expands from coast to coast, from east to west. We are reminded again of the pioneers of the game, the players, the builders, and the sponsors. We are there for the birth of our national golf associations, and for the beginning of the national championships like the Canadian Open.

Jim Barclay captures the high drama of the game over many decades, and in doing so he draws from the work of early writers, particularly Ralph Reville and Hilles Pickens, professional writers who helped preserve the history of the game. He also brings to this book the work of countless sports writers whose stories were found in newspaper clippings, on microfilm, in magazines, and in RCGA records. Thus, in this book we have an opportunity to go back to the turn of the century and to share the excitement and drama of the matches of some of our earliest champions – golfers like George S. Lyon of the Toronto Rosedale club who won eight national amateur championships, and New Brunswick's Mabel Thomson who would win the Canadian ladies' championship five times.

Author Barclay does not profess to be a humorist but the book has more than its share of humour and wit. Take, for example, the article by Lord Wellwood in the Badminton Library book *Golf*, published in Britain in 1890. Lord Wellwood asks whether there is a place for women in golf, and not very delicately answers his own question. ("If they choose to play at times when the male golfers are feeding or resting, no one can object.") Lord Wellwood may well be spinning in his grave these days as women march to new heights in national and international golf, but Barclay infers that His Lordship had a good reason to start spinning much earlier, as his words were absurdly out of date within a few years of the time they were written.

Then there is the story of the young man – a Scottish sailor – who found the Plains of Abraham an ideal spot to practise golf shots one day in 1854. The Canadian legend was that the sixteen-year-old was William Dibman, but Barclay's further research revealed his name was not Dibman after all, but Doleman, who in the 1860s and 1870s was the top amateur golfer in Scotland.

Barclay takes us through the Hagen, Hogan, and Snead years. We are there as a young dashing pants-hitching Arnold Palmer breaks through to win his first PGA tour event in the Canadian Open at Toronto's Weston Golf and Country Club in 1955. The author has us walk the fairways with many others, among them a young Moe Norman so shy he would hide in the bushes after winning, for fear he would be called on to make an acceptance speech; with a brash Nick Weslock (Nick the Wedge); with Pat Fletcher as he became the first Canadian in forty years to win our national championship; with Ada Mackenzie and an emerging Marlene Stewart Streit, with Sandra Post and Jocelyne Bourassa. And we meet a new generation who are about to engrave their names on national and international golf . . . But I must not give away too much of the pleasure that awaits the reader of this magnificent book.

This, then, is a book of champions and near champions. It is a story of small beginnings and exciting growth. We are reminded of the contribution made to the game by the early clubs and by the regional and provincial associations. We see the expansion of golf from east to west and we meet the true pioneers of the game. We are given a unique opportunity to march the fairways of time with some of the greatest figures the game has produced.

It is my view that this book will rank with the best of its kind. For golf in Canada it is an invaluable record. For those who love the game, it will be a delightful read.

INTRODUCTION

Golf is a private game. It brings the joys of experiment and discovery, the intellectual challenge of finding things out for yourself.

All that is equally true of the writing of golf history, for the history of no other sport has been woven into such an intricate and colourful fabric of legend, myth, and fact.

In this book, I have tried to untangle these skeins of legend, myth, and fact, and to tell the story of golf in Canada: where it came from, who brought it here, how and why it spread, how it has progressed, who were its champions and its leaders.

Canadian golfers who care anything about the history of the game will have heard of George S. Lyon, the great patriarch of our sport and the winner of the Olympic gold medal for golf in 1904. And Alex Dennistoun, the Sidey brothers, and Andrew Smith will be known to those who read club histories. But Tom and Andy Scott, Charles and James Hunter, W. Lindsay Creighton and the Dicksons, mean nothing to most golfers. Nor will they have heard of Ethel White, our leading woman golfer in the last century, or of those women who formed a Canadian Ladies' Golf Association long before the present one.

All these people were active many years before the country's first golf magazine, *Canadian Golfer*, could record them. These pioneers should be more to us than faces in yellowed newspapers. You don't have to prefer gas lamps to neon lights to believe that their deeds deserve to be recognized.

Canada had golf clubs from the early 1870s, fifteen years before the first club was formed in the United States. By the time Americans came to organize golf in the south, Canadians had been playing at clubs in Montreal, Quebec City, Toronto, Brantford, Niagara-on-the-Lake, and Kingston; Ontario and Quebec had already started interprovincial matches.

But for most of the 1870s and 1880s, golf in this country remained unheralded and unremarked. These were its obscure years, when newspapers gave more space to draughts, quoits, and speed-shaving and dog-swimming contests than to the royal and ancient game of golf. These were also golf's insecure years, when three of the six clubs in the country failed for lack of support, leaving less than two hundred golfers to soldier on.

Then, in the closing years of Queen Victoria's reign, a great flood of golf swept the English-speaking nations of the world. The game spread to our nation's capital and throughout the provinces of Central Canada. It crossed the Rockies into Vancouver and Victoria. A Scot carried it to Virden and Winnipeg and did his best to interest Regina. The North-West Mounted Police helped it get under way in Alberta. Montrealers carried it down east to New Brunswick, from where it spread rapidly to the rest of Atlantic Canada.

Joseph T. Clark was editor of Toronto's *Saturday Night* around this time. He wrote of the lady from a small country town dining with friends in the city. On being asked how she enjoyed her visit, she said:

> I never saw or heard of anything like it! I am an old woman and in all my experience, I never know of anything like that dinner last night. They asked me if we had a golf club in our town, and I said we had not.

ATTITUDES

IN GOLF

One of the earliest golf cartoons in Canada.

Then they began telling me what a fine thing it was, but soon forgot me and talked of nothing but golf, golf, golf. The women were just as bad as the men, and they all talked at once. After dinner there was music, but when the piano stopped, golf started again, and they were still at it when I left.

There may have been other sports that attracted as much attention – Mr. Clark noted – but none so thoroughly absorbed people's interest and enthusiasm.

Having fallen victim to golf, men quickly lost interest in all other forms of recreation. The game lured many away from cricket and yachting. Youths and octogenarians alike were struck by how easy a game it appeared, how difficult in practice, how impossible to give up. They discovered such truths as this: that a two-foot putt has about it a dreadful feeling of finality. It is not the loss of a dollar or a championship that concerns us, but that we might be made to look a fool, unable to do something a child could manage nine times out of ten with one hand and the blunt end of an umbrella. Golfers were also discovering what we know to be true today: that the appetite comes with the eating; that the games is healthful and character-building; that it plays constantly on the emotions – hope, fear, pride, shame, self-confidence, distrust of oneself. They discovered that a man can not *act* when golfing. After ten minutes on a golf course, a friend of twenty years will reveal sides of himself that you never knew existed.

The average golfer, they quickly found out, experiences in a good round of golf perhaps five minutes of intense satisfaction. Ninety bad shots can instantly be forgotten when a ball lands close enough to the hole to delight a professional. Of what other sport can that be said? At times like these, it is easy to believe that the Garden of Eden was a short par four, with no bunkers, no water, and one-inch rough on both sides of a velvet fairway.

When snow covered their courses, golfers would meet on the flimsiest of pretexts, to go over the new way of gripping the mashie and the cleek. A putter would come out, and new theories would be demonstrated by putting real balls into imaginary holes in the carpet.

All that was as true for women as it was for men. All that is as true today as it was then. The game still makes slaves of us all. In the fight between our will and golf, we have made no progress at all.

The game of golf has its hazards. The golf course architect will tell you that they were put there to be avoided, that the clever golfer will steer clear of them. To write golf history is to set out on a course bristling with hazards. Some of them cannot be avoided.

Take the question of the dates on which some of our golf clubs were organized. I think it can be shown beyond a reasonable doubt that some of Canada's early golf clubs are not as old as their members believe. Proud parents record exactly when a child is born, but the birth of a golf club is often minuted by its members many years after the event, when their memories are no longer reliable or too much influenced by their hearts.

There is no more dangerous hazard in the writing of golf history than expressing a view on the origin of the game: how it all started, and when, and in which country. I have skirted this hazard, leaving the debate to others.

Sometimes a piece of play has to be recorded, if only to show by how little championships may be lost. In 1900, Gordon Macdougall lost the 36-hole final of the Canadian Amateur at the second extra hole, when his ball stopped a quarter of an inch from the cup. A quarter of an inch short, after travelling six miles! But I have tried, with arguable success, to limit hole-by-hole narratives, no matter how important they may have seemed at the time, for there is little of use to be said about a golf ball flying through the air, or about how many strokes or what club was needed to land it on the green. But you will find something about the club itself, and how it has changed over the years; and about the ball, and why it will not travel further than the Authorities permit.

The authorities are dealt with, too. These are the people who do so much for us, but who remain hidden in anonymity. Not much is ever accomplished at their annual general meetings, but a great deal is talked about by a great many people, old friendships are renewed, the food and liquor is free, and no great harm is done to the country. Our oldest Authority, the Royal Canadian Golf Association, runs the game, makes the rules, and organizes the television spectaculars in which so few golfers compete for so many dollars. This Authority has come a long way since 1928, when its secretary required Board approval to purchase a new minute-book.

Which reminds us that money is an unreliable guide to the progress of golf. The first golf club in Winnipeg had a snug little clubhouse. It cost the members $385. They took it with them as they moved from one course to another, sliding it down a frozen river. Ten years later, with golf now established as more than a fad, the second golf club in Winnipeg splashed twenty thousand dollars on a palace. It burned down twice. The winner of the first Canadian Open championship in 1904 was given a cheque for sixty dollars. For the rest of his life John Oke was proud to be introduced as "a former champion of Canada." The winner of the 1990 Open was given a cheque for $209,000, and the men who tied thirty-fifth place got one hundred times as much as John Oke.

The Open has changed in other ways. Seventy years ago a handful of boy scouts were paid to be marshalls; now, we need four hundred volunteers. In 1904 a boy of sixteen played, wearing short pants, and took thirteenth place.

As for golf instruction, here is the only piece of advice you will find between these covers. The early-eighteenth-century English essayist, Hazlitt, wrote: "We never do anything well till we cease to think about the manner of doing it."

Before we get to the first tee, a word about content and nomenclature.

There were many fine provincial golfers and administrators who are not mentioned in this book unless they were also national figures. I hope that some day their deeds will be recognized by other golf historians.

When writing about golf clubs (the institutions) I have thought it less important to use the then current title of the club, than to be clear about which club I am writing. For example, I always give The Royal Montreal Golf Club the prefix *Royal*, although it did not acquire the right to use *Royal* until 1884. (Similarly for the other Royal clubs.) But I also refer to it as Royal Montreal GC, and sometimes as just Royal Montreal, when I think it better fits. Again, many golf clubs became golf and country clubs and changed their titles. I may go on calling them golf clubs, or GC, rather than switch to G & CC, or to CC, unless the new name refers to a different institution.

I usually refer to a club as having been "organized," but sometimes as having been "formed." I consider these words synonymous. Most clubs also became "incorporated," either when they were organized or some years later. For example, Royal Montreal was organized in 1873 but was not incorporated until 1896. I have looked upon the incorporation of a club as a legal nicety and have not made a point of noting these dates.

ACKNOWLEDGEMENTS

I am indebted to the governors and to the executive of the Royal Canadian Golf Association in many ways. The RCGA has sponsored the printing of this book. Without this financial guarantee it would probably have gathered dust as a manuscript. I value as much the RCGA's words of support when I was researching and writing. Honorary Life Governor Ralph Costello, chairman of the RCGA's Centennial Committee, has been a friend, advisor, and supporter from the beginning, and I am most grateful to him. The RCGA's most recent executive directors, the late Geordie Hilton and Stephen Ross, were as helpful as they were patient. My thanks to them, and to the man who hired them, Honorary Life Governor Bruce Forbes.

If the RCGA had not permitted me to act as its curator in the years 1983–86, I should never have had such easy access to its library of books, scrapbooks, minutes, and magazines at Glen Abbey. Honorary Life Governor James P. Anglin put this library together when the RCGA moved to Glen Abbey in 1975, but the work of collecting goes back many years. The present curator, Karen Hewson, was good enough to let me browse around at my leisure in the records.

Neither the RCGA nor any others have ever sought to have a say in the content of this book. I am solely responsible for the views expressed in it, as well as for the accuracy of all facts and for all omissions.

Marlene Stewart Streit and Ralph Costello were kind enough to write forewords to my book, and I am most grateful to them.

Many people took the time to talk to me over the past eight years, sharing their experiences and giving their views, among them Jocelyne Bourassa, Gordie Brydson, Judge Earl Caughey, Bud Donovan, Doug Farley, Bruce Forbes, Dick Grimm, Bill Kerr Sr., the late George Knudson, the late Fred Lyon, the late Tex Noble, the late Robbie Robinson, Sandra Post, Mike Riste, Jack and Aileen Salter (who, between them, must have more years of experience in the echelons of provincial and national golf than any other couple), Cathy Graham Sherk, Norm Smith, Marlene Stewart Streit, Bill Taylor (who gave me a new insight into some of the national golf figures of between the wars), Nick Weslock, and Dick White.

Any history of this sort relies heavily on the facts and views recorded by many writers who were there at the time. This book would have been impossible to put together without Ralph Reville, who should have written the first edition when he stopped writing, editing, and publishing his *Canadian Golfer* in 1933. And I owe a great debt to Hilles Pickens Jr., who took over *Golfer* and kept it going in one form or another until 1963. William and Michael Barber followed with *Golf and Club News*, which later became *Golf Canada*. More recently we've had *Score*, which brought out the writing and editing talents of Lorne Rubenstein, Lisa Leighton, John Gordon, and Bob Weeks.

I am indebted to dozens of other golf writers over the years. Most of those who wrote about golf in our newspapers and magazines before the First World War were anonymous; I suspect many were the secretaries of clubs. Had it not been for them, much useful information would have been lost. Some of these pre-war writers did not remain anonymous, like J. Lewis Brown, Joseph T. Clark, W. Climie, J. L. Foote, Stewart Gordon, Arnold Haultain, Charles Hunter, W. A. H. Kerr, Agnes Lambe, Fred T. Short, R. Stanley Weir; the initials M.G. probably stood for Madeleine Geale, and R. R. for Ralph Reville. And in the 1890s, J. Hutton Balfour of Royal Montreal wrote to the British magazine *Golf*, as did Alex Simpson of Royal Ottawa, with information that never appeared in any Canadian publication that I know of.

To the many others since, I say thank you, and that includes Allen Abel, Alan Anderson, Michael Bartlett, Dick Beddowes, Ted Blackman, Christie Blatchford, Charlie Boire, James Christie, Jim Coleman, Jack Cuthbert, James Davidson, Paul Dulmage, Milt Dunnell, W. H. Evans, Brad Ewart, Rick Fraser, Trent Frayne, Fred Jackson, Stuart Keate, George Laughlin, Andy Lytle, Rex MacLeod, C. W. (Baldy) MacQueen, Janet McWha, Jack Marks, Bill McCall, Ken McKee, Ken McKenzie, Marven Moss, Andy O'Brien, Tom O'Connor, Jim O'Leary, Arv Olson, Wayne Parrish, Rev. E. Leslie Pidgeon, Bill Roche, Lorne Rubenstein, Paul Rumstead, Roland Wild, Jim Vipond.

A number of clubs across Canada dusted off their old minute-books and let me examine their treasures. The Royal Montreal Golf Club suffered many of my visits, and also let me examine its fine collection of early British golf magazines. My thanks also to The Belvedere Golf and Winter Club, Charlottetown; Brantford Golf and Country Club; Halifax Golf and Country Club; Royal Ottawa Golf Club; Royal Quebec Golf Club; Toronto Golf Club; Niagara-on-the-Lake Golf Club; St. Charles Country Club, Winnipeg; Victoria Golf Club.

The archivists of provincial, city, and private archives across Canada, as well as those in the National Archives in Ottawa, could not have been more helpful. I thank them for putting up with me during my visits, for their patience in dealing with my correspondence, and for the many photographs they reproduced for this book. Their names appear in many of the photo credits. Patient, too, were the executives of the other national golf associations I pestered: Dave Colling of the Canadian Professional Golfers' Association, and Len Murphy and Jennifer McGuinness of the Canadian Ladies' Golf Association.

Herbert McNally and Jim Serba were kind enough to read some early chapters I had written on the origins of golf, and wise enough to hint that I scrap them. Thank you.

Mel Hurtig was the first to show an interest in publishing this book. Later, I was equally fortunate in meeting Douglas Gibson of McClelland and Stewart, and incredibly lucky in having Lynn Schellenberg as my editor – she guided me through the minefields of publishing, made countless judicious suggestions, and saved me from a thousand embarrassments.

GOLF IN CANADA

PART ONE

THE PIONEERS 1873 - 1889

(Over) *Alexander Dennistoun, president and captain of Royal Montreal, 1873–81.*

ACROSS THE ATLANTIC

GOLF IS A SCOTTISH GAME. SOME HAVE gone so far as to label it, not unkindly, a Scottish disease. Others see golf as embodying many of the traits of the Scottish character, requiring stoicism in the face of self-inflicted punishment.

Dr. Johnson was not a great friend of the Scots. He might well have described golf as a game with a stick, having a ball at one end, and a fool at the other. No matter that the kings and princes of Scotland played golf in the sixteenth and seventeenth centuries, as did Mary Queen of Scots right after the death of Darnley, and Charles I while waiting to be beheaded. They earned for the game the sobriquet of Royal and Ancient.

For over four hundred years, the Scots kept the game more or less isolated within their own borders. From time to time golf would infect neighbouring England; there were outbreaks near London and in Ireland in the seventeenth and eighteenth centuries; then a period of immunity before it struck again at Manchester in 1818, and, permanently, at North Devon in 1864. In the 1820s the germ was carried by Scots as far as Montreal, where it did not spread, and to India, where it remained for some years behind the walls of the Royal Calcutta Golf Club. In the 1850s it struck at Pau, in the south of France (where, as Henry Leach observed, a dog-leg hole did not become a "jambe-du-chien" but a "doc-lac"). All these outbreaks were contained. Unlike measles, golf was confined to a few isolated spots.

Then, in the late nineteenth century, having nurtured golf for over four hundred years, the Scots gave their gift to the world, carrying it to all English-speaking nations. At the same time, they gave the world the very finest of golf clubs and balls, in the days when these were made by hand. And the Scots produced the first teachers and champion players of the game, amateur and professional.

But did the Scots invent the game of golf? Were they the first to play it? We can not say for sure. The paternity of the game has been lost in antiquity. We know that the earliest references to golf appear in Scottish documents in the fifteenth century. The Scottish game of golf appears to have been born, or at least to have become popular, around this time.

But the identity of the name does not guarantee identity of the game. We cannot be sure that the game called *golf* in the fifteenth and sixteenth centuries had the essential characteristics of the game we play today. In those days, nobody in Scotland thought to write down a description of the game of golf (or if they did, we have not found it). They did not even tell us whether it consisted of hitting a ball with a club, cross-country, into a hole. The earliest reference to the hole being part of the game of golf dates to about 1636. By that time the Scots were using several clubs in the playing of the game. The earliest description of the methods used to strike a golf ball with a golf club appears in the writing of a Scot, some fifty years later. However, the Scots left little in the way of sixteenth- or seventeenth-century works of art to illustrate their social life and recreation. So their claim to golf is vulnerable to claims from others.

Golf Among the Midianities?

This illustration is from an eighteenth-century Scottish chapbook. The illustration is of "Joseph Sold Into Egypt." When he reproduced this in Golf Illustrated, *27 November 1903, Martin Hardie wrote: "No doubt . . . a higher critic in a German University could produce without difficulty an argumentative thesis to prove that golf was played by the Ishmaelites in the land of Midian."*

Other people in other countries were said to have been the first to play golf: the Irish, English, Dutch, French, Mongols, Chinese, Japanese, even the North American Indians. The discovery of any illustration that shows, among other things, someone striking a ball with a club, or someone wielding a club, or just a club bent at one end, is enough for someone to claim that this, then, was the beginning

of golf. But when we examine the other ball games of the thirteenth to eighteenth centuries that people claim were "early golf" or "early forms of golf," the evidence is not convincing. None has the same characteristics as the game played in Scotland. Some were played cross-country, but without the hole. Others may have had a hole, but there is no evidence that they were played cross-country. None, so far as we know, used several types of club.

The early writers on golf would have us believe that all classes of Scot, from common folk to kings, had long been addicted to the game. However, these same writers present us with evidence of costs so high that the common people could not have afforded to play.

The golfers in Scotland who founded the first club in 1744 came from what we would now call the upper classes. These "several Gentlemen of Honour, skillful in the ancient and healthfull exercise of Golf," petitioned the City of Edinburgh to put up a silver club for annual competition on Leith Links. They gave an assurance that the competition would be open to "as many Noblemen or Gentlemen or other Golfers, from any part of Great Britain or Ireland." But the entrance fee of five shillings was enough to restrict the entrants to men of means. Women had not yet taken up the game.

This competition is the first recorded one of its kind; it marked the beginning of club golf. These dozen or so gentlemen golfers were founding what was to become the Honourable Company of Edinburgh Golfers. They did not formally set themselves up as a club, as we would today, by electing office-bearers. But they did draw up a set of rules for playing the game, and they were recognized as a collective body of golfers by the City of Edinburgh. The Honourable Company remains the oldest golf club in existence.

Ten years later, its example was followed by golfers at St. Andrews.

By the end of the eighteenth century, golfers had established at least nine golf clubs in Scotland, which still exist as the Honourable Company of Edinburgh Golfers, the Royal and Ancient Golf Club of St. Andrews, the Royal Musselburgh Golf Club, the Royal Burgess Golfing Society of Edinburgh, the Bruntsfield Links Golf Club, the Royal Aberdeen Golf Club, the Crail Golfing Society, the Glasgow Golf Club, and the Burntisland Golf Club.

In Scotland, certain towns and districts have long been centres of golf, sending their sons and daughters to play golf in many parts of the world. Their names will keep cropping up when we come to look at Canada's early golfers, amateur and professional.

On the west coast, there is Troon, Prestwick, and Glasgow. On the east coast, there is Dornoch in the very north; Aberdeen further south; St. Andrews in the neuk of Fife; Carnoustie, in Angus; Leith, the port of Edinburgh and home of the first golf club; and, perhaps most important of all, the area just east of Edinburgh known as East Lothian.

This garden of Scotland – or "The Holy Land of Golf," as it calls itself – became the garden of golf. At the turn of this century the one parish of Dirleton held the courses of North Berwick, Muirfield, Gullane, Old and New Luffness, and Archerfield. (Canada's first amateur champion came from Old Luffness.) Some twenty clubs played over these courses, the most prestigious being the Honourable Company at Muirfield, and the club at North Berwick, where the prime minister, the Right Honourable Arthur James Balfour, was a member. Musselburgh, the largest town, was home to many famous professionals including the Willie Parks, father and son, and the family of Dunns. The Honourable Company moved from Leith to Musselburgh in 1836, then to Muirfield in 1892.

Lesser-known courses and clubs served the emerging ranks of the middle- and lower-class golfer. The game became more affordable from the middle of the nineteenth century, when golfers stopped playing with the old "feathery" ball (a leather case stuffed with feathers) and started using the cheaper ball made of gutta-percha. This encouraged the lower classes to take up the game. They formed their own artisan, or working-men's, clubs. As a rule, they played over the links of established golf clubs, and were subject to certain restrictions and conditions. The distinction between the artisan clubs and the most prestigious clubs, such as the Honourable Company, was quite clear. But between these two extremes, clubs emerged that provided for golfers at all levels of the social strata.

A great many artisan golfers became professionals in Canada in the early years of this century. We shall meet some of them later.

The growth of golf from the 1850s can probably be attributed to the introduction of the new, cheaper, and more durable golf ball. The gutta-percha ball could be remoulded by the player, was not liable to split open at the seams, and played much better in wet weather than the old feathery. Too, the game had now spread to England. The stage was set for the astonishing spurt in the popularity of golf which seems to have started in the second half of the 1880s.

By 1885, there were some 130 golf clubs in Great Britain and Ireland, about 70 per cent of them in Scotland. Then golf began to expand at a rate that has rarely been equalled by any other sport. "In 1885, golf was the eccentricity of a few; by 1890 it had become a general fashion." British golfer and writer Horace Hutchinson's statement is supported by the statistics. The number of golf clubs in Britain doubled in the short space of five years, 1885 to 1889.

Why did golf in Britain expand at such a remarkable rate during these late Victorian years? The overriding factor was probably the change in public attitudes and circumstances. In this period, mortality rates fell, cholera and typhus ceased to be endemic social threats, real wages increased, there was a great expansion in suburban railways and in tramways, or streetcars, and in the use of bicycles. Before the days of the automobile, golfers relied on local railways, tramways, and bicycles to get to the links.

Also, in 1887, Arthur James Balfour was appointed chief secretary for Ireland, at a time

ATLANTIC OCEAN

NORTH SEA

S C O T L A N D

Dornoch

Aberdeen

Montrose

Perth
Carnoustie
St. Andrews

North Berwick

Leith
Glasgow
Musselburgh
(East Lothian)
Edinburgh

Troon
Prestwick

NORTHERN
IRELAND

ENGLAND

IRELAND

Centres of Golf in Scotland with Links to Canada

0   40   80 km
0 10 20 30 40 50 mi

when this post was very much in the public eye. A member of an old aristocratic Scottish family, he had taken up golf late in life. The newspapers noted his addiction, and his political opponents ridiculed him for it. "James Golfour" became the subject of political cartoons. Perhaps for the first time, the word "golf" appeared on the front pages of the nation's newspapers, as in "Mr. Balfour playing golf at North Berwick," or "Mr. Balfour at St. Andrews."

The introduction of the British Amateur Championship in 1885 also gave golf a boost in England, since the second championship was won by Horace Hutchinson, an Englishman.

The role played by women in the spread and growth of golf has probably been understated. In his *A History of Golf* (1955), Robert Browning quotes a Mrs. Blanche Hulton as saying that "golf has been a factor of no small importance in the mental, as well as the physical, development of the modern girl." It is probably as true to say that the modern girl has been a factor of no small importance in the development of golf.

Golf's boom coincided with the emergence of the New Woman. A declining birthrate; the relaxing of mid-Victorian taboos and restrictions such as chaperonage; personal transportation in the form of the bicycle; the need for women in business (the typewriter conveniently came along at this time): all these factors contributed to the new-found and hard-won freedom of late-Victorian women.

In Britain, there were very few women golfers in 1885; by 1890, hundreds of clubs had women members and ladies' sections. But it is difficult to distinguish between cause and effect. Did women help make golf fashionable by playing it, or did they play golf because it had become the fashionable thing to do? Whatever, the main impetus came from the English, who made golf a family game. When families went on vacation, no longer would the husband take off and play golf while the

wife sat in the hotel with the children. Resorts soon had to provide a golf course for the family, or the family would go to ones that did.

These and other reasons also explain the boom in golf elsewhere, for by now the game had crossed the Atlantic. We shall follow it there, going back to its beginnings.

Canada was some fifteen years ahead of the United States in organizing clubs where the members played golf. But long before the 1870s, when this happened, people were bringing the implements of golf to this side of the Atlantic.

As with the origins of golf in Britain, legends and myths about early golfers in North America have been given a wide currency. We have been assured by writers that golf was being played in the seventeenth century in Albany, New York, and in the eighteenth century by the Company of Adventurers into Hudson's Bay, by the British troops under Wolfe, and by the Scottish settlers in South Carolina and Georgia.

The earliest reference to the game of golf being *played* in North America is found in a Montreal newspaper of 1826. The first golfer in North America to whom we can put a name played at Quebec City some thirty years later. The first active golf club – a club whose members played the game – was formed in Montreal twenty years after that.

Ralph Reville, the founder, publisher, and first editor of *Canadian Golfer*, propagated the myth that golf had been brought to Canada at the end of the eighteenth century by Scottish fur-traders – the men of the Hudson's Bay Company, or of the North West Company. It is about as romantic a beginning as you could wish for the game in this country.

Most of the North West traders were Scottish by birth or by parentage. Some of them had fought with Wolfe at Quebec, others had fled the United States as United Empire Loyalists. The North West partners would meet for several days each summer at the field headquarters at Grande Prairie to do business and to wine and dine. Peter C. Newman, in his *Company of Adventurers* (1986), notes that the men of the North West Company, and those of the Hudson's Bay Company, did play football (soccer) together. But if they ever played golf, they left no record of it.

Some years ago, Lieutenant-Colonel Peters, a former secretary of the Victoria GC at Oak Bay, drafted a history of his club. In his opening paragraphs dealing with early golf in North America, he makes this statement:

> . . . in the 1840s the game was played in Washington State by the officers of the Hudson's Bay Company before the United States took over this portion of British America. The British trading company's headquarters were near Fort Steilacoom, and the factor (agent) in charge sent for clubs and balls from Scotland. There was a 7-hole course near the north end of Lake Steilacoom and some 2 miles east of the present village of Steilacoom. When the United States took command of Washington, the small golf course was abandoned.

I was unable to determine from Colonel Peters the source of this information, which is so detailed as to be convincing.

In the 1830s, the Hudson's Bay Company set up the Puget Sound Agricultural Company and grew crops and bred cattle near Fort Nisqually, not far from the present city of Tacoma.

William Fraser Tolmie, a Scottish HBC trader and physician, was in charge at Nisqually, off and on until 1859, when he moved to Victoria. If any officer of the HBC laid out a golf course, then Tolmie would seem to be the most likely person. He was in Scotland in the period 1842–44, so he'd presumably had the opportunity to play the game.

If there ever was such a golf course, it would have been abandoned when United States immigrants moved into the area, in 1850.

The earliest recorded link between Canada and golf appears to be when a Mr. Philip Loch(e) of Montreal applied for membership in the Royal and Ancient Golf Club in 1788. I am indebted to the club's historian, William Burnet, for finding this piece of information, but we know nothing more about this gentleman.

The earliest-known reference to the game of golf being *played* in North America appeared in the *Montreal Herald*, in 1826. (Some writers give the date of the notice as 1824, but there is no microfilm record for that year.) In its issue just before Christmas, the newspaper carried this notice:

TO SCOTSMEN.

A FEW TRUE SONS OF SCOTIA, eager to perpetuate the remembrance of her Customs, have fixed upon the 25th DECEMBER and the 1st JANUARY, for going to the Priests' Farm, to

PLAY AT GOLF.

Such of their Countrymen as choose to join them, will meet them before TEN o'Clock, A.M., at D. M'ARTHUR'S *INN*, Hay-Market.

Steps have been taken to have CLUBS provided.

(The Haymarket is now Victoria Square.) This is clear and unequivocal. But, strangely, there is no mention of providing balls.

That Christmas, the daytime temperatures were above freezing – unseasonably high for Montreal – so there is no reason to suppose that these keen Scotsmen did not have their game of golf.

Priests' Farm was then two miles from the city. The name is still given to a piece of land north of Sherbrooke Street, just west of Côte des Neiges.

No doubt some of these Scots were fur-traders, others bankers with the recently formed Bank of Montreal. That week, the bank held a general meeting three days after Christmas, chaired by John Molson who, appropriately, had been born at a place called Spalding.

Perhaps the most storied legend in Canadian golf is that of William Dibman.

One day, in the late summer or early fall of 1854, a British ship docked at Quebec City to take on supplies. A sixteen-year-old Scottish sailor from Musselburgh came ashore to spend the day practising his golf on the Plains of Abraham.

The young man playing golf apparently did not go unremarked. Perhaps an enterprising

The Priests' Farm in West Sherbrooke Street, from a drawing by James Duncan, 1839.

reporter from a Quebec newspaper sensed a good story, spoke to the young sailor, made notes, asked him for his name. When the story later appeared in print, the youth's name was given as William Dibman.

With the passing years, the story of young Mr. Dibman playing golf on the Plains of Abraham became part of the folklore of Canadian golf. From time to time a newspaper or magazine would reprint the story. And, almost one hundred years after the young sailor's practice ashore, Robert Browning tells us about him in his *A History of Golf* – for by this time golf had become a popular game in Canada, and William Dibman had become a legend of some significance. He was the first person to play golf in North America to whom we can put a name. It was, however, the wrong name.

As T. M. Hutchison pointed out in *Canadian Golfer* in 1932, the youth's real name was William Doleman. On the printed page this may not look like Dibman, but if you scribble *Doleman* as though it were your signature – and I have tried this — the word might credibly be taken for Dibman.

Who was William Doleman? To have asked that question of a golfer of a hundred years ago would be like asking a golfer today if he has heard of Jack Nicklaus.

William was the third of four Doleman brothers, all golfers. In the 1860s and 1870s

he was probably the finest amateur in Scotland, which would have made him the finest in the world. Between 1866 and 1884, he was the top amateur in the British Open no less than nine times.

William Doleman gave up the sea soon after his ship escaped from Sevastopol in 1854, where it had been shelled by the Russians, and he became a businessman. But golf was his life. He played at Musselburgh, Aberdeen, and, finally, Glasgow. He was a leading player at the Glasgow Golf Club for over thirty years.

William Doleman died in 1918, probably unaware that his afternoon in the sun at Quebec City had made him a legend in Canadian golf.

The game of golf may have been played at other places in North America at an even earlier date than the 1826 game in Montreal.

William Doleman, who golfed on the Plains of Abraham in 1854.

What is probably the earliest reference to golf in North America appears in the written inventory of the effects of the Governor of New York, William Burnett, dated October, 1729. Among the items listed were: "Nine Gouff Clubs and 1 Iron . . . Seven Doz. Ball . . . " There is no evidence that the governor ever used the implements.

Robert Browning's *A History of Golf* quotes an advertisement for the sale of golf clubs and balls, which appeared in a New York publication, *Royal Gazette*, on 21 April 1779. This advertisement was probably directed at Scottish officers in New York who, the story goes, played golf during the American Revolution. Where they played is not known.

The best-documented legend is that of the golf clubs in South Carolina and Georgia, around the turn of the eighteenth century. It has been known for many years that some Scottish residents of Charleston and Savannah had organized in each of these cities a club to which they gave the name *Golf Club*. Newspapers carried notices inviting members to club meetings and annual reunions.

The only hint at what the members of these clubs might have been up to at their outdoor meetings appears in one notice in a Savannah newspaper inviting members "to meet at Mr. Gribbin's hotel on the Bay, to draw for finders and enter into other arrangements for the season." According to the Oxford English Dictionary, in the sporting world of 1800 a finder was "a dog trained to find and bring game that has been shot." In those days there were scores of clubs in this part of North America, many with names that gave no indication of their activities. Hunting clubs were abundant. So it seems likely that the golf clubs of Charleston and Savannah were social clubs for dining and conviviality, perhaps for organizing hunts, clubs given the title *Golf Club* by the Scots who founded them as a nostalgic reminder of the Old Country.

Golf, then, was not a game entirely unknown in North America before the first active golf clubs were organized on the continent, in Canada. But it was a game of little significance, one doubtlessly played fitfully by other people, in other places, and at other times, all unrecorded. There are tales of Canadians playing the game in the late 1860s and early 1870s. But these golfers went on to form Canada's, and North America's, first active golf clubs. Their stories form part of the histories of these early Canadian clubs.

2

CANADA'S FIRST SIX CLUBS: SUCCESS AND FAILURE

When the first golf club was formed in Canada in 1873, the Dominion was only six years old. Its population then of 3.8 million is about the number of people you will find today within twenty miles of metropolitan Toronto. All but 3 per cent lived in Central Canada (Quebec and Ontario) and the Atlantic provinces. Manitoba was three years old, and much smaller than the province we know today. British Columbia was a year younger. The provinces of Alberta and Saskatchewan were not to be created for another thirty-two years.

Cricket was the main sport of middle-aged gentlemen in Canada before golf came along, so the rise in the popularity of the one sport led to a decline in the other. At first, cricket prevailed, and golfers played mainly in the spring and fall (except in the plains of British Columbia, where the season started in the fall and finished in late spring).

Cricket was popular with the soldiers of the British garrisons in Quebec and the Maritimes probably as early as the second half of the eighteenth century, but it grew fastest in Ontario after 1850. It was a game confined largely to the higher classes of society, fostered by such schools as Upper Canada College and Trinity College. (*The Globe* saw it as a game "seasoned with snobbishness.") Around the turn of the century, there were cricket clubs in Charlottetown, Halifax, Saint John, Winnipeg, Calgary, Edmonton, Vancouver, and Victoria, as well as in many towns and cities in Central Canada. Like golf, cricket could be played by young and old. And, as in England, many middle-aged cricketers switched to golf.

The first phase of organized golf in Canada, covering the period 1873 to 1889, came in with a whimper, and left with a whimper. The game remained virtually unknown outside a close circle of relatives and friends of Canada's two hundred golfers.

The Royal Montreal GC, founded in 1873, was the first club in North America whose members played golf. But the club did not make a ripple in the sporting life of Montreal for some years. In the 1877–78 directory of the city, twenty-four sporting clubs are listed, including six lacrosse, four curling, and two cricket. Golf is not mentioned.

Within eighteen months of Royal Montreal's founding there was a club at Quebec City (1875), and within eight years, golfers had organized at Brantford (1880), Toronto (1881), and Niagara-on-the-Lake (1881). But even at their peak in the 1880s, these five clubs could not muster more than two hundred members between them. The three clubs in Ontario played against each other, as did the two clubs in Quebec. And in 1882 the golfers of Ontario played, for the first time, a team from Quebec. This was intended to be an annual affair. But there were only four matches in the decade, mainly because of apathy in Ontario, where the game struggled to survive.

A club was formed at Kingston in 1886. But it fell into desuetude after only two seasons. A year or so earlier, the clubs at Brantford and Niagara had also failed. This left only the Toronto GC to keep the game alive in Ontario. The two clubs in the province of Quebec grew at a steady rate in the 1880s, but their combined membership was less than 150.

The Canadian golfer of the time must have had serious doubts about the future of his adopted sport. His family had come to accept his addiction, but his friends still smiled at this odd, transplanted sport. Strangers on the horse-drawn Toronto streetcars would look at him inquisitively, perplexed by the bundle of sticks under his arm. So he took to leaving them in the hotel near the field he called his course. His red-jacketed figure shouting "Fore!" was not popular with the nursemaids on the slopes of Montreal's Mount Royal Park. And there were grumblings in Quebec City and in Niagara about the antics of these gentlemen beating the turf on two of our nation's historic battlefields.

Surrounded by golf as we are now, it is hard for us to imagine how rare a fellow was the Canadian golfer of the 1880s. How many of us would have carried on playing the game in the face of such wavering popularity and a seemingly hopeless future?

In *A History of Golf*, Robert Browning notes that the Rules of Golf Committee of the Royal and Ancient Golf Club laid down that the test of what constitutes a recognized golf club is that it should have duly elected office-bearers. Some of the early British clubs did not at first elect office bearers, so Browning proposed – and it has generally been accepted – that they be recognized as clubs from the date they held their first competition for a trophy.

In Canada, there is doubt as to exactly when some of our early clubs first elected office bearers or held their first competition for a trophy. So, quite arbitrarily, I have admitted other evidence of a club having been organized; namely, the date on which its members first played a match against another club, under the name of their own club.

The fact that golfers are known to have played the game in a given place can hardly be accepted as evidence that they had organized themselves into a golf club. As we have seen, a group of Scots golfed in Montreal in 1826, and other groups golfed in Brantford and in Halifax in 1873, but these cities have never claimed to have golf clubs dating back to these years.

When organizing themselves into a club, golfers could not have foreseen that the game of golf would one day become one of the world's great participatory sports, and that historians would want to know how and when it took root in a city. Few records were kept. Of the six early clubs, only Royal Montreal has a minute-book going back to its first meeting as a club in 1873. The other five clubs either did not keep minutes of their first meetings or the minutes have been lost or destroyed.

In the 1890s, when golf was expanding and obviously here to stay, golfers started to put down on paper their recollections of the 1870s and 1880s, with little to help them but their failing memories. Many of the facts they committed to paper were faulty. Today we have tools of research that were not available to them. Over the years, librarians have collected copies of newspapers and periodicals from various parts of the country and have put these on microfilm. But with the weight of their authors behind them, the errors of the 1890s became written in stone, to be copied by writers in this century. Of the dates of organization given above, only those of Royal Montreal and Kingston appear to be undisputed in twentieth-century literature. The errors have all been on the generous side, making the club older than it is. Pride in the seniority and antiquity of one's club probably explains this bias.

In the United States, the first golf clubs did not appear until the late 1880s; the Civil War had divided the country, and in the 1870s it was still preoccupied with the task of Reconstruction.

In Canada, the early golf clubs were formed in a new country, in the years following Confederation. But the birth of Canada's golf clubs had less to do with politics and economics than with the arrival of the right people at the right time. The clubs at Montreal, Quebec, Brantford, and Niagara were established shortly after the arrival (or return) of golfers who had recently played in Britain.

These clubs did not spring up independently. When we examine the background of the members forming the nuclei, we find that many of them knew each other well; some were related, others had long-standing business connections. The establishment of one club, to some extent, led to the establishment of another. The city which started it all was Montreal. The Royal Montreal Golf Club was the premier club in Canada. It would be hard to argue that it has not kept this proud place throughout nearly 120 years of existence.

On 24 May 1876, the Queen Victoria's Birthday Celebrations in Montreal were marked by the official opening of the road through the city's first public park on the slopes of Mount Royal.

The city corporation had fought hard for its park. Here was the largest, most cosmopolitan city in the newly formed country of Canada, the greatest commercial city in the Dominion, the historical seat of the fur trade, the home of the first bank in British North America, yet it had no public park for its 125,000 citizens.

As Montreal had grown, its houses had crept north from the St. Lawrence River to the slopes of Mount Royal. As mountains go, Mount Royal is tiny. Of volcanic origin, it stands no higher than six hundred feet above the river. By 1870 some private residences and the Hôtel Dieu hospital had already been built on its slopes. Residents had a fine view of the city, the river, and, in the distance, the mountains of Vermont.

Around 1870, the city started to buy up the properties on Mount Royal for a park, but the process was long and tedious. It was not until 1876 that the mayor could announce the completion of the park, with its two miles of road graded for horse-drawn carriages.

The Montreal *Gazette* reported the weather as fine, the crowd enthusiastic, on that twenty-fourth of May. Ten thousand people and twelve hundred troops congregated at the southeastern end of the park, on the open space known as Fletcher's Field, where Colonel Fletcher addressed the troops, and Mayor Hingston addressed everyone for some considerable time, after promising "a few, a very few words." With a frankness and an exactness seldom found in today's public official, Alderman Nelson confessed that the city had already spent $50,158.80 of the people's taxes in laying the road through Mount Royal Park. And with an eye to the future vote, Alderman David promised that Montreal would soon have a second public park, perhaps in Logan's Farm, one for those who lived in the *east* end of the city.

As the alderman was speaking, history was also being made in Quebec City. A team of four golfers from Royal Montreal was playing a team from the only other golf club on the continent, Royal Quebec. No doubt the Montreal club would have hosted this first interclub match had its course on Fletcher's Field not been in the process of being flattened by twenty-two thousand feet. So the honour of hosting the first inter-club golf match in North America went to Royal Quebec, as did the honour of winning it.

The Royal Montreal Golf Club had been formed by a small group of businessmen in November 1873. The drive and the inspiration came from Alexander Dennistoun (whose portrait appears on page 1), the man honoured as the club's first captain and president.

Dennistoun was then in his early fifties, and a commanding figure, standing some six feet three inches. He came from a distinguished Scottish family. The Dennistouns go back to the thirteenth century, and have royal connections with the Scottish kings Robert II and III. Alexander was born in Dumbarton, in 1821, but after his father's death the eldest brother sold the family estate and moved their home to Edinburgh.

Alex Dennistoun already knew Edinburgh, having been educated there, at Edinburgh Academy, and at Loretto School, Musselburgh. Since Musselburgh was one of the earliest centres of golf in Scotland, Dennistoun would at least have been acquainted with the game and might even have played it in his youth. Emigrating to Ontario around 1840, while still in his late teens, he is said to have entered the lumber trade. (Another account has him engaged in land speculation in New York before coming to Canada.) Living first in Peterborough, Ontario (where one of his several brothers was a farmer and county judge) he moved to Montreal in 1861. Five years later, he married a daughter of John Redpath of the Redpath Sugar Refinery.

Over the next thirty years, Alex Dennistoun and his wife appear to have spent as much time in Scotland as in Canada. And it was during one of these visits home that he had some success in competitive golf. He played not only at St. Andrews and Musselburgh, but also at Royal Liverpool GC. At Liverpool, he won the Silver Cross for the second-best scratch score in the spring competition of 1870. A year later, he tied for the Gold Medal. So it was as an accomplished golfer – and no doubt an enthusiastic one – that he returned to Canada in 1872 with his wife, their first visit in years, and took a house on McTavish Street, within walking distance of the new Mount Royal Park.

It is safe to say that a golfer is never keener to play than when he has just won a tournament, and never more frustrated than when he faces the future in a country without a golf course. The incentive for Dennistoun to form a golf club in Montreal is not hard to find.

Two other characters enter the scene, the brothers Sidey. At least three Sideys were members of Royal Montreal in its early years. But only two appear to have been in at the birth of the club – John G. Sidey, a Scot who had been in Montreal for some years, and his brother David D., who appears to have joined him in business in 1872 or 1873.

These three, Dennistoun and the two Sideys, were the most active of those early Montreal golfers. Dennistoun was to be elected the first captain and president of the club they formed, but John Sidey was to be similarly honoured in 1889–90.

The inaugural meeting was held in the Sideys' office on 4 November 1873. Joining Alex Dennistoun and the two brothers (David Sidey was elected treasurer) were five others, according to the minutes. William M. Ramsay, elected vice-president, was manager of the Standard Life Assurance Company; Joshua (Josh) Collins, elected secretary, ran an agency for dry goods; the Honourable M. Aylmer was a gentleman of leisure, and of the same family as Lord Aylmer, a former governor-in-chief of Canada; Hartland St. Clair Macdougall, a stockbroker, was born in Devonshire, England, and educated there; Philip Holland was a general commission merchant.

Having organized themselves into the Montreal Golf Club, the minutes record that they also agreed that the entrance fee and the annual subscription would be five dollars; that the number of members would be limited to twenty-five (which would bring in subscriptions of $125); that the rules of the Royal and Ancient Golf Club of St. Andrews would be followed; and that the hours of play would begin at 1:00 p.m. on Wednesdays and Saturdays.

(Being a member of a club with only twenty-four others, one could not go along and pick up a game at any time. Matches had to be arranged for fixed days and fixed hours, to ensure that more than one player turned up. In those days, the business world worked a ten-hour day, and a five-and-a-half or six-day week. The fact that golfers could schedule games for Wednesday afternoons has helped feed the myth that all golfers belonged to the leisured class, although it is more to the point that one did not need shorter working hours to play golf, but the flexibility to defer working hours to the evening or early morning.)

Those present at the inaugural meeting also decided that eight other gentlemen should be invited to be members. All sixteen are shown as charter members in a composite photograph put together by Notman Studios many years after the event.

Alex Dennistoun was very much an active president. We find him getting directly involved in ordering trophies from Britain, in arranging for the club's first professional to be sent over, and in organizing his duties when he arrived.

Dennistoun was also the club's finest golfer, which is no more than we should expect from a gold medallist at Royal Liverpool.

William Ramsay, Dennistoun's vice-president, was an Edinburgh Scot, forty years of age, who had come to Canada as a youth. He was remembered as a man of "kindly disposition, constant amiability and unfailing courtesy." Ramsay is said to have played golf with another of the sixteen charter members some years before the club was formed. Writing in *Outing* in 1898, John P. Roche assures us that banker Richard R. Grindley and William M. Ramsay could, if they so wished, tell us much of their golfing deeds on the fields of Logan's Farm, in the 1860s. (Logan's Farm became Logan's Park, now Lafontaine Park, just as Alderman David had promised in 1876.) But if Ramsay and Grindley golfed there, they probably did so after Grindley returned from a six-year stint in Halifax in 1871.

The Royal Montreal Golf Club, 1873-1973 also records that the brothers Sidey golfed on Fletcher's Field before they helped form the golf club.

A composite photograph of the members of Royal Montreal at their clubhouse, about 1881. Alex Dennistoun addresses the ball. Also wearing white helmets are, to the left, both hands holding a club, David Sidey; to the right, with a club under his arm, John L. Morris, who succeeded Dennistoun as captain; and, on his left, wearing white trousers, John Sidey.

What brought these men together in 1873 was apparently the return from Britain of Alexander Dennistoun and his wife, to settle down for the first time in Montreal, if only for a few years. And Dennistoun would be anxious to play golf, for he was then relishing success. The Dennistouns took a home at 30 McTavish. In 1873, they had new neighbours at No. 26 – Mr. and Mrs. Ramsay.

So, in the years 1871 to 1873, the paths of some of these men converged, some for the first time. This happened just as Fletcher's Field, on the slopes of Mount Royal, became the property of the city, a public park, and a stretch of ground on which they could play golf.

Of all these charter members, only Alex Dennistoun, the Sideys, Josh Collins, Hartland Macdougall – and, to a lesser extent, William Ramsay – appear to have become regular golfers, or to have taken an active part in the club's affairs. They were joined later in 1873 by J. K. Oswald, of Oswald Brothers, commission merchants and stockbrokers. Oswald was to become the club's secretary in 1875. (Alex Dennistoun's mother was Mary Ramsay Oswald. Could there have been family connections here?) The names of the others seldom, if ever, appear in the club's minutes or in the notices of its matches.

Royal Montreal had several courses during the twenty-three years it spent on the eastern slopes of the Mount Royal Park, on the land given the name of Fletcher's Field. These would have been rudimentary courses, with tees and greens almost indistinguishable from fairway, fairway from rough. Being part of a public park, Fletcher's Field could not be dug up for bunkers. The club's accounts for 1877–78 show that $6.05 was spent on "Preparing Green," and sixty cents on "Marking Flags."

Fletcher's Field was not a discrete area with fixed boundaries. It was the name given to the open land which lay between the wooded slopes of Mount Royal and what is now Esplanade Avenue, within the boundaries of Mount Royal Avenue on the north and the Hôtel Dieu hospital and Pine Avenue on the south.

If you look at maps of Montreal of the 1870s, you will be lucky to find one showing Fletcher's Field. But most maps show a Fletcher's Hill on the eastern slopes of the mountain, south of the Cartier Monument, near the tree-line, and opposite what is now Duluth Avenue. Fletcher's Hill is still there in Mount Royal Park, although part of it has been flattened for the site of a fire-alarm building.

Legend connects the name of the fields to the Colonel John Fletcher who spoke to the troops on the Queen's Birthday in 1876. This Scot came to Montreal as a young man, and he organized early fire services for the city, as well as the first rifle association in Lower Canada. There is no evidence that he owned any property on the slopes of Mount Royal, nor is there any evidence that he ever played golf. His name was probably given to the fields because he paraded his troops there.

The members of Royal Montreal laid out their original six-hole course in the south end of Fletcher's Field. The first tee (and later the first clubhouse) was probably on Fletcher's Hill. According to a club history published in 1923, "the players came downhill towards Pine Avenue for the first hole, then across the roadway, and returned paralleling the stone wall of the Hôtel Dieu." The roadway was to become Park Avenue, but in 1873 it was little more than a path.

Within a year or so the course was expanded to nine holes, using the northern part of the fields, up to Mount Royal Avenue, on both sides of Park Avenue. Then the city began to quarry on the eastern section of the course. At the same time, the buildings of the Mount Royal Exhibition (Montreal's Crystal Palace) began to encroach on the northern holes of the course. So the land east of Park Avenue (now know as Jeanne Mance Park) was abandoned and a new nine-hole course laid out to the west.

In those days, the members of Royal Montreal did not refer to their course as Fletcher's Field. To them, it was "the Park green" or "the green at the top of Durocher," Durocher being the main avenue running from Sherbrooke Street to the course.

The pressure to move to a new course was always there, since Fletcher's Field was open

The Prince of Wales Rifles on parade, 1885, with Fletcher's Field in the background, left.

to the public. The trials of playing on such a course were vividly described by the club's secretary, in his report to *The Golfing Annual* of 1888–89:

> Our green here is a public park, and therefore great care is required to be taken when playing, as there are so many people upon it, especially nursery maids and children, and should anyone be hurt I fear the city might step in and stop us. Our old country cry of "Fore!" is no use here. We have to wait quietly until people pass, or politely ask them to walk to one side. The park has been enlarged this autumn, a large piece of ground with trees being joined; so I trust next year all the children will go there for shade and leave us.

The players also had to put up with the aggravation of golf balls being stolen from fairways, and with troops exercising on Fletcher's Field. During army manoeuvres, the wheels of gun carriages rutted fairways and greens, which were also trampled by the boots of hundreds of soldiers and spectators.

The inaugural meeting had agreed to a limit of twenty-five members, subject to review. About sixty new members joined the club in the years 1882–84, when membership was closed and a waiting list established. In 1885, about fifty playing members went on a golf outing to Laprairie, and in 1888 the club reported its membership to be eighty-eight.

There were a number of reasons for the surge in membership. The club had opened its first clubhouse, although this was at first no more than a room attached to the new lodge of the Park Ranger. (In 1892, the club took over the entire lodge.) The first of the interprovincial matches in 1882 against the traditional rival, Ontario, gave the game more apparent purpose and more real publicity. The same could be said of the governor general's appearance for Royal Quebec in the interclub match a year earlier.

Significantly, the new members included Sir Alexander Galt and the mayor, Sir William Hingston. They joined other influential persons such as George A. Drummond, the club's captain and president, 1884–88.

George Drummond was yet another Edinburgh Scot, born in 1829. After graduating from Edinburgh University as an industrial chemist, he came to Canada to direct the technical operations of the Redpath Sugar Refinery. He married one of John Redpath's daughters and rose to be president of the company in 1880, when he also became a senator. Ultimately, George Drummond was to become one of the country's leading financiers, and was knighted in 1904, a year before he was elected president of the Bank of Montreal.

George Drummond is reputed to have been a keen golfer before leaving Scotland, and – with Alexander Dennistoun also married to a Redpath daughter – the only surprise is that he did not join Royal Montreal before 1875.

Finally, in July 1884, Her Majesty Queen Victoria was "graciously pleased" to grant the club the right to add the prefix *Royal* to its name. No doubt this honour was anticipated by many of the new members who joined that year, for membership was closed shortly afterwards and a waiting list established.

There do not appear to have been any French-Canadian members until the late 1880s; between then and 1901, at least ten joined the club, including judges Dugas, Girouard, and Rainville, and stockbroker-politician Louis-Joseph Forget, who gave his name to the large brokerage firm.

Although Oswald won the first club competition, held in 1875, it was a handicap event; Dennistoun was clearly the club's best golfer. He won the club championship – for his own Dennistoun Gold Medal – in 1880, the first year it was played for. The club's minutes record the players' average scores for that season, over eighteen holes, revealing that his average of 94.3 was some twelve strokes better than the next man's. If that score seems high, we should remember that it was made with long-nosed, wooden-shafted golf clubs and gutta-percha balls, on fairways and greens that had not been cared for by a greenkeeper.

In the 1880s, the Dennistouns moved to Edinburgh and made only the occasional visit to Canada. Alex Dennistoun, now in his sixties, continued to golf in Scotland. But in his one appearance in the British Amateur Championship – the first championship, held in 1885 – he got no further than the first round. He is probably the A. Dennistoun who attended the meeting of the Honourable Company of Edinburgh Golfers in 1892 and who argued that the club should not dispose of the clubhouse at Musselburgh. He died in Scotland in 1895.

It took George Drummond another twelve years to hone his game to club championship standard. In the meantime, the gold medal had been won no less than four times by another immigrant Scot.

The Reverend James Barclay (no relation to the author) arrived in Montreal in 1883, at the age of thirty-nine, to be the pastor of St. Paul's Church. A native of Paisley, this tall, muscular Christian had made a name for himself on the field of sport and in the pulpit. Educated at Merchiston Castle School and Glasgow University, he became one of Edinburgh's most popular preachers, and was honoured by invitations to preach before Queen Victoria.

The Reverend Barclay captained the Glasgow University cricket and soccer teams and led the Gentlemen of Scotland against England

The Reverend James Barclay, captain and president of Royal Montreal 1891–92, helped to start golf in other centres.

on the cricket field. He was also an enthusiastic curler. And he excelled at golf, where his strength lay in his long driving. Years after he came to Canada, the British magazine *Golf* carried the story of one of his first games at Musselburgh. He had a mighty drive at the first hole, which rather astonished a host of young caddies gathered around the tee. "Who is that?" asked one. "Well," said an older caddie, "folks say he's a minister. He says he's a beginner. But I say he's a liar."

The Reverend James Barclay was president and captain of Royal Montreal in 1891–92. He led Quebec against Ontario in 1887, when he had the distinction of being the only player on record to beat the renowned A. W. Smith in an interprovincial or interclub match.

Because of the constraints of golfing on Fletcher's Field, Royal Montreal moved in 1896 to a new course at Dixie, on the west end of the island. But Fletcher's Field was far from finished as a golf course. Surprising as it seems now, from all we know of its restrictions, it was taken over by a new golf club, the Metropolitan. Some Royal Montrealers may have had a sentimental attachment to the course, among them the Reverend James Barclay, who became a president of the new club. Its members played on Fletcher's Field until a few years before the First World War.

But we are ahead of ourselves. At Royal Montreal in the 1870s the golfing events of the year soon became the biannual team matches against the only other club on the continent, Royal Quebec.

One of the many myths surrounding early golf in Canada has the troops of the British Army introducing the game when they were garrisoned in Quebec in the late eighteenth century. But there is no evidence that these troops played golf before the civilians did in the 1870s. Claudette Lacelle's *The British Garrison in Quebec City as Described in Newspapers from 1764 to 1840* (1973) showed that the sol-

diers' main recreational activities were swimming, fishing, horse-racing, and cricket. There is no mention of golf. The troops introduced cricket into Quebec, cricket was their favourite sport, and it remained popular after they left in 1871.

No doubt James Stevenson, a native of Leith, and Charles Farquharson Smith, from Aberdeenshire, had discussed with fellow Scots in Quebec, at meetings of the St. Andrews Society, the possibility of introducing golf. They may even have tried golfing in Quebec a year or so before organizing themselves into a club. James B. Forgan had worked as a clerk in the Montreal branch of Smith's bank, back in 1873, and it seems likely the two knew each other. Forgan's father had the largest clubmaking business in St. Andrews.

James Stevenson, a founding member and first president of Royal Quebec, sketched about 1890.

We know he brought his clubs to Canada, and he could well have persuaded Smith to try them out.

The game of golf took firm root in Quebec City in 1875 during the visit of James Hunter, a twenty-six-year-old Scot from St. Andrews. He came to the city in the early summer of that year, reportedly to work for the Bank of British North America. Hunter had played golf most of his life and was now a first-class amateur.

When John L. Foote, of Quebec's *Morning Chronicle*, wrote to the British periodical *The Field* in November 1875, he said of James Hunter: "In July last a smouldering enthusiasm was rekindled by the appearance amongst us of an accomplished golfer, and we at once organised the Quebec Golf Club." (He used the work "rekindled," another hint that golf had been tried earlier.)

James Hunter was the catalyst for the founding of Royal Quebec in 1875; from a painting.

The James Hunter who inspired these neophyte golfers to form a club was married to Libby Morris, the only daughter and favourite child of Old Tom Morris, Keeper of the Green at St. Andrews.

The golfers of Quebec would have turned to James Hunter for all sorts of advice: how to lay out a twelve-hole course, make a sand tee, keep the green, cut the holes, interpret the simpler points of the rules. But he would have

inspired them most by his playing, by making a difficult game look easy.

To run it, the club elected a green committee, consisting of the captain, Farquharson Smith; a secretary-treasurer; and four committee members, including James Stevenson. Only later did the club elect a president, this honour going to the co-founder, Stevenson.

The number of members soon increased to twenty, most of them influential in banking, shipping, or the lumber business, exiled Scots or men of Scottish descent. They included Joseph Laird, Peter MacNaughton, C. Chaloner Smith, H. Stanley Smith, Peter McEwan, John Gilmour, James Gibb, Andrew Thompson, Herbert Price, and George B. Symes Young.

The club held its first tournament in October 1875. Under the heading of "Scottish National Game," the *Morning Chronicle* set the date as Saturday, the second day of October:

> The members of the Golf Club, lately organised in Quebec, meet today on their links, Cove Fields, for the first handicap competition, the first prize being a handsome silver medal . . . This is a fine, healthy, national sport, which has been hitherto totally neglected here . . . Those wishing to view the sports will require to be on the ground behind the Racquet Court at two pm. We learn that there is a Golf Club in Montreal, and it is the intention of this club to send them a challenge shortly.

But the competition was put off for two weeks, presumably on account of the weather. James Hunter won by nearly two strokes a hole over his nearest opponent, and was awarded a silver medal. He went round the twelve-hole course, with its rough new greens, in 64 strokes. Hunter also won the handicap prize, despite giving away 25 strokes in the round to his nearest challenger. This was apparently Hunter's first and last competition in Quebec.

James Hunter's contribution to the founding of Royal Quebec may have been minuted in the club's books, but all records before 1908 have been lost or destroyed by fire. When

Canadian golfers in the 1890s came to look back, some of them remembered the part he had played. They wrote of "Mr. Hunter, the son-in-law of Old Tom Morris." Some gave him the name Charles, perhaps confusing him with the Charles Hunter who helped organize a club at Niagara.

James Hunter appears to have left Canada later in 1875. His brother-in-law, Young Tom Morris, died in Scotland on Christmas Day, at the age of twenty-four, and his death may have been the reason for Hunter's departure. Or perhaps his task at the bank had been completed.

The name James Hunter crops up from time to time in Scottish golf, but there may have been more than one first-class amateur with the same name. A James Hunter had won the Club Medal at Prestwick St. Nicholas in 1871. The James Hunter of St. Andrews who won the Hall Blyth Gold Medal at Hoylake (the home of Royal Liverpool GC) in 1883 is almost certainly our man. His name was later associated with both Hoylake and Prestwick. When he returned to Scotland he apparently lived for a time in Prestwick; it was there that his son, W. Bruce Hunter, was born and learned to play golf.

James Hunter went out to Mobile, Alabama, in November 1885, likely on business. He died there in the following February, from heart disease, at the age of thirty-seven. A short notice of his death appeared in *The Field*:

> Of his merits as a golfer, accentuated as they were by his geniality of temperament and unfailing self-command under the most adverse circumstances, it is unnecessary to speak. Enough to say, they were sufficient to raise him to quite the front of players; and at St. Andrews, Hoylake, and Prestwick, as well as on other greens, his loss will be severely felt.

(In the 1885–86 edition of the Mobile city directory the only James Hunter listed is a timber exporter so he may have changed his profession by the time of his death.)

The first course of Royal Quebec was laid out on the common known as Cove Fields. These

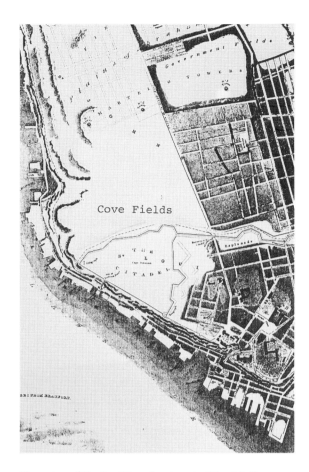

Plan view of Quebec City, showing the Citadel, Cove Fields, and the Plains of Abraham, from a map by Alfred Hawkins, 1845.

fields are some four hundred feet above the St. Lawrence River and just outside the west gate of the old, walled city. The British Army had used Cove Fields for nearly a century for recreation and exercises, but their departure in 1871 left the land sufficiently free for golf. The course was bounded on the east by the Citadel, on the north by the Grande Allée, on the west by a fence joining two Martello towers, and on the south by the cliffs overhanging the St. Lawrence River.

It is doubtful if golfers anywhere have ever played on land so deeply rooted in the history of their country. Jacques Cartier fortified the site in 1535; in 1608, Samuel de Champlain built a *habitation* at Quebec, so founding the city of Quebec; the Martello towers were erected by the British in the period 1802–23; the Citadel was approved by the Duke of Wellington and built in the period 1820–31. Only golf shots have ever been fired at these fortifications.

Just to the west of Cove Fields lie the Plains of Abraham, where the British under Wolfe defeated the French under Montcalm in 1759, and the French under Lévis defeated the British under Murray, a year later. Wolfe died on the Plains, as did Montcalm. Monuments to both stand today along the west boundary of the old golf course.

The members of Royal Quebec played on Cove Fields for forty years. Their links had some of the most picturesque golf holes in North America, and some of the most trying. The club's secretary wrote this for *The Golfing Annual* of 1888–89:

> Quebec green may be termed a "sporting" one in every sense of the word. It is more extensive and more diversified in character than that at Montreal, its hazards being old fortifications, deep gullies (which carry off the melting snow in spring), precipices, bogs, and moats; altogether a pleasant green, if for no other reason than for the immense variety of trouble which can be enjoyed (?) while at work on it.

The original twelve-hole course was soon expanded to fourteen, the last four being played twice to give the full round. A simple layout of this course is given in the club's written history, *Le Club de Golf, Royal Quebec 1874–1974.*

Writing in *Athletic Life* in 1895, Charles Hunter described the course as "the most extensive in Canada, being over two miles in length, and consists of sixteen holes, two of which are played over twice . . ." According to W. A. H. Kerr, writing in *Canadian Magazine* in 1901, "The course . . . consists of fifteen holes, the first three of which are played twice." So it would appear that various green committees experimented with a number of layouts.

Horace Hutchinson also referred to the links as "sporting." (In his day, to refer to a course as "sporting" was much like saying of a person that he was "doing his best.") But in *Famous Golf Links* (1891), Hutchinson was obviously taken by the history of the site:

. . . as the harmless golf ball whistles over the old French fortifications, the mind naturally reverts to the time when balls of a much more deadly description filled the air . . . The erratic golfer who ploughs furrows with his iron, may find he has unearthed one of the old round leaden bullets which did duty when Tommy Atkins was armed with brown Bess.

Horace Hutchinson also describes the course, hole-by-hole, each hole having a name. The first was played along the glacis (a gentle slope in the fortification) under the guns of the citadel. At the second, or Old Forts hole, the ball could be pulled over the cliffs, or heeled into the Sugar Bowl, masses of rock piled up like sugar lumps in a bowl. The fifth, or Cliff hole, was "just the sort of hole to impress upon the mind of the young golfer the fact that the game of golf is not a mere pastime, but a fine moral training." As for the seventh, or Eagle's Nest hole, he thought it "a good golfing hole, and may be done in two or ten, according to the fancy or capacity of the player." The next hole, Glacis, was remarkable for its putting green, which "for practical putting purposes might as well be situated on the roof of a house."

One hole was named Racquet Court. The club first used a small cottage as a clubhouse, later switched to the rooms of the Racquet Club, and finally moved to rooms in the Skating Rink.

Hutchinson sums up the course in this way:

> For the long clean driver, the Quebec links are a haven of rest, but for the duffer they are Pandemonium, from the first hole to the eighteenth. If the mid-green were not *quite* so rough, and if the putting-greens were a trifle larger and the least thing smoother, the Cove Fields, as a golfing ground, would be hard to beat.

Cove Fields was Canadian government defence property but, like Fletcher's Field in Montreal, it was open to the public. The club was given playing rights from year to year, until 1895, when the Ministry of Militia and

Defence granted it a twenty-one-year lease. In 1909, the club learned that the National Battlefields' Commission was planning to build a large conservatory on Cove Fields. The mayor of Quebec, Sir George Garneau (a member, later the president, of the club), advised the club to seek other quarters. But it was not until April 1915 that the members agreed to move to a new site on the St. Lawrence, northeast of the city, adjacent to the Montmorency Falls.

In the formative years of Royal Quebec, the three finest golfers to follow James Hunter were all young Scots who had golfed before coming to Canada. The Scott brothers, A. P. (Andrew) and T. M. (Tom) came to work for a Quebec bank around 1876 and joined the club then. Their names do not appear on any of the early trophies that have survived, but each won at least one medal for being club champion. They left for Toronto in 1881–82 and joined the Toronto GC, but remained members of Quebec, although seldom playing there.

Andrew Scott was arguably the second-finest golfer in Canada in the 1880s. The finest was, indisputably, A. W. Smith. A first-class amateur in his native country, Andrew Smith of St. Andrews was Canada's leading golfer from the time of his arrival in Quebec in 1881 until the emergence of George S. Lyon in 1898. He, too, kept on his membership of Royal Quebec GC when he was transferred to Ontario. His name appears only once on the club's early trophies. But it would have been in the nature of the man to not enter for the championship of the club, which he could have won quite handily. When living in Toronto, he often elected to play for Royal Quebec GC and for the province of Quebec. His contribution may not have been enough to swing the match in Quebec's favour, but it did put a better face on some of its defeats.

From 1875, with two golf clubs active in North America, the stage was set for golf more competitive than club championships and club handicaps. The interclub match was to become a prominent feature of golf in Canada and was to remain so until the 1930s, *the* social and competitive event in golf, just as the bonspiel was in curling.

The first interclub golf match in North America was a modest affair played on 24 May 1876. *The Field* carried a short account of the match, sent by Mr. Foote. It reads in part:

> The members of the Montreal Golf Club, keen for the sport, arrived by morning boat, and as they toiled up the hill, laden with the peculiar implements of their craft, might well have been mistaken for the advance guard of a besieging force, or a fresh lot of agriculturalists supplied with the oddest of tools.

(No doubt they followed the steep path up the hill used by William Doleman, some twenty years earlier.)

The teams played two rounds of the course, or 24 holes. Quebec won by 16 holes. For the record, these were the teams:

QUEBEC		MONTREAL	
Smith	0	Sidey	10
Nicoll	3	Sidey	0
McNaughton	11	Esdaile	0
Scott	12	Collins	0
Holes won	26		10

The Smith playing for Royal Quebec was probably Farquharson Smith; the Scott, one of the two Scott brothers.

The return match was played in Montreal in September, and this became the pattern of the annual home-and-away matches for some years – the spring match at Quebec, the autumn match at Montreal. In 1876, they played for a Challenge Trophy, and today the members of these two clubs still compete for the trophy, although only once a year. The winning team attached a silver ball to the trophy. The members of the winning team later competed amongst themselves for the honour of having custody of the trophy, the winner attaching a smaller silver ball to it.

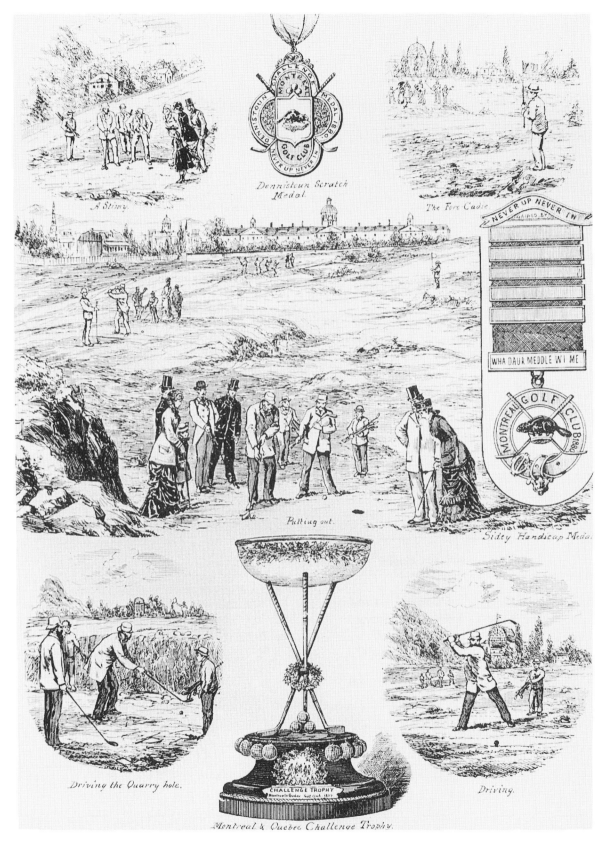

Interclub match between Royal Montreal and Royal Quebec, Fletcher's Field, about 1880, showing (bottom) the Challenge Trophy and (top) the Dennistoun Scratch (Gold) Medal.

The size of the teams was decided before each match, depending very much upon the number the visitors could muster. The winner was the team winning the greater number of *holes*, not the greater number of matches, so each match of eighteen holes had to be played to a finish. If Brown won six holes, Smith four holes, with eight holes halved, then Brown contributed two holes to his team's total.

There was a great deal of argument as to which was the fairer method of scoring, by matches or by holes. Despite this, there was never any question of converting to stroke play. Head-to-head golf was the essence of the game in these late Victorian days.

The courses at Fletcher's Field and Cove Fields had their own unique forms of hazards. Local knowledge of these meant that the home team usually won. In the first forty or so matches, Montreal won only four at Quebec, and Quebec won only four at Montreal.

Early in the 1880s, the two clubs were to join forces to meet the challenge of a new competitor. By then, organized golf had reached Ontario, and there was soon a demand for interprovincial competition. The three Ontario clubs which provided the opposition were all formed within the space of a year or so, the first at Brantford in 1880.

At least two young men golfed in Brantford in 1873, seven years before a golf club was organized. The town then had a population of only nine thousand, and it was not to become a city until 1877. But it did have a couple of banks, and one of these recruited two young clerks who had played golf in their native Scotland. They laid out a makeshift four-hole course over some common land to the south of the town in an area then known as Vinegar Hill, where a vinegar factory had once been sited.

James Darling had come to Canada from Perth, where he had golfed for some years. Neither he nor James Cran, the other clerk, was to stay in Brantford for long. Darling was sent to Halifax for a year, and after that he emigrated to the United States. Years later he recalled in *Canadian Golfer* his trip from Brantford to Nova Scotia:

> I remember going down the St. Lawrence on my way to Halifax, the many enquiries made as to what my clubs were for. We had to change to a small steamer to run the rapids, and having no cabin for this part of the trip, I was carrying the clubs in my hands. The boat was full of American tourists, and the strange clubs, especially the irons, seemed to excite their curiosity.

James Darling recalled that Alexander Robertson, the manager of the Bank of British North America in Brantford, had also played golf with him and Cran.

Robertson was born in St. Fergus, Aberdeenshire, in 1831. He came to Canada in his early twenties, joining his bank in Brantford as a clerk. By 1864 he was manager, a post he held for over forty years. When Brantford Golf Club was formed, Robertson was elected captain.

There is no evidence that golf was played in Brantford between 1873 and 1880. Alexander Robertson was no doubt aware that his coun-

Alexander Robertson, first captain of Brantford Golf Club in 1880.

terpart in Quebec City, Farquharson Smith, was golfing, as was their boss in Montreal, Richard Grindley. But Robertson obviously lacked the incentive or the support needed to establish a club in Brantford.

Two events took place around 1880 which probably led to the founding of a club in Brantford. In 1878, Alexander Robertson visited his native Scotland for the first time in many years. He would have found that golf had become a much more popular sport there. More important, W. Lindsay Creighton arrived in Brantford from Sarnia, to manage a branch of the Bank of Montreal. Creighton had come to Canada from Scotland many years earlier, at the age of seventeen. Creighton inspired the birth of the club, and the club remained active only as long as he remained in Brantford.

There is some doubt as to when the first Brantford Golf Club was formed. In the February 1920 issue of *Canadian Golfer*, Ralph Reville quoted this extract from a back issue of the Brantford *Courier:*

> A golf club (whatever that may mean) has been organized in this city, with the following as office bearers: A. Robertson, Captain; John H. Stratford, Treasurer; W. L. Creighton, Secretary; Henry Yates, Jas. Ker Osborne, J. Y. Morton, George H. Wilkes, Committee.

According to Reville – a Brantford man and at one time publisher of *The Courier* – this notice appeared in the 8 January 1879 issue. So the Brantford club's written history, understandably, shows 1879 as the founding date. (Unfortunately, there is no microfilm record of *The Courier* of 1879 or 1880 to settle the question.)

All other dates published before the turn of the century, and some after, show the club as having been organized in 1880. Take this extract from a Toronto *Globe* report on the second Brantford Toronto match. It appeared in June 1881, and is probably copied from a Brantford paper, which would have received the information from the club secretary:

Brantford, June 13. . . . The game of golf was first played in this city in 1873, but the present club was regularly organized last year. It and the one at Toronto are the only two clubs in this part of Canada.

The Golfing Annual of 1901–2 also shows the Brantford club as having been established in 1880, on 2 June. The records of the Bank of Montreal also support the 1880 date. They reveal that Creighton was not transferred from Sarnia to Brantford until May 1879. However, since this first Brantford golf club failed after a few years, its date of birth is perhaps only of academic interest.

With the exception of Creighton, the members of the club were long-time residents of Brantford. All were leading business or professional men.

Henry Yates had been chief engineer of the Grand Trunk Railway, and was a railway contractor during his membership. He died in 1894. Both his sons, Henry B. and Herbert R. Yates, were to be associated with golf clubs at Brantford and Montreal well into the twentieth century.

John H. Stratford came to Brantford with his parents in 1844, working first with his father in a pharmaceutical business. He later set up on his own, entering into a rewarding partnership with Henry Yates in railway contracting and other ventures.

George H. Wilkes, the son of the city treasurer, rose to become president of an Ontario railroad.

James Ker (or Kerr) Osborne was one of the founders and later a vice-president of the Massey–Harris Company, and he was also president of the Verity Plough Company of Brantford.

J. Y. Morton, known simply as "J. Y.", owned the local hardware store. An avid sportsman, he was to play golf on the Brantford links until a few years before his death in 1923, at the age of eighty-eight.

The club first played over a six-hole course laid out on Terrace Hill, a piece of land on the northern outskirts of the city, but the course was soon expanded to nine holes. (The accounts for 1881 – quoted in an article in *Canadian Golfer* in 1931 – show an active male membership of twenty-four, and assets of only $9.64, including six flags and posts valued at $1.29, and six tees – presumably teemarkers or sand boxes – valued at $1.50.)

There is no record of competitive golf at Brantford until the interclub matches against Toronto GC in June and October 1881. The club had no clubhouse. For the June match, it erected a marquee for lunch; in October, the teams had dinner at a local inn. Brantford won the first match by a margin of ten holes, but that was to be its only win for some time. Toronto recruited immigrant Scots from Quebec, the two brothers Scott and William Moffatt, and won at least the next five matches. By 1883, Brantford had the services of A. W. Smith, who was then working in nearby London. Smith won his match, but the Brantford club still could not field a team to match Toronto.

Over the next few years, members of these two clubs played for a trophy named the Brantford Medal. Then, unexpectedly, the Brantford club ceased to operate after the 1885 season. The reasons for the failure of the first Brantford Golf Club are given in the 1901 annual report of a later Brantford Golf Club:

> The rapid extension of the city which gradually overspread the old golf links, and the departure and also removal by death of several of the most enthusiastic of the old-time players, resulted in the game virtually dying out here for over ten years. Then came a rekindling of the golfing fever to some extent in the early nineties . . .

We know that the "rapid extension of the city" overran part of the club's course on Terrace Hill in 1884, when the new city hospital was constructed on the brow of the hill. Ironically, the hospital was financed by the club's treasurer, John Stratford, who also donated a seven-acre site on Terrace Hill. As for the "departure . . . of several of the most enthusiastic players," Creighton, the club's

secretary, and the force behind its creation, was moved in 1886 to his bank's branch in Kingston. Also, John Stratford died in 1888, at the early age of forty-seven. However, five of the other six members identifiable in 1885 became members of the second Brantford GC, organized in 1894.

The general attitude to golf in Canada in the 1880s is consistent with the failure of the Brantford club. The game was perceived as a passing craze that would soon die. It received little attention from the newspapers, which failed to comprehend its mysteries, just as they failed to learn its vocabulary.

There may have been another reason why the Brantford club failed in 1886. In that year, the tennis craze struck the town, and this was a game played by both sexes. In an article written six years later, *The Courier* reminisced:

> Originating in a small way in 1886, [tennis] has since arisen in popularity . . . [In 1886] a few people who were fond of tennis were invited by Mr. George H. Wilkes to make use of his lawn . . . and the next year the Brantford Lawn Tennis Club was formed. During 1887, the club, through the kindness of Mr. Osborne, were enabled to use his grounds in addition to those of Mr. Wilkes . . . Presidents have been G. H. Wilkes, J. Kerr Osborne . . .

Could it be that Messrs. Wilkes and Osborne transferred their allegiance from golf to tennis, effectively killing the golf club? (If so, they would not have been alone. Writing in the British *Golf Monthly* in 1921, Willie Park, the professional golfer and golf course architect, recalled that "in 1886, golf was at a very low ebb, and lawn tennis was then enjoying a boom." This was presumably just before the golf boom that started that year in Britain.) Or did Wilkes and Osborne switch to tennis only after golf was already seen to be dead?

People went on with other sports in Brantford. A Brantford Amateur Athletic Association was formed, with committees for lacrosse, baseball, bicycling, football, and shooting. Cricket and canoeing also prospered. That is not to say that all the citizens of the city were happy with what they had, if we can judge from this letter to *The Courier* in 1893:

Dear Sir:

What on earth is the matter with Brantford Sport? The lacrosse club is as dead as Julius Caesar. The baseball club seems to be incapable of hitting a balloon, much less a curve ball. The cricketers never forget themselves so far as to win a match, and the bicyclists seem to confine themselves principally to making fast time on the sidewalks. Won't some of our girls please come to the rescue and challenge the Cainsville girls to a game of skipping rope?

Yours, Sport

By now, golf was spreading to other parts of Canada, and the game was given a second chance in Brantford. In October 1894, *The Courier* reported: "Golf: An effort will be made to start a club in Brantford . . . some years ago there used to be quite a strong club in the city, and some of the old players are still available." Later that month a meeting

voted that "The Brantford Golf club, organized in 1880, be reorganized."

The second Brantford GC elected Alexander Robertson as captain. Its members included, once again, Herbert R. Yates, George and A. J. Wilkes, and J. Y. Morton. The club rented a house as a clubhouse and remained active until the end of the 1896 season, holding a number of well-attended competitions. Apparently, it then ceased to operate for a second time, after losing its course in the east end of the city.

In March 1898, *The Courier* reported yet another attempt to revive golf in the city: "A meeting was held last night at Kirby House to consider the formation of a golf club." A second meeting was held, and officers elected, including Herbert Yates as captain and Ralph Reville as treasurer. The members of the third Brantford GC played on farmland north of the city. But enthusiasm for the game had waned by the following year. The members complained that the course was inaccessible. A meeting called for March had to be adjourned because of poor attendance, and little or no golf was played that year.

The turn of the century saw an encouraging revival of interest. Years later, Ralph Reville was to praise the lady members of the club for having done so much for the club in

Sport in Brantford in 1899, showing the golf course and Ralph Reville (not Revell). Tennis probably contributed to the failure of the first golf club in 1886.

Brantford golfers and their caddies – a montage put together in 1899.

the early years of the century (without mentioning that the club had failed in the 1880s). From the date of its annual general meeting in 1900, the Brantford GC (the third or perhaps the fourth club to be given that name) has been, continuously, an active golf club.

The facts on the golf clubs at Brantford have been laid out at some length to illustrate that the fragile state of the game in the 1880s extended into the next decade. So far as we are able to judge so long after the events, it would appear that golf's failure to take firm root in the city was more due to the general apathy of its players than to the loss of a golf course. Brantford golfers were able to find a new course around the turn of the century, and another new course several years later. But, by then, the will was there.

Toronto Golf Club also lost its course to developers in 1888 but quickly found a new one. Its members were not going to be deprived of their game by the temporary lack of a field to play in, for golf had already securely captured their imagination.

The golfers who organized what is the oldest operating golf club in Ontario and the third oldest in North America, the Toronto Golf Club, probably started playing together around 1876. Since there is no record of the event, we can only speculate as to how and when golf reached Toronto. Nevertheless, the memories of the pioneers are consistent on at least one point: it was first played at the home of James Lamond Smith, an older brother of Charles Farquharson Smith of Quebec.

The brothers Smith came from a large and well-to-do family of landowners housed at Glen Millen, Lumphanan, Aberdeenshire. They had attended Marischal College in Aberdeen. James Lamond, born in 1822, came to Fergus, Ontario, around 1840, his father having bought him a piece of land. As a gentleman farmer and notary public, he lived in three houses in his twenty years in Fergus. The last of these, which he

called "Glen Lamond," was on the south side of the Grand River, where he owned a sawmill. The area has remained Glen Lamond to this day.

In 1861, Lamond Smith came to Toronto to manage the properties of the Bank of Upper Canada. When the bank failed in 1866, he went into business as a land broker and contractor. For most, if not all, of his remaining years in business, he was associated with Benjamin Morton, who had worked for the same bank.

Part of their investment was in land in York County, east of Toronto. It was here that Smith established his home, Ben Lamond Park. His property, which bordered the Kingston Road half a mile east of the post village of Norway, has long since been incorporated into the east end of metropolitan Toronto, where you will find a Benlamond Avenue. In the 1870s, the view of Lake Ontario to the south was unimpeded by tall trees, houses, or factory chimneys. To the west, a tree-lined, unpaved Kingston Road swept down from the heights of Norway, through the village, to the lakeshore. In the distance were the spires and roofs of Toronto, its population of 80,000 increasing at a rate of over 4,000 a year.

Charles Farquharson Smith, captain of the Quebec Golf Club, may have been the first to interest his brother in golf. One can imagine him visiting Ben Lamond Park, enthusing over his club's battles with Royal Montreal. Lamond Smith would be caught up in the excitement. He would see no reason why golf should not be brought to Toronto: a three-hole course would fit nicely into Ben Lamond Park, or six holes if he used his land on the south side of Kingston Road. A few exiled Scottish friends would surely join him. He would send for clubs and balls.

And that is apparently what he did. In June 1881 the Toronto *Globe* noted:

> Some years ago an effort was made to institute the royal game in Ontario. Since then, a few Scotchmen and others might be seen any Saturday afternoon enjoying that very popular pastime on the beautiful high lands of Benlamond, overlooking our city and Bay.

James Lamond Smith, who introduced golf to Toronto.

Robert H. Bethune, first captain of Toronto Golf Club in 1881.

The "few Scotchmen" would be friends and business acquaintances of Lamond Smith, including Robert Bethune and his brother George, Walter G. Cassels, Edmund B. Osler, and Robert Cochran. These men were later to organize the Toronto Golf Club.

Robert Bethune of the Dominion Bank had once worked for James Stevenson of Royal Quebec. Walter G. Cassels, who was employed in private banking, could trace his golfing ancestry back to his grandfather, a member of the Honourable Company of Edinburgh Golfers in 1808. Young Osler was a frequent visitor to Ben Lamond, his first wife being one of Lamond Smith's daughters. She had died in 1871, and he later married Anne Farquharson Cochran from Aberdeenshire, a niece of the Smiths. Edmund Osler was a stockbroker, among other things.

Robert Cochran (of Scarth, Cochran and Company, stockbrokers, estate and insurance agents, and general managers of the North British Investment Company) was an all-round sportsman, famed in local yachting, tennis, and billiards. He was Smith's nephew, and a brother of Anne Farquharson Osler.

In the late 1870s, these and other friends of Lamond Smith met to play golf over a rudimentary course laid out on the fields at Ben Lamond Park. They did not play regularly but "at rare intervals," to use the words of Stewart Gordon, a secretary of the Toronto GC in the 1890s.

Golf did not immediately take firm root in Toronto as it had in Montreal and Quebec. None of Smith's friends had played the game in Britain, so far as we know. They had no skilled player to instruct them and to inspire them with his skill. Toronto did not have an Alexander Dennistoun or a James Hunter. Too, the game of cricket had a much firmer hold on the middle-aged gentlemen of the province and of the city. The grounds of the Toronto Cricket Club were within walking distance of homes and offices. Golf at Ben Lamond Park involved a journey of four miles by horse-drawn tram or carriage over unpaved and dusty roads. When golfers came to organize the Toronto GC in 1881, they moved their course near to the Woodbine Driving Course, closer to the city. Montreal golfers could reach their course by walking up Durocher Street, Quebec golfers by walking through the St. Louis gate at the Citadel. As for Toronto's early golfers, Stewart Gordon aptly described their predicament when he wrote:

> Some bright September day might be seen a comfortable wagonette, with a party of respectable and apparently middle-aged gentlemen, wedged in with a great number of curiously shaped implements, faring eastwards to unknown regions.

Why, after dallying with the game for several years, did Toronto golfers decide in the spring of 1881 to form a golf club? The catalyst appears to have been the new club at Brantford. Golfers in Brantford would have been aware that a few played the game in the larger city, and no doubt delivered them a challenge. Robert Bethune took it up. He called a meeting, which formed the Toronto Golf Club and elected him captain of the Toronto teams to play against Brantford that year.

A notice in the 9 May 1881 issue of the *Toronto Daily Mail* invited all interested in golf to a meeting that night. It was headed: "Golf. Proposed Introduction of the Game in Toronto." If there were many exiled Scottish golfers then in the city, they do not appear to have turned out in large numbers. Those who attended the inaugural meeting of the Toronto GC in the North of Scotland Chambers did little more than formally establish a club. The *Mail* wrote of this May meeting: "Very little business was transacted beyond the election of officers, Mr. Bethune of the Dominion Bank being chosen president."

Apparently, Bethune's title was later changed to captain, and J. Lamond Smith was given the title of president, perhaps in recognition of his pioneering efforts at Ben Lamond Park. On 8 April, *The Globe* of Toronto reported the 1882 annual meeting and the election of these officers:

President:	J. Lamond Smith (re-elected)
Captain:	R. H. Bethune
Hon. Sec-Treas:	T. M. Scott
Committee:	Messrs. Gordon, Keith, Moffat, W. G. Cassels, G. S. C. Bethune

If the club kept minutes of its meetings in the 1880s, these have been lost or destroyed. The evidence suggests that the club did not keep minutes of the inaugural meeting of 1881. The club secretary of 1882, and those who followed him over the next twenty years, would often write that the Toronto Golf Club had been formed in 1882.

Tom Scott, elected honorary secretary-treasurer in 1882, beginning a long association with the club, came to Toronto from Quebec in the summer of 1881, too late to be a founding member. His brothers, Andrew and John, appear to have joined the club later in 1882.

Apart from the Bethunes, Lamond Smith, Walter G. Cassels, and E. B. Osler, it is likely that the others who played in any of the four matches against Brantford GC in 1881 were also founding members of the club. These included W. H. Lockhart Gordon (who had come to Canada in 1868 and was now a partner in a law firm); George Keith (a Scot and a Toronto merchant); William Moffat(t) (another Scot who had been a teller in a Quebec bank – and a member of Quebec GC – but who now worked in Toronto); and W. P. Darling (probably Walter, son of the Reverend William Stewart Darling who owned an estate close to Ben Lamond).

Four weeks after organizing in 1881, Toronto GC played against Brantford GC, the first of four such matches that year. These matches, and others against Niagara GC, continued (but less frequently than four times a year) until the clubs at Niagara (in 1885) and Brantford (in 1886) fell into desuetude. Toronto was invariably the winner, having in the brothers Tom and

Andrew Scott and – from late 1883 – A. W. Smith probably the three finest golfers in Canada.

The members also competed for the Brantford Medal and the Niagara Cup. These two trophies had been put up for competition between Toronto and the other two clubs. The winning club then put them up for internal competition.

During the first fourteen years of its life, Toronto GC appears to have played on at least three courses, none of which had more than nine holes. These were all laid out on farmland close to the Woodbine Race Course, south of the Grand Trunk Railway (now the CNR track) and bounded on east and west by Coxwell Avenue and Woodbine Avenue and on the south by farmland and two ponds. Reading over the early members' accounts of playing "at the Woodbine," it is not always clear to which course they were referring.

The first was laid out over land leased from a prosperous Norway farmer, Charles Coxwell Small. Small's farm was on the Kingston Road, across from the Woodbine Hotel, where some members kept their clubs. After the matches with Brantford, the players would lunch or dine at the hotel, then take a tallyho or horse-drawn tram west along Queen Street, past the racetrack, to the Union railway station. Late in 1881, the members considered using the grounds inside the racetrack, no doubt because the course on Small's farm was cramped, but nothing seems to have come of this.

The club played on this site until 1887 or 1888. When reporting the club's activities to *The Golfing Annual* of 1888–89, secretary Tom Scott wrote that no account could be given of the club's golf course, since the members "have been turned off their ground by building speculators. They have arranged for a new ground which they expect will be ready for next sea-

Toronto from the Kingston Road, about 1880. This would be the view from Toronto Golf Club.

son." Plans for the sub-division of Small's property had been filed as early as 1882.

In the years 1887–88, the Toronto newspapers gave no news of their local golf club. They continued to report on golf in Quebec and to carry the odd article on golf, so apparently the sport was still considered newsworthy. But nothing can be written of a club with nowhere to play.

In 1889, the *Mail* reported members playing "on the beautifully situated ground of Mr. G. W. Clendennan, opposite the Woodbine race course, which he kindly allows to be used as Links by the golf club." This was only a temporary measure. By 1890, the club had settled its course on sixty-four acres of land leased from Molson's Bank, further north on Coxwell Avenue. Here it was to remain for the next twenty-three years. The first course on this site was a short one. In 1890 *The Globe* reported that its longest hole was about 250 yards.

When the club incorporated in 1894, the land was bought from the bank by the Fernhill Land Company, a company established by the executive of the club. A year later, the Fernhill Links – as they came to be known – were

Walter G.P. Cassels, captain of Toronto Golf Club 1894–1908, golfing at the club around 1897.

extended to eighteen holes, following the conveyance to the club of sixteen acres of land owned by Walter G. P. Cassels, captain of the club from 1894 to 1908. Cassels had owned the property between the railway track and what is now Cassels Avenue. You will find today a Golfview Avenue running south from Cassels.

The club also acquired several buildings with the property. One was converted into a clubhouse; another served as a house for George Cumming when he arrived from Scotland to be the club's professional. (The clubhouse stood on the brow of the hill, where Gainsborough Road joins Wembley Drive.)

The earliest published layout of the Fernhill links of Toronto GC is dated 1898, when the club hosted the Canadian Amateur championship. It shows an eighteen-hole course of 4,601 yards, short by modern standards, but not abnormal in the days of the short-flying gutta-percha golf ball. The ravine and creek to the east of the clubhouse are still there, to the east of Wembley Drive. But the creek now runs underground in what were the lower slopes of the course, and the ponds have long since been drained.

The membership of Toronto GC, when first formed in 1881, was no more than fifteen, all men. They played twice a week, on Wednesday afternoons and Saturdays. For the next ten years the membership apparently did not exceed the thirty-five reported by the secretary in 1888. Two years later, the opening competition attracted only a dozen golfers, but this was considered "a large turnout of players." The opening competition of 1893 brought out twice this number, and there were half as many again in the following year.

When the club took over the Fernhill property and reorganized, in 1894, it also increased its membership limits to 150 men and 120 ladies. By now, golf had become a fashionable sport in Canada.

I have said that Toronto golfers probably started playing together at Ben Lamond Park in 1876. Several articles published around the turn of the

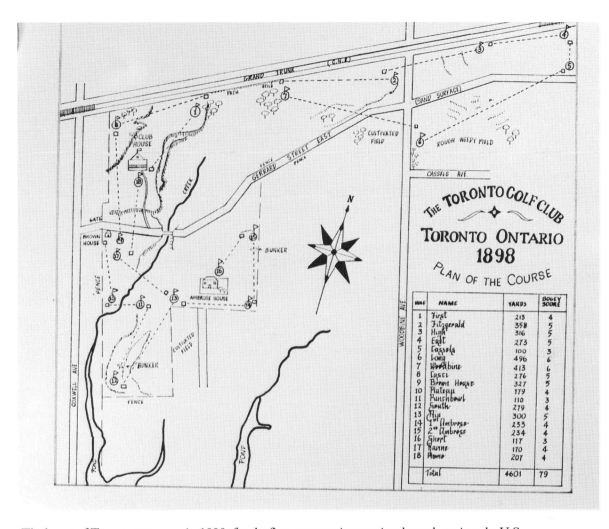

The layout of Toronto GC course in 1898, for the first amateur international match against the U.S.

century cite this date, but these same articles show the club being formed in 1882. These include an article in an 1895 issue of *Athletic Life* written by Charles Hunter, captain of the club in 1889, and one by Stewart Gordon published by the American magazine *Golf* in 1898. Gordon was then the secretary of the club.

Niagara-on-the-Lake is a quaint, old-style village, nestling amid groves of pleasant shade and fruit trees, right on the brink of blue Lake Ontario. Here the wealthy of the land build to themselves houses, and try to keep cool during the summer months. Those who have no house, throng the many hotels, or arrange with the rural inhabitants to be kept at a rea-

sonable temperature, at so much per head during the torrid season. The summer population play golf, tennis, bowls, drive, ride, bike, fish, sail, row, eat, drink, flirt, make love, marry, dance, swim, go to church, play poker, and in fact do about anything that a summer man or woman, of reasonable means, could or would do anywhere else, only more so.

– *The Daily Mail and Empire*, Toronto, 22 August 1896

This historic town, settled by United Empire Loyalists in the late eighteenth century, has had many names. When a golf club was formed there in 1881, it was given the name then current, Niagara.

By the late Victorian years, Niagara (not to be confused with Niagara Falls) had become a popular summer resort for the people of Toronto, Buffalo, Rochester, and other cities on the Great Lakes.

What is remarkable about this early club is that its successor – Niagara-on-the-Lake GC – today golfs over the same piece of land used in 1881, which makes this nine-hole course the oldest surviving links in North America. Like all courses, it has changed over the years. Its greens have been moved, its holes lengthened, new bunkers built. But the fairways remain where they were over a century ago, inside a tight rectangle of land bounded by Lake Ontario, Fort Mississauga, and the stately homes of Simcoe and Front streets, five generations old.

Fort Mississauga was built as a temporary field work during the War of 1812, near the junction of Lake Ontario and the mouth of the Niagara River. Never completed, it was abandoned by the military in the 1860s. At one time the golf course – the Mississauga Links – had

its second green inside the earth dykes surrounding the fort, and its third tee on top of one of these dykes.

What is equally surprising is that some of today's older members recall the man who first brought golf to Niagara in the 1880s and who, at the time of his death in 1931, was reckoned to be Canada's oldest golfer.

J. Geale Dickson came from a prosperous local family. He spent some years away from Niagara as an officer in the Loyal North Lancashire Regiment in England, where he took up golf. On his return to Niagara around 1880, with the help of Ingersoll Merritt he laid out a few holes for golf on the Fort George Common, across the road from the family home in John Street. He and Merritt moved their course to the Mississauga Common on the other side of town, at the same time expanding it to the nine holes which came to be known as the Mississauga Links. These two men were joined by

J. Geale Dickson, one of two brothers who were founding members of the Niagara Golf Club. This photograph was published at the time of his death in 1931.

Charles Hunter, a founding member of Niagara Golf Club in 1881, photographed in 1896.

other golfers, among them Charles Hunter and Walter G. Cassels from Toronto.

Charles Hunter, a Scot described as "kind, genial and witty," had played golf some twenty years earlier, before coming to Canada. He was the Ontario representative of the Standard Life Assurance Company. Hunter lived in Toronto but made Niagara his home in the summer, and he reported to the general manager of Standard Life, who happened to be William Ramsay of The Royal Montreal Golf Club.

Walter G. Cassels, a founding member of the Toronto GC, also summered at Niagara.

We have been left with one account of a match played over the Mississauga Links around 1880 by Geale Dickson, Charles Hunter, Walter G. Cassels, and three others who were to help form the Toronto GC – Robert and George Bethune and Robert Cochran. This appears to have been a congenial gathering of sportsmen engaged in a leisurely round on an otherwise empty course, for we are told that "a pony cart followed them from hole to hole, laden with every possible beverage which the human tongue could desire." After the morning round, they lunched all afternoon, then dallied over cigars, "by which time it was too late to renew the contests of the morning."

It was about this time that Geale Dickson's twin brother returned from service as an officer in the Queen's Own Hussars and Dragoon Guards. Robert H. Dickson – usually referred to as Captain Dickson – became the first captain of the Niagara Golf Club.

There is no contemporary record of the organizing meeting of the club. If minutes were kept, they have been lost or destroyed. Janet Carnochan's *History of Niagara* (1914) states that the club was formed in 1877. (She also describes its picturesque appearance: ". . . the black man with roller, shears and cart, the caddies lazily or eagerly searching for a lost ball, the scarlet coats, white waist shirts, the graceful swinging movement in a long drive . . . ") Around the turn of the century, the members claimed that the club had been founded in 1881, and there is some evidence to support

this. This is the date printed on the programs of the Niagara International Golf Tournament, which started in 1895. An article in the Toronto *Globe* of April 1882 refers to the Niagara GC in terms that suggest at least a year's history. This article also comments favourably on the Mississauga Links:

> The golf course at Niagara is perhaps unsurpassed, and bids fair to become the St. Andrews of Canada. Its central position, ease of access by rail or steamer, and large area, combine to make it one of the best that could be selected for matches between other clubs on neutral ground.

Both Dicksons played in the first interprovincial team match at Royal Montreal in 1882, and again in 1883 when the Niagara club was host. The Niagara GC played against the Toronto GC for the Niagara Cup, and no doubt it had matches with Brantford.

This first incarnation of the Niagara GC survived for only four seasons. It died after the 1884 season, apparently through lack of interest. Golf had not yet reached the United States, so American visitors to Niagara were not familiar with the game.

By the time Charles Hunter and the Dicksons formed the second Niagara GC in 1894, many of the American visitors to the town had become golfers, keen to follow their sport on vacation. The golden years of the Niagara GC were about to begin.

If golf in Victorian Canada was to grow and prosper, it needed more apostles like W. Lindsay Creighton. He appears to have had an ability to inspire others to take up the game and to organize. Within a year of his arrival in Brantford, he had enjoined local businessmen to form a club. And when he left the city, the club foundered. Shortly after his arrival in Kingston, the city had a golf club, with Creighton as captain. And when he left Kingston, two years later, this club also failed.

The committee that helped Creighton run the Kingston GC from 1886 comprised: John Bell Carruthers (Kingston born and bred, a merchant, and president of the Kingston and Montreal Forwarding Company, Carruthers was the club's secretary-treasurer in 1886; he was to become a long-serving member of the second Kingston GC and, for many years, its captain. His wife also captained the ladies' section in the 1890s); Lieutenant Colonel William Henry Cotton, commandant of the Royal School of Artillery; Colonel Oliver, also of the Royal Artillery; Dr. Grant, a local physician; and F. Brownfield.

A city of 16,000 in 1886, Kingston had never quite recovered from being dropped as the capital of the United Canadas. Until 1870, when the Imperial troops were withdrawn, it continued to be a large military centre; substantial fortifications had been erected as late as the 1840s.

The course of the Kingston GC was laid out on Barriefield Common, next to the Royal Military College, and under the guns of the historic Fort Henry. The course had thirteen holes, the five holes on the Barriefield Hill being played twice to complete the round.

In Creighton's time, the club does not appear to have played against any other club; the nearest competitors were at Toronto and at Montreal, over 150 miles away. But Creighton and Colonel Cotton played for Ontario in the interprovincial match against Quebec in 1887. After Creighton left, the club was disbanded.

The second Kingston Golf Club was organized in April 1891 when a group of golfers – most of them from the Royal Military College – met in Colonel Cotton's office at the Tête du Point Barracks. Colonel Cotton was elected captain, H. J. Hewat, the new secretary-treasurer.

The founding force behind this second Kingston club appears to have been Hewat, an East Lothian man. In his *The Golf Book of East Lothian* (1896), the Reverend John Kerr writes of the Kingston GC that it was "founded six years ago by a gentleman, who, when a boy, attended the public school at Dirleton."

A note in an 1898 issue of the American magazine *Golf* also pins the medal on Hewat. "The Kingston Club was originally organized in 1886, lapsed for a time, and was revived in 1891, mainly through the efforts of Mr. H. J. Hewat, now of the North Jersey Country Club." Hewat remains an elusive character. Having put up a trophy for competition, he left Canada for the United States.

And what of Creighton? In the fall of 1888, his bank transferred him to Quebec City. Well-known to Quebec golfers, having played in three interprovincial matches against them, he no doubt joined Royal Quebec GC. He was never to play as a member on Cove Fields. He died in the following April, at the age of forty-four.

3

THE FIRST INTERPROVINCIAL TEAM MATCHES

THERE HAVE BEEN THREE SERIES OF men's amateur interprovincial team matches in the history of Canadian golf. The first series consisted of four matches played between Ontario and Quebec in the period 1882–87. Then, after a lapse of four years, the two provinces went at it again, more or less continuously between 1892 and 1921, the years of the First World War excepted. In the final match of this series, Manitoba and Alberta entered a team. After another lapse of five years, in 1927 we started the present series of matches for the Willingdon Cup, with all provinces eventually competing. In the first two series, the size of the team was largely determined by how many players the visiting team could field. In the Willingdon Cup matches, each province sends a team of four.

No doubt encouraged by his team's successes against Brantford, Robert Bethune of the Toronto Golf Club proposed to Royal Montreal that a match be arranged between their two provinces. He offered to bring an Ontario team made up of Toronto, Brantford, and Niagara players to Montreal in 1882. Montreal accepted the challenge. Early in October of that year, teams of nine met at Fletcher's Field, Quebec captained by Alexander Dennistoun, Ontario captained by Robert Bethune.

The teams paired off according to their standing in their province (as determined by the captains), the number one man in Quebec, Dennistoun, meeting the number one man in Ontario, A. W. Smith. Each match was played to a finish over eighteen holes (two rounds of the course). Quebec won by 37 holes to 19. But the results of the individual matches illustrate just how superior Smith (playing out of Brantford) and the two Scott brothers were to the rest of the field. Between them they accounted for 18 of Ontario's 19 holes. In spite of his ground advantage, Dennistoun lost to Smith by the surprisingly wide margin of 10 holes. But Dennistoun was nearly twice the age of Smith, who was in his thirties and at his peak.

We are told that "the Ontario team accepted their defeat with that good humour which is characteristic of golfers." The teams lunched and dined at Royal Montreal's new clubhouse, where they met the mayor, members of the Montreal Corporation, the Park Commissioners, and other influential citizens. As was the custom, the evening was enlivened by speeches and songs.

The return match was played at the Niagara club a year later, the players going over by lake steamer from the wharf in Toronto. Quebec fielded nine players, only three of whom had been in the winning team a year earlier. Ontario won easily by 30 holes.

Teams of seven a side met at Royal Montreal in 1884, Ontario winning by 17 holes to 12. The Scott brothers and A. W. Smith (now play-

ing out of Toronto GC) accounted for all of Ontario's holes.

There was no match in 1885. It should have been played at the Toronto Golf Club, but apparently Toronto's course was not considered fit for such a match, and Royal Montreal had suggested it be played for the second straight year at Montreal. Ontario declined, citing the high cost of travel, but a smallpox epidemic in Montreal probably had as much to do with the cancellation.

Whatever the reason, financial or otherwise, there was no match in 1886. In 1887, travel costs and the demise of the Brantford and Niagara clubs aside, Ontario did not appear to have any difficulty in raising a team. It sent fourteen players to Montreal, two of whom were from the new club at Kingston.

Quebec simply overpowered the Ontario side, to the extent that even the seemingly invin-

PLAYERS IN THE INTERPROVINCIAL MATCH ON TORONTO CLUB GOLF LINKS, SEPTEMBER 30TH.

FIGURES IN BACK ROW.—Professor Cappon, Kingston; V. C. Brown, Rosedale; C. A. Maston, Toronto; F. G. H. Pattison, Hamilton; G. T. Brown, London; S. Gordon, Secretary Canadian Golf Association and Toronto Golf Club; Dr. F. C. Hood, Rosedale; F. P. Betts, London; R. McCann, Montreal; A. Brodie, Quebec; L. Brown, Montreal; W. J. S. Gordon, Montreal; A. Z. Palmer, Montreal; W. B. Scott, Quebec; F. Stancliffe, Montreal. SECOND ROW.—G. S. Lyon, Champion of Canada, '98; W. A. H. Kerr, Champion of Canada, '97; W. W. Watson, Captain Montreal Club; A. J. Piddington, Montreal; A. W. Smith, Toronto. FRONT ROW.—T. D. Law, Toronto; W. H. Blake, Toronto; J. P. Taylor, Montreal; G. S. Gillespie, Quebec, Champion of Canada in 1896.

The Ontario and Quebec teams in the interprovincial match played at Toronto Golf Club in September 1898.

cible A. W. Smith fell to the Reverend James Barclay of Royal Montreal, the first defeat of Smith on record. The score of 57 holes to 17 would have been much worse had Andy Scott not come in with a 10-hole win for Ontario.

The failure of the Kingston club after the 1888 season left Toronto GC by itself in the province, and it was having difficulty in finding a permanent course. This probably explains why there were no matches for four years.

With two new clubs in the province by 1892 – Royal Ottawa and the second Kingston GC – Toronto GC again had some support. Too, its own membership was expanding. However, it was still without a decent course, and the 1892 match was again played at Royal Montreal. With so many new golfers on its side, Ontario was easily overwhelmed. Andy Scott gave the province its only 2 holes against Quebec's 53.

With the exception of three missed years – and the years of the war – this second series of matches continued to be played until 1921. Teams ranged from twenty a side to only four

(when held in Quebec City). From 1896, the matches became part of the Royal Canadian Golf Association's Annual Meeting. From 1906, the result was determined by individual matches won or lost; in 1921, by the aggregate of stroke play.

In 1921, when the Canadian Amateur championship was held in Winnipeg, Manitoba and Alberta entered a team against Ontario. (Quebec did not send enough players to make up a team.) Manitoba won, and Alberta was second, much to the surprise of golfers in Central Canada.

In the first and second series of matches played over the period 1882 to 1921, the honours were fairly evenly divided between Ontario, with fourteen wins, and Quebec, with eleven. After 1921 the matches appear to have been discontinued for the very good reason that the members of Western clubs could not afford to send players every year to the RCGA's Annual Meeting in Central Canada. This problem, as we shall see, was to be solved in 1927.

4

CHAPTER

BANKERS TO THE FORE

WHEN WE EXAMINE THE BACKGROUND of Canada's pioneer golfers, we find a predominance of bankers of Scottish descent. Some of them were young inspectors or accountants, others were tellers or clerks. In Canada, they found a land and a profession rich in Scottish tradition, receptive to Scottish customs, and eager to adopt a Scottish game.

In later years, bankers carried golf in their baggage as they moved from one bank branch to another, even from one province to another. They were, if you like, golf's gypsies. To call them golf's missionaries would be to endow them with a spirit they would not have recognized in themselves. They had not set out from Scotland to bring golf to Canada, or to spread golf in Canada, but to do their job, which was to operate the nation's banks.

The archetypal eighteenth- and nineteenth-century Canadian banker is a dour Scot who had brought with him to Canada his Scottish banking practices and a keen nose for money-making. In fact, it has been shown that Americans outnumbered Scots in Canada's early financial community. Too, the Scottish origin of the Canadian banking system is apparently largely a myth

(sceptical Scots should read *Canada's First Bank* [1965] by Merrill Denison). Nevertheless, in the 1870s, Canada's banks were thick with Scots and with others of Scottish descent. In the period of growth following Confederation, there was a boom in business and commerce; between 1868 and 1874, twenty-eight charters for new banks were granted by the Dominion parliament. To help cope with such growth, Canadian banks recruited in Britain, where wages were lower than in North America. Many of the new managers, accountants, tellers, and clerks were hired in Scotland. And many of these Scots were, inevitably, keen and proficient golfers.

In the late nineteenth century, branch managers and clerks of a Canadian bank were among the few who could afford the time and the money to play golf in a club and who had the required standing in the community. Their place in the social structure of the Canadian town of the 1870s and 1880s was described in this way by David R. Forgan (one of the St. Andrews Forgans) in an article in the *Journal of the Canadian Bankers' Association* in 1899:

A bank manager is always a leading man in any Canadian town or city, and is placed on

42

an equal footing, socially, with those who have been successful in life in other pursuits.

The relative status of the bank clerk was even more striking:

> . . . the bank clerk has no difficulty in obtaining social recognition, on being moved to a strange town. In this respect he is far more fortunate than a young man in a mercantile situation, and the society he commands is always the best a town affords.

This assessment is confirmed by events. When the governor general, the Marquis of Lorne, captained Royal Quebec against Royal Montreal in 1881, his team of ten included the general manager of a bank, one branch manager, and five bank tellers or clerks.

The governor general, the Marquis of Lorne, who played for Royal Quebec against Royal Montreal in 1881.

As for the leisure needed to play golf, David Forgan had this to say:

> . . . the advantages of a banking life are almost too well known to be mentioned at all. A bank clerk, in most towns and cities, commences his work at nine o'clock in the morning, and is usually out and away by four. In contrast to this, the hours spent in labour by the commercial clerk – from seven until six, and sometimes longer – seem very long indeed.

Finally, on the matter of money:

> . . . there is no business in which the mediocre man is paid as well as in banking.

So the bank employee appears to have had all the prerequisites for membership of a golf club: the social status, the leisure, and the money.

Two bankers, R. R. Grindley and Wolferstan Thomas, were charter members of Royal Montreal. They had little to do with the founding of the club, nor were they very active members, so Royal Montreal can not be dubbed a bankers' club. But bankers organized the clubs in Quebec, Toronto, Brantford, and Kingston, and made up the greater part of the teams for the early interclub and interprovincial matches.

James Hunter, sent to Quebec by the Bank of British North America, rekindled an enthusiasm for the game in his fellow bankers, and fellow Scots, Farquharson Smith and James Stevenson. Among the first members of Royal

The Junior Bank Clerk

Even in the 1920s, when this cartoon appeared, the junior bank clerk was stereotyped as a golfer.

Quebec were three other bank managers and three bank tellers or clerks, all Scots or of Scottish descent.

Bankers dominated early golf in Toronto. Of the ten who played for Toronto GC against Brantford in its first year, seven worked (or had worked) for banks in the city. In 1881, golf should have found no more fertile ground in which to plant its seed than Toronto's colony of Scottish-Canadian bankers, some of whom had their roots in Scotland's golfing counties or had relatives who had played the game in the Old Country.

The three brothers Cassels, Walter G., Robert, and Richard, born at Leith in the teens of the century, individually emigrated to join banks in Canada. In 1931 Robert's grandson, R. C. H. Cassels, wrote of them in *Canadian Golfer*:

> I do not know whether they played golf in Scotland, but I think it probable that they did, because most people in Scotland played the game and also because their father was a member of the Honourable Company of Edinburgh Golfers, to which he was admitted in December, 1808.

Robert Cassels, the first to emigrate, was for many years the manager of the Bank of British North America at Quebec City. He may have played golf in Canada, but he died a year after the Toronto GC was organized. His son and grandson were to become presidents of the club.

His brother, Walter G., came to Canada in 1845, also to the Bank of British North America. He had a spell with the Bank of Hamilton, became general manager of the Gore Bank, and later turned to private banking. The third brother, Richard, was a branch manager with the Bank of Upper Canada when it failed. He, too, probably turned to private banking.

Walter G. Cassels was a founding member of Toronto GC in 1881, and played in at least three of Toronto's matches against Brantford that year. He also helped form the club at Niagara. Walter G. and brother Richard, together with their nephew (Robert's son, Walter G. P. – later

Sir Walter) were three of the ten who attended the first annual general meeting of the Toronto GC in April 1882, when Walter G. was elected to the committee.

The three Cassels brothers worked for the Bank of Upper Canada at the same time as Lamond Smith and his son-in-law, Edmund

Edmund B. Osler, a founding member of Toronto Golf Club and originally a Canadian banker.

(later, Sir Edmund) Osler, so all three probably golfed at Ben Lamond Park. Over the years, the Cassels and Osler families were to give long and distinguished service to their club and to golf. Between them, they were to provide five captains, four presidents, and five honorary presidents for the men's section of Toronto GC, as well as two presidents for the Royal Canadian Golf Association.

Robert Bethune, general manager of the Dominion Bank (which became Toronto Dominion), was the first captain of the Toronto GC; his brother, George, of the Farmer's Loan and Savings Company, was a founding member. Bethunes had long been associated with the home of golf, St. Andrews. In the sixteenth century, two Bethunes (or Beatons or Betouns, two spellings of the same family's name) were archbishops of St. Andrews, as well as powerful political figures and advisors to King James V. The brothers John and Henry Bethune were two of the twenty-four original members of the Royal and Ancient Golf Club of St. Andrews in 1754. Over the years, the family has provided five captains for the Royal and Ancient.

Robert Bethune of Toronto GC and James Stevenson of Quebec GC helped in the birth of the Canadian Bankers' Association. The two were long-time friends, having much in common besides their profession and an enthusiasm for golf. Robert Bethune was a quiet, modest man, a church warden – as befitted a son of the Right Reverend Bishop Bethune – and a "practical advocate of innocent and healthful recreation," being a keen curler and an all-round cricketer as well as a golfer. He was well-read; his family thought of him as "the bookish banker." In 1866, Stevenson picked him to be inspector of the Quebec Bank, so the two also worked together for four years, until Bethune left for the Dominion.

James Stevenson was something of a dilettante, could paint a good picture in oil or watercolours, and was a fine judge of engravings and bronzes. He modestly declined the presidency of the Canadian Bankers' Association in 1893 but was elected an honorary president.

Daniel Robert Wilkie, another of Scottish descent, had also worked for Stevenson in the Quebec Bank, before becoming general manager of the Imperial Bank of Canada. Wilkie was an early member of the Toronto GC, but does not appear to have played in an interclub match until 1885.

Into this established colony of Toronto Scots came a number of new young Scottish bankers. Some of them had been members of artisan golf clubs in Scotland. None of them was to rise higher in his profession than branch manager, but together they were to give golf in Toronto what it needed – a few skilled players, experienced in club golf. Four of them had been members of Royal Quebec. (If we did not know Robert Bethune to have been a gentleman, we might suspect him of enticing them away from banks in Quebec, so they could golf for Toronto.) Tom Scott came first, transferring from the Bank of British North America in Quebec to be a teller in Robert Bethune's bank in the summer of 1881. He was to serve as secretary-treasurer of Toronto GC for eight years, ranking as the club's, and the province's, third-best player.

Second place would have gone to his brother, Andrew (Andy), who moved from Quebec to join George Bethune in 1882. The third brother, John, possibly came straight from Scotland to the Dominion Bank that same year. W. P. Sloane had also been in a Quebec bank before moving to Toronto and transferring from Royal Quebec to Toronto GC.

The finest player to join the Toronto club about this time was A. W. Smith. As we shall see, Smith did as much as anyone to raise the status and standard of golf in Quebec City and Toronto.

In one of the early matches between the Toronto GC and the Brantford GC, no less than ten of the sixteen golfers worked for banks. In Brantford the pattern had been much the same as in Toronto; bankers were the first to play the game, the organizers of the club, the first officers. W. Lindsay Creighton, manager of the Bank of Montreal, was the force behind the club and became its first secretary. Alex Robertson, manager of the Bank of British North America, became its first captain. When Creighton's bank moved him to Kingston, he promptly formed a club in that city.

Some immigrant golfing bankers moved from Canada to the United States, helping to plant the game there. (In America, poet Walt Whitman recognized the link between the profession and golf when he wrote:

"I sing the song of the Bankers' Association. . . / Men, and large men who walk all over a ten-acre lot batting the Scotch elusive high ball. / Batting it with brasseys, mashies, lofters, cleeks, soles, bulgers, spoons and many waggles. . . . ") The best known were the Forgan brothers, James and David. Their father, Robert Forgan, was head of the noted clubmaking business at St. Andrews.

In March 1873, at the age of twenty, James Berwick Forgan came from a Scottish bank to the Bank of British North America in Canada. In his *Recollections of a Busy Life* (1924), he tells of how he was sent to work in the Montreal office of the general manager, R. R. Grindley, at a salary of $600 a year (plus a bonus of $100, because he could speak schoolboy French and sing "La Marseillaise" in its original language!). After a few months, he was transferred to Halifax, where he later joined the Bank of Nova Scotia. He rose to be its first inspector.

David R. Forgan left the Clydesdale Bank in St. Andrews to join his brother in Halifax. Both were later enticed to the United States, where

Thomas A. (Tom) Scott, another of the three, and secretary of the Toronto Golf Club 1882–89.

they became bank presidents. David Forgan also helped to found the Onwentsia Golf Club, in Chicago. He would come back to Canada as a member of a United States amateur golf team in 1898.

In 1873, James Forgan played golf in Halifax, on the fields of the South Common. Two of his playing companions, also young Scots, were in the same bank. One was the James Darling who had earlier played at Brantford. The other was J. J. Morrison, who rose to become manager of his bank in Hamilton. He was a charter member of the Hamilton GC and for many years its secretary-treasurer, captain, and president. In 1918, *Canadian Golfer* said of Morrison's contribution to golf in Hamilton:

Andrew (Andy) P. Scott in 1895, one of the three Scott brothers who came as bank clerks to Canada in the period 1875–82. In the 1880s Andy was the second-finest golfer in the country. Note the long St. Andrews back-swing.

> To his enthusiasm, wise counsel and unselfish efforts, not a little of the great success of the Royal and Ancient game is attributable, and also to no small extent its vogue in neighbouring cities and towns.

J. J. Morrison, a banker golfer at Halifax in 1873, later a founding member and president of Hamilton G & CC.

Many other Scottish bankers contributed to the rise and spread of golf in Canada, and we shall meet some of them later. As the sport became more popular, their efforts were diluted by golfers of other professions, notably lawyers. In the West, land agents, grain dealer, ranchers, and the North-West Mounted Police also had the time and the wherewithal needed to take up the game. But it is doubtful if any other single profession has contributed as much to Canadian golf as has banking.

Andrew W. (Andy) Smith came to Canada from Scotland late in 1881, to work for the Quebec Bank. As a member of the Toronto Golf Club, he was Canada's finest amateur golfer until the emergence of George S. Lyon in 1898.

Smith learned his golf at St. Andrews, Scotland, where he was born and educated. He first came to prominence as a golfer at the age of twenty-six, when he won both the Spring Meeting and the Scratch Medal of the Glasgow Golf Club, which he had recently joined. "Curl" Smith – as he was known in Scotland – went on to win a number of club and provincial events in Glasgow, including the Tennant Cup in 1880 and 1881. This was a scratch, stroke-play competition, open to any amateur in Britain, although most of the competitors came from clubs in the west of Scotland.

Upon his arrival in Quebec, Andy Smith joined the Quebec GC. He was a member there for only a year or so before his bank transferred him to London, Ontario, which had no golf club. To get a game, he had to travel by train to Brantford. Another year later his bank moved him to Toronto. He joined the Toronto GC, of which he was to become secretary-treasurer for the years 1890–95.

Today we can measure the success of an amateur golfer in Canada by the number of provincial and national championships he or she wins. We can not do the same for Smith. In his day, there were no provincial tournaments, and the Canadian Amateur was not held until 1895. By then Smith was past his best. He died in 1901, at the age of fifty-two.

The records of his club championships have mostly been lost or destroyed, but in what records we have, he is shown as winning every scratch event in which he played. Sometimes the margin by which he won shows just how superior he was to the other golfers of his day. In 1890, he won the scratch event at the Quebec GC – where he had retained his membership – by a margin of 32 strokes over 36 holes. His handicap at Quebec GC was then *plus* 15, the next best player being scratch. At Toronto GC, he does not appear to have been rated better than plus 3.

He played in nine of the twelve interprovincial matches held between 1882 and 1899, usually for Ontario. He was beaten only once, by the Reverend James Barclay of Royal Montreal, in 1887.

Year	Playing for	At	Smith	Opponent
1882	Ontario	Montreal	Won by 10 holes	Alex Dennistoun Royal Montreal GC
1883	Ontario	Niagara	Won by 8 holes	H. S. Smith Royal Quebec GC
1884	Ontario	Montreal	Won by 5 holes	G. W. F. Carter Royal Montreal GC
1887	Ontario	Montreal	Lost by 3 holes	Rev. James Barclay Royal Montreal GC
1892	Quebec	Montreal	Won by 2 holes	Tom Harley Kingston GC (Harley won the first Canadian Amateur Championship)
1893	Ontario	Ottawa	Won by 11 holes	Hon. Geo. Drummond Royal Montreal GC
1894	Ontario	Montreal	Won by 9 holes	F. Stancliffe Royal Montreal GC
1895	——	——	Smith Playing in U.S. Open	——
1896, 1897	——	——	Smith in Scotland	——
1898	Quebec	Toronto	Won by 2 holes	George S. Lyon Rosedale GC (Lyon won Canadian Amateur, 1898)
1899	Quebec	Ottawa	Won by 7 holes	Vere C. Brown Rosedale GC (Brown won Canadian Amateur, 1899)

There were no interprovincial matches in the years 1885, 1886, and 1888 through 1891. In 1896, Smith went on a long vacation to Scotland, and when he returned it was as the representative of the Gutta Percha Manufacturing Company.

He played once in the British Open, in 1879, when he was the leading amateur. In 1897, he was beaten in the fourth round of the British Amateur by A. J. T. Allan, the eventual winner. He also played twice in the U.S. Open: in 1895 he tied for third place, in a field of twelve, and a year later he again tied for third in a field of thirty-six. In both years he was the leading amateur. (No Canadian was to finish higher in the U.S. Open until Dave Barr tied for second in 1985.)

Smith was remembered in Scotland with affection, as one of its leading artisan players. Writing in *Canadian Golfer* in 1931, R. C. H. Cassels of the Toronto Golf Club recounts how he visited Ben Sayers's shop at North Berwick, in 1899:

. . . when the old club maker saw the name "Toronto" on my club, he said to me, "You'll know Curl Smith." When I told him that I did, he held forth at length as to the quality of his game and various matches which he had taken part in at St. Andrews.

Andrew Smith and George Lyon seem to have shared the honours in the few times they met in match play, but this was near the turn of the century, when Lyon was only just emerging as Canada's leading golfer and Smith was past his best. Their closest match was in the quarter-finals of the Toronto club's Osler Trophy in 1900. *Saturday Night* magazine wrote this of their encounter:

> Golfers who visited the Toronto links on Saturday were given a rare treat. One of the closest and most interesting matches ever witnessed in Toronto was played between A. W. Smith and George Lyon . . . At the end of the 18th hole, Smith had pulled down Lyon's lead and tied the match. It was then agreed to play 4 more holes to get a decision, the result of this being also a tie. Both players took a little refreshment and again repaired to the links, playing the 1st, 8th, 9th, and 18th holes to cut the knot, Lyon winning on the last green.

It is useless to speculate as to which was the better golfer. Smith was at least as far ahead of the golfers of the 1880s and most of the 1890s as Lyon was of the golfers of the next twenty years. There were times when both men were the beaten favourites, having experienced that inexplicable fall from form that hits all champions from time to time. All we can say for sure is that Smith could play well enough to defeat any other player of his time, and no man can do more than that.

Andrew Smith's contribution to golf in Canada led *Saturday Night* to label him, in 1900, "The Father of Golf in Canada." Strictly speaking, he had no hand in the birth of the game in this country. But a father's responsibility is also to nurture, to educate, and to inspire. In that sense, Smith was a true father of our golf. The historian of his old club in Glasgow called him "our unapproachable model and mould of form." He had, by all accounts, the classical St. Andrews swing, which was envied and copied in Canada. There was no such term as "Junior Development" in late Victorian golf, but Smith did more than anyone to encourage the junior members of his clubs to learn the fundamentals of the game. In 1891, J. Hutton Balfour of Royal Montreal wrote of him in a letter to the British magazine *Golf*:

Andrew W. (Andy) Smith, Canada's finest golfer from the time of his arrival in 1881 until the emergence of George S. Lyon in 1898. He is seen here in his slimmer years.

The junior members of the Quebec club showed up well, thanks to the attention given to them by Mr. A. W. Smith, one of their members, who walks round the course instructing them. It is to be hoped the Montreal members will show better in the autumn by making good use of their professional's services.

Witnessing a good player serves not only to instruct and improve those who already play but also to attract new recruits. In 1891, Smith played a series of matches against Davis, the professional at Royal Montreal. After watching Smith win the play-off, a reporter wrote: "As a result of this match, there are several gentlemen applying for membership to both clubs, having got bitten." But if he was a golfer to be copied, he was also a golfer who instilled in others a proper sense of humility. "New players," someone wrote, "are not likely to be puffed up with vainglory so long as they have before them a standard of enviable, and also unattainable, golfing prowess as Mr. A. W. Smith."

George Lyon wrote of him in 1906:

> I have never taken lessons from a professional, but have been very observant of other players, and in that way picked up many valuable points. I played a good deal with Mr. A. W. Smith, and from him got many useful hints. He was always willing to help anyone who asked him, from the good player down to the tyro. I believe he was one of the prettiest players I ever met. His style was in my judgement almost perfect.

The world of golf in the nineteenth century was a very small world, even in its home, Scotland. The link between James Hunter, Andrew Smith, William Doleman, and others illustrates just how small it was.

James Hunter, who inspired the golfers of Quebec to form a club, and Andrew Smith, who inspired them by his playing six years later, were both born in St. Andrews, in 1849. Smith – perhaps Hunter too – schooled and played golf with Young Tom Morris, son of Old Tom, the Keeper of the Green at St. Andrews.

Hunter and Smith both joined Scottish banks. Andrew Smith remained a bachelor, but James Hunter married Young Tom's sister, Libby. When Young Tom died in 1875, Andrew Smith was nominated in Glasgow to collect for the memorial fund, and James Hunter came home from Quebec.

When Andrew Smith played in the first Tennant Cup at Glasgow Golf Club in 1880, the leader after the first round was William Doleman. Smith overtook him in the second round and went on to win. He won again in 1881, several months before he, too, left for Quebec.

This William Doleman was the fellow who had come ashore at Quebec in 1854 to practise his golf on Cove Fields. Two decades later, James Hunter helped organize the golf club at Quebec and won the club's first competition over the same Cove Fields. And five years after that, his friend Andrew Smith arrived in Quebec to continue where Hunter had left off.

After Smith left for Canada, William Doleman went on to win the Tennant Cup three times. He would have won more often had it not been for a father and son, David and Robert Bone. Seven times the cup went to the Bone household. By the time the Bones, too, left for Canada – where Robert was to become a leading golfer in British Columbia – William Doleman was too old to think of winning again.

Doleman and Smith had fought for the cup over the course of the Glasgow Golf Club, in Alexandra Park. This park is in a district of Glasgow known as Dennistoun and had been part of the Dennistoun estates. These estates belonged to the family of Alexander Dennistoun, who had organized the Royal Montreal Golf Club and who played against Andrew Smith in interprovincial matches in Canada.

For many years Andrew Forgan of St. Andrews looked after the golf greens and the clubmaker's shop at Alexandra Park. His nephews James and David Forgan – and perhaps Hunter – went to the same school as Smith, and, like him, came to Canada as young bank clerks. David Forgan played for the United States, and Andrew Smith played for Canada, in the first international golf match between the two countries, in 1898.

In the 1890s, one of Andrew Forgan's star pupils in his workshop at Glasgow was young George Cumming, learning his trade as a club-maker. In 1900, Cumming came to Canada, to be the professional to the Toronto Golf Club. Andrew Smith, until recently the honorary secretary of the club, was there to greet him. Did they ever talk, I wonder, of James Hunter, William Doleman, Andrew Forgan, and the other folks back home? We know that Andrew Forgan did, when he came to Canada some years later . . . but that story can wait.

Andrew Forgan was seen at most championships in Central Canada in the years following the First World War.

PART TWO

COAST TO COAST 1890 -1899

(Over) *Dr. Charles S. Haultain, a surgeon in the NWMP, the first president and club champion of the Macleod Golf Club.*

GOLF BOOMS
EAST AND WEST

ONLY A FOOL, OR A VERY WISE MAN IN a great imaginative leap, could have reflected on the state of Canadian golf in 1890 and forecast its astonishing growth within a few years. Of the six golf clubs formed since 1873, only three had survived. Their combined membership was less than two hundred, absurdly low by today's standards, and hardly enough to keep alive one small club with a nine-hole course.

But anyone with a keen sense of the sporting scene in Britain would have been aware of this new sport, golf, which was growing fast and threatening to usurp tennis as the summer sport of the affluent. That being so, it was only a matter of time before the same happened in Canada. In 1890, most of Canada's 4.8 million people – those outside of Quebec, that is – thought of themselves as overseas British. The well-to-do in the cities of Ontario, and in the English-speaking communities of Quebec, followed closely the fashions and fads of the Old Country. They took up golf for the same reasons as the British: there had been a change in public attitudes, a swing towards

participatory sports; working hours were gradually being reduced; railways, tramways, and the bicycle now provided a means of getting to and from golf courses; and news of the British sport, played with such enthusiasm by Arthur James Balfour, found its way into Canadian newspapers.

Canada also had its New Woman. Here, as in Britain, golf grew rapidly as women started to play. Most of the new clubs in Canada had ladies' sections; the older clubs – Royal Montreal, Royal Quebec, and Toronto – formed such sections in the early 1890s.

This new enthusiasm for golf manifested itself in several ways. Not only did golfers organize new clubs across the country, but many joined the three existing clubs, tripling their memberships. And a surprising number of these keen new golfers were young people who had previously scorned the game. J. Hutton Balfour of Royal Montreal wrote to the British magazine *Golf* in November 1892:

We have been having a lively time at Golf during the past few weeks, and present appearances would tend to show that some people who used to consider the game only fit for old men, now begin to see its merits, and we look for a regular boom next year . . .

Next year was 1893, when Royal Montreal's membership was to grow to nearly 250, from something like 100 at the beginning of the decade. Women made up just under half of the membership.

Growth was proportionately greater at Toronto GC, which had historically been much smaller. It was helped by the electrification of Toronto's streetcar system, starting in 1892, and had probably been spurred by an article in *The Globe* of 17 May 1890. This three-column article on "The Game of Golf," including illustrations, is probably the first time the game appeared in the headlines of a North American newspaper. "How many people in the city know of the existence of the Toronto Golf Club," the paper asks, "or know anything of the game its members play? Golf! What is it?" The article goes on to answer its own questions, noting that in England golf was making rapid strides in popularity and could name among its votaries "many prominent statesmen and litterateurs."

In November 1894, Toronto's *Evening Telegram* carried a story on the club, which read in part:

> . . . there are [now] one hundred and fifty members, and the waiting list is two-thirds as large as the whole membership. Last year (1893) it would have been an easy thing for any man who was not undesirable to have joined the club. But with the opening of the spring came a wave of popularity for the game and the applications began to pour in at such a rate that the list was soon filled up.

"The Game of Golf" as it appeared in The Globe, *17 May 1890, probably the first illustrated article on the game in a North American newspaper. The views are of the Toronto Golf Club grounds just east of Coxwell Avenue.*

By the end of 1895, the club had expanded its course to eighteen holes, had a clubhouse "second only to the Forest and Stream Club of Montreal," and had further boosted its membership to 270, nearly half of them women.

In the same period, Royal Quebec had more than doubled its membership to ninety, and its strong ladies' section had played several matches against the ladies of Royal Montreal.

As might be expected, most of the new golf clubs formed in the 1890s were in the provinces of Quebec and Ontario, where Canadian golf had its roots. (Some 92 per cent of the country's population lived in Central Canada and in the Atlantic provinces.) In 1891, golfers revived the Kingston GC, and in 1894, the club at Niagara. There were, as we have seen, various attempts to get golf started again in Brantford. More significantly for the game, golfers organized in the nation's capital.

Mr. Hugh Renwick of Lanark, Scotland, came to visit his sister in Ottawa, in 1891. The Renwicks had long been members and benefactors of the Lanark Golf Club in Scotland. At the Ottawa St. Andrews Society, Hugh Renwick met many Scots, some of whom he already knew, among them John Thorburn, then in his early sixties.

Thorburn had been born and raised in a place with the unlikely name of Quothquan, only a few miles from Lanark. After graduating from Edinburgh University, he taught in the Grammar School at Musselburgh, where one could not live without becoming acquainted with the game of golf. Curling, however, was his first love. After coming to Canada in 1856, Thorburn became a leading figure in curling circles, latterly in Ottawa (where he was employed for a time as the headmaster of the Ottawa Grammar School). At the time of Renwick's visit, Thorburn was chairman of the Board of Civil Service Examiners.

Renwick persuaded his fellow countrymen in Ottawa to take up golf. John Thorburn chaired the organizing meeting of what was to become

John Thorburn, who helped bring golf to Ottawa, photographed about 1874.

the Royal Ottawa Golf Club. By one account at least (in *Canadian Golfer*, 1917), he was also elected the club's first president, although the club's handbook shows this honour going to the Honourable Edgar Dewdney, Minister of the Interior.

The club acquired some fifty acres of rolling farmland overlooking the old Rideau rifle ranges, and hired the professional of Royal Montreal, William Davis, to lay out a nine-hole course on grounds known as Sandy Hill. Royal Ottawa quickly outgrew its course and, in 1896, took a lien on land on the Chelsea Road. Along with the ground, the club acquired a stone farmhouse, which was converted into a comfortable clubhouse. Three years later, the club purchased the 108 acres for about eight thousand dollars, and built itself a twelve-hole course.

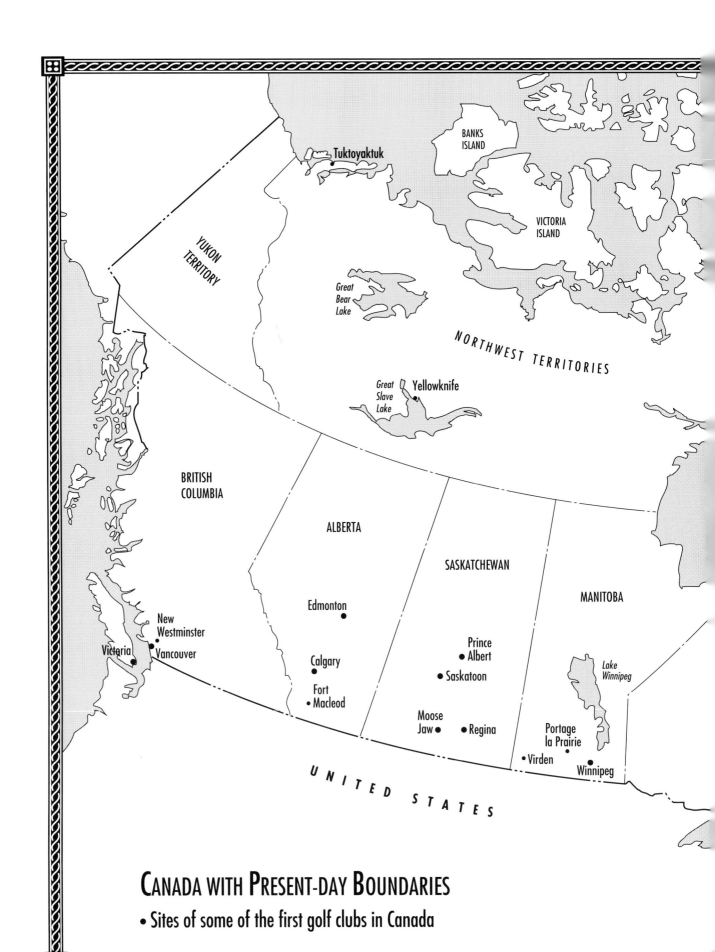

CANADA WITH PRESENT-DAY BOUNDARIES

• Sites of some of the first golf clubs in Canada

BAFFIN ISLAND

HUDSON
BAY

ATLANTIC OCEAN

NEWFOUNDLAND AND LABRADOR

QUEBEC

St.
John's

ONTARIO

PRINCE
EDWARD
ISLAND

Sydney

Murray Bay

NEW
BRUNSWICK

Charlottetown

NOVA
SCOTIA

Quebec City

Fredericton

Truro

Dartmouth

Woodstock

Halifax

Lake Superior

Montreal

Saint
John

Ottawa
Kingston

St.
Andrews

Lake Michigan

Lake Huron

Toronto
Brantford

Lake
Ontario

Niagara-on-the-Lake

Lake Erie

0   200   400 km
0 100 200 mi

Part of Royal Ottawa's land was found to hold the ingredients of high-quality cement. The club was offered, and accepted, twenty thousand dollars for the property, in 1903. So it moved again, to its present site on the Aylmer Road, Quebec. By this time its membership was up to 300, justifying a full eighteen-hole course.

Royal Ottawa had no sooner been organized in 1891 than it replaced Royal Quebec as the third-most influential institution in Canadian golf. It was to promote and play host to the first Canadian national championships, held in 1895.

Hugh Renwick did not forget that he had been largely responsible for the founding of the Ottawa club. In 1906, he presented it with a unique trophy. It was said to be a duplicate of the original bell given to the Royal Burgh of Lanark by King William the Lion, in 1166, for annual horse-racing.

With a waiting list at the Toronto Golf Club, it is not surprising to find golfers forming a second club in the city. At an enthusiastic meeting held at Moore Park in April 1893, golfers decided to import immediately clubs and balls from Scotland, and to establish the Deer Park Golf Club. The Reverend James H. White, recently arrived from Scotland to be the young minister of the Deer Park Presbyterian Church, was the moving spirit behind the club, and its first captain.

The members laid out a short, makeshift, nine-hole course in Moore Park.

In June, 1895, the Toronto Lacrosse and Athletic Association (TL & AA) announced that it had formed a golf club and was arranging for additional land around its grounds in Rosedale on which to lay out a course. This would encourage a membership increase of about 100, the club noted, "as the golf spirit is strong in the northern part of the city."

In September, the Deer Park GC amalgamated with the newly formed golf section of the TL & AA, to form Rosedale Golf Club. The new club laid out an eighteen-hole course adjacent to the lacrosse and cricket grounds in Rosedale, between what is now Binscarth Road and Summerhill Avenue, south of the railway tracks. This gave the golfers access to the TL & AA's clubhouse.

The clubhouse of the Royal Ottawa Golf Club, shortly after its opening by Lord and Lady Minto in 1904.

For years Rosedale struggled to squeeze eighteen holes into an area large enough for only a dozen. It was cramped, even by Victorian standards. *Canadian Golfer*, in 1916, recalled some of the problems:

> The play at two holes was in full view of the occupants of the "bleachers" of the Lacrosse Club, who never failed to pay their respects to the golfers. The jollying, jeering and broad witticisms from a few hundred brazen throats proved the undoing of many players whose nerves were not of the strongest type.

Too, a dairyman had the right of pasturing his cows on the links. Legend has it that many a ball finished up as cattle-fodder.

Regardless, the Rosedale club prospered. Within a few years it was a thriving organization of some 270 members, more than a third of them ladies. But with the formation of the Lambton club in 1902, many Rosedale members – including its president, M. McLaughlin,

and its finest player, George S. Lyon – joined the luxurious new venture to the west of the city. "The prospects for Rosedale and its continuance became enshrouded in uncertainty," a member wrote, many years later. But golf was growing so fast that the members' worries were unwarranted.

In 1909, an expanding city forced a move. The club bought land and built itself a championship course, at the top of Mount Pleasant Road, where it remains.

In 1894, Toronto Hunt formed a golf section, although it did not construct its nine-hole course in the east end of the city until 1897. Most of its golfing members were also members at other Toronto clubs.

High Park, the third active club in the city, opened for play in 1896. The club occupied its course north of Grenadier Pond for over ten years, building itself a fine new clubhouse as late as 1904. Three years later, congestion in the park forced a move to Port Credit, at which

The opening of the new clubhouse of the High Park Golf Club, Toronto, in May 1904. Within three years the club had moved to Port Credit and become Lakeview Golf Club.

time the name of the club was changed, first to High Park Golf and Country Club, then, a year or so later, to Lakeview Golf Club (now a public course).

In 1898, some twenty of the staff and students of the University of Toronto formed a golf club. The first captain was Professor Robert Ramsay Wright, a Scot from Fife. Within a year or so, membership had quadrupled, and the seven-hole course on the university playing fields had been increased to eleven holes. However, within a few years new buildings had encroached on the course, and it had to be abandoned in 1903.

Finally, what sounds like a public course seems to have been opened in 1899 in the east end of the city. In July, a notice in *The Daily Mail and Empire* advised readers that a nine-hole course had been opened near Bain Avenue, with a green fee of fifty cents. Its story remains a mystery. That is the only reference I have seen to this course; it may have been in the Don Valley.

Toronto, then, started the 1890s with only one golf club of less than fifty members, all male. It finished the decade with five clubs, having something like eight hundred members between them, a third of them women. It was the busiest golf centre in Canada.

During the same period, golfers organized some twenty new clubs in the province, outside Toronto, including the successors to the clubs at Niagara, Brantford, and Kingston. Golf became a recognized sport at Hamilton, London, Barrie, Simcoe, Berlin (Kitchener), Cobourg, Kincardine, Orillia, Oshawa, Peterborough, Collingwood, Napanee, Penetanguishine, Port Hope, Preston Springs, Perth, and Smith Falls. (As in every province, some of these clubs were later reorganized into new clubs using the same name.)

The clubs at Cobourg, Port Hope, and Niagara (the town soon to be renamed Niagara-on-the-Lake) were largely resort clubs, supported by summer visitors from Toronto and the

Great Lakes cities of the United States. At least one resort hotel had a course – the Maplehurst Inn, Muskoka.

Hamilton had a large colony of Scots, so it is surprising to find the city without a golf club until 1894. By all accounts, the leading spirit behind the formation of the Hamilton Golf Club was Senator Donald MacInnes. He had previously laid out a private course for his friends. Among the few who helped him organize the new club was Alexander Ramsay, elder brother of William Ramsay, a founding member of Royal Montreal. Alexander Ramsay was also in the insurance business, with Canada Life. He was to become president of the Hamilton club.

Its first twelve-hole course was formally opened in October, when four players described by *The Hamilton Spectator* as "experienced" played what the paper called a "four-handed match." They were, it seems, all Scots: Senator MacInnes, F. G. H. Pattison, T. H. Macpherson, and the mayor, A. D. Stewart. Although Pattison was the finest player of the four, he lost that day; in 1898, he was to be runner-up in the Canadian Amateur Championship. J. J. Morrison, another founding member, later club president, was one of the three young bank clerks who golfed at Halifax in 1873.

Hamilton's first course was laid out near the corner of Barton and Ottawa streets, next door to the Hamilton Jockey Club, which was used as a clubhouse on opening day. Following the custom of the time, the club gave names to its twelve holes. It is not hard to guess which were the most difficult: All's Well, Bunker, Trouble, Railway, Short, Ladies Drive, Paradise, Turning, Orchard, Purgatory, Hide and Seek, and Homeward Ho!.

A number of ladies also tried their hand on opening day, and some took up the game immediately. This was the beginning of the Hamilton ladies' tradition of service to women's golf in Canada. The club was to provide several of our finest women golfers in the early years of the new century, and would become the first headquarters of the Canadian Ladies' Golf Union.

The club moved to a new course after a year or so, laid out on a farm in what is now Aberdeen Avenue.

Legend has it that a member of the Toronto Golf Club, lawyer William Hume Blake, visited friends in London, Ontario, in the spring of 1894. Included with his luggage was a golf bag with a few clubs and balls. He so impressed his friends with his dexterity in handling the implements that they established the London Golf Club in September.

Blake's mother was a Cronyn, from London, Ontario. A London lawyer, Verschoyle Cronyn, was elected president of the new London GC. Frederick P. Betts, a law partner in Cronyn and Betts, was the club's first secretary. Within a year he was also the club's leading golfer, playing off scratch. (His brother Hyla was soon to catch him.) He was one of a few outstanding pioneers of golf, and not only in London. He often summered at Murray Bay, Quebec, and was one of its early golfers. (He played with a chief justice by the name of Taft, who later became president of the United States.) In the early years of this century, Frederick Betts was looked upon as something of an authority on golf.

Other pioneers in London golf were George T. Brown, Sir George Gibbons, Colonel Peters, and Charles Somerville (he played off something like 30, did the father of Canada's future champion).

George Brown became one of the club's top golfers, with a fine record at the early Canadian Amateur championships (where he never won the title) and at the Niagara International Tournament (where he did). At one Niagara tournament he beat the redoubtable Andy Scott of Toronto GC, a result that was greeted with disbelief in Toronto.

The club laid out a rough nine-hole course on the military parade ground – also known as Garrison Common and as Carling's farm – a piece of land offered by the commandant of the corps of infantry stationed at London.

At the same time, a London Ladies' Golf Club was formed, with its own course, and with Mrs. George C. Gibbons as president and Mrs.

H. E. Gibbs as secretary. Both clubs were later absorbed into The London Hunt and Country Club, organized back in 1885.

The Perth Golf Club (now know as Links O' Tay) claims that it was founded in 1892 and that its course has been in continuous existence longer than any course in Canada. This claim was staked in *Perth Remembered* (1968) and given some currency in 1989 by *The Globe and Mail*'s reference to the course as "the oldest nine-holer in Canada." But in the 1918 CPR booklet *Golf in Canada*, the club shows itself as established in 1903, and in the 1923 edition of *Fraser's Golf Directory and Year Book*, it gives the date of 1902.

The *Perth Courier* apparently first mentions golf in an issue of 1900, noting much local interest in the local golf course. The inference is that it had only just been laid out, and there is no mention of a golf club. On the evidence available so far, the club might date itself to 1900, but hardly any earlier.

As to the antiquity of the course, there are several older ones, including the nine-holer at Niagara-on-the-Lake (1881) and Victoria's course at Oak Bay (1893). However, the Perth club does have a distinctive claim to fame: it once had a unique clubhouse – part of an old factory that had helped to produce the biggest cheese in the world.

The province of Quebec did not experience the same growth in golf as Ontario. For many years the game was to remain almost exclusively a recreation of the English-speaking minority in the province, which was concentrated in Montreal and the Eastern Townships. But not completely so. In 1896, some golfers organized a second club in Montreal, the Metropolitan, and some French-Canadians took up the game and joined.

Metropolitan took over Fletcher's Field when Royal Montreal moved out to Dixie. Within a short time, its membership was over 200, including some former members of Royal Montreal.

The American magazine *Golf*, in an issue of 1898, carried a few lines on the Metropolitan club, including these: "Most of the members are French, but the list comprises a few habitues of the old grounds, who found it difficult to suddenly wrench themselves from the pleasant associations of the past." There are no membership lists available today, but an examination of newspapers around the turn of the century reveals the names of some fifty golfers who played for Metropolitan in interclub matches. Only five appear to be French-Canadian, which seems a surprisingly low number, although it may be explained by the fact that the most experienced members would have been chosen to play for the club, and the French-Canadian members were new to the game.

The problems of having a public park and parade ground as a golf course persisted. In 1904, a Montreal newspaper reported that "the inspection of the Fifth District Garrison by the Earl of Dundonald on Fletcher's Field put the Metropolitan Club out of business for the afternoon." The Metropolitan clubhouse (the old park ranger's house) burned down in 1909, and at about this time the Montreal parks department appears to have put the club permanently out of business.

The Westmount Golf Club became the third club in, or close to, the city. Organized in the spring of 1900, it had a membership of 120 by the summer, nearly half of them women. It had two nine-hole courses in its short life, the first one of only 1,700 yards being on the side of the mountain, and the second situated on farmland west of Victoria Avenue.

The Reverend James Barclay of Royal Montreal was president of the Metropolitan GC for a spell; William Ramsay of Royal Montreal helped found the Westmount club, and was its president in 1903. The Westmount club did not survive the First World War.

In the Eastern Townships, within the span of a few months, golfers formed two clubs within walking distance of each other. An old St. Andrews player, D. L. Herbert, started a club at Lennoxville in 1896. A handful of golfers at Sherbrooke laid out a course and started golfing early that same year, but did not organize until 1897. The enthusiast behind this club was apparently A. J. Ready, manager of the Merchants Bank, who had previously golfed at Cove Fields, Quebec.

The proximity of these two clubs did much to guarantee their success. Within two years they each had more than forty members, including those of ladies' sections.

It is hard to say exactly when the Murray Bay Golf Club was formally organized. This watering-hole on the St. Lawrence, some seventy-five miles below Quebec, had been popular for many years with holidayers wishing to escape the summer heat of the cities of New York, Ontario, and Quebec.

Visitors staying at summer cottages, or at the local hotels, probably started golfing in the early 1890s. By one account, the Reverend James Barclay had a hand in planting golf in Murray Bay and in forming a club there in 1895. The game soon became so popular that the nine-hole course had to be enlarged to eighteen. Members of the club at the turn of the century included the Reverend Barclay and Alex MacPherson of Royal Montreal; Major Sheppard and W. A. Griffith of Royal Quebec; W. A. H. Kerr, W. H. Blake, and a young R. C. H. Cassels, all of Toronto GC. The club would play challenge matches against Royal Quebec and, not surprisingly, would usually win.

The Ile d'Orleans Golf Club claims on its score card that it was founded in 1868, which would make it the oldest golf club in the country. In its spring issue of 1989, the Quebec historical periodical *Cap-Aux-Diamants* repeats the claim that the anglophones who summered in St. Petronille (the nearest village on the island to Quebec City, as the crow flies) laid out a three- or four-hole course and formed a club. But the article also admits that the club was formed by members of Royal Quebec. That would give it a date later than 1875. It is easy to see why the golfers of Royal Quebec would want to golf on this beautiful island. But until we have more contemporary evidence, it is not possible to put a date on this club (which still plays over a nine-hole course on, I believe, the original site).

To the nineteenth-century golfers of Quebec City and Montreal, "the West" was Ontario, the interprovincial matches between Quebec and Ontario taking on the nature of a friendly rivalry between East and West.

Beyond Ontario lay the prairie province of Manitoba, which had come into Confederation in 1870, although as a smaller province than today's. Between Manitoba and British Columbia lay the sparsely populated North-West Territories, out of which were to be born, in 1905, the two other prairie provinces of Alberta and Saskatchewan.

The first Canadian golf course west of Brantford of which we have record was laid out at Stony Mountain in 1889. Stony Mountain was then a village of some two hundred people, about fifteen miles north of Winnipeg. It was, and still is, the site of the provincial penitentiary. The *Manitoba Free Press* reported in 1889

Lt.-Col. Samuel Bedson, warden of the Stony Mountain penitentiary near Winnipeg, who may have formed the first golf club in the West in 1889.

that the Warden, Lieutenant-Colonel Bedson, had laid out a nine-hole course and formed a golf club, presumably having been coerced by a Scottish inmate: "Taken all round, the Stony Mountain link is a hard one: knolls, bunkers (sandpits), ploughed land, burnt prairie, bushes, and long grass all helping its diversity." Three other persons are named in the article, but there is no evidence that they organized a golf club with an elected committee.

Golf at Stony Mountain seems to have died before 1894. In 1925, golfers in Stony Mountain formed the Assinawa Country Club, proclaiming at the time that this marked the revival of the pioneer golf club of the province. The Assinawa CC – now defunct – put on display an antique golf club said to have been made by a local mechanic for the first Stony Mountain golfers.

By 1894, Winnipeg was no longer the booming frontier town of the 1880s. The city of 27,000 had settled down to less spectacular growth and quiet respectability, confident of its place as the commercial capital of the West. The Grain Exchange and the banks closed early in the afternoon, and to a large extent lawyers and real-estate men could make their own working hours. There was a nucleus of middle- and upper-class businessmen with the means and the time to take part in a summer sport other than cricket, canoeing, riding, and shooting.

Few golfers have taken up the game with more earnestness and expedition than did the golfers of Winnipeg. On 20 June 1894, an itinerant Scot recently arrived in the city, John Harrison, wrote to the *Free Press* offering to help form a golf club, and to supply clubs and balls. A native of Musselburgh, East Lothian, Harrison had just come from Virden, then no more than a village on the CPR line, two hundred miles to the west. He had already organized a small golf club in Virden a year or so earlier.

The response to Harrison's letter was immediate and enthusiastic. Within three weeks, two meetings had been held, a pro-tem committee elected, a constitution drawn up, and on 7 July the Winnipeg Golf Club was formally established.

The first president was William Bain Scarth, president of the Board of Trade. A Scot from Binscarth in the Orkneys, Scarth had come to Canada as a youth. Since he had never been a member of a golf club, he accepted the presidency reluctantly, and only when it was pointed out that hardly a man present – Harrison being one exception – knew an iron from a driver. A real-estate company, the Norwood Improvement Company, offered the club the use of land at no cost. While a course was being laid out, the neophyte golfers took to the cricket ground for practice.

The nine holes of the Norwood links were opened for play on 14 July, within four weeks of Harrison's letter. By that date, there were seventy-seven members, a third of them women. But only a few had the implements of play. The stock of clubs and balls had been bought from the club at Virden and an order had been placed with a supplier in Toronto. On 20 August, a supply of cleeks, drivers, irons, and putters arrived from the East, together with twenty dozen balls, sent by William Scarth's brother, a member of Toronto GC.

On the day it opened, Winnipeg golfers claimed that their course would "compare favourably with any in America." (Who amongst them had seen another golf course, Harrison excepted?) In Winnipeg, this incomparable course lasted only four weeks. By the middle of August the Norwood links had been abandoned for a better site off Portage Avenue. This was to be the club's home for ten years.

This nine-hole course of only two thousand yards was flat and featureless, had few hazards, and was constantly being revamped in an attempt to add some variety. In 1896 a second nine was added for the ladies. At first a marquee served as a clubhouse, the ladies serving ice cream, tea, coffee, and lemonade. (A second tent offered "other liquid refreshment.") In 1895, the club splashed $385 on a clubhouse, to which they added a bicycle shed a year later. The *Free Press* reported that members became very attached to their "little red clubhouse."

Real estate was always a problem with the club, but not for the want of skilled advisors.

The first president, William Scarth, was land commissioner for the Canada North West Land Company, and a friend of Lamond Smith, Cochran, and Osler, of Toronto Golf Club. Other members included L. H. Smith, commissioner of Dominion government lands, Lauchlan A. Hamilton, land commissioner of the CPR in Winnipeg, and Walter R. Baker, executive agent for the CPR in Winnipeg.

Baker and Hamilton were to distinguish themselves later by service to golf in the East. Baker became president of Royal Montreal (1915–21) and a founding member and first president of the Canadian Seniors' Golf Association in 1918. Lauchlan Hamilton, having retired and gone back east, helped form the Mississauga Golf Club and became its very active president.

With the exception of John Harrison, who left in 1896, the club had no golfers of national ranking in its first thirteen years. Charles P. Wilson was possibly another exception. In the 1890s, he and Professor McDermid of the Deaf and Dumb Institute shared the club's championships. They both played off scratch, but that meant only that they could score in the middle 80s.

The Winnipeg GC had no other clubs within a reasonable distance until the Brandon GC

Charles P. Wilson was an early member of the first Winnipeg golf club in 1894; he became a VP of the Royal Canadian Golf Association in 1921, when the Amateur Championship was held in Winnipeg.

was formed in 1900. So it arranged matches in the northern United States, against Minikahda GC at St. Paul/Minneapolis, Minnesota, and Fargo GC in North Dakota.

Early in 1906, the property at Portage Avenue was purchased for development, and the club lost its course. To add to its misfortunes, only thirty-six members renewed their membership, the others having joined the new St. Charles Country Club. Some members were for closing the club, but a few struggled on, encouraged by an influx of immigrants from Ontario and Britain, which added some forty new members. It moved its course to near where it had started, in Norwood. There it survived, gloriously, until 1946.

Having returned to Norwood, it renamed itself Norwood Golf Club, in 1914. In 1909, some of its members had formed a new club, which they named The Winnipeg Golf Club Limited, with its course at Bird's Hill, just outside the city. But the members of Norwood insisted to the end that *it* was the premier club in the city.

The man who planted the seeds of golf at Virden and Winnipeg came to Manitoba in his late twenties. He farmed for about ten years before coming to Winnipeg. When invited to St. Paul, Minnesota, to help lay out a golf course in 1896, he was hailed by the press as "John Harrison of Musselburgh, Scotland, the champion and most skilled player in that country." That same year, he had tried to get golf started in Regina, but without success. He then left Winnipeg, to test himself as a professional in the United States.

The Winnipeg club sent a consignment of clubs and balls to a new club formed at Portage la Prairie in April 1896, with a Lieutenant-Colonel Anstruther as its president. The members were reportedly laying out a links on the eastern side of town.

In 1900, a Dr. Gillies, superintendent of the local asylum, and N. Marquis, of the Bank of British North America, had a club under way in Brandon. It had twenty members, none of whom had golfed in Britain. They played a number of matches against Winnipeg GC, in the early years of the century.

In the month Royal Montreal was playing its first match against Royal Quebec, the North-West Mounted Police (NWMP) were putting the finishing touches to Fort Calgary.

Six years later, when golfers in the East were playing in the first interprovincial match, Calgary was no more than a collection of tents, log buildings, and wooden shacks. By 1883, the CPR had arrived. A year later, the town of Calgary was incorporated, the second town, after Regina, in the North-West Territories.

When golf came to Calgary in 1895, the population was only four thousand, largely of British or Ontarian origin. The British influence was strong. Many of the ranchers came from the British landed gentry, many of the NWMP officers from British Army stock. So it is not surprising to find cricket, hunting, and polo the popular forms of recreation among the better-off citizens.

The Calgary Golf and Country Club conservatively dates itself back to 1897. But newspaper reports of the day show that golfers had organized in Calgary two years earlier. In April 1895, a small band of enthusiasts met and formed the Calgary Golf Club, with Justice Scott as its president.

The local newspapers paid no attention to the game until a challenge match in 1898 caught the public's fancy. J. H. Wilson, a Scot with the Imperial Bank (and a member of Royal Montreal a year earlier), was backed by his fellow club members to beat Mackenzie Grieve, from out of town, who claimed he was the champion of Wales. The stakes were one hundred dollars a side. A large crowd, many of them seeing golf for the first time, saw Wilson win.

It is not clear who brought golf to Calgary. William Toole seems as likely a person as any – if any one person was responsible. He had been in Winnipeg for five years as a land agent for the CPR, and could have played at the Winnipeg GC. His arrival in Calgary as a CPR district

The members of Calgary Golf Club, October 1899.

land agent coincided with the birth of the club.

William Toole went on to become the club's captain and president, as well as one of its better players around the turn of the century. And the Toole family were to serve the Calgary club over several generations. But in the early years, he, Justice Scott, John Young, and another judge, Horace Harvey, were equally strong supporters.

Several Critchleys – English ranchers outside Calgary – joined the club, and Oswald Critchley was vice-president in 1899. His greatest contribution to golf was fathering a son who became Brigadier-General Critchley, CMG, CBE, DSO. In the 1930s, "Critch" was a noted British amateur golfer. Later, he became director general of the British Overseas Airways Corporation.

In a town expanding as fast as Calgary, the club had to move its course every few years just to keep ahead of new building. The first course was probably sited just south of what is now Palliser Square. Around 1899, part of the course and the clubhouse (carried on the books at its cost price of seventy-five dollars) was moved further south. In 1902, a nine-hole course was laid out north of the Elbow River near 4th Street and 17th Avenue S.W., and this was expanded to eighteen holes by 1906. These links were all on leased land.

To pay for these moves and alterations, an entrance fee of one dollar had been introduced in 1899 for new members, the annual subscription remaining at three dollars for men and one dollar for ladies. Ladies made up a third of the membership from the beginning. They may have served tea in the clubhouse, but they were also keen and active golfers, playing for their weekly gold, silver, and brass buttons. The men, too, had their weekly button competitions. But Alberta now had several golf clubs, notably in Fort Macleod and Edmonton, and the first Alberta championships provided stiffer competition.

Golf probably came to Fort Macleod in the summer of 1895. In August of that year, the *Edmonton Bulletin* reported that "Macleod has a golf club," but this probably meant only that some residents of the Fort had taken up the game.

The *Macleod Gazette* reported the inaugural meeting of 30 September 1895, in the rectory of the rural dean, the Reverend Hilton. The other founding members were Inspector Gilbert Sanders of the NWMP; Charles E. D. Wood, editor and publisher of the *Gazette*; and Dr. Charles Haultain, a surgeon with the NWMP. We are told that Staff-Sergeant Heap of the NWMP "volunteered" to act as the pro-tem secretary.

The members elected Dr. Haultain president and appointed a committee of four to lay

Inspector Gilbert E. Sanders of the NWMP, a founding member of Macleod Golf Club in 1895, and president of Calgary Golf and Country Club in 1914.

Dr. Charles S. Haultain, a surgeon in the NWMP, the first president and club champion of the Macleod Golf Club.

out a golf links "at some point to be decided upon by them." By the third week of October, the committee had fixed on a course and had recruited many new members. The *Macleod Gazette* had problems with language when reporting the first competition held that week:

> The enthusiasm which was displayed over golf when it first made its appearance here still keeps up. Almost every day parties, sometimes small, sometimes large, are seen wending their way towards the links to enjoy a game . . . Dr. Haultain still holds the highest score of 52. He also holds the record for the longest put [sic] the score being 75 yards.

Charles Haultain probably introduced the game of golf to the residents of the Fort, since golf was in the Haultain blood. This branch of the Haultain family came to Canada in the

1870s from India, where the father was an officer in the British army. Theodore Arnold Haultain, a brother, was a member of the Toronto GC and later wrote some fine pieces on the game, including his book, *The Mystery of Golf* (1908), the first study of its psychological challenges. Charles had probably golfed at Toronto with his brother. A cousin, Frederick W. G. Haultain, had been the first lawyer in Fort Macleod. He was later to become the accepted premier of the North-West Territories, and the president of Regina Golf Club. In 1899, a W. G. Haultain was on the committee at Macleod GC. This would have been Wilmot Haultain, Frederick's brother. Wilmot had a varied career as a Manitoba rancher and as an engineer with the CPR. For twenty-five years he was the registrar of the Regina land-registration district.

Charles Wood had been a partner of F. W. G. Haultain, and before that he had a spell in the NWMP.

Inspector Gilbert Sanders, from Yale, British Columbia, had been schooled at King Alfred's in Yorkshire, and at the Royal Military College, Kingston, but long before these places had golf courses. The monocled Sanders was to become a much respected president of Calgary Golf and Country Club. His daughter married into the Toole family, which gave equally distinguished service to this club.

The enthusiasm of these early Macleod golfers was captured in an article that first appeared in a Winnipeg paper in the 1890s. This article was quoted in a local history, *Fort Macleod – Our Colourful Past* (1977). It reads, in part:

> . . . for golf enthusiasm, pure and simple, the Macleod Golf Club stands supreme. It is positively alarming and the infection seems to spread; from the oldest member to the newly elected novitiate the one topic is golf and golfing interests . . . At first, little or no notice was taken of the few who were seen armed with curious-looking clubs, wending their way towards the then very crude grounds that were made to serve as "links."
>
> The casual observor would report having seen these men striking attitudes, twisting themselves into corkscrew positions and, after making wild swoops into the air, would then wander apparently aimlessly into the next concession "casting their eyes down to the ground" and after an intermission of some twenty minutes, venture a repetition of their strange antics. They were simply regarded by [the] community as eccentric . . .
>
> The course is undulating and consists of nine holes, being about two and a half miles around; formidable bunkers in the shape of ploughed ground [have to be] surmounted not infrequently. Hazards formed by water courses there are more [none?] but this is not surprising, a Macleod man not having much use for water, other than his morning tub.

Charles Haultain soon set the record for the original nine-hole course at 43. But the layout was changed too many times in the first year or so to compare this score with those shot later.

The first two courses of the Macleod GC were in the east end of the town, close to the Old Man's River. The club moved to its present site on the west side of town early in the new century.

By 1897, the club had over fifty members, a third of them women, an excellent record for a town with less than one thousand citizens.

In 1896, the Hudson's Bay Company, through its local agent, Chipman, put up a silver cup "to assist in encouraging the playing of golf in Southern Alberta." The competition was open to members of any club south of Mosquito Creek, which joined the Little Bow River some fifty miles north of Fort Macleod. By this time, there were small golf clubs at the Peigan Reserve, North Fork, Lethbridge, and Pincher Creek, each perhaps with no more than five or six players. It had been hoped that some of these would enter. But, in the end, only six players from Fort Macleod took part. The winner, after a play-off, was Dr. Haultain. He was hailed as the Amateur Champion of Southern Alberta, which I suppose he was. His 109 for eighteen holes was another course record.

In the 1897 championship, the last man in the field of eight did not finish. We are told that "owing to the continued exposure to the rain having rendered Mr. Mathews' clubs useless, he was unable to finish his fourth round." His problem was probably more serious than wet grips. In those days, wooden clubs often had leather inserts on their faces, to protect them, and these soaked up moisture.

In this championship, Dr. George Kennedy looked as though he would tie for the lead when he lost his ball down a gopher hole. It says much for these Prairie golfers that they stuck to the rules of the R & A, and did not permit him to drop another ball without penalty. Clearly, there are no gopher holes at St. Andrews.

The Macleod Golf Club was not to become one of the great clubs of Alberta, but it did have its moments of glory. In 1919, the Prince of Wales played over its new course west of the town. The Fort Macleod History Book Committee refers to the club as "Royal Macleod Golf Club," probably on the strength of this visit, but there is no evidence that the club was granted the right to the *Royal* prefix.

Edmonton, a considerably larger town with almost double the population of Fort Macleod, did not have a golf club until 1896, a year after Calgary and Fort Macleod established theirs. It seems likely, however, that some of its cricketers and baseball players had taken up golf before this. A local store, Carpenter and Vaudin, was selling golf equipment in April 1896 and would hardly have stocked up on these long-delivery items without a visible market.

Unlike Calgary, Edmonton had not gathered around itself the same elitist society of ranchers, although its population of 1,700 was also made up largely of British and Ontarians. As early as 1891 these people had organized clubs for the British games of rugby, cricket, and tennis, as well as for the Canadian game of lacrosse. They had also laid out a racetrack and a sports ground.

The first president of the Edmonton Golf Club, R. A. Ruttan, may well have been the man who brought golf to the town. He was working in the Dominion Land Office in Winnipeg when golf hit that city, and an R. Ruttan was listed as a member of the Winnipeg GC in 1894. Ruttan came to Edmonton in July 1895, so the timing fits. But his role as the town's first golfer can only be conjecture. Other golfers visited Edmonton from time to time. Justice David Scott, who had helped start golf in Calgary, visited as a district judge. The ubiquitous NWMP, who had sponsored golf in Fort Macleod, kept coming and going. Inspector A. E. Snyder was a founding member at Edmonton, as were former Mounties Chalmers, McNicol, and Dr. Braithwaite.

In 1895, the *Edmonton Bulletin* had noted the formation of a golf club in Macleod, but the first indication that the game had spread to its own city came in this item in its issue of 6 April 1896:

> A meeting to organize a golf club was held in S. S. Taylor's law office on Saturday afternoon last. Fourteen persons were present,

and about thirty have signified their intention of joining. A committee consisting of Messrs. Ruttan, Turnbull, Edmiston, Lay and Jackson was appointed to draw up a constitution and by-laws, to invite members and to look up grounds.

The club held its inaugural meeting two weeks later in the office of McNicol (by now a local accountant and commission agent), electing a president (R. A. Ruttan) and a vice-president (Alex Taylor). Three of the committee, Chalmers, Slocock, and de Roux, were prominent cricketers who did not give up this game when they took to golf.

In its first year or so, the club probably had no more than twenty members, including a few ladies. During the season they practised Monday to Friday; on Saturday they competed for gold, silver, and bronze buttons.

The Edmonton GC had the most distinguished clubhouse in the West. Its first five-hole course was laid out on the river flats below Hardisty House (better known locally as the Big House), the one-time home of the chief factor of the Hudson's Bay Company. The club took over the house, with its two storeys and its balcony. One of the earliest photographs we have of golf in the Prairies shows the members of the club at their magnificent nineteenth hole. The clubhouse had to be incinerated in 1906, following an outbreak of smallpox.

A year later, the club had to move its course further west, when the government of the new province of Alberta decided to build its legislative assembly on the land. The club's new seven-hole course, later expanded to nine, was only a stop-gap. By 1912, the Hudson's Bay Company had sold the land to the city for a park, so new property was purchased on the river, some eight miles upstream. The club now reorganized as the Edmonton Country Club. The city, in its wisdom, took over the old course, converting part of it into Victoria Park Golf Course, Canada's first public golfing facility.

Members of the first Edmonton Golf Club at their clubhouse, the former Hardisty House.

The links of the Edmonton Golf Club, 1900.

Organized golf came to Saskatchewan in 1899, six years before Saskatchewan became a province. At the turn of the century, its population was about 90,000, of whom 82,000 lived in rural communities and only 8,000 in towns like Regina (the seat of the Territories' government and the headquarters of the NWMP), Saskatoon, Moose Jaw, Prince Albert, and Swift Current. There were no cities in Saskatchewan. You needed 5,000 people to be a city.

About 50 per cent of the population had British roots. Many of them were Scots. In Regina, the Sons of Scotland set itself up in 1896, held Caledonian Games, and helped to revive the curling club.

The ubiquitous John Harrison, having successfully planted golf in Virden and Winnipeg, tried to do the same in Regina. *The Leader* of 19 March 1896 carried a notice of a meeting to organize a golf club. But Harrison was not the active catalyst he had been elsewhere, and there is no evidence that golfers formed a club.

In 1899, John Kelso Hunter, a local civil servant, was one of several who considered that the time was now right to organize. As the new golf club's provisional secretary, he canvassed the town for members, got permission to use some Canada North West Land Company property as a course, and had Lieutenant-Governor Forget agree to be the club's honorary president.

The charter members of the Regina Golf Club met in May, electing F. W. G. Haultain president and Hunter secretary-treasurer. They included R. S. Barrow, manager of the Union Bank; Rogers and Green, local merchants; Peterson, the Deputy Commissioner of Agriculture; Mackenzie and Johnstone, barristers; Peters, a civil servant; Gilpin Brown of the NWMP; Greentree, an accountant in the Bank of Montreal; and J. A. Kerr, a local hardware merchant who had laid in a supply of clubs and balls for his fellow members.

Some of the moving spirits behind the Regina Golf Club were certainly familiar with the game and had probably played it before.

J. Kelso Hunter, first secretary of Regina GC.

John Kelso Hunter, a lawyer in Regina's land titles office, had come to Canada in 1892 from Glasgow, Scotland. In 1899, he was in his early thirties. He was to remain the club's secretary-treasurer for fourteen years, and was then made an honorary member. It was Hunter who laid out the club's first nine–hole course.

Robert Barrow was born and bred in Quebec City and no doubt witnessed golf on Cove Fields. Other charter members had names that suggest a Scottish background.

In its first year, the club was beholden to the Canada North West Land Company, which gave the club the right to lay out its first course on company land, just north of the Wascana Creek, in an area now bounded mainly by Albert Street and College Avenue. The company also made an empty house on Retallack Street available as a clubhouse.

But the Regina club, and golf in the city, owes as great a debt to the NWMP. When the club's first course became infested with cows

Commissioner Perry of the NWMP, a member and good friend of the Regina Golf Club during its formative years.

and mosquitoes, in 1901, Assistant Commissioner Perry offered the club the use of a course and a clubhouse at the barracks, where he and his daughters soon took up the game. In 1906, when the club moved once again, Perry formed an officers' golf club at the barracks.

Alexander Angus, manager of the local Bank of Montreal, joined the club around 1902. In 1906, he was elected president, a post he held until 1920. Under his leadership, the club moved back to the site of its original course and built a new clubhouse. Among its new members was Scottish banker W. S. Gray. When the club organized a provincial championship in 1908, Gray was the first winner, with J. Kelso Hunter runner-up.

In 1911, Commissioner Perry came to the rescue of the Regina club again. When it lost its third course to an expanding city, he invited it to take over the NWMP course at the barracks, which it did. It has been there ever since.

These constant moves and a wish to get away from the city led some members to plan the Wascana Country Club, offering golf, tennis, and other sports. Outside the Wascana club-

The clubhouse of the Regina Golf Club at the RCMP Barracks course, about 1923.

house today stands a plaque honouring the men who were its charter members on 16 June 1911.

By the time the Wascana club had been formed, golf clubs were to be found at Saskatoon (1907), Prince Albert (1908), Sedley (1908), and Moose Jaw (1910). The town of Qu'Appelle has claimed that it, too, had a golf club in 1899, but I have not been able to confirm this.

Golf first came to the Northwest Territories in, I believe, 1947, when it reached Yellowknife, more than six hundred miles north of Edmonton. This city was a product of the gold rush of the 1930s. Yellowknife golfers boast of this advantage – in the summer they may play golf for twenty-four hours a day, if they are so inclined.

Like courses in the Middle East, the Yellowknife course was all sand, with doormat tees and oiled "greens" (or browns) and a rough of tundra and bog. Golf architect Stanley Thompson happened to visit the course in 1948, but could not suggest any improvements. ("Why put in bunkers? The whole course is a sandtrap.") Hazards included mosquitoes and black flies, and – at one time – ravens that made off with the ball. (Golfers were permitted to carry .22 rifles or shotguns.)

Golf at midnight on the Yellowknife course.

The unique clubhouse of the Yellowknife Golf Club.

For a few years, Yellowknife GC had a unique clubhouse – I say that without fear of contradiction. In 1949, an RAF DC-3 crashed near the course, and the members hauled part of the fuselage to the course. When this makeshift clubhouse was removed, Giant Mines donated a building to take its place.

Yellowknife is not our most northerly golf course. In 1974, a bunch of enthusiasts laid one out on an island at Tuktoyaktuk. Most of the original players were Inuit who had watched the Canadian Open on television.

The intricacies of its place names reveal the British roots of Canada's most westerly province.

British Columbia had been formed by the union of two British crown colonies. The one on the mainland had been christened New Caledonia by the Hudson's Bay fur traders, but Queen Victoria preferred the name British Columbia. She also named its capital New Westminster. The other crown colony, Vancouver Island, had taken its name from the British sea captain who had helped put it on the map. Its capital was Victoria, after the queen.

When the province was formed by the union of the two, it assumed the name of the mainland colony, British Columbia. But its seat of government was in Victoria, on the island. To further complicate matters, what was to become the prominent city of the mainland was given the name Vancouver.

With the completion of the trans-Canada railway, the population of its terminus, Vancouver, rapidly overtook that of Victoria. By the time organized golf reached these cities in the early 1890s, both had some fifteen thousand citizens, three-quarters of them of British stock.

True to their roots, the people of the province played soccer, cricket, and tennis, as well as the Canadian lacrosse and the American baseball. But the love of the wealthier citizens was the sea.

We do not know for sure when golf reached B.C. or in whose ship. But Captain Cook, who was acquainted with the game, was among the first to lay outside eyes on Canada's Pacific shores, in 1778. The United States Golf Association's museum has a painting of the captain standing with a golf club in his hand, his ship *Endeavour* in the background. The painting is said to represent the captain at Sandwich. But since the Sandwich in the south of England did not have a golf club until the late nineteenth century, this is obviously Cook at the Sandwich Islands (since renamed the Hawaiian Islands). Cook went ashore there in January 1778. In March, he sailed up the west coast of North America, seeing what is now Vancouver Island, anchoring in what is now Nootka Sound. On an earlier voyage in 1770, he had anchored at Botany Bay, Australia. Here, the naturalist Joseph (later Sir Joseph) Banks went ashore and played golf, a fact recorded in Banks's biography by author Hector C. Cameron.

So it is perhaps not stretching a point too much to say that Cook was the first golfer to see the attractions of the province.

The golfers of the British Columbia coastal plain and island have this great advantage over other Canadians – their climate is such that they can golf for twelve months of the year, time and money permitting. But in the beginning, golf was a winter game. Cricket and sailing, and the cows grazing on the course, kept it a winter game for some years.

Today's Vancouver Golf Club was not organized until 1910. It is the second club to bear this name.

For a full account of the first club in Vancouver, we are indebted to one of its early members, Francis M. Chaldecott. Born in Surrey, England, in 1863, Chaldecott practised law in England before coming to British Columbia in 1890. He was admitted to the B.C. Supreme Court in 1891. If he had played golf in England, he makes no mention of it.

In 1921, he published a note giving his account of early golf in Vancouver, revising this in 1935. He shows a Vancouver Golf Club in continuous existence from 1892 to 1899. During this time it underwent two reorganizations and moved its headquarters twice, but it always had regularly constituted committees to run its affairs.

The moving spirits behind the formation of the club appear to have been the Bell-Irving brothers, Henry and Duncan. They were born in Lockerbie, Dumfriesshire (a village brought to the world's attention in 1988, when a sabotaged plane crashed there). Duncan was the first to come to Vancouver, in 1883. Educated at the universities of Glasgow and Heidelberg, he became Vancouver's first doctor and one of the first staff at the city's hospital. His brother, Henry, arrived two years later. As a twenty-nine-year-old civil engineer trained in Germany, Henry worked on the CPR railway. By the time we meet him on the links, he is making his fortune in fish-packing with his Anglo B.C. Packing Company, which was soon to be the largest sockeye company in the world.

Dr. Duncan Bell-Irving called a meeting in November 1892, and a dozen or so local professional men and merchants formed the Vancouver Golf Club. For his pains, Duncan Bell-Irving was elected secretary, but there is no record of the other office-bearers.

In its short life of eight years, the club played over three courses, all of nine holes. Duncan Bell-Irving, T. S. C. Saunders, G. A. Hankey, Henry Hulbert, and F. M. MacIver-Campbell laid out the first course on the flats at Jericho, overlooking English Bay. (Thomas Saunders is better known as an international cricketer, but he had probably golfed in Toronto, where his brother was a member of the Toronto Golf Club.)

The Dalgleish house, which became the clubhouse of Jericho Country Club.

At Jericho, John Moody Dalgleish, a Scot who had a lease on the property, gave them unsolicited but welcome advice. With nostalgic tears in his eyes, Dalgleish admitted that the process of laying out a golf course reminded him of his boyhood days in St. Andrews. As Chaldecott describes it, this course was a pretty rudimentary affair:

> The fairways were mostly sand, but the greens were passable. Drift logs were strewn everywhere and had to be hauled to one side so as to make the fairway about two hundred feet wide. A badly played stroke would often result in the ball coming to rest under a pile of drift logs . . .

This course was literally washed away during a gale in the winter of 1894.

The club laid out its second links on the grounds of the Brockton Park Athletic Club, in Stanley Park, a short course of less than eighteen hundred yards. City regulations forbade Sunday play. What is more, the course encompassed the cricket and lacrosse fields, and golfers had to yield to players of these sports. All were in danger of being struck.

After three years of this, the club moved to the north shore of the Burrard Inlet, between the Lynn and Seymour creeks. Here they laid out a course on the old Moodyville Rifle Range, at a cost of thirty-five dollars. ("The only impediment was an occasional cow"). The first clubhouse in 1892 had been a small, two-roomed shack, bought from fishermen. Now the thirty or so members (not including wives and daughters, who were honorary members) could use the Moodyville Hotel.

The club played at the Moodyville links until June 1899. Then, for reasons not given by Chaldecott, the club disbanded. Perhaps it lost its course again or its members became disenchanted, put off by having to take a ferry to get to the course.

That there was still a demand for a golf course in Vancouver is clear from the several attempts to revive the club over the next few years. In 1902, CPR agreed to lay out a golf course on its property. Many of its executives were, or were to become, keen golfers. Richard Marpole, born in Wales, was superintendent of construction and operation of CPR's Pacific division. Under his supervision, Chaldecott and Dr. Graham Colin Campbell started to construct a course at Point Grey. But the CPR's land department put the project on hold, and it was eventually abandoned.

Two years later, in July 1904, encouraged by promises from over 130 prospective members, another unsuccessful effort was made to revive the old club, by, amongst others, Chaldecott and Campbell Sweeney, Superintendent of the Bank of Montreal in British Columbia. (Sweeney's son was later to marry Violet Pooley, the province's finest female player of her generation.)

More than a year later, in November 1905, a group of enthusiasts started to lay out a course at Eburne, near the present Vancouver airport, but this scheme, too, was discarded. In the meantime, another group was having more success.

The Jericho Syndicate Limited was incorporated in June 1905 as a holding company for the planned Jericho Country Club. *The Daily Province* reported that the 123 members of the syndicate "agreed on a favourable location, subscribed the required funds to purchase the freehold premises, construct and finish the club house, lay out grounds, make the golf course, and do all dyking, draining, road making and other preliminary work."

The syndicate leased sixty-nine acres of land, part of the Admiralty Reserve at Jericho, near where the first course of the Vancouver Golf Club had been in 1892. It laid out a nine-hole course, bought and reconstructed the old Dalgleish house as a clubhouse, and opened for play in 1907. Many of its members were those who had tried unsuccessfully to organize a club in previous years. Harry Abbott was the first president of the new club; Chaldecott, Marpole, and James Waghorn (a former Winnipeg golfer) were on the committee. Jericho Country Club was to be a leading club in the province until it lost its course and disbanded during the Second World War.

Dr. Duncan Bell-Irving, one of two brothers who introduced golf to Vancouver in 1892.

Campbell Sweeney, the pioneer Vancouver golfer who tried to re-introduce golf to the city in 1904, was to become father-in-law of Violet Pooley Sweeney, B.C.'s finest woman golfer in the early decades of this century.

One colourful tale has golf being played at Beacon Hill, Victoria, some years before the Victoria Golf Club was organized. In 1943, a Vancouver newspaper cited Harry Pooley, KC, a former attorney general of the province, who claimed that he had helped to lay out a golf course on Beacon Hill, in 1889. The inspiration – Pooley tells us – was a character named Wastie Green, "an odd but highly educated chap" who had once been tutor to the Prince of Siam. Under the direction of the retired and knowledgeable Mr. Green, Harry Pooley and Heben Gillespie laid out a course of seven holes. Green's golf clubs were said to have been put on display in the window of T. N. Hibben and Company's stationery store in Victoria with the sign: "These are golf sticks, the national game of Scotland."

Such is the legend. The source is unimpeachable; the name, Wastie Green, too improbable to be a fiction. Harry Pooley, born in 1878, would only have been ten or eleven at the time.

In or about 1921, when Francis Chaldecott was writing of early golf in Vancouver, he tried to establish where golf had first been played in the province. He met or corresponded with Colonel G. E. Barnes, an Edinburgh Scot who had been with the Royal Marine Artillery in Victoria, whose officers used the United Service Club. Barnes recalled that he and a fellow officer, Templer, arrived at the local barracks in August 1893 and laid out a golf course in October. Barnes claimed they first played over the United Service Club links in late 1893 or early 1894. The golf section of the United Service Club (or the United Service Golf Club) appears to have been formed early in 1894.

In 1922, the club moved its course to Cadboro Bay, renaming itself Uplands Golf Club. J. D. Peden authored an informative history of the club in 1982.

Neither Barnes nor Chaldecott mentions golf being played in Victoria before 1893. Chaldecott wrote: "Sir Frank Barnard is certain that no golf was played in Victoria before the spring of 1893, and certainly there was no organized club before that date." Those civilians who played golf in or about the spring of 1893 were those who organized the Victoria Golf Club in November of that year.

The Victoria Golf Club, organized on Vancouver Island in 1893, suffered none of the vicissitudes of the Vancouver club. There are several fairly obvious reasons for this. For one thing, the older city of Victoria had already settled into a period of stability and slow growth. There was little fear of its golf course at Oak Bay being swallowed by commercial or residential expansion. For another, the course was no temporary affair likely to be washed away by the tide. It is still there. It has always been one of the most attractive in the country.

The nature of Victoria was quite different from the fast-growing railway terminus on the mainland. As a summer resort for tourists, it offered fine scenery, English country roads, and just about every form of summer sport. Too, Victoria society was quite distinct from that of the mainland. Originally a Hudson's Bay town established by Scottish fur-traders, its character was now unmistakably English. It was developing into the type of society which S. W. Jackman describes in his book *Vancouver Island* (1972):

> . . . a large proportion of the population was made up of a very special strata of British society. Oak Bay, Duncan and Maple Bay, for example, had a high proportion of retired naval and military officers, and also colonial civil servants. These people perpetuated an "English" way of life which, however, was not exactly the same as in England itself. Rather it tended to be a somewhat nostalgic and unreal re-creation. Tea, cricket, the Church of England, tweed suits and the like were all carefully preserved . . . They never really became a part of Canada.

The very "English" nature of Victoria is noticeable in the backgrounds of those who formed the Victoria Golf Club. Whereas the clubs in Quebec and Ontario had been organized largely by immigrant Scots and Canadians of Scottish descent, many of the early members of the Victoria club had their roots in England and had been educated there. Most came from the ranks of the local aristocracy, the sons and daughters of well-known and well-to-do families – the Tyrwhitt-Drakes, Luxtons, Wards, Priors, Wilsons, Langleys, and the like. Already members of the yacht and cricket clubs, they took to golf only a few years after it had become a popular sport in the Old Country – which to them meant England.

The club they formed, the Victoria Golf Club, remains the oldest surviving golf club west of Ontario, and the oldest on the west coast of North America. The course laid out in 1893 is the oldest in Canada to have been in continuous operation. (The Niagara course is older, but was used as a camp during the First World War.)

The club owes its existence to two or three enthusiastic golfers. Sir Richard Musgrave, a native of Waterford, Ireland, came to B.C. in 1885. He married a daughter of Robert Dunsmuir, a Scot from Ayrshire and one of the richest patriarchs of the city.

Harvey Combe, born near Guildford, England, in 1860, was educated at an English public school, Charterhouse, and came to B.C., where he was Registrar of the Supreme Court, in the late 1880s. He discovered golf while vacationing in England and came back to the province with a set of clubs and a determination to share the joys of the game with his friends.

The land at Oak Bay that was to become the golf course was part of the large estate of Joseph D. Pemberton, the province's first surveyor-general. Many years after the event, Pemberton's daughter recalled that three young men – Musgrave, Combe, and Charles Prior – called to see her father, seeking permission to golf on his land at Oak Bay. Permission was granted. This was probably in the spring or summer of 1893.

On 7 November, Sir Richard Musgrave chaired a meeting of prospective golfers, who "resolved to form themselves into a Golf Club to be styled the Victoria Golf Club." Some of them may have golfed in Britain: Richard Musgrave and George Alan Kirk, who may have golfed while in the Royal Navy; Arthur P. Luxton, who had been born and bred in Devon; William A. Ward, who had completed his education at a school next to the Royal North Devon Golf Club; Judge Brian Tyrwhitt-Drake, who had been educated at England's Charterhouse, and whose family were prominent golfers in England; and George Gillespie, who had been born in Quebec City, educated in Scotland, and had spent his formative years with the Royal Bank of Scotland in Edinburgh.

Lieutenant-Governor Dewdney agreed to be the club's first president (he had served in the same capacity for Royal Ottawa in 1891). The members of the Pemberton family were made honorary members, since the land was theirs. Several of them golfed at the club and, in later years, helped to run its affairs.

The members laid out their own course and looked after its construction. The ground leased from the Pemberton family amounted to some 190 acres bordering on the Juan de Fuca Strait. This was rough grassland, used for grazing, thick with brush and gorse and strewn with rocks. It had to be cleared by hand, under the supervision of members. As for labour, the club's accounts record that "two chinamen work[ed] on links for 11 days at $2.50 a day = $27.50."

The grand sum of twenty-two dollars was spent on construction equipment: a garden roller, wheelbarrow, stampel, spade, trowel, and two rakes. Another ten dollars went on twelve flagpoles, nine sand boxes (to hold sand for tees), and two dozen flags.

Over the next two years, a further stretch of land was cleared, part of it so wooded that trees had to be felled and uprooted. By September 1895 the club had eighteen holes in play, the first course of this size in Canada. What is now Beach Drive crossed some of the fairways, so that golfers had to play over the road, which constituted one of the major hazards, for both golfer and passer-by.

In the 1894–95 season, about $70 of the club's $360 income went on the wages of two part-time groundsmen. As membership increased from sixty (forty men, twenty women) to eighty (fifty men, thirty women) and as entrance fees and annual dues went up, the club could afford to spend about three hundred dollars in the season of 1899–1900. A trifling sum to spend on an eighteen-hole course. Perhaps better than any words, these figures give us an idea of just how rough and ready, how close to their natural state, these early Canadian golf courses really were.

By 1900, the course measured some 4,900 yards. It was then, and has remained, one of the most picturesque golf courses in the world. Rudyard Kipling visited Oak Bay in 1892, and again in 1907, and had this to say of it:

> You must take all the eye admires most in Bournemouth, Torquay, Isle of Wight, The Doon, Sorrento, and Campo Bay; all reminiscences of the Thousand Islands, and arrange the whole around the Bay of Naples with some Himalayas for background.

Many of the holes were laid out along the shoreline. The golfer could see to the south the Olympic Mountains of Washington, and to the south and west the blue-green waters of the Juan de Fuca Strait; to the east, Haro Strait, the Juan de Fuca Islands, and, on a clear day, the peak of Mount Baker. A poor round of golf has many consolations on such a course.

There is a tale that the first locker-room – if you can call it that – was a box once used to ship a piano to the Pembertons. In 1894, a clubhouse (called "the pavilion") was erected at a cost of fifty-five dollars, and as much again was spent on paint and furnishings.

Most members came to the club by streetcar. "The Golfers' Special" ran from downtown Victoria to within a five-minute walk of the club.

The golf season was October to May. For many years, the club could not use its course in the summer months, since the Pembertons rented out the grounds for grazing. When constructing the course, the members had got rid of the long grass by setting fire to it. The Pembertons naturally enough forbade this, and thereafter it had to be kept short by grazing or cutting. A proposal to spend $130 on the latest in cutting machines – a thirty-inch, horse-drawn Pennsylvania mower – must have been defeated, for shortly afterward a local butcher was given grazing rights for his sheep.

The course of Victoria Golf Club with Trial Island in the background, early in this century.

In any event, the rocks on the course would have blunted the blades of any mower. These were to be a continuing problem, leading the club to adopt a local rule, whereby "If a ball be against rock (rock including all stone) the player may lift his ball and drop it a club's length behind the spot where it lay, with the loss of a stroke, or a club's length behind the spot where it entered the hazzard [sic] with the same penalty." In those days, hazards were all-embracing, and not confined to bunkers and water hazards.

A few experienced Scottish golfers joined the club in the early years. F. H. Maitland Dougall was a member within a day or so of the inaugural meeting, went on the committee, and soon held the course record with an 85. He was the son of Admiral Maitland Dougall of the R & A. (The Admiral is best remembered for having won the Royal & Ancient Autumn Medal in 1860. This was played in a gale, and he stepped onto the first tee having spent the previous five hours in a lifeboat, helping a ship in distress.) The son, F. H., was also well-known at St. Andrews and in English golfing circles. Among other events, he won several scratch prizes at the Royal Liverpool Golf Club, between 1876 and 1884 (playing in the same events as James Hunter, of Quebec fame, and Alex Dennistoun of Royal Montreal).

Another St. Andrews man was soon to equal Maitland Dougall's course record. William E. Oliver, the Dominion Surveyor, joined in October 1894. He was to win many club competitions, as well as the B.C. Amateur Championship in 1895 (when it was first held) and in 1896. Yet a third St. Andrean, Dr. F. H. Stirling, became a member around 1898. But he was not to win his one and only B.C. title until 1907. By then, Harvey Combe had overtaken both Oliver and Stirling as the club's and the province's leading male golfer.

Harvey Combe was the club's and the province's outstanding male golfer before the First World War. Mrs. Charlotte Combe became one of the leading women golfers in the province, as did their daughter, Nora (later Mrs. Hew Paterson).

William E. Oliver of Victoria Golf Club, the first B.C. amateur champion in 1895.

Harvey Combe won the B.C. Amateur Championship nine times between 1897 and 1909. Strangely, he never did win the championship of the Pacific Northwest Golf Association (PNGA). He came to prominence at about the same time as George S. Lyon in Ontario, and was, like Lyon, a self-taught golfer who had taken up golf late in life. Combe was to B.C. golf what Lyon was to golf in the East. But he was constrained by geography from taking part in Canadian national championships, so the two never did meet.

Combe was the secretary of the Victoria Golf Club in 1900 and then – more or less full-time – from 1905 to 1918. He died in 1922, at the age of sixty-two.

Mrs. Charlotte Margaret Combe was the club's finest player in its formative years. Gradually Mrs. Langley, and then one of the Miss Tyrwhitt-Drakes, came to share with her the club's and the province's golf honours. Between them, these three were to win eleven out of the thirteen B.C. Ladies' championships held between 1895 and 1907.

In the PNGA championships, Victoria's women were much more successful than its men – Miss Drake (1901), Mrs. Langley (1908), and Nora Combe (1910 and 1911) winning this title. What little opposition they had inside the province (before the Jericho Country Club got under way in 1907) was at the United Service Club. It was here that the province's most famous player of the pre-First World War era started her golf. We will meet later with Violet Pooley Sweeney.

A well-known Fifeshire golfer, H. Thomas Peter wrote his *Reminiscences of Golf and Golfers* (1890) while living with a relative in or near Victoria. In 1895 he wrote a short account of the Victoria Golf Club in a letter to a friend. When publishing his letter that year, the British magazine *Golf* referred to the Victoria golfers by their initials, but "O" is almost certainly William Oliver. Tom Peter wrote in part:

> The links are about three miles out of town, at a suburb called Oak Bay, and the electric tram goes within a mile of them, so one gets easily to them at a charge of five cents . . . I went out . . . to see them, and was agreeably surprised. The course has nine holes and good turf at this season, but there is still a want of bunkers. However, the public road is crossed twice which is bunker enough for many. One sees some peculiar styles. One chap, in putting with an iron, had one hand on the leather, and the other down on the socket, giving him a droll shape. I saw two really good players, a young fellow, O——, who is from Edinburgh, and came here a year ago, and has the true golfing style . . .
>
> I retired into the "pavilion", as the Golf-house is called here, and had tea and bun given me by one of the lady players; so I fared well . . . Clubs and balls from the old country have been imported. The clubs are mostly of Forgan's make – some by Tom Morris, and another man, Ayres I think. In shape, the wooden clubs differ a good deal from what I was accustomed to – shorter in the face and dumpier – they seem good tools. The cleeks and irons are very like what they were; the balls ditto. . . .

Golfers were active in New Westminster on the mainland from the middle of the 1890s to at least the early years of the new century. In September 1894, the secretary of the Victoria Golf Club was asked to get in touch with the golf clubs at Vancouver and New Westminster, to invite them to subscribe towards a B.C. championship cup. There is no record of their response.

Again, in April 1895, the *Victoria Daily Times* recorded the scores at "The New Westminster Links," including that of R. P. Sharp,

The streetcar "Golfers' Special" that ran from Victoria to the Oak Bay course of Victoria Golf Club. Some of the golfers on this car seem to be carrying their clubs loose, not in a bag.

a noted B.C. architect. And in their book, *New Westminster: The Royal City* (1958), Barry Mather and Margaret McDonald record that at New Westminster's Moody Park golf was one of several sports being enjoyed in 1903, so there was a golf club, or at least a golf course, in that city around the turn of the century. But its members do not appear to have taken part in any of the B.C. championships under the name of the New Westminster club.

The three provinces of Nova Scotia, New Brunswick, and Prince Edward Island joined the confederation of Canada between 1867 and 1873, and are now referred to as the Maritime provinces, or the Maritimes.

The island of Newfoundland remained a British colony until 1949, when it became Canada's tenth province. Together with the Maritime provinces, it makes up Atlantic Canada.

For many years the main cities of the Maritimes were garrisoned by British troops. Around 1870, these troops were withdrawn, with the exception that they stayed on in Halifax, Nova Scotia, as they did in Victoria, B.C. And, as in Victoria, the troops in Halifax introduced and perpetuated the British summer sports of cricket and tennis. If they played golf before 1896, there seems to be no record of it. After this date, the servicemen stationed in the Maritimes, together with officers from visiting warships, provided competition for local golfers.

Thirty years before golfers organized themselves into clubs, a few practised their game on the shores of the Atlantic. In the 1930s, a claim was put forward on behalf of John White that he was "the originator of golf in the Maritime Provinces." White came to Saint John, New Brunswick in 1862, a young Scottish bank clerk looking for a job. He first worked for an auctioneer, before setting up his own furniture business. John White had played golf in his home town of Lundin Mill, Fifeshire. Naturally, he brought his clubs to Canada, one of them, inevitably, bought from Old Tom Morris at St. Andrews.

John White practised on the sand flats at Saint John when the tide was out, since the few acres of farm land in or near the city were too much in demand to be used for sport. When the Saint John Golf Club was formed in 1897, he joined. Until well into the 1920s, his red-jacketed figure played over its fairways, often in a foursome with his daughter, granddaughter, and great-grandson.

In Nova Scotia, as we have seen, James B. Forgan and two other junior bank clerks practised their golf over the South Common at Halifax, in 1873.

It has also been claimed that golfers were playing at St. Andrews, N.B., before the Algonquin Golf Club was formed in the spring of 1895. At about the same time, golfers organized the first Sydney Golf Club in Cape Breton, Nova Scotia. Golf then spread rapidly. There were soon clubs at Halifax (1896), Saint John (1897), Fredericton, N.B. (1897), and Woodstock, N.B. (1899). The earliest club in Prince Edward Island was the Charlottetown club (1902); in Newfoundland, golfers are said to have been playing before the turn of the century, but they did not organize the Bally Haly club until 1908 or later. Since the first Sydney club failed after a few years, the oldest continuous club in Atlantic Canada appears to be the Algonquin club at St. Andrews.

St. Andrews-by-the-Sea is a popular resort on the Atlantic, close to the border with Massachusetts. To this day, its population is no more than two thousand. Many people have retired there, attracted by its slow pace of life. The atmosphere has, or had, an English flavour, not unlike that of Victoria, B.C. The Algonquin Golf Club was, from the beginning, a resort club, depending largely on summer visitors.

The town of St. Andrews was rediscovered as a tourist attraction in the 1880s. When the CPR took over the local railway in 1890, several CPR officers – among them Van Horne – built summer houses at St. Andrews. It soon acquired a faithful clientelle of visitors, some having their own houses or cottages, others staying at the CPR's Algonquin Hotel: Americans from New England and New York, Canadians from Quebec and Ontario as well as from the Maritimes.

In the early 1890s, golf was spreading in the environs of Boston and New York, and the Americans who came to St. Andrews had a natural need to play their newly acquired sport when on vacation. The same could be said of Canadians. So a golf course was constructed in response to the demand. In retrospect, we can see that the town would hardly have prospered as a resort in the way it did, without golf.

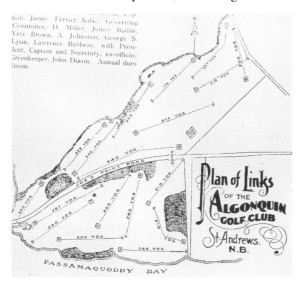

A plan of the course of the Algonquin Golf Club in 1898.

A photograph captioned "Golf Links at Peacock's Farm," and probably taken of the Algonquin course in the early years of this century.

The Algonquin Golf Club was organized mainly by the efforts of a few men, including the Reverend James Barclay of Montreal. In 1894 or 1895, he took his clubs to St. Andrews, one of his favourite resorts. He was soon joined by other Montreal enthusiasts, notably Frederick Stancliffe. In the early summer of 1895, the Reverend Barclay and W. P. Winch of Boston laid out a few holes in front of the Algonquin Hotel, and the hotel guests and others started to play there. Many years later, Earl Stinson of St. Andrews recalled caddying on this five-hole course as a boy, and he fixed the date as 1889. But there is more compelling evidence, in the form of articles published in the American magazine *Golf* in 1898, that the course's first year was indeed 1895.

This first course was soon abandoned as being too short, and too dangerous to passers-by, because of flying golf balls. Later in the same year, the Reverend Barclay and Winch, together

A CPR advertisement for the Algonquin.

with two other Bostonians, T. R. Wheelock and R. S. Gardner, laid out a new nine-hole course on grazing land at St. Joe's Point, overlooking the scenic Passamaquoddy Bay. At the same time, the players organized themselves into the Algonquin Golf Club. Winch was elected president, Wheelock, secretary and treasurer.

Within two years, the club's membership was over one hundred, and the course had been expanded to eighteen holes and 4,320 yards. A scenic course, to be true, but one with little variation in the length of its holes; sixteen of the eighteen measured 200 to 287 yards. But after CPR bought the property in 1905, the Algonquin course never looked back.

Some of the finest golfers in eastern Canada and the United States summered in St. Andrews-by-the-Sea, including several members of the Forgan family, then in Chicago, so the Algonquin Golf Club could field a for-midable team. Its matches were played mainly against Saint John. Typically, in 1900, these clubs played three times, Algonquin winning them all. In-deed, it went through the series of four-somes (or four-balls) without losing a match.

The sight of golfers playing at St. Andrews may have prompted sportsmen in Saint John to take up the game, as they did in 1897. It seems just as likely that the persuasion came from Fred T. Short.

Born and bred in New Brunswick, Short had been sent by his employer, the Bank of British North America, to work for its branch in New York. He helped form the Staten Island Golf Club, and became such a keen golfer that he was fined for playing at the club on a Sunday. When the bank transferred him back to Saint John in 1896, he joined a long list of golfing missionaries employed by this far-sighted institution. He became a leading advocate of the game in the province, so that his name pops up from time to time in connection with a number of clubs over the years.

Land was scarce in Saint John, so Short and his friends had difficulty in finding a suitable ground on which to play. In April 1897, together with William H. (later Senator) Thorne

and George West Jones, he drove golf balls over the fields of the Millidge farm (a mile from the city centre) to reassure the farmer, Mr. Millidge, that golf was no menace to live-stock. That accomplished, they rented grazing land on which to lay out a nine-hole course. In May, they called a meeting of some twenty prospective golfers and organized the Saint John Golf Club.

Elected president and captain was William Thorne, who owned one of the largest hard-ware companies in the Maritimes. The vice-president, John Douglas Hazen, QC, a member of an old loyalist family and former mayor of Fredericton, later became premier of the province. Members included Hugh Hazen Hansard, who was later to join the Department of Railways and Canals in Ottawa and become a prominent golfer at Royal Ottawa; Robert R. Ritchie, QC, one of the leaders of the bar in Saint John. (Ritchie is notable for having "On 31 Dec. 1900, discharged all the prisoners in the city and county jail, in order that the peo-ple of the city might commence the new centu-ry with empty cells." And with empty pockets, one is tempted to add.)

Then there were the McAvitys, who were to have a long association with the club. The brothers Tom and George ran a hardware and sporting-goods business in the city, which was one of the first to sell golf equipment. George was also in pulp and paper, and in the N.B. Coal and Railway Company, of which he later became president. John A. McAvity, Tom's son, became a leader of golf in the city and president of the Saint John club. (He was close to being "The Father of Golf in Saint John," opined *Canadian Golfer* when he died in 1931.)

The club rented a cottage as a clubhouse, and this was decorated by the enthusiastic ladies' section, which put on an evening of entertainment to raise the funds. A crowd of some four hundred attended the formal open-ing of course and clubhouse in mid-July. Legend tells of Hugh Hansard holing his opening drive, which would have made this a remarkable hole-in-one. But his ace was accomplished two weeks before the opening day. Nevertheless, I have never come across an earlier hole-in-one in the Canadian press.

The Millidge farm could lease the club only enough land to accommodate a nine-hole course of 1,700 yards, lengthened to 2,000 yards in 1899. Although thick with natural hazards such as rocks, trees, and brooks, the course was hardly challenging. So it is all the more surprising that Mabel Thomson was able to teach herself golf on what was no more than a par three layout. But she did, and with no small success. Miss Thomson was to become Canada's first great national woman golfer. But in 1897 Mabel was no doubt quite happy to be the club's first lady champion.

By 1913, the rubber-cored ball had made this short course outdated. The club bought land at Riverside Heights, laid out a new course, and renamed itself the Riverside Golf and Country Club, which it remains to this day.

Teams from Saint John played against the club at St. Andrews and – with more success – against those at Fredericton and Woodstock. They also played against the British North Atlantic Fleet. In 1903, the British *Golf Illustrated* reported sailors as having played ten matches against Saint John golfers. "The most interesting game was that between Miss Mabel Thomson, lady champion of Canada, and Midshipman Lubbock. Miss Thomson was one up on her opponent."

Fred Short helped a Major Memming lay out a course at Fredericton in the fall of 1897. The old racecourse, or driving park, in the city had fallen into disuse some years before, when it seemed likely that a railway would be built. But the railway went elsewhere, so the citizens decided – responsibly, it would seem – to construct a golf course instead.

Golfers organized the Fredericton Golf Club in September 1897, the men playing their opening game on the twenty-seventh of the month, the ladies four days later. The members of the club included professors Dixon and Davidson, two of the several members of the staff of the University of New Brunswick who had been smitten by the game. The club's first

president, Thomas Carleton Allen, was a lawyer and a former mayor of the town.

The course in the old driving park had one unusual hazard – part of it was still in use as a rifle range. But it was probably its flatness, and not its danger, which made the members move to a field on Waterloo Row. Later still, in 1916, the club acquired the property west of the town, where it enjoys golf to this day.

A Presbyterian minister, the Reverend G. D. Ireland, is said to have brought golf to Woodstock in 1897, leading to the formation of a golf club two years later.

George Ireland, born in P.E.I. in 1866, was educated at McGill University, then at the Montreal Theological College, graduating in 1897. He was the pastor at St. Paul's, Woodstock, from 1898 to 1911. Since he introduced golf to the city on his arrival, he obviously had played the game in Montreal, perhaps as the guest of one of Royal Montreal's several golfing ministers.

Golf was brought to Sydney in the spring of 1895 by a native of Nova Scotia returning from a business trip. Walter Crowe had not been to Scotland but to the United States, where, it seems, he had been invited to a golf club. On his return to Sydney, he managed to interest a few friends, among them the Reverend E. B. Rankin and three lawyers, James and David Hearn and F. I. Stewart.

Walter Crowe, a solicitor, was born in Truro, Nova Scotia, in 1861, and took his law degree at Dalhousie University. He went on to be the mayor of Sydney (1897–1903).

Crowe and his friends laid out a nine-hole course of some 2,300 yards in Victoria Park, which was then being used for pasture. In October, they met and formed the first Sydney Golf Club. The Reverend Rankin was elected president of the club (or its captain), Stewart was elected the vice-president, and Walter Crowe, the secretary-treasurer. The indications are that the club started with only a dozen or so members, but it flourished for a few years before running into difficulties with

Walter Crowe, who brought golf to Sydney, N.S.

its course. Like so many other clubs of this era, Sydney Golf Club relied on grazing cattle to keep the grass short on the fairways, and permission to graze cattle on its course was soon withdrawn. What is more, cricket was undergoing a revival, and baseball was becoming increasingly popular. Both sports sought space in the park, forcing the golf club to narrow its fairways and to lay new putting greens. It became obvious that the club would have to find new grounds or go to the wall.

In 1903, a few members of the club laid out a new course at Lingan Bay, on land offered by the Dominion Coal Company. It seems likely that Walter Crowe had a hand in this, since he acted for this company, but the general manager of the company, H. J. McCann, is also credited with arranging the deal. The tale is told that he and two friends went to Lingan on McCann's buckboard, taking a tape measure, nine empty tomato cans, and a mid-iron. Having laid out the first nine of what soon became an eighteen-hole course, they formed the Lingan Country Club, while still

retaining their membership in the club in Sydney, where they played when cricket and baseball permitted. The two clubs competed for a cup for a few years, until the Sydney Golf Club went out of existence.

Just before the First World War, the Dominion Coal Company found it needed the land used by the Lingan club, so the club had to lay out a new course on its present site. The club had a ladies' section from the beginning, although with only a handful of members until after the First World War.

The Halifax Golf Club (often referred to as Ashburn) was organized in 1896 and is the oldest continuous club in Nova Scotia.

It was said of late nineteenth-century Halifax that it had more admirers of amateur sport than did any other city in the Maritimes, if not in Canada. For many years the city had been a British garrison town and naval station, the headquarters of the Commander-in-Chief of British North America. The presence of these services had much to do with the popularity of cricket, polo, croquet, archery, sailing, and boating. But for some reason the army and navy officers did not get around to playing golf until the closing years of the century.

If you stand on the western ramparts of the Halifax Citadel, you may still see part of the North Common, but the fields of the South Common, where James Forgan and his friends practised their golf, lie under buildings.

When organized golf took root in Halifax, it did so at Studley, further from the city core. Judge Croke (later Sir Alexander Croke) had purchased a thirty-acre estate to the west of the city. He named it Studley, after his English home. In the 1890s, the fields were being used by the Studley Quoit Club. And it was here that Lieutenant-Colonel Anstruther-Duncan and Captain Collins, who presumably had picked up the essentials of the game in their travels in the services, laid out a nine-hole course for golf.

The Halifax Golf Club was organized at a meeting in April 1896. There exists in the city archives a summary of the early minutes of the club. On the first page we read that:

Meeting held at Church of England Institute 17 April 1896 to take steps towards formation of a Golf Club. Rev. Thomas Fowler acted as Chairman, Mr. Murray as Secretary. The Studley Grounds were leased for the sum of $150.00. Caretaker engaged for $6.00 a week. A house in Le Marchant St. was rented from Mrs. Gibbs from May to October for a sum of $25.00.

The meeting went on to elect a president and captain, Lieutenant-Colonel Anstruther-Duncan; a vice-president, Reverend Fowler; and a secretary-treasurer, W. B. Torrance. (By a strange coincidence, a Lieutenant-Colonel Anstruther was busy organizing a golf club in Portage la Prairie, Manitoba, in the same month.)

The committee included Professor Walter Charles Murray, a New Brunswick man, who had been educated at Edinburgh University; Charles Archibald, a native of North Sydney, who had moved to Halifax in 1894, joined the Bank of Nova Scotia, and later became its president; Dr. George Campbell, a proud descendant of the Campbells of Argyll, who was born in Truro in 1861. Campbell and the Reverend Fowler were prominent members of the North British (that is, Scottish) Society in Halifax.

W. B. Torrance was probably one of the Montreal Torrances, a prominent family in that city. If so, he was related by marriage to both Alexander Dennistoun and William Ramsay of Royal Montreal.

Army and navy officers supported golf in Halifax much as they did in the other garrison towns of Kingston and Victoria. In Halifax, they joined with the civilians in organizing the club. Naval officers from visiting warships were offered monthly memberships at the enticing rate of $1.00 each – normal green fees were $1.00 *per week*, or $2.50 per month, annual dues $10.00.

The nine-hole course at Studley was only 1,818 yards in length, the longest hole being 283 yards. Today it would be rated at about 29 strokes. Nevertheless, after two years of play, nobody had broken 50. Although it had no sand bunkers, its natural hazards – stone walls, trees, bogs, long grass, ditches, roads, and ponds – obviously made it more difficult than its length would suggest.

In the spring of 1900, the club secured new grounds closer to the city and laid out a longer nine-hole course. This has been referred to as the Collins Field course and also as the Gorsebrook course of the Halifax Golf Club. The Collins Field belonged to the family of that name. Among the builders of Nova Scotia (having immigrated from England in 1744), the Collins have been described as merchant princes of their day, possessing the largest fortune in British North America. The Gorsebrook estate, with its rolling fields and parks, was part of Collins Field.

Once established there, the membership of the club grew steadily from forty to over a hundred. Whereas the club had only four lady members in 1898, by 1901 it had ten times this number. The occasional home-and-away match was played against the Saint John Golf Club, but until the formation of clubs at Truro (1903) and Dartmouth (1913), the main opposition came from army and navy officers stationed in Halifax and from the officers of visiting warships. Occasionally the navy would bring along its band, making the day a social event as well as a golf tournament.

The Collins Field course was still short, even by the standards of the day. By 1919, after ingenious manipulating of the available space, it had been stretched to only 2,266 yards, the longest hole being 375 yards. In 1922, the club reorganized as the Halifax Golf and Country Club, bought land west of the city, a property known as Ashburn, and laid out a new, championship-length, eighteen-hole course.

"All the land is low and plaine, and the fairest that may possibly be scene, full of goodly medowes and trees." So said Jacques Cartier, on becoming Prince Edward Island's first tourist in 1534.

Some of these goodly meadows were transferred into links for the Charlottetown Golf Club, in 1902.

The members of Halifax GC about 1900.

At the turn of the century, P.E.I. had a population of 103,000, with about 10 per cent living in the province's only city at the time, Charlottetown. The summer sports were cricket, tennis, fishing, and sailing. (In 1903 the city had a Lawn Tennis Ice Cream Committee, whatever that did!)

We need not seek to find the route by which golf reached Canada's smallest province. By the turn of the century the game was prospering only a few miles away in New Brunswick and Nova Scotia. Sportsmen from the Island must have been aware of this new game of golf. No doubt they tried it on the mainland before organizing themselves into a club.

An Island Scrapbook (1933) mentions a golf club being formed in 1893, but gives no details. At least one other later publication has used this date, but when Fred Short of Saint John wrote on the clubs of Eastern Canada in an article published in the American magazine *Golf* in 1898, he made no mention of a Charlottetown Golf Club.

The CPR booklet *Golf in Canada* (1918) and the 1923 edition of *Fraser's Golf Directory and Year Book* show the Charlottetown club as having been established in 1902, and this information would have been solicited from the club. The author of *Golf Gleanings Old and New* (the history of the Maritime Seniors' Golf Association, published in 1953) believes that Charlottetown golfers first played over a few holes laid out on the exhibition grounds in 1902 and organized a club later that year.

On 9 April 1903, the Charlottetown *Guardian* noted that "a meeting of the Golf Club takes place this evening in the Office of Messrs. Peters and Ings at 8 o'clock – Members are requested not to forget it." This suggests that the club was a going concern by the start of the 1903 season. Also, by June 1903, local merchants Dodds and Rogers were advertising a full line of golf goods.

Charlottetown was a small, close-knit community, in which in their everyday amusements premiers mixed with local lawyers and merchants, many of them from families long established in the province. The names Haszard, Longworth, Pope, Ings, and Weeks were to Charlottetown golf what the names Osler, Bethune, and Cassels were to golf in Toronto.

Lawyers were predominant among the club's leading members. Justice Robert Rowan Fitzgerald was the club's first president. Justice Francis Longworth Haszard was the premier of the province (1908–11) and the club's second president. He and A. Ernest Ings, William Weeks, Duncan C. McLeod, Alexander Warburton, A. A. Maclean, all lawyers, were among

the twenty or so early – and probably founding – members. (The Goff Brothers, owners of a local shoe store, do not seem to have been golfers, which is rather a pity.)

There were no outstanding players among the early members of the club. The club's first Match Book, written in a find hand, has been preserved. It dates from August 1903, when a score of 119 for two rounds of the nine-hole course won the monthly handicap for Percy Pope. (He and A. E. Ings were the two scratch players.) A Miss Brown came in with a score of 68 (presumably for nine holes) to put her well ahead of the ladies' pack.

F.L. Haszard, long-time president of Charlottetown GC, photographed in 1916.

The second page of the original match book of Charlottetown Golf Club.

A member, Fred Hyndman, held the agency for the Standard Life Assurance Company, amongst many others. In June 1903, he persuaded the company to put up the Standard Challenge Cup for annual competition, and this became the main event of the year for the men. In 1903, an eighteen-hole score of 135 was good enough to qualify for the match-play rounds. A fair crowd of townspeople turned up to witness the play that year, leading *The Guardian* to congratulate the club on bringing golf to the city (another indication that the club had only recently been formed). It also noted that "the outside of the Club House has been stained, the roof green and the walls terra cotta."

The Charlottetown club was the only golf club on the island until the mid-1920s, so for interclub competition it had to rely on matches against the sailors of visiting warships and the mainland clubs such as Halifax, Truro, Sydney, and Saint John. Charlottetown was usually defeated pretty decisively, even over its own course. This course was known as the Belvedere Links (today the club is known as the Belvedere Golf and Winter Club). The club may have started playing on the exhibition grounds, but by 1903 it had a nine-hole course laid out on land rented from an Alexander Beazeley, who called his estate Belvedere.

Although Newfoundland did not become a province of Canada until 1949, we should record that its first golf club was probably organized some forty years before this.

Paul O'Neill, in his book *The Oldest City* (1975), credits the city of St. John's as having active golfers before 1900. They are said to have played over a course in the west of Buckmaster's Field, and a Golf Avenue is still there as evidence of its existence. Mr. O'Neill writes: "There was no suitable course in the town, however, until 1908 when a group of people purchased Colonel Haly's farm on Logy Bay road." (Colonel Haly was an aide-de-camp to Governor Cochrane in the early nineteenth century.) He goes on to say that Bally Haly was organized as a proper golf club in 1917.

Other sources have claimed that the present Bally Haly Golf and Curling Club was organized earlier, in 1902, but it is not clear if golf was one of its activities as early as that. Like so many clubhouses in Canada, Bally Haly's twice went up in smoke, in 1937 and in 1957.

The Bally Haly clubhouse in 1917.

CHAPTER

THE ROYAL CANADIAN GOLF ASSOCIATION

AT A MEETING IN OTTAWA IN JUNE 1895, several Canadian golf clubs agreed to form an association. The Canadian Golf Association was formally constituted in September of that year, when it elected its first office-bearers. The right to the prefix *Royal* was granted by Queen Victoria in June 1896.

The founding members of the RCGA numbered only ten clubs: eight from Ontario and Quebec, the Victoria Golf Club from British Columbia, and the Winnipeg Golf Club from Manitoba. Ninety-five years later, over 1,300 clubs from across Canada are members of the RCGA.

The role and structure of the RCGA has changed considerably in the intervening years. Conceived as a national organization, it was soon perceived as serving the interests of golf in Central Canada to the detriment of the other provinces. It became more truly national in the 1920s, when faced with the threat and reality of a Western Canada Golf Association. The RCGA's problems were Canada's problems: how to meet the needs of minorities; how to overcome regional prejudices, the vast expanse of the country, the high cost of travel.

Until 1938, the RCGA had to compete with provincial golf associations for members. In that year, a club belonging to a provincial association automatically became a member of the RCGA. As a result, RCGA membership more than doubled. Income, however, did not go up until 1948. In that year, a club stopped paying a flat membership fee to its provincial association, but extracted from each of its senior male members the sum of one dollar yearly, half of which went to the RCGA.

A much bigger leap in income came in the late 1970s, from the profitable Canadian Open. The money enabled the RCGA to acquire new headquarters at Glen Abbey, with a championship golf course, open to the public. Within a few years, income from the course was matching income from the Open.

The RCGA exists to provide services to amateur golf in Canada. For most of its life, the association's lack of money restricted these services. In the 1990s, the money is there, and the challenge would now seem to be to determine where, and how best, to direct it.

94

This chapter deals with the birth of the RCGA, and with its *modus operandi* before the First World War.

In 1890, only three golf clubs were active in Canada: Royal Montreal, Royal Quebec, and Toronto. There was no national or international golf in North America, and very little interclub golf in Canada. Royal Montreal and Royal Quebec still held their biannual team matches, but Toronto Golf Club had no club to compete against in the province. The interprovincial matches between Quebec and Ontario had been held only four times in nine years.

Interclub matches, and interprovincial matches for that matter, did not require a golf association. Three golf clubs were quite capable of looking after matters of common interest.

All that changed in the space of the next five years. By the end of 1895, there were golf clubs in Montreal, Quebec, Toronto (two), Ottawa, Barrie, Simcoe, Brantford, Niagara, Winnipeg, Vancouver, Victoria, Kingston, Hamilton, London, Calgary, Fort Macleod, Sydney, St. Andrews, and Murray Bay. The time had clearly come for national championships and for some national body to run them.

The first golf associations, or unions, had arrived with the 1890s. The Irish golf clubs established the Golfing Union of Ireland in 1891, and the ladies in Britain established their Ladies' Golf Union two years later. Although there were county golf unions in England by 1895, neither England nor Scotland had a national union. Instead, custom had established that the management of the game be left to the Royal and Ancient Golf Club of St. Andrews, this being the historic seat of the game. The Royal and Ancient was the authority on the rules of golf. An R & A committee, made up of delegates of those clubs where the championships were played, ran the British Amateur and Open.

The clubs in the United States early recognized the need for an association of clubs. With typical American thoroughness, they did something about it.

In 1894, two U.S. golf clubs organized separate tournaments, open to amateur golfers. Each club hoped that the winner of its tournament would be recognized as the first amateur champion of the United States. The Newport Golf Club of Rhode Island held an open, stroke-play tournament in September. Not to be outdone, the St. Andrews Golf Club of Yonkers, N.Y., invited amateur golfers to a match-play tournament in October. For reasons we need not go into, neither winner came to be recognized as the national champion.

The general confusion over these tournaments confirmed the need for a national organization to run national events. In December 1894, the representatives of five prominent U.S. clubs met and formed a governing body for golf, naming it the Amateur Golf Association of the United States. But since its purpose was also to look after the professional interests of the game, it changed its name in January 1895 to the American Golf Association. This also proved unsuitable. The word *American* might be construed as *North American*, encompassing *Canadian*. So in March 1895 the name was changed again, to United States Golf Association (USGA).

The example of their American neighbours probably did much to persuade Canadian golfers that they, too, needed a national championship and a national body to run it.

If there had been any reluctance in Canada to organize an association and hold national championships, this attitude changed over the winter of 1894–95. A newspaper had reported that three leading Canadian players had been denied entry to the Newport tournament, being members of clubs "on the wrong side of the line."

It turned out that this report was wrong. A. W. Smith of Toronto Golf club had withdrawn, as had Frederick Stancliffe of Royal Montreal. The third golfer, W. W. Watson of Royal Montreal, wrote to the newspaper to say that not only had he played at Newport, he had been warmly welcomed by its members. If this report did nothing else, it created an awareness among Canadian golfers that their cousins across the border were a step ahead of them in organizing national golf.

Then came word of the American Golf Association. There is no evidence that Canadian golfers formally complained about the use of the word *American*. (Who, for that matter, was to complain on their behalf?) But there would be many in Canada ready to put the worst interpretation on any American venture. The bad feelings over the Fenian raids and the Civil War had not entirely disappeared. And if some Canadian golfers viewed with suspicion the use of the *American* in the title of this new organization, they were probably right to do so. The British magazine *Golf*, in its issue of 25 January 1895, reported the secretary of the U.S. association as saying: "It has not as yet been decided whether or not the National Association will take in the Canadian clubs of Toronto, Hamilton, Ottawa and Quebec." In his *Fifty Years of American Golf*, H. B. Martin confirms that the USGA did indeed consider inviting Canadian clubs to join:

> The question arose about admitting Canadian golf clubs to membership. Admitting them seemed the likely thing to do as there were so few clubs in existence then that any first class club in North America was a valuable acquisition . . . It was decided that first winter, after due deliberation however, to confine the issue to the United States. That was when the name was finally changed to the United States Golf Association. . . .

It is probably no coincidence that the movement towards a Canadian golf association started in February 1895, when the organization across the border was still calling itself *American*.

The first step was taken by Royal Ottawa. This club had grown rapidly in membership and prestige since its establishment in 1891. Its secretary, Alex Simpson, was a recent and enthusiastic convert to golf, as well as a fast-improving player. He persuaded the committee of his club that Canada needed an association of golf clubs, if only to organize a national championship, and that Ottawa should take the lead.

A. Simpson of the Royal Ottawa club, organizer of the Ottawa Tournament, the first Canadian Amateur Championship, in 1895.

In February 1895 he wrote to Royal Montreal, and presumably to those other clubs in Canada of whose existence he was aware, proposing that they form a Canadian Golf Club Association and that they have their members compete that summer for a national trophy, which the honorary patron of Royal Ottawa, the governor general, Lord Aberdeen, would be pleased to donate.

The response appears to have been encouraging. However, Royal Montreal suggested that the organizing meeting and the national championship be left until September, to coincide with the interprovincial meet in Toronto between Ontario and Quebec.

Its advice was not heeded. Perhaps Mr. Simpson was impatient; perhaps he feared that Royal Ottawa would be forced to play a diminished role at an interprovincial meet in Toronto. He wrote a second letter in March, saying that the majority of clubs seemed to favour an early meeting.

Royal Montreal had replied, offering to host this first meeting of the golf association, when a third letter arrived from the busy Mr. Simpson. The meeting would be held at Ottawa on the weekend of Queen Victoria's birthday, the twenty-fourth of May. There would be a full week of golf: handicap events; long driving and pitch-and-putt competitions; an exhibition by British professionals; a match against the American golfers who had been invited. The main event would be for the Aberdeen Cup, which would go to the first Amateur Champion of the Dominion. During the week, the Canadian clubs would also formally organize themselves into a Canadian Golf Association.

Royal Montreal noted that its offer and advice had not been accepted. But its committee was then preoccupied with matters of some importance – the need to move from Fletcher's Field. At its suggestion, however, the Ottawa Tournament, as it came to be called, was put off until the first week in June, so as not to clash with Royal Montreal's match with Quebec, traditionally held on the weekend of the queen's birthday.

The Ottawa Tournament was a success, but not quite the grand event that Mr. Simpson had promised. Only five Canadian clubs sent a total of some thirty players; the Americans declined; and the two British professionals then touring America, Douglas Rolland and Willie Park Jr., were apparently persuaded by a more lucrative offer to continue with their round of exhibition matches in the United States. However, with the promise of prizes totalling five hundred dollars, some of the crack golfers of the Royal Montreal, Kingston, Toronto, and Niagara golf clubs came to Ottawa, June 4–7, 1895.

In the first Canadian Amateur Championship, Thomas M. Harley of Kingston Golf Club beat Alex Simpson of Royal Ottawa Golf Club by 7 and 6 in the 36-hole final. Harley's name went on the Aberdeen Cup, and he was given a gold medal.

The earliest RCGA minutes that still exist are those of 1912. I have not come across any report of exactly what business was transacted at the Ottawa meeting, other than two reports in Ottawa newspapers published at the time, and two reports in the British magazine *Golf*, published in July 1895 and July 1896. There appear to be two different and somewhat contradictory accounts of what took place. The reports agree that a Canadian Golf Association was in place after the meeting in Ottawa but differ on the matter of its first office-bearers.

There is no dispute over the fact that on the sixth of June delegates from the five clubs at the Ottawa Tournament (Royal Montreal, Royal Ottawa, Toronto, Kingston, and Niagara) met and confirmed their support for a Canadian Golf Association. But some members of the

The governor general, the Earl of Aberdeen, who presented his Aberdeen Cup to the first winner of the Canadian Amateur Championship. He was educated at St. Andrews University, and he and his sons were enthusiastic golfers.

press, and the governor general, Lord Aberdeen, were under the impression that the Canadian Golf Association had indeed been formally established, with elected office-bearers, during that meeting of the clubs. The *Ottawa Daily Free Press* on 8 June carried a report on the tournament, written the day before (the italics are mine):

> When the Governor-General arrived at the Marquee, Lt.-Col. Irwin introduced His Excellency to the large company and thanked him for his presence as well as for the practical interest he had shown in the game.
>
> His Excellency in reply said he always felt at home in the precincts of the ancient game of golf, one of the national games of Scotland. He congratulated the winners, the club *and the newly formed association.* . . .
>
> Previously, the centre of attraction was the final struggle *for the championship of the Canadian Golf Association which was only formed last night with Lt.-Col. Irwin as first president.* With the honour goes the Governor-General's silver cup, which must be won three times in succession before becoming private property, the winner each year being entitled to a gold medal, while the runner-up gains a silver medal.

(At the beginning of the tournament, the same newspaper had reported that the Amateur Championship of Canada would be restricted to amateur members of clubs "associated or affiliated with the Canadian Golf Association." This implies that the clubs attending had previously committed to becoming associated or affiliated with the CGA, and that the CGA was firmly in place before the tournament.)

An article on the Ottawa Tournament appeared in the 5 July 1895 issue of the British magazine *Golf*. The final paragraph reads: "During the tournament, a Canadian Golf Association was formed, mainly on the lines of the United States Golf Association." This confirms part of the report in the *Daily Free Press*.

However, a second Ottawa newspaper, the *Evening Journal*, carried this report after the Ottawa Tournament:

"The Canadian Golf Association" is the name of an organization formed . . . here yesterday. It was decided that the annual meeting of the association should take place at the time and place of the interprovincial golf match. Col. Irwin and Mr. A. Simpson were appointed Chairman and Secretary pro tem.

This appears to be the more plausible version of what took place. In the minutes of Royal Montreal there is an entry dated 27 September 1895 referring to the interprovincial match then being held at the Toronto Golf Club. It reads: "After the match a meeting of the clubs present was held and the Canadian Golf Association was formed, and the officers for the ensuing year appointed."

The newspaper reports of the interprovincial match at Toronto Golf Club on 27 September 1895 make no mention of a meeting of the CGA. But a note in the British *Golf* of 3 July 1896 gave the following information on the then current officers of the association, and these would be the ones elected in September 1895.

President:	Hon. George A. Drummond [Royal Montreal]
V.P.'s:	Lt-Col. D. T. Irwin [Royal Ottawa]
	John Hamilton [Royal Quebec]
Hon. Secy/Treas:	W. C. J. Hall [Royal Quebec]
Members:	Charles Hunter [Toronto/Niagara]
	Lt.-Col. Cotton [Kingston]
	J. F. Kirk [Deer Park/Rosedale]
	J. L. Morris [Royal Montreal]
	F. P. Betts [London]

The same note records that: "Her Majesty has been graciously pleased to grant the petition of the Canadian Golf Association for permission to use the prefix Royal."

This note was published on 3 July, so the petition was probably granted in June. We have no record of how the petition was made. No doubt it went through the office of a sympathetic governor general. After all, he had been in at the birth. So far as I know, the RCGA is the only golf association to be honoured in this way.

Finally, we should note that the list of past presidents of the RCGA (which started appearing at the turn of the century, when Lieutenant-Colonel Irwin and others were still alive) shows the Honourable George A. Drummond, and not Irwin, as the first president. The records also show him as the president for 1896, the year *following* his election, a practice the RCGA followed until 1921.

The Canadian Golf Association was born at a time when Canadian golf was in its infancy. There was no golf periodical to record CGA events, and the press took scant notice of this new game, so the pioneering efforts of Royal Ottawa, and of Lieutenant-Colonel Irwin and Alex Simpson, have been dealt with rather perfunctorily by those who have written on the history of golf in Canada.

We now come to the question of which clubs were the founding members of the RCGA.

On 7 June 1895 the British *Golf* recorded that: "Montreal, Quebec, Toronto, Winnipeg, London and Kingston have acquiesced in the proposal [by Royal Ottawa, to form a Canadian Golf Association] and other clubs are expected soon to follow the lead thus given."

By the time the CGA was *formally* constituted on 27 September 1895, when it elected its first office-bearers, Niagara GC and Rosedale GC were also members, since these clubs also provided office-bearers. Only these eight clubs (that is, all but Winnipeg GC, for obvious reasons) provided players for the September interprovincial team match between Quebec and Ontario.

The minutes of the Victoria Golf Club of 29 August 1895 state that the club had become "an affiliated club to the Canadian Golf Association." On this evidence, Victoria Golf Club should be added, to make ten founding members of the CGA: Royal Ottawa GC, Royal Montreal GC, Royal Quebec GC, Toronto GC,

Senator George Drummond of Royal Montreal, the first president of the RCGA in 1895.

Kingston GC, Niagara GC, Rosedale GC, London GC, Winnipeg GC, Victoria GC.

That does not necessarily mean that these ten clubs were the only founding members on 27 September 1895. Other clubs (like Winnipeg and Victoria) not represented at the September meeting may have been granted membership. The earliest list I could find of the member clubs of the RCGA appeared in the U.S. magazine *Golf* in April 1898:

Associate Members: Cobourg, Hamilton, Kingston, London, Niagara, Royal Ottawa, Toronto, Rosedale, Royal Montreal, Royal Quebec, Winnipeg.

Allied Members: Oshawa, Lennoxville, Murray Bay.

To compete in the Canadian Amateur, one's club had to belong to the RCGA. Three members from Lennoxville Golf Club played in the Amateur at Quebec City in 1896, and F. G. H. Pattison of Hamilton Golf Club played at Royal Montreal in September 1897: so one can assume that these clubs had joined the RCGA by these dates.

The list of members in 1898 was put together by Fred Short of Saint John, in an article on "The Golf Clubs of Canada." He notes the non-members – Kincardine, Simcoe, Fredericton, Algonquin, Saint John, Sherbrooke, Halifax, Vancouver, and Victoria – but his list by no means covers all the clubs in Canada.

Apparently, Victoria Golf Club had quit the RCGA by 1898. By that time the club was engaged in matches with U.S. clubs. Soon it would help form the Pacific Northwest Golf Association.

We do not know what else was agreed at the Ottawa meeting on 6 June, but it seems likely that Lieutenant-Colonel Irwin and Alex Simpson were asked to draw up a draft constitution for the CGA. This would be circulated to all prospective members before the interprovincial match in September, at which meeting the CGA would approve the constitution and formally establish itself and elect office-bearers, in accordance with the requirements of this constitution. The secretary of the RCGA later wrote to the British magazine *Golf*, which published the objects of the RCGA in September 1896. They were:

> . . . to promote interest in the game of Golf; the protection of the mutual interests of its members; to establish and enforce uniformity in the rules of the game by creating a representative authority; its Executive Committee to be a court of reference as a final authority in matters of controversy; to establish a uniform system of handicapping; to decide on what links the Amateur and Open Championships shall be played.

At first glance, the reference to an Open championship seems strange, since the Canadian Open was not held until 1904. But the RCGA had copied these objectives, word for word, from the constitution of the USGA, and the USGA did organize an Open from 1895.

The earliest constitution of the RCGA I have been able to find was published in 1918. It is a constitution adopted on 28 September 1901, with by-laws adopted on 25 April 1901, revised on 1 July 1914. The objectives are essentially the same as in 1895, but the RCGA now undertook "to arrange and control the Amateur, Ladies' and Open Championships, the Interprovincial matches and other matches and competitions."

These objectives were no doubt an earnest expression of what the executive committee hoped to do for golf in Canada. But the evidence points to the executive concerning itself almost exclusively with the running of championships, for at least the first twenty years of the RCGA's existence. These championships did much "to promote interest in the game of golf," so this particular objective was achieved. The RCGA did not set up its first standing committee, the Rules of Golf Committee, until 1916, and did little or nothing to promote national handicapping until the 1930s. Even then, the impetus came from the golf associations of Quebec and Ontario.

There were very good reasons why the RCGA did not meet all its original aims. It was run by a small body of volunteers, each with his own profession to follow or his own business to run. The first permanent, but part-time, secretary-treasurer was not appointed until 1920. The vast expanse of the country, the high cost of travel, low membership and low revenue – all these factors made it difficult for the RCGA to provide services to clubs across Canada. But there was little demand for such services until after the First World War. Golf was there to be enjoyed. The playing of the game was much more important to the thousands of new, stumbling, golfers than the finer points of the rules or the intricacies of handicapping. Under the circumstances, the

RCGA did an excellent job. Golf grew rapidly in Canada. Championships were keenly fought. The traditions of the game were preserved. And a few men and women, players and administrators, started to write a new chapter in the history, legend, and myth of Canadian golf.

After 1895, when it was part of the Ottawa Tournament, the Canadian Amateur Championship (the "Amateur") was the main event in a week-long tournament which came to be held annually around Dominion Day in July. The tournament was referred to as the "Annual Meeting" of the RCGA. It should not be confused with the annual general meeting (the AGM) held during the same week, for the purpose of electing office-bearers and conducting other business.

The Amateur and the other golfing events of the Annual Meeting were open to any male amateur golfer whose club was a member of the RCGA. All the golfer had to do was turn up the night before and register. In the events before the First World War, he was assured of a game, regardless of handicap. About a hundred players might attend the meeting for at least part of the week, but only thirty to sixty would play in the Amateur.

As well as competing for the Amateur, players could take part in such events as:

- the interprovincial team match between Quebec and Ontario. (Ten players selected for each side; eighteen holes, match play.)
- the Annual Handicap, by far the most popular event of the week since everyone was a favourite to win. (Two rounds of eighteen holes.)
- the interclub team match.
- the consolation events, for those knocked out in the first round of the Amateur.
- miscellaneous events, such as long-driving, putting, or pitch-and-putting competitions.

From 1904 until 1910, the Canadian Open Championship was tagged onto the end of the Annual Meeting, as a sort of afterthought. But from 1911, in order to spread the burden among the organizers, the Open was played at a different time and venue. If the Amateur was held in the East (which meant Quebec), the Open was held in the West (which meant Ontario).

Holding the Open at the end of the week of the Annual Meeting is a measure of its insignificance in the eyes of Canadian golfers until after the First World War.

A measure of the importance the RCGA attached to the Amateur is the method used to select RCGA presidents. The clubs attending the AGM would first select the club to have the honour of hosting the next Annual Meeting. The president (or past president) of this club would be elected president of the RCGA for that year. The secretary-treasurer of the RCGA would also come from this club or from a club in the same locality. This made very good sense. Getting the club and the course ready for the Annual Meeting could then be left safely to the president of the host club and his committees.

There were exceptions to this method of choosing RCGA presidents. In September 1895, the Honourable George Drummond of Royal Montreal was elected the first president of the RCGA, but the Amateur in 1896 was held at Royal Quebec. Drummond's election was no doubt a recognition of his long service to Canada's premier club. In the following year, the positions were reversed, John Hamilton of Royal Quebec being RCGA president in a year when the Amateur was held at Royal Montreal. With one other exception, the RCGA chose its presidents in this way until 1921.

Finally, from 1901 the RCGA also ran a Canadian Ladies' Championship. This was usually held in September or October, the venue alternating between Quebec and Ontario. The Canadian Ladies' Golf Union (founded in 1913) went along with this until 1924, when the ladies took over their own event.

The number of RCGA member clubs appears to have grown to twenty by 1902, to thirty-three by 1905, but was only one greater by the beginning of the First World War. The membership represented about a third of the clubs in Canada.

Towards the end of the First World War, the annual membership fee was waived, since the RCGA had cancelled its national championships and could provide no services. This partly explains why, by 1918, membership had jumped to sixty-two clubs, more than half the clubs in the country.

Another likely reason for this sudden interest is the emergence in 1915 of Canada's first golf periodical, *Canadian Golfer*. As we shall see, *Canadian Golfer* became the official organ of the RCGA and of the Canadian Ladies' Golf Union, and did more to promote the RCGA than any other medium.

The RCGA constitution established two categories of member. An allied club was required merely to be a regularly constituted golf club in Canada. An associate club was also required to have a golf course, a clubhouse, and at least twenty-five members.

An allied club paid a membership fee of five dollars a year, and was allowed one delegate and one vote at the AGM. An associate member paid ten dollars a year, and was allowed two delegates and votes in proportion to its senior male membership. The large clubs could, therefore, have dominated the RCGA by virtue of their large membership; and they did, but benignly and democratically, or so it would appear. Although it can be argued that the RCGA appears to have been formed almost exclusively for the benefit of the large city clubs in Quebec and Ontario, the members of these clubs were, almost exclusively, the ones who gave their time and money to the successful running of the RCGA. In the period before 1920, four clubs – Royal Montreal, Royal Ottawa, Toronto, and Lambton – provided between them eighteen of the twenty RCGA presidents. This meant, in effect, that they also provided their courses and clubhouses for the Annual Meeting.

PART THREE

AMATEURS SUPREME 1900 - 1918

(Over) *Mabel Thomson in 1905, on her way to her third of five championships.*

7
CHAPTER

THE EARLY CHAMPIONSHIPS

A WEEK BEFORE THE OTTAWA TOURNAMENT in June 1895, word got out that the city engineer was about to lay a new railway track along Charlotte Street, leading to the Royal Ottawa Golf Club.

The club's president, Lieutenant-Colonel D. T. Irwin, accompanied by two aldermen, hastened to city hall, pulled rank, and the roadwork was deferred. No doubt Irwin let it be known in the proper places that the governor general could not be expected to abandon his carriage and clamber over the rubble of a dug-up street. The first Amateur Championship of Canada went ahead as planned, and on the afternoon of 7 June Lord Aberdeen presented his cup and the gold medal of the Canadian Golf Association to the winner, Tom Harley, of Kingston Golf Club, who defeated Alex Simpson of Royal Ottawa by 7 and 6 in the 36-hole final of this first Amateur.

They came from the same neck of the woods, did this lord and this carpenter. Lord Aberdeen had been coached at Musselburgh Golf club, a mile or so from the home of the man who received the cup. In Britain he had his own private golf course, and he had been

Thomas M. Harley of Kingston Golf Club, first winner of the Canadian Amateur Championship in 1895, seen with the Aberdeen Cup and his winner's medal.

105

Captain of the R & A in 1885. Tom Harley was born in 1855 in Aberlady, East Lothian (still one of the prettiest villages in Scotland), the son of Captain George Harley. He was in his late thirties when he came to Kingston, Ontario, in the early 1890s, to practise his trade. He helped Kingston win several matches during the few years he stayed in Canada.

Harley's name crops up several times in the Reverend John Kerr's *The Golf Book of East Lothian* (1896), which also carries a photograph of him holding the Aberdeen Cup. A contributor recalled: "When I started the Luffness Links Golf Club in 1867, the few golfers that were about Aberlady took up the game again at once . . . The best of the young players were Tom Harley, Peter and James Hunter . . . " (The latter is no relation, so far as I know, of the James Hunter of Royal Quebec.) Tom Harley won a number of scratch prizes there, including the Hope Challenge Cup in 1876, 1877, and 1880, and the Hope Challenge Medal (open to all East Lothian golfers) in 1875, 1877, 1879, and 1880.

F. P. Betts, KC, of London Hunt, recalled in *Canadian Golfer* in 1929 the impression Tom Harley had made over thirty years earlier:

> In person he was a man of medium height, weighing about 170 lbs. He had a very florid complexion, was clean shaven, and spoke with a typical Scotch accent . . . He was a thoroughly good and sound golfer – in some respects quite remarkable. He was particularly efficient with his cleek, which he played in quite a remarkable manner, getting a long, low ball with a very considerable run; his control of the club was wonderful . . .When he made a cleek shot, [it was] as if the ball were a sentient thing, knew where the hole was, and was making for it. I have time and again seen him drive long shots (well over 200 yards), with his cleek, among the rocks and hummocks of the old Kingston course, and the ball run 50 yards or more, along the ground . . .
>
> Mr. Harley was a most unassuming and modest man, thoroughly straightforward and reliable, and well-liked by all who knew him – a fine type of Scotchman.

Tom Harley lost his Amateur title when playing over the Royal Quebec course for the first time, in 1896. After that, he more or less disappeared from sight. There were rumours he had gone to the United States as a professional. But in fact he had returned to his native village. Many years later, around 1930, a Canadian who had seen Harley play happened to be golfing on an East Lothian course when he spotted an old man with a very familiar swing. By then, Tom Harley would have been about seventy-five. But his golf swing was still as identifying as his fingerprints.

Canadian golfers remembered Harley as much for his good fellowship, fine sportsmanship, and his willingness to help others, as for his classical swing. He was a graceful loser. In the second round of the 1896 Amateur, he was one down with two to play, when young Stuart Gillespie laid him a stymie, Gillespie's ball lying between Harley's and the hole. A reporter of the match tells us what happened:

> Mr. Harley examined the situation and jocularly asked if some gentleman in the audience which followed the match would not kindly come across and play that stroke for him; he then attempted the almost impossible stroke, and the moment his ball passed the hole, he wheeled around, nodded to Mr. Gillespie, walked over and shook him by the hand.

Tom Harley died in 1943, at the age of eighty-eight, and is buried in the old section of the Aberlady churchyard. The local death register confirms that he was "at one time golfing champion of Canada."

As few as eight golfers competed in the first Canadian Amateur in 1895, and only two more entered a year later. This was not an encouraging start for what was to become Canada's premier golfing event. But a new championship is not always an instant success. The lure of tournaments such as the British Open stems from a tradition established over years. Many seeking to win are as attracted by a sense of the past, by a need to add their

AT THE GOLF TOURNAMENT.

A cartoon from the Toronto Globe *at the time of the 1898 Amateur Championship. Messrs. Smith, Kerr, Brown, Taylor, and Hood were five of the team of ten that competed that week in the first amateur international against the United States.*

names to a long list of legendary golfers, as by anything else.

After its modest start, the Canadian Amateur gradually became a great national event. Before the late 1920s, however, it could hardly be characterized as "national." The twenty championships held before the First World War attracted only a handful of golfers from clubs outside Ontario and Quebec. The members of the Victoria, Calgary, and Winnipeg clubs in the West and of the Halifax, Saint John, and Algonquin clubs in the East would have been eligible, since these clubs were members of the RCGA for at least some of those years.

It is more difficult to explain the indifference of so many fine golfers from clubs in Ontario and Quebec towards the Amateur. Men who could be counted upon to turn up for inter-club matches would not always enter for the Amateur, even when it was being held in their home city. Canada's oldest golf clubs, Royal Montreal, Royal Quebec, and Toronto, might have been expected to provide the greatest number of entries for Canada's premier event, but they often disappointed by providing so few. Royal Quebec may be excused; apart from Stuart Gillespie and W. A. Griffith (the winner and runner-up in 1896), this club had few players of national stature. But first-class

players from Royal Montreal, such as Fred Stancliffe and the Honourable George Drummond, did not play in either of the first two Amateurs. Nor did A. W. Smith of Toronto Golf Club. (Smith and three other Toronto players were in court during the week of the Ottawa Tournament, and found guilty of playing on a Sunday. In 1896, Smith was in Scotland.)

In 1905, Percy Taylor and other top players of Royal Montreal did not enter. Taylor was especially criticized for not being there to defend his title. This Amateur was held at the Toronto Golf Club, yet only six members of the club entered. In contrast, Lambton entered eight. This in an era when there was no handicap limitation for entrants.

Again, at the 1906 meeting, all the players from Royal Montreal and all but two from Toronto GC left after the handicap event, before the start of the Amateur. Lambton put a large number into the field, five making their way to the last sixteen.

In the following year at Lambton, Royal Montreal had one entry, Toronto Golf Club three, in a year when players from Peterborough, St. Catharines, London Hunt, Outremont, Hamilton, and Mississauga all qualified for the last four rounds. *The Montreal Daily Star* remarked: " . . . there were none of the promising players of the Montreal clubs, a matter commented upon about the club house verandah. Ottawa sent sixteen players to Toronto . . . and this spirit was appreciated here."

The cost and inconvenience of travel can not wholly excuse these absences, since players from other clubs were willing to travel further. If there is any explanation for this apathy, it probably lies in the nature of the championship. It was an individual event, in a day when team spirit and club spirit were still dominant.

Having noted the absence of so many members of Canada's two leading clubs, it bears repeating that Royal Montreal and Toronto Golf Club were two of the staunchest supporters of the RCGA in other ways. Between them they provided twelve of the twenty venues for the pre-war Annual Meetings. And those of their members who did compete in the Amateur did exceedingly well, taking fourteen of the forty places in the pre-war finals.

The Canadian Amateur was a match-play event until 1969, although frequently it had stroke-play qualifying rounds. Until 1903, from eight to twenty-five golfers competed; from 1904 to 1914, anything from thirty-four to sixty-five were entered, depending on the venue and the month of the meeting.

From 1896 to 1903, the Amateur was held in late September, the traditional time of the interprovincial matches between Quebec and Ontario. In 1904, the event was moved to the week of Dominion Day. This enabled the RCGA to hold the popular handicap event on a public holiday, the first of July, a move that brought out a number of golfers who would not otherwise have attended. But the intense heat during the 1911 Annual Meeting persuaded the RCGA to revert to September. (Temperatures of over ninety-five degrees were recorded. People were sleeping in the streets. Ice was at a premium.) However, when only thirty-four competed at Royal Montreal in 1912, September was again abandoned for Dominion Day.

The RCGA constitution permitted only players from RCGA-member clubs to compete in the Amateur. In 1912, British champion Harold Hilton visited Canada, and the RCGA executive voted to suspend the by-law for a year to enable him to compete. Although Hilton did appear in exhibition matches in Montreal and Ottawa, he could not stay for the Amateur. Two other visitors, one American and one British, competed, but did not get far.

In 1914, the by-law was again suspended and a general invitation issued to all "English and American players in good amateur standing with their respective Associations." This led to four American entries; Brice Evans of Boston was runner-up in this last Amateur before the war.

Some of the competitors in the first few Amateurs were survivors from the 1870s and 1880s, golfers of the old school who had nurtured the game in Canada, all the while being laughed at for their idiosyncracies. The players at Ottawa in 1895 were W. W. Watson and W. A. Fleming of Royal Montreal; A. Simpson and A. Z. Palmer of Royal Ottawa; T. M. Harley of Kingston GC; C. Hunter of Niagara GC; A. P. Scott and G. F. Carter of Toronto GC.

After the turn of the century, few of the old school played, being no match for the new generation. But you will still find their names in the lesser events.

The story of these early championships is largely the story of one man, George S. Lyon. Playing out of Rosedale Golf Club until 1902, when he joined Lambton Golf and Country Club, Lyon was eight times a winner and twice a runner-up. His achievements will be dealt with later.

George Lyon's sweetest victories in the Amateur he acknowledged to be those against his brother-in-law, F. R. (Fritz) Martin, of Hamilton Golf and Country Club. Martin twice won the Amateur and was twice runner-up, a record in pre-war championships second only to Lyon's. Fritz Martin was reckoned to be the greatest left-handed golfer in North America. He is the only left-handed golfer ever to win the Canadian championship.

The left-handed Martin making his approach shot to Lambton's "Punch Bowl" in his final against Lyon in 1907 – he lost by 3 and 2.

George S. Lyon, left, *and his brother-in-law, F. R. (Fritz) Martin, Canada's two finest amateurs in the early years of the century, seen with the referee when they met in the Amateur final of 1910. Martin won at the 37th hole.*

No one defeated George Lyon more often. Martin's victories over his brother-in-law included a hard-fought Amateur final in 1910, which he won at the 37th hole. And when Lyon went for the U.S. Amateur title in 1905, it was Fritz Martin who knocked him out in the first round. The two would surely have met more often in the final of the Amateur had there been seeding of the draw. In 1903, they met in the first round; in 1905 and 1912, in the second.

Seeding of the draw was a controversial matter in those days. In 1905, Lyon had met R. S. Strath and had defeated him by the sweeping margin of 12 and 11. Strath was a good club golfer, but not of national calibre. He reached the finals largely through the luck of the draw, which put the best golfers in the same half as George Lyon. Thereafter, the matter of seeding was left to the RCGA. It was given the power to modify the draw when, in its opinion, "a change would result in improving the excellence of competition." If the executive ever did change the draw, then the changes were not made public. With proper seeding, Lyon and Martin would hardly have met in the second round in 1912.

Frederick Richard Gunning Martin, to give him his full name, was born in 1869, in Seneca Township, Haldimand County, Ontario. His grandfather had emigrated from Ireland some thirty-five years earlier. Fritz Martin attended Upper Canada College, which has been described as "the nursery of all that is best in Canadian sport." There, he became a fine rugby player, a skilled oarsman, and an international cricketer. In competition he met other cricketers who had turned to golf, including the Bethunes and the Saunders of Toronto, W. A. Henry of Halifax, H. H. Hansard of Saint John and Royal Ottawa, and his future brother-in-law, George S. Lyon.

Martin made his career as a lawyer in Hamilton. In the spring of 1898 he took up golf in a perfunctory way, joining the Hamilton club. By 1902, he was playing the game seriously. In that year he made his way through the rounds of the Canadian Amateur to beat R. C. H. (Bertie) Cassels at the 36th hole of the final.

SKETCHES AT THE GOLF CHAMPIONSHIPS—MR. "BERTIE" CASSELS, OF TORONTO.

Runner-up in 1902, R. C. H. (Bertie) Cassels, sketched at the 1905 Amateur.

Quebec City as William Doleman would have seen it.   A painting by H. Clerget, "Quebec 1854," showing, top left, the Citadel and the Plains of Abraham. AUTHOR'S COLLECTION.

A putting green on Royal Quebec in 1894; a painting by R. W. Rutherford. COURTESY ALAN J. MCCREADY, MCCREADY GALLERIES, TORONTO.

Canadians sent these postcards in the early years of this century. Cards mailed before the First World War took a one-cent stamp.

Golf Links — Royal Muskoka Hotel — Lake Rosseau Ont.
"On Grand Trunk Railway".

COURTESY DON FINLAYSON.

View from the Manoir
Richelieu Golf Club,
Murray Bay, Que.

COURTESY DON FINLAYSON.

Club House, Golf Links, Banff Springs.

Queen's Royal Hotel Golf Club-House, Niagara-on-the-Lake, Ont., Canada

St. Stephen, N.B. Golf Club.

COURTESY DON FINLAYSON.

Cataraqui Golf Club - Kingston Ont.

AUTHOR'S COLLECTION.

COURTESY DON FINLAYSON.

COURTESY DON FINLAYSON.

Westmount Golf Club House, Montreal

AUTHOR'S COLLECTION.

THE COUNTRY CLUB, SHERBROOKE, P.Q., CANADA

AUTHOR'S COLLECTION.

*A CPR poster of the Algonquin hotel, St. Andrews,
N. B.* COURTESY CP CORPORATE ARCHIVES.

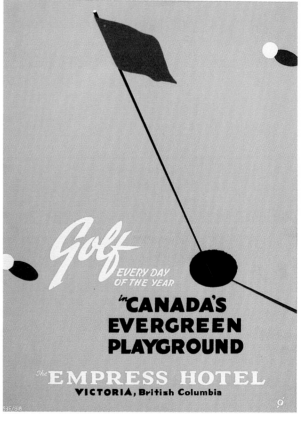

*A CPR poster for the Empress Golf Tournament,
Victoria, B. C.* COURTESY CP CORPORATE ARCHIVES.

At the time, this was looked upon as a great victory for the West, Hamilton being the most westerly club to breed a champion. He was a fine stroker of the ball, swinging in a much more orthodox way than his brother-in-law. He was long off the tee, and a fine putter.

Fritz Martin was twice runner-up in the Amateur before snatching the title from George Lyon in 1910, on the 37th green.

The contests between the two were to be repeated in Seniors' golf. But again George had the better of their encounters, and Fritz won the championship of the Canadian Seniors' Golf Association only once, in 1927. He died in 1934.

W. A. H. (Archie) Kerr of Toronto Golf Club was the only other double winner of the Amateur before the war. Born and bred in Montreal, Kerr was educated at the Royal Military College, Kingston, where, like Lyon and Martin, he developed into an all-round athlete. One of Canada's finest rugby football players, he also excelled at tennis, skating, and hockey. After studying at Osgoode Hall, he was called to the Ontario bar in 1893. A year later, he joined Toronto Golf Club.

A stylish player, with few weaknesses, Kerr's handicap came down rapidly, from nine in 1895 to scratch by the beginning of 1897, when he was the club's top player. In that year he won his first of two Amateur championships, beating T. R. Henderson of Royal Montreal in the final. Two up after eighteen holes, Kerr won easily by 5 and 4.

An unofficial ranking of Canada's top amateurs showed Archie Kerr third behind Lyon and Martin. Tragically, he was to die suddenly in April 1908, when only thirty-six. His memory is perpetuated at Toronto Golf by the Archie Kerr Memorial Trophy, put up by his father-in-law, D. R. Wilkie, an early member of the club.

On the way to his second Amateur win in 1901, at his home club, Archie Kerr beat in the semi-final a George Lyon recovering from a violent fever, and in the final, Percy

W. A. H. (Archie) Kerr, winner in 1897 and 1901.

Taylor of Royal Montreal. There was a keen rivalry between Toronto and Montreal, and the Quebec contingent had great hopes that Taylor would carry the trophy back after its four years in Toronto. But he lost at the 36th hole.

John Percy Taylor was then a fast-improving player. His father, John, had been an early member of Royal Montreal and its second captain and president. Rowing was Percy's first love. As a member of the Lachine Rowing Club he was virtually unbeatable, winning over fifty paddling prizes. He turned to golf in 1896, at the age of twenty-six, and applied himself to the game with a fierce intensity. By the time he met Kerr he had already won his club's championship four times. His strength

Percy Taylor, winner in 1904.

lay in his approaching and putting. One reporter of his final with Kerr had this to say of him:

> Mr. Taylor is a remarkably cool and careful player, and although this was not his first appearance in a championship event, he showed a wonderful improvement since last year, and is certainly one of Canada's strongest players. With the exception of his driving, his style is quite orthodox. He does not attempt to follow through, and his putting is a bit tedious to watch. Had he been more sure in his long approaches, he would have won the match.

Percy Taylor's deadly precision in the short game was probably at its peak when he defeated George Lyon for the Amateur title in 1904, playing over his home course.

An incident during the final and recorded in his club's history serves to demonstrate how attitudes to national championships have changed. All square after the morning round, Taylor went home for lunch and to change. His wife asked him to fetch water from the lake. Taylor rowed his boat out a fair distance, filled the container, and, on his way back, tipped the boat over. Not in the best of moods, he changed again, and set off for the first tee. The ducking did no harm to his game. One up at the 20th, he never lost his lead to Lyon, and went on to win by 3 and 2.

Having won the Amateur championship, Percy Taylor seems to have lost interest in national golf. He did not even turn up to defend his title in 1905. But at Royal Montreal, he won the Dennistoun Gold Medal, emblematic of the club championship, for ten years in a row.

A stockbroker for most of his life, Taylor died in 1931, at the age of sixty-one. The Montreal Stock Exchange closed for over six hours to allow members to attend the obsequies.

Before the First World War, Stuart Gillespie (he also appears in print as Stewart) of Royal Quebec was the only other player to reach the final of the Amateur at least twice. He won the title over his home course in 1896, a slightly built young man of only twenty. This made him the youngest player to win, until Donald Carrick came along nearly thirty years later. It was exceptional to find a twenty-year-old playing golf in Canada before the turn of the century, never mind one good enough to be national champion.

There is a temptation to attribute his victory to his home-course advantage. But he discounted any such explanation by reaching the final again, at Royal Montreal, three years later. Shortly afterward, Stuart Gillespie left Canada for the United States, and Canada lost its finest young golfer.

Vere Brown knocked out two former champions, Lyon and Gillespie, when winning the Amateur in 1899. Although born in England, he took up the game at Toronto's Rosedale club, and so is another home-bred champion.

Vere Brown reached the semi-finals when defending his title in 1900 and again in 1903. In 1911, the Canadian Bank of Commerce transferred him to Winnipeg, to be superintendent of its western branches. He served as the western representative on the RCGA executive and was invited to join the Rules of Golf Committee when it was formed in 1916. After the war, he left to join a bank in the United States.

In 1909, Edward Legge came to Toronto from Glasgow as a young lawyer. He joined Toronto GC, and, six months later, he walked away with the Canadian Amateur championship, having led the qualifiers by no less than seven strokes. Prominent in sports since the years he went to grammar school, Legge had attended Aberdeen University and golfed for the university team. In 1904, as a member of the Aberdeen Victoria Golf Club, he was the first winner of the Aberdeen Golf Links Cup. Shortly after winning the Amateur, he went to work in Winnipeg. He did not play in another national championship, but he did win at least one Manitoba title.

On the outbreak of war, Legge joined the army as a private. He survived the war but never did return to Canada. His photograph hangs in Winnipeg's Elmhurst club: he helped in the laying out of the club's first course on Bird's Hill.

George Hutton of Beaconsfield put up a good fight against George Lyon in the semi-final of the 1910 championships before going down at the eighteenth. A year later "the wee Scotsman" won the title. (He came from Edinburgh, being yet another of those Scottish bankers.) In 1913 or 1914 the Bank of Montreal transferred him to Chipman, Alberta, which put an end to his career in national golf. But he joined Edmonton's Mayfair club as a non-resident member and played in several provincial tournaments in the early 1920s. He led the qualifiers in the Alberta Amateur of 1924, but lost in the semi-finals to Douglas Lougheed, father of the future premier. He also played in the 1933 Amateur at Shaughnessy Heights. I wonder how many in Vancouver knew he was a former champion of Canada?

One of Canada's home-bred champions to have take up golf as a boy, Alec Wilson of Royal Montreal won in 1908. In the early years of the century, he spent summers with his parents at Little Metis, Quebec, on the south shore of the St. Lawrence. There he played at the Cascade Golf and Tennis Club, organized in 1900 and popular with many Montreal families.

Wilson's final against Fritz Martin was attended by several hundred spectators. Those who had witnessed previous Amateur finals rated this one second to none in excitement. Wilson was 4 up with only nine holes to go. Martin fought back till Wilson was dormie 1.

Edward Legge, winner in 1909, and (right) *Glen Moss, runner-up.*

The feeling was that Wilson would crack, but he played coolly for his half and a win.

Geoff Turpin was another champion who started golfing as a boy at Cascade, and another Royal Montrealer. He was a twenty-six-year-old stockbroker when he defeated Gerald Lees in 1913, after one of the hardest-fought finals before the war. It is a sign of the times that Turpin was looked upon as a youngster, his victory a surprise to many because of his relative youth. The more observant George S. Lyon rated Turpin the best amateur in Canada and forecast his victory.

Lees was 2 up at the 18th, after "performing like a machine . . . his accurate approaching and putting was wonderful to see," according to an Ottawa newspaper. Several hundred spectators followed the pair in the afternoon, a large gallery for those days. Lees appeared to succumb to nerves in the afternoon, lost his lead, and never recovered. Another stylish player, Geoff Turpin was to reach the final of the first Amateur held after the war.

Although Tom Reith never won the Amateur, he was, technically, the most accomplished golfer to come to Canada in the early years of the century. On his form, he should have won both Amateur and Open at least once, but his best performance in terms of results was in 1906, when he came second in the Open to the professional Charlie Murray. In the Amateur, he never got further than the semi-finals. His failure to win the Amateur is as surprising as Phil Farley's a generation later.

Of Reith's style, Ralph Reville of *Canadian Golfer* had this to say: "When he was going well, there was nothing more perfect than his swing, both with wood and iron, and it was a pure delight to watch him play . . . He was especially a master with the irons."

As a youth in Scotland, Reith held the course record at the Victoria Golf Club in Aberdeen. By 1895, he was playing off plus 3, and was a member of the Aberdeen University golf team. He later played in this team alongside Edward Legge.

Within months of coming to Montreal in 1905, to be a professor at Montreal High School, Reith had joined Beaconsfield and won an invitational amateur tournament at Royal Montreal. The 1906 Canadian Amateur at Royal Ottawa was his first. It was not an auspicious debut. Another young Scot, John Morgan, defeated him 5 and 4 in the first round. Yet two days earlier, Reith had gone twice round the course in 169. This was not only good enough to win the gross prize in the handicap event, but was one stroke lower than the professional Charlie Murray needed to win the Open later in the week, over the same course.

Reith led this Open for most of the way, but finished in a tie for second place, one stroke behind. This was to be the story of his career in Canadian golf. He was one of those players who excelled in stroke play, but who did not have whatever it takes to win in the head-to-head combat of a match. Tom Reith returned to Scotland around 1934 and died there a few years later.

Of the others who never won, Gerald Lees, with his much-admired swing, was one of Canada's most talented golfers. He first played out of the Outremont club in Montreal, but later moved to Royal Ottawa. Great things were forecast for him, and there was a great sadness in eastern clubhouses in 1915 when the news came that he had been killed in France.

In the 1900 Amateur, Gordon Macdougall of Royal Montreal gave George Lyon the hardest-fought struggle of any of the finals he was to win. An account of their match in the *Montreal Witness* tells us as much about how golf was perceived in 1900 as it does about the players:

> . . . it was splendid in every sense of the term, exciting to a degree, and resulting in a great deal of really excellent and brilliant play. Those who profess to sneer at golf, and see in a match of the ancient and royal game nothing but a couple of athletes in flannels chasing a couple of little white balls about a field, followed by a crowd composed

of summer girls in walking skirts and golf capes, and of men in knickerbockers and red jackets, would have changed their minds as to the amount of interest to be derived from a good game of golf had they been present on the Dixie links yesterday afternoon. For it was in every sense an afternoon of real, clean, royal sport. A rank greenhorn could not help growing enthusiastic and excited.

Lyon was 4 down at the 28th hole, and it looked as though the spectators were to see the surprise defeat of the favourite. But he won the next four holes. All square at the 36th, the match went to sudden death. At the 38th, Macdougall's putt stopped on the lip of the cup, after Lyon had sunk what was to be the winner. Which led the Montreal paper to observe:

> . . . after driving the little balls for six miles, against head winds, across stiff cross guts [sic] and before tricky "fish-tails", over meadow land, ravines, kopjes, "bunkers", sand patches, ditches, brooks, bushes, railway tracks, and what not, the winning of the match finally depended upon the failure of one ball on a certain stroke to roll a small fraction of an inch further to its objective.

The newspaper world was finding out that such is golf. The fault lay not with the ball's failure to roll that extra quarter of an inch, but with the player's failure to stroke it a quarter of an inch further.

When national championships were discontinued at the beginning of the First World War, most of these golfers were still reckoned to be among the finest in the country. In July 1915 *Canadian Golfer* published a list of Canada's top eighteen amateurs. The judges were two or three well-known but anonymous players, said to be thoroughly competent to choose fairly. Their selection had to be made "by the standard of the Canadian championships," so they could not consider the many fine players in the West and in the Maritimes who had never played in the Amateur or in the interprovincial matches (still confined to Ontario versus Quebec).

Nevertheless, it is likely that the top five would have kept their ranking had this been truly national. They were, in order of merit: Lyon (Lambton); Martin (Hamilton); Reith (Beaconsfield); Legge (St. Charles); Turpin (Royal Montreal); Moss (Toronto); D. Laird (St. Charles); Hutton (The West); Grier (Royal Montreal); Adams (Hamilton); W. Laird (St. Charles); Blackwood (Toronto); Cassels (Toronto); Wilson (Royal Montreal); Gray (Rosedale); More (Toronto); Dawson (St. Charles); James (Lambton).

Four of these golfers were members of the St. Charles club in Winnipeg, but all had made their names when golfing in Toronto.

We have already met Legge. On his way to his championship in 1909, he was given a rare fight by William G. Laird and only escaped at the 21st hole of their quarter-final match. Bill Laird was a young Fifer (Carnoustie and Monifieth), stood six feet four inches in his cleats, and could outdrive any amateur in Canada. Upon immigrating in 1906, he joined the Toronto Golf Club. He won several local tournaments, including the championship of the League of the Lower Lakes and the Lambton Open Amateur of 1909, in which he defeated Legge in the final. That same year, he was the leading amateur in the Canadian Open. To reach the quarter-finals of the Amateur, he had to dispose of both George Lyon and George Hutton.

Ed Legge and Bill Laird gave us the stuff that legend is made of. When playing for Ontario in a four-ball, best-ball, against Quebec, the pair found themselves 4 down with five to play. They won by covering the last five holes in 15 strokes.

Bill Laird was transferred to Winnipeg where he, too, became a provincial champion. Determined to win the Amateur, he came east at his own expense to compete at Ottawa in 1911. He led the qualifiers, setting a new amateur record of 77, but was knocked out in an early round of match play. He was never to get another chance. Like so many of his generation, Bill Laird was killed in the First World War.

The seventh man on the list, Douglas Laird, came to Winnipeg and joined St. Charles at about the same time as Legge and Bill Laird (no relation). Born in New York, Douglas Laird captained the Princeton golf team around 1904. When his father returned to Canada, young Laird joined Toronto GC. He fought his way to the final of the 1906 Amateur, only to meet George Lyon at his best. An erratic golfer, brilliant when he could control his urge to go for length, Douglas Laird was to do well in the early Manitoba championships.

The last St. Charles man on the list, Dudley Dawson, had learned his golf as a youth at Rosedale. Joining Lambton when it was organized in 1902, he was soon one of its rising young stars. He worked for that great nursery of Canadian golf, the Dominion Bank, which transferred him first to Peterborough, then to Winnipeg. He had reached the semi-finals of the Amateur in 1904, but that was to be his best performance. Out West, he captured the Manitoba Amateur championship in 1907, 1909, and 1910. In later years, Dudley Dawson returned to Toronto and rose to be general manager of his bank.

Of the others, Bert Adams of Hamilton Golf and Country Club (he started his golf at Simcoe) never gave of his best in national championships until a Senior. For years he more or less dominated golf in Hamilton and district, proving an able successor to Fritz Martin. Winning the Niagara International trophy in three successive years probably did as much as anything to rank him in tenth place.

Robert M. (Bob) Gray Jr. of Rosedale was later to become one of Canada's most respected golfers, but his national successes came as a Senior. William More built up a record at Toronto GC second to none, but national competition never seemed to bring out his best golf. Much the same can be said of Wilfred James of Lambton. Charles Grier of Royal Montreal was just then beginning to make a name for himself. His best was yet to come, in the post-war championships. R. C. H. (Bertie) Cassels had been on the scene since the early 1900s, giving Fritz Martin a fright in the final of the 1902 Amateur. But Cassels became better known as an administrator, the long-time solicitor to the RCGA, its first expert on the rules of golf, and, in 1922, its president.

In looking back, what seems most surprising about the early Amateur championships is that the first champion, Tom Harley, was the only winner in fourteen years (until Legge in 1909) to have learned the game in Britain. The greatest name not to appear on the Aberdeen Cup is that of A. W. Smith. Too, T. B. Reith's name should have appeared on the trophy at least once. The same can perhaps be said of F. G. H. Pattison, of Hamilton. A Musselburgh man, he had played for Cambridge in the second match against Oxford in 1879 (defeating the great Horace Hutchinson). Pattison came to Canada to work as a fruit farmer at Winona, Ontario, with his best golf behind him, and he had to settle for runner-up place in the 1898 Amateur. Like so many golfers of his time, he had to learn how to cope with George S. Lyon but, like them, never did.

GEORGE S. LYON:
THE GRAND YOUNG
MAN OF GOLF

IF YOU HAD ASKED ANY CANADIAN SEVENTY years ago who would be judged the most electrifying, most colourful, most inspiring golfer of this century, the answer would have been unequivocal: George S. Lyon.

It is a fact that no male golfer has so dominated amateur golf in this country for so long. Certainly, no golfer has been more respected or beloved. George Lyon's career in national and international golf is surpassed only by that of Marlene Stewart Streit, and if there is any other contender for George's title, then it has to be her. Imagine what a treat it would have been to watch him partner Marlene in an international foursome!

George Lyon's record in amateur golf has not been equalled by any Canadian male golfer:

Canadian Amateur champion: 1898, 1900, 1903, 1905-7, 1912, 1914
Canadian Seniors' G.A. champion: 1918-23, 1925-26, 1928, 1930

U.S./Canada Seniors' G. A. champion: 1923, 1930-32
Olympic Games, 1904: gold medal and Olympic Cup for golf.

George Lyon was also runner-up in the 1910 Canadian Open, and in the 1906 U.S. Amateur championship.

What George Lyon did for Canadian golf, Bobby Jones was to do for American golf twenty years later. Both were modest men, respected as gentlemen, admired as sportsmen, feared and envied as competitors. But there the similarity ends. Jones developed from a boy star to a national champion when in his early twenties. Lyon did not take up golf until he was in his late thirties. The Jones swing was a thing of beauty; the Lyon swing an impossible marriage of baseball and cricket, in its time described variously as "a coal-heaver's swing" and "the swing of a man cutting wheat with a scythe." Never one to be racked by doubts or conflicting theories, George Lyon believed that the ball should be smote hard, and that the method of smiting was of little consequence.

George Lyon was a man of boundless good spirits who brought great gusto to the game. At home and abroad, he established rich bonds of friendship with other golfers, bringing great credit to Canada and to the club he helped found at Lambton, whose name became known throughout North American golf. (The story was told of the Canadian visitor to New York who bought a Toronto newspaper and asked the newsboy if he knew where Toronto was. "Yessir," the boy replied, "Toronto is done located about seven miles from Lambton.")

Lyon became renowned as an international sportsman, first as a cricketer, then as a golfer. At the Olympic tournament, the Americans could make nothing of this man, the Chicago *Telegram* seeing him as a "veteran whose sinews are of iron and whose temperament is as phlegmatic as that of an Algonquin Indian." At the age of forty-six, he beat their own champion, Egan, who was less than half Lyon's age. But it was Egan who was exhausted after their 34-hole final, and Lyon who walked on his hands the full length of the clubhouse.

His colourful excursions in such events caused pages to be written in the Canadian sporting sheets, helping to bring golf to the attention of thousands who had never heard of the game. George Lyon caught the interest and imagination of all. He is remembered as a man who played golf for the sheer enjoyment of it, as one who loved to win with deep and untrammelled sincerity, but who knew how to win graciously, how to lose gracefully. Above all, he was a man who hewed to the written and unwritten rules of the game.

George was also the dominating spirit in the clubhouse. "Wherever George Lyon sat was the head of the table," Ralph Reville wrote of him. Thousands of golfers in Canada, Britain, and the United States, at one time or another, joined him in his inimitable rendering of "My Wild Irish Rose" and "Mother Machree."

Finally, as an example of the charisma of the man, of the way in which spectators came to fall under the spell of his sheer good nature and sportsmanship, here is an account from the New York *Tribune* of the astonishing scene after he had lost to Eben Byers in the final of the U.S. Amateur, in 1906. (Byers had already made his way to the clubhouse.)

> [As Lyon] turned to leave the green, there was a remarkable scene. The onlookers blocked his steps, and those nearest shook his hand and patted his back, while the hundreds who couldn't reach him, began to clap hands. The women were as noisy in applauding as the men, and if not clapping they were waving their handkerchiefs or parasols. Lyon, although the color of a boiled lobster from the sun, blushed to a deeper shade, and doffed his cap five or six times. It was a scene unprecedented at the championships. "Speech, speech," yelled some of the applauders . . . As he ducked away, Lyon answered with a laugh, "I hope I gave my friends a run for their money."

George Lyon did not play golf until shortly after his thirty-seventh birthday, in 1895. This fact has been mentioned so many times over the years that we are inclined to look upon him as something of an oddity. But he was no such thing. In his day, golf was only becoming a popular sport in Canada. In the 1890s, it was not unusual for men and women to take up competitive golf when well over thirty, and to outperform their juniors. Harvey Combe of Victoria, B.C., was only four years younger when he took up golf at about the same time as George Lyon, to become the champion of the Canadian West Coast.

In the British *Golf Illustrated* of February 1906, Lyon told how he came to the game:

> My first experience of golf was in the fall of 1895; I only played a few times, however, before winter set in; but I took up the game quite enthusiastically in the spring of 1896. I was first induced to play . . . by Mr. John

Dick . . . a member of the Rosedale Golf Club. . . . I was up at the Rosedale Cricket Ground waiting for some of the players to come up for [cricket] practice, when Mr. Dick came along with his golf clubs and said to me, "Come with me, Lyon, and have a try at golf."

I felt like saying to him, "Tip-cat," but, of course, not wishing to be rude, I did not. Still, I had a sort of contempt for the game, though I had never played it . . . Well, we went out to the tee, and he teed a ball and gave me a driver and told me what to do. I remember I drove a fairly good ball, and then when I came up to it he gave me an iron and told me to play at the flag. I will not say any more about my short game, as I fear I took too many strokes to be counted. Besides, I cared little for what was called the short game. We went to the second tee, and again I drove a fairly good ball, and this seemed to please me, so I kept going from one hole to the other until I had gone over the then full course of nine holes, and, like all other beginners, I caught the fever there and then. I asked to be proposed as a member the next day and was in due course elected, and from that day to the present, it would be hard to find a more enthusiastic golfer.

In 1896 and 1897, he played cricket in the summer, golf in the spring and fall. In the first round of the Canadian Amateur in 1897, George Lyon shocked everyone by defeating the title holder, Gillespie, by no less than 7 and 5 over eighteen holes. In the second round, he put out W. W. Watson of the home club, at the eighteenth. But he went down in the third round to an experienced Scot, T. R. Henderson.

In 1898, he played cricket as usual in the summer but practised his golf for two weeks before the Amateur. Lyon went through the pack with little difficulty, taking the final from the Cambridge Scot, Pattison, by 12 and 11. So, within three years of holding a golf club in his hands, George Lyon had become the Canadian amateur champion.

This was the first of a long string of victories, for George Lyon was to dominate Canadian

George S. Lyon, in the front centre, a member of the Canadian cricket team that played Lord Hawke's eleven in 1894.

amateur golf until the First World War. Even in the 1920s, he was a very hard man to beat. His record of eight wins in the men's national amateur championship of his country has never been equalled in Canada, and it matches that of the noted British golfer who was his contemporary, John Ball.

When George Lyon won his third successive Amateur in 1907, he became the outright owner of the Aberdeen Cup. (The cup, alas, has disappeared. His son Fred Lyon told me that it sat for years on a shelf in the Lyon household with George's many other trophies.)

He was to add a second string of titles in Senior golf, winning the Canadian Seniors' Golf Association championship ten times, the U.S./Canada Seniors' title four times. (In his day, the only Senior events were those for members of golf associations.)

George Lyon won his first three national titles as a member of Rosedale Golf Club. When Lambton was organized in 1902, he became a charter member. He captained the club for twenty-three years. He also captained Canadian international teams against the

George S. Lyon in 1898, shortly after he took up golf.

Olympic golf champion, St. Louis, 1904.

The grand old man in the 1930s. Note the six clubs in a stovepipe bag.

United States and, as a Senior, against the United States and Britain.

He was chairman of the RCGA's first Rules of Golf Committee in 1916 and went on to be RCGA president in 1923.

George Lyon twice tried his hand at the British Amateur. In 1905, he lost in the third round; in 1908, in the fourth.

No victory brought him more recognition than his winning the gold medal at the St. Louis Olympic Games in 1904. This was the first time, but not the last, that he was to offend the purists with his style. Nor was it the last time he was to shock the cream of U.S. golfers with its effectiveness.

It is doubtful if any event has created more suspense, excitement, and exhilaration among Canada's golfers than George Lyon's winning the gold medal at St. Louis. And it is hard to think of any single event which has done more for the game in this country.

In those days, the Olympics were the product of a world of golden afternoons, unclouded by politics and commercialism. "Open to the Amateurs of the World," the golfing program proudly proclaimed, which meant true-blue amateurs of sufficient means and substance.

Lyon was then forty-six. He had to play twelve rounds of golf in six days. He suffered acutely from summer catarrh, or hay fever, and the weather in St. Louis in September can be hot and humid, and aggravating to hay fever. Lyon was one of three Canadians in a field of seventy Americans, which included their national champion. He had never before seen the course of the Glen Echo club. Its fairways were flanked by thousands of partisan Americans, rooting for their favourite sons. The final was played in a tropical downpour.

Had George Lyon lost, these are some of the factors that might reasonably have been put forward to explain why. But he won. He won with vigour and grace, and in a manner that not only captured the hearts of Canadians but left him with many life-long friends and admirers in the United States.

There was nothing of the fluke about his victory. On his way to the final, he took on the champions of France and the U.S. Pacific Coast. In the final, he defeated Chandler Egan, the U.S. amateur champion. Egan had only recently won his title by defeating Walter Travis, the American who held the British title. This led some writers in Canada to hail Lyon as "the Champion of the World." Which was nonsense, of course. For one thing, the British did not take part in the Olympic tournament at St. Louis. Admittedly, they had been invited. But their absence discounts any claim that this Olympic event was a test of the world's best golfers. George Lyon, with characteristic modesty, admitted as much in an article he wrote for the *Toronto Daily Star*: "Now I would just like to say here that though the winning of this trophy carries with it the title of champion of the world, I am not foolish enough to think I am the best player in the world . . . but I am satisfied that I am not the worst."

The course of the Glen Echo Country club is situated on high ground, in those days some twelve miles from St. Louis. It was just over 6,100 yards long, which made it of championship length. It had most things that a good golf course should have – trees, a ravine, a brook, undulating ground. George Lyon wrote in the *Star*: "I never played on a course where I had to play so many down hill lies." Too, its greens were only a year old and difficult to read.

Before the tournament, George Lyon went largely unnoticed by the American players and press. If his name came up at all, it was usually in a comment that he was one of three competitors from outside the United States. Walter Travis, the American holder of the British title, did not compete, claiming that he was off form. The local favourite was Stewart Stickney of the St. Louis Country Club. The new U.S. national champion (who was also the western champion), twenty-year-old Chandler Egan, came from the Exmoor club in Chicago. He was the clear favourite to win at Glen Echo. A good, all-round player, with a classical swing, Egan was an exceptionally long hitter. Frank Newton of Seattle, "the Scotch wizard" and champion of the U.S. Pacific Coast, was favoured by many.

The eighty or so entrants were reduced to thirty-two by two rounds of stroke play on the Monday. Stewart Stickney led the qualifiers with a 163. Chandler Egan came seventh, equalling the amateur course record of 78 in his second round. George Lyon put together an 84 85–169 to tie for ninth spot.

The Toronto *Star* correspondent noted that "scores were not particularly good, owing to heavy rain on Sunday, which made the ground very soft, and the balls in many cases stuck half an inch deep in the soft earth." There were no great surprises. All those fancied to win were somewhere in the top sixteen. But there were a few heartbreaks. One player from New Jersey ruined his chances before he left the first tee. The Chicago *Evening Post* told of his catastrophic start:

> Dr. W. F. Shaw, of Westfield, Mass., developed the worst case of hard luck ever seen at a big tourney. He traveled from Friday night until this morning to play in the Olympian championship, arriving at the club just as his name was called. With one stroke he killed his chances of qualifying. His drive struck a tree, the ball bounding back into the hedge to the right of the tee. His next was into the tennis court. Batting along like a disappointed man, the doctor finally got out ten yards in front of the tee in seven strokes. His eighth was into the rough, and the spectators said good-by to his chances.

Lyon and Egan were drawn in separate halves of the draw, but at the time this had no significance to the experts. Stickney or Newton – in Lyon's half of the draw – were considered the most likely to meet Egan in the final.

Each round comprised 36 holes, 18 in the morning, 18 in the afternoon. George Lyon was given a hard fight in the first round, although he eventually beat his man by 5 and 4. In the second round, against Stickney, Lyon set a new course record of 77, all putts holed, and was no less than 8 up after the morning round. He went on to whip Stickney by 11 and 9. "The greatest surprise of the day," many experts wrote, among them a reporter from the *Toronto Daily Star*, and they began to look more closely at this forty-six-year-old man with "the coal-heaver's swing."

Lyon was now the oldest competitor left in the tournament. In the third round, he brought further dismay to St. Louis by knocking out the left-hander, A. B. Lambert, the champion of France and now a member of Glen Echo. "Lyon's driving was as steady as clockwork, and his control over the ball was perfect . . . while his nerves seemed of steel, so easy and resourceful was he in his putting," reported the *Star*.

George Lyon had now reached the semi-finals. Here he ran up against his toughest opponent to date. His battle with Newton was described by one observer as "the most desperate set-to of the tournament." When it was all over, George Lyon agreed, in an article written for the *Star*:

> I will never forget the battle royal we fought. Mr. F. C. Newton of Seattle, the champion of the Pacific coast was, without doubt, to my mind my strongest opponent. He is a young man, of good physique and average height, and has a good free swing . . . Nearly all through the match it was one up or one down or all square, and right up to the thirty-sixth hole it was anyone's match. I had to hole a nine-foot putt on the last green to win . . . I am inclined to think that had Newton won from me, he would have also defeated the national champion [Egan].

Throughout the tournament, Lyon's driving was described as phenomenal. He was the only man consistently to reach the first green, 276 yards from the tee. At the 25th hole against Newton, he drove all of 300 yards – by some accounts 325 yards. Normally good but not outstanding on the green, he managed to save himself several times by holing long and critical putts. At the 30th hole, Newton (1 up)

drove into the creek. The Chicago *Evening Post* observed: "Newton's iron nerve now gave way . . . You could almost imagine you heard his nerves rend like the tearing of a canvas sheet. The observant ones then remarked 'Newton is done.' So it turned out." One up coming to the last hole, Lyon hit a long straight drive, while Newton half-topped his. But Newton recovered, forcing Lyon to sink that nine-foot putt for the match.

Before the final, Egan was still favoured to win. "Lyon is playing against the man of the year," one U.S. newspaper reassured its readers. It was unthinkable that this twenty-year-old national champion, the epitome of style, could fall victim to a man with such an unwieldy swing. But the experts outside Canada were always underestimating George Lyon.

In the final, Egan was very late in arriving on the tee, as he had been in his semi-final. If he thought this would unnerve his opponent, he was in for a shock. George Lyon attacked him like a whirlwind, was 4 up after five holes, and 3 up at the turn, which he reached in 37 strokes. Thereafter, Egan whittled away at Lyon's lead, reducing it to one hole at the end of the morning round.

That round had been played in what was described by one as "a pitiless, cold, northwest rain," by another as "cyclonic conditions." Most greens were flooded in parts. Unable to putt, the players often had to chip the ball over puddles of casual water. The *Sunday Record-Herald* of Chicago described the play at the seventh green in the morning: "Casual water stood in pools on the green, and Tom Bendelow, as manager of the gallery, borrowed a broom from a street car conductor just over the fence and swept the water away. The rain came down almost as fast as the green could be swept. . . ."

Lyon went round in 80 to Egan's 81. The American champion had won the long-driving competition before Lyon arrived at St. Louis but now found himself consistently outdriven by the older man. Unable to control his long game, Egan was often wild off the tee. Perhaps he swung too hard, trying to keep up. This was to be his undoing in the afternoon.

The end of the match was described by the Chicago *Telegram*:

> Two down, three to go, [Egan] seemed to lose his last ray of hope. A more weird exhibition of golf he never displayed than on the way to the thirty-fourth deceptive green. His tee shot was sliced into the rough, his next went to a tree to the right of the country and his third also went wild, striking another tree. Lyon, who had pulled out a long, telling drive, followed with a fine second and was on the green in three, only two feet from the flag. Holing in 4 to Egan's 6 [Lyon] became the possessor of the massive Olympian cup and the heavy gold medal trophies considered to be the greatest prizes ever offered in the game of golf.

Egan took his defeat with good grace, admitting that he had been outclassed by Lyon, whom he described as "one of the cleverest players I have met."

The Olympic Trophy.

The last word to Frank Newton, quoted by Seattle's *Post-Intelligencer*:

> . . . Lyon [is a man of] remarkable physical endurance. He is an old cricketer, and that helps a great deal in golf. He makes the most remarkable and accurate drives that I have ever witnessed . . . At the conclusion of the game when the rest of us were tired out he walked on his hands the full length of the club dining room at St. Louis.

In Canadian cities where golf was more than a word, newspapers reported George Lyon's progress through the Olympic tournament, day by day. Some even carried on their front pages news of how he stood at the time of going to press ("Lyon at Noon Was Ahead of Newton"). The *Free Press* of Winnipeg – the city then had only one golf club – gave its readers the same hole-by-hole account of the matches as carried by the press in Toronto.

There would be occasional mention of the other two Canadians who had accompanied Lyon to St. Louis, neither of whom had qualified. A. W. Austin, president of Lambton, had won the *fourth* flight consolation prize; his son, Albert E. (Bert), came home empty-handed.

The news of George Lyon's victory reached Toronto over the wires of the Associated Press,

A sketch of Lyon's Olympic Gold Medal.

at some time between seven and eight o'clock on the Saturday evening. Those still at the Lambton clubhouse held a spontaneous celebration. The club's secretary, Harold Muntz, sent a telegram, which, in true Olympian spirit, recognized both wins: "To A. W. Austin . . . heartiest congratulations to Lyon and yourself." On the Monday, the train from St. Louis stopped at Lambton to pick up – perhaps literally – a large number of club members, before making its way to Union Station. Unless distance lends enchantment, this would seem as fine a day as any to have been there.

In the weeks that followed, George Lyon was fêted by his club and by the city of Toronto, whose civic leaders presented him with a silver fruit dish. Among the numerous letters of congratulations was one from the leader of the opposition, R. L. Borden.

George Lyon's victory brought hope to middle-aged golfers everywhere. And it made news of a game that was not yet a household word in Canada. Time now to take a closer look at the man who did much to make it so.

George Seymour Lyon was born on 27 July 1858, in the village of Richmond, some twenty miles south of Ottawa. He was educated at the local grammar school.

Around 1880 he settled in Toronto, working in the insurance business. (In May 1931, when he retired as chief agent of the Sun Insurance Office, Toronto, he was said to have given this company over thirty-seven years of loyal and faithful service.) He also joined the Queen's Own Rifles of Canada in 1881, as a reservist, and served through the North-West Rebellion of 1885, first as a corporal, finally as a sergeant. His regiment was among those who made the famous two-hundred-mile march from Swift Current to relieve the besieged town of Battleford.

From his youth, George Lyon was an outstanding athlete. To him, sports were not only healthful and character-building, they were the very essence of life itself. He played football, hockey, and tennis; when only eighteen, he held the Canadian pole vault record of 10 feet 6 inches. In 1886 and 1887, he captained the insurance baseball team in the Commercial League of Ontario and was considered to be one of the best amateur players in the country. From the early 1880s, he played cricket, first for East Toronto, later for Parkdale and Rosedale; he was capped eleven times by Canada, at least once as captain, in matches against teams from Britain and the United States. In 1894, when playing for Rosedale Cricket Club against a combined Toronto Peterborough side, he carried his bat for 238, said to be a record in first-class cricket until Don Bradman bettered it in 1934. George Lyon also curled in teams that captured the Walker Trophy, the Canada Life Trophy, and the coveted Ontario Tankard.

When in his mid-forties and fifties, at the peak of his golfing career, he was a stocky, well-muscled 180-pounder, standing just under five feet eight inches. He had tremendous strength in his arms, legs, and thighs, all of which helped his golf. A 1906 newspaper reported him to have "plenty of girth to his shoulders, giving evidence of good lungs. His out-of-door life is evident in his browned face, and his forearms when cleared of shirtsleeve for a match exhibit two bronze models." He was, by the same account, a holy terror to play against. "Once he has played his stroke, off he goes like a steam engine, and if his opponent will follow at the same gait he will soon learn that he has a pace maker who will walk him off his feet."

In 1891, George Lyon married Annette Mary, daughter of Frederick Martin of Toronto. They had five children; their two sons both became first-rate golfers.

The great sorrow of George Lyon's life was the death of his elder son, George S. Jr., known as Seymour, who had been injured at the third battle of Ypres. Seymour recovered sufficiently to become one of Canada's finest young golfers, leading the qualifiers in the 1919 Amateur. But he died suddenly in 1925, from a pneumonic condition brought on by his war wounds.

The other son, Fred – the first winner of the Ontario Junior championship in 1924 – later became a governor of the RCGA. Fred died in January 1987.

In after-golf singsongs, George Lyon so often gave voice to "My Wild Irish Rose" and "Mother Machree" that many believed his family came from Ireland. In fact, he was part Irish, part Scottish. The Lyons were pioneers of Upper Canada, and their story is as romantic as any you will find in the history of the settlement that became Ontario.

George Lyon's paternal grandfather, Captain George Lyon, was born in Perth, Fifeshire, in 1789, son of Baillie George Lyon of the Strathmore Lyons. Captain George appears to have lived in Inverurie, Aberdeenshire, before coming to British North America as a lieutenant in the 100th Regiment of Foot, to fight in the War of 1812. One of his sons, Robertson Lyon (the father of George S.), married into an Irish family, the Maxwells. And George S. Lyon married Fritz Martin's sister. So, with an Irish mother and wife, it is not surprising that George Lyon should give vent to Irish songs.

To George Lyon, his finest achievement was not his Olympic gold, nor any of his eight victories in the Canadian Amateur. He believed he played his finest golf in 1906, at Englewood Golf Club, New Jersey, when taking second place in the U.S. Amateur. He must also have been pleased to defeat for the second time his opponent in the Olympic final, young Chandler Egan.

This time, Egan could not make the excuse that he was over-golfed, as his friends had claimed in St. Louis. He was again a clear favourite. As for Lyon, the critics had obviously forgotten how he had foxed them two years earlier. "No one except the Canadian thought he had a ghost of a chance," the *Toronto Daily Star* reported.

A gallery as large as the final's followed Egan and Lyon when they met in the second round. As it became obvious that their man Egan was not going to have an easy win – might even be defeated – the armchair experts noted Lyon's style, and later ridiculed it.

Lyon won at the 20th.

In the final, George Lyon met Eben M. Byers. Having defeated Walter J. Travis, Byers was now the odds-on favourite for the title. Although Lyon never made any excuse for his loss to Byers, it is a fact that Byers had an experienced caddie, a professional from his home club of St. Andrews, Yonkers, whereas Lyon was given a boy of fourteen, a mere bag-toter. We will never know what difference that made, but it could have been worth the single stroke separating the two men after 36 holes of match play.

Over three thousand spectators followed the match. According to the *Star* they were "kept at boiling heat all the time, both as regards the closeness of the game and the temperature of the day, which was close up to 90 degrees."

Lyon started as he had at Glen Echo. Three up at the ninth, he was pulled back to 1 at the eighteenth. He went round in 77 to Byers's 79. In the afternoon, Byers quickly took over the lead, was 1 up at the 35th hole, and halved the final hole to win.

The New York *Tribune* saw the finalists in this light:

> Young Byers, trim in knickerbockers and with a style modelled on the methods of classic St. Andrews and Sandwich, was in contrast in every way to the stocky, grey-haired, old-time amateur cricket player, who stood in flannel trousers and white shirt as if to bat or bowl. He golfs as a baseball player does, hitting and poking, instead of swinging with freedom and follow through, but Lyon made shots with fine results . . . "He reminds me of a baby elephant," said one stickler for style.

Although George Lyon did not capture the U.S. title, he captured the hearts of the spectators, as witness their spontaneous show of affection for him on the final green. "It was a scene unprecedented at any major championship . . ." Exceptional indeed. But so was the man.

Two years later, the Olympic Games were held in London, England, so George Lyon went over to defend his title. But the Royal and Ancient and the Olympic committee could not agree on a number of things, the British competitors withdrew, and the golf event was cancelled. There was talk of awarding the gold medal to George Lyon as the undefeated champion, but he would have none of it.

From early in this century, George Lyon was an honorary member of over twenty golf clubs in Canada. You will find him playing for Lambton in an interclub match, the next week for Toronto Golf Club in the League of the Lower Lakes. But he was a Lambton man. The officers of the club presented him with his portrait by a well-known Canadian artist, E. Wyly Grier. Another portrait hangs in the St. George's Golf and Country Club, Toronto, where he laid the foundation stone for the clubhouse in 1929.

If you look at the handsome face, wrinkled by the wind and sun of so many fairways, it is not too difficult to imagine those keen blue eyes concentrating over a putt on the last green at Englewood, or Glen Echo, or at his beloved Lambton.

In his later years, he served the Canadian Seniors' Golf Association as charter governor, chairman of the tournament committee, and always as captain of the international teams.

In 1930, when he won both the Canadian and U.S. Seniors', the members of Lambton put up the George S. Lyon Cup. This has been competed for ever since by teams from Ontario clubs.

George Lyon suffered acutely from hay fever. And in 1911, when he had to withdraw from the Canadian Amateur, it was said that a recurring problem with his eyes would soon bring an end to his competitive career. He went on to play for another twenty-six years, and to shoot his age from his sixty-ninth birthday, with one exception – when he was seventy-eight, he did not play much golf

because of a wrist injury. The story of this injury, and how it affected him, was touchingly described by the Toronto *Star*:

> . . . the agony of waiting for the shattered wrist to mend took its toll on Mr. Lyon . . . he seemed to age from then on . . . with his arm in a sling, he would haunt the golf courses of the district and chat with all his friends, and always the question would be "how's the wrist, George, and when do you think you'll be able to play?" He would move over to the club's putting green and stab at a few balls with his one good hand . . . hoping and waiting for the day when he could again swing a golf club.

He was out and about again in 1937. In one game, he needed a par 4 for a 78, one less that his age, but took a 6 for an 80. Uncharacteristically, he had looked up when playing a chip shot.

George Lyon suffered a stroke at Christmas, 1937. He died in May 1938.

This merry, modest, much-beloved man was the inspirative figure in Canadian golf for over thirty years. Simple in his faith, in his songs, and in his long devotion to the royal and ancient game, he put Canadian golf forever in his debt.

When young Chandler Egan took the U.S. championship from the much older Walter J. Travis in 1904, a poem (after Kipling's "Recessional") appeared in an American golf magazine, praising youth. ("Youth will not, can not, be denied.") But this particular youth was to be defeated by George Lyon, later that year. A poet of the Lambton club did not let this go unheralded:

> Boast not thy Youth. A Veteran tried
> to test thy skill, to call thee forth.
> A Veteran from the hardy North
> said "Youth may often be denied."
> The Olympic laurel must be gained.
> This sport on age puts not a ban;
> the Youth went down before the Man,
> and Lyon stands where Egan reigned.
> "Lest we forget – lest we forget."

CHAPTER

THE FIRST PROFESSIONALS AND THE CANADIAN OPEN

Are there not enough professionals in Canada (together with the best amateurs) to have an open Canadian championship event? This would prove interesting, and could be held at the same time as the amateur championship, and there would be at least five or six professional entries. As it stands now, the pro's do a great deal for the game in the matter of coaching etc., but beyond this have no particular interest in the game here.

– *Saturday Night*, 19 June 1900

WHATEVER IT MAY HAVE THOUGHT of the suggestion that it organize an Open championship, the RCGA wisely waited for four years. The amateurs already had their own national championship. Why should they play in another, against the same competitors plus the half dozen professionals then in the country?

But even as these words were being written, they were being overtaken by events. In the early years of this century, golf in Canada was growing rapidly in just about every province. The long-established clubs were full, with waiting lists, and city golfers had been forced to organize new clubs. These were all fairly large and prosperous, with members who needed and demanded professional help, in all sorts of ways.

The visit to Canada in 1900 of the top British professional, Harry Vardon, encouraged many to take up the game. At exhibition matches in Montreal and Toronto he made golf look so easy. He also set new standards for those who thought they were playing well by showing them otherwise. This was altogether a new game they were witnessing, one of easy grace and frightful accuracy. Perhaps they, too, could play like Vardon, given a skilled instructor. For all these reasons, the number of professionals in Canada had increased fourfold by 1904, when the first Open was held.

In Britain, the title of "professional" or "club professional" was popularized with the spread of the game to England. The man employed by a Scottish golf club to tend to the needs of its members and to its course had traditionally been given the title of "Green-keeper" or "Custodian of the Green." For his wage of one pound (about five dollars) a week, he was expected to control a squad of caddies and to be keeper of the green, or golf course. This meant little more than cutting the grass, reseeding divot marks, filling tee-boxes with sand, and cutting the holes on the greens. For a fixed fee, he would also repair golf clubs, remould gutta-percha golf balls, and coach the members by playing with them.

At a large club, the greenkeeper might have up to a dozen men to help him: three or four clubmakers, a caddie master, a groundsman, and labourers for the course. But a small club might be able to afford only one man, a jack of all trades.

As evidence of a gradual change in the status of the professional in Britain, many of them were now abandoning their traditional trousers and dressing like amateurs, in plus-fours (knickerbockers) and stockings, following the example set by Vardon. Nevertheless, in his own country, the British professional was still viewed as very much of the working class; *Golf Illustrated* defined a professional as "a golfer who spits on his hands." He still knew his place, which was in his workshop or locker-room, not in the clubhouse.

Much to his astonishment, he found himself treated like an equal in North America. When touring North American clubs, Vardon and Willie Park Jr. were invited to lunch with members. Having worked for some time in America, professional Bernard Nicholls complained about having to lunch in the professional's shop when he came back to England. The British press reported Vardon as making a mint of money out of his North American tour, as much as ten thousand pounds (or fifty thousand dollars).

These reports fired the imagination of British club professionals. There was every incentive to immigrate to Canada and the United States at the turn of the century. Golf there was growing, wages were better, and they could expect to be treated more as equals than as servants to the members.

In 1881, the Royal Montreal club had brought over William Davis, a Scot then working as an assistant professional at the Royal Liverpool GC, Hoylake, England, where Alexander Dennistoun was well known. This golfing Columbus was only seventeen or eighteen at the time. Royal Montreal engaged him for the playing season starting in April 1881, at a guaranteed wage of one guinea per week (about $5.25). In those days, professionals would coach members by playing with them; pupils were expected to learn by example. For playing a round of nine holes with a member, Davis was allowed to charge the equivalent of twenty-three cents, but a third of this went back to the club. He was also expected to make and repair clubs and balls, for an agreed fee.

The professional Columbus, William Davis of Royal Montreal.

Davis also agreed that "it shall be part of my business to put and keep the Green in order, as well as the putting holes." And it was because of this clause that the deal between Royal Montreal and its first professional came unstuck.

To Davis, the clause meant that he would supervise a groundsman, such as the Mr. McNulty (or McAnulty) the club had hired in the past. But to the club and its captain, it meant that Davis would do the work of McNulty – would cut the grass and care for the course – when he was not repairing clubs or coaching.

This was not an unreasonable request. Royal Montreal, remember, had only twenty-five members. It could not afford the luxury of both a professional and a groundsman, as could Royal Liverpool with its five hundred members. But Davis refused. At Royal Liverpool he had not been expected to do such menial chores. Royal Montreal and its professional were at odds. Neither would yield. In October 1881, the club offered Davis to Royal Quebec, but Quebec was not interested. So the club told Davis it would pay his passage back to England.

Davis did not leave Canada. He found work for the winter and, in June 1882, again offered to serve Royal Montreal as a coach and a clubmaker, but not as a working greenkeeper. The club did not yield, and Davis was on his own. (Most accounts have him returning to Britain after this, but they fly in the face of his own statement, in a letter in 1895 to the British magazine *Golf*, that he was in North America continuously for fourteen years. He may have taken a job in a bank, since he appears to have done this during his first winter or two in Montreal.)

Royal Montreal made do with only a groundsman on its payroll until Davis rejoined the club in 1890. By this time, the club's membership had tripled, and it could now afford both a professional and a groundsman. Davis's duties included supervising the greenkeeper.

During his second term with Royal Montreal, Davis turned his hand to laying out courses. In 1891, he laid out the first course of the Royal Ottawa Golf Club. The members of the newly formed club at Ottawa also bought a supply of his clubs.

Davis also laid out a course at the Shinnecock Hills Golf Club in Long Island, which claims to be the first club in America to have its course laid out by a professional. For many years, Willie Dunn was credited with laying out Shinnecock in 1891, but there is irrefutable evidence that Willie Davis did the job, including a letter written by J. Hutton Balfour of Royal Montreal, to the British magazine *Golf*, published in November 1891. Balfour wrote: ". . . Next request we had was from several gentlemen in Long Island, New York, that we would permit our professional to go there for a month to lay out a green and instruct them; this we gladly did, and a good eighteen holes [sic: there were twelve] have been laid out . . ."

In November 1892 Davis discussed the lay-out of a course with the about-to-be-formed Newport club. Early in the following year, Newport made him an offer, and he left Montreal for Rhode Island.

As golf grew rapidly in Canada in the 1890s, so golf clubs, old and new, had need of professional help, if only to keep members' clubs in good repair. There were no private clubmaking firms in Canada, as there were in Britain.

The overriding need for a skilled man to make and repair clubs probably explains why Royal Montreal rehired Davis in 1890. When he left the club after the 1892 season, the club offered his job to Tom Harley, no doubt impressed by his showing in the interprovincials. But Harley declined, and the club then sought help from Alex Dennistoun, by this time living in Scotland. He sent them another Scottish professional.

Bennet Lang had made his name as a clubmaker rather than as a player or teacher. In their book *Golf in the Making*, Ian T. Henderson and David Stirk describe him as "a specialist in hand-made woods which were made to measure to suit each individual client . . . He was, also, a roving craftsman locksmith and a violinist, and apparently quite an entertaining character." He stayed in Montreal for only the 1893 season.

We can only guess at how the other early clubs – Royal Quebec, Brantford, Toronto, Niagara, and Kingston – managed without a skilled clubmaker for so many years. Presumably they found a local carpenter able to reshaft clubs.

Royal Ottawa was the second Canadian club to hire a professional. It brought over Alfred Ricketts from England, in 1891, the year the club was formed. Ricketts helped Davis lay out the club's first course and laid out the second by himself. When he left after five years, to go to Albany Golf Club in New York, he was replaced by a J. Devine, from an unknown source.

Meanwhile, Royal Montreal had engaged its third professional in as many years. Tom Smith of Carnoustie had been an assistant to George Fernie at Yarmouth, England. A year later, Toronto Golf Club hired Smith's brother, Arthur, but he left the club in 1899. And yet another Smith, Harry, came over for the 1898 season to the Hamilton GC. (When Harry Smith left Hamilton, Arthur Smith's young assistant, Nicol Thompson, took over.)

Toronto's Rosedale club made the most unusual choice for its first professional. David Ritchie was born in St. Andrews, in 1874. As a boy at Madras College (a junior high school), he had developed into a proficient golfer. His family immigrated to Canada when he was fourteen. Following his father's death, in 1890, young Ritchie found work in the office of Dr. Brebner, Registrar of the University of Toronto. And when Brebner joined Rosedale, he naturally turned to Ritchie for advice and instruction. This led to Ritchie's appointment as the professional to Rosedale in 1896, a job that financed his own studies for the ministry at the Old Knox College, University of Toronto. On graduating in 1904, "Davie" – as he was affectionately called by the Rosedale members – left the club to continue his studies at Glasgow University. He took a graduate

Davie Ritchie of Rosedale appears to have had a two-handed palm grip and a not very elegant swing.

degree in theology, at the same time winning the golf championship of the United Free College in Glasgow.

The Reverend David Ritchie returned to Canada. In 1909, playing out of Francis, Saskatchewan, as an amateur, he won the open stroke competition in the Saskatchewan championships. A year later he won the Saskatchewan amateur championship. In the 1920s, he returned to western Ontario and laid out two or three golf courses there.

Other new clubs had greenkeepers before the turn of the century but, so far as can be determined, these were greenkeepers in the modern sense of the word, not teaching professionals or clubmakers. In British Columbia, Victoria GC employed two men, Norman and Clayton, as groundsmen, in 1895. And an R. M. Clayton (the same Clayton?) was greenkeeper to Halifax GC two years later. London GC had a George Kibbler, Oshawa a John Lenton, Saint John a T. Richardson, Sherbrooke a Norrey Belknap, all listed as greenkeepers, and probably no more than that.

But John M. Peacock, greenkeeper at the Algonquin club, St. Andrews, N.B., in the late 1890s, did develop into a full-fledged professional. Peacock was at Algonquin until about 1938, making him at the time the longest-serving professional in Canada. He spent his winters at Pinehurst Golf Club in the United States. It appears that the Peacock family came over from Ayrshire in the 1820s, to farm in St. Andrews. When the Algonquin club took over part of their land around 1896, to expand the golf course, John went along with the land. He probably did little more than look after the course, until the Scottish professional-turned-golf-architect, Donald Ross of Pinehurst, visited Algonquin in the early 1900s, to revamp the course. It was then, presumably, that Peacock came to spend his winters at Pinehurst and picked up the art of club-making.

Peacock remained a shadowy figure until I had the good fortune to meet Judge Earl Caughey, now retired and living at St. Andrews. As a boy, Judge Caughey caddied at Algonquin and knew John Peacock well.

Judge Caughey tells of a rather strict, severe, man. The Judge recalls that during the summer of 1928, when he was working as a bellhop at the Algonquin Hotel, he had a hole-in-one. He asked Peacock to certify his achievement, to be told, "It will cost you a bottle of whisky," more than a bellhop could afford.

Canada's nineteenth-century professionals seldom had the opportunity to play each other. For his first ten years, Davis was the only professional in North America. "My time is so taken up in [the] workshop and in giving lessons that I have no time to practise the game," he complained.

In 1896, the two brothers Smith, Arthur and Tom, made the trip to Niagara, to play two professionals from U.S. clubs. But Arthur became seasick on the crossing from Toronto, and the brothers lost.

In 1898, Arthur Smith played Ritchie, in home-and-away matches. "The first game between two pro's of any note that has been seen on the greens of this city, and a goodly number of spectators were on hand . . . about 100 people," reported the Toronto *Globe*.

Launcelot Cressy Servos was probably our first home-bred professional. He was, without a doubt, our most eccentric.

The Servos family were United Empire Loyalists who helped found Niagara-on-the-Lake in the late eighteenth century. Launcelot picked up golf alongside the Dickson boys and played in some of the Niagara International Tournaments. Although he never won anything (unless off handicap) he met George Wright, of Wright and Ditson of Boston, and in 1898, when he was nineteen, Wright got him a job as a professional in New England. For a few years, Servos made a living selling Wright and Ditson equipment on the road, while teaching golf, playing for money, and laying out golf courses in the southeastern U.S. (including the first at Miami and Bellair). By the time he came back to Canada in the 1920s, he was no match for the playing professionals of his day but appears to have made a living teaching. His book, *Practical Instruction in Golf* (1905), came out in a revised edition in 1938. In it, he claims to have lowered over two hundred course records, but I imagine many of these were at courses he had just laid out.

Servos was of a literary bent; he wrote a romantic novel (not recommended) and an opera, which was broadcast over CKCL radio in 1929. When he died, penniless, in a Toronto rooming-house in 1969, at the age of ninety, he left a trunkful of worthless German marks and a will of thirty pages and twice as many clauses. One clause bequeathed a billion dollars to a Servos Association of Professional Golfers; another called for the building of a twenty-storey golf centre. He was, as I have said, our most eccentric professional.

At the end of the 1890s, then, Canada had six club professionals that we know of: Tom Smith of Royal Montreal, Arthur Smith of Toronto, J. Devine of Royal Ottawa, David Richie of Rosedale, John Peacock of Algonquin, and Nicol Thompson of Hamilton. Only Peacock was to stay for more than a year or so into the new century, although Nicol Thompson – having left Hamilton for the U.S. – was to return and be the professional there for many years. The Smiths and Devine left behind no anecdotes, established no legends, and are little more than shadowy figures in Canadian golf.

In the short space of five years after the turn of the century, the face of professional golf in Canada changed profoundly. Those years witnessed an influx of young recruits from Britain. And in these same years, the first of Canada's home-bred professionals began to emerge.

Some of these newcomers did not stay long in Canada. The Canadian season was short, which meant finding another job in the winter. Not surprising, then, that a few of them left for the warmer climate and the higher money of the United States; others disappeared from the records entirely. But the best of them stayed, to lay the foundation of modern golf professionalism in this country. And, by 1904, there were enough of them to justify holding a national championship in which they could play against each other for money.

Before having a closer look at these men, and where they came from, a word about the Canadian Open Championship in which they competed.

In the fall of 1903, the RCGA appointed a committee to devise a plan for making the Annual Meeting more interesting. The committee recommended, among other things, dropping the interprovincial matches (they were dropped for two years) and introducing a 36-hole medal-play championship open to the world and carrying the title of open champion of Canada. As a result, the first Canadian Open was held as a one-day affair tacked onto the end of the ninth Annual Meeting of the RCGA, held at Royal Montreal on the Dominion Day weekend of 1904.

The Open was originally given the title of "The Open Golf Championship of Canada." But this proved too much of a mouthful for newspaper editors, and within a few years it became simply "The Canadian Open."

Ten professionals and seven amateurs competed in the first Open, which was a 36-hole, stroke-play event, played in one day. In 1907, this was increased to 72 holes, played over two days. By 1909, entries had increased to about thirty, and they remained at this level until after the First World War.

As its name implies, the event was open to all, but in those years there were few entries from outside Canada and in some years none at all. The record foreign entry of five was in 1912, when professionals from U.S. clubs took three of the first four places.

Until 1939, the Open was held at a club in Central Canada. As a result, there were few entries from clubs outside Quebec and Ontario before the First World War. By 1914, a handful of clubs in the West employed professionals, but only those from Winnipeg made even the occasional trip to the Open. A professional from the West Coast would have had to take a couple of weeks off work to come to the Open, and then he would have had to win just to cover his expenses.

The total prize money in the first Open was $170, divided between the top six players. Professionals received this in cash, amateurs in plate. The winner also received a gold medal, the runner-up a silver medal, from the RCGA. The prize money was increased to $225 in 1905, and to $265 by 1909, when the winner took $100. This was about half the purse of the U.S. and the Mexican Opens. It was also less than the prize money at some second-rate events in the United States. There was little to attract the U.S. professional to the Canadian Open unless he happened to live in the Great Lakes area, where his travelling costs would be low.

The scoring in the Open depended more on the state of the course than on its length, although the lengths of the courses then considered championship courses were much more varied than today.

The course of the Toronto GC measured only 5,125 yards when George Cumming won the 1905 Open, with a 36-hole score of 148, whereas the Royal Ottawa course measured 6,310 yards when Charlie Murray won in 1906. Murray's high score of 170 was attributed more to the poor state of the greens, which had suffered from winter kill. Other pre-war Opens were won with average scores per round of anything from 73.7 to 78.5.

Admission for spectators was free until 1923. Far more attended the Amateur than the Open, which would be doing well if it managed to attract a few hundred.

Of the pre-1900 professionals in Canada, only Tom Smith of the Metropolitan and Outremont clubs in Montreal played in the first Open of 1904. Six of the other nine professionals had come to Canada since 1900; the remaining three were local recruits. The winner, John H. Oke, had been brought over

John Oke of Royal Ottawa, winner of the first Open.

Nine of the ten professionals who played in the first Open, Royal Montreal, 1904. The only recognizable faces are those of Cumming (third from the left), *James Black* (fifth from the left), *and Oke* (third from the right).

from England by Royal Ottawa only a few months before the Open. Born near the Royal North Devon Club, his name appears in British professional tournaments as early as 1899, when he was a nineteen-year-old assistant to J. H. Taylor at the Mid-Surrey Golf Club. When this slightly built young man (five feet seven-and-a-half inches, 145 pounds) left Mid-Surrey for Canada, he was said to be "a very fine player and a lad of excellent character."

The *Toronto Daily Star* considered Oke rather lucky to win by two strokes at Royal Montreal: "The weather was miserable, and the conditions did not contribute to accurate golf. Oke had the advantage of being first away, so that he had the best of the greens." Having the best of the greens probably meant avoiding the heelmarks of previous players. Greens did not drain well in the early 1900s, and they took longer to recover in wet weather.

Oke was well down the field in the 1905 Open. When he returned to England in the following year, he irritated the newspapers in Canada by referring to himself as "The Open Champion of Canada." He played in many British tournaments, but never distinguished himself, before he immigrated to the United States in 1915.

It rained again during the second round of the 1905 Open at Toronto Golf Club, "to an extent that prevented ladies and their friends watching the play of the saturated late starters." We are not told if the winner, George Cumming, was an early or late starter. Perhaps the newspaper men had other things on their minds. One paper recorded that "the Press were the guests of the Royal Canadian Golf Association during the meet – up to a limit! The steward of the ultra-fashionable golf club was authorized by the RCGA to see that no reporter exceeded a certain limit.")

Cumming's second round of 72 was the lowest of the tournament, and he won by a margin of three strokes. This was to be his only Open win, although he was to come second in 1906, 1907, 1909, and 1914. This man's contribution to Canadian golf can not be mea-

sured by his success as a player, but by his role as a teacher, golf architect, and leader of men.

More than any other man, George Cumming led the way to modern golf professionalism in Canada, by his example and by his training.

The Toronto Golf Club brought Cumming from Scotland in 1900, giving him an old house on the golf course for his home. He then embarked on what was to be a life-long vocation.

There was no sense of any grand design when Cumming started out in 1900. The club did not set out on a pre-arranged plan to recruit and train in Cumming's workshop a continuous stream of Canadian professionals. What happened did so by chance, one event leading to another. But it is a fact that between 1900 and 1950, some twenty-five to thirty assistants passed through his workshop, a number which no other professional in Canada can even approach.

These assistants became the disciples of the Cumming teachings. They went on to serve many other clubs, taking with them George Cumming's values, standards, and methods, and passing them on, in turn, to their assistants. They established, if you like, the first dynasty in our professional golf. In this way the stamp of George Cumming was imprinted on many teachers, and on many pupils. He rightly deserves the title given him as early as 1910: The Dean of Canadian Professionals.

This finest of teachers had the finest of trainings. George Cumming was born in Bridge of Weir, Scotland, in 1879. When he was ten, the Ranfurly Castle Golf Club opened on the outskirts of his village, an event which was to shape his life. As a son in a working-class family, he had to find work after school hours and on weekends. A powerful, well-built lad for his age, he got a job caddying for the gentlemen who came down by train from Glasgow. He was attracted by the club's workshop, with its tool-bench, saws, rasps, awls, ball-press, its smell of oil, leather, and hot glue. Willie Campbell of Musselburgh was the club's professional at the time. He gave the boy jobs in his workshop, showed him how to put new leather grips and binding on a club. When the course was quiet, Cumming would golf with a borrowed club, swinging in the style of Campbell. By the time he was thirteen and ready to leave school, his mind was made up: he wanted to be a golf professional.

Willie Campbell knew the Forgans, and he arranged for George Cumming to be taken on as an apprentice to Andrew Forgan, the son of the founder of the firm. Forgan was "Custodian and Club maker" to the celebrated Glasgow Golf Club, which could afford a large clubmaking shop and staff as well as a teaching professional and a greenkeeper. George Cumming joined Andrew Forgan's workshop in 1892. There, he was to learn not just the art of clubmaking, but also how to look after a course and a club and its members.

While working with Andrew Forgan, Cumming helped him lay out a golf course at Murdoch Castle, a lesson that was to stand him in good stead when he turned to golf course architecture.

Forgan thought highly of his pupil. Years later he wrote of George Cumming in *Canadian Golfer*: "George was a diligent apprentice, and learned to make a good club. His favourite work was making brassie spoons. He was a great teacher then, and was champion of the shop. There were a dozen of us then . . . George left me for Dumfries, where he built up a reputation not yet forgotten. . . ."

After his years at Glasgow, the Forgans sent Cumming to be professional to the Dumfries and Galloway Golf Club, which had a nine-hole course and a hundred members. He was to remain there for four seasons, combining the training of the Forgans with his own natural aptitude for getting on well with people. In the summer of 1899, the secretary of the Toronto Golf Club, Stewart Gordon, was visiting his old home at Dumfries and played golf with Cumming. He was obviously impressed by what he saw and heard. In October, Toronto made Cumming an offer. He accepted and left for Canada in March 1900.

The George Cumming swing was to be copied by many.

George Cumming was to endow Canadian professional golf with something more than his technical knowledge of the game and its implements. He gave the vocation a nobility of purpose. He set standards of decorum. He had acquired a trait common to the finest of the old Scottish professionals, an ineffable mixture of humility and pride that both exuded and exacted respect. He knew exactly how he wanted to deal with club members and how he wanted them to deal with him.

The written history of the Toronto GC recounts that he entered the clubhouse at Dixie only twice in his career. Fred Lyon told me that Cumming was the only leading golfer, amateur or professional, never to address his father, George S. Lyon, in public by his first name, but always as "Mr. Lyon."

George Cumming had an outstanding record as a tournament golfer, as measured by his consistency rather than by his number of outright wins. In eleven pre-First World War Opens, he had only one victory (in 1905), but he also had four second places. His total prize money of $430 made him the leading money-winner in this period. (Contemporary golf statisticians, of course, never measured success in that way.)

Cumming often seemed to play best when behind. Two strokes down after the first round in 1905, he made these up and more, to win by 3. A year later, he made up five strokes in the final round to lose by only 1. In 1914, his four-strokes recovery was again one too few for a tie.

George Cumming made his name as a teacher. Countless amateurs learned or improved their game under his tuition and remembered how his wise counsel, his stress on the discipline

George Cumming and six former assistants at the Canadian Open, Rosedale GC, 1912. Left to right: *Charlie Murray, Willie Bell, Frank Freeman, Karl Keffer, Albert Murray, Willie Freeman, George Cumming.*

At Royal Montreal in 1913 the winner was Albert Murray, sitting cross-legged on the extreme right. Standing behind him, far-right to left, are James Black, Charlie Murray, Karl Keffer, Davie Black. With the straw hat in the back row is joint runner-up Nicol Thompson. George Cumming is second from left, standing.

of body and mind, also helped them in their business careers. In the 1920s and 1930s, he was particularly proud of his "ladies." When one of them won a provincial or national title – which was often – she would telephone George first with the news.

The same can be said of the other gifted professionals of the day, notably Charlie Murray of Royal Montreal, in the east, and Davie Black of Shaughnessy Heights, in the west. They were outstanding club professionals, whose teaching went far beyond instruction in how to swing a club.

In a memoir written in 1945, Cumming recognized these professionals as having been his assistants: Charlie Murray, Albert Murray, Karl Keffer, Frank Freeman, James Clay, Willie Freeman, Willie Bell, Norman Bell, David Hutchison, Kernie Marsh, Dick Borthwick, Willie Lamb, Davie Spittal, Gordon Brydson, and his son Lou Cumming. But others worked in his shop over the years, among them James Blair, J. Hines, Sydney Lingard, James Martin, Charles Nixon, Nicol Thompson, R. J. Sansom, L. N. Senour, and J. Simpson.

It is not always clear exactly when some of these men worked for George Cumming, and what were their duties. In those early years, a professional would take a number of caddies into his shop for training. Having caddied beyond their fifteenth birthday, these youths lost their amateur status. In tournaments, they would be shown as professionals playing out of the club where they worked, although at the time they might be employed there as anything from assistant professional to greenkeeper, clubmaker, caddiemaster, groundsman, or caddie. So you will find Karl Keffer listed as playing out of Toronto GC in the 1905 Open. At the time, he was probably a caddiemaster, or a clubmaker apprenticed to George Cumming. He was not recognized as an "assistant" to Cumming until 1907.

To further complicate matters, some of Cumming's assistants were farmed out to other clubs for the peak summer months, as part of their training and to help them make a living. In the newspapers of the day, these assistants are sometimes shown as playing out of Toronto GC and sometimes out of the club to which they were temporarily assigned.

All of Cumming's assistants before 1913 were caddies who lived close to Toronto GC, in or near the village of Norway.

The Murray family, immigrants from England, settled in Norway. Charlie Murray, born in 1880 in Birmingham, came to Canada as a young boy. He caddied at the Toronto club from the early 1890s and picked up the rudiments of clubmaking from Arthur Smith. George Cumming appointed him as his first assistant in 1900. As part of his training, Charlie Murray was farmed out to the golf clubs at Cobourg and Peterborough, before going as professional to Outremont and then Westmount, both in Montreal. While at Westmount, he was "discovered" by Royal Montreal and signed to be its professional, in November 1904.

Charlie Murray was to serve Royal Montreal until his unexpected death, following an operation, in 1938. More of an extrovert than Cumming, this tall, well-built, exuberant man was to become as renowned and as highly regarded as his teacher. The Royal Montreal history records that he was imbued with the same principles of conduct:

> His high standards of golf sportsmanship and skill, his careful deportment and courtesy in his relations with Club members, while also full of humor and fun, the stern discipline of his pro shop, all contributed to the Club's standards and reputation.

Charlie Murray was Canada's finest tournament professional until the mid-1920s. "Like his speech and personality, Murray's three-quarter swing was clipped, terse and dependable," *Canadian Golfer* said of him. In the teens of this century, he was scoring in the 60s, a feat then quite rare. His record in the Open is exemplary. He won in 1906 and 1911, and lost in a play-off with Tommy Armour and J. Douglas Edgar, in 1920.

He never came lower than sixth in any of the Open championships held before the First

World War. His victory in 1906 at Royal Ottawa came with rounds of 84 and 86, by far the highest scores ever to win the championship.

Charlie Murray won again when the Open was next played at Royal Ottawa in 1911, lowering the average score by over six strokes per round. But he almost threw this championship away in the third round. His 84 included an inward half of 46 strokes.

Charlie Murray was about as keen on fishing, hunting, and shooting as he was on golf. He would spend his winters as the professional to a club in Florida, where he was as much loved as at Montreal.

Charlie's younger brother, Albert, was born in Nottingham, England, in 1887. Albert also caddied at Toronto, and when he was fourteen he joined Cumming's workshop to learn the art of clubmaking. In 1903 he became Charlie's assistant, first at Westmount, then at Royal Montreal. Three years later, Royal Quebec took him on as its professional, when he was only eighteen.

Albert had a smaller build than his brother and had none of Charlie's ebullience. He was never to settle for long at any one club, moving from Royal Quebec to Outremont, and from there to Kanawaki, then to the Country Club of Montreal and to Beaconsfield. He later became a proficient and busy golf-course architect, following in the footsteps of his first master, George Cumming.

Albert Murray played in the first Open when he was only sixteen and wearing short pants. I think we can say, unequivocally, that he set a fashion that has never been copied. He finished thirteenth in a field of seventeen.

By 1908, he was in long pants, and playing much better. His opening round of 74 at Royal Montreal led the field, and he was never caught. He hit every fairway in the 72 holes, "the most consistent driving game seen at Dixie in many a long day, sure in his approaching and accurate on the greens," reported the Montreal *Gazette*. He finished with a score of 300, to win by four strokes. Only twenty at the time, Albert Murray remains the youngest golfer ever to win the Canadian Open Championship.

Albert's victory came as a great surprise to the pundits. He had never figured as a likely champion. After the first day, when he led Sargent by one stroke and Cumming by two, his opponents were still the favourites. In the last round, when he took 41 to the turn, the wise ones shook their collective heads and agreed that he had finally cracked. Not for the last time, they were hopelessly wrong. Albert covered the next seven holes in 27 strokes, had a back nine of 36, beating the field and the prophets of his doom. "A mere boy," said *The Gazette*. "Few golf victories have been more surprising." (In the final round, Charlie Murray was so anxious over Albert – who was in the twosome behind – that his own game suffered, and he blew to an 82.)

Albert Murray was to win the Open again, in 1913, while the professional at Kanawaki. Jack Burke of Philadelphia was then the almost unknown professional at Fort William GC (Thunder Bay). He had a two-stroke lead after the first day, with a 147. Murray caught him early in the third round when Burke putted so badly that he took 43 to the turn. Murray went on to win by six strokes, with the then record score of 295.

A feature of the 1913 Open had been the deadly approaching and putting of Nicol Thompson, the professional at Hamilton Golf and Country Club. In the four rounds he had no less than twenty-one 3s. He and Burke shared second place, for which each received $62.50 and a silver medal from the RCGA.

This was the closest Nicol Thompson came to winning the Canadian Open. He was another who had started his career as a caddie at Toronto GC, in the days of Arthur Smith. Having picked up the rudiments of clubmaking, he became professional to the Hamilton GC in 1899, when Smith's brother, Harry, left that club after one season.

Nicol Thompson went back to work with George Cumming at Toronto for the 1902 season, probably to round off his skills as a clubmaker and teacher. He returned to Hamilton as its professional in 1903 and soon left for the

Birmingham GC, Alabama, but by 1912 he was back as Hamilton's professional, a post he held until 1945. In his first Canadian Open in 1912 he finished fifth and won ten dollars. His only success in national golf was to be the CPGA Championship of 1922.

Like other Thompson boys, Nicol was of a stocky build, and he had a short, fast swing. But he was an excellent teacher. Hilles Pickens wrote of him in 1954 in *Canadian Sport Monthly*: "He had every shot in his bag. His record for developing fine players was probably only equalled by his contemporary, the late George Cumming of the Toronto Golf Club."

The fourth former Toronto GC caddie to make a name for himself in national professional golf was Karl Keffer, winner of the Canadian Open in 1909 and 1914. He is shown in some Ontario directories of the early 1900s as a carpenter, perhaps because he repaired clubs in George Cumming's workshop.

Born in Tottenham, Ontario, in 1882, Keffer moved before he was five to a house overlooking the course of the Toronto Golf Club. As soon as he was strong enough to carry a bag he became a caddie. Picking up the game in his spare time, he early showed his promise as a golfer by winning the first caddie tournament held by the club. (The two Murrays and Nicol Thompson were three of the other players.) On the advice of George Cumming he took up golf as his profession. An unidentified newspaper clipping in his scrapbook carried these facts on Keffer, written at the time of the 1914 Open:

> In 1907, after having duly served his initiation series [service?] as a caddie and gradually mastering the rudiments and masonic conditions surrounding the game, he entered the shop of George Cumming to learn the art of club making, and to have his knowledge of the game cultivated under his guiding eye . . . Hockey and baseball were his favorite sports [as a boy] and he was no mean artist at either one, as some of the old Norway and Balmy Beach boys can testify.

This is the only time I have seen it suggested that there were, in 1914, "masonic conditions surrounding the game."

When the Open was held at Toronto Golf Club in 1909, Keffer became champion by beating his teacher, George Cumming (the first- and second-round leader) by three strokes, with a total of 309. *The Globe* described the scene:

> The first to congratulate him was George Cumming, who now has the proud position of having trained three champions, besides having himself won the honour. Keffer was then seized by his confrères and carried shoulder high from the grounds. The win is an extremely popular one, and as there was nothing in the element of fluke about it, is all the more deserved. The outstanding feature of Keffer's game was its machine-like accuracy, which argues well for his nerves.

In 1910, Karl Keffer joined the Albany GC, New York, as its assistant professional. A year later he returned to Canada to become professional to Royal Ottawa. He served this club until his retirement in 1943, with a break for service in the First World War.

Karl Keffer has this added distinction: he remains the only Canadian-born player ever to win the Canadian Open. And he was to win once more, in 1914, the last Open before the war. Again, this was a two-man struggle between Keffer and Cumming. In the third round, Keffer's record-breaking 72 gave him a seemingly impregnable five-stroke lead. But George Cumming then played "one of the best fighting games ever seen in Canada," according to *The Toronto Daily News*.

Keffer was out early and the leader in the clubhouse. Facing a strong wind for the last nine holes, Cumming whittled away at the deficit. He came to the last hole needing a par 4 to tie, on a hole where he normally made a 3 (the eighteenth at Toronto Golf Club). "His drive from the tee provided him with a nice approach, but he was short. From almost the edge of the green he left himself with a comparatively easy putt for a golfer of his calibre, but 'never up, never in' and he lipped the cup taking five."

To the list of golfers who dominated the Canadian Open before the First World War – Cumming, Keffer, and the two Murrays – we should add the name of Percy Barrett.

Born in Huddersfield, England, in 1880, Barrett was not a Cumming product, but a protégé of Harry Vardon at Ganton, on whose recommendation he was invited to be the first professional at Lambton in 1903. Barrett lacked the personality of a George Cumming or a Charlie Murray, and although a popular professional at Lambton, he never established himself as warmly in the hearts of members.

His fellow professionals reckoned that Percy Barrett was their finest striker of a ball. He was perhaps the longest driver of his day, one of his carries from the tee in the 1904 Open being measured at some 240 yards. Such ability does not always lead to victory, as Barrett's experience shows. Nevertheless, in the first eight Opens he had a fine record for consistency. In the years 1904 through 1911, he won once (1907), was second twice (1904, 1905), and had four third-places. All of which earned for him the princely sum of four hundred dollars in prize money. In 1905, he came third in the U.S. Open.

When Barrett won at Lambton in 1907, it was again a case of a professional winning on his own course, a more common occurrence in the early days of golf than it is today. The weather, too, had more influence in the days when the leaders did not go out together, and when courses did not drain so well. A sudden downpour could easily flood fairways and greens. Golf umbrellas and rain gear were almost unheard of. In 1907, Barrett was caught by rain in his final round:

> The Lambton man was steady and brilliant, and while his final round was an 80, the fault lay with the weather not with the players, and the probabilities are that if the storm had held off the winner would have

Percy Barrett of Lambton, winning the Open in 1907.

reached home with a 77 card and have been at least five strokes better than his nearest competitor, Cumming . . . Hendrie was swamped by rain . . . A. G. Gill [an amateur] whipped four balls into the water and sent his caddy back with his clubs . . . Davie Black got the full benefit of the downpour that threatened to flood out the course.

In every generation there are fine golfers of whom it can be said they should have

"Wee Davie" Black, the pride of Shaughnessy and the West.

won national Open championships but didn't. Such a golfer was Davie Black, an experienced professional who came to Canada from Troon, Scotland, in 1905. Employed first by Montreal's Outremont and Ottawa's Rivermead club, he is best remembered as the long-time and much-loved professional at Shaughnessy Heights, Vancouver (1920–45).

Described on his arrival in Canada as "a short chunk with a good natured face and a jolly laugh," the professional who came to be known as "Wee Davie," or "The Wee Iron Man," endeared himself to golfers on the West Coast.

Davie Black golfed with an easy, graceful swing. But he is more often remembered as a bold and accurate putter. He specialized in putting, and probably gave more putting lessons than any Canadian professional before or since. In *Canadian Golfer* in 1934, George Boeckh recounted the time he and Bill Taylor played Davie over Shaughnessy, and their best ball was nowhere good enough. Davie took six putts in the first five holes, and was 3 up. He finished with a 66, including only 26 putts. "Taylor and myself were treated to the most devastating exhibition of putting we had ever been privileged to witness," claimed Boeckh.

Davie Black never quite lived up to his promise in the Canadian Open. In 1911, he came from behind to take second place to Charlie Murray. But in other years he was no better than fourth.

It was quite a different matter in the CPGA championships, where Davie was a four-time winner. He seemed to be playing his best golf in 1920, at the very time he left for the West Coast. Once there, it was an expensive matter to come back east for the Canadian Open and CPGA championships. There is no saying what further nationals he might have won had their venues been in the West.

There were many other professionals who never became national figures but who were well known in their provinces. You might find their names on old wooden-shafted clubs or in early minute-books. Few of them stayed at one club for long. The golf professional had no tenure in those days; he was hired from season to season. Come November, except on the West Coast, he had to find a winter job in the southern United States (with no guarantee that his Canadian club would rehire him in April of the following year) or set up a winter golf school in his home city. So you will often find a professional's name linked to many clubs in Canada, usually in the same province.

Some of the others who worked for George Cumming in the first twenty years of this century were Frank and Willie Freeman (Frank had several seasons at Hamilton and Rosedale; Willie is probably best remembered as the first professional at Toronto's York Downs), the brothers Bell (Willie, Norman, and Percy), and Kern, or Kernie, Marsh ("a quiet boy, not easily excited," said the Toronto *Star*, when he played in the 1914 Open. He is remembered as the teacher of Sandy Somerville and Jack Nash).

French-Canada had not taken up golf in a big way in the early years of the century. The first French-Canadian professional to compete in the Open was A. Desjardins, who played out of Brockville in 1914. Over the next few years the name A. Desjardins mysteriously turns up as professional to a number of clubs at the same time. There were in fact three brothers, all professionals, with the names Aime, Andrew, and Albert. I am indebted to Aime's son, Andrew, who helped me disentangle who worked where and when.

When Royal Montreal moved to Dixie in 1896, the club's professional had to recruit a new bunch of caddies. Aime Desjardins, born in Dorval in 1890, became one of these caddies. In time, he came to work in Charlie Murray's shop, learning the trade of clubmaking. Aime Desjardins was later professional to a number of clubs in the Laurentians.

His brother Arthur's career was closely intertwined. When Aime left Laval-sur-le-Lac in 1925 to go to the Alpine Inn at St. Margarets, Arthur appears to have left the Alpine Inn to

Aime Desjardins in 1919, probably the first French-Canadian professional.

take Aime's place at Laval.

The third brother, Albert, played out of the St. Jerome club in 1931, and then probably went to the United States.

There were also a few professionals in the West. In 1901, Winnipeg Golf Club – at that time the only golf club in the city – brought over twenty-two-year-old Albert Kam from England to be its first professional and clubmaker.

The newly formed Jericho Country Club of Vancouver hired Kam in 1906 to help lay out its course. He must have impressed the members of the club, for they kept him as their professional for several years. During this time he seems to have spent his winter months in Vancouver (the golf season there) and the summer months in Winnipeg. He returned to Britain early in the war.

Albert Kam came east to play in the Canadian Opens of 1911 and 1913 but he finished well down the field.

N. Stevens was an assistant to Albert Kam at Winnipeg for a few years before the war. He turns up later as the professional to clubs in Regina. He left to go to the United States in 1917.

Victoria Golf Club took on an L. S. Jacobs in 1902 (he was probably British, and the L. S. Jacobs who played in the 1909 U.S. Open), but he lasted only a couple of seasons, The club shared its next professional, Jack Moffatt (he came from the Waverly Golf Club in Portland, Oregon), with the St. Charles Country Club in Winnipeg, since the two clubs had different playing seasons.

Alex Duthie and Jimmy Huish were the first professionals in the West to have the status of the likes of George Cumming and Charlie Murray in the East – not in terms of playing ability, perhaps, but in terms of the respect and affection in which they were held by golfers in their province of British Columbia.

Duthie was "a formidable scratch player" at the Carnoustie Golf Club, a stonemason who left Scotland in 1903 "to better himself in the new Colonies," as the British magazine *Golf Illustrated* put it at the time. After working at his trade in New Zealand, Australia, and South Africa, Duthie arrived in North America, and was the professional at Waverly for several seasons after Moffatt. Following a short stint with the United Service Club, he embarked in June 1910 on what was to become a thirty-two-year career with Vancouver's Jericho Country Club. It was Duthie who persuaded the club to expand its course to eighteen holes in 1923, and who laid out the new course.

Jimmy Huish, a Musselburgh man, came over to be an assistant at Victoria Golf Club in 1910. But he worked at Victoria for only a season of so, helping the club's professional meet the heavy demand for coaching. After

Jimmy Huish (right) *with the president of his club in the 1920s.*

spells with the United Service Club and Royal Colwood, Jimmy Huish joined Vancouver GC in 1919. Later he was to spend fifteen years (1926–40) with Marine Drive GC, Vancouver.

The lean, good-natured, unflappable Huish was one of the world's philosophers. As an after-dinner speaker he could quote Omar Khayyám, Robert Burns, and Kipling with equal facility. Few professionals have had such a hold on their membership.

The immediate pre-war years were not good years on the Prairies; wheat prices were down, business was poor, unemployment was high. It was not a time to be investing money in golf instruction, and consequently the number of golf professionals in Saskatchewan and Alberta could be counted on the fingers of one hand.

The first professional to a club in Saskatchewan appears to have been W. A. (Bill) Kinnear, who had picked up the art of clubmaking at Leven and St. Andrews in Scotland. He came to Saskatchewan to follow his trade as a carpenter. The members of the newly formed Saskatoon Golf Club heard of this Scot who had played golf, and hired him in 1910 to lay out its nine-hole course next to the exhibition grounds in the city. He was then taken on as professional and clubmaker.

Bill Kinnear was to remain in Saskatoon until shortly before his retirement in 1949. During this time he laid out the fine course of the city's Riverside Country Club, and was also professional and greenkeeper to this club for many years. As a clubmaker, he was much in demand until wooden-shafted clubs went out of fashion in the 1930s.

Two professionals, Fred Foord and Arner Tollifson, arrived in Saskatchewan in the spring of 1913, Tollifson to be professional to the Wascana club, Foord to the Regina club. Both stayed only a year or so. Tollifson had started as a caddie in Chicago in the late 1890s, and his buddy may have come from the same city.

When Tollifson left, he probably handed over the care of the Wascana club and course to W. H. (Bill) Brinkworth. This charismatic, jovial fellow was to become one of the grand old men of golf in the Prairies. A Regina directory shows Brink (as he came to be known) as a coach with the RNWMP in 1914, and as a golf professional from 1915, facts noted by Mickey Boyle in his history of golf in Saskatchewan, *Ninety Years of Golf* (1987). An unpublished history of Wascana Country Club suggests that Brink worked there from 1911.

Brink was to serve Wascana as a professional until 1925. He moved around a number of clubs, including Swift Current's Elmwood, Moose Jaw's Citizen, and the Edmonton Golf and Country Club, first as its greenkeeper,

then as its professional. In the 1930s, Brink became "The Squire of Jasper" – the professional at Jasper Lodge.

None of these early Western professionals, with the exception of Kam and Stevens of Winnipeg, played in the Canadian Open. (Davie Black also played, but before coming west.) Those on the Pacific Coast had ample opportunity for tournament golf, including the championships organized by the Pacific Northwest Golf Association. Davie Black won the PNGA Open championship in his first year at Shaughnessy and again in 1922. In 1924 he won the Washington State Open. But a West Coast golfer would have had to win the Canadian Open just to cover his travelling expenses.

Only a few clubs in the Maritimes could afford a full-time professional before the First World War. Private Pringle of the Royal Garrison Regiment served as the professional to Halifax GC in 1903; Martin Conway served the same club from 1904 until 1915, and was later the professional at the Brightwood club, Dartmouth. But during this time, he farmed out his services to a number of clubs, including Charlottetown and Digby, when his own club could spare him.

Harry Hampton, from Carnoustie, was the professional at Lingan Country Club in 1912, when he also offered his part-time services to Charlottetown. None of the professionals from down east were to make a name for themselves in national competition.

Before the First World War, the Canadian Open was dominated by Canadian professionals. The American challenge did not come from home-bred U.S. professionals, but from Scottish and English-born professionals employed by U.S. clubs. The low prize money offered in Canada kept their numbers down; for U.S.-based professionals, coming to the dark north was hardly worth the candle.

Alex Robertson, originally a clubmaker at St. Andrews, came up from Buffalo Golf Club to compete in Toronto in 1905, as did R. Tait of Erie, Pennsylvania.

Daniel Kenny, who replaced Robertson at Buffalo, had once been professional to North Berwick GC, Scotland. Kenny played in the Canadian Open in 1907, and in 1910 he won the championship "playing brilliantly in a baffling breeze." He joined the newly formed North Toronto GC a year later and unsuccessfully defended his title. He appears to have left Canada before the war.

NUMBER OF TIMES COMPETITORS FINISHED IN THE TOP SIX, SO SHARING THE PRIZE MONEY.		
	competed	in top six
Charlie Murray	11	11
George Cumming	11	9
Percy Barrett	11	8
Davie Black	10	7
Karl Keffer	8	4
Albert Murray	10	4
George Sargent	4	4
Nicol Thompson	3	3
George S. Lyon (amateur)	7	3

The 1912 Open at Rosedale GC was a portent of things to come. From the other side of the border came three of the hottest golfers in the United States, and they took three of the first four places.

George Sargent, who had been the professional at Royal Ottawa, won. Runner-up was J. M. (Long Jim) Barnes, a Cornishman who was the professional at Tacoma Country Club.

Alex Smith, a Scot from Carnoustie, took fourth place, two strokes behind George Cumming, who managed to break up this American triumvirate. Smith's best golf was behind him. He had twice won the U.S. Open and been runner-up three times.

The weather at Rosedale could not have been worse for the first round of this Open. High heat and humidity gave way to heavy rain. Sargent, a quiet, unassuming young man, shot a 72, for a one-stroke lead over Cumming. He increased his lead to five strokes in the afternoon, but not without some lucky breaks. At the thirteenth, he pushed his ball into the woods, where it hit a tree and rebounded to the fairway.

Although nobody took much notice of him that day, Walter Hagen, the nineteen-year-old assistant at the Country Club in Rochester, played in his first Canadian Open. He finished in eleventh place. Hagen was later to remember his first visit to Canada. In his biography, he wrote:

> Karl Keffer met me at the dock and we went to the Rosedale Golf Club where he introduced me around. I thought it mighty friendly of a former champion to take so much trouble for an unknown like me and I certainly appreciated it.

Of the nineteen Canadian professionals who played in the 1912 Open, eight had been pupils of George Cumming. But with only four entries, the British–American contingent had taken three of the first four places. If ever there was a time for Canadian golfers to be asking themselves: "Why? And what holds the future?" it was surely that day at Rosedale.

When the championship moved to Royal Montreal in 1913, Sargent obviously felt he could not afford to make the long trip to defend his title. His first-place prize money, after all, had been only one hundred dollars.

Until 1910 the Canadian Open was just one event of the RCGA's Annual Meeting. The leading amateurs who played in the Open did so in a week when they were also competing in the Canadian Amateur, the interprovincial team match, the annual handicap, and other events. Even the fittest of them must have suffered from physical and mental fatigue. Not surprisingly, no amateur was to win the Open.

Only George Lyon and T. B. Reith seriously challenged the professionals. Lyon came third in 1904. He was runner-up at Lambton in 1910 when his second-round score of 71 set a new amateur course record, equalled only by the home professional, Barrett. After the third round he was tied with Kenny, but he lost four strokes to him in the final round. *The Globe* concluded that "Mr. Lyon lost his chance when he required eight strokes to go down at the sixth hole, one which is not at all difficult for him in five and one which he took in three in the second round."

Tom Reith was runner-up in 1906 but seldom competed thereafter. Increasingly, the Canadian Open became an event for professionals. In 1914, only five amateurs competed in a field of thirty-two.

On 7 July 1911, during the Canadian Open at Royal Ottawa, some twenty Canadian professionals met and organized the Canadian Professional Golfers' Association. This was to be, although not intentionally, exclusively a Central Canada organization until after the First World War.

The early minutes and other records of the CPGA have been lost or destroyed. But during the First World War, the association's long-time secretary-treasurer, Karl Keffer, laid out its objects in a letter published by *Canadian Golfer*. These are presumably the objects formulated in 1911:

- to promote interest in the game of golf.
- to protect the mutual interest of members of the association.
- to hold meetings and tournaments periodically for the encouragement of the younger members.
- to act as agents for assisting any Professional Golfer or Assistant to obtain employment.
- to carry out any other objects that may be determined upon from time to time.

George Cumming was elected captain of the CPGA, Percy Barrett the vice-captain, and Arthur Russell the honorary secretary-treasurer.

Karl Keffer took over from Russell in 1914 and was to be the CPGA's main spokesman until he gave up the post in 1929. He was elected the association's first president in 1938.

In its early days, the association also elected each year as honorary president the president of the club where the CPGA championship was held.

Canadian professionals still dominated the Canadian Open when the CPGA was formed in 1911; the Open prize money was too small to attract many entrants from the United States. But Canada's professionals knew that they lacked tournament experience. The CPGA championship, first held in 1912, was one step towards correcting this. P. D. Ross, president of Royal Ottawa in 1909 and 1910, put up the P. D. Ross Cup for the winner.

Only fourteen professionals and assistants went for the first CPGA title, over the Mississaugua course, on the day before the 1912 Open at nearby Rosedale. Charlie Murray won by a stroke over 36 holes. ("He won by a point," according to one Toronto newspaper.)

Nineteen turned out for the 1913 and 1914 CPGA championships. Davie Black won in 1913, his first of four CPGA titles, before he took off for the West Coast. Charlie Murray took 46 for the last nine holes that day at Beaconsfield, which was not "the lowest score turned in for the half course during the day," as a newspaper would have us believe, but the highest score. An A. Desjardins (no club reported) played that day – the first French-Canadian professional to join the CPGA. This was probably Aime, working at the time in Charlie Murray's shop at Royal Montreal.

In 1914, Willie Bell went round Lakeview in 72, to lead by three strokes after the morning round. But this big, strapping youngster from Scarboro Golf Club lost confidence in the afternoon, to finish second to his old teacher, George Cumming.

There is no record of the amount of prize money, which was probably put up by equipment manufacturers and the host club. In 1914, Cumming also received a gold watch donated by the Carter Seed Company. This was to be the last CPGA championship until after the First World War. But those professionals not in the forces were to compete with each other during the war, raising considerable amounts for charities.

Canada's professionals were a much-respected group, a fact captured in this piece written by a Montreal sportsman, Captain J. Reid, and published in a Montreal newspaper during the 1913 Open:

> It was pleasing, too, to notice how well-braced up, tidy and keen, the professional golfers appeared, as in succession they paired off from the tee beneath the verandah. Golf is a fine, healthy, clean sport, and it reflects itself in the appearance of its professional players. They contrast well with many of the other branches of sport. They are good craftsmen too, in the art of club-making, to master which a long apprenticeship is necessary. They are abstemenious, well-spoken, and courteous, and one has only to keep his ears open to hear how popular from the many greetings all are.

10

HARRY VARDON IN CANADA

His first question was as to the danger arising from the herds of buffalo which he understood frequented our Golf links. After I had explained to him that buffalo were absolutely extinct in North America, with the exception of a few solitary specimens in captivity, he evidently felt relieved, and it seemed an additional solace to him when he learned that Indians were about as scarce in the United States as Druids in England.

— Mr. Josiah Newman, editor of the American magazine *Golf*, as reported in the British magazine *Golf Illustrated*, March 1900

WHEN HARRY VARDON MADE HIS FIRST visit to North America, he was what we would now call a hot property. He had won the British Open in 1896, 1898, and 1899. He had just beaten the pride of Scotland, Willie Park Jr., in a series of matches, and by a wide margin. His reputation as a golfing machine was already made and had preceded him across the Atlantic.

The concept of turning oneself into a golfing machine by practice, practice, and yet more practice, had much appeal to the American mind. American golfers did not want to believe that the Vardon swing was some innate gift. He told them what they wanted to hear. To be a top-class golfer, you had to work long and hard.

There was much speculation as to the terms under which he had agreed to spend six months touring North America, during which time he was supposed to play exhibition matches, go back to Britain for the British Open, and then return for more exhibition matches and the U. S. Open.

Josiah Newman of *Golf* reported the terms to be that Spalding would use its best endeavours to arrange exhibitions for Vardon, each to pay him $250, Vardon covering all his own expenses. In exchange for Spalding's services, Vardon agreed to the use of his name on a brand of Spalding clubs, the manufacture of which he, Vardon, would superintend.

All this is now quite commonplace, but in 1900 the idea of being paid for lending one's name to a set of golf clubs was quite new and startling. The British did not know what to make of it. But they were proud of their man. He was, after all, a professional, and a fine, modest fellow to boot. And he *was* in the game for the money.

Vardon's tour of America was a great success. When playing head-to-head matches, he was apparently beaten only once, on a course in Florida on a surface that must have been quite foreign to him. But to make a match of it he usually played against the better ball of two local professionals or of two leading amateurs, and he did lose a few of these. In an otherwise successful year, he lost the British Open title to J. H. Taylor. But the second part of his American tour does not seem to have been any the worse for this.

By the time he reached Canada in late September, he was a tired man. And he had yet to play in the U.S. Open, which was scheduled for October 4 and 5 at the Chicago Golf Club.

Harry Vardon arrived at the Queen's Hotel, Toronto, on Friday, 21 September, prepared to play a 36-hole match against the better ball of George S. Lyon and Vere Brown over their own course, Rosedale.

For days, the press had been referring to "The most important fixture that has ever been brought about in Canada." Delegations, they reported, were coming from Hamilton, London, Orillia, and Cobourg; the course record of 73 was in danger; there would be a record number of spectators; the club would be selling badges for the match at one dollar each.

The Globe also reminded spectators of their responsibilities:

> For the guidance of those who have not been in the habit of attending golf matches it will be well to remember that absolute silence must be maintained when the players are addressing or making their strokes. The same advice applies to the camera fiends, as the snapping of the Kodak spoils many a good shot.

At four o'clock on Friday morning, half a dozen men and a team of horses were out rolling and cutting the course by lantern. On the Friday afternoon, Vardon played over the links with the club's secretary, Baxter, but this knowledge was kept to a few, and there were no outside spectators.

On the Saturday, playing for only the second time on the course, Vardon beat the better ball of George S. Lyon and Vere Brown by 5 and 4, over 36 holes. The players completed both rounds, Vardon shooting 72 73–145, Lyon 161, and Vere Brown 169.

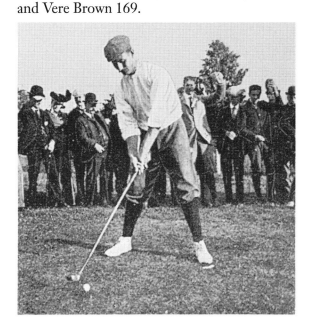

Harry Vardon driving at Rosedale, 1900.

Vardon's 72 was one stroke lower than the course record held by the club's professional, Ritchie. Lyon did not play at his best, and Vere Brown was even more off his game. But the three to four hundred spectators had come to see Harry Vardon. To the surprise of the Toronto *Mail and Empire* reporter, "There was a very large proportion of ladies among the spectators, and many of them were present during both rounds, walking the long distance as resolutely as their escorts."

From the tee, Vardon was no better than Lyon; or, at least, he was no longer, and not conspicuously straighter. But his shots to the green, his recovery shots when needed, his short approach shots, his holing of long putts over the lumpy greens – these were what won him the match and the admiration of those who were witnesses to this entirely new way of playing the game.

After the match at Rosedale, the club's president gave a dinner for Vardon at the National

Club in Toronto. If British newspapers ever reported this, there would have been a few raised eyebrows in that country's clubhouses.

On the following Tuesday, the Montreal Stock Exchange closed early so that brokers could witness the spectacle of Harry Vardon playing golf at Royal Montreal.

The club had opened its doors to members of the other two city clubs, Westmount and Metropolitan. Invitations also went out to two hundred special guests. And leading members of the Toronto, Ottawa, and Hamilton clubs were there, having come to Montreal for the Canadian Amateur due to start the following week.

Vardon arrived on the 9:50 p.m. train from Toronto, accompanied by the tour manager, S. C. Cox of Spalding, and Tom Wall, Spalding's Canadian representative. Next morning, a Montreal newspaper described Vardon's drive to the club as "in the order of a triumphant procession." The same paper devoted one column to the match, giving equal space to a list of the dignitaries who had received invitations. For this was more than a golf match: this was a fashionable function, one of the social events of the year. Among those present were Sir William and Lady Van Horne; R. B. Angus, of the Bank of Montreal, and Mrs. Angus; The Honourable George and Mrs. Drummond; Sir William and Lady Hingston; the Stephens, the Labatts, the Maltbys, and a string of Macdougalls.

Vardon was again playing against the better ball; in the morning round, that of two professionals, George Cumming of Toronto GC and Tom Smith of Royal Montreal; in the afternoon, that of Percy Taylor and Gordon Macdougall, Royal Montreal's two leading amateurs.

In the first match, Vardon went round in 77, to lose by 1 hole to Cumming (81) and Smith (79). In the second match, Vardon's 71 bettered the old course record by 8 strokes, good enough to beat the amateurs' better ball by 5 and 4.

Vardon's visit to Canada appears to have triggered two reactions. His criticism of the courses on which he played – and it is not clear to whom he vented these complaints – forced Canadian clubs to take another look at the architecture and maintenance of their links. Secondly, by his example, he showed where and how matches are won and lost. Canadians could match him for

Vardon at Royal Montreal, 1900.

distance, but were vastly inferior in accuracy when playing to the green. The two points were clearly connected. Open, poorly bunkered fairways do not put a premium on accurate play.

Saturday Night wrote in September of his match at Rosedale:

> Vardon has come and gone, carrying away with him his usual victory, and leaving us wiser and perhaps sadder golfers. Beyond doubt, he demonstrated his ability as a player of the first order, though handicapped by the roughness of the course, which he criticized in no gentle terms. Those who stay at home don't quite realize the conditions of Canadian courses as compared with those of England and the States . . . His criticisms both as regards courses and players in Canada hit the nail on the head, and will doubtless do good.
>
> It is not now so hard to explain the defeat of our players by the Statesers over the lat-ter's good courses. The home-bred players cannot be surpassed at the long game, but when it comes to fine approach work and putting, they drop below zero. There is no incentive to accurate work in this branch in Canada, as compared with England and the States, as so much has to be left to chance.

Harry Vardon's later visits to Canada, in 1913 and 1920, did not have the impact of the first. In 1913, he and Ted Ray came to Toronto shortly after losing the U.S. Open to Francis Ouimet. They played at Lambton and Toronto Golf, before going out west to Winnipeg and Victoria. There is a photograph in the Victoria clubhouse showing Vardon and Ray with amateurs Harvey Combe, A. Vernon Macan, and Biggerstaff Wilson. In 1920, Ray and Vardon played over the Scarboro course and at Royal Montreal. (Ray had just won the U.S. Open from Vardon, who was a close second. They came to Canada after playing ninety-five exhi-

Harry Vardon and Ted Ray visited Victoria GC in 1913 and are seen here with leading B.C. amateurs. Left to right: *Ted Ray, Biggerstaff Wilson, A. Vernon Macan, Harvey Combe, Harry Vardon.*

bition matches in the United States.) At Winnipeg, the pair played at least three matches, one against Jack Cuthbert and Tom Gillespie, at that time the two leading amateurs in the province.

Only one reporter of Vardon's first visit to Canada in 1900 captured the excitement of the moment; of how it felt to watch the finest golfer in the world display his skills. Theodore Arnold Haultain, who was to publish his *Mystery of Golf* in 1908, wrote a lengthy analysis for the Toronto *Mail and Empire*. At the time, Haultain was private secretary to Goldwyn Smith. He wrote, in part:

> . . .There is nothing in the man himself – his build, his physique, or his muscular power – to account for the perfection of his play. It was just simply the utmost development of what physiologists are also in the habit of calling the "muscular sense," the sense that determines how much force is requisite for wielding a fork, a stick, a pen, or – as in Vardon's case – a putter or a cleek. I venture to think that it is upon the perfect development of this sense, through years of practice, that Vardon's success is due . . .

Vardon's play was a pure aesthetic pleasure to behold. The trajectory of his drive, low at first, with a terrific velocity, and a distinctly audible whizz, rising higher and higher with lessening speed, and magnificent curve, was a thing to stir the emotions; and the ball, as it rose into the clouds, hung for a moment in the firmament, then dropped with parabolic swerve plumb on the green, gave you an emotional thrill only to be compared to that evoked by a work of art. Philosophically, the pleasure was the same; it appealed probably to the same ganglionic centres as those affected by beautiful colours or harmonious sounds.

11
CHAPTER

CLUBS AND BALLS IN THE WOODEN-SHAFT YEARS

WHEN THOSE HARDY MONTREAL golfers played over Priests' Farm at Christmas 1826, what sort of clubs and balls did they use?

The wooden-headed clubs of the early nineteenth century were sleek, often elegant, with long shallow heads, sweeping oval necks, and long, tapered wooden shafts. They have come to be known as "long-nosed" clubs. Their heads might be made of beech, apple, or holly; their shafts of the exotic woods of ash, orange wood, greenheart, lemon wood, or split hickory. If the players used irons at all, they would have been heavy, coarse, and thick-shafted, with smooth faces. The golf ball of the period was the feathery – a capsule of leather stuffed with feathers. When dry, it could be driven perhaps 180 yards; when wet, it responded like a sponge.

By the time Canada's golfers had organized themselves in the 1870s, sleek, long-nosed clubs were still being used, but the feathery had long since been replaced by the gutty.

The gutty was made from gutta-percha, a leathery, water-resistant substance obtained from the latex of various Malaysian trees. On heating, gutta-percha becomes plastic; on cooling, it hardens. In the second half of the last century, it came to be used for such things as underwater cables, as well as for making chewing gum and golf balls.

When the gutta-percha golf ball first came on the market, in 1848, it was joyously welcomed by golfers. It cost half as much as a feathery, could be made ten times as quickly, and did not soften in the rain. *Hail Gutta Percha! precious gum!/O'er Scotland's links lang may ye bum*, sang the poet William Graham, at the autumn meeting of the Innerleven Golfing Club, in 1848.

There are conflicting accounts of who invented the gutty. In his *Reminiscences of Golf and Golfers* (1890), H. Thomas Peter claimed "the credit of having first brought them [gutties] to the notice of the golfing world, and this at the Spring Meeting of the Innerleven Club in 1848." He had seen them on sale in a basement toy shop in David Street, Edinburgh. In a letter to the British magazine *Golf*, published in August 1891, Tom Peter described what happened when he tried out the ball:

> The ball was . . . quite round, without a mark upon it, and instead of paint was coated with a sort of "size." I expected great results from it, but, to my chagrin, on striking it fairly, instead of rising and flying as a good ball ought to do, it ducked and bobbed along the ground, more like a performance of hop, skip, and jump. . . .

Later, when he had scraped the size off the ball, "it flew beautifully, going much further than I expected." In scraping the size off the ball, he had given its surface a crude form of dimple. In such ways, golfers learned that a new gutty would not fly long and straight unless its surface was nicked or otherwise roughened. The old feathery had not needed this treatment. Its stitched seams gave it a rough surface from the day it was made.

Ballmakers made gutties from gutta-percha supplied in sheets, ropes, or rods. They softened a piece of gutta-percha by immersing it in hot water, rolled it into a round form by hand on a board, then hardened it by immersing it in cold water. The ball was, as Tom Peter described it, "a nasty, dirty, brown." The ballmaker then gave it several coats of paint, by pouring paint into the cup of his hand and rolling the ball in his palms. The ball was then put on a shelf to cure for six months, for reasons that are not clear.

Once ballmakers discovered that nicking a ball made it fly farther and straighter, they took to indenting its surface with the sharp end of a hammer. An experienced ballmaker could give a ball some three hundred indents in under three minutes. So uniform were the indents on a "Forgan Hand-Hammered" ball that it sold for a penny premium over the usual price of a shilling (twenty-five cents).

Near the end of the century, when balls were made in moulds instead of being rolled

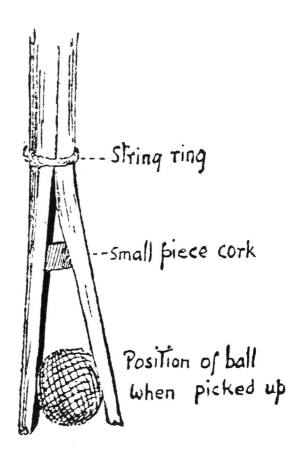

An implement used by ball-snatchers, 1899.

by hand, the mould was indented to give the surface of the ball a bramble appearance.

The gutty had many advantages over the feathery. It did not go soggy in wet weather. Neither did it burst open at the seams, strewing feathers over the green. Its scars were readily fixed by remoulding. A club professional would do this, exchanging a new ball for a scuffed ball plus a few cents. Many golfers learned how to remould their own gutties. By the 1890s, as golf was exploding in Canada, do-it-yourself kits were on the market. A gutty could be remoulded several times, but it did lose a fraction of its original weight each time as a result of the trimming.

The great weakness of the gutty was its inability to stand up to extremes of weather. It softened in very hot weather. This was never a problem in Scotland, seldom a problem in England, but at the peak of the North American summer the gutty would fly off the face of the club like a lump of chewing gum.

Few balls were made from pure gutta-percha. Golfers and ballmakers experimented with the ball, adding lead shot, or moulding the ball around cores of various materials, such as wood, ball-bearings, or cork. Composition balls were turned out, made of mixtures of gutta-percha and a variety of materials, including Indiarubber. These attempts to make the ball less crackable in cold weather, and to withstand better the blows of the club, met with limited success. Among the most durable of the composite balls were the "Eclipse" and the "Agrippa," both sold in Canada. The Eclipse was made for the North American climate. It was, as its makers put it, "popular in the colonies."

By the time Royal Montreal had hired Willie Davis as professional in 1881, gutties were being made in moulds. The club probably bought all its balls in Scotland, relying on Davis mainly for remoulding. The club's minutes show that he was paid fourpence (about seven cents) for "making up a ball." With a new gutty costing twenty to twenty-five cents, remoulding was obviously worthwhile.

By the turn of the century, in Britain, ball-making had virtually left the professional's shop and entered the factory, but the Canadian market was still much too small to justify domestic manufacture. Indeed, it was only towards the turn of the century that Spalding, and Wright and Ditson, started making balls for the much larger U.S. market. Canadian companies such as Hingston Smith Arms Manufacturing Company, Winnipeg, imported balls for sale to clubs. And in cities where golf clubs had been organized, sporting goods stores had balls on sale by the middle of the 1890s.

By 1900, the Maponite ball was on the market. Its composition was kept secret. It did not need curing, did not soften or crack, and stood up well to the club. It was probably heavier than the normal gutty, since it flew better in a cross-wind.

There is no saying what success the Maponite might have had if the rubber-cored ball

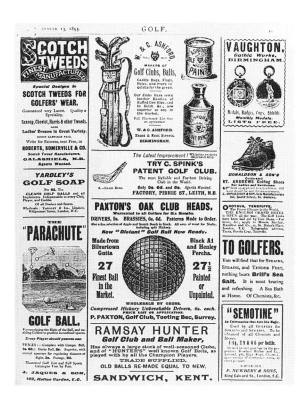

A page of ads from the British magazine Golf, *September 1895, includes paint for your golf balls and "Semotine" for your sprains and strains.*

had not come on the market about the same time. The editor of the British magazine *Golf Illustrated* reported in November 1899:

> I hear that Goodrich, the Golf ball maker of Boston, is to bring out a wonderful ball next season. Its composition is a secret, but it is whispered that it can be driven out of sight, if only it is fairly and squarely hit. If this be true, we shall have to lengthen our courses; but what shall we do about lost balls?

No other single event in the history of golf has so quickly changed the playing of the game, and the face of the golf course, as the introduction of the rubber-cored ball, essentially the ball we use today. And it is equally true that no other event has brought more enjoyment to the average golfer. At the turn of the century, he was driving the gutty about 160 yards off the tee, using a new ball, or a remoulded ball, for each round (if he could afford it), worrying about it softening in hot weather or becoming too brittle

A feathery.

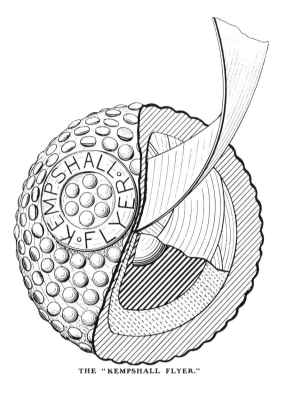

THE "KEMPSHALL FLYER."

A rubber-cored ball of the early 1900s.

A Forgan "hand-hammered" gutty of the late Victorian years.

in cold. Overnight – or so it seemed – his life was changed. Summer or winter, his ball flew 30 yards farther. Badly topped, it went nearly as far. He could use the same ball, round after round. His scores were consistently in the 90s, and now and then he might even break into the 80s. No matter that his friends were doing the same. No matter that his handicap was not

coming down. He was now driving the ball to places on the course hitherto reached only by the club professional. This is what the game of golf was all about. Welcome, twentieth century!

The ball that so changed his life was the Haskell. Coburn Haskell was an American businessman and a golfer. The idea came to him to wind elastic yarn round itself to form a ball. He and Bert Work of Goodrich did this by hand, encasing the ball of elastic yarn in gutta-percha. When they tested the ball on a course, they found that a professional could drive it out of sight.

The idea of using Indiarubber instead of gutta-percha was not new. But the problem with solid Indiarubber was its softness and lightness. Stretched rubber tape or thread, wound tightly, was harder and denser. But if golf balls were to be produced in this way, a method had to be found of doing the job mechanically. John Gammeter, an inventive genius from the Goodrich tool shop, developed a machine capable of winding elastic around a solid gutta-percha or rubber core at high speed.

They applied for a patent in August 1898 and were granted it in the following year.

The Haskell ball came on the market early in 1901. But the Gammeter machine had not been perfected, so supplies were limited. In North America, the ball was accepted with little question, being looked upon as a natural development to be expected from a continent that sponsored and rewarded entrepreneurial genius. At the U.S. Amateur championship in September 1901, all the talk centred on the relative merits of the rubber-core and the gutty. Walter Travis played the Haskell, used only one ball all week, and won. He found he could keep up with players who would normally have outdriven him by at least thirty yards. What is more, he had never putted so well, which put paid to the stories that the Haskell was a difficult ball to handle on the green.

This was only one of the faults that the British were to find with these early Haskells. Or, at least, some of the British; for the golfers in the country were very soon divided into two camps. The majority of professionals were against it. To some extent, their opposition was a matter of self-interest, since they made a good part of their living out of remoulding old gutties. But many of them sincerely believed that the rubber-core took much skill out of the game and made it too easy for the mediocre golfer.

THE NEW AMERICAN GOLF BALL.

The new American rubber-cored ball (left) *being ridiculed by three old British gutties: "He's a bit of a bounder, I admit, and he can't putt for nuts…"*

Professional Sandy Herd, after condemning the new ball, used a Haskell in the 1902 British Open, and won it for the first and last time.

Some prominent and influential British amateurs crusaded against the Haskell on a number of grounds. They were concerned that the form and make of implements were coming to dominate golf. They feared that courses would now be outdated; too short, with hazards in the wrong places. They accused the new ball of being too lively, and gave it the sobriquet of "bounding billie."

The traditionalists and the professionals (through the British PGA) sought to have the rubber-core banned from the 1903 British Open. When that failed, they sought to have the golf ball standardized, by having the Rules of Golf Committee set down how it should be made and how far it should fly. They quickly ran up against formidable opponents to standardization, among them the Prime Minister, the Right Honourable A. J. Balfour.

Many who had been sceptical about the claims of the Haskell soon came to support the new ball, mainly on the grounds that it lasted longer and hence was cheaper. What is more, it made golf easier for the average golfer, and therefore more enjoyable. As for legislation making the rubber-core illegal, Horace Hutchinson had the last word: "If legislation says that golf is not to be played with a Haskell, the world will play the Haskell and leave golf to be played by the legislators."

Eventually, the ball *was* standardized, but not until 1921.

In 1902, another rubber-core came out as a rival to the Haskell. The Kempshall ball had a truly Indiarubber core, enclosed in gutta-percha, bound with elastic, with an outer cover of gutta-percha. It was soon followed by the Kempshall Flyer, which had a centre of celluloid, bound with a layer of fine quality rubber tape. The Flyer was followed by other balls, in which every material imaginable was tried

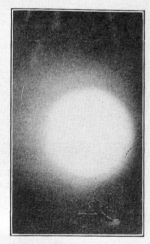

An ad for a radio-active ball in 1918, in an age of ignorance.

as the centre. Improvements came so rapidly that, within a few years, the old gutty had been abandoned, even by the traditionalists.

In Canada, the rubber-core was in such short supply that it was not generally available to golfers until late 1902 or early 1903. As in the United States, a black market quickly developed, with Haskells going for $2.50 each, about five times the retail price. And, as in Britain, the debate over its use started before the ball was properly on the market. In July 1902, *Saturday Night* had this to say:

> If, then, the ball, and not the player, is to become the determining factor in a competition, it will be necessary to handicap a golfer according to the ball with which he is playing, just as cyclists were handicapped when they first used pneumatic tires or highly-geared safeties . . . Some genius will have to calculate the advantage of the Haskell or Kempshall ball . . .

Some of the quantifiable evidence of the advantage of the rubber-core in Canada comes from the results of long-driving competitions. In 1898, J. G. Averill won the long-driving competition at the Niagara International Golf Tournament with three drives averaging 181 yards; when the results were next published, in 1905, Fritz Martin won with an average of 241 yards, and had one drive of 271 yards. Martin had obviously switched to a rubber-core by 1905.

Too, players who had previously scored in the 80s suddenly started scoring in the 70s. In the medal competitions at Toronto GC, W. A. H. Kerr won the low gross with 82, 82 in May and October 1901. In May and September 1902, he won with 74, 73. In the same competition, Stewart Gordon came down from 85, 85 to 80, 78. Thereafter, the club started to lengthen its course.

When the 1903 season opened at Victoria Golf Club, B.C., Harvey Combe shot a new course record of 75, and nine players were in the 80s, scores that were quite unprecedented.

At Winnipeg GC, a new course had been opened in June 1901, so comparisons are impossible. But at the opening of the 1903 season, "Ramage did the most sensational work with the driver, sending the ball nearly 250 yards on one drive." One suspects that Mr. Ramage had found himself a rubber-core.

The new ball brought changes to Canadian courses. But around the turn of the century, many courses were, coincidentally, being lengthened and bunkered to make them better tests of golf. Clubs were also recruiting more members and expanding the number of holes for play. So changes were under way before the rubber-core came on the market to make the courses even more outdated. In 1904, George Lyon had this to say in an article in the Montreal *Standard*:

> No money is being spared by the various clubs in Canada to improve their courses . . . The rubber cored ball demands a much more difficult course than the gutta percha ball. It is only fair that a straight player should be advantaged by his skill; and without a much more difficult course than that which formerly obtained – that is, a course without more bunkers – the player who drove the ball to the side has as much of an advantage as the straight driver.

The courses used for national championships were all lengthened, and made more difficult in other ways, within a few years of the arrival of the rubber-cored ball.

Toronto GC lengthened its course from 4,610 yards to 5,125 yards in time for the 1905 Canadian Amateur and Open, but it was still too short. What is more, there were a number of places on the links where the player could drive well off line and not be in any hazard or rough. More land was acquired, and the course expanded to around 6,000 yards by 1909.

The Lambton course was being laid out at the time the new ball was coming on the market. Nevertheless, the club resolved to tighten the course by adding bunkers, with the declared intention of making Lambton "the most difficult course of its kind in Canada . . . to induce players to make straight drives." The course measured 6,025 yards.

Royal Montreal's new site at Dixie had a nine-hole course, measuring only some 2,500 yards in 1896. Three new holes were added before the 1902 championships, when the first six holes were played twice to give an eighteen-hole round. "By national championship standards, the course was only a makeshift," the club admits in its written history. In the spring of 1902, the club bought an adjacent farm and laid out a new eighteen-hole course of 5,665 yards.

The then recently constructed course of Royal Ottawa GC, at 6,310 yards, was the longest in Canada and well-equipped for the first generation of rubber-cored balls.

By the teens of the century, however, manufacturers were producing a ball in which the elastic thread was wound more tightly, giving a smaller and denser ball, one which flew even farther. Faced with the choice of lengthening courses or limiting the distance a ball would travel, golf's rulemakers chose the latter. They did this by stipulating in 1921 that the ball should be not less than 1.62 inches in diameter and not more than 1.62 ounces in weight. This was the size of the Canadian ball until 1948, when it was changed to 1.68 inches.

A full account of the old Scottish clubmakers and ballmakers is given in Henderson and Stirk's *Golf in the Making* (1979). This first book of its kind is already a classic of golf literature. In their book, the authors distinguish between clubmakers, who made wooden-headed clubs, and cleekmakers, who made irons (cleek being the name given to an early form of iron-headed club). In mid-Victorian times, the average golfer carried perhaps six clubs, all but one or two of these having wooden heads. The trend towards more clubs, and more irons, started later in the century. But as late as 1890

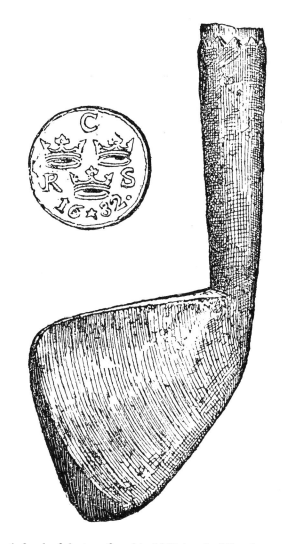

A sketch of the iron found in 1891 in a building in Leith. It was found along with a coin dated 1682 and was believed to be of a similar date.

the Toronto *Globe* defined a whole set of clubs as comprising only six, namely, the playclub, the putter, the spoon, the sand-iron, the cleek, and the niblick or track-iron.

The Dicksons of Leith were club and ballmakers in the seventeenth and eighteenth centuries. They were the first to make clubs renowned for their quality of craftsmanship. But it has been often said that Hugh Philp was the Stradivarius of clubmakers. Born in Leith in 1782, he was appointed clubmaker to the R & A in 1819. A Philp club, with its slender shaft and graceful head, is much prized by collectors.

Robert Forgan was the first clubmaker to become known worldwide. He was Philp's nephew. A carpenter by trade, he joined his uncle's business in 1852, and took over four years later, when Philp died.

When Forgan took over the clubmaking shop, he had only one assistant. By 1900, the firm of R. Forgan and Son had over fifty men in the workshop overlooking the R & A clubhouse. Forgan was the first Scottish clubmaking firm to build up a large export business, when golf spread to North America. By 1900, you could find many Forgan clubs on sale in Canada.

Forgan was the largest of the clubmaking firms, but there were others of equal skill. Among these were the McEwans of St. Andrews; the Morrises of St. Andrews, including Old Tom Morris; the Patricks of Leven; the Dunns of Musselburgh; and the Willie Parks of Musselburgh.

A corner of the Forgan workshop, St. Andrews, in 1895. The bearded gentleman is Robert Forgan, founder of Robert Forgan and Son, Ltd.

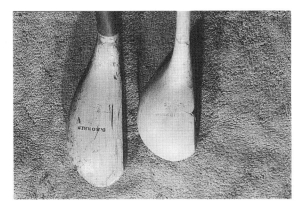

A long-nosed driver or playclub made by Old Tom Morris, alongside a driver made by R. Simpson early this century.

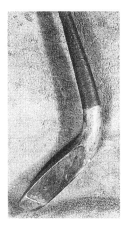

A side view of the playclub.

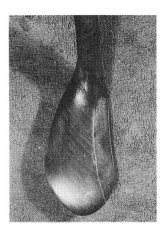

A long-nosed spoon by Old Tom Morris.

The cleekmakers did not become so well known. But the names of Stewart of St. Andrews, Gibson of Kinghorn, and Anderson of Anstruther could be found on wooden-shafted irons wherever golf was played.

Until the early 1890s, the clubmaker shaped his club by hand. For the head, he could choose the woods of beach, apple, or holly; for the shaft, ash, orange or lemon wood, green-heart, lancewood, or split hickory.

The wood came in planks, five or six inches thick. The clubmaker cut these into short blocks for clubheads, laboriously shaping the blocks by hand, using frame-saws and rasps. In this way, he turned out wooden clubs with a variety of purposes, and with names like play-club (or driver), baffy, brassie, and spoon. Just as there are now woods numbered up to nine, so there were short, medium, and long spoons.

As demand outstripped supply in the early 1890s, human inventiveness came up with rotary machines that could do much of the work previously done by hand. The clubmaker blocked out the rough head with a bandsaw. He placed the rough head in the rotary machine, which turned out a neatly shaped driver head in a minute or so, from a metal model. Another machine cut out the cavity for the lead at the back and a space for the horn that protected the clubface. Yet another machine cut out and tapered the shaft.

In this way, clubs that had previously been made by the dozen could be turned out by the thousands. In the middle of the nineteenth century, Robert Forgan had to arrange with the captain of a ship trading with Quebec to bring home the odd plank or so of hickory. By 1900, the firm of Forgan and Son was buying shafts cut on the square in America in consignments of twenty thousand at a time. The demand for clubheads could not be met by the supply of the traditional beech and apple-wood in Britain, so harder woods, such as persimmon, were imported from North America.

Clubmaking firms also shipped mass-produced heads to club professionals overseas, including those in Canada. The Canadian professional still had to fix the shaft to the head, gluing and binding the joint. He then sandpapered and polished the head, fitted the cloth and leather, and stamped his name on the clubhead. He might also file the clubface to a preferred angle of loft, or adjust the lead weight, to meet a particular member's needs.

These machine-made clubs did not have the individuality or charm of hand-made clubs, but they did have a uniformity that many hand-made clubs lacked. And they were cheaper to make, requiring much less labour. The capital cost of the cutting machines could often be recovered in months. Those who preferred a genuine hand-made club could still have it from one of the traditional clubmakers, but at a premium.

Just before the cutting of clubheads was largely taken over by machines, the shape of the wooden clubhead changed. The long-nose disappeared. The new clubhead was shorter, wider, and deeper, very much like today's clubhead. It was given the name "bulger," since its face was slightly convex. As a rule, the new club had a more upright shaft. The long-nosed club may have been ideally suited to playing the feathery, when the player stood further from the ball, his arms extended. His stroke was more of a sweeping motion, with the clubhead going around the body rather than around the shoulders.

These typical dimensions of the old and the new clubhead are taken from *Golf in the Making*:

	Long-nose	Bulger
Head: length	5"	4"
width of face	2"	2 1/4"
depth of face	1"	1 1/4"
Length of shaft	45"	42"

The change from long-nose to bulger was complete within a few years. A well-known British amateur, Edward Blackwell, went to

California in 1886; when he returned to Britain in 1892, he found his wooden clubs outdated.

There was a more gradual change in the method of fixing the shaft to the clubhead. Traditionally, the head and neck of the club had been cut out as one piece. The neck was fixed to the shaft by means of a spliced (or scared) joint, which was glued and bound with whipping. The neck and the lower end of the shaft, when spliced together, had an oval shape, not a round one. About the turn of the century, the bottom of the shaft began to be rounded, and socketed into the head, without a scare.

From the early 1890s, the head was made from a multiplicity of materials as well as wood – vulcanite, Xylonite, celluloid, brass, iron, aluminum, and steel. Do not think that "metal woods" are an invention of the 1980s.

Steel shafts were also tried, but without any great success.

Most of the well-known Scottish clubmakers turned out irons as well as woods. But the cleekmaker specialized in iron-headed clubs. Stirk and Henderson concluded that early irons were made by blacksmiths, hammering bars of heating iron into the required shape round a mandrel, which gave form to the socket (or hosel) of the clubhead.

Later in the nineteenth century, iron clubheads could be mass-produced by drop-forging. In this process, a heavy hammer was dropped on a die (in the shape of a clubhead) filled with molten mild steel. In both methods of making the clubhead, the wooden shaft was fitted into the hosel, the top of which had serrated teeth (or nicks) to help hold the clubhead to the shaft.

The cleekmaker, then, if not a blacksmith, relied on smiths to supply his crude iron heads, which he would file smooth, shaft, and stamp with his name and logo.

The early Canadian professional had even less to do with the iron clubs "made" in his shop. He would buy most of his clubheads in bulk from a Scottish cleekmaker, such as Stewart; shaft them; and add his name to that of the cleekmaker's name or logo. Nevertheless, Canadian professionals had to learn how

to make and repair wooden-shafted woods and irons, as part of their apprenticeship. The professional's workshop was kept pretty busy until the early 1930s, by which time mass-produced steel-shafted clubs started to out-number the old hickories.

As we have seen, the Canadian golfer in 1890 carried something like a playclub (or driver), a putter, a spoon – all wooden-headed – and a sand-iron, a cleek, and a niblick or track-iron, with a head not much bigger than a crown: three wooden and three iron-headed clubs. The golfer of 1920 would carry a driver, a brassie, a spoon, a driving iron, a mid-iron, a mashie-iron, a mashie, a mashie-niblick, a niblick (now with a much bigger head), and a putter: three wooden and seven steel-headed clubs.

STOPUM MASHIE-NIBLICK.
This deep-grooved "Stopum" was legal in 1921.

The market being so small, balls and clubs were not manufactured in Canada until after the First World War — except for those turned out in professionals' shops – so everything had to be imported.

Increasingly, the United States came to replace Britain as the main supplier. The import duty on U.S.-manufactured golf balls was 27.5 per cent, as against 15 per cent for the British balls. The high duty, and the booming demand after the First World War, led Spalding to open a factory at Brantford, in 1921. Here it manufactured all its most popu-

An ad in Canadian Golfer *for the Spalding "50".*

lar balls, from the most expensive (at seventy-five cents), the Fifty and the Forty, to the cheapest (at fifty cents), the Glory Dimple, the Baby Dimple, the Corker Dimple (a ball that floated on water), and the Red Dot Mesh – the mesh referring to its square dimples. The Fifty was Spalding's flagship, so to speak. It was the ball used most often by professionals. In 1921, it had a hand in winning the Opens of Canada, U.S., Britain, and France.

For the first time, the size and weight of golf balls was being standardized by the rules of golf, so that other smaller and heavier (more tightly wound) Spalding balls had to be discontinued in 1921, because they were flying too far.

In time for the opening of the Canadian golf season in 1923, Spalding brought out its most durable of lines. The Kro-flite, made in

Canada and selling for seventy-five cents, had a tough new cover and was noted for its longevity. It was guaranteed not to cut for 72 holes. In 1935, the Kro-flite was made one of the longest balls – so Spalding claimed – by the injection of extra liquid into the core after the ball was made. ("The new needling process adds 7 to 10 yards more distance.") The price of the needled Kro-flite remained seventy-five cents – but this after an economic depression that had seen the price of the best balls fall to fifty cents.

In the 1928 Canadian Open, the company was able to boast that 151 of the 165 entrants and 64 of the 69 qualifiers, including the winner, Leo Diegel, used Spalding balls.

Two other U.S. companies made their Canadian headquarters in Brantford just after Spalding, although at first they imported balls from the U.S. to warehouses. Within a few years, Wright and Ditson and A. J. Reach became A. J. Reach, Wright and Ditson of Canada Limited.

The Canada Golf Ball Company of Toronto also started to make balls in its own factory in 1922. This company's Pioneer, National, and Plus Four appeared for a number of years. These balls were advertised as being made completely in Canada, from first-grade materials. Around 1928 the company brought out a Fly-Rite, which was said to have the durable qualities of the other hard-cover balls then on the market.

In 1921, S. M. and M. S. Glassco, together with professional Nicol Thompson, all of Hamilton, established The Shur-Put Golf Ball Company, with the intention of making a low-priced golf ball.

If you went to your professional for clubs, you would be assured that these were "hand-made," but not necessarily hand-made all the way from the rough plank of wood, or molten steel, to the finished article. Frank Freeman of Rosedale advertised in 1915: "All my Clubs are hand made and finished. I get all my heads from England and Scotland." And in England and

FRANK FREEMAN

Professional to the Rosedale Golf Club, Toronto

A Golfer is judged by his Clubs. All my Clubs are hand made and finished. I get all my heads from England and Scotland. All Golf Bags sold by me are hand made. I always keep in stock all kinds of Maxwell Irons and the best makes of Golf Balls. A trial order solicited

FRANK P. FREEMAN

WM. M. FREEMAN

Professional to the Lambton Golf and Country Club, Lambton Mills, Ontario.

A fine line of Wood and Iron Clubs always kept in stock, also all Golf requisites. The most careful attention given to properly "fitting" and suiting golfers and their needs. All Clubs hand made and finished and guaranteed.

WM. M. FREEMAN

Canadian clubmakers advertise in 1915.

Scotland, the wooden heads were probably cut out by machine, the iron heads shaped by a die.

Some clubs hired clubmakers who were to become as well-known to their members as the club's professional. Charlie Macdonald joined Vancouver's Shaughnessy Heights as a clubmaker in 1913, after working for eighteen years for Ben Sayers in North Berwick. His handiwork became well-known on the West Coast. But even Charlie would probably buy the shafts and heads for his woods from one of the many block-making companies which had sprung up in the United States.

In the 1920s, the Golf Shaft and Block Company of Memphis, Tennessee, reputedly had the largest plant for turning out clubhead blocks for professionals. You could buy nearly finished heads in a variety of woods, including persimmon, ash, and dogwood. A Canadian

clubmaker didn't need to go all the way to the United States for his shafts. In the 1920s, D. Ackland and Son of Winnipeg sold "Arrow X L" brand shafts made from the finest Tennessee hickory.

The first of the large club manufacturers to open a factory in Canada appears to have been Spalding, which set up a production line in St. Catherine Street, Montreal, either just before or during the First World War. By the end of the war it was turning out by the thousands its machine-made Gold Medal range of woods and irons. Spalding hired four local professionals for the winter months as supervisors and finishers. One of them was James Black of Beaconsfield, noted as a clubmaker.

But most of Spalding's clubs were imported from its factories in the United States, until later in the 1920s, when it made its steel-shafted Kro-flite clubs at Brantford.

Scottish-born John Martin was, I believe, the first Canadian to set up a clubmaking firm in Canada. His father James had come over to be a clubmaker to George Cumming in 1922. John and Jim Jr. followed two years later. John was an assistant to the Rosedale and Bayview clubs in Toronto, before forming the Craftsmen Golf Company in Newmarket in 1926, along with his father and brother. Here they manufactured by hand and machine what they claimed were the first 100 per cent Canadian-made clubs. Two years later, they started the Martin Golf Company, with its factory in Sherbourne Street, Toronto. This company made clubs for many local professionals, leaving the professional to stamp his name on the finished article. The Martin company was bought out during the Depression years and reappeared as the Adanac Golf Company, which also had the franchise for Forgan and MacGregor clubs in Canada.

John Martin formed the Professional Golf Company, in 1934, in partnership with Canadian professionals Gordie Brydson, Willie Lamb, Arthur Hulbert, and Jimmy Johnstone. In 1937, Martin moved over to run the golf department for Campbell of Canada. But we are now well out of the wooden-shaft years,

Spalding's Bobby Jones steel-shafted clubs, made at Brantford, were best-sellers in the early 1930s.

although a few golfers did not make the change. The rules of golf had been changed in Canada in May 1925, to permit the use of steel-shafted clubs. They had already been legal for a year in the United States.

The Par Golf Company of Kenora, Ontario, was set up in the mid-1920s. It made the Par putter, patented by the Kenora club professional Jack Vernon and available in hickory or steel shaft.

The golfer of 1890 might have had a caddie to carry his or her six clubs underarm; by 1920, for ten clubs, a golf bag was essential.

Where and when did golfers start to use a golf bag for carrying their clubs? Ralph Reville put this question to Andrew Forgan in 1916, when that gentleman was staying in Montreal. Forgan remembered seeing a member of the Glasgow Golf Club using a black cloth bag for his clubs soon after 1870, but thought that bags did not go on the market until the early 1880s.

The 1923 history of Royal Montreal reproduces a photograph taken in 1885 of some fifty golfers awaiting the train for Montreal after golfing at Laprairie. They have no golf bags. They or their caddies are carrying the clubs loose.

In 1896, Julian Sale Leather Goods of Toronto's King Street claimed to be the only manufacturer of golf bags (or "caddie bags") in Canada.

The first golf tees were made by hand. The golfer or caddie slapped a handful of earth or damp sand on the ground, pressed it into the shape of a small cone, and placed the ball on top. In the early days, caddies scooped wet sand from bunkers, carrying it in their pockets, but in Canada, before the turn of the century, golf clubs were providing sand boxes at teeing areas. The neat golfer might use a wooden or brass tee-mould to shape the tee, but the process was still time-consuming, messy, and unhygienic.

Whether made by caddie or golfer, sand tees always looked as though they *must* slow the speed of the clubhead. Golfers had the vexed feeling that too much of their energy was being wasted in scattering sand over the teeing area.

Golf scientists had been experimenting for years but had found nothing to replace sand. Then, in 1921, Dr. William Lowell of New Jersey came out with the first commercially successful artificial tee. It was a simple wooden peg, not unlike the tee of today.

With success came competition. Imitators began to flood the market with artificial tees of various shapes, lengths, and colours, made from all sorts of materials: wood, aluminum, steel, fibre, and celluloid. They were advertised in Canada with all the hoopla and razzmatazz normally reserved for the promotion of film stars: "shaped to fit snugly between the fingers . . . brilliant in color, smooth to the touch . . . handsome black and yellow . . . made from the finest birch, beautifully finished in bright yellow lacquer . . . particularly well built, good alike to the eye

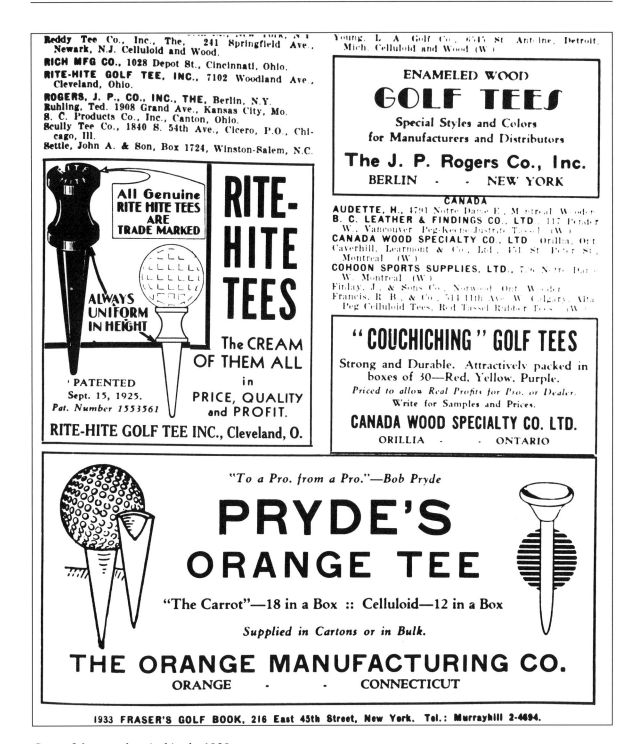

Some of the tees advertised in the 1930s.

and club . . . with assorted heads; red, yellow, blue and purple."

The Yello tee was wood and yellow. The Carrot had the shape and colour of its name. The Peg was popular with the ladies, who were said to choose a tee for its looks. The Peg came in three sizes: regular, long, and extra-long. The Anchor Blade had a razor-edged stem, to reduce earth resistance. The Super Aluminum tee was enamelled red or yellow. The Rich tee was of hickory. The Rite-Hite gave you the right height, and the Ivoris was made of pyroxalyn by French Ivory Products of Toronto, and came in four colours.

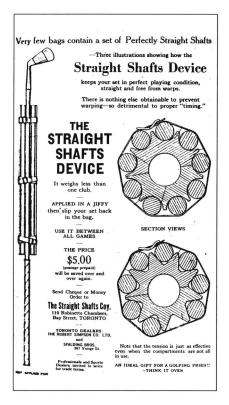

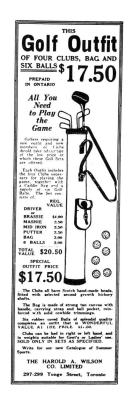

Kept your shafts straight, but not the ball.

Well-oiled shafts lasted longer.

A set of clubs, with bag, in 1922.

Some peg tees were moulded or cut in one piece; others had wooden heads and metal stems; and others were two-part celluloid.

With the introduction of the two-part celluloid tee, golfers felt the tee had come full circle, and that life was just as difficult now as it had been with sand. This tee was made in two parts, glued together; a one-inch stem, white, red, or blue, pointed at one end; and a saucer-shaped head, blue, red, or white. When the ball was struck, the tee separated into its two parts – inevitably, but not by design – and the two parts had to be found and glued back together.

In the days of the wooden-shafted club, shafts had a tendency to warp. The Straight Shafts Company of Toronto sold the Straight Shafts Device, which fitted inside the bag and was guaranteed to keep shafts from buckling. The Golf Club Press, produced by another Toronto

company, was intended to keep your clubs straight during storage in the winter months.

Shafts also had to be oiled. Imperial Oil's Ioco Liquid Gloss cleaned heads and protected them from rust; it also protected shafts from moisture.

The Golf Ball Stencil Company of Montreal was one of several that made a ball marker. Shaped like a large nutcracker, this device embedded your name in the surface of the ball and was of great usefulness in a day when balls cost something like three times today's price, in real terms.

In 1925, the Golfocycle Manufacturing Company of Montreal patented a single-wheeled pull-cart. The invention of a Montreal man, the Golfocycle was featured in *Popular Mechanics* of Chicago. But after this brief announcement, nothing more was heard of it. The pull-cart as we know it today did not appear until after the Second World War.

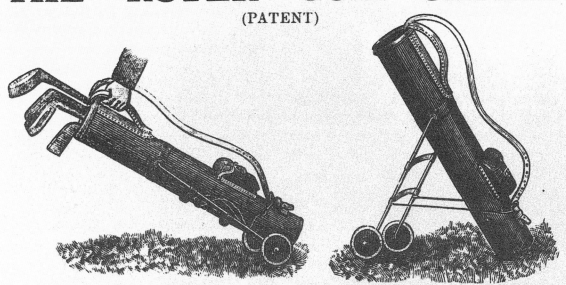

THE "ROVER" GOLF CADDIE
(PATENT)

GOLF WITH EASE AND COMFORT.

This Caddie relieves the player or his caddie of entire weight of clubs and so minimizes fatigue. It will convey an unusual number of clubs without feeling extra weight, and other kit, such as mackintosh. The carriage (with wooden wheels and rubber tyres) is easily detached, and bag can be used separately when so required. Positively light in weight, and can be stowed in ordinary-sized locker.

Wholesale : F. H. AYRES, 111, Aldersgate Street, London, E.C.
Retail : THE ARMY AND NAVY CO-OPERATIVE SOCIETY, LIMITED, 105, Victoria Street, London, S.W. ; and all other dealers.

An early form of pull-cart, sold in Britain around 1900.

12

ENTER THE LADIES

THE BADMINTON LIBRARY BOOK *GOLF*, published in Britain in 1890, had a piece on women and golf, written by Lord Wellwood. His Lordship debated three delicate matters: the right of women to play golf at all; their right to play the full round of eighteen holes; their right to attend matches as spectators.

He concluded that women did have the right to play, but on a very short course. Women, he argued, could not be expected to drive a ball more than seventy or eighty yards. He argued this not because he doubted their ability to drive further, but because they could not do so without raising the club above the shoulder. And the posture and gesture needed to raise the club, he pointed out, would not be particularly flattering to someone wearing female dress.

What if women *did* want to play eighteen holes on a full-length course? Let them play, by all means. But within limits. "If they choose to play at times when the male golfers are feeding or resting, no one can object . . ."

What seemed to concern his Lordship the most was the right of women to be spectators: "If they could abstain from talking while you are playing, and if the shadows of their dresses would not flicker on the putting-green while you are holing out, other objections might, perhaps, be waived."

So far as we know, Lord Wellwood wrote these words in all seriousness. He may not have been representative of all male golfers, but he represented more than a chauvinistic fringe.

Yet even as these words were being written in the late 1880s, the New Woman was fast emerging from her Victorian cocoons. Cocoon*s*, in the plural, for she was escaping from the physical protection of many layers of petticoats, as well as from the protective attitude of mid-Victorian society. For many years she had been treated as something fragile and readily given to fainting or to the vapours if made to exercise.

Within the space of a few years, Lord Wellwood's words were absurdly out of date. By 1893, British women had organized a Ladies' Golf Union and held their first national golf championships. The winner was Lady Margaret Scott who, a year earlier, had won a club competition in which all the other players were men.

As we shall see, women golfers in Canada started to organize ladies' clubs as early as 1891. But woman's perception of herself was slow to die. At the third annual meeting of the

JUST LIKE A WOMAN.

COUNTRY GROCER — "Oh, no; a girl can't carry home a pair o' shoe strings or a package o' tea — has to hev'em delivered; but I notice she kin always manage to lug a bag o' them golf-sticks.

— *Judge.*

The woman golfer has often been the butt of cartoonists; this appeared in Canadian Magazine *in 1900.*

National Council of Women held in Montreal in May 1896 (the founder was Lady Aberdeen, the local president Mrs. George Drummond), a Dr. Elizabeth Mitchell spoke on "Recent Development of Athleticism Among Women and Girls." The Montreal *Gazette* reported her words:

> [She] expressed the opinion that sweeping, dusting, and bedmaking, were the best of indoor exercises, and many young women, she said, would find most of their aches and pains vanish if they would only do house-maid's work every morning regularly. Anything in the way of sports that went on in the open air was to be preferred to indoor gymnastics, but care should be taken that there be no competition, no prizes, no public exhibition, as the nervous strain induced by such was too much for many girls.

No competition, no prizes, no public exhibition! What would she have thought of the

Handicap Enough !

"What is your handicap, Mrs. Montgomery?"
"Hush! Here he comes."

But she later got her own back.

women golfers – some of them no more than girls – who, five years later, would be competing day after day, at times through freezing rain, for the Ladies' Golf Championship of Canada?

The liberation of the Canadian woman from petticoats and her perception of her own fragility was hastened by the coming of the bicycle. "Wheels," as they were called, came to her at about the same time as golf. The male attitude towards women cyclists appears to have been the same as the male attitude towards women golfers. In an article entitled "The Evolution of the Lady Cyclist," published in *Massey's Magazine* in 1897, Grace E. Denison looked back on her experience of the past six or seven years.

> The whole world (excepting the makers) balked at the bicycle – at least, for women's use. Men must have been at the bottom of this attitude which made the world look foolish, for I don't recall any decided pose of the sort against man as a straddling enthusiast, nor any protest whatever, previous to that first shipment of English wheels for ladies to Canada. Talk about the landing of the Pilgrim Fathers on Plymouth Rock! Believe me, that the disembarkation of the first woman's bicycle was the real event of this or previous ages.

The lady cyclist had to change her costume to accommodate her sport, as had the lady golfer.

> Before the proper and conventional garb was invented, evolved, or what you will, we struggled through a maze of short skirts, long skirts, divided skirts, strapped skirts, into which we were hobbled by bands of elastic, like cows; heavy skirts, with leaden sinkers in the hem . . . light skirts which caused us modest agonies whenever the stormy winds did blow, and led to letters being written by proper minded old ladies of both sexes to the daily papers.

The same strapped skirts, hobbled by bands of elastic, and often held down by metal weights in the hem, were used by the first lady golfers.

The rapid growth of golf in Canada in the early 1890s coincided with women taking up the game. Did women make golf fashionable by taking it up, or did they take it up because it had become the fashionable thing to do?

A contemporary observer seems to believe the former. The history of Royal Montreal quotes the club captain of 1894–96, John L. Morris, as saying that it was "only since the advent of the Women's Golf Club in Montreal that men have evinced a genuine interest in the game." This may have been said in a spirit of gallantry, as the author of the book points out, but I prefer to think that Mr. Morris had hit the nail on the head, or the ball on the sweet spot.

For some years before Canadian women formed ladies' golf clubs (to be more precise, ladies' sections of existing golf clubs) they had taken part in the social events of the clubs to which their husbands belonged. In the 1880s, they would help organize the luncheons and afternoon teas, although the dinners at night were strictly for the men. The records of the Brantford GC for 1881 showed women paying an annual subscription of one dollar each to be a member of the club.

There is no record of women in Canada playing golf in the 1880s. But it would be surprising if some had not tried their hand on the links for a year or so before deciding to organize in the 1890s.

Starting in 1891, the ladies of the three most senior clubs in the country – Royal Montreal, Royal Quebec, and Toronto – formed ladies' golf clubs, elected officers, and soon had their own clubhouses.

The women played over the same course as the men, but usually from forward tees. The expression "ladies' tees" was not used in the 1890s. People talked about "the short course" or "the ladies' course." The London Ladies' Golf Club was one exception to this generality. Organized in October 1894, it had its own course adjoining the course of the London Golf Club. And new clubs, such as Lambton, often laid out a separate nine-hole course for the ladies. National championships, however, were played over the men's course.

The wives of members of the premier club in the country were the first to organize themselves into a club for ladies. According to the club's history, at its annual general meeting in 1891, Royal Montreal voted to "admit ladies and boys as members of the club . . . on payment of an annual fee of $2.00." On 17 December, Mrs. W. W. Watson was elected the first lady member of the club. Early in 1892, the twenty-four members of the Royal Montreal Ladies' Golf Club elected Mrs. George A. Drummond as their first president. In October of that year the ladies played their first competition, thirteen members taking part. (The winner shot 150 for eighteen holes.)

By the end of 1893, the ladies had their own rooms in the clubhouse and made up nearly half the membership of the main club. Over the next seven years, their numbers appear to have fluctuated between 80 and 150. In the early days, teas were more popular than tees. The club's history comments: "They enjoyed each other's company but, by and large, they didn't really play much golf. Or if they did, it wasn't often mentioned . . . [The] game, itself, was of compelling interest to only a few."

This is confirmed by the paucity of reports on women's competitions until the late 1890s. One of the winners of an early competition was Lillias (Lilly) Young. She was presented with a red silk belt having a large silver buckle engraved with "Royal Montreal Golf Club" and the motto "far and sure"; it is now in the RCGA museum.

One source reports Royal Quebec as having a ladies' club in 1892. It was certainly organized before the summer of 1893, when it arranged to play its first interclub match against the ladies of Royal Montreal. But some of the Montreal team could not play on the date proposed, so the match was put off until the following year.

This first interclub match in North America between teams of women golfers was played over Cove Fields, Quebec, on 31 May 1894. An account of the day's proceedings appeared in the British magazine *Golf* in June.

MONTREAL VS. QUEBEC LADIES

. . . The morning opened with splendid weather, and the bright costumes of the ladies, in contrast with the fresh spring grass, made a lovely picture. Nearly all the members of the Quebec Ladies' Golf Club were present, and a large number of spectators, who took the keenest interest in the game throughout. Each couple was accompanied by a gentleman, a member of the Quebec Golf Club, who acted as a scorer. Unfortunately, the weather proved fickle and rain fell towards the end of the game. The result of the match was in favour of the Quebec ladies by 33 holes. A return match will be played in the fall in Montreal . . . After the conclusion of the match the victors entertained their guests to a most delightful banquet at the Chateau Frontenac, where covers were laid for about seventy-five persons.

The ladies of Royal Montreal had probably never seen a golf course other than their own, a reasonable excuse for their loss. But on the return match over their own course they did no better, going down by 42 holes to nil. Not until the fourth match, a year later, did Montreal win at home.

The male golfers continued to keep score for the ladies. The minutes of Royal Montreal reveal that the ladies "do not feel fully qualified to perform such an onerous task."

Toronto GC admitted women members in May 1894, and within a year they numbered 100 out of a total membership of 270. Tuesdays and Thursdays were set aside for lady golfers, but the secretary of the club does not appear to have informed the press of the results of their competitions until 1897. By this time, the Toronto ladies were engaged in combat with the ladies of Rosedale.

If anything, women golfers played more interclub golf than men. At the turn of the century, the hub of interclub golf was Toronto. Twenty or so golf clubs were within easy reach of each other by tram or train and could be visited in a day. Matches were played mainly in the early and late summer. In July and August, all golfers who could afford it – which meant all golfers – left the city heat for the cool courses of Cobourg, Port Hope, Muskoka, Niagara, Murray Bay, or St. Andrews, N. B. But in other months the Rosedales were forever taking on the Fernhills (as the ladies of Toronto GC were known) or the Morningdales (the ladies of High Park GC) or the ladies of Hamilton. The Bracondales (the ladies of Spadina GC) took on anyone, until their club was dissolved in 1902.

Ninety years ago, visiting a nearby club in the same city was not the simple job it is today. In 1898, a team of fifteen ladies from Rosedale went to play the ladies' team at High Park, some six miles distant as the crow flies. The Rosedale team met at Union Station, no doubt getting there by electrified streetcar. They travelled by train to Sunnyside Station, where they were met by horse-drawn buses "which took the visiting team via the picturesque old Indian Road to the clubhouse."

In April 1897, the ladies of Toronto GC invited a joint team of ten Montreal and Quebec ladies to play a joint team from Toronto and Rosedale. The match was played over the Toronto GC course on the first of June. The press gave only a few lines to the event. "The ladies representing the Montreal and Quebec Club played a friendly match with the ladies from the Toronto and Rosedale Clubs, and scored a victory by 3 holes, on the Toronto Golf Links."

The combined Montreal and Quebec team had indeed won by 17 holes to 14. A luncheon and a dance were held on the day before the match, and an afternoon tea and dinner were held after the match, attended by "smart society in its prettiest frocks." The Toronto GC had arranged with the Grand Trunk Railway for the Montreal train to stop at the top of Coxwell Avenue, so that the visitors did not have to make the trip by horse-drawn coach to Union Station.

This event cannot properly be called the first ladies' interprovincial match. There were other clubs in both provinces whose members were not even considered.

The ladies' interprovincial match of 1899; Quebec and Ontario at Royal Montreal's course at Dixie.

In a return match played over Royal Montreal's new course at Dixie, in October 1897, Ontario defeated Quebec by 30 holes to 23. The press labelled this match "interprovincial," but again there is no evidence that other clubs knew anything about it.

The two leading scorers were Ethel White of Toronto GC (52 for the nine-hole course) and Muriel Bond of Royal Montreal (55). The 52 was a ladies' course record, but on a relatively new layout. In the match, Ethel White also beat Royal Montreal's star player Lillias Young by 6 holes. Miss Young was to win the first national championship in 1901, so Ethel White's defeat of her is most commendable.

Miss White emerges as quite the outstanding golfer of her day in Central Canada. She seems to have been invincible in interclub matches. In 1898, she defeated the leading player of Royal Ottawa by 13 holes and was the only winner in a match against Philadelphia.

In September 1899, Ethel White married a son of the Chief Justice of Ireland and left to make her home there. Her team-mates were devastated. Here is *Saturday Night*:

> Miss Ethel White's marriage . . . will leave the golfers of the Fernhill Club inconsolable. Few in America can play a better game of golf than she, and none can play a prettier or more graceful game. The club will lose in her their chief strength, and just how without her they will hold their own against the other clubs, which are rapidly climbing up to the top as it is, will indeed be a problem difficult of solution. . .

These interprovincial team matches continued until 1900, apparently without any suggestion that they be extended to include an individual national championship, such as the men had.

The first step in this direction was taken by the Toronto Golf Club. It proposed that the interprovincial match at Toronto in October

Ethel White (addressing the ball) of Toronto Golf Club had all the makings of a national champion when she left Canada for Ireland in 1899.

1900 include a long-driving, pitch-and-putt, and individual stroke-play competition, open to the lady members of all recognized clubs in Canada. This was agreed, and the tournament was duly held on 10 and 11 October. Over fifty ladies from the Royal Montreal, Royal Quebec, Royal Ottawa, Toronto, Rosedale, High Park, Hamilton, London, and Saint John clubs took part (although *not* "from every place in this country where 'ye royal game' is played," as one newspaper would have us believe).

The stroke-play competition of 18 holes was won by Mrs. John Dick with – as one paper put it – a "a score of 100 for the 18 ends." Mrs. Dick was later to play her golf out of Lambton, as was her daughter Muriel, but in 1900 she put herself down as coming from the Rosedale, Toronto, and High Park clubs. She was taken to three extra holes by Miss Hodgins of Toronto GC, so her victory was a narrow one.

In the long-driving competition, we meet for the first time Canada's first great national champion, Mabel Thomson of the Saint John GC, N.B. Again, a play-off was needed. Mabel Thomson and Miss Towne of Royal Montreal both drove the old gutty ball 162 yards. On the extra drive, Mabel won with 160 yards.

The next day, Ontario won the interprovincial match by 50 holes to 32, after which "lunch was served on dainty little flower-decked tables, some being on the verandah and others in the dining room." The ladies from Quebec left on the evening train, "which stopped at the links for their convenience," said the Toronto *Globe*.

The ladies' championships before the First World War were started in 1901. Organized by the RCGA, the championships were run on similar lines to the men's. Although the format changed from time to time over the years, this program for 1907 is typical:

Monday: Annual handicap event, over 18 holes. The gross scores were used for the interclub competition and also as the qualifying scores for the Ladies' Championship of Canada. The lowest 16 qualified.

Tuesday: Ladies' Championship, first round. Consolation competition, first round.

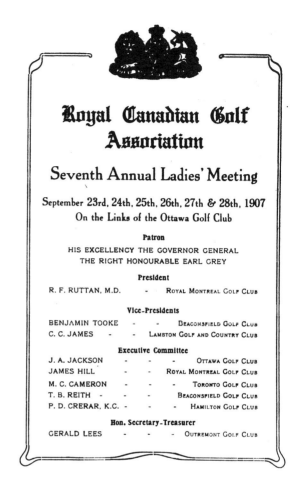

The program for the 1907 Ladies' Championship.

Wednesday: Long-driving competition. Ladies' Championship, second round. Consolation competition, second round.

Thursday: Approaching and putting competition. Ladies' Championship, semi-final. Consolation competition, semi-final.

Friday: Ladies' Championship, final. Consolation competition, final. Interprovincial team match, Quebec v. Ontario.

Saturday: Mixed foursomes.

The venue for the pre-First World War ladies' championships rotated between Royal Montreal, Toronto, Royal Ottawa, Lambton, and Rosedale. Visiting golfers would stay either at the host clubhouse – which in those days had bedrooms – or with members of the host club.

Anything from forty to seventy competitors attended the meet. With few exceptions – but these were very important exceptions – they came from the large, city clubs of Montreal, Toronto, Quebec, Ottawa, and Hamilton. The championships were open to all RCGA member clubs. However, as with the men, the exigencies of geography prevented the women golfers of the Prairies and British Columbia from taking part. Of the hundreds of competitors in the thirteen pre-war championships, not more than two or three came from clubs west of Ontario, and not more than five or six came from clubs in Atlantic Canada.

Just as the men's Canadian Amateur was a close amateur event (open only to members of Canadian clubs) until 1913, so was the ladies' event. In 1913, three well-known British women golfers visited Canada, and the ladies' championship was made an "Open" so they could compete. In other words, between 1901 and 1912 the ladies were competing in what was later called the Canadian Ladies' Amateur Close Championship. The record books list these championships as "Open," which they were not.

The ladies held their championships in the fall, after the Canadian Amateur and the Canadian Open, so that the task of running them fell on the shoulders of the newly elected RCGA executive.

Canada can be cold in the fall. It can also be wet. Many of these early tournaments were settled in torrential rain, on muddy fairways and soggy greens. The grim determination with which these young ladies ploughed their way cheerfully through the most appalling conditions to complete their matches flies in the face of much that was then being written about the fragility of the female spirit. What would Lord Wellwood or Dr. Elizabeth Mitchell have made of this, taken from a report in the Toronto *Globe* on the final of the first Canadian Ladies' Championship, in 1901:

> A worse day for golf could scarcely be conceived. During nearly the entire match a cold drizzling rain fell, against which neither umbrellas nor waterproofs availed. Both Miss Thomson and Miss Young were clad in warm white sweaters, but scorned hats and gloves.

And in *The Mail and Empire*:

> [The downpour] transformed . . . the links into something almost approaching a bog. The teeing grounds were a sea of mud, while the putting greens were soft and sodden to a degree that made accurate putting an impossibility.

Here, the 1903 semi-finals as reported by the Montreal *Gazette*:

> Conditions for yesterday afternoon's play were about the worst possible. The pairs set off in a driving rain and before the first hole was reached everybody was soaked through. The wind drove in from the lake, whipping the rain about in a manner that was decidedly uncomfortable to face. In spite [of this] a fairly large gallery witnessed the match between Miss Harvey and Miss Thomson.

Again, *Saturday Night* on the 1908 championships, when "rain in blinding sheets" deterred only six of the seventy golfers:

> There were many ladies who were not at all pleased when the rain began to fall briskly just as they were about to play off from the first tee, and then poured steadily throughout the whole afternoon. "It hasn't rained a drop for six weeks," one lady exclaimed, "and yet the very moment our annual championship begins, here comes a downpour! Why didn't it rain last week or last night?"
>
> "A number of clergymen prayed for rain last night," mildly interposed another lady.
>
> "I shan't forgive them, then," retorted the first.
>
> But they played – the ladies played, rain or no rain, and owing to the unfavourable conditions and the crowded state of the course, most of them were from three to four hours in the wet. Here and there one of them would drop out and scurry for the clubhouse and a pot of hot coffee – abandoning all hopes of the championship in favour of her dripping sisters. Under the circumstances the

qualifying round was less a test of golf than a test of endurance and luck. . . .

Looked at today, the scores in these early championships seem high. In the first year, 1901, Lillias Young of Royal Montreal, the eventual winner, was the sole player to break 100 in the qualifying round. The qualifying score for the match-play rounds was 107. When next held at Royal Montreal, in 1903, four players scored in the 90s. But by then the ladies were using the rubber-cored ball, and driving it 20 yards farther.

In 1909, Violet Henry-Anderson shot an 85 at Royal Montreal, her home course. So the trend towards lower scoring continued until the championships were stopped by the First World War.

These ladies won the championship, or reached at least two semi-finals, before the First World War:

	semi-finals	finals	wins
Mabel Thomson (Saint John)	9	6	5
Dorothy Campbell (Hamilton)	3	3	3
Florence Harvey (Hamilton)	7	4	2
Lillias Young (Royal Montreal)	3	2	1
V. H-Anderson (Royal Montreal)	2	2	1
Muriel Dodd (England)	1	1	1
Muriel Dick (Rosedale)	5	2	0
Evelyn Marler (Royal Montreal)	2	1	0
Frances Phepoe (Hamilton)	2	1	0
C. McAnulty (Montreal Victoria)	2	1	0
Muriel Bond (Royal Montreal)	2	0	0
Effie Nesbitt (Woodstock)	2	0	0
Florence Greene (Royal Montreal)	2	0	0

Lillias Young was probably the most experienced of our early lady champions. By 1901, she had been golfing for nine years. In that year's final, Mabel Thomson outdrove her, but Lillias Young's pitching and putting were superior, and her short game gave her victory.

Miss Young did not defend her title at Toronto in 1903. In fact, she was to take part in only four championships – 1901, 1903, 1905, and 1909, all held over her home course at Royal Montreal. In three of these she reached the semi-final. But Mabel Thomson was to defeat her 3 and 2 in her second and last final, in 1905.

Mabel Thomson of Saint John, New Brunswick, had by far the finest record in those pre-war championships. From 1901 to 1908 she reached every semi-final, was six times a finalist, five times the champion. She was the first outstanding woman golfer in Canada, the Ada Mackenzie, the Marlene Stewart Streit, of her day.

Mabel Thomson's early successes in national golf are all the more astonishing given how little competitive golf she had played and how seldom on a full-length course. Already a first class tennis player, she took up golf at the age of twenty-three. She joined the Saint John Golf Club, N.B. (now the Riverside Country Club) when it was organized in 1897 and became its first lady club champion.

Its course was then a short 1,700 yard nine-holer. The club had no professional, and even by the standards of the day only one first-class male golfer, H. H. Hansard. So Mabel Thomson was essentially self-taught.

She first came west to play in the ladies' tournament organized by the Toronto GC in October 1900. Mabel Thomson and another woman golfer from Saint John (her chaperon?) were the only two competitors from outside Quebec and Ontario. She was not among the leaders in that first, unofficial, national championship for women, so her fifty-cent entrance fee went for naught. But after lunch she paid twenty-five cents and smote a golf ball 160 yards to win the long-driving competition.

From the few photographs we have of Mabel Thomson with a golf club in her hand, we can deduce a two-handed palm grip. The right hand is so much under the shaft that it would offend the purists of today. But it gave her the draw and the distance for which she was noted. There is a hint, too, of the intense concentration that shows on the face of Marlene Stewart Streit.

As a golfer, Mabel Thomson's strength lay in her long, raking wood shots. After her win in 1907, *The Montreal Daily Star* was exuberant:

> Her driving was a revelation, and her clean, bow-shaped rakers straight down the course were worthy of any professional, and justly aroused the gallery to bursts of hearty applause. Not only was her long game truly remarkable, but in approaching and putting she showed great judgement, and strong masterful control, and it is safe to say that Miss Mabel Thomson's winning of the championship of 1907 will linger long in the memories of those fortunate enough to witness this glorious match.

At the first official ladies' championships in 1901, she had been runner-up to Lillias Young. Her semi-final opponent, Florence Harvey, wrote in *Canadian Golfer* in 1915:

> When she has lost, Mabel Thomson has scorned excuses; when she wins she does it in her own tactful way . . . She may have beaten you by 6 and 5 or so, but you have that nice feeling just the same . . . She is one of the most modest and generous sportswomen that ever handled a club.

When Mabel Thomson won her fifth championship in Toronto in 1908, no one could have foreseen that this was the end of her reign. Since 1905, she had won four national titles in a row, setting a record that was to last for fifty years, was playing with confidence and great skill, and looked invincible. Her kingdom seemed as secure as the majesty of her play. "Miss Thomson almost has the rank in ladies' golf occupied by Mr. George S. Lyon in men's golf," quoth *Saturday Night*, partly in praise, partly in prophecy. Already a six-time winner, George Lyon won two more national titles, plus ten as a Senior. For Mabel Thomson, the 1908 win was her last in national golf.

She did not succumb to a better player, nor to one of those sudden and inexplicable losses of form that have so often struck at champions. She was beaten by injury. She had not let the news be broadcast that somehow, just before the 1908 championships, she had injured her ankle and had almost been forced to withdraw. Much more serious than first imagined, this injury did not keep her from playing the game, but it so restricted her play that it effectively ended her short but brilliant career in Canadian national golf.

Injury or no, she was unstoppable at Lambton in 1908. She first won the qualifying round by five strokes. Only two players in a field of the finest women golfers in Canada could shoot within thirteen strokes of her. In the quarter-finals of the championship "the ease with which Miss Thomson disposed of Miss Defries, the Lambton crack, astounded those who had been following the play," wrote the *Toronto Daily Star*, after her 8 and 7 victory.

She did not defend her title in 1909, her ankle injury, no doubt, keeping her away. In 1910 she was knocked out in the semi-finals and a year later she failed to qualify. In the first round of the 1912 championships one newspaper reported:

> Miss M. Thomson commenced playing a wretched game, and a spectator annoyed her quite a lot and caused her to miss shots to such an extent that she was two down and three to go, but she came back and bravely fought out the game and won the last three holes and the match from Mrs. Rodgers.

So at least her fighting spirit had not left her.

The facts on Mabel Thomson's record in Maritime golf are hard to establish, since she was playing before the days — and the written records – of the Maritime Golf Association. The New Brunswick Hall of Fame credits her with three Maritime Ladies' Golf Championships, in 1905, 1906, and 1911. Writing in 1915, another credible source – Florence Harvey, a close friend and the first secretary of the Canadian Ladies' Golf Union – credited her with nine, and with winning the tennis championship almost as often. Despite her injury, Mabel Thomson was good enough to reach the final of the Maritime event in 1924, and the semi-final in 1925.

Mabel Thomson's father owned a steamship, sat on the board of the Bank of New Brunswick, and was the commodore of the Royal Kennebecasis Yacht Club. So, as with most women players of her day, she came from a well-to-do family.

But she also had in her the blood of the New Woman of her day. Her mother, the former Louisa Donald, was president of the National Council of Women of Canada in 1902, and represented Canada at meetings of the International Council of Women. She must have been very proud of her daughter. Mabel Thomson was among the first to demonstrate that women would not fall to pieces or suffer from pelvic disturbances from exercise more vigorous than passing the beanbag.

She also did much to change men's views on the woman golfer. In 1906, having watched Mabel Thomson drive 199 yards and reach a 370-yard hole in two shots, a Canadian male writer had to admit that there was a prodigious rattling of dry bones in the dusty gallery of men's beliefs: "The day of the male gloater is dead." Women's golf was no longer something to fill in the time between a late breakfast and afternoon tea.

Outside of her native New Brunswick (she was inducted into its Hall of Fame in 1975) Mabel Thomson's achievements lived only in the record books, until the RCGA inducted her posthumously into the Canadian Golf Hall of Fame in 1985.

Just as golf is a matter of timing, so the difference between everlasting fame and oblivion in golf is a matter of timing. Mabel Thomson was perhaps too early. She was the queen of Canadian golf at a time when the people writing and reading the news were, with few exceptions, so ignorant of the fine points of the game as to expect a paragraph on the pleat of a lady's skirt, and a sentence on her skill as a golfer.

Mabel Thomson died in 1950. In that year, a sixteen-year-old girl, Marlene Stewart, played in her first Canadian Ladies' Championship. *La reine est morte. Vive la reine.*

Mabel Thomson in 1905, on her way to her third of five championships.

Florence Harvey won her first of two titles in 1903.

Overshadowed as a golfer by Mabel Thomson, Florence Harvey of Hamilton was yet a fine player with an outstanding record. The First World War brought out her equally fine qualities as an organizer, fund-raiser, and humanitarian.

She was to write eloquently and eulogistically of her fellow women golfers and about the CLGU she managed. But she wrote nothing about herself, so we know little of her early life. She was born in England and came to Canada with her parents, who settled in Hamilton. She had a younger sister, Laura, also a skilled golfer but not quite in Florence's class.

Miss Harvey took up golf at the Hamilton club around 1900 and quickly became one of the club's top players. Soon she was ranked in the club as second to Frances Phepoe, so her defeat of Miss Phepoe in the second round of the 1902 national championships was the surprise of the day. Miss Harvey had been four down with six to play; she fought back stubbornly to win, 1 up. A reporter noted that "a week ago, nobody would have said that Miss Harvey would have beaten Miss Phepoe, because the talent agreed that Miss Phepoe was about sure to win the championship."

Thereafter, Florence Harvey was to replace her clubmate as Hamilton's top player. She was also to become the second most consistent player in these pre-war national championships. She reached the semi-finals seven times, the final four times, and was twice champion. (Miss Harvey also won the Ontario Ladies' Championship in 1904, 1906, 1913, and 1914, facts not shown in today's record books.)

She was not an instinctive golfer, like Mabel Thomson, but rather slow and deliberate in assessing and making her shots. As in her life, she was a determined player. "She fought with guts," sums up the phrases used to describe her matches. When winning her first title in 1903, she was deemed by the experts to have been rather lucky in knocking out Mabel Thomson

in their semi-final match. Two down going to the sixteenth, Miss Thomson picked up her ball on the sixteenth green, under the impression that she had lost the hole and the match, when she had a makable putt to win the hole and keep the match alive. With commendable sportsmanship, Florence Harvey invited her opponent to replace the ball without penalty, which she did not do.

In 1904, the weather was kind to the ladies, but this did not result in one of the best finals. Florence Harvey was never behind and took only two and a half hours to dispose of Miss McAnulty. (Miss McAnulty, we are told, wore a gun-metal grey sweater, was very nervous at the outset, and started with a triple bogey. Florence Harvey, in a white sweater, played with great coolness.) Miss Harvey's win was easier than the score would suggest. The match was played to a finish since the holes counted for the inter-provincial team match, and she won by 3 holes, going round Toronto's 4,900-yard course in 97, five strokes less than her opponent.

Her finest achievement in later championships was in reaching the final in 1913. This was the first event open to foreign players. In the semi-final, Florence Harvey defeated Violet Pooley, a golfer from Victoria, B.C., who had done most of her golfing in England. But in the final, she went down to the British champion, Muriel Dodd.

Five times a semi-finalist, twice the runner-up, three times winner of the provincial title, Muriel Dick of Rosedale and Lambton was perhaps the finest of our pre-war women golfers from a club in Central Canada never to win a national championship. She was the daughter of the John Dick who had persuaded George Lyon to take up golf. Her mother was also a fine golfer and had been runner-up to Mabel Thomson in 1902.

Young Muriel was viewed as a potential champion in 1898. Wrote *Saturday Night*, when she played for Rosedale against High Park:

Among those who came close, Mrs. John Dick . . .

. . . and daughter Muriel Dick, both of Rosedale and Lambton.

The prettiest thing on the links was Miss Muriel Dick, a lithe, grey-eyed little maid of twelve or thirteen with a head of thick tumbling brown curls, on the top of which sat very jauntily a black and scarlet tam matching a suit of scarlet cloth braided in black. She played against Miss Scott, and gave every promise of some day being an exceedingly good golfer.

In 1901, she won the long-driving contest, when only fifteen or sixteen. Her driving was fully equal to Mabel Thomson's in distance, and more accurate. Her "full St. Andrew's swing," as it was labelled, was the product of Davie Ritchie's teaching at Rosedale.

There was no seeding in those early championships, with the result that potential finalists often met in the early rounds. Muriel Dick was knocked out by Mabel Thomson in the first round in 1906. They met again in the next year's final, and again Muriel Dick gave

the champion a hard fight. Three down after five holes, she took Mabel Thomson to the eighteenth, which Miss Thomson won with a triple bogey. Two years later, again in the final, Muriel Dick had the misfortune to meet Violet Henry-Anderson, recently arrived from England, and was defeated by 5 and 4.

Frances Phepoe was another Hamilton girl, and another who had little to show in the way of national medals for a remarkably consistent performance.

She made her debut in the 1900 inter-provincial match, when she defeated Mrs. Sparks of Royal Ottawa by 7 holes. In the 1902 championship, she shot an 84 over the Toronto GC course. "A better exhibition of golf has never been given by any lady on a Toronto links," according to one observer.

Frances Phepoe led the field in the championship qualifying rounds in 1902, 1903, 1906, and 1907, and was second in 1905. The championship draw was unkind to her. It put her against Flo Harvey in the second round in 1902, and against Mabel Thomson in the first in 1903. So she did not make it to the semi-finals until 1906.

In that year's qualifying round she went round a lengthened Toronto GC course in 89 to lead Miss Thomson by three strokes. When winning her first-round match, she shot an 88, and she knocked a stroke off this when winning in the second round. A run of 89, 88, 87 was spectacular golf in the early years of this century. In the final, she took Mabel Thomson to the 21st hole, and again shot an 88 for the round. Consistently outdriven by the Saint John player, Frances Phepoe made up for this with clever and consistent work with her irons. But that was not good enough. On the 21st hole, a 600-yard monster, Mabel Thomson's length was too much for the Hamilton girl.

Frances Phepoe's father was a bank manager, who moved his family to Montreal in 1909 and to Vancouver a few years later. Frances Phepoe joined Royal Montreal and won the scratch medal in four consecutive years. After the war, she was one of the leading players at Vancouver Golf Club, being runner-up to Violet Pooley Sweeney in the 1920 Pacific Northwest Championship.

There were other fine home-bred players in these pre-war years, notably the Royal Montreal quartet of Evelyn Marler Boulton, Muriel Bond, Mrs. Clarendon Mussen, and Florence Greene.

Two players from smaller clubs, Effie Nesbitt of Woodstock and C. McAnulty of Montreal's Victoria, were always hard to defeat in national championships. And Lady Sybil Grey, wife of the governor general, was good enough to qualify for match play in 1911 and 1913, but she got no further than the first round.

The standard of women's golf in Canada in the first decade of this century, fast improving, was still well below that in Britain. The first British player to test the merit of our home-taught women came to Canada in 1909.

Violet Henry-Anderson had taken up the game as a child in her native Scotland, playing first at St. Andrews, then, from 1893, at Blairgowrie, Perthshire. She was a Scottish internationalist when she came to Montreal with her family, joining Royal Montreal. In her first Canadian championship in 1909, held at her

Violet Henry-Anderson of Royal Montreal looked as though she would be champion for years when she won in 1909.

home club, she simply overwhelmed the others in the qualifying round, coming in with an 85, nine strokes ahead of the field. Significantly, she also won the approaching and putting competition. For it was in the short game that British golfers were so vastly superior to Canadians.

In the championship proper, neither her team-mate Lillias Young in the semi-finals nor Muriel Dick in the finals was any match for her.

Pity the Canadian golfers! No sooner had the domination of Mabel Thomson been undermined by injury than Violet Henry-Anderson arrived, looking as though she would be defending her title for years.

If that was the general prophecy in 1909, then the prophets were quickly proved wrong. For yet another Scottish girl came to Canada, who was to prove virtually unbeatable, even by Violet Henry-Anderson.

The earliest reference to Dorothy Campbell I have come across in a national periodical dates back to June 1899. She had just won the

The much-travelled Dorothy Campbell, the Scottish and U.S. champion who also won the Canadian Ladies' in 1910–12, and then left us.

scratch prize at North Berwick, with a score of 63. The British magazine *Golf Illustrated* commented: "Miss Dorothy Campbell is an exceedingly promising young player, being only sixteen years of age. She has a very lazy style, is a long driver, and good on the green."

This was the beginning of an astonishing career. When it was over, Dorothy Campbell Hurd had accumulated 750 prizes in golf, some of them from winning these major championships: British Ladies' (1909, 1911), Scottish Ladies' (1905, 1906, 1908), U.S. Ladies' (1909, 1910, 1924), Canadian Ladies' (1910, 1911, 1912).

She was the first golfer to win the British, U.S., and Canadian titles.

Dorothy Campbell came to Hamilton in 1910 and left in 1912 for Pittsburgh, where she married Mr. Hurd. During these three years, it was not a question of who would win the Canadian Ladies' Championship, but who else would reach the final, and by how large a margin would she lose.

In 1910, Dorothy Campbell and Violet Henry-Anderson took the first two places in the qualifying round and met in the final, Miss Anderson losing by 2 and 1. When Dorothy Campbell went round the Toronto GC course in 82 strokes, a newspaper thought "her play would have astounded anyone . . . bad lies did not feaze her at all." Her approach shots, as we would expect, were the basis of her success. When defeating Muriel Dick by 5 and 3 in the semi-final, she was said to be off her game.

In 1911, Dorothy Campbell and Violet Henry-Anderson were again the top two qualifiers, but Miss Henry-Anderson was unaccountably knocked out in an early round of the championship, leaving Florence Harvey to be Miss Campbell's victim in the final, to the tune of 7 and 5. "Miss Campbell seems invincible on any links," was the consensus of the local press.

In 1912, the luck of the draw brought Dorothy Campbell and Violet Henry-Anderson together in the first round, and the former won by 5 and 4.

Few of the spectators were aware of the drama that preceded their meeting. After the qualifying round, Dorothy Campbell took ill. Violet Henry-Anderson and Effie Nesbitt were up the greater part of the night waiting on her, giving no thought to themselves, to how tired they would be, or how it would affect their golf in the first round.

But the 1912 championships are noteworthy for more than this unselfish act of benevolence. In the quarter-finals, Dorothy Campbell was given a hard fight by a new young player from Mississaugua GC. The headline of the *Toronto Daily Star* of 10 October 1912 was the first of many that would appear in Canadian newspapers over the next thirty years: "Spectacular Golf by Miss Mackenzie."

This was Ada Mackenzie's first national championship. She was then one month short of her twenty-first birthday, but was relatively new on the scene. Against Dorothy Campbell she played some superb golf, to be 3 up at the turn. Miss Campbell pulled her back to 1 at the sixteenth hole. At the seventeenth, a one-foot putt would have given Ada Mackenzie victory and the biggest upset in the twelve-year history of the ladies' championships. But she missed the putt by over an inch.

Still in with a chance, she sliced her drive at the 18th into long rough, and sliced again at the 19th. The headlines record the result: "Newcomer Has a Grand Chance to Beat Miss Campbell, But Nerve Fails." But the same newspaper concluded that "next year, with more experience and less nerves, she should be a most serious contender for the honours."

In that next year, 1913, the championship was "opened" to admit four players from Britain.

Muriel Dodd (later Mrs. Macbeth), Gladys Ravenscroft (later Mrs. Dobell), Maureen Harrison, and Violet Pooley (later Mrs. Sweeney) had come over to play in the Canadian and U.S. championships. The first three were among the half dozen finest players in the British Isles.

Muriel Dodd was the current British champion and would play for England until 1926.

Gladys Ravenscroft had been the British champion in 1912, was to win the U.S. championship in 1913, and would be an English internationalist until 1930. Maureen Harrison had been the Irish champion for three consecutive years, 1910–12.

With Dorothy Campbell now in the United States, Muriel Dodd and Gladys Ravenscroft were joint favourites to win the Canadian title. But they met in the third round, when Muriel Dodd won. She went on to meet Flo Harvey in the final, but the Canadian girl was no match for her and went down by 7 and 6. Two pieces from the Toronto *Star* describe the ways in which British women golfers were superior to their Canadian sisters before the First World War:

> Nearly all our Canadian ladies handle their irons wrongly. They take a full swing with them, as with a wooden club, and sweep the ball instead of hitting it. It was beautiful to see how Miss Dodd or Miss Ravenscroft would get her wrists into her iron or mashie approach. They never played one of these shots without taking a piece of turf to give the shot direction . . .
>
> The finish which characterizes the iron shots of the English ladies is equally characteristic of their wooden club play. They all play with a full easy swing except Miss Harrison, who likes only a three-quarter swing, but who hits very hard . . . All four English ladies showed wonderful judgement in their approach putting . . . They all hit the putts with the centre of their club head, with a true, clean stroke. They do not chop the putt or adopt any freak stand. Their work on the green is very business-like.

And what of Ada Mackenzie? She was knocked out in the second round by Mrs. Barlow of Philadelphia. Her time had not yet come.

The author of the piece in the Toronto *Star* refers to "all four English ladies" in the 1913 championship. He could be forgiven for supposing that Violet Pooley, too, was British born and bred. Her recent golf record showed her winning tournaments in England, as well as going far in the British championships. She played golf in the British way: not remarkably long off the tee, but accurate, with great economy around the greens. She may also have picked up some of the accent of the upper-class English, to whom golf was "goff," and bunker "bunka."

But Violet Pooley was Canadian, born in Victoria, B.C. She is arguably the finest Canadian player never to win our national ladies' title. Since she was to play so little national golf in Canada after the war, we will examine her record now.

Violet Pooley's father, Charles Edward Pooley, a lawyer turned statesman, emigrated from England in 1862. He sat in the B.C. legislature for some twenty-five years, during which time he was twice elected Speaker. It has dutifully been recorded that Violet's sister married the second son of the sixteenth Earl of Derby.

Her brother Harry introduced Violet to golf on the United Service Club's course, when she was only nine. She played there for a year or so. Then, like most children of her class, she was shipped off to school in England, where she never handled a club.

In 1905, one year back in Victoria, Violet was persuaded to make up the number for the United Service Club team in the B.C. championships. This eighteen-year-old girl had never been on the Oak Bay course of the Victoria Golf Club, but she played well enough to become the B.C. lady champion. A month later she came back from Portland, Oregon, with the championship cup of the Pacific Northwest Golf Association, competed for by the clubs of B.C., Oregon, and Washington.

Thereafter, until the end of the First World War, Violet Pooley appears to have spent almost as much time in England as in Canada. In the early years she was completing her education. Later, having married Lieutenant Sweeney of Vancouver in 1915, she went to join him in England, where she became an ambulance driver. But when in British Columbia, she could usually be counted on to win either the B.C.

or the PNGA title. One or other of these came to her in 1905, 1908, 1909, 1910, and 1914. In three of these years she won both.

After the war, Violet Pooley Sweeney continued to dominate Pacific golf.

But she had probably played her best golf in England. In 1911, a combined Canadian–U.S. team was judged competent to play a team made up of the *reserves* of the home countries of England, Scotland, Wales, and Ireland, a team known affectionately as "The Rubbish Heap." Violet was one of only two to win against The Rubbish Heap. She then startled the gallery by reaching the fourth round of the British Ladies' Championship. During that summer in England, she won four tournaments.

Back in England again in 1913, she came second in the celebrated Golf Illustrated Gold Cup, before winning two lesser events. Again she surprised the experts by reaching the semi-finals of the British championships, the first overseas player to do so.

Her game was characterized by a very short back-swing and a tremendous follow-through. But it was around the green that she excelled. A leading British player wrote of her: "It is to Violet Pooley that we should go to learn how to play the perfect pitch-and-run shot."

Her country's geography was unkind to Violet Pooley Sweeney, as it was to other western golfers. The spectators of Canada's national championships were to see her compete only twice, in 1913 and in 1935.

In 1913, her friend Florence Harvey played above herself to defeat her in the semi-finals, 1 up.

She entered the championships again in 1935, when they were held for the first time in B.C., at her home club, Jericho Country Club. Although she was then of an age to be a senior golfer, she led all other B.C. golfers in the qualifying round. Again she reached the semi-finals of match play, but lost at the seventeenth hole.

Two trophies bearing her name are awarded annually in B.C. to junior golfers, for whom she was to do so much.

That, briefly, is the record of this woman who was for so many years the queen of the

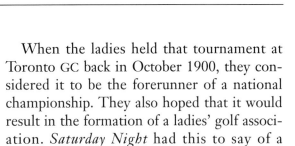

Violet Pooley, about 1913.

Pacific Coast. But we shall meet her again when we come to the founding and development of the Canadian Ladies' Golf Union.

The ladies did not organize their present Canadian Ladies' Golf Association (CLGA) until 1913, and for some fifty years gave it the name Canadian Ladies' Golf Union (CLGU). But there is evidence that they formally instituted a golf association many years earlier.

When the ladies held that tournament at Toronto GC back in October 1900, they considered it to be the forerunner of a national championship. They also hoped that it would result in the formation of a ladies' golf association. *Saturday Night* had this to say of a meeting held on the second day:

> The ladies of the two provinces [Ontario and Quebec] have at last taken action to form an association. A meeting was held on the 11th [October] and the organization was practically formed, as the gathering was very representative. The feeling of a number of clubs that were not represented will, however, be ascertained. At all events the step has practically been taken and the Ladies' Golf Association of Canada is an assured fact, with the following officers for 1900–01: President, Mrs. MacDougall (Montreal); Vice-President, Mrs. Sweny (Ferndale); Secretary, Miss Bond (Montreal). The details of the association are as yet in embryo, but the lines followed by either the Ladies' Golf Union of Great Britain, or the Metropolitan Women's Association [of New York] will be adopted. It is to be hoped that meets under the auspices of the association will be made attractive and interesting, and that an event will be slated for which our United States cousins will be eligible.

Mrs. MacDougall (or Macdougall) was the president of the ladies' section of Royal Montreal.

Two weeks later, the same magazine reported that "the Ladies Association is quietly assuming form, and by the spring will doubtless be in a state of completion. Mrs. V. C. Brown of Toronto has the affairs of the Association well in hand."

Alas for these hopes. It was to be another thirteen years before women golfers organized the Canadian Ladies' Golf Union. What went wrong in 1900 has not been recorded. The ladies at the turn of the century may have doubted their ability to run their own affairs. Just as likely, the men talked them out of it.

The RCGA appears to have changed its constitution specifically to permit it to organize national events for the ladies, and it also appears to have formed a ladies' section of the RCGA, although we have no minutes of the RCGA (since these have been lost or destroyed) to substantiate this. We do have it on record, however, that on 28 September 1901 the RCGA constitution was amended, so that its objectives now read: " . . . to arrange and control the Amateur, Ladies' and Open Championships, the Inter-Provincial and other matches and competitions."

Three weeks after this revised constitution was adopted, the first Canadian Ladies' Championship was held at Royal Montreal. The invitations came from "the Ladies' Branch of the RCGA, Montreal." But one newspaper reported that "although the tournament is held on the Royal Montreal links, it is managed by the executive of the Canadian Ladies' Association, of which Mrs. R. W. Macdougall, of this city, is president and Miss Bond of Montreal, secretary."

That is the last report I have come across that mentions this early ladies' golf association. There is no reference to it in any historical article I have read on the CLGA.

The ladies tried for a second time in 1913, organizing their present association along the lines of the Ladies' Golf Union (LGU) of Britain.

The LGU was one of the earliest golf associations. Irish male golfers had formed an association of golf clubs in 1891, but there was no similar organization for men in England, Scotland, or Wales until the 1920s.

The R & A was accepted as the governing body for men's golf in Britain. But not by all golfers. In the 1890s, a few golf administrators objected to the apparent autocratic behaviour of the R & A. One of these was Laidlaw Purves, a respected golfer in the south of England. He referred to the R & A as "a great oligarthy of an ancient and venerable club ruling over the golfing world." The R & A was undemocratic, he argued; individual clubs had no say in the running of the game or in the formulation of its rules.

Purves was also disenchanted with the way in which clubs established handicaps. Usually, the best player in the club would be made scratch, and the handicaps of others would be based on their scores relative to the score of this player. So a scratch player in one club could become a ten handicapper if he or she moved to another.

Laidlaw Purves was a member of Wimbledon Golf Club, London. So, when the members of the Wimbledon Ladies' Golf Club wanted to organize a national ladies' championship, they turned to him for advice. In April 1893, with Purves as their influential sponsor, the women members of some fifteen British clubs organized the Ladies' Golf Union with these objects: To promote the interests of the game of golf; to obtain a uniformity in the rules of the game by establishing a representative legislative authority; to establish a uniform system of handicapping; to act as a tribunal and court of reference on points of uncertainty; to arrange the Annual Championship competition and to obtain the funds necessary for that purpose.

The incongruity of the handicapping system had also struck Issette Pearson of the Wimbledon Club, who was to become the first secretary of the LGU (1893–1921). With the help of Purves, the LGU got over this problem by doing what we do now, although we now use more exact methods. It set up a system for establishing the "par" of a golf hole, and of a golf course, as a measure of its difficulty. The difference between the par of a course and a player's best average score became that player's handicap. Women golfers who had zero handicaps (that is, who were scratch) at small, provincial clubs now found themselves with handicaps that gave them a fair chance when they competed in regional or national handicap competitions.

Florence Harvey of the Hamilton G & CC was well acquainted with the good work of the LGU. She knew Issette Pearson and other officers of the LGU, having visited Britain to play in the British championships. She kept in touch with her English friends and followed the progress of the LGU through its annual handbooks. It became obvious to her that Canadian ladies needed a similar organization.

Florence Harvey had staunch supporters in Mabel Thomson of Saint John, who had also competed in the British championships, and in Violet Pooley of Victoria, who had played most of her golf in Britain. They seized their opportunity when English golfers Muriel Dodd and Gladys Ravenscroft came to the Canadian championships at Royal Montreal in 1913.

On the evening of 28 September, Flo Harvey called a meeting in the Montreal clubhouse. No doubt the British ladies explained how the LGU worked and promised the LGU's support to any Canadian venture. So the Canadians voted to organize a Canadian Ladies' Golf Union, with Florence Harvey as its honorary secretary.

Toronto had more ladies' golf clubs than any other city, so it seemed only fitting that the Union's first president should be Miss

Frances Campbell of the Toronto Golf Club. She had been a generous hostess to women golfers visiting the city. The Duchess of Connaught, wife of the governor general, later consented to be patroness to the Union. One of her first acts was to put up a gold trophy for the ladies' championship. (The original trophy had been won outright by Dorothy Campbell in 1912.) The new trophy was, at least in theory, the property of the RCGA, the body that administered the championships.

By 1913, the ladies' golf unions of Scotland, Ireland, and Wales had become affiliated to the LGU. The CLGU became another affiliate. It could not accept the LGU's constitution in toto, since the organizing of the ladies' championships in Canada was still the responsibility of the RCGA. But in some respects the CLGU was more independent than the LGU, which had a man chair its meetings until 1925.

The ladies who organized the ladies. Seen in front of Lambton's clubhouse in 1913, just before or after the formation of the CLGU, are left to right: standing, *Maureen Harrison of Ireland and Violet Pooley of Victoria;* seated, *Muriel Dodd of England, Florence Harvey of Hamilton, and Gladys Ravenscroft of England.*

Frances Campbell, first president of the CLGU.

National championships apart, Florence Harvey tried to organize the CLGU along the lines of the LGU. And she proved to be a most able administrator.

The CLGU had two vice-presidents: Mrs. Ricardo, a leading player in Victoria, and Mrs. Ella Murray, of Halifax GC. The executive in the head office at Hamilton – Miss Harvey's house – consisted of herself, the honorary secretary and the driving force behind the organization; Mrs. Mitchell, honorary treasurer; and Miss H. Bankier, corresponding secretary.

Because of the wide expanse of Canada, Florence Harvey set up three separate divisions of the CLGU: Edith Bauld of Halifax GC looked after the Maritime Division (nine clubs); Frances Scott of Hamilton GC and Mrs. Philbrook of Regina GC looked after the Middle Division (Quebec, Ontario, and the three Prairie provinces, a total of twenty-four clubs); Violet Pooley of Victoria GC looked after the Pacific Division (four clubs). The divisions were further subdivided into districts, and district managers were appointed.

The establishment of the CLGU meant that Canada's women golfers were represented nationally, coast to coast, at least ten years before the men.

The ladies' sections of golf clubs paid annual dues of between ten and twenty dollars, depending on their membership. The money went towards the cost of administering the CLGU (mainly postage) and of medals, which the CLGU bought from the LGU for member clubs.

The most unifying act of the CLGU was the establishment of a standard system of handicapping women golfers in Canada, based on the "pars" of golf courses. It set up a National Pars Committee, whose function was to see that member clubs established pars according to the LGU method, and to have these pars ratified by the LGU in London, England. For many years this method survived the empirical test of utility – it worked.

In 1914, the CLGU determined the par of a hole and a course mainly from its length. Under 160 yards a hole was a par three; under 345 yards, a par four; under 480 yards, a par five; 480 yards and over was a par six. But local pars committees would play over the course and adjust these pars, taking into account factors such as the placing and the difficulty of its hazards. These adjusted pars would be vetted by members of the CLGU's National Pars Committee. Here are some typical pars established for women golfers: Charlottetown, 80; Halifax, 74; Saint John, 74; Royal Montreal, 78; Lambton, 81; Rosedale, 79; Beaconsfield, 78; Hamilton, 79; Sarnia, 76; and Victoria, 78.

With handicaps based on the pars of courses, the member clubs of the CLGU grouped their golfers into a Silver Division (scratch to 20) and a Bronze Division (21 to 36). The CLGU encouraged clubs to organize monthly handicap competitions (monthly medals). Winners received silver or bronze medals, or buttons, which the CLGU bought from the LGU. Clubs that ordered a dozen medals were awarded an LGU spoon to be used as a further prize.

Clubs were awarding silver and bronze medals for scores very close to par, which suggests that the system was working well. That seemed to be the opinion, too, of golf clubs. The new method of handicapping was invariably greeted with enthusiasm. The wonder is that men playing at the same clubs waited another twenty years or so before adopting a similar system.

The CLGU, then, was a vibrant, growing organization by 1915, when the First World War forced many of its committee members to disperse, and the CLGU to turn its resources to raising funds for war charities.

13

OTHER TOURNAMENTS, EAST AND WEST

IN THE EARLY YEARS OF THE CENTURY, golfers had more than national and provincial events to keep them up (or down) to scratch. Four such events, in the order in which they took place, were The Niagara International Golf Tournament, the Pacific Northwest championships, the League of the Lower Lakes, and the Lambton Tournament. Only the Pacific championships survived the First World War.

In 1894, when golf was becoming an increasingly popular sport in Canada and the United States, the Niagara Golf Club was resuscitated, mainly through the efforts of one of its original members, Charles Hunter, who had bought a house in Niagara. There is evidence, too, that the Dicksons, who had been away from the town for some years, had now returned.

The first golf clubs had been organized in the United States in the late 1880s, so many of the American visitors to Niagara were now familiar with the game and became members of the Niagara GC. In fact, by 1896, there were more American than Canadian members, although many of the Americans played for only a month or so in the summer.

The great days of the revived Niagara GC began in 1895, through the efforts of Charles Hunter. At various times he was captain and president of the club; always he was its main visionary. "From their accessibility and proximity to the American shore, and direct tourist route to Niagara Falls, the links bid fair soon to become the Golfing St. Andrews of Canada," he wrote in an 1895 article, perhaps hoping the club might become so merely by his predicting it.

Hunter first put out an open invitation to the newly formed American Golf Association to hold an all-American championship at

Niagara GC, "where the game may be played in plain view of both nations' flags." When the American association became the USGA, he knew that his offer had been rejected. So he organized the Niagara International Golf Tournament.

The Niagara International was probably the first of its kind in the world of golf. It had events open to amateur golfers of all nations – which meant in practice the United States and Canada – and it had events for lady golfers. In later years, entries were restricted to members of clubs belonging to the RCGA or USGA. This did not mean that the RCGA sanctioned the tournament. In 1896 it announced imperiously, in the manner of Victoria herself, that "it has not extended its sanction to the competition; it was not consulted. Nor, for that matter, has it expressed its disapproval."

The tournament of 1895 more or less set the pattern for future years. On the first day, an open handicap event, 18 holes of stroke play, and a long-driving competition. On the second and third days (and a fourth if needed), 18 holes of match play for the silver International Challenge Trophy, put up by the Queen's Royal Hotel. On the final day, there was a 9- or 18-hole stroke-play event for the ladies and sometimes a money match between a few professionals.

Over the years, a number of famous names came to be inscribed on the International Challenge Trophy. The first winner, in September 1895, was an American, Charles B. Macdonald. A few weeks later he was to win the first U.S. amateur championship. George Lyon has his name on it twice, A. W. Smith once, and Macdonald was to win again in 1907. Two Canadians won in three successive years each: Douglas Laird (1904–6) and A. A. Adams (1908–10). The records of the women winners are not so complete, but they included Miss Phepoe of Hamilton and Miss Bedomme of London.

For many years the winner of the International Challenge Trophy was hailed by the Niagara press as "The Champion Golfer of America." Charles Hunter probably did noth-

Andy Smith of Toronto GC defeated Ransom of the U.S. in the 1898 Niagara International.

ing to correct this. Being hailed as the first champion of America would have appealed to that other Charles, Macdonald. (Macdonald had close family ties with Niagara. He and his mother were both born near what is now Niagara Falls, Ontario.)

The first Niagara International was held 5–8 September 1895. I do not believe this was an "International Championship Tournament between Canada and the United States," as Macdonald says in his book *Scotland's Gift: Golf* (1928), or a team competition between the two countries, as H. B. Martin implies in his *Fifty Years of American Golf* (1936). Nor was it, as advertised in the Niagara newspapers of the time, a tournament that would test the relative strengths of Canadian and U.S. golfers. Of the Americans who played, only three or four were of national status. The same can be said of the Canadians. They came from the Toronto GC: A. W. Smith, H. M. Mickle, Charles Hunter (also president of Niagara); from Niagara GC: the Dickson brothers, Bertie Dickson, and A.

Cleveland Lansing; from Royal Ottawa: A. Simpson; and from Kingston GC: Tom Harley. Only Smith, Harley, and Simpson would have been ranked among the top ten in Canada.

Of the match between Smith and the American Livermore, it was said that "a more keenly fought battle has never been seen on Canadian links." Livermore survived seventeen holes by brilliant scrambling, but he was defeated at the last hole.

The final was between Macdonald and Smith, as skill and form demanded, for they were clearly the two best players in the field. Their match was all square at the seventeenth. At the last hole, Smith put his ball over the cliff, tried to recover and failed, and conceded the match. Feelings ran high among the spectators of this final. If we are to believe Macdonald's account, his forecaddie was paid five dollars to lie over Macdonald's ball so that no one would tamper with it.

Madeleine Geale of Niagara (65 for nine holes) triumphed over Mrs. Chatfield Taylor of Chicago (71) in the ladies' competition. Only four or five ladies appear to have played.

In 1896, few prominent Toronto golfers attended the tournament, which led to a bitter complaint by the Niagara newspaper. The surprise winner that year was Bertie Dickson, the seventeen-year-old son of Captain Dickson who had been coached by A. W. Smith at Toronto GC. This was to be his finest hour, for his name never again appears as a winner in the records of Canadian golf. He also won a gold medal put up by Hiram Walker.

At the end of the 1896 tournament, there took place "the first meeting of representative Canadian and American professional golfers," claimed the Niagara paper. Arthur Smith (of Toronto GC) and his brother Tom (Royal Montreal) took on Horace Rawlins (from the Utica GC, and winner of the first U.S. Open) and William Tucker (of St. Andrews GC, N.Y.). All four had at one time been professionals in Britain.

Arthur Smith was handicapped by seasickness on his way over by lake steamer from Toronto. Straight off the boat, he put his first

Bertie Dickson, surprising winner of the Niagara International Challenge Trophy in 1896.

drive into Lake Ontario, for an 8. Tucker won $150, Rawlins $75, which is more than they would have won in official prize money with a first and second place in any Canadian Open before 1919.

The first tournament in 1895 was played over 18 holes, made up of the nine-hole Mississauga Links and another nine-hole course laid out on the Fort George Common at the other side of town. The competitors were taken by horse-drawn bus between the two courses. This arrangement was considered unsatisfactory, so in 1896 the Fort George Links was expanded to eighteen holes, using land scarred by the ruins of the fort. The names given to some of the holes bear witness to the military setting: Rifle Pit, Magazine,

Half Moon Battery, Fort George, Officers' Quarters, Barracks.

There is a special piquancy in the choice of Niagara (or Niagara-on-the-Lake, its name today) for the first friendly battle between American and Canadian golfers. And a strange irony in the use of the Fort George Links. For, in the War of 1812, American troops had set fire to the town and destroyed Fort George and all but a few of the town's buildings.

The significance of the site was not lost on the local residents in 1896, when the Fort George Common was taken over for golf. "We will soon have the edifying spectacle of golf being played on what should be one of the most sacred spots in our Dominion . . . and by an American club," wrote one Niagara citizen. He was assured that the club was in fact Canadian, despite its large American membership.

When the Niagara GC moved to the Fort George Links, it took over the commissariat officers' quarters as its clubhouse and handed over the Mississauga Links to the ladies. In 1904, a second golf club was formed – the Niagara Tennis and Golf Club – and this new club also used the Mississauga Links.

Both clubs flourished for some years. In 1901, His Royal Highness the Duke of Cornwall and York (the future King George V) was made an honorary member of the Niagara GC during a visit to the town, where he stayed at the Queen's Royal Hotel with his future queen. In the 1930s, the club added the prefix "Royal" to its name for at least a year, but there is no evidence that it was ever granted a royal charter.

The First World War brought an end to the Niagara International Golf Tournament. Both links were inundated with army tents and paraphernalia for most of the war. Only the Mississauga Links was to survive. It remains to this day a relic of late Victorian golf.

Prevented by their isolation from taking part in Canada's national championships until the late 1920s, B.C. golfers found solace and

The program for 1901.

international competition in the championships of the Pacific Coast. These events gave them a chance to meet and compete against golfers from American clubs who were similarly cut off from the USGA's events in the East. The Pacific Northwest Golf Association championships started in 1899 and, but for three years during the Second World War, have been held ever since.

The Victoria Golf Club played its first match against a U.S. golf club in April 1895. A six-man team journeyed to the state of Washington to meet a team from the Tacoma Golf Club. This was not match play, however, but a stroke-play team competition. The scores for eighteen holes were astonishingly high, even by Victorian standards. The foul weather was probably to blame. Harvey Combe's 97 was the lowest score by 22 strokes. Tacoma won, 741 strokes to 753.

This team match was the first between a Canadian and a U.S. golf club and may well have been the first international golf team match to be played anywhere.

Even in those early days of the Victoria club, Harvey Combe was clearly the man to beat. In the handicap event he was made to play off plus 10, shot 94 100–194, and, not surprisingly, did not win.

This was the first of several interclub matches over the next few years. Victoria invited the clubs of Tacoma, Waverly (Portland), Vancouver, Seattle, and San Francisco to send members to its spring meeting in 1897. Some thirty men and women came from Tacoma and Seattle, competing also in the B.C. championships.

Undoubtedly such meetings between golfers from different clubs planted the seed of an association. But it is not clear which club was responsible for the first step. In January 1899, the secretaries of three clubs, Tacoma, Seattle, and Waverly, wrote a joint letter to the other clubs in the Pacific northwest, inviting them to send two delegates to a meeting in Tacoma at which a golf association would be formed. The meeting on 4 February was attended by delegates from Tacoma, Seattle, Victoria, Waverly, and Walla Walla. The outcome was the organization of the Pacific Northwest Golf Association (PNGA), with C. B. Stahlschmidt, the secretary of Victoria, as its first president. The objects of the PNGA were to promote interest in the game of golf in the Pacific northwest, to bring about uniformity in the rules and handicapping, to prescribe the times and places for holding championship meetings, and to do any and all things to further the welfare of its members.

The founding members were Victoria GC, Seattle GC, Tacoma GC, Waverly GC, Walla Walla GC, and Spokane CC. Clubs were expected to subscribe fifty cents a year per male member, rather than a flat annual membership fee. All clubs that had golf courses in the state of Oregon or Washington or in the province of British Columbia were eligible.

There is no evidence that the PNGA, in its early years, did anything more than the RCGA to standardize methods of handicapping. Like the RCGA, its role was mainly one of arranging tournaments. Its first annual meeting was held in Tacoma in April 1899. The two main events were the men's and ladies' individual championships, originally determined by eighteen holes of match play (fourteen for the ladies, at first), but there were the usual minor events common to most tournaments of the day, such as long-driving, putting, and pitch-and-putt.

Strangely, the two finest players in Pacific Canada around the turn of the century were never to win the PNGA Amateur. Victoria's Harvey Combe won the B.C. Amateur nine times, but got no further than the semi-finals of the PNGA. William Oliver, twice B.C. champion, reached the finals of the PNGA in 1901, to be defeated by a clubmate, A. H. Goldfinch. But C. K. Magill (1906), R. N. Hincks (1912), and A. Vernon Macan (1913) all upheld the honour of Victoria by winning in the years before the First World War. Victoria's ladies did much better than the men. They had registered ten wins by 1915, including three by Violet Pooley. She was to make the PNGA title her own private property after the war, with another four victories in the 1920s.

These PNGA championships gave Canada's West Coast golfers the international experience they were denied by not being able (because of geography) to attend their own national championships. The competition was fierce. A multiple winner of the Amateur title was the same Chandler Egan who had met George Lyon in the 1904 Olympics.

The PNGA grew rapidly after the First World War. The championships held in Vancouver in 1920 were attended by over two hundred golfers, so that two courses had to be used. In the newly introduced Open, Shaughnessy Heights' professional, Davie Black, recently arrived from Ottawa, carried off the championship for the first time.

From 1899, Toronto Golf Club played in an annual tournament with a handful of U.S. clubs from cities around the Great Lakes. The Brantford club also played, from around 1908.

Vera Ramsay Hutchings of Vancouver, six times winner of the Pacific Northwest championship, seen here playing to the flag in a match with Mrs. F. Jackson of Victoria around 1930.

The Brantford team in the League of the Lower Lakes meet at Buffalo in 1908. Back row: Allan Ellis, Alex Moffat, W. Hastings Webling. Middle: Judge Hardy, Ralph Reville, John Hewitt, George McKee. Front row: Percy Thornton, Billy Griffith, Stanley Schnell.

The tournament came to be called the League of the Lower Lakes. The clubs did not play against each other weekly or monthly for points, so the word "league" is perhaps misleading. The league appears to have been disbanded during the First World War.

The Toronto GC had been playing home-and-away matches against Rochester GC since 1896. In October 1899, the four U.S. clubs at Rochester, Buffalo, Detroit, and Cleveland met in team competition, the winner to meet Toronto. But this first meeting soon developed into an annual one in which the clubs played against each other in a tournament that lasted for several days, with the Toronto club one of the participants.

The 1907 tournament followed a typical format. It was played at the Detroit Country Club, between teams from Toronto, Buffalo, Detroit, and Rochester. Representing Toronto GC were George S. Lyon, Vere Brown, W. H. Blake, H. H. Betts, S. Temple Blackwood, and S. A. Rowbotham. The teams met in knockout match-play competition, each match being played to a finish, since the winner was determined by the holes won (as in Canada's early interprovincial matches). On the first morning, Detroit defeated Rochester, Toronto defeated Buffalo. In the afternoon, Detroit defeated Toronto by two holes, to win the team cup.

On the second day, the top thirty-two players in the team matches went on to individual match play. In 1907, George Lyon led the qualifiers with 81 91–172. (The 91 was the result of heavy rain; his ball was eight times buried in the mud. In those days you played the ball as it lay, mud and all.) In the final, on the fourth day, George Lyon defeated G. T. Curtis of Rochester, by a score of 5 and 4.

There was much rivalry between the U.S. clubs. Rumour had it that the clubs would go so far as to entice rival clubs' players into leaving one city so that they would be eligible to play for another.

Next to the RCGA Annual Meeting, the Lambton Golf Tournament came to be looked upon as the premier golfing event in Central Canada. It was inaugurated almost as soon as the club had a course to play on. Until the First World War, it remained one of the social and golfing events of the year. The American golf writer A. W. Tillinghast (later to become a renowned golf course architect) played in the 1906 Lambton Tournament and was runner-up to Canada's Fritz Martin in the main event. He wrote of the week in flattering terms. ("I think the Canadians are prone to make more of country club evenings than we. The red coat about the house in the evening is almost a necessity . . .")

The Lambton Tournament lasted for a full seven days, Saturday to Saturday (excluding Sunday), with every conceivable type of competition for amateur men, women, mixed, and interclub. The tournament was just one more inspiration of Lambton's inspiring president, A. W. Austin.

Albert William Austin (president of the RCGA in 1907 and 1910) was the first in Canada to transpose an innate entrepreneurial spirit from the world of business to the world of golf. He was a man cast in a rare mould. At fourteen, he went to work for Robert Bethune in the Dominion Bank, cleaning pens, filling inkpots, sweeping floors, lighting morning stoves, getting up in the wee small hours of the morning to do so. But this is not a rags to riches story. Albert's father, James Austin, was the founder of the bank and its first president.

In 1880, Albert W. Austin left Toronto for Winnipeg, a city then in the throes of a boom. Still only twenty-four, he set up his horse-drawn Winnipeg Street Railway Company, incorporating in 1882, with the support of his father and Edmund B. Osler. He partly electrified the system four years later, giving Winnipeg the first commercially operated electric streetcars in the country.

In 1894, he was squeezed out of this business, for reasons that need not concern us. But the land he held showed him a 5,000 per cent profit. Back he came to Toronto. He joined the boards of the Dominion Bank and the Consumers' Gas Company, later becoming their presidents.

The Dominion Bank had been the unwitting sponsor of early golf in Ontario, so it was inevitable that Albert Austin should be smitten. Around 1897, he fired his first tentative shots over a few holes laid out next to the family home, Spadina, which still looks down the avenue of the same name. (Part of his private course is now occupied by the Casa Loma.)

In 1900, Austin persuaded a few friends to help him organize the Spadina Golf Club. This was only a makeshift. Albert Austin was planning a greater leap in the dark. He was about to bet his money and his reputation on what his heart told him to be fact – that golf had a promising and exciting future.

The Lambton Golf and Country Club, which he founded in 1902, was innovative from its conception, breathing new life into Canadian golf. For the first time in Canada, a club showed so much faith in the future of the game as to plan and construct in advance of its opening not only a championship golf course, but a clubhouse fully equipped with lounges, dining and reception rooms, kitchens, and bedrooms for scores of members. Within a year it also had a nine-hole course for the ladies.

After a year, a $100-share in Lambton was selling for $250, and the club had a waiting list.

Albert Austin also had the insight to recognize that first-class competitive golf was the quickest route to higher standards in the country. Fully convinced of the worth and wisdom of his belief, he put Lambton to the test with all the zeal of a missionary. The week-long Lambton Tournament, open to all amateurs of good standing, was first held in 1906.

A prelude to the Lambton Tournament. A. W. Austin and guests in 1904. Back row: *Florence Harvey (Canadian Champion), Mrs. C. E. Griscom (chaperon).* Middle: *Mabel Thomson (ex-Canadian Champion), Miss G. M. Bishop (U. S. Champion), Miss F. C. Griscom (ex-U. S. Champion), A. W. Austin (president of Lambton).* Front: *George S. Lyon, Miss Lottie Dod (Britain).*

It drew a field second only to the meet of the RCGA. In Central Canada at least, winning the Lambton Challenge Cup was the next best thing to winning the Canadian Amateur.

The presence of the ladies made the tournament the social event of Ontario's golfing calendar. But Austin had already given the ladies something more competitive than mixed foursomes. He had earned for himself the title of "Golf Father" to Canada's women golfers. In 1903, he had chartered a private railway car and taken a party of their finest – the finest in the East, that is – to an invitational tournament at Philadelphia's Merion Golf Club.

The top U.S. players were there, as was Rhona Adair, the British Champion. Of Mabel Thomson, Florence Harvey, Muriel Dick, Mrs. John Dick, Evelyn Cox, Florence Greene, and Frances Phepoe, only Miss Phepoe made her way through to the match-play rounds.

A month later, Austin had Rhona Adair as his guest at Lambton, where she beat the best in Canada by ten strokes over eighteen holes.

In 1904, he sent his railway car to pick up a team of U.S. ladies for an unofficial international at Lambton.

In 1907, he took another Canadian team to compete in the Women's Western Golf Association championships at Chicago. The WWGA elected him an honorary member, the first man to be so recognized.

For the male membership, Austin and his Lambton committee promoted interclub golf on a grand scale. Interclub matches had already become an outstanding feature of golf in the days before the First World War. In the early 1900s, it was not unusual to find a team of twenty-five Lambton players, led by George Lyon, engaged in a match at Rosedale, on the same day that a second string of twenty-five Rosedale players was engaged in battle at Lambton. The Lambton club also hired railway cars to transport the players and their equipment, and at least once toured other clubs in Quebec.

In all these ways, Albert Austin stands out as one of the most innovative of the RCGA's early presidents.

THE YEARS OF THE FIRST WORLD WAR

THE OUTBREAK OF WAR IN AUGUST 1914 caught Canada's golfers unawares, as it did most of the world.

The summer had been good to the game. Golfers broke records on many courses. In July, George Lyon won his eighth Canadian Amateur title and looked fit enough for another eight. But this was to be the last RCGA Annual Meeting for five years.

Canada entered the war on 4 August, the day Britain entered the war. No mandate was asked for or needed. The ties with the Old Country were too close to require debate. Many took the view that the war would be over by Christmas. "I am confident that the Olympic games will be held in Berlin in 1916, in spite of the impending war," said James G. Merrick, the Canadian delegate to the Olympic Congress in Paris, on the morning of 4 August. "The war is not likely to last more than four months."

On that day, Rochester was top of the International Baseball League, two games up on Baltimore and thirteen ahead of Toronto. The stock market took the outbreak of war in its stride; brokers reported that stocks were steady in light trading. The technical position of the market was said to be strong.

The expected rumours and scares floated in the air. A man was found with ninety-six sticks of dynamite. CNR denied that one of its bridges had been blown up.

On 10 August, Willie Bell, the big, powerful professional from Scarboro, shot a 72 to take a two-stroke lead in the CPGA championship at Toronto's Lakeview. But George Cumming caught and passed him in the next and final round to win.

On 13 August, eighty golfers played in the annual interclub match between Toronto and Lambton.

Next morning, players teed-up in the first round of the Canadian Open. And on the following afternoon, Karl Keffer, soon to be Corporal Keffer, snared the Open title for the second time.

By 18 August, some 225 men had been accepted for the Princess Patricia's Canadian Light Infantry, "the Princess Pats"; many had served in the South African war. There was now talk of switching the 1916 Olympics to Sweden. The Germans, it was said, would be

"too badly mussed up" to be in any shape to handle the events.

On 21 August, a ladies' golf competition was held at Niagara-on-the-Lake, probably the last before both courses were taken over for military training camps. On the same day, a twenty-two-year-old professional won the U.S. Open. This was the first of Walter Hagen's four titles.

Come the end of August, the newspapers were running full-page lists of the names of volunteers signing up. It was now thought more likely that the Olympic games would be switched to the United States.

Corporal Karl Keffer, twice an Open winner and the first secretary-treasurer of the CPGA.

By the middle of September, the news from Europe was discouraging. The ladies' championships were cancelled. The annual match between Toronto and Rosedale was called off. Some were even conceding that the Olympic games might not take place at all.

In Canada, as in Britain, the first shock of war was followed by the almost complete cessation of amateur sports. It was felt that men and women should be applying all their energies to the war effort.

This well-intended decision was quickly reversed. Politicians were the first to point out that there was no good reason why participatory sports such as golf should be stopped. On the contrary, they should be encouraged. The country needed workers healthy and fit, mentally and physically. British Prime Minister Lloyd George, one of the busiest men in the world, set an example by playing golf whenever possible at Walton Heath, near London. Canada's prime minister, Sir Robert Borden, and several of his war cabinet golfed whenever they could find the time.

In Quebec and Ontario, and to a lesser extent in the Atlantic provinces, almost all interclub matches were cancelled for the duration. But not in the West. The leading clubs and golf associations in the Prairies and British Columbia played to their regular schedules, almost without exception. This was by no means a measure of the West's contribution to the war effort. If anything, the western provinces had more men in khaki per capita than did the eastern provinces. The West's was the more prosaic approach. After all, if golfers were to be encouraged to keep fit by playing golf, they might as well play in matches against other clubs.

With so many young golfers away from home, it would have been unjust and unpopular to have continued with national events. So the RCGA cancelled its annual meets – the Amateur, Ladies', and Open championships. Its executive committee met only four times in as many years.

The prime minister Sir Robert Borden sets an example by golfing in wartime.

In place of its Annual Meetings, the RCGA sponsored exhibition matches and club competitions for war charities, in many of the principle cities across Canada. It encouraged clubs to organize "Patriotic Days" as a means of raising money for the Red Cross and other charities. Every leading Canadian amateur and professional still at home contributed his or her services to exhibition matches.

The recently formed CPGA also organized charity matches across the country. For the first time, spectators to golfing events across

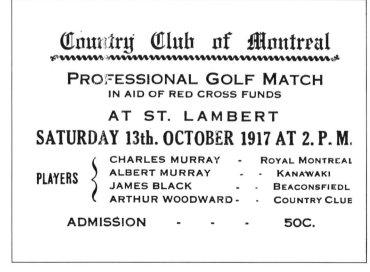

Tickets for two professional Patriotic matches during the First World War, when spectators across Canada were charged for the first time.

Canada were asked to pay an entrance fee of a dollar, which went to the Red Cross. The charity matches brought professional golf to clubs that were not on the circuit for the Canadian Open. What purported to be the first professional four-ball ever at Royal Quebec was played over its course at Montmorency Falls in 1915. The Murray brothers played Arthur Woodward and the Quebec professional Quesnel.

In the same year, the Murrays played against Karl Keffer and Davie Black over Ottawa's Rivermead, the admission fee going to the 207th and 230th battalions. The match attracted some three hundred spectators, including the prime minister. Many were seeing golf for the first time. Some spectators had never even heard of the game. The patriotic motive brought out many people who would not otherwise have walked a hundred yards to witness a game of golf.

To the professionals, these were not just exhibition matches. When they could, they practised hard over the course where the match was to be held. Not only were they playing for no fee, they also met their expenses out of their own pockets. The Murray brothers paid their own way to Ottawa. Black and Keffer each contributed five dollars towards the fund. A gallery of four hundred attended the return match at Royal Montreal.

On the lighter side, the women golfers of Kanawaki held a "Kaiser Bill" competition. An effigy of the German emperor was erected in front of the first tee. Ladies were charged ten cents for three chances of driving a ball at the Kaiser. A silver spoon went to the lady with the most "knock downs."

Later in the war, the government asked the public to observe "Gasless Sundays." Golfers were particularly hit. Many courses were miles from residential areas, and getting to the links without an automobile was a hardship. The situation in Winnipeg in October 1918 was recorded by the *Free Press*:

As far as sport was concerned, yesterday was decidedly a gasless Sunday. In this connection, the golfers suffered patriotically in the general effort to conserve gasoline, for not a buzz wagon was to be seen at any of the golf courses except a very small number that had arrived over night for the week-end at the Winnipeg and Elmhurst courses. Not a car was seen on the Bird's Hill road going to or from the Pine Ridge, Bird's Hill, or Elmhurst course.

With so many professionals, greenkeepers, and clubhouse staff away on active service, members took a new interest and pride in the management of their club's affairs and in the care of their courses. Some clubs, Rosedale among them, brought in sheep to graze on the courses and keep the grass short.

Clubs were urged to use spare land for growing vegetables and crops, in response to Lloyd George's cry from Britain, "The Plough is Our Hope!" Toronto's Lakeview club ploughed some of its fairways for food production, and its members devised new ways of playing the course.

The Canada Food Board suggested that "golfers organize Production Handicaps, in which every member of the club should compete. The losers in each successive round should be compelled to do so many hours cultivating or hoeing."

To mark the approaching end of the war, the RCGA organized a Thanksgiving Day Drive, a field day held at the courses of some fifty member clubs in October 1918. A total of over $30,000 was raised for the Red Cross. The RCGA prizes, in the form of honour flags, went to the London Hunt Club, which raised over $5,000 (or $36 per member), Picton GC ($22 per member), and Victoria GC ($17 per member). The tournament at Victoria's Oak Bay links was "the biggest thing in golf pulled off in British Columbia since the war." Entries and attendance exceeded any of the meetings of the PNGA.

Canadian Golfer recorded with pride that the golf clubs of Canada raised more for patriotic purposes than did any other branch of sport, amateur or professional. It also recorded

The honour flag awarded to clubs for raising money for war charities.

the magnificent work done by Florence Harvey and the CLGU during the war years.

As we have seen, the ladies of the CLGU were just getting into their stride when the First World War came along and all national and most provincial ladies' championships were cancelled. Canada's women golfers were not to hold a national championship for six years.

The CLGU soon diverted its energies from establishing pars and handicaps to the business of raising money for war charities.

Early in the war, Madge Neill-Fraser, a Scottish internationalist, died of typhus while on ambulance duty in Serbia. The death of this popular young golfer touched everyone. She had been known to the Canadian girls who visited Britain, and Violet Henry-Anderson

had played on the same Scottish team. The LGU established a Madge Neill-Fraser Serbia Hospital Memorial Fund.

The raising of money for war charities, and specifically for the Madge Neill-Fraser fund, gave Florence Harvey yet another mission to which to dedicate her already busy life. As a measure of her local success, the town of Hamilton purchased sixteen hospital beds and an ambulance in Madge Neill-Fraser's name.

At the same time, Miss Harvey, the great communicator, did her best to keep the CLGU from disbanding. "Until the war is over, we must simply hold the CLGU together," she wrote to member clubs. Officers of the CLGU became widely scattered: Mrs. Ricardo left Victoria to return to her native England; Violet Pooley (now married to Lieutenant Charles Sweeney) went to live in England to be near her husband; Frances Campbell had to give up the presidency; district managers resigned because of work or when their husbands were transferred.

Women golfers still held interclub competitions during time off from volunteer war work. The CLGU purchased a supply of "Queen's Work for Women Fund Medals" through the LGU and sold the medals to clubs for local competitions. When a club bought twelve medals, it got a free silver spoon, also for competition. Entry fees went to the Neill-Fraser fund or another of the many war charities.

The Halifax Ladies' Club held a field day for the Golfer's Fund in Aid of Belgium Sterilizers, in the summer of 1915; its cheque was the largest from any golf club in the Empire. Other Canadian clubs raised enough money to donate beds to British hospitals.

Florence Harvey administered all of this. By her personal canvass and through the CLGU, she raised several thousand dollars for the Neill-Fraser fund. At the same time, she was nursing her aging parents. When both parents died, she gave up her post as secretary of the CLGU, in February 1918. No longer tied to Hamilton, she volunteered as a chauffeur for the Scottish Hospitals and asked to be sent to Serbia. On 12 February, she wrote her last

The ladies still played charity matches. Here is the Hamilton team that played Toronto GC and Rosedale in 1915, left to right back, Miss Morrison, Florence Harvey, Miss M. Scott; *front,* Frances Scott (the winner) *and Mrs. Margaret Kathleen Rowe.*

Queen's Work for Women Fund Medals

The ladies competed for these wartime medals, supplied by the LGU.

report to the editor of *Canadian Golfer*. "Just a line in haste. Got my overseas orders today. Sail next week. Good luck and Au Revoir."

Florence Harvey became attached to the First Serbian Army and drove an ambulance at Yalek, on the Serbia–Greek border. Her daily runs took her from the front line, over treacherous mountain roads, to the base hospital. Later, she moved to Belgrade and was put in charge of a hospital fund-raising drive.

Too frequently, those who have written about the early days of the CLGU have given the impression that little was accomplished between 1913 and 1919. But much was accomplished. That is why Florence Harvey's portrait now hangs in the Canadian Golf Hall of Fame.

The Great Communicator: Florence Harvey, first secretary of the CLGU, on her way to Serbia during the First World War.

The war was nine months old when Ralph Reville launched his *Canadian Golfer* in May 1915. This was Canada's first golf magazine. It was to survive until the Second World War.

It seemed a strange time to be bringing out a new golf magazine, during a global conflict, and Ralph Reville admitted he had serious reservations about his plans. But his supporters included senior people in government, right up to the prime minister, and he was finally persuaded to go ahead. As we have seen, the political leaders of the day encouraged citizens engaged in the war effort to take an active part in sports such as golf.

Ralph Reville was a keen golfer, with an infectious enthusiasm for the game. Born in Witney, England, in 1867, he came to Brantford as a youth in 1887, along with his brother. They worked for their uncle, Thomas

Ralph Reville, whose Canadian Golfer *was such a success.*

Hastings Webling, our poet laureate.

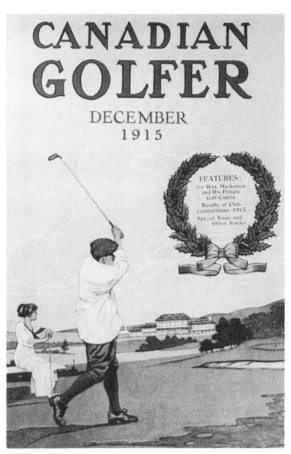

The cover of Canadian Golfer, *December 1915.*

Lemmon, who owned *The Courier* in Brantford. Ralph ultimately became part-owner (with his brother), editor, and publisher of *The Courier*, and a member of the Brantford Golf Club.

In the early years of the century, he wrote the occasional article on golf for Toronto newspapers. His informed analysis of the play and players of the day stood out in sharp contrast to the tedious hole-by-hole narratives of his fellow journalists. When he sold his interest in *The Courier* in 1913, leading golfers urged him to start Canada's first golf magazine.

The first on Ralph Reville's list of subscribers to *Canadian Golfer* was the governor general, His Royal Highness, the Duke of Connaught and Strathearn; the second was the prime minister, The Right Honourable Sir Robert Borden.

Canadian Golfer was an instant success, in style, content, and circulation. Its reputation grew quickly, and it soon became the official

organ of the RCGA and the CLGU. Many golfers in Canada first became aware of the existence of those organizations through the pages of the *Golfer*.

A leading American journalist of the time noted that there was no better way to judge the life of a sport in a country than by the periodicals that that country supported. Judged by this standard, he said, "golf in Canada is fairly thrilling with life and progressiveness."

This was to be the oft-repeated judgement of Ralph Reville and his magazine. He brought to golf journalism an intimate, chatty style that none of his contemporaries in other countries could match. As a contributing and managing editor, he reported regularly on what was happening in golf clubs across Canada, relying on friends and acquaintances to supply him with information.

Reville also gave his informed opinion on the state of the game. He agitated for reform, chastised those who paid insufficient attention to etiquette, rules, and traditions. He advocated Canada-wide championships, and exhibition games for the Red Cross, spoke out for a national system of handicapping, more municipal golf courses, and the right of women to organize their own championships. By enlisting correspondents in the West, he introduced to each other golfers who would never meet other than through the pages of his magazine.

Canadian Golfer had readers in other countries and it brought international recognition to Canadian golf. "It is one magazine which stands apart from the general run of publications," wrote a former president of the USGA. "The *Canadian Golfer* is a model which many of our British golf papers might well imitate," wrote Lord Alness, from Edinburgh. And in the opinion of the U.S. Burke Golf Company, "The *Canadian Golfer* is the best golf journal we receive."

The magazine came out monthly, with up to one hundred pages of information on golf across Canada. It had next to nothing in the way of golf instruction, but carried articles on a variety of subjects, including greenkeeping, the rules of the game, the organization of new clubs, the construction of new courses. It carried accounts of provincial and national championships and of the annual meetings of clubs. If you had a hole in one, your name appeared in the magazine.

But it was a different and smaller golf world in 1915. There were, remember, only about 115 golf clubs in Canada when the *Golfer* first came out, less than a fifteenth of the number we have today. More significantly, there were only about thirty thousand golfers; we now have something like seventy times that number.

The brutal realities of the First World War were never spoken of in *Canadian Golfer*. Ralph Reville saw the war as a conflict of ideals, its horror to be camouflaged in euphemisms. He referred to the war as "the greatest game of all," in which men often "walked down their last fairway" or "played their final shot."

But now and then he could not sidestep the truth. In 1917, he published a roll call of

Canada's golf clubs, showing that some 3,500 members were on active service and that already some 150 had been killed and hundreds more wounded. Among those who gave their lives were Captain Gerald Lees of Royal Ottawa, the honorary secretary-treasurer of the RCGA in 1913; his clubmate Alec Frazer, of whom much had been expected in the (cancelled) 1914 Amateur; Sergeant W. G. (Bill) Laird, of Winnipeg's St. Charles, a semi-finalist in the 1909 Amateur; and Gordon Southam of Hamilton, a fine, all-round sportsman of whom great things had been expected in post-war golf. The roll of casualties did not spare any club, in any province.

Ralph Reville ("Rafe" at his club) was made an honorary member of the Brantford Golf Club in 1934, having been for thirteen years its captain. He remained a governor of the Canadian Seniors' Golf Association until his death in 1957.

The assistant editor of *Canadian Golfer* was another English-born writer, W. Hastings Webling, a Brantford man who shared Reville's love of golf and cricket. Webling was the poet laureate of Canadian golf. Most issues of the *Golfer* carried at least one of his short poems on the game, which were usually humorous, reminding us of our foibles, but were now and then serious, reminding us of the frustrations and glories of the game. He published three small volumes of his work: *Fore: The Call of the Links* (1909), *On and Off the Links* (1921), and *Locker Room Ballads* (1925). The last-named has some fine illustrations by C. R. Snelgrove.

In 1933, a Montreal publisher, Hilles Pickens Sr., bought *Canadian Golfer*. His son, Hilles Jr., was soon to become its editor. The new *Canadian Golfer* lost the chatty, informal style of its first editor. But Canadian golf had probably outgrown Ralph Reville. He could no longer keep in touch with a family of clubs that was by now five times larger than it had been when he had started writing in 1915.

Canadian Golfer ran until 1943. What with a shortage of news, newsprint, money, and advertising, Hilles Pickens could no longer keep it alive as a separate publication. It became one

Hilles Pickens Sr., pictured here in 1933, when he took over Canadian Golfer *from Reville. His son, Hilles Pickens, right, took over as editor of* Canadian Golfer.

section of his *Canadian Sport Monthly*. The move was intended as a wartime expedient but lasted until 1963.

Young Pickens, once he had cut his teeth on the magazine, was to prove a worthy successor to Ralph Reville as a chronicler of Canadian golf. A journalism graduate, a fine amateur golfer, he became "one of Canadian golf's most ubiquitous figures," and one of our most percipient of golf writers. For some twenty-two years he was the honorary secretary to the Province of Quebec Golf Association. He died in 1975, at the age of sixty-three.

With so many golfers away in the services, with so many restrictions on travel, and with so many other things on people's minds, it would have been understandable if the number of golfers had declined during the First World War. True, a few clubs did fail because of the loss of members. But on the whole, the war years witnessed a remarkable growth of the game in Canada.

This phenomenon appears to have been the continuation of a surge in golf's popularity that started just before the war. The surge was to develop into an unprecedented boom as soon as the war was over.

As we have seen, golf was virtually unknown in Canada until the 1890s. The game then captured the interest of groups of men and women across the country. The number of golf facilities increased from three in 1890, to about fifty by the end of the century. Despite this growth, the sport was still insignificant in terms of the numbers of players.

For the first thirteen years of the new century the game continued to grow, with some years being better than others. An influx of immigrants in the early 1900s added many new golfers, mainly in Central Canada and Manitoba. In the years 1900 through 1906, less than a handful of new clubs were formed west of Ontario; in the years 1907–12 there were at least a dozen. A downturn in the economy in 1912–13 may have been the cause of a levelling-off in those years, although there does not seem to be any consistent relationship between the health of the nation and the health of the game.

A number of clubs organized around the turn of the century had disappeared by the First World War. Still, by the beginning of the war we can name about 110 clubs, double the number in 1900. (There were undoubtedly more clubs, uncounted, hidden away in the smaller towns.) Nearly half the nation's golfers were in Ontario, which had established itself as the main golfing province. Ontario had some fifty clubs, Quebec about twenty; Prince Edward Island still had only one; the other provinces had between five and ten clubs each.

Memberships had also increased. For a few of the large city clubs, it was more a question of *permitting* the membership to rise.

Most of the country's golf clubs were in or near cities, or in the popular resorts that served cities. Golfers came mainly from the ranks of commercial and professional men and their families – lawyers, bankers, insurance and real estate men, stock and commodity brokers.

Probably about thirty thousand people were golfing in Canada by 1914, a quarter to a third of them women. They came mainly from the middle and upper classes. The readers of the country's newspapers would have been quite right in believing that golf was an exclusive and expensive sport. The newspaper photographs were usually of the most affluent clubs, showing large clubhouses, with automobiles parked outside; well-dressed ladies and gentlemen could be seen sipping drinks on the verandah, or being attended to by a retinue of servants or caddies.

However, while it is true that some city clubhouses were palatial, with twenty or thirty bedrooms, which bachelors might rent for the season, married men for the weekend, such clubhouses were in the minority before the First World War. The great majority were modest buildings, often huts or farmhouses that went with the land leased for the golf course. "It is not that golf really costs so very much. It is only that people who have not played it imagine it must be [expensive]," wrote an anonymous correspondent to *Canadian Golfer* in 1915.

But in most places it *was* an expensive sport. In 1914, a city club might ask for an entrance fee of one hundred dollars and an annual subscription of fifty dollars. Golf balls cost four times what they cost today, in real terms. Golf

clubs were relatively cheaper, but they needed more frequent reshafting and repair. Caddies were almost mandatory at the large clubs, as was wining and dining after the game.

Golf was also exclusive. There was only one public course in Canada (in Edmonton) although many clubs allowed visitors to play for a green fee.

Things started to look brighter in 1914. Late in the previous year a young American amateur, Francis Ouimet, had taken on and defeated two top British professionals, Harry Vardon and Ted Ray, in a play-off for the U.S. Open. Ouimet's "shots heard around the world" had made the headline news in every country where golf was played, and undoubtedly led to a surge of interest in golf in the United States and elsewhere. Too, in 1913 our women golfers organized themselves into the CLGU, further promoting the game.

Whatever the reasons, the year 1914 saw the beginning of a renewed interest in golf, leading to further increases in the number of clubs, courses, members, and players.

With Canada now at war, with some 10 per cent of the nation's golfers in the armed forces, one would have thought that this renewed interest would have been short-lived. Quite the contrary. During the years 1915–18, some twenty-six new clubs were organized, and the membership of many clubs soared.

A few clubs did close because of the war, some permanently, but usually because their courses had been taken over for new housing projects. Among these were the clubs at North Toronto and Kingston. The club at Macleod, Alberta, was reported to be *non est* during the war. The courses at Niagara were commandeered for military camps. Some of the small Prairie clubs that had apparently disappeared by 1919 may have failed during the war.

For many clubs, the war years saw a dramatic growth in membership. Saskatoon GC reported in 1917 that its golf course had never been so busy. Winnipeg's Elmhurst GC opened for play in 1915 and soon had a waiting list of 250. The same city's Assiniboine club, opened in 1917, saw its membership jump from 60 to

160 in the first year. Winnipeg's Norwood added 140 new members in 1918. "Every man, woman, and child in Winnipeg is golf crazy," wrote a western correspondent. On the other hand, as a new Edmonton Golf Club was being formed in 1917 to play over the municipal links, Edmonton Country Club was reporting that its membership had fallen from four hundred, in 1913, to less than a hundred. But there were few such stories.

It was much the same in the East. Toronto's Lakeview GC added seventy new members in 1915, and by the end of the war it had a waiting list for the first time. Essex G & CC added fifty new members in 1915. "Golf was virtually dead in Simcoe a couple of years ago. Today the Norfolk G & CC has a membership of over 300," said the club.

Reports from professionals in all parts of the country attested to the phenomenal new interest in the game. This from the pen of Ralph Reville, in July 1918: "There is not a pro who is not booked up for lessons from early morning till dusk every day of the week. They are having the most successful season ever recorded in Canada. Never was there such a demand for golf goods." He estimated that the number of golfers in Canada increased by about five thousand in that year alone.

Many factors contributed to the growth of the game in wartime: reports of the prime minister playing golf for relaxation; the introduction of Daylight Saving Time, which made evening golf possible and popular; the war-stimulated boom in salaries and wages that meant that more people could now afford the game; a lowering of class barriers; the growing independence of women, many of whom worked in offices and factories for the first time; and the new magazine *Canadian*

Canadian soldier golfers in Britain; front left is Robert M. Gray Jr. of Rosedale GC; front right, A. Vernon Macan of Victoria GC. Macan was to lose his left foot in the war.

Golfer, which provided a new bond between golfers across Canada. While he was recording the remarkable wartime growth of the game, Ralph Reville was also doing much to further this growth.

The imminent end of the war brought a new stimulant: servicemen and women returning from Britain, having golfed there for the first time, wanted to play in Canada.

In December 1917, *Canadian Golfer* carried a short article entitled: "The Returned Soldier and the Game of Golf," written with great prescience by Ralph Reville:

> There can be no question at all that the returned soldier will be a very important factor in the future of the game of golf in Canada. Word comes from overseas that converts to the game by the hundred are being made amongst the forces in training in Great Britain. Golf has always been more or less a favourite sport amongst the officers of the regular regiments, whilst every club in the United Kingdom numbers on its membership list many retired officers who find golf supplies the ideal recreation, both mentally and physically. Soldiers everywhere take very kindly to the Royal and Ancient. . . .
>
> In every training camp in England, Canadian officers and men alike are taking up the sport and every spare afternoon finds them on the neighbouring links. When they come back they will of a certainty be ardent missioners [sic] of golf throughout the Dominion.

When the Canadian forces had arrived in Britain, they had been sent to training and transit camps, mostly in the south of England. The areas of Salisbury Plain and the south coast were thick with golf courses. One Canadian camp at Shorncliffe, a village contiguous with Folkestone, was within easy reach of the golf clubs of Folkestone and Hythe. Not too far away were the courses of Dover, Deal, and Sandwich. Camps were later set up at Bramshott and Witley, in Surrey.

The Canadians used Bramshott Camp until 1919 and for a time it was also the headquarters of the Canadian Training Division. In the 1916–17 season, Canadians contributed more than half the money taken in by membership subscriptions to the Hindhead Golf Club, Bramshott. Ralph Irwin-Brown, the club's historian, estimates that some five hundred members of the Canadian forces joined the club that year.

This was the experience of only one of the many golf clubs near Canadian army camps, but there is evidence that it was quite typical. The Mayor of Hastings wrote to the British magazine *Golfing* in 1918, congratulating the members of local clubs on maintaining the links in prime condition, "and providing play for military men, mostly Canadians, stationed there." Again, in September 1918, *Canadian Golfer* reported: "Many Canadian golfers have pleasant recollections of the golf course at Folkestone on the south coast of England, which presents the last chance for a round of the links before crossing to France . . ."

In all these ways, many Canadians took up golf for the first time during the war, some at home, some in Britain. They were to fuel an astonishing explosion in the game in the 1920s.

PART FOUR

THE GOLDEN YEARS BETWEEN THE WARS 1919-1944

(Over) *Sandy Somerville playing in the 1933 Canadian Open at Royal York* GC *(St. George's* G *&* CC*)*.

15

TWENTY YEARS
OF CHANGE

IT IS PROBABLY UNWISE TO MAKE PREDIC-
tions about any sport. But it is inconceiv-
able that golf in Canada will ever undergo
more change in the space of twenty years than
it did between the wars.

It was a turbulent time in the country's history. The post-war depression gave way to a
few years of prosperity, as the world drew on
Canada's resources. Then came the Great Depression and the long years of drought on the
Prairies. Recovery was slow. It took a second
world war to put the country back to work
again.

The health of golf could not help but be
affected by the sickness of the country. Yet we
can not say that, as the country went, so always
did the game of golf, for it was during the
uncertain years of the early 1920s that golf
knew exactly where it was going: Up, up, and
up again. The game prospered. It grew and it
spread at a rate that has never been equalled
since. From being mainly an urban sport, an
exclusive and expensive pastime for commercial and professional men and their families, it
spread to all sorts of occupations in all sizes of
communities – rural hamlets, villages, and

towns. Rural Canada showed that the game
could prosper outside large and expensive
country clubs and outside Central Canada. The
Prairie provinces soon had more golf facilities
per capita than Ontario and Quebec. The
growth and spread of the game in the Prairies
in the early 1920s was perhaps the most astonishing feature of golf in the interwar years.

But more vital to the future of the game
was the growth in the number of public golf
facilities. In 1918, there were only three public golf clubs in Canada, owned by municipalities. Golfers who joined these clubs paid only
a monthly or seasonal fee to play the game
and were not asked to buy a share in the club
or to come up with a prohibitive entrance
fee. Twenty-one years later, in 1939, there was
hardly a city in Canada that did not have at
least one public golf course, perhaps even a
pay-as-you-play. Thousands of people were
now able to try the game for a round, a week,
or a month, to see if they liked it, and many
converts were won.

As golf grew and spread in Western Canada,
the dominance of Ontario and Quebec golfers
came to an end. But national championships

A crowd around a Tom Thumb course in Montreal. Left to right: *Odie Cleghorn, Babe Siebert, Walter Grant, James Patton, Margery Kirkham, S. F. Tilden, Red Mackenzie, Gordon B. Taylor, Doris Taylor, Bill Taylor, Art McPherson (the winner with a 41).*

that were truly national were slow in coming. Of the twenty-one Amateur championships held between the wars, seventeen were held in Central Canada, three in the Prairies, and one in British Columbia.

After much agonizing, the RCGA found a way of sending the top four amateurs from each province to play in the national championships, regardless of where they were being held, at little cost to the player. The inter-provincial team matches for the Willingdon Cup almost immediately acquired a prestige of their own. The matches also helped to make the Amateur a truly national event, but not before the Prairie provinces had formed a Western Canada Golf Association and organized their own championships.

Indicative of the growth of golf during these years was the establishment of so many new provincial golf associations, whose func-tion was to promote interest in the game, par-ticularly among small clubs not members of the RCGA, to develop competitive golf within the province, and, generally, to control the game. Later, some of them were to develop provincial handicapping.

The Prairie provinces already had their own golf associations, as did the Maritime provinces as a group. There were district associations in Quebec and Ontario, but, after the war, first the Montreal and District GA (formed about 1912) and then the Toronto and District GA (1914) expanded into provin-cial associations, Quebec in 1920, Ontario three years later. British Columbia clubs orga-nized the BCGA in 1922.

Although the Maritime Provinces GA contin-ued to hold regional championships, the three provinces finally formed their own associations; Nova Scotia in 1929, P.E.I. in 1932, and New

Brunswick in 1934. (In 1937, the latter two amalgamated into the N.B.–P.E.I. Golf Association, only to split again in 1971.)

Of the other district golf associations formed in the same period, the Northern Ontario GA (1926) was the largest.

Reorganized in 1919, the Canadian Ladies' Golf Union had provincial branches from coast to coast by 1928. It managed to escape the problems of regional dispute faced by the RCGA, although its championships were no more national in character. Lack of funds kept it from organizing nationwide interprovincial team matches until 1934.

Ontario continued to dominate national golf, but British Columbia gradually replaced Quebec as the main challenger. In 1924, *Canadian Golfer*'s ranking of the nation's top ten male amateur golfers did not include one from B.C. But by 1937, B.C. amateurs were ranked first (Ken Black) and third (Stan Leonard), and six of the top ten lived west of Ontario.

The years between the wars saw the passing of the old guard and the coming of the new. The last of the old amateurs, George S. Lyon, fought to the end. I wonder how many golfers in the 1930s, anywhere, managed to shoot their age as often as he did?

In the early 1920s, it looked as though the Thompson brothers – Frank, Bill, and Stanley – would dominate amateur golf for a decade. As it turned out, the Thompsons served only as a bridge between the old and new. A new bunch of exciting young golfers came to the fore who were to make the 1930s the golden years for amateur golf in Canada. Youth supreme! became the cry of the day.

Few of the previous generation had played golf from childhood, whereas it seemed that this new generation had been born club in hand. Don Carrick, Canadian Amateur champion at the tender age of eighteen, was the first to set new standards of scoring. Over the next eight years he was followed by Sandy Somerville, Jack Cameron, Gordon Taylor Jr., Freddie Wood, Jack Nash, Gordon B. Taylor, Phil Farley, Ken Black, Bob Morrison, Stan Leonard, Bobby Reith, and Bud Donovan.

They broke, and broke again, all sorts of records. Hilles Pickens (who took over *Canadian Golfer*) dubbed them "the boys of '32," for it was in 1932 that they all played together in the Amateur championship.

These young gladiators seemed to be clashing constantly in the summers of the 1930s. They met for national and provincial tournaments. They would go to Jasper for the Totem Pole, to Banff for the Prince of Wales Trophy, to Victoria for the Empress Hotel tournament, to Murray Bay for the Manoir Richelieu Shield, and to Kent House, Quebec, for the Duke of Kent Trophy. The American threat was omnipresent. But so long as Somerville, Carrick, Black, Leonard, Farley, and Taylor were in the field, the country could rest assured that the Canadian championship had a good chance of staying at home.

If the interwar years belonged to any two golfers, they belonged to C. Ross (Sandy) Somerville of London, Ontario, and Ada Mackenzie of Toronto.

An advertisement for Golf Week *at the Manoir Richelieu, 1934.*

Golf at one of the Muskoka resort hotels, 1927.

Sandy Somerville's record of six Amateurs has been surpassed only by that of George S. Lyon. Somerville went one better than Lyon by winning the U.S. Amateur, although George's Olympic win ranks equal. In 1950, Sandy Somerville was named Canada's finest golfer of the first half of this century. Such titles are questionable in concept, as Sandy would be the first to admit. How can we say that he was a better golfer than George Lyon when they competed in different generations? Both men played well enough to establish a clear supremacy over others of their times. No golfer can be asked to do more than that.

Of women golfers born and bred in Canada, Ada Mackenzie reigned more or less supreme throughout the 1920s and 1930s, winning four Open and six Close national titles. But for her, the Americans would have completely dominated our Ladies' Open championships.

If we could feel satisfied with the way our amateurs met the American threat, the same can not be said for our professionals in the Canadian Open. The 1920s and 1930s were the years of Walter Hagen, Leo Diegel, Tommy Armour, and – from 1938 – Sam Snead. In the early years of the Second World War, it looked as though our own talented Bob Gray Jr. might wrest the title from the Americans. He came close but in the end was just not good enough.

The CPGA championships were taken over by a new crop of immigrant professionals in the middle of the 1920s: Andy Kay, Willie Lamb, Jimmy Johnstone, Lex Robson. But in the 1930s our new home-bred stars came to the fore: Stan Horne, Jules Huot, Bob Gray Jr., Gordie Brydson, Bill Kerr.

The years between the wars saw the last major change to the implements of golf. The steel shaft replaced the hickory, leading the way to graduated sets of clubs, mass-produced. Cleeks, jiggers, mashies, and niblicks gave way to irons, numbered 1 to 10. Much was gained in the process, much was lost. The affection for one's set of clubs quickly disappeared.

Golfers experimented with deep-grooved irons and concave faces on their wedges. Both were eventually ruled illegal.

For the first time, we had a standard golf ball. To be more precise, we had two standard golf balls, one for North America and one for Britain, since the legislators could not agree. The ball that floated on water soon became a collector's item. So too did the small, dense, tightly wound ball of 1920, which, some said, threatened to fly so far as to make our golf courses a thousand yards too short.

Our courses improved immeasurably in design and in upkeep. In the 1920s, Canada produced perhaps the greatest of an excellent crop of golf architects in Stanley Thompson. His legacies of Jasper, Banff, Capilano, and St. George's rank with the finest in the world.

Our present system of handicapping and course rating was born between the wars. The authorities also tinkered with the rules, on both sides of the Atlantic.

The amount of space newspapers devoted to golf increased substantially after the First World War. Ralph Reville observed in *Canadian Golfer* in 1918: "A baseball fan has nothing on a golfer when it comes to reading about the game, and keeping tabs on records and incidents and the doing of the star players generally, both amateur and professional." By the end of the period, most large newspapers had their own golf writers.

We were reminded that golf was an ancient royal game when the Prince of Wales (later King Edward VIII, later the Duke of Windsor) travelled across Canada in his private railway car, in 1919 and again in 1927. In 1919 he came as a duffer who played golf only with members of his entourage. This selectivity helped to preserve the dignity of his office; it would not do for the royal whiffs to be witnessed. At Lambton, the club's professional, Willie Freeman, caddied for the prince, but in those days there was no question of Willie selling his story to the newspapers. By 1927, the Prince appears to have been a more proficient golfer. This time he played at seventeen courses, from Royal Quebec to Victoria. The same secrecy and obsequiousness surrounded him, as in "The *Canadian Golfer* is privileged by special permission to reproduce the official list of courses played by the Prince personally." He now golfed with club presidents, but members were discouraged from following his four-ball. The press was not permitted to witness him playing golf, but a correspondent of *The Globe* was later taken over the course at Laval-sur-le-Lac and shown where the Prince's drives had landed.

The Prince of Wales at Calgary G & CC, 1919.

Lord and Lady Willingdon, with Albert Murray (far left) and future RCGA president, G. H. Forster (far right) at Beaconsfield GC, with club president Dr. Fred Tooke (centre), 1930.

Golf instruction began its inevitable climb to popularity in our magazines.

The boom in golf between the wars saw the heyday of the schoolboy caddie. Many came from families where the money they earned caddying was needed to help make ends meet. The city boy would finish his morning paper-run and head for the nearest club, looking to make thirty cents a round. Looking, too, to become as good a golfer as any he caddied for. (*Canadian Golfer* noted that "every urchin was joined by other small urchins who brandished clubs alarmingly near each other's heads, in a vain endeavour to master in a few moments the art of the perfect swing.")

Clubs organized caddie camps, to teach the boys discipline. The annual caddie competition soon became the event of the year for the youngsters, surpassing even the Open. Here is *Canadian Golfer*, in 1926:

> Over one hundred caddies of the Toronto Golf Club participated in the annual caddie matches last week. They had a great day of it.
>
> After the championship, the boys were given a dinner by the club. The pie-eating contest, which has been a feature of the match for many seasons, was won by Andy Brown. After a decidedly poor round of golf, Brown met all comers in the dining room. After the dinner, the lad won the contest by eating ten large slices of blueberry pie.

(Will Andy Brown, wherever you are, please stand up and take a bow.)

Most old fans of the game remember the 1930s with nostalgia. To them, the game had a charm and simplicity long since lost to commercialism. It was played for the most part in the true spirit of amateurism, as part of a small, exclusive world, in a setting of champagne and iced tea, hampers of cold cuts, watercress sandwiches, corks popping, gusts of laughter, the distant click of the Kro-flite, the cries of "good shot"; a world of multi-coloured skirts, ribbons, blazers, white flannels, straw hats, striped tents flapping, bright parasols shading the summer heat.

These, then, were the golden years of the golden people between the wars. Golf will never see their likes again.

In this advertisement for Canada Dry, the Del Monte at Pebble Beach typified the good life of the 1920s.

16

CHAPTER

GROWTH AND THE PUBLIC COURSE

IN THE YEARS BETWEEN THE END OF THE First World War and the Depression, golf in Canada grew and spread at a rate that has never since been equalled. The number of golfers increased from some 50,000 to four or five times that number. We can identify some 130 golf clubs in Canada in 1918. By 1926, this number had increased to over 500; by the end of the decade it was nearer 600.

The growth in golf seems to have been a continuation of the boom of 1914, but it gathered momentum after the war. As the working week was reduced and real incomes went up, more people had the time and the money for recreation. They wanted to participate in sport, not just to spectate. And with better roads and cheaper automobiles, they no longer had to rely entirely on streetcars or trains to get to the golf course.

As the demand for golf increased, more and more clubs ran up against something not experienced before – overcrowding. Their facilities became overloaded, and they had to stop taking on new members. J. Lewis Brown had this to say, in 1920, of the golfing scene in Quebec:

. . . the outstanding feature of the local season . . . is a deep under current for a splendid revival of the game. The great drawback is lack of accommodation. Nearly all the clubs have waiting lists of incredible length, and they are besieged daily with applications for membership. Even five day memberships in some of the clubs have failed to assist to any noticeable extent. It is next to impossible to get into any of the clubs that have been playing for more than two or three seasons, but fortunately there are a number of new clubs being organized which to some extent will relieve the situation.

Memberships doubled or tripled in the 1920s. In 1920, the large Toronto clubs had to introduce starting-time sheets for the first time. And, on busy days, four-ball matches were given precedence over singles (that is, pairs) and foursomes. Only the economic depression at the end of the decade was to put a stop to this expansion, and to render waiting lists obsolete.

The First World War liberalized many attitudes, including those towards Sunday recreation. The work week for most was still

221

five-and-a-half or six days, so Sunday was the only day when working people could enjoy favourite sports. Increasingly, Sunday became a day of recreation, as well as of religion.

The playing of games on the sabbath had always been a matter of fierce debate in Scotland, as in Canada. Even to this day, the Old Course at St. Andrews is closed on Sundays.

In May 1895, four members of the Toronto Golf Club – V. F. Cronyn, J. F. Edgar, W. J. S. Gordon, and A. W. Smith – were taken to court and fined five dollars each for playing golf on a Sunday. The crown relied on a statute that made it unlawful to play shuttles, ball, football, racquets, or any other noisy game on a Sunday. The defence contended that golf was not a noisy game and appealed. The appeal was heard in September and the four were acquitted. The judge ruled that golf was not a game of ball similar to those proscribed by law: it was not a noisy game, like football or baseball.

The Lord's Day Alliance of Canada wanted to see all games banned on Sundays, including golf. It was largely responsible for the Lord's Day Act of 1907, aimed at restricting Sunday trade, work, and recreation. There is no indication, however, that the law stopped those who wanted to play golf from playing. The golfers' only concession was not to use caddies, or at least not very young caddies, on Sundays.

These changing attitudes undoubtedly had much to do with the growth of golf in Canada during and after the First World War. But the battle for Sunday continued to rage across the country. In 1917, shareholders of Waterloo G & CC were asked to vote on opening the clubhouse for golfers on Sunday. The 117 ballots cast showed a majority of only one for opening.

The city of Winnipeg's dichotomy over Sunday golf was probably typical of the split in other communities during the 1920s. The Manitoba Conference of the United Church had condemned the playing of golf on the sabbath. It had an articulate spokesman in Dr. C. W. Gordon, better known as Ralph Connor,

"The Sabbath Breakers." Sunday golf was long forbidden in Scotland.

the novelist. ("Those who devote their time to golf on Sunday cannot be relied upon to advance the cause of our holy religion.") By 1926, he had few supporters left. "Agitation against Sunday golf and other harmless pursuits has done more damage in the province of Manitoba than the pursuits themselves," countered Judge Stubbs of the County Court.

Some saw the banning of golf on Sundays as the class problem of the times. Said Alderman Simpkin: "There was no agitation to prohibit Sunday golf until the workers took it up . . . The Lord's Day Alliance are trying to take away the working man's opportunity to play golf." He had a point. By then, Winnipeg had two public courses, and they were full every weekend.

The last word goes to the *Winnipeg Tribune* in June 1926. "Unless they can show that golf is an anti-social, unhealthy, dangerous pursuit, the Puritans will not make headway against Sunday golf. And if it is these things, then it shouldn't be played at all." Naturally, no one could show that golf was any of these things.

The figures illustrating the rapid growth of golf in Canada in the early 1920s are, if anything, understated. When golfers organized themselves into a club, they were under no obligation to report doing so to anyone, so the provincial association, as well as the RCGA, would often be unaware of a club's existence.

For a few years after the First World War, Ralph Reville tried to keep track of the number of clubs in each province. But in 1924 he had to acknowledge that his figures were low:

The total of 352 does not represent all the golf clubs in the Dominion, although it does represent all the important ones. There are many small places in the West and British Columbia which recently established, or are establishing, courses. So it is a conservative estimate that there are now in Canada well over 400 clubs.

Understated or not, the *Canadian Golfer* figures (in box below) are the best we have. They do illustrate better than words the dramatic growth in Canadian golf in the post-war years.

Number of Golf Clubs in Canada									
	Alta.	B.C.	Man.	N.B.	N.S.	Ont.	P.E.I.	Que.	Sask.	Total
May 1919	9	8	9	7	8	46	1	18	8	114
May 1920	14	13	13	6	7	60	1	20	9	143
May 1921	17	17	13	7	9	71	1	21	12	168
May 1922	22	20	19	7	11	86	1	32	30	228
Mar. 1923	53	25	26	8	11	101	1	37	30	292
May 1924	56	26	35	8	13	116	1	49	48	352
Jan. 1925	56	30	39	9	13	125	1	53	47	373
Sept. 1926	64	37	68	11	18	143	3	60	105	509
Apr. 1927	65	36	60	11	18	153	3	54	109	509
Dec. 1931	56	49	71	13	20	194	3	73	112	591
1936	66	44	54	16	26	189	7	94	71	576
1954	37	50	39	21	20	177	—	98	56	498

The figures for 1936 are taken from Fraser's International Golf Year Book; *those for 1954, from an RCGA survey. P.E.I. and Newfoundland are grouped with N.B. in 1954.*

In all provinces, the progression from 1919 to 1926 was undoubtedly much smoother than is shown by these figures.

✕

In 1918, golf in the Prairies was limited to urban centres, with a few exceptions. It is unlikely that the handful of small clubs in southern Alberta, near Fort Macleod, survived the war.

Within eight years of the end of the war, Alberta had expanded from twelve (my figure) to over sixty clubs. Small rural towns with populations of only two or three hundred laid out nine-hole courses.

By 1926, Manitoba had sixty-five clubs, Winnipeg leading with sixteen. It vied with Calgary for the distinction of being "the golfiest city in North America," with the greatest number of clubs per capita.

But it was in the least populated of the three Prairie provinces, Saskatchewan, that there was the most widespread addiction to golf. During the war the number of golfers in Saskatchewan probably doubled, but that meant only an increase from one thousand to two thousand. Four new clubs sprang up in the first year after the war, and another twenty-five or so appeared by the middle of 1923.

The next reliable number of clubs is the figure produced by the Saskatchewan Golf Association in 1926. It named 103 clubs. This, remember, in a province that at the time had a population of less than one million, only half the size of present-day Toronto. About half of the clubs had fewer than fifty members, and some had as few as five. They sprang up in small rural communities all over the southern half of Saskatchewan, in the farm belt.

How did golf first arrive at these small rural centres? Who carried it there? How did it spread from one community to another?

In an article published by *Canadian Golfer* in May 1923, Jackson Walton (a former Saskatchewan Open champion) speculated on how it might have reached a typical, but fictional, prairie town in Saskatchewan.

His Gopher Hill has a population of three hundred. It has a couple of banks, a real estate and insurance agency, a pool room, a garage, a livery, some barns and grain elevators, and a large frame hotel.

The ladies of Gopher Hill, he hypothesized, are kept busy enough with their socials. But the men of Gopher Hill have little to distract them but the pool room. All this changes when a Sandy Macpherson comes to live in Gopher Hill, transferred there by his bank.

The Bowness club in Calgary opened just before the war.

The Canadian Purple Sage: putting at one of the smaller clubs in the Prairies.

Sandy (a Scot, naturally) goes out on the prairie to practise his golf. Within a week, others are borrowing his clubs and are smitten. They lay out a nine-hole course and The Gopher Hill Golf Club is under way, with fifty members, and an annual subscription of ten dollars. The news spreads, and within a few months there is scarcely a town in the district without its own golf club.

"Joking apart," Jackson Walton concludes, "it would be impossible to overestimate the value of golf as a means of diversion in the average prairie town."

It was probably not by chance that Jackson Walton chose a young Scottish banker to be his golfing missionary. Scottish bankers continued to help golf prosper, as they had forty years earlier. C. J. Kidd, the Scottish manager of the Bank of Commerce in Hardisty, Alberta, wrote to *Canadian Golfer* in 1922:

Remembering many happy days spent on Norwood course in Winnipeg a few years ago, I renewed my association with the game . . . on our rough prairie at Hardisty – last year. At first there was much good-natured chaff, which was followed by curiosity, resulting in my being joined by half a dozen friends taking up the game. By the end of the season we had an organized club of some forty members. We now have no less than one hundred members and have organized committees – "grounds", "social", etc., and every member an enthusiast.

Prairie golfers competed in golf leagues that were formed after the war. The village of Lemsford – population thirty-seven – had a golf club with only six members. In 1920, its team of four was good enough to win the championship of the Swift Current district, against eleven other clubs. It successfully defended its championship in 1921. Lemsford could well have been the smallest community in North America to own a nine-hole course.

The Swift Current golfers were typical of those in the prairies. When they needed a course, they gave no thought to consulting golf architects and construction companies but took on the job themselves. An Associated Press reporter was much taken by their enthusiasm:

Three citizens who obtained permission to use a piece of prairie invested five dollars in shovels and picks, donned overalls and began to dig out a course for themselves. They made three holes, and induced some fellow-townsmen to try their luck over the rugged fairways from the earthen tees to the sanded greens.

No western boom was ever greater than that of the Swift Current Golf Club, for within a few weeks, there were a hundred members, all willing workers. They kept delving into the virgin prairie until eighteen holes were completed, and then they chipped in and bought the land, some 400 acres. Using a farm house for a club house, they began to improve the course with bunkers, a watering plant and a rustic gateway.

This was published at about the time golfers were forming the Elmwood club in Swift Current.

One remarkable victory was recorded in the interclub matches between these small towns. In 1924, six Kerrobert golfers visited Biggar to play for the Dark Cup. This was a team match, decided by the total number of holes won by each side, so that all matches had to be played to a finish. With one match to go, Kerrobert was seventeen holes down.

"How do we stand?" asked McMullen, the last Kerrobert player, as he walked into the clubhouse after his match.

"We need seventeen to tie, eighteen to win," came the downhearted chorus.

"We have 'em," cried McMullen. He handed in his card, showing he had won all eighteen holes against his luckless opponent.

Golf was slower to bloom in British Columbia. The Victoria GC and the United Service Club prospered on Vancouver Island. The nine-hole course of the Jericho Country Club opened for play in 1907 and met Vancouver's needs for several years.

The years 1910 and 1911 saw the founding of two celebrated clubs, still with us today.

The Vancouver G & CC opened its first six holes a year after it was formed in 1910. Its course, bowling green, and palatial clubhouse were carved out of forest, overlooking the picturesque Fraser Valley, at Burtquitlam (a hybrid of Burnaby and Coquitlam). It stood on the old Burnaby Lake line of the B.C. Electric Railway. CPR started to lay out its Shaughnessy Heights course in 1911 and completed it a year later, naming the club after the company's former president, Lord Shaughnessy. Situated on a hilltop inside the city boundary, the original Shaughnessy course and clubhouse became a showpiece.

Victoria added a third club in 1913. The rolling hills, oaks, and evergreens of Royal Colwood overlooked the bay some eight miles east of the city. The course became well-known to golfers throughout Canada in the 1930s, when Victoria's Empress Hotel held its annual winter tournament.

During the 1920s, golf grew nearly as rapidly in British Columbia as in the Prairies. But with most of the province mountainous, and therefore ungolfable, the game could not spread to the same extent. Most of the new clubs were, naturally, where the great majority of the people lived: in the lowlands of the east coast of Vancouver Island and the lowlands of the lower Fraser Valley. The two large cities of

Shaughnessy Heights Golf Club, Vancouver, about 1922.

Vancouver and Victoria dominate this region, where golf can be played all year round.

By 1929, greater Victoria had six courses, and there were half a dozen others on the island. The BCGA has on record a description of the club formed in 1927 at Port Alice, Quatsino Sound, in the northwest corner.

At one time a barge was anchored at the shoreline and used as a No. 8 tee-off. Across the creek and in the area of No. 7 and No. 8 greens, the Japanese community had their graveyard. Etiquette demanded that your ball should be picked off the fenced burial area.

St. Paul's Anglican Church was built in 1927 when the initial golf course clearing took place. Eventually the course surrounded St. Paul's. So, there was an unusual hazard for a golf course . . . a church in the middle of the fairway. You could either go around the church or over it. Needless to day, wire screen had to be put over the near side windows . . . At one time, the frugal committee acquired some goats to crop the greens . . .

In the low-lying land of the mainland, including the greater Vancouver area, there were soon a dozen fine golfing facilities. Further up the coast, golfers of the pulp and paper town of Powell River formed a club in 1922.

Golf also grew and spread in the two other southern regions of the province: the first a region of rolling hills, thousands of feet above sea level, where most of the population lived in cattle- and fruit-farming valleys such as the Okanagan; and the second, the mountainous southeast Kootenay–Columbia region, where mining is the important industry. In these inland regions, golf is not a winter sport.

In the Prairies, the game had spread to wheat farmers and the traders who serviced them. In B.C., fruit farmers, miners, and pulp and paper workers took up golf. They often had to carve their courses out of forests. Men

Lining up to play at Oak Bay, Victoria.

working for the Cominco company laid out the first course at Kimberley. They cleared out dense bush, filled in swampland with fallen trees and old logs, hauled twenty loads of earth a day to cover rocks on the fairways. In 1920, a writer to the New York *Herald Tribune* gave this description of the course at Hedley:

> The employees of the mine and the townspeople have laid out a nine-hole course on the hills. The only artificial features are the sand greens. Sage brush forms the turf; hills, rocks, trees and dwarf cactus furnish the hazards. The winner of the hole has the honour of driving the rattlesnakes off the next green. Caddies are unknown, so no short sports can delegate them the job of driving the bears off the fairway. All the crack golfers are not club professionals or well-to-do amateurs. A mill mechanic, Murray (good golf name) goes around consistently near 70.

These were truly the pioneering days of golf in the West. If you have ever helped lay out the first holes for golf in a foreign land, you will know the feeling of pride and pleasure such simple courses give to their amateur architects.

The province of Quebec had been the birthplace of golf in Canada in the 1870s. But, by the turn of the century, Ontario had replaced it as the country's premier golfing province. By the end of the First World War, nearly half the nation's golfers were in Ontario.

Several of the early Toronto clubs had been forced to move out of the city – including Toronto GC and Rosedale – or forced to close, the value of their land having become too great – Highlands, High Park, Spadina. New facilities had sprung up in or around the city, notably at Scarborough, Weston, Port Credit, and Mississauga.

Some of the new courses in the province were at resort hotels, where city golfers from Ontario and the United States learned how to survive a summer away from their home clubs.

The popular Muskoka area had seven courses by the end of the First World War.

The nation's capital had acquired a second major club in 1910, Rivermead GC, which, like Royal Ottawa, had its course at Aylmer, Quebec.

Given its Scottish roots, golf was understandably a recreation adopted mainly by English-speaking Canadians in the first quarter of the century. This restricted its growth and spread in Quebec. Royal Quebec became progressively more French-speaking. As we have seen, Montreal's Metropolitan was said to have been predominately French-Canadian, but it closed around 1909. A club had also been formed on Ile d'Orleans; but the first prominent French-Canadian club was Laval-sur-le-Lac, near Montreal, organized in 1917. With this exception, the new clubs organized before the 1920s were in the English-speaking areas of Montreal, Hudson Heights, Sherbrooke, Lennoxville, and Magog, and at other resorts frequented by English-speaking golfers. The Montreal area had a number of fine clubs, including Beaconsfield, the Country Club of Montreal, Mount Bruno, Outremont, Kanawaki, and Whitlock.

After the war, the game grew and expanded rapidly in Ontario and Quebec, but from a much larger base than in the West. In one year alone, 1922, Toronto added five new clubs, to bring its total to seventeen: Thistledown, out beyond Weston; York Downs, on north Bathurst Street; Thornhill, on Yonge Street; Uplands, just north of Thornhill; and Cedar Brook, north of the Kingston Road. Thereafter growth slowed, but new courses continued to appear through the years of the Depression, and very few closed.

The Maritime provinces showed the least inclination to be gripped by the golf fever that swept the rest of the country after the First World War. Nevertheless, the game grew at a steady, if unspectacular, rate.

By the war's end, in Nova Scotia the original Halifax club had been augmented by the nearby Brightwood club at Dartmouth, and golfers had organized at Lingan, Truro, Yarmouth, Amherst, and Digby. Soon after the war, Halifax GC moved to a new site at Ashburn and became a country club, and new clubs sprang up in half a dozen towns.

In New Brunswick, the Saint John GC had moved to Rothesay and renamed itself Riverside G & CC. The original Fredericton GC had been reorganized in 1916. Moncton's

Truro Golf Club around 1914.

two early clubs had amalgamated, under the name of Riverdale GC, with a new course formally opened in 1919. (In the 1940s it became the Moncton G & CC.) The club at Woodstock was still active, and clubs had been formed in St. Stephen (1904) and in Sackville (1909). The Algonquin club at St. Andrews, now with twenty-seven holes for golf, was more popular than ever with vacationers from Central Canada and the United States. Over the next ten years or so, the number of clubs in the province doubled.

Prince Edward Island managed to get along with only the Belvedere links of the Charlottetown GC until 1927, when a club was organized at Summerside. But by the early 1930s it had no fewer than seven golf courses. Some were obviously rudimentary facilities laid out to attract summer visitors who might be golfers.

By 1930, Ralph Reville reckoned there were, at a conservative estimate, some 150,000 golfers in Canada, or over three times the number at the end of the First World War. This figure should probably be nearer 200,000, if we include the occasional, public links golfer. For, by 1930, Canada had a number of public courses, all doing a record business. Whereas a large private club might have provided a course for six hundred golfers, a public course probably had a clientele of two to three times that number. The public links were gradually bringing golf to thousands who could never have afforded it otherwise.

At the end of the First World War, all but a few of the golfing facilities in Canada were owned or leased by private clubs or by resort hotels. To play golf regularly in or near a city, you had to join a club and pay a stiff entrance fee or buy a share in the club. You also had to pay annual dues to cover operating and maintenance costs.

Most golf clubs welcomed visitors, particularly on weekdays when the course was not crowded, charging them anything from fifty cents to one dollar for a round of eighteen holes. City clubs usually required visitors to be introduced by a member, or at least to be a member of another recognized club.

Many of the large resort hotels also owned golf courses where hotel guests could play free of charge. Casual visitors might be charged the going rate of fifty cents a round, or one dollar a day.

With only a few exceptions, then, Canadian golf clubs were privately owned. However, we would now classify most of them as "semi-private," since they did allow non-members to play at certain times.

In the matter of public golf courses, Canada differed quite dramatically from Scotland and the United States. In these countries, a large number of golf courses were owned by a city or a town. The public could use them without charge, or for a small "green fee." A city might construct such a course in a city park, in much the same way as it would construct a playground for children. The local taxpayer was financing or subsidizing the local golfer, a practice rooted in the origins of the game in Scotland, where providing a course for golfers was looked upon as essential a public duty as providing paths for walkers or roads for carriages. Local golfers were free to organize their own clubs and run their own tournaments on public links.

Despite the example of Scotland, there were only three municipal courses in Canada at the end of the First World War: in Edmonton, Calgary, and Saskatoon. The privately run Edmonton Golf Club (1896) had its first course on land owned by the Hudson's Bay Company. In 1907, the Alberta government bought the property and the club moved a few yards west to a new site, still on Hudson's Bay land. In 1912, this piece of land went to the city of Edmonton and the club moved again. By this time it had renamed itself Edmonton Country Club.

The city wisely included the club's former course in its Victoria Park, expanding it from seven to nine holes. The Victoria Park golf course thus became the first municipal golfing facility in Canada. It had not been open for play long in 1914 before a group of golfers formed a new Edmonton Golf Club to play over this public course. The club selected its own committees and even hired its own professional.

The city of Calgary opened a municipal course in 1915, complete with a clubhouse, showers, lockers, and dining room. Within a year, well over two hundred golfers belonged to the Calgary Municipal Golf Club.

Golfers could join these new clubs in Edmonton and Calgary by paying modest annual dues, but they were not required to pay an entrance fee or to buy a share. Visitors could play for as little as thirty-five cents for eighteen holes.

Saskatoon also had a form of municipal course. The private Saskatoon Golf Club

Canada's first public golf course at Victoria Park, Edmonton.

The following pages show a selection of covers from Canada's golf magazines through the years.

AUTHOR'S COLLECTION.

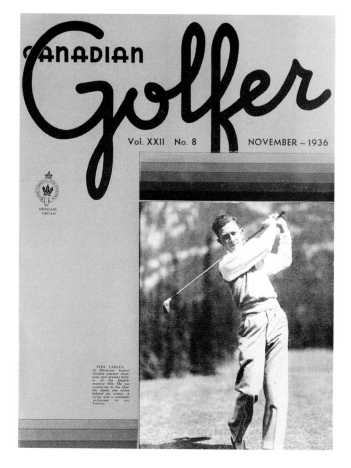

AUTHOR'S COLLECTION.

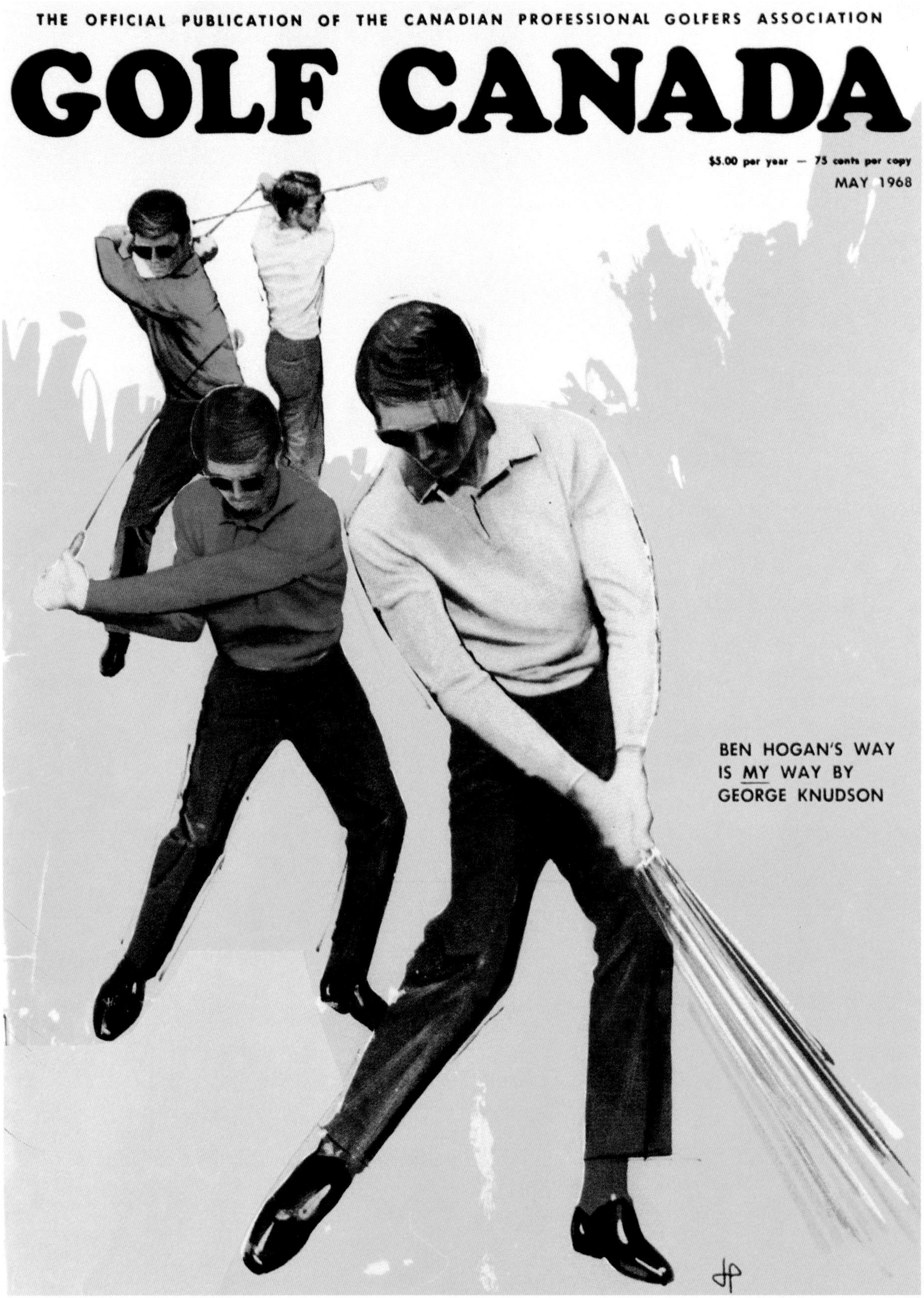

AUTHOR'S COLLECTION.

COURTESY *SCORE.*

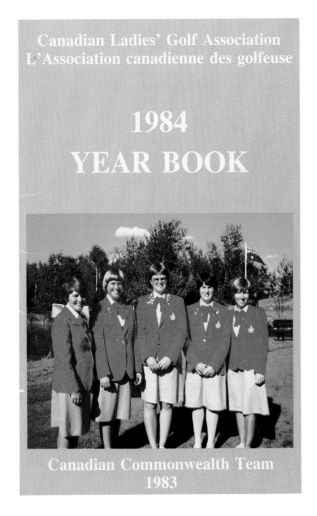

COURTESY CLGA.

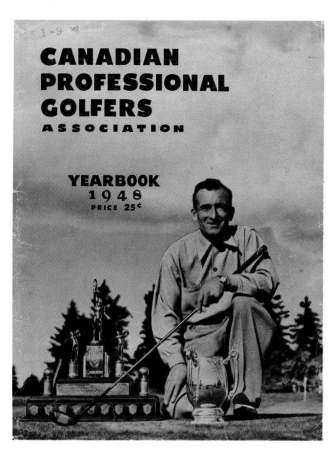

Courtesy CPGA.

Courtesy CPGA.

CANADIAN

GOLF REVIEW

St. George's Golf & Country Club
Islington, Ontario

Scene of the 1968 Canadian Open — June 20th to June 23rd, 1968

OFFICIAL PROGRAMME AND PUBLICATION OF THE ROYAL CANADIAN GOLF ASSOCIATION

Courtesy RCGA.

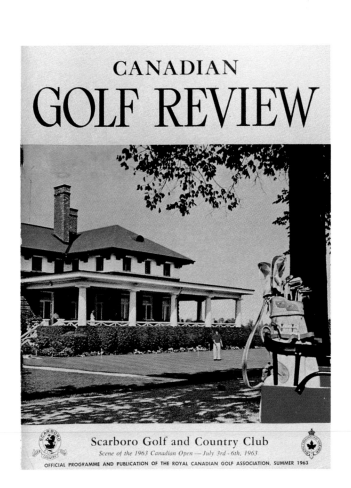

CANADIAN

GOLF REVIEW

Scarboro Golf and Country Club
Scene of the 1963 Canadian Open — July 3rd - 6th, 1963

OFFICIAL PROGRAMME AND PUBLICATION OF THE ROYAL CANADIAN GOLF ASSOCIATION, SUMMER 1963

Courtesy RCGA.

Green Master

The Official Publication of CGSA

ENVIRONMENTAL COURSE DESIGN

Course design and architecture play an important role in golf's continuing contribution to more effective environmental management

Greenmaster, *the publication of the Canadian Golf Course Superintendents' Association.* COURTESY CGSA.

played on a course laid out on city land. In 1914, the city made it a condition of renewing the lease that the course be opened to the public at a green fee of twenty-five cents a round or an annual fee of twelve dollars.

Public course golfers in Edmonton, Calgary, and Saskatoon were spared the expense of a hefty entrance fee. Too, their annual dues were only about half of what they would have been as members of private clubs.

Strangely, there were no municipal golf courses in Central Canada, where the game had started. Why municipal golf courses should have taken root in American cities, but not in Canadian cities, is not easy to explain.

The English writer, Henry Leach, visited the United States in 1913, and in his book *The Happy Golfer* he attributed the growth of municipal golf in the United States to the Americans' keen desire to excel. "Some Americans of great golfing experience, not confined to their own country, have not hesitated to say that they will 'make America the greatest golfing country in the world.'" (If that was indeed their aim, then they have surely succeeded.) This may also explain why English and Canadian golfers did not push for more public courses. England *was* the greatest golf-

ing country in the world, early in the century. There was no need to encourage the public to excel. And, in those days, the precepts of English golf had more influence in Canada than the precepts of American golf.

There was, however, a small but persistent lobby for municipal golf in Central Canada. New Scottish immigrants, accustomed to playing over public links at home, were dismayed to find none in Canada.

In his editorials, Ralph Reville constantly argued the case on behalf of the many golfers who could not afford the luxury of a private club. He correctly saw the public golf course as "a certainty of the future."

He found a strong supporter in W. M. Stuart, the assistant managing editor of the Montreal *Standard*. It was a sad commentary on the state of civic affairs in Montreal, Stuart observed, that the largest city in British North America had no public course: "The writer personally knows of half a score of young men, the majority of whom are employed in banks at the usual bank clerk's salary, who have come to Canada from the other side of the water where they were rated as first class club players and who owing to the lack of the necessary funds are unable to enjoy their favourite

Saskatoon Golf Club, a thriving club in the West.

game." Stuart was in favour of re-opening Fletcher's Field as a public course. But there was little hope of that happening so long as the game was almost exclusively a sport for the English-speaking. In 1916, he correctly forecast that "ten years from now there will be many municipal golf courses in the country."

Supporters of municipal courses did not do their case any good by claiming that these courses, being self-supporting, would be no burden on the taxpayers. Edmonton and Calgary officials claimed that their cities made a profit on their municipal courses. They ignored the fact that the cities were not charging rent for the land.

In the summer of 1920, private enterprise, and not the municipality, gave Toronto its first two public courses. Ralph Connable was the general manager in Canada of the Woolworth Corporation and a prominent member of the Lambton G & CC. He had lived in Buffalo, which had a municipal course, and was determined to see a municipal course in Toronto.

Connable was so sure that a public course could be built and operated successfully that he offered to cover, personally, any first-year loss, if the city would open a course in High Park. The city council said the park was too crowded already. Then anywhere else, said Connable.

When the council continued to dither, Connable took it upon himself to form the Humber Valley Golf Corporation and plan an eighteen-hole public course at the mouth of the Humber River. Golfers would be able to reach the course by streetcar.

Connable recruited a strong board of directors, including George S. Lyon, Stanley Thompson (then emerging as a world-class golf course architect), and George Cumming, who laid out the course. Connable leased 135 acres of land at a nominal rent from the real estate company, which was owned by a friend and Lambton colleague, R. Home Smith.

The project was swamped with success. By early 1921, over 1,400 applications had been received from Torontonians keen to join the Humber Valley Golf Club, which had no entrance fee and annual dues of only ten dollars.

Spurred by this response, Connable started looking for land in the east end of the city, before the ground had even been broken at the Humber. This time, not one but two white knights offered to help. Businessmen A. E. Ames and A. H. Cox owned adjacent properties at Glen Stewart, in Scarborough, overlooking the lake. There, Ames had already laid out his own private nine-hole course. Ames and Cox handed over their properties to the Humber Valley Golf Corporation for a nominal rent, and the corporation soon had twelve holes ready for play. The Glen Stewart Golf Club opened in May 1921.

About two weeks later, just forty days after the first sod had been turned, ten holes of the Humber Valley course were opened for play, the other eight holes five weeks later.

From the day they opened, the Glen Stewart and Humber Valley courses were crowded. In 1921, two thousand golfers applied to join either of the two clubs, or about double the number they could handle in that year. At the time of its annual general meeting in the spring of 1924, Humber Valley Golf Club had 1,783 members, many of them with restricted hours of play. It had a waiting list of twelve hundred. (About one thousand members turned up for its annual general meeting, which must be a record for a golf club in Canada.) Club members were specifically requested to respect the club's property "and to promote an atmosphere of moral cleanliness."

Ralph Connable had shown beyond doubt that there was a demand for public golf and that, given the will, private enterprise could meet the demand. Given, also, generous benefactors, for the cost of building and operating the courses could not have been met if Home Smith, Ames, and Cox had charged the going rate for the lease of their land. Be that as it may, Ralph Connable had achieved what he set out to achieve. The city of Toronto no longer rested with the opprobrium of being one of the richest and most sport-loving centres on the continent with no facility for public golf.

The success of Humber Valley and Glen Stewart encouraged other Ontario cities to go

James McDiarmid, "father of municipal golf in Winnipeg."

for municipal courses. Hamilton's Chedoke Civic Golf Club was opened in 1922; the Thames Valley Golf Course in London, and the Arrowdale Golf Club in Brantford, a few years later.

In 1923, Connable met with the City Park Board and civic officers of Montreal. He persuaded them to lay out a public course in Maisonneuve Park.

In Alberta, where public golf began, Lethbridge had opened a municipal links in 1918, the third in the province.

The matter of a public golf course for Winnipeg was brought before the Winnipeg Parks Board by Bill Laird before he left for the war, in which he was killed. In 1916, the Parks Board decided to lay out an eighteen-hole course in Kildonan Park. In the event, it was not opened for play until the spring of 1921.

Kildonan was a fine course, laid out by one of the city's veteran golfers, James McDiarmid, who came to be dubbed "The Father of Municipal Golf in Winnipeg." The facility was also a great success. In its first season, it was crowded from dawn till dusk. The fact that it rented out 55,000 sets of golf clubs in a

The clubhouse at Winnipeg's Kildonan Park.

season suggests that many of its players were new to the game.

In 1920, a joint committee of businessmen and city aldermen looked at where to build a municipal course in Vancouver. (The chairman, Robert Bone, was one of the Bones of Glasgow Golf Club.) Over the winter of 1921–22, two hundred men worked on clearing the ground for a course in Hastings Park. It was a sign of the times that the men were drawn from a labour camp set up in the park for the unemployed. It housed seven hundred men. A few were skilled civil engineers and surveyors, thrown out of work by the immediate post-war depression. The Hastings Park Municipal Golf Course was not opened for play until 1925.

In 1926, Canada's first "pay-as-you-play" course, the St. Andrews Estates and Golf Club of Toronto, was opened by private enterprise. This was sited on Upper Yonge Street, only half a mile or so from the city limits and accessible by streetcar. Unlike the municipal courses, which charged modest membership fees, this course did away with the concept of a club membership fee altogether. A golfer paid for each game played, nothing more. Some 26,000 rounds were played over St. Andrews in its first year, to make it a financial success. The course had been laid out by Stanley Thompson, and was so highly praised that it was chosen for the Canadian Open in 1936 and 1937.

By 1927, then, Canada had some thirty public courses in play, most of them municipally owned, and had caught up with the United States in terms of public courses per capita. There are many club golfers today who started their golfing careers on a public course. Hundreds of thousands of golfers who can not afford the ever-increasing entrance fee and annual dues of city clubs could not play the game at all were it not for inexpensive public facilities, most of them "pay-as-you-play." Canada's public links have developed many great players who would probably never have joined private clubs.

Back in 1923, Jack Cuthbert (then the amateur champion of Manitoba) said it all in the *Winnipeg Free Press*:

How much the vastly increased popularity of the game is due to this venture [Winnipeg's municipal golf course] cannot easily be estimated, but there is little room for doubt that many of the hundreds, who are now among the city's most ardent enthusiasts, were first inveigled into playing at the Municipal course.

Of all the changes wrought to the face of golf between the wars, the introduction of public courses did most for the well-being of the game. In North America, public links golfers now outnumber club golfers by something like four to one.

The dramatic increase in the number of clubs in western Canada led to renewed demand that the national championship live up to its name, for the Amateur was in no wise national.

For its first twenty-five years, the RCGA had little incentive to be a truly national organization. It served golf clubs in Ontario and Quebec, where the great majority of the nation's clubs were, and where the national championships were held.

The clubs in the Maritimes apparently accepted this state of affairs and ran their own regional tournaments. The clubs in British Columbia also realized that geography was not on their side. But having helped organize a Pacific Northwest Golf Association, golfers on the coast had something more competitive to shoot for than club and provincial titles.

The golfing balance of power between east and west started to shift right after the First World War. When the RCGA was formed in 1895, only 10 per cent of the nation's population of five million lived west of Ontario; by 1920, four times as many people lived in the West, making up some 22 per cent of the nation's population of nearly nine million.

By the mid-1920s, the Prairie provinces had as many clubs as Central Canada, although fewer golfers. Reflecting this new strength, the clubs in the Prairies demanded some say

Past Presidents Royal Canadian Golf Association

PAUL MYLER
Hamilton Golf

R. C. H. CASSELS, K.C.
Toronto Golf

C. A. BOGERT
Toronto Golf

FRANK A. ROLPH
Lambton Golf

W. W. WALKER
Royal Montreal

W. E. MATTHEWS
Royal Ottawa

S. B. GUNDY
Rosedale

Some past presidents of the RCGA.

in where Canada's national championships were held, particularly the Amateur.

Until the Second World War, for a Canadian club to be awarded the Amateur was to be given the jewel in the RCGA's crown, a nod that acknowledged one's course was considered a championship course, a wink that said one's clubhouse was considered fit for the elite of Canadian golf. What is more, having the Amateur at one's club or in one's city meant that local golfers could play in Canada's pre-

mier tournament without the inconvenience and high cost of travel.

Up to 1920, the Canadian Amateur had always been awarded to clubs in Central Canada, so that a *total* of three or four golfers had entered from clubs west of Thunder Bay and not many more from clubs east of Quebec City. The RCGA had not planned it that way. It was made inevitable by the geography of the country.

As early as 1911, Winnipeg GC had threatened to split with the RCGA and form a Western Canada golf association. At the end of the First World War, this threat was renewed. The RCGA perceived such a move more as a threat against the integrity of its Amateur championship, than as one against its authority as the governing body for golf in Canada. R. C. H. Cassels of Toronto GC wrote in *Canadian Golfer* in 1919:

> If the RCGA continues to hold the championship meetings in Ontario and Quebec, exclusively, the result is almost certain to be that a new association will be formed in the West, which association will hold its own championship meeting . . . There will be no real championship of Canada, but merely a championship of each of the different associations.

As a solution, he proposed that the RCGA divide into four or five districts and organize district championships. The district semi-finalists would then compete in the Amateur championship "to be held in a city not further west than Winnipeg, nor further east than Montreal."

The response was not encouraging. Wrote Vere Brown from Winnipeg: "I am inclined to think that the West and East are too far removed geographically to justify hope that an ordinary meet of the RCGA held in Winnipeg would be much more largely attended from Ontario and Quebec, than the tournament now held at alternate Eastern points is attended by players from the West." He was to be proved correct.

When the RCGA awarded the 1921 Amateur championship to Winnipeg, the results did not serve well the cause of Canada-wide championships. The event was marked by the entire absence of golfers from British Columbia and the Maritimes, and a slim representation from Quebec, which did not even enter a team for the interprovincial match. The holder of the Amateur championship, C. B. Grier of Royal Montreal, did not even show up to defend his title.

R. C. S. Bruce of Winnipeg, first president of the Western Canada Golf Association.

Naturally, there was a great deal of resentment in the West at the indifference of Quebec to the first national event to be held at a Western club.

As a further step towards reconciliation, the RCGA brought more Western representatives onto its executive committee in 1922. Traditionally, the ten-man executive committee that ran the affairs of the association had been selected from those clubs in Central Canada that hosted the national championships. Now, one seat was awarded to the Maritimes and three seats to the West (one each to Winnipeg, Calgary, and Vancouver).

None of these steps hit at the root of the problem. Within the RCGA two irreconcilables were at work: a desire to make the Amateur truly national in character, and a need to do this without paying the expenses of amateurs who had to travel far to play in it. So the three Prairie provinces elected to run their own Western Canada championships. The officers of the Manitoba and Alberta golf associations took the lead in promoting the Western Canada Golf Association, organized in 1923.

British Columbia declined an invitation to join, so the WCGA became an organization of the three Prairie golf associations, with the following executive: President, R. C. S. Bruce, Norwood GC, Winnipeg; First VP, Lorne Johnson, Wascana CC, Regina; Second VP, Tom Gillespie, Calgary G & CC; Secretary-Treasurer, A. Innes Mackenzie, Alcrest GC, Winnipeg. The committee included Sir Frederick Haultain.

Bruce had come to Winnipeg in 1911 to work for the Manitoba Government Telephones. Previously a member of Royal Musselburgh, he joined Winnipeg GC and was largely responsible for its survival. He guided the club through its difficult years to see it flourish under its new name of Norwood GC.

He also helped organize the Manitoba Golf Association and was its president. Although a strong advocate of a Western golf association, he remained one of the best friends the RCGA had in the West: "I am sure that with the hearty co-operation of the provincial associations – and that is assured from the West – a National Association both in name and in fact, will be attained."

Bruce made it clear at the outset that his WCGA was designed only to foster competitive golf in the West and was not out to usurp the authority of the RCGA on other matters. (There was never any question of the WCGA adopting a confrontational stance like that of the Western Golf Association in the United States, which for years had an acrimonious relationship with the USGA, and went its own way in changing some of the rules of golf.)

The first WCGA championships were held in September 1924, at Saskatoon. Thereafter, each Prairie province took its turn at being host. The championships consisted of an Amateur, an Open, sometimes an event confined to professionals, sometimes a team event, all held in conjunction with the host province's own championships.

The WCGA did what it set out to do. It raised the standard of golf in the Prairie provinces by providing competition keener than amateurs and professionals could find within their own provinces.

This did not mean that the Western provinces gave up their bid to have the Canadian Amateur held regularly at a western venue, but they realized this would only come about if the leading golfers from each province could somehow be reimbursed for travelling to the Amateur. This idea was first muted by the RCGA's secretary, B. L. Anderson, in a series of articles published in *Canadian Golfer* in the last quarter of 1925. Anderson made these points: the Amateur championship should be contested by players selected by provincial or regional golf associations, although open to other players; there were already precedents in amateur sport for paying the travelling expenses of selected players. The members of the British Walker Cup team had their expenses paid when they travelled to the United States; the money could be raised by a tax of only thirty-five cents a year on each member of a club belonging to a provincial or regional golf association.

The matter of paying the expenses of players came to a head in 1926 at the RCGA's Annual General Meeting. The response from R. C. H. Cassels, as legal advisor to the RCGA and member of the Rules of Golf Committee, was immediate and unequivocal:

Whatever the views of the individual delegates may be as to the payment of expenses, St. Andrews has ruled that it is not legitimate for a player, to take part in a tournament, to accept any part of his expenses. Any person so doing would lose his amateur standing.

As secretary of the RCGA, B. L. Anderson could hardly express his own views at the meeting, but others could. George S. Lyon was present, as was William J. Thompson, secretary of the Ontario Golf Association. They reminded the meeting that the expenses of the British Walker Cup team were paid, with the approval of the R & A, because they travelled and played *as a team*. Said Lyon: "If it is possible to have a team, or an Inter-provincial team, of, say, four, or five, or six players go to the tournament, you would be quite within your rights to pay their expenses, but they would have to pay their own expenses after the [team] match was over."

Could not the RCGA revive the interprovincial team matches, dropped in 1921, which had traditionally been held in conjunction with the Canadian Amateur? This would enable each province, within the R & A guidelines on amateur status, to pay the travelling expenses of a team to the interprovincial matches, and hence to the Canadian Amateur.

In effect, that is what was done. The interprovincial team matches were revived in 1927. The governor general, Lord Willingdon, later presented a cup, so that these came to be known as the Willingdon Cup matches.

In 1927, three provinces sent teams, in 1928, five provinces, and in 1929, six. The expenses of the four men making up each team were pooled, so that distant provinces, such as British Columbia, did not suffer unduly. The RCGA shared the cost with the provincial associations. In this way, the Canadian Amateur became, for the first time, a truly national event.

Why had this not been done sooner, say in 1919, when the RCGA looked at ways of making its championship more representative? The answer given in 1926 was that in 1919 there were no golf associations in Quebec, Ontario, and British Columbia, and the payments to players had to be made by the provincial associations they were representing.

But that is not strictly the whole answer. There had also been a change in attitudes by 1926. The payment of travelling expenses to amateurs, even as teams, would have been repugnant to many of Canada's golf administrators in 1919. It may have been slightly less so in 1926. But the Canadian Amateur had to be saved. This, then, was the solution of last resort.

R. C. S. Bruce should have been at this historic meeting in 1926, as Manitoba's representative on the RCGA executive. When he could not attend, Charles Harvey came in his place. Harvey spoke eloquently on behalf of the West. Three years later he was elected president of the RCGA, the first president from a province outside Ontario and Quebec.

The 1929 Canadian Amateur Championship at Jasper, Alberta, was only the second in thirty-five years to be held outside Central Canada. It was a much different affair from the Winnipeg Amateur of 1921. Six provinces entered teams of four for the interprovincial matches, ensuring that the entries for the Amateur included the finest golfers from East and West. The Jasper Amateur was probably the first having the right to call itself "national."

Acting on Charles Harvey's suggestion, the RCGA agreed that every third Canadian Amateur should be awarded to the West. Western venues were chosen three times in the 1930s, although the 1939 Amateur at Edmonton's Mayfair had to be cancelled because of the war.

Even as the West was making its case, the award was diminishing in stature. The Canadian Open was replacing the Amateur as the golfing event of the year. The 1989 Amateur was held at the Oakfield G & CC in Halifax, but only a few lines were devoted to it in *The Globe and Mail*, our national newspaper. That would have been unthinkable in the 1920s.

17
CHAPTER

LADIES COAST
TO COAST

THE CANADIAN LADIES' GOLF CHAMPI-onships, last held in 1913, were revived in 1919.

In the intervening years, women's golf had grown in numbers and stature, to some extent reflecting the changing attitudes of society towards women in sport brought about by the war. But much of the credit must go to Florence Harvey and the CLGU. Her newsletters in *Canadian Golfer* found their way into homes and clubhouses across Canada, bringing women golfers closer, encouraging others to play.

Florence Harvey had given interclub matches a new and nobler sense of purpose – raising money for war charities. By 1919, however, the ladies were ready to resume their national championships.

A visitor to these early post-war tournaments who had not seen women's golf since 1913 would have noticed that skirts were shorter, halfway to the knees. They were also lighter and brighter, and were worn with blouses in a dazzling array of colours. Boots had given way to shoes, more or less: rubber-soled shoes if the ground was dry, leather-soled and studded if the ground was wet.

The visitor could easily have mistaken the championships for a six-day glorious garden party, one of the great social events of the year. The new governor general, Lord Byng of Vimy, might be there, with Lady Byng, and not just to present the prizes, but to walk round the course, keen golfers as they were. And if Lord and Lady Byng weren't present, then the prime minister, the Right Honourable Arthur Meighen, with Lady Meighen, might be seen at the dinner dances for five hundred guests.

Early Ford automobiles would chug up to the clubhouse, transporting early flappers. Afternoon tea on the lawn was a treat not to be missed, if you wanted to hear how Effie was doing in the fourth consolation event. Or even the sixth consolation event, for the ladies were there to play competitive golf the entire week, and the CLGU and the host club put up dozens of prizes, which could be viewed during the week by going to the men's billiard room. The men had given up not only their days on the course that week, but also their locker-room.

The main prize would be presented to the new champion at the closing dinner on the Saturday night. Almost a decade earlier, in 1911,

Dorothy Campbell had won outright the original trophy put up by Lady Grey. The Duchess of Connaught, the patroness of the CLGU in 1919, put up the Duchess of Connaught Gold Cup to replace it. Each winner of the Ladies' Open held the cup for a year, and was given a gold medal to keep. For the first time in 1920, she would also have her name inscribed on the championship shield bought by the CLGU, which showed the winners since 1901.

While all the ancillary events would be taking place, the real struggle for the ladies' championship of Canada would be followed by some five hundred spectators. Only thirty-two of the hundred or so entries would qualify for the 18-hole match-play event, with its 36-hole final on the Saturday.

Most of those eliminated in the qualifying round, or in the early match-play rounds, would compete in the consolation events. Others would caddie for sisters or friends still in the competition.

There were no social barriers to preclude any woman in Canada from competing in the ladies' championships. But she did have to belong to a golf club affiliated to the CLGU, and she did need a CLGU handicap of not more than 24 (reduced to 20 in 1921, and to 15 five years later). Too, it was almost a necessity to know a member of the host club who could put her up for the week or arrange for her to share a bedroom in the clubhouse. In the national championships held between the wars, it seems there was only one competitor who was a member of a municipal golf club: Mrs. Murdoch of the Humber Valley GC, Toronto.

The geographical barriers were more evident. From 1901 to 1925, the national ladies' championships were held in Montreal or Toronto or Ottawa, once in Hamilton. In 1926, 1933, and 1937 they were given to Winnipeg; in 1935, to Vancouver. So while national in name, most of them were regional in practice, since many women could not afford the time and money to travel across Canada to play golf.

The men got around this problem in 1927 by organizing interprovincial team matches – that paid team expenses – to coincide with

their national Amateur. But a lack of funds prevented the CLGU from doing the same until 1934. In that year, Ontario, Quebec, British Columbia, and Manitoba each sent their top four women golfers to Scarboro. If any championship could be said to be the first truly national championship, this was it. Significantly, it was won by Vera Ramsay Ford, of the Shaughnessy Heights club, Vancouver. She was one of a few who would occasionally make the journey east.

Although travelling great distances to compete deterred Canadian golfers from the West and the Maritimes, it did not discourage some of the top players from the United States and Britain. From 1901 to 1912, the Canadian ladies' championship had been a Close affair. If a woman wanted to play, her club had to be a member of the RCGA. In 1913, the entry conditions were relaxed so that three visitors from the British Isles, Misses Dodd, Ravenscroft, and Harrison, could play. It had been the intention of the newly formed CLGU to open up the championship permanently. But the RCGA restricted the 1919 championships to members of CLGU clubs, to give Canadian women golfers a year's grace before facing international competition.

In 1920, the championship was thrown open to all women golfers from Britain and the United States who were in good standing with their national golf associations. This move was welcomed by Canada's leading women golfers who, on the face of it, would seem to have the most to lose. Florence Harvey echoed their views when she wrote: "Until we can defend it successfully, let the Canadian National title be held by an outsider, so long as it brings us better players to compete with, from whom we can learn much."

As it turned out, only one foreign player came to Hamilton in 1920. Alexa Stirling of Atlanta was a three-time winner of the U.S. ladies' title. She now added the Canadian championship to a long string of honours.

Next year, at Ottawa, it was an altogether different story. British champion Cecil Leitch, her sister Edith, and another British internationalist, Doris Chambers, stopped over in Ottawa on their way to the U.S. championships. Alexa Stirling came up from Atlanta, bringing with her Mrs. Gavin, an English golfer then living in New York, who had won the British title in 1916.

Alexa Stirling and the two Leitch girls made their way to the semi-finals, together with a clever little left-hander from Beaconsfield, Molly McBride. To everyone's astonishment, including her own, Molly McBride defeated Edith Leitch. And having done so, she openly apologized to a player who would have beaten her nineteen times out of twenty. (Her guilt was compounded by the fact that Edith Leitch had earlier shown her how to correct some weak spots in her game.) But Molly McBride was no match for Cecil Leitch in the final. So, for the second time, the championship went to Britain.

As a result of all of this, the year 1922 saw yet another innovation, one that was to prove controversial for most of its forty-six-year life: the Canadian Ladies' Close Championship.

In introducing a second national event with entries restricted to members of CLGU clubs, the CLGU acted with the best of intentions. But it also acted on the premises that there would always be a number of American or British players eager to play in the Canadian championships and that Canada's women golfers could meet the mental and physical demands of two national championships in two weeks. For these had to be played back-to-back, the Ladies' Open and Close. Some golfers were already unwilling to travel long distances to one national championship in a year, never mind two a month or so apart. So, between the wars, the Open and the Close were held in the same city, at different courses, with only a Sunday's rest in between.

There was much to be said for a Canadian Close championship. Many women who did not play in the Open turned out for this tournament. But when it was held one week before the Open, as it sometimes was, it clearly did more harm than good. No golfer, man or woman, could be expected to retain his or her concentration, to say nothing of physical strength, for two weeks of match-play golf.

Having won the Close championship in 1927, a tired Ada Mackenzie played uninspired golf in the Open that followed, and lost.

In 1931, the defending Close champion, Margery Kirkham, played for six days in the Open, was defeated in the final, then went on to play stale golf for five days in the Close. She lost. Holding the Open immediately before the Close was a favour only to those knocked out early in the Open.

There were years when no leading American or British players came to the Open. Since all the arrangements had been made with the host club, the Open and Close championships went ahead, with identical or nearly identical fields. Take the 1926 events, held in Winnipeg. The semi-finalists in the Open at Elmhurst were Ada Mackenzie, Helen Paget, Vera Ramsay Hutchings, and Cecil Smith. The semi-finalists in the Close at St. Charles were Ada Mackenzie, Helen Paget, Vera Ramsay Hutchings, and Dora Virtue. In both the Open and Close finals, Ada Mackenzie defeated Helen Paget, by an almost identical margin.

These seemingly absurd situations provided ammunition for those who wanted to scrap the Close. But in retrospect, it is fairer to dismiss Winnipeg as an anomaly, a reasonable cost to pay for the pleasure that the Close gave to so many golfers.

If the first Close championship in 1922 proved anything, it was that women golfers were quite capable of running their own tournaments. But when the CLGU suggested that it should also take over responsibility for the Ladies' Open, there was more rattling of dry bones within the RCGA.

R. C. H. Cassels, KC, a former president and a stickler for the written word of the RCGA's constitution, was strongly opposed to any change: the RCGA's mandate required it to be responsible for the running of the ladies' championships. However, a compromise was reached at the RCGA's Annual General Meeting in 1924, when it was resolved that "this Association meet the wishes of the officers of the Canadian Ladies' Golf Union by naming ladies suggested by them on a Committee of the Royal Canadian Golf Association for the purpose of conducting the Canadian Ladies' Championship Tournament for 1924."

That may have been the intention. In fact, the ladies of the CLGU virtually took over the running of their Open from 1924. When the RCGA revised its constitution in 1948, it made no mention of ladies' championships.

Before we look at some of the women champions between the wars, a word about the general level of scoring.

Drawing conclusions from a comparison of scores at the beginning and the end of these two decades is a process fraught with hazards. Changes to courses and the state of the weather can distort the truth. But one gets a general impression that better equipment and improved skills led to scores being lowered by something like ten strokes a round in championship golf.

In 1919, an 88 won the qualifying round at Beaconsfield; in 1928, the lowest score at the same club was 78. The course was longer and more heavily bunkered in 1928, but its greens were in better condition.

The introduction of steel shafts, legalized in Canada in 1926, probably did more for women than for men. In 1919, Ada Mackenzie came second in the long-driving competition, her longest single drive being 200 yards. When she won the same competition in 1929, her best drive was 34 yards longer. There is no proof that she had changed to steel by 1929 but it seems likely that she had.

In the 1990s there is no Close championship, and the Open is now called the "Canadian Ladies' Amateur Championship." The word "amateur" was not needed between the wars, since Canada had no playing professionals who were women. For the sake of both simplicity and historical accuracy, I will refer to the two championships as the Open and the Close. Again, for reasons of historical accuracy, I consider the championships of 1901 through 1919 as having been Close, which they were, with the exception of 1913.

The statistics for the years 1919 through 1938 are given below. These show the names of the winners and of those who reached the semi-finals of the Open or Close at least three times. The statistics for the Close are in parentheses:

	Number of Times							
	Semi-finalist		Finalist		Winner		Medallist	
Ada Mackenzie	8	(11)	6	(8)	4	(6)	7	(3)
Alexa Stirling Fraser	8		4		2		4	(1)
Glenna Collett (U.S.)	3		2		2		3	
Maureen Orcutt (U.S.)	2		2		2		2	
Sydney Pepler Mulqueen	4	(4)	1	(2)	1	(2)	1	(1)
Margery Kirkham	4	(3)	4	(3)	1	(1)	1	(3)
Mrs. W. A. Gavin (U.S.)	2		2		1		—	
Helen Hicks (U.S.)	2		2		1		1	
Dora Virtue Darling	1	(3)	1	(1)	1		—	(1)
Mrs. John Rogers	1	(1)	1	(1)	1		—	
Virginia Wilson (U.S.)	1		1		1		1	
Helen Payson (U.S.)	1		1		1		—	
Cecil Leitch (England)	1		1		1		1	
Vera Ramsay Hutchings Ford	3	(4)	—	(2)	—	(2)	1	(2)
Frances Scott Gibson	2	(4)	—	(2)	—	(1)	1	
Helen Paget	1	(4)	1	(3)	—	(1)	—	
Mrs. Eric Phillips	2	(1)	1		—		—	
Mrs. E. W. Whittington	—	(3)	—	(1)	—		—	
Irene Jolin Horne	—	(1)	—	(1)	—	(1)	—	
Heather Leslie	—	(1)	—	(1)	—	(1)	—	

Alexa Stirling won her first Open in 1920, as a U.S. citizen, and before she became Mrs. Fraser. She played in the Close only once.

Ada Mackenzie is usually credited with winning five Open and five Close championships. In fact, her 1919 win was a Close.

The names of pre-First World War champions will not be found in this list. Three-time winner Dorothy Campbell Hurd now lived in the United States. She played in the Canadian Ladies' Open in 1923, but the eventual winner, Glenna Collett, knocked her out in round three. She tried again in 1925. This time, Toronto's Sydney Pepler Mulqueen put her out in the same round.

Several of the younger pre-war players went on to make a name for themselves. Frances Scott Gibson (in the record book as Mrs. Hope Gibson, later as Mrs. Gordon Ferrie) rather surprisingly won a gold medal only once. Effie Nesbitt of Woodstock continued to play in the CLGU championships long after time had overtaken her game. (Her good work on the CLGU Pars Committee earned her plaudits from the LGU in England.) And then, of course, there was Ada Mackenzie.

"This plucky little girl played to the best of her ability," a newspaperman had written of her when she had appeared in her first national championship in 1912, one month before her twenty-first birthday. Had she not missed a one-foot putt on the seventeenth green at Rosedale, she would have eliminated the Scottish, British, and Canadian champion, Dorothy Campbell, in the third round. What is more, the cup presented to Dorothy Campbell by Lady Grey would never have left Canada in 1912, but would have become the property of Marlene Stewart Streit in 1956 . . . But golf is a game of ifs. Ada missed the putt, and that is that.

Ada Mackenzie went on to become indisputably the finest woman golfer Canada produced in the years between the wars. She was as much loved and admired by women golfers as George Lyon was by the men, and had many of the same characteristics: a love for all sports, for fair play, for winning (but not at all costs), for never giving in, for being gracious in victory as in defeat, for never making excuses.

Her record in women's national golf in Canada, below, has been bettered only by Marlene Stewart Streit, to whom she gave much encouragement when Marlene was just beginning her career, over a generation later:

Canadian Ladies' Open Champion: 1925, 1926, 1933, 1935.
Canadian Ladies' Close Champion: 1919, 1926, 1927, 1929, 1931, 1933.
Canadian Ladies' Senior GA Champion: 1955 through 1960, 1962, 1965.

In the United States, Ada Mackenzie twice reached the semi-finals of the women's amateur championship, in 1927 and in 1932, and was the medallist in 1927.

Ada Charlotte Mackenzie was born in the west end of Toronto on 30 October 1891, one of four children of a well-to-do family, including her twin brother, George. She was educated at Toronto's private Havergal Ladies' College (1903–11). There, she developed into an all-round athlete, captaining the hockey, tennis, basketball, and cricket teams. For two or three years, she served as a sports instructor to the same school.

Ada Mackenzie's father was a Scot, a keen and proficient club golfer, as was her mother. They were members of the Highlands Golf Club, which was organized in 1901, with a course in West Toronto Junction. At Highlands, Ada picked up the rudiments of the game. When only thirteen, she played in her first match, taking the place of her mother in a mixed foursome. She and her father won the prize for the low gross. When Highlands was disbanded in 1905, her parents moved (along with many other members) to the Mississaugua club, where Ada became a junior member. "I started golfing when women were supposed to know more about a cook stove than a niblick," she told a reporter many years later.

After three or four summers on the links, often playing with her father and his friends, Ada Mackenzie became closely attached to

A youthful Ada Mackenzie of Mississauga Golf Club, winner of the Rosedale Field Day, 1917.

the game. Early in 1912, she took lessons from the club's professional, Willie Locke. He urged her to enter for the national championships at Rosedale. Hence her encounter with Dorothy Campbell.

During the war years, she went to work for the Canadian Bank of Commerce, but played enough golf to win several club championships at Toronto GC and at Mississaugua. She also had a few golf lessons from George Cumming at his winter school, where he coached her in her mashie (or mid-iron) play. Then, for a week before the first post-war Close championship at Beaconsfield, she placed herself in the hands of the new professional at Mississaugua, Pritchard. He rapidly rounded her game into championship form.

Ada in 1932.

Ada, driving, with Britain's Joyce Wethered.

With a CLGU handicap of 6, Ada Mackenzie was one of several fancied players going into the 1919 championships. She went through the field with relative ease, but Kate Robertson of Beaconsfield gave her a fight in the final. Outdriven by 10 to 20 yards, she took Ada Mackenzie to the nineteenth green before losing to superior putting.

This was the first of many national titles to come her way. But for five years, even Ada Mackenzie could do nothing against the best of the Americans.

The American challenge to Canadian women golfers started with the first post-war Open of 1920. Over the next few years, the invasion of American and British girls continued to be so strong in numbers and quality that no Canadian won the Duchess of Connaught Cup until Ada Mackenzie in 1925. This win in the Open confirmed her place as Canada's leading woman golfer.

The 1925 Open at Royal Ottawa attracted the cream of America's ladies, with the notable exception of the championship holder, Glenna Collett. Dorothy Campbell Hurd came up from her new home in Philadelphia. It was generally predicted at the beginning of the week that she and Alexa Stirling Fraser (who was now married and playing out of Royal Ottawa) would be left to fight it out for the title.

Ten Americans and twenty-two Canadians qualified for the match-play rounds. Significantly, Alexa Stirling Fraser led the qualifiers with an 83. Ada Mackenzie's 85 nipped third-placed Dorothy Campbell Hurd by a stroke. After two days of rain – yes, the weather continued to be unkind to the ladies – the course was playing long, although in good condition.

Sydney Pepler Mulqueen of Toronto GC, the destroyer of so many hopes in ladies' championships, disposed of Dorothy Campbell Hurd in round three. This assured, more or less, a Fraser–Mackenzie final.

Both finalists had reasonable excuses for playing below their best. Alexa Stirling Fraser had undergone a severe operation a year earlier and had played little competitive golf since. Ada Mackenzie's preoccupation with launching her Ladies' Golf and Tennis Club had kept her off the course. But there is no doubt whatsoever about the reason for her fine victory of 5 and 4. Practice and more practice had brought her short game – approaching and putting – to a level where she could match any British or American golfer. On fourteen of the thirty-two holes played in the final, she was down in one putt or was conceded her first putt. She three-putted but once. That was to give her the edge over Alexa Stirling Fraser in 1925, since both ladies were hitting the ball about the same distance off the tee, averaging over 200 yards.

It was a particularly important win for Ada Mackenzie and for Canada. It brought the Canadian Ladies' Open title to this country for the first time; it showed that foreign stars were not invincible.

Ada Mackenzie successfully defended her title in 1926, and she also won the Close. The venue that year was Winnipeg. It was an unpopular choice with the American girls, and none turned up for the Open. Despite the brave face put on by the CLGU, it had to admit that the Close was superfluous that year. Both events had almost identical, and parochial, fields, since two-thirds of the thirty-six qualifiers came from Winnipeg or Toronto. Only one came from the province of Quebec, only one from British Columbia. The first CLGU championship held west of Ontario may have succeeded in bringing the ladies' championships to the Prairies, but it also attracted the weakest Open field to date.

In the Open, Ada Mackenzie defeated Helen Paget by 8 and 6 in the final. The Close was almost a repeat of the Open – three of the same semi-finalists, the same finalists, and an almost identical win by Ada Mackenzie over Helen Paget, by 7 and 6. Ada went on to complete her final round in 77 strokes. At the time, this was said to be the lowest score ever shot by a woman in the West.

Ada Mackenzie had to wait seven years for her third Open victory. In the intervening years, the title went to Americans, five times out of six.

In 1933, the venue was again Winnipeg. Again, no Americans turned up. Again, the Open championship was largely duplicated in the Close. In both events, Ada Mackenzie defeated Mrs. Bearisto of Winnipeg in the semi-finals, Margery Kirkham of Montreal in the final.

The Open was played over Pine Ridge, soggy with rain. Neither the usually strong

The 1930 Ladies' Open. Left to right, *Glenna Collett (U.S.), Simone Thion de La Chaume (France), Bernice Wall (U.S.), Ada Mackenzie, Helen Payson (U.S.), Edith Quier (U.S.), and Virginia Van Wie (U.S.).*

Mrs. Bearisto nor Margery Kirkham put up any sort of fight. Ada Mackenzie tended to be wild off the tee that week, but the rest of her game was almost faultless. This was as one-sided a final as had been seen in years, with Ada winning by the same margin as in her previous victory in Winnipeg, 8 and 6.

She achieved the double for the second time, but her margin in the Close over Margery Kirkham was only 3 and 1 (over 18 holes).

Her fourth and last Open win came two years later. In Vancouver there were more Americans in the field, but none of the stars from the eastern U.S. This championship was history-making in its excellent representation from across Canada. The CLGU had introduced interprovincial team matches in 1934, so four players from each province could now be sent to the championships with their travel expenses paid. For the first time in women's golf, east went west. This brought out Violet Pooley Sweeney, who had last played in the Open of 1913. After defeating Toronto's Sydney

Pepler Mulqueen, she was herself knocked out, but not before proving she had lost few of her old skills.

Most of the 1935 final between Ada Mackenzie and Mme. Ragene Dagenais of Montreal was played in a downpour. Only six spectators braved the pelting rain to watch the morning round. They saw Ada go to lunch 4 up. In the afternoon, Mme. Dagenais made a brave start, taking the first hole, but from the sixth her game went to pieces; off-line drives, shanked irons, missed putts. As the weather improved, more spectators appeared, but they were to see little of the match. Ada Mackenzie was playing relentless golf, setting par and not the score of her luckless opponent as her target. She won the sixth, seventh, ninth, tenth, eleventh. *Canadian Golfer* reported:

> The end of the match came so quickly that even the two finalists didn't know it was over. They started to walk towards the twelfth tee when someone in the gallery started to

applaud the victory. Suddenly realizing that it was "all over," Mme. Dagenais laughed, shook hands and congratulated her opponent.

Ada Mackenzie's six Close championships came in 1919, 1926, 1927, 1929, 1931, and 1933. The Close was not held in 1928 and 1932, so Ada won in every year but one (1930) in the period 1926 through 1933.

All this is merely the statistical support for the claim that Ada Mackenzie was by far the finest woman golfer produced by Canada between the wars.

Ranking her internationally is more difficult. Two of her four wins in the Open were accomplished in Winnipeg, one in Vancouver, where the low turn-out of American women detracts somewhat from her victories. In the years when the American and British challenge was at its strongest, Ada Mackenzie's record hardly places her in the top echelons of international golf. In 1925 she won, in 1924 she reached the finals, but in eight years she did not make the semi-finals. Overall, her record in the Open is not quite up to the standard of the young American-born girl who became a Canadian upon her marriage in 1925 – Alexa Stirling Fraser.

Ada Mackenzie was also a successful businesswoman. In 1924 she launched her Ladies' Golf and Tennis Club of Toronto, raising the money by an issue of bonds and shares. It is not a club exclusively for women, but one in which women have priority when it comes to hours of play, in contra-distinction to most other clubs that restrict the hours when women may play. This club was not born of pique, but of practicality. A businesswoman is, after all, as entitled as a businessman to play golf on Saturday morning. Ada made her point in an article in *Canadian Golfer*, in 1924:

> The idea of forming such a club originated some years ago when I was in England. Realizing the opportunities that were open to English girls to enjoy the game and learn it from childhood up, it occurred to me that such a club would give our girls a chance . . . The business girl, teacher or parent can at their leisure make use of our new club, and spend delightful week ends when desired.

In spite of local cynicism – mainly from men – she quickly raised some $40,000 through a bond issue, and the club was under way. Today, it has over six hundred members.

In 1930, she launched a more personal venture, Ada Mackenzie Ltd., a quality sportswear store in Toronto. Her niece, Phyllis Ball, has recalled that this venture was inspired by Ada Mackenzie's own unfortunate experiences with women's golfwear, which was useless in wet weather.

There is record of one misadventure in the rain. In 1925, she played in the U.S. ladies' championship at St. Louis. In her second-round match, Ada was 2 up at the thirteenth, when heavy rain began to fall. Her knitted frock was quite unsuited for wet weather, and it slowly stretched to her ankles. More important, she was wearing rubber-soled, unspiked shoes, as she usually did on dry summer days. She sent to the clubhouse for her spikes. But by the time they arrived she had lost three holes and could only halve the last two to finish 1 down.

Ada Mackenzie was, in a way, a trailblazer. She showed Canadian girls the way to victory, one they could follow, if they were prepared to work hard, to believe in themselves, even to the extent of venturing south. She was inspirational, without being intimidating. All this without losing her fine sense of humour, the twinkle in her eye. She never married. "Too busy," she said. Diabetes weakened her in her later years. After several heart attacks she died in January 1973. These words were written for her memorial service:

> She will always be remembered not only for her championships and honours, but also for the encouragement and help she gave to everyone with whom she came in contact. None of the younger generation of golfers will forget the trouble she took to give them advice on the game, or the example she set of the highest ideals of sportsmanship.

Her record is on display at the Canadian Golf Hall of Fame, alongside that of her friend Florence Harvey. In 1975, some of her many friends started the Ada Mackenzie Memorial Foundation, which raises money to help a number of good causes.

Keenly fought but friendly, the battles between Ada Mackenzie and Alexa Stirling Fraser were few in number but, nevertheless, highlights of women's golf in Canada between the wars.

Despite her sturdy appearance, Alexa Stirling Fraser was not very strong, which may explain why she did not compete in the Close championship. Perhaps she felt that two weeks of competitive golf would have been too much for her. But perhaps she also wanted to leave some of the cream for others. In any case, the two met only in the Open.

A meeting between them became an event of national importance in the world of golf.

As players, they were clearly superior to all other Canadians in the field. Both were vulnerable to defeat by others but had reserves of concentration and perseverance that saw them win after being several holes down in a match.

Of the two, Alexa Stirling Fraser has the more impressive record. In ten appearances in the Canadian Ladies' Open between 1920 and 1938, she reached the semi-finals eight times, the finals four times, and won twice. (This record for consistency has been bettered only by Marlene Stewart Streit.) Of her four clashes with Ada Mackenzie, she won three. Before becoming a Canadian in 1925, Alexa Stirling had won three U.S. ladies' titles. In 1920 she held both the U.S. and Canadian titles.

In 1932, the CLGU ranked Alexa Stirling Fraser Canada's top woman golfer. They gave her a plus 1 handicap, two strokes lower than her friend and opponent Ada Mackenzie.

Born in the United States of a Scottish father and an English mother, Alexa Stirling Fraser played out of the Royal Ottawa Golf Club for

U.S. champion Alexa Stirling first won the Canadian title in 1920.

Alexa at the time of her marriage, 1925.

most of her competitive golfing life. Her brilliant record has generally been overshadowed in Canada by Ada's, but that would not have concerned this modest woman. She was happy to stay in the background with her family and let her record speak for her.

Alexa's father, Dr. S. W. Stirling, had golfed in Edinburgh before moving to Atlanta, Georgia, where he was the British correspondent (something akin to a consul). In Atlanta, Alexa Stirling grew up alongside Bobby Jones. Both were junior members of the Atlanta Athletic club, both were coached by Stewart Maiden and acquired his Carnoustie swing.

She won the U.S. title in 1916, when only nineteen. There were no championships in 1917 or 1918, but she held on to her title in 1919 and again in 1920.

During the war years, she, Bobby Jones, and two others raised $50,000 for charities by playing together in exhibition matches. But Alexa Stirling also drove a truck for the Women's Motor Reserve Corps.

Queen Alexa – as they called her in Atlanta – met Dr. Wilbur Grieve Fraser at the Royal Ottawa Golf Club when she came up for the 1921 Ladies' Open. They became engaged in 1924 and married a year later. Alexa Stirling Fraser settled in Ottawa for the rest of her life, enriching Canadian golf with her personality and skills.

She was an outstanding violinist. "I prefer playing the violin to playing golf," she told O. B. Keeler, Jones's biographer. Never a strong girl, she often found a week of competitive golf as much as she could stand. A serious operation in 1924 kept her away from tournament golf that summer. Thereafter, she limited her appearances in national championships.

Her golf swing had been firmly rooted by Stewart Maiden and was much admired and envied. She was, by the unanimous consent of the experts of the day, the finest swinger of a club on either side of the Atlantic.

The first Mackenzie–Stirling meeting was in the Open of 1922. The draw was not seeded, so they met as early as the second round. Their match captured almost the entire gallery at the

Toronto Golf Club. The qualifying round had been delayed because of torrential rain, so the course was playing several strokes longer than its 6,400 yards and its ladies' par of 79. Even so, both got off to a scrappy start. They reached the turn all square, but needed 44 strokes to get there. Seven of the nine holes had been halved.

The golf improved in the second nine. Ada Mackenzie took the lead at the tenth, increased it at the twelfth. But Alexa Stirling often played her best golf when behind, and she did so now, squaring the match by winning the thirteenth and fifteenth. They were still all square on the eighteenth green. Here Ada Mackenzie misjudged her long approach putt, leaving herself a nine-footer. She missed. Rather than ask her opponent to hole out from about two feet, she picked up, conceding the match. They had rounds of 84 and 86. This was considered fine golf in 1922, given the playing length of the course.

Alexa Stirling went on to the final, where she lost 2 down to Mrs. Gavin, the former British champion then living in New York. (Although it went to the eighteenth green, their final took only two hours to play, a sad reflection on today's snailpacers. It was virtually over when Miss Stirling tangled with the bushes of the seventeenth hole, The Graveyard.)

In 1925, at Ottawa's Rivermead, Alexa Stirling led the qualifiers of the Close championship, but played only to help Royal Ottawa in the team competition and did not go on to the match-play rounds. Her 77 was six ahead of Ada Mackenzie, who in turn was five ahead of the others.

In the following week, at Royal Ottawa, she fell to Ada in the final. As we have seen, Ada Mackenzie's win was the first by a home-bred Canadian in the Open, and also marked the first time that a player was to win the Open and Close in the same year.

Alexa Stirling Fraser had to wait two years for her revenge. When she met Ada Mackenzie in the 1927 Open, Ada was completing a marathon of golf. Both had gone to the U.S. championships at Cherry Valley, Long Island. Ada won the qualifying round with a record-tying 77. Then she and Alexa fought their way to the semi-finals, where they lost. After a weekend's rest, Ada played in the Close at Toronto GC and won.

Another day's rest, and it was off to Lambton for the Open. So when she met Alexa Stirling Fraser in the third round (there was still no seeding of players), she was playing something like her tenth round of competitive golf in twelve days. On a rainswept course with waterlogged greens, Ada clearly wilted and lost to the tune of 5 and 3. But Alexa got no further than the semi-finals that year. She was the last Canadian to fall in a field loaded with strong American players.

Ada was the holder when the two met in 1934, for the fourth and last time. Alexa had not played in the Open for two years but had lost none of her ability to win. In the qualifying round, her driving was noticeably off. When she mentioned this to George Cumming – the championship was at Toronto GC – he advised her to change her woods. This she did, perhaps going to steel shafts. Her distance and accuracy both improved. Nevertheless, she had to fight her way through every round, notably her semi-final match against the formidable Vera Ramsay Ford of Vancouver.

Her final against Ada Mackenzie was also an uphill battle. One down after the morning round, she lost another in the outward half in the afternoon. To this point, Ada's game had been steady as a rock. Suddenly she was hit by one of those inexplicable falls from form. The match went to sudden death.

When the 37th was halved in two brilliant 4s, the gallery had visions of this final being the longest in the history of the championships. But just as suddenly it was over. Two poorly played shots at the next hole left Ada with no hope of recovery. Fourteen years after Alexa Stirling won her first Canadian Ladies' Open Championship, Alexa Stirling Fraser won her second.

So, of the four Mackenzie–Stirling meetings in the Open, Alexa Stirling won three. However, when the holes won and lost are added up, it is evident that only two holes

separated them after playing some 103 against each other in national match-play events.

There have been several great nurseries of women's golf in Canada. Hamilton Golf Club, with professional Nicol Thompson, was perhaps the first: it gave us Florence Harvey, Frances Scott Gibson, and Mrs. Kathleen Rowe. In 1915, these three were the only women golfers in Ontario with single-figure handicaps.

George Cumming turned out a clutch of fine women golfers between the wars: Sydney Pepler Mulqueen, Mrs. Whittington, the sisters Cecil and Maude Smith, and Margaret Walsh Gouinlock all reached at least the semi-finals of the Open or Close, sometimes more than once.

George Cumming followed the progress of his ladies with a parental interest. The club's history reveals that he would telegraph his good-luck wishes when one of them was in the running for a championship, and his congratulations when they succeeded. And they would telephone him, so that he would be among the first to know if they won. Their swings were so identical and so distinct from others that a "Cumming girl" could be identified from a distance.

(I met and spoke with one of them, Mrs. Gouinlock, in 1987, nearly seventy years after she joined Toronto GC. "George taught us to swing the way *he* swung," she recalled. "In those days we took the club so far back over the right shoulder that the shaft pointed to the ground. And on the follow-through, the shaft pointed to the ground over the left shoulder.")

Sydney Pepler Mulqueen was the most successful of the Cumming girls. Playing over her home course in the 1922 Open, she tied Ada Mackenzie as leader of the qualifying round, and was one of two Toronto girls who fought their way to the semi-finals (the other was Joyce Hutton).

For the next twenty-five years, Sydney Pepler Mulqueen was always a tough nut to crack in any championship. Her great length

Two Cumming girls of Toronto Golf Club, left to right, *Miss Cecil and Miss Maude Smith, in 1929.*

Sydney Pepler Mulqueen, a leading national golfer for over twenty-five years.

off the tee, and her ideal golfing temperament, helped her defeat Dorothy Campbell Hurd in the 1925 Open. It is surprising to find that she reached the final of the Open only twice, and was only once the champion.

At Royal Ottawa in 1938, the field included Scottish internationalists Nan Baird, Jessie Anderson, Mrs. Williamson, and Mrs. J.B. Walker, and Ireland's Clarrie Tiernan, all British Curtis Cup players. The favourite to win was Jessie Anderson, ranked number two in Britain, but she lost to the Irish girl in the semi-finals. In the other semi-final, Sydney Pepler Mulqueen took an early lead over Mrs. Walker, held on grimly, lost her lead, but squeaked into the final at the last hole.

There were few who felt the Canadian could match the strapping Irish girl in the final. When it started to rain in Ottawa on the day of the final, the odds on her winning further in

creased. But Mrs. Mulqueen played the game of her life. She went round in 76 in the morning, to be 2 up. In the afternoon, the Irish girl's booming drives pulled her back to 1. The Canadian went to the eighteenth (or 36th) hole 1 up. On this 595-yard hole Mrs. Mulqueen showed she was a worthy champion. After her second shot she was still 200 yards away, her opponent 150. Not a good long-wood player, she had taken a 6 on this hole in previous rounds. But this time she lofted a 4-wood to the front of the green. It was a daring and brilliant shot, much appreciated by the gallery of six hundred. Two putts gave her the championship.

Her two successes in the Close came thirteen years apart. In 1923, young Sydney Pepler had defeated Ada Mackenzie by 3 and 1 in the final. "Seldom has a more perfect game been seen than that shown by the new Champion," exulted *Canadian Golfer*. Her long game, particularly with the irons, was more than a match for Ada. George Cumming had coached her specially for these championships and had travelled to Royal Montreal to see her win. In 1936, it was Dora Virtue Darling who fell to her immaculate long game at Beaconsfield, by the same score.

The province of Quebec had not produced a winner in the ladies' championships since Violet Henry-Anderson in 1909, when two young women appeared on the scene in the late 1920s who were soon to correct that: Margery Kirkham and Dora Virtue.

The sorrel-headed Margery Kirkham had first come to the notice of astute observers in 1927, when she was eighteen and still at Montreal High. Great things were expected of her.

When her family moved to California, Margery joined the San Gabriel Club near Los Angeles and was coached by its professional. Back in Montreal after a two-year absence, she showed that this spell of competitive golf in California had rounded off her game.

Four leading golfers from Quebec in 1931, left to right, *Margery Kirkham, Dora Virtue, Mme. Ragene Dagenais, Eileen Kinsella.*

In the 1930 Close, Margery Kirkham led the qualifiers at Mount Bruno CC with an 83 and breezed through the rounds to the final. Ada Mackenzie was in the other half of the draw. But the expectations of a Mackenzie–Kirkham final were upset by Cecil Smith (a "Cumming girl") who defeated Ada in the third round.

Cecil Smith was ahead for most of her final with Margery Kirkham, by anything from 1 to 3 holes, but Margery squared the match at the sixteenth, and sank a 12-foot putt at the seventeenth to go ahead. Both players made a mess of the last hole, a medium-length par four. When it became obvious on the green that she had little hope of winning the hole, Cecil Smith generously conceded.

This was the first of a series of excellent championships for Margery Kirkham, who played out of the old Forest Hills club. In the 1931 Open she eliminated Alexa Stirling Fraser, but she could not hold the American Maureen Orcutt in the final.

In the 1932 Open, hitting the ball long and straight, she defeated in the semi-finals the last

of the five Americans who qualified, Bernice Wall. In the final against Mrs. Eddis of Rosedale she was behind for most of the morning round but eventually won by 3 and 2.

In the final of the 1936 Open, Margery Kirkham was defeated by another Quebec golfer, Dora Virtue Darling. Dora played out of the Whitlock GC, Hudson Heights, where the Darlings are as much an institution as the Oslers at Toronto. This woman's climb to national fame had been long and sometimes frustrating. Back in 1924 she had given Helen Paget a fight and a fright in the semi-finals of the Close, before three-putting to lose on the eighteenth green. A year later, she and Ada Mackenzie led the qualifiers, but again she failed to get far in match play.

By 1936, Dora Virtue Darling had won the Quebec ladies' title four times. Although small and slim in stature, she was the most powerful striker of a ball in Central Canada. It may have been her recent defeat in the Quebec finals that caused her to attack Royal Montreal's course so vigorously in the Open that year. In the semi-finals she played some

Margery Kirkham, Ladies' Open champion in 1932, driving from the first tee at Beaconsfield in 1933.

Dora Virtue Darling of Whitlock GC, winner of the Ladies' Open in 1936.

of the finest golf of her career against America's Marion Miley. Three down at one point, she fought back to be 1 up at the ninth and to win by 3 and 2.

In the final against Margery Kirkham her stylish, powerful swing served her superbly. She was 4 up after nine holes, and held on to win by 4 and 2.

Dora Virtue Darling did not play competitive golf in 1937. But all to a good cause. Twenty years later, her daughter Judy was to win her first of five consecutive Quebec ladies' titles.

Of the leading players in the West, Vera Ramsay Hutchings (later Mrs. Ford) and Mrs. John Rogers were the most frequent visitors to the championships in the East. But even these two competed in less than half the nationals held between the wars.

Vera Ramsay of Leatherhead, England, played for her country against a U.S. ladies' team when she was only sixteen. During the war, she was a driver to the Women's Royal Air Force for four years. In 1919, she married Harold Hutchings, a well-known Winnipeg sportsman whom she had met in France. Settling in Winnipeg with two children gave her very little time for golf until 1922. In that year, she went to Victoria and won the ladies' championship of the Pacific Northwest Golf Association (beating in the final an old English friend, Violet Henry-Anderson, Canadian Ladies' champion of 1909).

Vera Ramsay Hutchings did exceptionally well in her first essays into the Canadian championships. She was three times the medallist, a semi-finalist in the 1923 Open and Close, and the winner of the 1924 Close. Her 1924 win made Canadian golf history. This was the first national title, women's or men's, to go to a member of a club west of Ontario (the Winnipeg Golf Club).

A year or so later, Vera moved to Vancouver, but she still came to the occasional national event.

The Scarboro course was much like her home course, Shaughnessy, and she came to Scarboro in 1934 to win her second Close title. In the finals, she met Margaret Walsh Gouinlock, who could match her length off the tee. The two were all square coming to the last hole but one. Here, Mrs. Gouinlock drove the ball 240 yards into the creek, to lose

Vera Ramsay Hutchings of Winnipeg, winner of the Close in 1924.

the hole. That seemed to unnerve her, for she pushed her tee-shot badly at the eighteenth, to lose by 2 down.

"Mother of two, fine badminton player, athlete *par excellence*, and most popular member of Winnipeg's golfing fraternity." Thus was described Mrs. John Rogers of the St. Charles CC, the 1937 Open champion.

The 1937 championships were the third to be held in Winnipeg. Predictably, none of the leading Americans made the trip. But this time, many top Canadian players also called off, including Ada Mackenzie, Alexa Stirling Fraser, Sydney Pepler Mulqueen, Mme. Dagenais, and Dora Virtue Darling (the holder was about to be, or had just become, a mother). In fact, no past holders of the Open or Close title played at Winnipeg that year. The small field resulted in the highest qualifying score for years – 101.

The final shaped up as a battle of East versus West. Two steady if unspectacular golfers made their way through: Mrs. Rogers of Winnipeg and Mrs. Eric Phillips of Lambton. Mrs. Rogers carried her steady play into the final. Four up after the morning round (with an 81) she won the first three holes in the afternoon. Mrs. Phillips occasionally played some brilliant shots in an attempt to reduce the deficit, but it was not her day. The title went to Mrs. Rogers by 8 and 7.

Having won the Open title, Mrs. Rogers went on to prove that her fine performance was sustainable. In the following week she worked her way into the final of the Close. She was narrowly beaten by her clubmate, Heather Leslie.

Without wishing to take anything away from this young player's fine performance, it has to be said that no champion has ever had a greater stroke of good fortune in the opening round of a championship. Going to the last hole, Heather and her opponent were all square. Unaccountably, Heather took 5 strokes to reach the green and was still far from the pin. Her opponent, Mrs. K. C. Allen of Calgary, was just off the green in 3. The odds were that Heather would take a 7, and that Mrs. Allen could go for an easy 6, a possible 5, to win. But golf is unpredictable, often cruel. No doubt smote by some mental glitch, Mrs. Allen's game suddenly went all to pieces. She took five more strokes to get down. Heather Leslie, about to concede, found herself the winner.

The semi-finalists in the Ladies' Open at St. Charles CC, 1937. Left to right, *Mrs. C. H. Shuttleworth of Hamilton; the runner-up, Mrs. Eric Phillips of Lambton; the winner, Mrs. John Rogers of Winnipeg; and Mrs. Harold Soper of Montreal. Inset is Heather Leslie, winner of the Close.*

The Winnipeg girl fully deserved this stroke of luck and her title. She had twice won the Manitoba title, once by defeating Mrs. Rogers in the final. She did so again in the national Close. Their match was a dogfight, in which the golf progressively got worse. One up coming to the eighteenth, Heather Leslie made no mistakes on the last hole, and won by 2.

Frances Scott of Hamilton (later Mrs. Gibson, then Mrs. Ferrie) had reached the semi-finals of the first Ladies' Open back in 1913, only to be defeated by the eventual winner, England's Muriel Dodd. In 1922, as Frances Scott Gibson, she was to win the Close.

This exceptionally accurate iron player had few weaknesses. Only her lack of confidence prevented her from carrying off many more titles. In the final at Lambton, she outdrove and generally outplayed Helen Paget of Royal Ottawa, who had been one of the surprises of the week.

She always seemed to be in the thick of things at the Close championship, so it comes as a surprise to find that she reached the finals only one more time, in 1924. *Canadian Golfer* obviously thought the same of her. In 1930, Ralph Reville wrote: "The Close Championship since its inception has been more or less dominated by Mrs. Gordon Ferrie of Hamilton and Miss Ada Mackenzie, of Toronto."

Frances Scott Gibson, of Hamilton G & CC, in 1922.

Helen Paget was a student of professional Davie Black, when Davie was at Rivermead during the First World War, and the youngest member of the club when she started to win competitions.

Not a long hitter, she made up for it with a marvellous short game. When her name came up in the 1930s, however, it was not in the context of her Close title of 1925, but for her play in the 1927 Open at Lambton. She was the sensation of the week. To understand why, we need to look at the stature and record of the person she eliminated.

Glenna Collett had taken over from Alexa Stirling as the top U.S. woman golfer. Her six victories in the U.S. ladies' championship remains a record to this day. She had won the Canadian Ladies' Open in 1923 and 1924. When overwhelming Ada Mackenzie in the 1924 final, she had demonstrated that ranking golfers no longer played to the green; they played to the pin, a lesson Ada Mackenzie never forgot.

Glenna Collett came to the Canadian Ladies' Open again in 1927 and shot a 77 to lead the qualifiers by five strokes. She looked odds-on to take the title for the third time. But in the second round, the spectators witnessed one of the most astonishing upsets in the history of the event.

The Collett–Paget match was a dual between a long driver plus superb long-iron player, and one equally skilled at pitching and putting. Not more than a handful of spectators followed them on the first few holes, for Helen was not given the ghost of a chance. She had qualified with an 89, twelve strokes more than Glenna. She had only just scraped through her first round.

Not a bit daunted, she set after the unbeatable Glenna Collett, hanging on to her like a terrier.

When word reached the clubhouse that Helen Paget was only 1 down at the turn, the gallery began to collect. And when she sank a 30-foot putt to square the match on the fifteenth green, the cheers caused many others to leave the matches they had been following. This putt apparently unnerved her American opponent. At the sixteenth, Glenna Collett topped her drive into a bunker. The steady Miss Paget seized her opportunity, and went to the seventeenth 1 up. But her short game could not make up for her lack of distance off this tee. The match was squared, with one hole to go.

At Lambton's eighteenth, a slightly uphill 230-yard hole and a par four for the ladies, Glenna Collett nearly drove the green. But again Helen Paget's short game rescued her; her approach shot finished less than four feet away. In trying to respond, Glenna Collett chipped

Edith Bauld, unbeatable in the Maritimes.

well past the hole. She needed two putts to get down. Apparently without a trace of nerves, Helen Paget stroked her four-footer into the cup for a 3. For the first time on Canadian soil, Glenna Collett had been defeated.

"My goodness, am I the champion?" she asked on the seventeenth green. Yes, indeed. Irene Jolin Horne of the Regal Golf Club, Calgary, was to be the only member of an Alberta club ever to win the Close championship. She did so in 1935, defeating Cecil Smith Gooderham of Toronto GC in the final by 2 and 1.

Her win was not without its ironic twists of fate. Irene Horne had played well in the Open held the week before at the Jericho CC, Vancouver. Her centre-shafted putter (a make known as "Cash-In") had performed well, but not spectacularly. In the Close at Royal Colwood the officials ruled the putter illegal. (It

had been accepted in the Open probably because of the entries from the United States, where that type of putter was legal.) So Irene Horne borrowed a standard putter, and used it with such precision that it won her the title.

Irene Jolin did not take up golf until 1926, which was about the time she married golf professional Roy Horne. She was to win the Alberta ladies' title six times in the period 1929–37. She had an ideal temperament for golf and, although of average build, was also a most powerful hitter.

Edith Bauld of Halifax was to the East Coast what Violet Pooley Sweeney was to the West. She dominated golf in the Maritimes from just before the First World War until well into the 1930s, to the extent that she decided to give up competitive golf in 1929 and 1930. According to her sister, "she felt she was discouraging others from playing, since she always won."

Edith Bauld was an all-round athlete. In her youth she was proficient at tennis, swimming, riding, rowing, ice-dancing, and badminton (in 1926 she reached the final of the ladies' doubles in the Maritimes).

She took up golf in 1910, at the age of twenty-four, joining the Halifax Golf Club. The published records are not complete; nevertheless, they show her winning the Maritime ladies' title no less than ten times between 1921 and 1935, as well as several Nova Scotia titles.

Edith Bauld was a stylish player and could hit the ball a long way. But her strength was her short game. She was one of those golfers who are admired and feared by fellow competitors. Yet, in the national championships, she never did as well as expected. She first played in 1911 but did not get far, although the experience led to her visiting Britain in 1912 with Florence Harvey and Mabel Thomson. She tried again for several years after the First World War. Her best performance was in 1920, when she tied Alexa Stirling for second place in the qualifying round of the Open, then reached the quarter-finals of match play.

Margaret Esson, Saskatchewan's "Puddin'," after winning the provincial title in 1936.

In 1949, the Maritime Ladies' Golf Association presented her with its championship cup, noting that "as her name is engraved on the cup's side in ten places, she should receive this historic trophy as a keepsake."

Edith Bauld served for many years on CLGU committees and had a hand in organizing the Nova Scotia Ladies' Golf Union in 1928.

This grand old lady of Maritimes golf died in 1962.

Now and then a new young star would brighten up the sky, cause us to look and wonder, then seemingly disappear over the horizon.

In 1937, sixteen-year-old Margaret Esson came out of Saskatchewan to take everyone by storm. She had already made her mark in provincial golf. A year earlier she had won the Saskatchewan Ladies' Championship, no mean feat for a schoolgirl of fifteen years and two months, the youngest ever to win a ladies' provincial title. In the 1937 Close at Winnipeg's Niakwa, she became the youngest ever to reach the quarter-finals.

This could quite easily have been the end of the Margaret Esson Cinderella story. But no. This young lady had only whetted our appetites. In 1938, she came to Royal Ottawa to compete in the Open. When she qualified easily with an 85, one or two keen observers started to take note.

Margaret Esson was by then seventeen, a slim, 110-pound five-feet-five-inch chubby-faced girl, affectionately known as "Puddin'" in her home town. Her home town was Rosetown, about one hundred miles from Saskatoon. Rosetown had a nine-hole course, with sand greens. Now and then, Margaret Esson would travel the distance to Saskatoon to get some experience of putting on grass. At other times she had to be content with putting into tomato tins at home.

In the first round of the 1938 Open, she came up against British Curtis Cupper Nan Baird, former Scottish and British champion. Any Glasgow bookmaker would have given you odds of one hundred to one against this slip of a girl from Rosetown. But in that innocent state that knows nothing of nervousness, Margaret Esson threw two quick birdies at Nan Baird, plus a string of pars. Before the Scottish girl knew what had hit her, she was out of the championship, beaten by 6 and 4.

In the second round, Margaret Esson met Winifred Evans of Vancouver, who had just defeated the favourite, Ada Mackenzie. Puddin' smacked the ball well over 200 yards straight down the middle, hit her approaches to within a few feet, and in the thirteen holes it took to dispose of Miss Evans was three over 4s.

This was too hard to believe, too good to miss. By the time Margaret Esson stepped onto the first tee to play another British Curtis Cup player, Mrs. Walker, she had attracted the largest gallery of the week. Some four hundred spectators hemmed her in, trying hard to be not too partisan. The crowd distracted her. She played mediocre golf to the turn, and was 5 down. Then back came her smile, she relaxed, won three holes, and the crowd had visions of tomorrow's headlines. But at the sixteenth – which she needed to win – she struck a bunker, and that was it. Mrs. Walker, by 4 and 2.

Margaret Esson was the leading player in Saskatchewan for six years. She married Bill Elliott, who became president of Regina's Wascana Club. It is comforting to see the name Margaret Elliott as runner-up, Saskatchewan Ladies' Senior Championship, 1978, 1981.

The Canadian Ladies' Golf Union had been re-organized at an enthusiastic meeting held in Toronto in December 1919. Those attending came mainly from clubs in Toronto, Ottawa, London, and Hamilton. Before leaving for South Africa, Florence Harvey handed over her work to a new committee, organized in much the same way as the pre-war committee, but with new titles and new faces:

President: Mrs. Ella Murray, Toronto
VP of Eastern Division: Mrs. McGregor Mitchell, Halifax
VP of Midland Division: Mrs. Beverly Robinson, Montreal
VP of Western Division: to be elected later
Hon. Sec.-Treasurer: Dora Faulkner, Toronto

An executive committee, consisting of members of Ontario clubs, was also elected. So was the CLGU's very important Pars Committee, comprising Edith Bauld of Halifax, Frances Scott Gibson of Hamilton, Violet Pooley Sweeney of Vancouver, and Mrs. Bartle Armstrong of Winnipeg. The first three – perhaps Mrs. Armstrong as well – had visited Britain and were familiar with the LGU system of parring courses.

Ella Murray, President of the CLGU, in 1922.

With the departure of Flo Harvey, the headquarters of the CLGU moved to the Toronto homes of its secretary and president. (It was to stay in Toronto until 1971.) Annual and semi-annual meetings were usually held at golf clubs or in city hotels, executive meetings at private homes or in such places as the Diet Kitchen on Bloor Street or the Inglenook Tea Rooms on Spadina. Thus the CLGU became a Toronto-based organization at about the same time as the RCGA. Some people accused both of being Toronto-biased. If they were, it is understandable: about half the country's golfers, men and women, belonged to clubs in Ontario.

The first post-war meeting of the CLGU, in December 1919, took place nearly three months after the first post-war ladies' championships. With a new committee in place, the CLGU's lost leadership was quickly restored. Its new president was to be no figurehead. Ella Murray soon realized that the Union could not be run efficiently if so much detail remained in the national office. (Even during her hectic years in wartime Hamilton, Flo Harvey had insisted on personally checking the handicap calculations made by the thirty or so member clubs.) Ella Murray immediately set about decentralizing the CLGU. She wanted to see provincial branches set up with their own officers, pars committees, and handicap committees. The national office would run the national championships, liaise with the LGU in London on matters of policy and on such things as changes to the rules and the methods of parring and handicapping.

Ella Murray had already proved herself an able administrator when she'd been in charge of the old Maritime Division of the CLGU. During her ten years as national president she accomplished what she had set out to do: branches were established across Canada, the membership of the CLGU increased sixfold, and the CLGU took over the running of the Ladies' Open and started a Ladies' Close championship. She put up with thousands of miles of travel, meeting with golfers in every province, cajoling, negotiating, convincing them that her vision of the CLGU was the right one. In the process, she became known and respected as one of the most skilled golf administrators in Canada between the wars.

The efforts of the CLGU were directed towards forming provincial branches. Quebec ladies established a branch in 1921, Manitoba ladies in 1922, British Columbia ladies at about the same time. There was no immediate need for an Ontario branch; the membership of the CLGU was so small (about forty clubs) that the national office could handle the affairs of the province. But by 1926 national membership had tripled and an Ontario branch was organized.

The ladies down east had set up their own Maritime Ladies' Golf Association in 1921. Ella Murray, accompanied by Helen Paget of Ottawa and Mrs. Whittington of Toronto, went to the Maritime championships in 1925. The three persuaded the officers of the MLGA to form a separate organization, the Maritime branch of the CLGU. (This branch began to split up into provincial branches after the Second World War.)

The ladies of Regina had written as early as 1923 to say that they hoped to form a Saskatchewan branch. But it was 1926 before they succeeded.

The last province to hold out, Alberta, was given the executive squeeze in 1928. A deputation of four made the trip across the Prairies: president Ella Murray; the new secretary, Mrs. Margaret Kathleen Rowe; the Quebec provincial champion, Helen Paget; a top Ontario golfer, Evelyn Mills. The pressure worked. When in Calgary, the four visitors attended the organizing meeting of an Alberta branch.

Therefore, by 1928, the CLGU could boast of having branches from the Atlantic to the Pacific. In 1929, it went a step further, when the Bally Haly club of St. John's, Newfoundland (not yet a province of Canada) became a member.

As these branches were formed, they took over the task of running the ladies' provincial championships. Previously, these had been run by the men's association and, before there *were* men's associations, by the clubs in the province.

In 1921, with a view to encouraging branches to hold provincial ladies' championships, the national office offered to supply each affiliated branch with a silver bowl for the winner. Ontario, Quebec, and the Maritimes took advantage of the offer in 1922, although the MLGA did not formally become a branch until 1925. The Manitoba branch accepted a year later, but it is not clear when the British Columbia branch accepted. Saskatchewan and Alberta agreed a year or so after they organized.

In the years between the wars, the CLGU's membership increased at about the same rate as the RCGA's. At the end of the First World War it was about 30 clubs. It increased to 47 by 1921; to 67 by late 1922; to 111 by 1925 (it now had member clubs in every province); to 176 by 1929; and to 265 by 1940.

The membership fees of the CLGU had been set up in much the same way as the RCGA's, and varied with the number of ladies in the club. Clubs with 100 lady members or less paid annual dues of $5; clubs with more than 400 members paid $25. Clubs between these two extremes paid $10 or $20, according to membership. This yielded an income of only $2,000 a year by 1939. Another $300 might come from advertising space in the CLGU's year book. (Originally called the Red Book, it appeared sporadically from 1922, but regularly from 1931 until the Second World War.) Little wonder, then, that the CLGU had to find other ways of funding the interprovincial team championships when these were started in 1934.

The decision to start a Close championship in 1922 did not sit well with some individuals within the CLGU. The Close was to be a bone of contention until it was dropped in 1969. The debate at the AGM of 1925 was probably typical of what took place at other meetings over the years. The matter so threatened to dominate the agenda of the 1925 meeting that

a second general meeting had to be held in the following February. Those who spoke in favour of two championships – including Ada Mackenzie – pointed out that with so many Americans entering the Open, Canadian women relied on the Close to give them some much-needed national experience.

The proponents of a single championship had an equally good case; it was nonsense to ask golfers to play competitive golf for two weeks on end, and it would also be quite impracticable to hold two championships a month or so apart, the cost of travelling being what it was. To hold only a Close "would be thoroughly unsporting and fatal to future development by eliminating outside entries." The words are those of Margaret Kathleen Rowe, who was soon to become the long-serving and influential secretary to the Union. When she got up to speak, the meeting seemed to be fairly evenly divided on the matter. But

Mrs. Edwin Crockett, President of the CLGU, and Mrs. Margaret Kathleen Rowe, Secretary, at the Ladies' Open in Vancouver, 1935.

she made an impassioned appeal to the ladies, adroitly turning the vote on the matter into a vote of confidence in Ella Murray. ("If this meeting does not vote by a large majority for continuing the two Championships, they would show a lack of faith in our President . . . and her executive, who have worked so long and faithfully, spending many hours in consideration of this important question," and so on.) She won their hearts, if not their minds, by 34 votes to 1.

But that was by no means the end of the matter. Whenever the championships were held in the West, the American entry was so small that the Close became a repeat of the Open. This led to cries that the Close should be abandoned. It had to be dropped in 1928 so that the Open could be played on a date that did not clash with the U.S. ladies' championships, and in 1932, because of the Depression. And in 1938, CLGU president Mrs. Edwin Crockett agreed to drop it for that year. Why? A general lack of interest, and a need to conserve our ladies' energies for a match against the British Curtis Cup team. But the Close was to survive the Second World War, and to be the subject of debate for another twenty years.

In 1926, the RCGA decided to revive the interprovincial team matches for men. This move was seen as a means of sending players from the provinces to the Canadian Amateur and – so long as they went as a team – of paying their travelling expenses.

At the 1926 Annual General Meeting of the CLGU, Mrs. Douglas Laird of Manitoba suggested that the ladies do the same. But whereas the RCGA could finance the provincial teams with the proceeds of the Canadian Open

championship gate (or nearly so), the ladies would have to seek the funds from member clubs. A special levy of something like fifty cents per lady member would be needed. The matter was shunted aside to a subcommittee. By the time this committee reported, the nation was facing the Depression. It was not a good time to be asking people for more money.

By 1934, the clouds were thinning. The CLGU established a Canadian Team Fund Committee. It encouraged branches to raise money by raffles, sweepstakes, and by levying fees of twenty-five to fifty cents for playing in provincial tournaments. The committee was so successful that by 1939 the fund stood at $6,000.

The first ladies' interprovincial team matches were played as part of the Close championships at Scarboro in 1934. British Columbia, Quebec, and Ontario sent teams of four. Ontario won by the small margin of 3 strokes over Quebec, thanks to an 80 by Ada Mackenzie, so that Ontario was the first name to go on the shield presented by the RCGA for this new event.

In 1938, the last interprovincial before the war, all seven branches entered teams. The ladies' championships had become truly national.

A final word on Florence Harvey. After living in South Africa for eighteen years, she went to England for the Second World War, where she worked in the ARP (air raid precautions) before finally coming home to Hamilton. She met many old friends when she attended the national championships in 1963, 1964, and 1965, and was given a fine reception by the hundreds who attended the CLGU's fiftieth-anniversary dinner in 1963. This woman who did so much for golf in Canada died on 7 July 1968, four months before her ninetieth birthday.

18

THE THOMPSONS' TAKEOVER BID

THE FIRST AMATEUR AFTER THE WAR, held at Lambton in June 1919, was given the title of the Peace Year Championships.

As had been customary, competitors did not enter ahead of time but merely presented themselves the day before and registered with the RCGA secretary. Anyone whose club was a member of the RCGA could enter for the Amateur, regardless of handicap. So the RCGA was quite unprepared for the 230 golfers, more than double the pre-war number, who turned up that June. With limited accommodation, Lambton had to erect tents on its lawns, but there were no complaints from the enthusiastic brotherhood. However, since just about everyone wanted to compete in the Amateur, the RCGA warned that the next year there would be a handicap limit of 20.

Among the 120 who played in the Amateur were a number of pre-war stalwarts: Fritz Martin, Dudley Dawson, Anthony Adams, Tom Reith, Geoff Turpin, Douglas Laird, and Robert M. Gray Jr. And George S. Lyon was there to defend his title.

In the end, none of these was to do well in the 1919 Amateur. The winner was a newcomer, William McLuckie, of whom we will hear more later. Among the also-rans were three brothers making their first appearance in national competition.

The RCGA had an added feature in the Peace Year meet – the Soldiers' Competition, open to all men who had served in uniform. The winner was a virtually unknown young golfer by the name of Frank Thompson. His brother Stanley had already made his mark by being runner-up to Seymour Lyon in the qualifying round of the Amateur. And yet another brother, Bill, one of those fancied to win the Amateur, reached the semi-finals. This, then, was the introduction to Canadian national golf of three of the five Thompson brothers. In the early 1920s they came to dominate amateur golf and to be dubbed "The Amazing Thompsons."

On looking back, it is hard to find any family that collectively has left more of a mark on the golfing scene. R. F. (Frank) Thompson and W. J. (Bill) were to win the Amateur –

Frank twice, in 1921 and 1924; Bill in 1923. Stanley came close many times. But his skill as a golfer has been overshadowed by his genius as a golf architect. From 1919 to the late 1920s, the three Thompsons were always a threat to the new generation of amateur golfers then trying to make its mark.

In all, there were five Thompson brothers: Nicol (born 1881), Mathew (1886), Bill (1891), Stanley (1893), and Frank (1898). We have already met Nicol, the long-time professional to Hamilton G & CC. Mat went to Winnipeg early in his working life, playing most of his competitive golf out of the Elmhurst club. As an amateur, he was runner-up in the 1919 Manitoba championship.

The trio of Bill, Stanley, and Frank played out of Toronto's Mississaugua club. Bill, a lawyer, had made a name for himself by winning a few local tournaments, such as the Field Day for Soldiers' Comforts at Scarboro in 1916 and the Patriotic Day Open held at the same club in June 1918. Stanley and Frank were virtually unknown in 1919, both having enlisted early in the war.

In May 1919, when Mississaugua played Lambton, Frank Thompson caused quite a stir by beating George Lyon by 4 and 3. When Frank won the Soldiers' Competition a few weeks later, Ralph Reville, with his usual perspicacity, described him as "a golfer with all the earmarks of a coming champion . . . He has style plus, drives a very long distance for one so young, and has a fine short game, too, that gives infinite promise for the future."

Frank was then twenty-one. It is a sign of the times that in 1919 he was considered a long driver "for one so young." Golf in Canada was still a game played mostly by older men in their thirties to seventies.

Frank did not disappoint the editor of *Canadian Golfer*. In the 1921 Amateur at Winnipeg, he beat a veteran Scot and the 1920 finalist, Tom Gillespie of Calgary, on his way to a victory over Charlie Hague, another Calgarian.

Thompson's toughest match was his semi-final against Percy Shaw of Toronto's Weston club, a fine match player of the 1920s. After the morning round, Frank Thompson was 3 down and playing with none of his customary vigour. By the afternoon, his whole mood had changed. He attacked the hole with his usual panache, squared the match at the 23rd, and won by 1 up at the last hole. The story behind Frank's comeback in the semi-final is recorded in the history of the Mississaugua club. His brothers Bill and Mat had taken him to another club for lunch, to take his mind off golf.

The Thompson–Hague final was as tense. Hague had also been through a tough semi-final against A. A. (Sandy) Weir, a veteran Winnipegger, who took him to the 36th hole.

There was a general expectation that both Thompson and Hague would produce listless golf, having given of their best to get to the final. Not so. A gallery of two thousand saw as exciting a final as you could wish for. Thompson used his mashie-niblick (or 7-iron) to good effect, "playing his shots to the pin with

Bill Thompson, Amateur champion in 1923, was later a golf administrator.

The Thompson brothers in 1923, left to right, *Frank, Mathew, Nicol, Stanley, Bill.*

a back-spin which actually at times causes the ball to drop back." He won, but only at the second hole of sudden death.

The Mississaugua history also records the problems Frank was having when he was on his way to his second Amateur title in 1924. In the third round, he met C. C. (Happy) Fraser, the winner in 1922. Again, Frank was not playing his usual game.

> . . . Frank was subconsciously trying to compete with Happy Fraser, whose style was to joke with the gallery. W. J. felt it was a losing situation. He advised Frank to play the eighteen holes in total silence, shutting out Happy, his antics and the crowd. He did. He won.

Frank Thompson was then only twenty-six years of age, too young to be classified as one of the old school golfers. He and his brothers were a bridge between old and new. In the 1924 final, Frank met and defeated the finest

of the new school, C. Ross (Sandy) Somerville, giving "a magnificent exhibition of dogged, determined golf."

The Thompsons had all mastered the pitch-and-run shot. Bill won his 1923 Amateur title with his accurate driving and his shots to the green. Nicol, Bill, and Stanley were stocky and well-built, often described as "chunky." Frank was taller and the most stylish, but some observers considered Stanley the finest golfer of the lot. Who knows what championships Stanley Thompson might have won had he spent more time playing golf and less time designing golf courses.

It has been said of many golfers that they were better in stroke play than in match play. This was said of the Thompsons. Indeed, if you examine the records of the three Thompson brothers in the two national stroke-play events – the Open and the qualifying rounds of the Amateur – it is hard to understand why, between them, they won only three Canadian amateur titles:

1919 – Stanley is second in the Amateur qualifying round, Bill is fifth, but only Bill makes it to the semi-finals. In the Open, Bill is the leading Canadian amateur, ahead of all but two Canadian professionals.

1920 – Bill leads the qualifiers for the Amateur (over 36 holes). Stanley is third.

1921 – Frank wins the Amateur. There are no stroke-play qualifying rounds, but Bill wins the Silver Bowl for the lowest gross prize in the Handicap Competition, with Frank second. In the Open, Frank is the leading Canadian amateur, ahead of all but one Canadian professional.

1922 – Bill leads the qualifiers for the Amateur, and again reaches the semi-finals.

1923 – Bill wins the Amateur. Stanley leads the qualifiers, with Bill second. In the Open, Frank is the leading amateur.

1924 – Frank wins the Amateur. Bill leads the qualifiers, Frank ties for second.

1925 – Stanley leads the qualifiers for the Amateur with a record score of 146. In the Open, Bill is leading amateur.

1926 – Bill leads the qualifiers for the Amateur, Frank is second, Stanley ties for third.

1927 – Frank is runner-up in the Amateur. Stanley is third of the qualifiers.

At the beginning of the First World War, Bill Thompson was twenty-three, Stanley a month short of being twenty-one, and Frank some five years younger. None of them appears to have played in any district or national competitions, probably because none could afford the time and the money.

The father, James Thompson, immigrated to Canada in the early 1880s, from Ecclefechan, Scotland, with his wife and two children, Nicol (listed as Nicholas in the 1891 census) and Marion. He is said to have registered himself as a "ploughman."

The family settled near Markham, north of Toronto. Around 1893 the father took a labouring job in the railway repair yards of East Toronto, moving his family – now numbering six or seven – to a house next to the course of the Toronto Golf Club, where the boys became caddies. Surrounded by such future national champions as Karl Keffer and the Murrays, the boys picked up the rudiments of the game while earning money to help pay for their board and education.

Mathew went to school in the village of Norway with Karl Keffer and left for Winnipeg when he was about twenty. Bill took a job with a baker and confectioner before studying law at Osgoode Hall. He became the Clerk of the County Court, Toronto, before going into private practice. He helped organize the Ontario Golf Association in 1923 and was its honorary secretary from 1926 to 1935. Stanley, and probably Frank, went through the same high school as Bill (Malvern Collegiate), caddying after school and on weekends.

The Thompson brothers came from what was essentially a working-class family, to which the cost of a golf club membership would have been prohibitive. Too, the boys may have caddied beyond their fifteenth birthday, so losing their amateur status, at least temporarily.

Bill Thompson was a keen student of the game. His ideas on how a golf ball should be struck are found in his book *Common Sense Golf* (1923). Thompson tried to get away from teaching the swing in parts, viewing this as the pernicious practice it is. He also advised the beginner to start with only a handful of clubs, instead of a full set. He practised what he preached. When winning the Amateur in 1923, he carried only seven clubs in his bag. Bill Thompson died suddenly in 1935, after several years of ill health. He was in his forty-fourth year.

The golfing skills of the Thompson family were passed on to the next generation. In 1932, four Thompsons qualified for the match-play rounds of the Canadian Amateur: Frank, Stanley, and two sons of Nicol – Nicol Jr. and Joe. Young Joe led the qualifiers. Alas, all the Thompsons ran up against their match-play jinx; not one got further than the first round. Fiery little Nicol Jr. went on to become a professional, like his father. He had a somewhat erratic but colourful personality, as well as the gutsy, fighting spirit of all the Thompsons. In the second round of the 1935 Amateur, Hugh

Jaques, a mighty hitter of the ball, blasted Joe Thompson off the course and was 4 up with seven holes to go. Joe won the next five holes in a row and held on to win.

Little Joe Thompson became an air-gunner in the Second World War. He was killed in action.

Mat's son, Bill, played Willingdon Cup golf for Manitoba in the 1940s. He worked for a time with his uncles Stanley and Frank at the Cutten Field GC, near Guelph, before becoming a professional in Manitoba and B.C.

In the first post-war Amateur, William (Bill) McLuckie of Montreal's Kanawaki GC survived the torrid weather of Lambton to defeat the 1913 champion, Geoff Turpin. But his victory was no sinecure. At one time he was 3 down to Turpin and had to come up with a brilliant string of 3s to win at the 37th hole.

Bill McLuckie had one of the smoothest swings in Canadian golf, a product of his teachers, for McLuckie was yet another of the Cumming school of golf.

Born in the east end of Toronto around 1889, of Scottish parents, McLuckie went to

school with Karl Keffer and Mat Thompson. He, too, became a caddie at Toronto Golf Club, where he mimicked Cumming's style. For many years he forsook golf for baseball, but when his company transferred him to Montreal he went back to golf, joining the Outremont GC and later Kanawaki.

Although McLuckie's great strength, imperturbability, and tenacity made him a good match player, he never quite regained the form that won him the 1919 championship.

Geoff Turpin of Royal Montreal reached the semi-finals again in 1920. This time he was defeated by clubmate Charles Grier, who went on to win the title.

The 1919 Amateur champion Bill McLuckie with Charlie Murray in a cartoon by LeMessurier of the Montreal Star.

Charles Grier, left, Amateur champion of 1920, with runner-up Tom Gillespie.

Charles Grier was born in Montreal in 1888 but educated at Toronto's St. Andrews College, where he developed into an all-round athlete and an outstanding boxer. In 1904 he joined Montreal's Westmount club and had his first lessons from Charlie Murray. When Charlie left to join Royal Montreal, young Charles moved with his teacher. He had been playing first-rate golf for some years before the war, and, but for his war service as a gunnery officer, would probably have been a force in national golf before 1920.

Another Montrealer won in 1922. C. C. (Happy) Fraser had also taken up golf as a boy at Montreal's Westmount GC. He switched to Kanawaki when this club opened, and put himself in the hands of its professional, Albert Murray.

Fraser developed a smooth and easy style, very much in keeping with his personality. An excellent spirit, he would chat and joke his way around the golf course, somewhat in the manner of Trevino, hence the nickname "Happy" or "Hap" by which he was usually known. Jack Cameron played with him and against him in later years and had this to say:

> In his best golfing days, Happy Fraser studied his opponents shrewdly and carefully. He imparted to them the feeling that he was always going to hit the ball exactly where he wished. His whole appearance, even though he was apparently laughing and joking, was one of confidence, and after being fooled once or twice, the contestant began to realize that Happy was most dangerous in a tight corner, and laughing.

In the 1922 Amateur, Fraser stormed his way to the final. In the third round he knocked out clubmate McLuckie by winning the first seven holes, a new experience for the unfortunate champion of 1919.

C. C. "Happy" Fraser, Amateur champion in 1922.

But in the final, when he met Norman Scott, he appeared to have met his match. Happy Fraser would probably have been defeated but for a misfortune that befell *him* late in the afternoon. The story reveals much about the character of both men.

Coming to the 165-yard 34th hole, Fraser was 1 down with three to play. Fraser put his tee-shot on the fringe of the green, close to a bunker. In order to line up his putt, he went down into the bunker. Without thinking, he picked up a scrap of paper lying on the sand and tossed it aside.

At that time, the rules of golf did not permit players to touch loose impediments in a hazard, so the referee awarded the hole to Norman Scott. Sportsman that he was, Happy Fraser did not protest the ruling, even by a glance, but picked up his ball immediately. On the other hand, Scott, sportsman that *he* was, protested his being awarded the hole on what was, to his mind, a technicality. But the referee was R. C. H. (Bertie) Cassels, president of the RCGA and soon to be chairman of the Rules of Golf Committee. He was adamant. Fraser had contravened the rule and that was the end of it. Fraser was now dormie 2.

It was in the nature of the man that Happy Fraser shrugged off the incident with a smile. A rumour spread through the gallery, however, that Scott had *called* the penalty on Fraser, and there were murmurings of disapproval. Poor Scott was demolished. He sliced his drive at the 35th, and lost the hole. Fraser sank a sliding six-footer to square the match at the 36th. He went on to win the first hole of sudden death, and the championship was his.

At the presentation of prizes, Cassels explained to the crowd that Scott had *not* asked that Fraser be penalized. The crowd cheered. But their understanding came too late.

There was no question in the minds of those who witnessed the 1922 final that Norman Scott would have won but for that small scrap of paper. This stylish player had first revealed his skills in 1913, when he reached the semi-finals. He again made the last four in 1925, but was never to go further.

Happy Fraser was a popular winner. His smooth style was the envy of many a young hopeful. Few could match him as an entertainer at the 19th hole. He went on to be a force in Quebec golf until well into the 1930s. In his second Amateur final, in 1926, he went down to an unbeatable Sandy Somerville.

These three immediate post-war champions – McLuckie, Grier, and Happy Fraser – had this in common: they had taken up golf when still in their formative years, and had placed themselves in the hands of a professional. They were also products of George Cumming, or of his one-time assistants, Charlie and Albert Murray, as were the Thompsons. For the rest of the decade we were to see a new breed of champion from a younger school.

19

SANDY SOMERVILLE AND THE BOYS OF '32

ONE MAN CAME TO DOMINATE CANAdian amateur golf in the two decades between the wars, just as George Lyon had in the two previous decades. The redoubtable Charles Ross Somerville – better known as Sandy – at first glance appears to have been the very antithesis of Lyon. You would never find him leading the boys in the singing of "Mother Machree" or walking on his hands in a clubhouse. Indeed, he came to be known as Silent Sandy, and was often characterized as dour.

Somerville's style was also the antithesis of Lyon's. In Sandy, Canada had no "baby elephant," but as fine a piece of well-oiled, human golfing machinery as you would hope to find anywhere. He swung a golf club with grace and controlled power, using a perfectly timed turn of the body, and not just his powerful arms and shoulders, to give him his great distance off the tee.

But Somerville and Lyon had much in common. They were both all-round sportsmen and particularly fine cricketers. Both were modest men, wearing the champion's crown with the proper blend of pride, dignity, and humility. In

their own country, they were an inspiration to legions of golfers, winning an affection that came close to adulation. In the United States and Britain they were highly respected as men and as golfers.

But whereas the U.S. and British critics had looked askance at George Lyon's unorthodox but effective swing, they were lost in admiration of Somerville's style. The critical eye of Britain's Bernard Darwin looked Somerville over and had this to say of him when he reached the semi-finals of the British Amateur:

> Style is a matter of individual taste, and I rank Somerville very high in the category of stylists . . . He brings to mind the description of an old cricketer, 'Elegance, all elegance, fit to play before the king in his parlour'.

Sandy Somerville won his first Canadian Amateur Championship in 1926, and went on to win another five before the Second World War. He also won a fistful of provincial titles, and countless others in Canada and the United States. But he was not the first of this new breed to make it to the top. Another brilliant young golfer had been one pace ahead of him. For a time it looked as though he might challenge Somerville for the title of Canada's finest amateur golfer in the years between the wars. His name was Donald Carrick.

When this rangy, dark-haired, athletic giant captured the public's imagination and the Canadian Amateur Championship in 1925, he became the first of our golfers to spring in a season from a schoolboy champion to champion of the country. He was eighteen at the time, and remains the youngest male golfer ever to win a national championship in Canada (other than those for juniors).

In 1925, Don Carrick was already a veteran golfer. At fifteen, he had won the club championship of Scarboro GC; at sixteen, the Ontario Junior Boys' Championship by the whopping margin of 11 strokes over thirty-six holes. A year later he reached the finals of the U.S. Western Junior Championship. In 1925, at eighteen, he was a runner-up in the Ontario Amateur and Ontario Open.

Don Carrick, Amateur champion in 1925 and 1927.

A product of St. Andrews College, Toronto, Carrick was another all-round athlete: boxer, footballer, hockey player.

Don Carrick first captured attention in 1923, when he was sixteen. In the Canadian Amateur, he fought his way through the first two rounds before meeting the experienced Scot and Manitoba champion, Jack Cuthbert. Their ding-dong battle attracted a large gallery. Although Cuthbert won by 4 and 3 (over 36 holes), Ralph Reville acknowledged that "to get so far in such a field is a feather in the cap of this young golfing giant, whose future will be followed with much interest by all keen students of the game."

In the Canadian Open, Carrick was the third-placed amateur, topped only by Frank and Bill Thompson. All this, remember, at the age of sixteen!

Don Carrick was one of a new breed of Canadian-bred golfer. Although they matured over sixty years ago, we can probably label them the first of the modern school. They differed from previous generations in that they had taken up golf while still schoolboys and had been coached by club professionals. When we look at the top amateurs before the First World War, we find George S. Lyon, Vere Brown, and Fritz Martin, who took up golf in their late twenties or their thirties.

Some of the players who came along just before, and just after, the war – Geoff Turpin, Charles Grier, Norman Scott, Happy Fraser – had also taken up golf as schoolboys and been coached by professionals. But the new breed, of which Don Carrick was the first to rise to the top, had another distinguishing feature. They had a new perception of golf. They saw it not as a game requiring a long apprenticeship lasting into one's twenties, but as a game to be mastered as a teenager.

Previously, teenage golfers were conditioned to believe they had no chance of doing well in the Amateur. Golf's administrators nourished this perception. Why else would they have introduced provincial and national junior championships, with an age limit of twenty-one? Clearly, to encourage competition between young men of twenty and less who believed they had no chance of defeating their seniors. So Carrick, Somerville, and the other young men of their time had to break through an age barrier, more perceived than real.

This new breed of golfer was also remarkable in its addiction to practice. We know little about the number of hours our early champions spent on the practice fairway or putting green. But the late-Victorian and Edwardian attitude towards amateur sports suggests that they spent very little time there. When George Lyon gave up cricket to practise his golf for two weeks before winning the 1898 Amateur, this was so unusual as to warrant mention by the press.

The easy-flowing, rhythmical, seemingly effortless swing common to almost all top golfers today was not suddenly discovered in the 1920s. But in the 1920s a large number of boys who had been taught from childhood to swing this way suddenly became young men. The term "grooved swing" was not then used, but that is what these new young golfers had in common. Their swing also had the advantage of being aesthetically pleasing, and of appearing to be easy to copy.

Many fine young golfers came on the scene in the mid-1920s, but it is to Carrick and Somerville that memory clings. These two were the giants of their day. At their best, there was little to choose between them. Both had been coached by former assistants of George Cumming: Carrick by Newell Senour at Scarboro, Somerville by Kernie Marsh at London Hunt. Of the two, Somerville was probably the longer driver and the more consistent, Carrick the more daring and adventuresome, with an edge in iron shots to the green and in putting.

Carrick also had the indefinable charisma of a Seve Ballesteros or a Greg Norman that attracts the spectator and adds colour to the game. He went for everything with a confidence and a fearlessness that, to some eyes, bordered on recklessness. He seemed to thrive on competition and all that went with it – the roar of the crowd and the clash of combat. Both he and Somerville came to have the over-

powering effect on opponents that George Lyon had had twenty years earlier.

In the 1927 final against Frank Thompson, Carrick uncorked a brand of golf that was simply unbeatable. "Even a Bobby Jones could not have held him," in the opinion of Ralph Reville. His morning round of 70 included a triple-bogey 7, and a double-bogey 5. He made up for this with no less than nine birdies. Poor Thompson found himself 5 holes down. In the afternoon, Carrick played well within himself, placing his iron shots dead, and rattling his putts boldly into the back of the cup. He won by 9 and 8.

In that championship, Carrick became the first man ever to lead the qualifiers and to win the title. His qualifying score of 67 74–141 was 7 under par, and a record for the Amateur. To break 70 in the 1920s was a rare feat. (I believe only one man had ever shot in the 60s in the Amateur. Marcus Greer of Grand' Mère was said to have had a 68 when winning his second-round match in 1920, but we can not be sure that he putted out every hole.)

Carrick's nine birdies in the morning round of the final would be hailed as an outstanding accomplishment today. In the 1920s, it was unheard of.

There was an aura of magnificence about the clashes between Somerville and Carrick, for here we had the two supreme amateurs of their day meeting in friendly but fierce debate. In the three years, 1925 to 1927, they faced each other in seven championships, provincial or national. Carrick won five of these encounters.

Their finest battle was perhaps the 36-hole semi-final of the 1927 Amateur at Ancaster. All square at the eighteenth, they were never separated by more than a hole until the end. Carrick won the 32nd hole to go 1 up. At the par-three 34th, Somerville's ball hit a rake, which not only stopped it from going into a bunker, but also deflected it onto the green, to give him a half. His opponent's piece of luck did not unnerve Carrick. At the 500-yard 35th hole, he hit two magnificent shots to reach the green and laid his first putt dead for a birdie. Somerville could do nothing to better this.

Don Carrick was also a top-class football player and a skilled boxer. At the University of Toronto in 1927, as inter-collegiate boxing champion of Canada, he won against the pick of U.S. naval and military colleges.

He did not defend his Canadian Amateur golf title in 1928. Instead, he directed all his energies to winning Olympic honours for Canada as a light heavyweight. In the 1928 Olympics at Amsterdam, he won his first-round match, but in the second round he was beaten on points by the eventual Olympic champion.

The Olympics behind him, Don Carrick next concentrated on his education at Harvard Law School. Serious golf was put aside while he applied his mind to his studies; he spent little time at practice, and put his competitive edge on hold.

Winning championships did not come naturally to Don Carrick, any more than it does to any top golfer. His earlier successes were not the result of some innate gift, but of long hours on the practice fairway under the eyes of Senour.

In 1933, he again took to the practice field at Scarboro. He also changed his clubs. For years he had remained faithful to hickory shafts and had sworn he would never change. But in the spring of 1933 he played in an invitational at York Downs with Phil Farley, Fred Hoblitzel, and Bill Taylor, three long hitters with whom he could usually keep up. They had switched to steel and consistently outdrove him. He discarded his hickories the very next day.

Carrick did not play in that year's Canadian Amateur, since to do so would have meant taking time away from his law office, but he won the Ontario Amateur. All the old skills were there; they required only honing.

Having proved that to himself, Don Carrick played no more first-class competitive golf. Golf became his pastime and his continuing pleasure. He set out to apply himself to his law business with the same assiduity and earnestness that he had given to golf and to boxing.

Don Carrick's short but sparkling essays into our national golf have been overshadowed by those of the more famous Sandy Somerville. Carrick epitomized, as did Somerville, the spirit of the true amateur golfer. He twice won the amateur championship of Canada. His first win proved that he could do it; his second, that it was no fluke. After that, what more did he have to prove!

In the days before an amateur championship was viewed as a stepping-stone to a professional career, it was not unusual for amateurs to retire from championship golf at their peak. Bobby Jones, to whom Don Carrick was often compared, is perhaps the best example. Joyce Wethered, the great British woman golfer of the same era, is another. And Sandy Somerville himself, as we shall see, won his six national titles, then withdrew. Perhaps reaching the moon twice should be enough for any person. Too, the mental and physical strain of championship golf is enormous. To win their titles, Carrick and Somerville often had to play twelve rounds of golf in six days.

In an article published in *Canadian Golfer*, "Some Reflections on the Amateur of 1931," the Reverend E. Leslie Pidgeon closed by writing this, which is as true today as it was sixty years ago:

> The attitudes of concentration and control [demand] a high degree of self-mastery. This inward discipline is golf's most valuable by-product …
>
> Golf has reached such a high point of skill that one wonders if a young man can really excel in the game and in anything else. To the amateur it must ever remain an avocation rather than a vocation: it must fit its devotees for life work rather than be a substitute for what is the real business of life. We must, therefore, encourage our young men whose skills we admire and achievements we cheer, to make the game, as well as its principles, subservient to their higher manhood.

No golfers lived up to these precepts more faithfully than Donald Carrick and Sandy Somerville.

. . . the City of London gave him a public reception such as is seldom given to any one. Thousands took part in the turnout in his honor and he was given the freedom of the City and presented with the Key and when asked by Mayor Hayman to ask for anything and it would be granted, he promptly asked for a school holiday for the children. . . .

George S. Lyon (who had gone to St. Louis in September 1904 to wrest the Olympic gold medal from American golfers) wrote these words, in *Golf and Sports Illustrated*, of Sandy Somerville, who went to Baltimore Country Club in September 1932 to wrest the U.S. amateur championship from a later generation of American golfers.

From the late 1920s through the 1930s, Sandy Somerville stood on top of Canadian amateur golf as firmly as George Lyon had between 1898 and the First World War. The statistics show why these were Somerville's years:

Canadian Amateur Champion: 1926, 1928, 1930, 1931, 1935, 1937
United States Amateur Champion: 1932

During these years, Sandy Somerville had an intimidating effect on his opponents. He had that quality that distinguishes the player who knows he should be champion from the player who accepts the inevitability of second place.

He set about his opponents with a "grim, silent precision," the outstanding feature of his golf from the beginning. "A phlegmatic, cold-blooded golf fatalist," added the Reverend Pidgeon in *Canadian Golfer* after Somerville's win at the 38th hole over Carroll Stuart in the semi-final of the 1928 Amateur.

But Sandy Somerville was a warm, kindly, unassuming man, and we should not confuse cold-bloodedness with heartlessness. He had the gift – mostly innate, partly acquired – of extreme stoicism in the face of the worst possible breaks, of being able to shrug off a bad hole, confident in the knowledge that he had the skill, and that his time would come.

Those who knew him never confused his silence on the fairway with unfriendliness.

Some sections of the press dubbed him "Silent Sandy" and "The Silent One." Bill Blainey, an American player he defeated on his way to the U.S. national title in 1932, had this to say of him a few months later in *Golf and Sports Illustrated*:

A great deal has also been written about his reticence toward conversation. I for one wish to contradict this belief. I had known Sandy for some time previous to our meeting at Baltimore and this perhaps may have something to do with it, but at any rate during our match Sandy upheld his end of a very enjoyable conversation which to me made our match more like a friendly day of golf upon which nothing depended rather than a match in a National Championship.

The truth is that he had little time for foolish questions from those who interviewed him, no more than Jack Nicklaus has today. Always polite, but less concerned with preserving an image in the days before images were relayed live by television, Somerville could afford to answer the press briefly.

When asked by a New York editor to comment on the fact that Johnny Goodman, whom Somerville had defeated in the final of the U.S. Amateur, had purchased a new set of clubs, had taken off weight, was now driving fifteen yards farther, and was reportedly "out gunning for Somerville," Sandy answered with characteristic modesty: "Nice boy, Johnny. I was a bit lucky to beat him at Baltimore." That is not what the editor wanted to hear. Head-lines cannot be fabricated from answers like that.

What the press often took to be Somerville's hostile silence was no more than his super-concentration, essential to his success. When asked for his most important advice to golfers, he answered: "This – that the first law, the second, the third law of golf, is concentration. Let all else be forgotten . . ."

Sandy Somerville's father, Charles Ross Somerville Sr., came to London, Ontario, in the 1870s, and was able to retire as a successful businessman while Sandy was still a schoolboy. Charles Somerville rendered considerable public service as a member and chairman of local boards, was elected mayor of London in 1918, and re-elected in 1919. He was an early member of the London Golf Club and an enthusiastic supporter of golf in the city. He took his son to Pinehurst, later to Scotland, where the two of them golfed together.

Although he played golf at the age of seven, the game was not Sandy Somerville's first love. His school, Ridley College, was the nursery of

Sandy Somerville as a boy golfer; on the right, golfing at Dornoch, Scotland.

Sandy as a Senior golfer.

cricket in Canada and turned Sandy into a first-class batsman. He held the highest score for a school cricketer in Canada – 212 not out. Later, he was to tour England with a select Canadian eleven and, in 1921, to play in the last international cricket match against the United States. (His cricket swing would occasionally creep into his golf, to spoil the odd shot.)

At the university of Toronto he also made a name for himself on the football field, and in London he was regarded as one of the finest amateur hockey centres in the country.

Only gradually did Somerville commit himself to golf. When still a schoolboy, he became

a pupil of Kernie Marsh, the professional at the London Hunt Club. Assiduous practice under Marsh's keen eye saw the young Somerville improve, but he did not pick up the finer points of the game as quickly as his good friend Carrick.

In the 1924 semi-finals of the Amateur we catch our first glimpse of Somerville's imperturbable spirit. One down after the morning round, Somerville fought back. He squared the match at the 21st, and went on to win rather easily by 4 and 3.

The experts took a closer look at this well-muscled, medium height, broad-shouldered, sturdily built, and well-nigh nerveless youth. But against Frank Thompson in the final he could not match a faultless display of pitching and putting, although he outdrove Thompson by thirty yards.

Somerville's first Canadian Amateur title came in 1926, at Toronto GC. Throughout the week he had given an exhibition of long iron and wood shots never before seen from an amateur in Canada. Consistently 300 yards or more off the tee, he outdrove and out-putted the title-holder, Don Carrick. His 4 and 3 win in the final over a tired Happy Fraser came as something of a let-down.

Somerville lost the 1927 semi-final at Ancaster to Carrick, after a homeric struggle. But it was in the interprovincial matches held that same week that he proved himself to be mortal.

The last two holes at Ancaster then measured 500 yards and 425 yards, neither of them particularly tight or tricky. At the seventeenth, Somerville put his ball in the bushes, tried to dig it out, and in no time at all suffered the ignominy of an 11 on his score card. At the eighteenth, a ball in a bunker also proved difficult to extract, and he was lucky to escape with a 9. Twenty shots for two holes. "It's nae fair, but it's gowf!"

The spectators who followed him around probably remembered only his long and accurate driving, especially at the 345-yard tenth hole, where he was pin-high off the tee.

Around this time, his style was described in this way in *Canadian Golfer*:

The mechanics of his stroke are faultless. His stance is more open than that of many good golfers; but that is quite orthodox. He uses the long "V" grip, never allows his right elbow to wander from his side, and never hits from the top. His club starts down slowly and maintains a perfect acceleration. There is entire absence of jerk and there is no apparent effort to hit – the sweeping away of the ball is just an incident in a perfect, complicated unity.

Finals do not always provide the most exciting golf or bring out the best in champions. Such was the case in 1928, at Summerlea, when the only golfer to draw out Somerville's remarkable qualities of concentration, precision, and nervelessness was Carroll Stuart of Ottawa.

Stuart was a neat, precise player, notably so with the short irons. He had acquired the unusual habit of lifting and dropping the clubhead behind the ball at the address, instead of the usual waggle (by all accounts, not unlike our Richard Zokol today).

In the morning, Somerville went round in a fine 72, but found himself 1 hole down. The lunch-time prediction in the clubhouse was that Stuart would not survive long in the afternoon, one of the hottest August days on record. However, the match was all square as they went to the 210-yard seventeenth (or 35th) hole. Here, Stuart sank a 20-foot putt over an undulating green. If we can believe one observer, Somerville's face was pale for the first time in the tournament. But otherwise it was expressionless. He went boldly for the half, but his ball struck the back of the hole, jumped in the air, and came to rest on the edge.

To go 1 down with a hole to go, and to a 20-foot putt, is enough to knock the stuffing out of any golfer. But champions in the mould of a Somerville do not react like *any* golfer. At the long par-four eighteenth, Somerville unleashed a tremendous drive of over 300 yards, well past Stuart's. He put his second on the green to win the hole easily, and went on to win the match at the second hole of sudden death, a 440-yard uphill par four, where his extra length off the tee was decisive.

Of Somerville's play, one reporter noted: "He is playing extremely poor golf for me. There is nothing to say about it, except that every stroke is perfect, and that makes poor copy."

When Somerville won in 1930, his finest hour again came in the third round, against the American, Connolly. Playing listless golf in hot humid weather, Somerville was 6 down with 12 to play. Thereafter, Somerville appeared to wake up from a bad dream, and the spectators witnessed one of the finest comebacks in the history of the Amateur. He won 7 of the last 12 holes to go on to the next round by the barest of margins.

In the following year, Sandy Somerville simply dominated the field to retain his title.

Observers of the golfing scene noted that Somerville's superiority over the nation's best golfers had increasingly become mental rather than technical. It was not that Somerville was invincible, but that his opponents came to believe he was, which is much the same thing in the end. The Reverend Pidgeon wrote in 1931 in *Canadian Golfer*: "He wins because he can control his conscious process in particularly trying moments and situations . . . He is unique because he can generally maintain his perfection under conditions to which others succumb." And when he lapsed, momentarily, his power of comeback was another indication of this control.

When he lost a vital match, it was usually as the result of a few inspired shots by his opponent. In the 1934 Amateur final at Laval, Scotty Campbell of Seattle defeated him by holing his ball from off the green for a deuce at the seventh; sinking a 30-foot putt at another short hole; holing a tricky 10-footer to win at the 36th. Somerville played sub-par golf in the afternoon round but could do nothing against such snatches of good fortune.

Illness cost him the 1936 championship. Although it was not generally known, he was pounds underweight, and appeared almost resigned to the loss of the title he had won for the fifth time the year before. He went out in the semi-finals to Fred Haas of New Orleans.

In the 1937 season he seemed determined to show the experts that he was a long way from being through as a top-flight player. He won practically every event he entered.

In the Amateur, Phil Farley produced the best golf of the week, until the final. Two up against Somerville after the morning round, he looked all set for his first national title. But Somerville cut his lead to 1 at the 27th. At the next hole came one of those strokes that can only be put down to a mental lapse. Playing a 7-iron to the green, Farley lifted his head and flubbed it. Somerville squared the match, took the lead at the 30th, had another birdie two holes later, and scrambled a half at the 34th to win his sixth and last Amateur championship.

Somerville produced a few outstanding shots when he had to, over the closing holes. But his relaxed attitude towards this final sent mixed signals to the critics. Some saw this as an inner confidence that he could continue to win as he wished; others, that the desire to win had gone.

This was to be the end of the Somerville hold on the Canadian Amateur. His war service took him overseas. When he returned as Major Somerville, MBE, golf became his pastime. He never again entered for the Canadian – or Ontario – championships.

But as a senior in the 1960s, he fought many a battle against old opponents Jack Cameron, Phil Farley, Jack Nash, and Gordon and Bill Taylor to become a four-time champion – or joint champion – of the Canadian Seniors' Golf Association, as well as a two-time winner of the U.S.–Canada Seniors' trophy. He was also president of the RCGA in 1957.

Winning the U.S. Amateur Championship at the Five Farms course of the Baltimore Country Club in 1932 was the zenith of Sandy Somerville's career. It would probably have given him as much satisfaction had he won the British Amateur (in 1938 he reached the semi-finals). In the 1930s there was little to choose between these two great tests of golfing skill and endurance. But whereas three Americans had won the British Amateur, only one foreigner had ever been successful in the U.S. – England's Harold Hilton, in 1911. Many Canadians had tried, including Somerville himself, but only George S. Lyon had ever got as far as the finals, and that was back in 1906. So Canadian golfing history was made on that Saturday in September 1932, when Somerville defeated Johnny Goodman of Omaha by 2 and 1 in the 36-hole final.

Sandy Somerville did not come to Five Farms as "an unknown," as at least one golf writer of the 1960s would have us believe. He was well-known to, and highly respected by, everyone who mattered in U.S. golf. He came to Five Farms with the reputation of being the most dangerous of foreign entrants, and these included the visiting British Walker Cup team.

At least one American fancied Sandy Somerville to win the U.S. Amateur in 1932. Can you imagine the furore today if the referee of a national tournament was known to have bet on one of the finalists and won $180? Yet not an eyebrow was raised in 1932, when the *Toronto Daily Star* reported that the referee of the Somerville–Goodman match admitted he had put his money on Somerville. The referee was Bobby Jones. In the 1930s, Bobby Jones did not have to defend his integrity or his motives.

Sandy Somerville had prepared himself well for the U.S. Amateur. All season he had persevered with the large American ball, perhaps forfeiting the Canadian title as a result. He came to Five Farms three days before the tournament.

The early rounds of the championship gave him no trouble. In the second round he defeated Jack Westland, a former U.S. Western Amateur champion. In the first 36-hole match he defeated Bill Blainey, a highly ranked U.S. player. Even his semi-final against Jesse ("Siege Gun") Guilford, champion in 1921, was a fairly easy win by a margin of 7 and 6.

The final was quite another matter. Johnny Goodman, twenty-two, had been dubbed "Giant Killer," having knocked out two Walker Cup stars before defeating the title-holder,

Francis Ouimet, in the semi-final. Full of confidence, he attacked Somerville and the course with all the vigour of youth. Their match was close. Fortunes shifted suddenly and dramatically, but with never more than two holes between the players. In thirty-four holes they never spoke a word to each other, a sign of concentration rather than unfriendliness. And in the end, Somerville's greater power of concentration gave him victory.

In the final, each player was escorted by two Baltimore City policemen, carrying service revolvers and handcuffs, presumably to protect the players against overenthusiastic spectators.

Somerville started the final as a duffer would, topping his drive 125 yards down the fairway. When Goodman did the same with his second, they were both lucky to get their pars. Thereafter it was tough, gritty golf, with Somerville sinking a 50-foot putt at the eighteenth to go to lunch 1 up.

The morning's play was marked by four stymies, three of which certainly determined the outcome of the holes. At the second, Goodman laid Somerville a stymie that could not be circumnavigated or jumped. At the tenth, Somerville got around a half-stymie, but failed to sink the putt. Later it was his turn to fox Goodman. On the twelfth green, Goodman failed to jump Somerville's ball with a 4-iron. On the thirteenth, he was given no chance when his ball finished eight feet from the flag, with Somerville's, on the same line, only two inches from the hole.

In the afternoon, Somerville went 2 up at the second hole (the 20th of the match). But Goodman came back with a spectacular run of birdies at 3, 6, 7, and 9. Somerville was now 2 down, with only nine holes to go.

As the players stood on the tenth tee, an unruly crowd held up play by encroaching on the fairway. Somerville smoked his first cigarette of the day and spoke to his friend Jack Nash. Goodman sat on his haunches and ruminated. When the crowd had cleared, Goodman hit what was described as a "dooser" – straight and very long. Somerville threw down his cigarette, opened his shoulders, and smashed one past him. That was the beginning of the end. Goodman hit a poor second, losing the hole to a par. On the eleventh (29th), Somerville's tee-shot finished in the rough under a weeping willow. Goodman sliced into the spectators, hitting a girl on the cheek. Somerville hit a perfect second, and lay dead for a par. Goodman's second hit a woman. On in four, he conceded. The match was all square.

Trying to play safe at the dog-leg twelfth (30th), Goodman missed the green with his second. Somerville did not play safe. He soared one high over the oak trees, cutting the dog-leg, and was 1 up. (To Bobby Jones, this was the shot that won the title.)

On the sixteenth (34th) Somerville went dormic 2 with a 25-foot birdie putt, while Goodman frittered away strokes on the fairway. A par on the short seventeenth gave Somerville the title.

All week, Somerville had taken the breaks, good and bad, with no change in expression. His first smile came on the 35th green when Johnny Goodman shook his hand. In spite of this – perhaps because of this – his win was well-received by a naturally partisan crowd. It took him thirty minutes to make his way through a wall of autograph hunters to the presentation. The newspapermen wanted to know why he looked so sour during the match. A stranger in another country should be quiet, he explained. He did not want to appear to be talking his opponent out of a match, he explained.

The USGA was unprepared for a foreign champion. No one could find a Union Jack. The Toronto *Star* reported that "they made up for this, however, by singing the Maple Leaf and Alouette."

In 1904, George Lyon had come home from St. Louis to be met by the joyous crowds at Union Station. It was characteristic of Sandy Somerville that he slipped quietly into London by motorcar. The Havemeyer Trophy was brought back from Baltimore by another London group. Fittingly, it included Kernie Marsh, the London professional who had done so much to mould the young Somerville's game.

Somerville wins the U.S. Amateur, 1932, and is congratulated by loser Goodman.

As a result of his win, Sandy Somerville was invited to the inaugural Masters at Augusta, in 1934. After playing a practice round with Bobby Jones, he made another piece of golf history. He had a hole in one, the first to be recorded in the Masters and only the second in his career.

Mention of Bobby Jones is a reminder that he always looked upon his defeat of Sandy Somerville in the 1930 U.S. Amateur as vital to his achieving the Grand Slam that year (he won the U.S. and British Amateurs and Opens). Twenty-four years later, he wrote in *Canadian Sport Monthly* of the crucial point in their match:

> We were both on the green of the seventh. I was about eight feet from the cup, Sandy only seven. I putted first and sank. Somerville missed his 7-footer. I then holed a 15-footer for a three on the eighth and a 20-footer for a deuce on the ninth.
>
> While the newspapers made but little mention of that seventh hole incident, I have

always looked upon it as the break that made the Grand Slam possible. Had I missed my 8-footer, Sandy probably would have sunk his 7-footer and the tide of play might have gone the other way. Somerville was that good.

Sandy Somerville was one of the first to be inducted into the Canadian Golf Hall of Fame.

The 1932 Canadian Amateur at Lambton was a meet of very special significance to amateur golf in Canada, although this only became evident some years later. It brought together for the first time an abundance of young talent who were to make the 1930s the golden years.

From Ontario came Sandy Somerville, Don Carrick, Phil Farley, Jack Cameron, Jack Nash, Fred Hoblitzel, Fred Lyon, Gordon Taylor Jr., the two young Thompsons, Joe and Nicol Jr., together with their veteran uncles, Frank and Stanley.

From Quebec we had Gordon B. Taylor and brother Bill, Hugh Jaques, Gordon McAthey, E. A. Innes; from Manitoba, Bobby Reith; from the Maritimes; Gint Cain; from British Columbia, the flaxen-haired Ken Black and the very talented, long-hitting, Stan Leonard. Hilles Pickens later christened them "the boys of '32."

Many who played at Lambton that year later looked back to the first day of the tournament with no sense of nostalgia and with something less than affection. On Monday 8 August, the field of some 120 golfers set out in pairs at 8:30 a.m. to play the *two* 18-hole qualifying rounds. These had to be completed in one day.

Something like 240 pairs, playing championship golf, are hard to squeeze into less than twelve hours of daylight, even with no hitches. At Lambton, there were numerous hitches. Several competitors were in the century class. One shot 107 in his second round. Another handed in a card of 97 98–197, which can be applauded only for its consistency. This, despite the fact that the entry conditions specified a handicap limit of 10.

The defending champion, Sandy Somerville, also ran into trouble in the first round, coming in with an 80. Starting his second round at 6:00 p.m., he finished an astonishing 73 by moonlight. Others were not so lucky on the dusking greens. Many could not see well enough to finish at all.

By nightfall, the officials had lined up automobiles, their headlights on, behind the eighteenth green and along the eighteenth fairway. Others carried lanterns and candles. George Lyon knew Lambton like the back of his hand, and played the last three holes from memory and imagination. Finishing 6, 6, 6, he missed the cut by three strokes. (So did Bill Taylor of Kanawaki. "I played the last hole by the light of automobile headlights," he recalled fifty-six years later.) George was in no singing mood that evening, but he gave the RCGA officials his views on moonlight golf.

Few of these boys of '32 were well-known outside their own provinces. In the early match-play rounds their sensational play kept the galleries of several thousand highly enthused.

In the first round, the four Thompsons were all eliminated, although Joe had led the qualifiers. The Thompson match-play jinx was thus perpetuated. In the second round Phil Farley went out at the 38th, after a bitter battle with Stan Leonard; Sandy Somerville eliminated the hope of the Prairies, Bobby Reith; Don Carrick was in trouble too often, and lost to the Quebec favourite, Gordon B. Taylor.

In the next round, Taylor had no difficulty in disposing of Leonard 8 and 7. As the week progressed, it became clear that he or the American William Gunn Jr. were the men to beat in their half of the draw. With Somerville in the other half, most people hoped for a Somerville–Taylor final. That was not to be. Jack Cameron (playing out of Mississaugua) accomplished a long-held ambition by defeating Somerville 3 and 2 in their semi-final match. (Sandy had been unusually short off the tee all week, and seemed unable to control the ball. He made no excuses. But the Lambton professional, Andy Kay, revealed that Somerville had been playing with the larger American ball, in preparation for his assault on the U.S. Amateur.)

In the other semi-final, Gordon B. Taylor shot a 69 in the morning round to be 8 up against Gunn, and he won by 12 and 10.

There was a strange irony in the meeting of Gordon B. Taylor and Jack Cameron in the final. They had spent the week as the house guests of Fred and Mrs. Hoblitzel. The two finalists slept in the same room and ate together. Both were underdogs in their semi-final matches but fought their way to the final. That week they formed a fast friendship that was to last for the rest of their lives.

Both Taylor and Cameron were long hitters. Several times in their final they drove the ball over 320 yards. But Cameron used more body-turn in his swing. The penalty for this was less accuracy. In the end, that was to make all the difference. He could not control a drive that hooked and sliced. He fell behind at the second hole and was never able to catch up with his straight-shooting opponent.

Four up after the morning round, Taylor went on to win by 5 and 3. The rhythm of his swing provided the basis for his championship. In *Golf and Sports Illustrated*, Gilbert Reid had this to say after the final:

> Both have orthodox swings, with Taylor exhibiting a rhythmical hit which is unrivalled in this writer's mind by any player in the game today. His perfect timing gives the appearance of effortless hitting, and for that reason his tremendous distance amazes the average observer. For such a long hitter, his control is indeed remarkable. With his irons

Gordon B. Taylor, winner of the moonlight Amateur in 1932, is still one of the sweetest swingers.

Taylor makes the average shot to the green appear absurdly simple, and his putting touch never once lapsed during the entire week of play.

Born in Montreal in 1910, Gordon Baxter Taylor was another champion golfer who excelled at other sports. Throughout his schooldays he played on the football, basketball, and hockey teams. Later, he played hockey for the Montreal Royals. He won the Quebec fancy diving championship and was considered a prospective Olympic diver.

Gordon B. Taylor (the middle initial distinguishes him from Gordon Taylor of Toronto) started golfing as a youth at the Hermitage Golf Club, Magog, Quebec. Like his older brother W. D. (Bill), he played his first competitive golf out of Montreal's Summerlea club, but in 1930 he joined Kanawaki. Although he had tried his hand in the Amateur as early as 1928, he was virtually unknown outside Quebec when he came to Lambton in 1932.

Gordon B. Taylor was timing his swing as sweetly half a century after his win at Lambton in 1932. It won for him the club championship of Kanawaki in 1931, and the championship of the Mount Bruno club some fifty years later. (Has this been equalled by anyone?) I had the pleasure of playing with him at Mount Bruno in the late 1970s, and have never seen a golf ball fly so far when struck with such apparent ease.

Taylor went out to Shaughnessy in 1933, but his putter was not kind to him and he lost his title.

A naval officer in the Second World War, Gordon B. Taylor became an able golf administrator, presiding over the RCGA in 1959. He was elected to the Canadian Golf Hall of Fame in 1987.

The runner-up at Lambton, Jack Cameron, was never to win the national title. He was another product of St. Andrews College, Toronto. And he, too, was another all-round athlete, an Olympic hockey goal-tender and a badminton player of national repute. Jack Cameron was often seen on the fairway in shorts, although he wore plus-fours at Lambton. (That may have been a mistake. He started in plus-fours at the Amateur in 1933. One down at lunch to Jimmy Todd, he changed into shorts and defeated Todd in the afternoon.)

Before we leave Lambton, we should look at some of the other "boys of '32." Gordon B. Taylor and Ken Black were the only two Canadians to emulate Somerville and Carrick and win the national Amateur.

When Ken Black won in 1939, he had a titanic struggle in the semi-finals to eliminate a player he had first met at Lambton – Phil Farley.

In Farley we have a golfer who epitomizes the cruel irony of golf and its major championships. For some twenty years, from 1935 to 1954, his name appeared in the rankings of Canada's top amateurs. Had there been rankings in the early 1930s, you would have found his name in them. No other amateur who came to the top in the 1930s remained there for so long. In 1939, he was ranked number one, jointly with Somerville.

Some leading amateurs, like Somerville, chose to retire early from competitive golf. And perhaps Phil Farley would have taken himself off the cutting edge of national golf sooner than he did had fate been kinder to him. But fate dictated that in twenty-five years of trying, he was to win just about everything in amateur golf in Canada but the national championship. In the record books you will find his name as the winner of the Ontario Junior, six Ontario Amateurs, two Ontario Opens, and two Quebec Amateurs. Eight times he was low Canadian amateur in the Open; eight times he represented Canada, including twice as a Senior. In 1942, he defeated a field that included professionals Bob Burns, Willie Lamb, Dick Borthwick, Bill Kerr, Bob Gray, Gordie Brydson, and Jimmy Johnstone, to win the Ontario Open by four strokes over 36 holes. This may have been his finest performance ever. But in the records of the Canadian Amateur, his name appears only as the runner-up in 1937, 1949, and 1951.

Phil Farley came to golf in 1922, as a ten-year-old paid ten cents an hour for picking stones on Toronto's Cedar Brook course (later Cedar Brae) when it was being constructed. He graduated to being a caddie when the course opened later that year. Local legend has it that he was the boy designated to approach the club's president and negotiate a deal whereby caddies could play the first and eighteenth holes before normal tee-off time. After a year or so of caddying, he so impressed the members with his golf that he was accepted as a junior.

This slim, curly-haired, compact, 130-pound golfer with the infectious grin could hit the ball farther than fellows four inches taller and seventy pounds heavier. When asked after winning the Ontario junior at the age of eighteen for his advice to young golfers, he said: "Don't bother about distance from the tee. Don't study distance, study timing. Look at me. I'm just 130 pounds, but I can lam 'em out with the best of them, because I'm a timer." He was self-taught. Success came to him only as the result of long hours on the practice tee. School holidays would see him spending upwards of six hours a day at Cedar Brook, working on his game, mainly his putting and approaching. He also had a burning ambition to be Canada's finest amateur, but never to the extent that golf was to become the be-all and end-all of his life, or that winning was all that mattered. No one was to give more back to the game than Phil Farley.

From the time the Ontario Junior title fell to him in 1930, and the Ontario Amateur, in 1931 (making him the only person to hold both titles at the same time), he seemed destined to win everything in golf. His strength lay in his short game. But the Canadian Amateur was to elude Phil Farley.

In 1937 he frittered away holes in the semi-final, which he won, and in the final, which he lost. In his final against Somerville, the gallery of eight hundred saw him flub that important 7-iron shot at the 28th. Over the next few holes his shots to the green were so tentative that the ball was never close enough to give him a reasonable chance of a birdie. And his

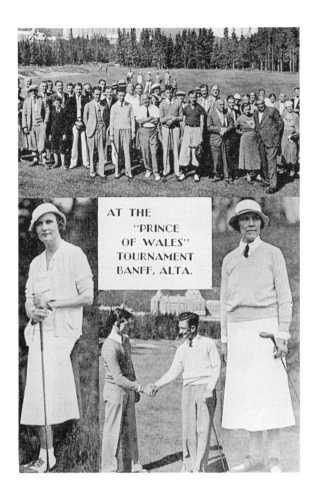

The Banff Springs Prince of Wales tournament in 1933 attracted a number of golfing celebrities: left, ladies' winner Ms. W. R. Desburey of Winnipeg; loser Bobby Reith shakes hands with winner Phil Farley; among those in the front row top are Bud Donovan and Sandy Somerville.

putting, too, started to let him down. The problem was mental. He was always nervous when playing in a tournament. "It just stays in my stomach and knots," he admitted. Somerville probably knew that he had won as much by his superior mental and physical stamina as by anything else. Accepting the winner's trophy, he graciously admitted that if there were some way of sharing it, "I'd be delighted to have it that way, Phil."

Phil Farley was exhausted, mentally and physically, by this final. Hours after it was over, he was discovered sleeping on a bench in the locker-room with a blanket over him.

Two years later he went to Mount Bruno, ranked jointly with Somerville as the country's

top player. Again, he frittered away his semi-final lead over Ken Black, when the match and the championship seemed to be his. He lost at the 25th. Black's marvellous recovery shots seemed to be more than Farley could bear.

In 1935, his job as a salesman of golf equipment took him to Montreal for four years. Playing out of the Marlborough club, he won the Quebec Amateur twice, and represented Quebec (three times) as he had Ontario (twelve times) in the Willingdon Cup.

Once back in Ontario, he joined Scarboro and carried his quest for the Amateur title into the post-war years. He was to captain the Canadian team in the first Americas Cup matches. He was also to become one of the country's most respected and admired golf administrators, heading up the OGA, and the RCGA in 1967.

Jack Nash was another whose name appeared for some twenty years in the top ten national

Phil Farley and Jack Nash after one of their many battles, in 1935.

golf rankings, although not consistently. He played out of London Hunt, usually in the shadow of Somerville, who was ten years his senior. Nash and Farley disputed many a title. "The two bantam-weight Goliaths of Canadian golf" someone dubbed them in the early 1930s.

Next to Jack Cameron, Nash was probably the finest combination of badminton player/golfer in Canada. In golf, he had to content himself with several provincial titles, until he became a senior.

In the years between the wars, British Columbia emerged to become a force in national golf. By the early 1930s its amateurs were challenging the domination of Ontario and Quebec in the interprovincial matches for the Willingdon Cup. By the end of the decade, two of its home-bred golfers, Stan Leonard and Freddie Wood, were on their way to becoming the leading professionals in Canada.

That is not to say that, hitherto, the province's amateurs could not match Central Canada's. There is no saying what national honours Harvey Combe and Vernon Macan might have won. But by the time B.C. players could legitimately have their expenses paid to play in the Willingdon Cup (and hence the Amateur) Combe was dead, and Macan, who lost a foot in the war, was past his best.

British Columbia did not enter a team for the Willingdon Cup until 1929, when the Amateur was held at Jasper. It was then that golfers outside B.C. got their first look at Freddie Wood. He was one of a string of young B.C. golfers about to enliven the golfing scene, but the first to make his mark in national golf.

The strange and unpredictable events of the Amateur at Jasper have been recorded but never explained. Why did Canadian golfers from the East fail so miserably in their bid for the championship? Not one of four national champions – Somerville, Carrick, Frank Thompson, Happy Fraser – survived the third round.

The biggest upset of the tournament was the first-round defeat of the favourite, Somerville, by Cecil (Cece) Colville of the Glen Oaks club, Vancouver. A slight youth, Cece had been a finalist in half a dozen events on the coast but had never won anything of note.

B.C.'s winning Willingdon Cup team of 1934, left to right: *Stan Leonard, Bob Morrison, Dick Moore, Ken Black.*

Less of an upset was the first-round victory of Freddie Wood over Happy Fraser. The Kanawaki player had been off form for a year or so. But when Freddie disposed of Don Carrick in the second round, the reporters who had flocked to Jasper as guests of CNR decided it was time to take a closer look at this young man.

The Scottish-born Wood had taken up golf while a caddie at the Vancouver G & CC, back in 1919. He won his first city caddie championship in 1924, but had no provincial titles when he became the sensation of the Jasper Amateur. He was then a clerk in a Vancouver store and able to golf only on weekends. "Unsung and unheralded, he came to Jasper. He left there virtually the uncrowned king of Canada." So lyricized Ralph Reville, and his sentiments were no doubt shared by many at the time, for Freddie Wood not only eliminated two former champions, he also upheld the country's golfing honour. While Somerville and the other cracks from the East were wilting, Freddie fought his way to the semi-finals, the only Canadian to do so. Once there, he put up a gallant fight against Eddie Held. But Held won, going on to become the first American golfer to carry off the Canadian Amateur Championship.

During the week, Freddie Wood showed that he possessed a sound game and an excellent golfing temperament. In his match against Carrick, he was 2 down after the morning round, but gave no sign that he was intimidated by the two-time champion. In the afternoon, he wore Carrick down with a display of faultless, steady golf.

In his semi-final against Held, he nearly pulled off another surprise win. Like so many matches of its kind, this one hinged on a lucky break for the eventual winner. Held was 1 up on the 34th tee. His drive was heading for an area of deep rough and rocks when it hit a spectator and dropped into the short grass. Perhaps unnerved by this rub-of-the-green, Wood lost the hole. At the next hole, Held got the half he needed to win.

Why did the cream of the East all go sour at Jasper? What happened to our four ex-champions that they should all go down so ignominiously? The temptation is to blame the nature of the course, the environment, and the 1920s equivalent of jet lag. The well-bunkered course at Jasper, one of architect Stanley Thompson's jewels, is 5,000 feet up in the Rockies. The ball flies farther in Jasper's rarified atmosphere. The judgement of distance and club selection is made even more difficult by the mountainous backdrop.

What is more, the greens at Jasper were of creeping bent, a turf then seldom found in the East. They proved difficult for most golfers to read, being slower against the grain. Admittedly, these were problems that all golfers faced. But place any group of golfers on a strange course, in unaccustomed circumstances, in an environment that affects them physiologically, and you'll find distorted scores. Some golfers adjust more quickly than others.

The golfers from the East also had the excuse that they had travelled to Jasper as part of a tour laid on by CNR. The "Special Tour de Luxe" left Toronto on 10 August, with golfers, wives, and newspaper reporters. It picked up the Winnipeg contingent and arrived at Jasper on 17 August, a day or so before the championships. How could they be expected to play well after being cooped up in a train for a week?

Unfortunately, such excuses fly in the face of the facts. The three leading Canadians in the qualifying rounds of the Amateur were Don Carrick, Frank Thompson, and Sandy Somerville. So much for alibis.

The greatest B.C. golfer of them all, Stan Leonard, first played in the Amateur in 1932, at Lambton. This wiry, seventeen-year-old youth with the terrific pivot and whiplash wrist action shot a 147 in the Willingdon, a score bettered only by Fred Hoblitzel of Ontario. But he did it with good, steady golf, without anything lucky or spectacular apart from his slashing swing.

In the second round of the '32 Amateur he met Phil Farley. Their match turned out to be one of the outstanding encounters of the week. For 36 holes, these two serious-demeanoured lads fought on even terms. Leonard was already notoriously long off the tee. But Farley's short game kept him alive until the 38th hole, where he cracked with a double-bogey 5. Both players were worn out by the strain of the match. So Leonard's usual fire was quickly extinguished in the next round by Gordon B. Taylor.

Stan Leonard and Sandy Somerville met only once in the national Amateur. In 1935 at Ancaster, where it rained every day, the two clashed in the semi-finals. Leonard had won his second B.C. title that year and was fancied by westerners to win the national title as well. His great propensity for practice had polished his game.

Leonard could now outdrive Somerville, and at Ancaster he did. But Somerville was more than a match in accuracy. He came to the 36th hole 1 up. Their match now took on some of the aspects of a circus. A deep fog had settled on the course. Visibility was so poor that forecaddies had to be sent out to listen for the balls landing. Leonard somehow managed to get a par 4, which was good enough to square the match. At the first hole of sudden death, however, his 280-yard drive was off line, although he could not tell just how far off line. Somerville was nearly as long, but his drive was straight. He had no difficulty in finding the green with a short iron on this 375-yard hole. But Leonard's ball had strayed so far that he was faced with playing a 4-wood through a blanket of fog to a green he could not see. His ball finished in a greenside trap. He exploded out, and was now lying 3 to Somerville's 2.

Both balls were about fourteen feet from the hole. To determine who was away, the referee (A. A. Adams, that fine amateur of the 1910s and 1920s) measured the distance from Leonard's ball to the hole, then from Somerville's ball to the hole. Unaccountably, in measuring Leonard's distance, he heeled and toed his way over the soft, damp turf on a direct line between the ball and the hole, when he should have taken pains to avoid this line. If Leonard saw footprints in the turf, he said nothing. He missed the putt, and the match was over.

Ken Black was the finest amateur of his time to come from the West Coast. For some years in the 1930s he was ranked the top amateur in the country. This son of the old Scottish professional Davie Black was born in 1913, in Montreal.

Ken Black first came to the Canadian Amateur in 1931, one of B.C.'s Willingdon Cup team, a rosy-cheeked youth of eighteen. Although overshadowed that year by team-mate Bob Morrison, even then Black was showing his fine touch with the short irons and putter. In 1932 he won the B.C. Open against a field of top western professionals. At the Lambton Amateur the ball did not run well for him, and he went out in the first round.

The 1933 Amateur was played over Black's home course, Shaughnessy. The B.C. and Vancouver championships had been held there earlier in the year, to familiarize B.C. golfers with

Ken Black at the age of three, playing at Rivermead GC.

the course. The strategy seemed to work. Vancouver golfers Ken Black, Dick Moore, Stan Leonard, and Jack Matson occupied four of the first five places in the qualifying rounds. Somerville and Carrick had not come west, but defending champion Gordon B. Taylor was there, together with Happy Fraser, Jack Cameron, and Phil Farley. (George Hutton of Prince Rupert, B.C. entered, but did not qualify. I wonder how many recognized him as the young Scot who had won the 1909 Amateur while stationed in Montreal?)

Ken Black was at the peak of his form. He fought his way to the final, to meet Albert (Scotty) Campbell of Seattle. That week, Campbell had one of the finest putting touches ever seen at Shaughnessy, and Black did well to hold on until the 33rd hole.

Over the next four years, Ken Black played much better golf than his fortunes in the Canadian Amateur would indicate. Although frequently the leading scorer in the Willingdon Cup, he reached the Amateur semi-finals only once, in 1936. That was the year of his greatest triumph. Ironically, it did not come against Canadian amateurs but American professionals.

The victory of Ken Black in the Vancouver Jubilee Open of 1936 has to be one of the most sensational in Canadian golf. Here we had a twenty-four-year-old amateur pitting his skills over 72 holes against one of the strongest professional fields ever assembled in Canada. The $5,000 prize money had attracted U.S. professionals Lawson Little, Horton Smith, Tony Manero, Byron Nelson, Orville White, Jimmy Thompson, Ralph Guldahl, Macdonald Smith, and others.

The tournament was held at Shaughnessy, a plus for both Blacks, father and son. In the first round, Freddie Wood (by then a professional) led with a 67. A 70 in the second round let him hang on to his lead, jointly with Orville White. Old Davie Black was one stroke back, tied with Ralph Guldahl.

Wood stayed in front after the third round with a total of 207, but he had several Americans on his heels. The leading amateur, Ken Black, was five strokes back, tied with Byron Nelson.

In the final round, Nelson got hot. He shot a brilliant 66 (six under par). His total of 278 overtook Freddie Wood, Tony Manero, Macdonald Smith – all in the clubhouse. He appeared a certain winner.

Word came from out on the course that Ken Black had made the turn in three under par. "That's good," someone said, "Ken will be low amateur."

The officials started to brief Byron Nelson on the closing ceremonies, while spectators crowded him for autographs.

Another flash from out on the course – "Ken Black is five under at the twelfth" – brought the comment: "If he stays at five under, he'll tie for third place."

An increasing number of spectators left the clubhouse to go cheer their local hero. They saw him birdie four more holes between 13 and 17. At 18, he missed a birdie when his ball stopped two inches short.

Ken Black had shot ten birdies, one bogey, for a 34 29–63, or nine under par. His total of 275 beat Byron Nelson's by three strokes.

Ken Black remains the only Canadian amateur ever to win a PGA tournament – which this was. His performance ranks as one of the finest by any Canadian golfer.

His success in the Jubilee Open was the result of four excellent rounds of golf, one of them spectacular. When he won the Canadian Amateur in 1939, he had to play twelve rounds of golf, each of them better than that of his opponent.

The foreign invasion of Montreal's Mount Bruno club that year was reckoned to be the strongest in the history of the Amateur. The field included the American defending champion, Ted Adams, and the British Walker Cup player, John Langley.

The championship was really decided by the result of the Farley–Black encounter in the semi-final, which had all the excitement and drama of a final. Farley had a morning round of 69, to be 1 up, both he and Black playing virtually faultless golf. There was little in it until Black went ahead for the first time at the 32nd. Then high drama at the next hole. Black's putt for a half stopped on the lip of the cup. As the players walked off the green, and before Black's caddie could reach the ball, it fell into the hole. This seemed like a death blow to Farley. He pitched an easy third shot over the back of the next green, and Black was dormie 2. But Farley won the 35th, and at the 36th he seemed about to tie the match when he was only ten feet from the cup in 2, with Black's ball well through the green, lying on bare earth. But Black pitched up dead with his niblick (which he named "Jimmie"), Farley missed his ten-footer, and the match was over.

In his final against Henry Martell, Ken Black was never pressed. A 68 in the morning saw him 5 holes up, and he won handily at the 30th. In the last five rounds he was never over 71.

Ironically, Black and Martell were to meet again in the next Amateur final, which, because of the Second World War, was not until 1946.

Henry Martell (left) and Ken Black, who were to share the 1939 and 1946 Amateur championships.

During the war, Ken Black was probably at the peak of his playing career. In 1941, he took on American and Canadian amateurs and professionals to win the Western Canada Open at Shaughnessy from Leonard and Wood. In a practice round he duplicated the course record of 63 he had set in the Jubilee Open of 1936.

In his time, Ken Black probably did more than any other golfer to make B.C. a force in national golf. He was elected to the Canadian Golf Hall of Fame in 1988, to join former team-mate Stan Leonard and his erstwhile foes, Somerville, Farley, and Martell. His father, Davie, had been posthumously elected, making the Blacks the first family to be honoured in this way.

In 1935, the B.C. Golf Association selected Ken Black and Dick Moore to be members of the first Canadian amateur golf team to tour the United Kingdom. As the 1933 and 1934 B.C. Amateur champions, they were the obvious choices.

The curly-haired Richard L. (Dick) Moore, born in Victoria, B.C., of English parents, is most often remembered as the player who gave Sandy Somerville such a hard time in the fourth round in 1935. In anticipation of this match, he decided to sharpen his powers of concentration (in the Somerville manner) by hardly talking to anyone, even his room-mates, for several days.

He was a member of the storied B.C. team of Black, Leonard, Moore, and Morrison, the second to win the Willingdon Cup for the province, in 1934.

The Prairie provinces had to wait until 1946 before one of their amateurs, Henry Martell, won the national championship. Yet Alberta had been the first province outside Central Canada to provide a finalist. In fact, it provided two. Tom Gillespie was runner-up in 1919, Charlie Hague in 1920.

Tom Gillespie emigrated from St. Andrews, Scotland, to Winnipeg before the first World

HO HUM!

DICK WON THIS SAME CHAMPIONSHIP WHEN HE WAS 19 - AT OAK BAY IN VICTORIA. STAGED A COMEBACK AFTER SEVEN YEARS.

Dick Moore, a top B.C. golfer from the 1920s to the 1940s, after winning his second B.C. championship in 1934.

War. He is probably the T. Gillespie who played for the university of St. Andrews against the university of Aberdeen in 1896. If so, he would have played against Tom Reith of Beaconsfield.

Gillespie was Manitoba's amateur champion several times before he moved to Calgary. He was to win the Alberta Open title before enlisting in the services.

In 1919, on a visit to Scotland, Tom Gillespie won the coveted gold medal at the autumn meeting of the R & A. This marked him as an amateur golfer equal to any in Canada.

One of Gillespie's friends at Calgary G & CC was an American, Charlie Hague, who had taken up the game in Canada. Back in 1907, Hague had won the first Alberta Amateur championship, and he had won it several times since. At Winnipeg in 1920, he emulated Gillespie's success in reaching the last stage of the national Amateur. But Hague's final against Frank Thompson was a much more dramatic affair. The perspiring, mosquito-bitten gallery of two thousand was on edge to the very last hole.

Hague was a neat, compact player, then in his mid-thirties, whose strengths were his putting and an ideal temperament for match play. At Winnipeg, he could not match Frank Thompson's short game.

Charlie Hague moved to California in 1924, and was lost to Canadian golf.

The inimitable Jack Cuthbert was perhaps the finest of the 1920s school of Prairie amateurs. Yet this fine Scottish-born golfer only once reached the semi-finals of the Canadian Amateur.

"Cuthbert has done more for golf in the Middle West than any other man. He is a stylist, and many a young Westerner has to thank him for first inculcating in him the love of the game." So wrote the western correspondent of *Canadian Golfer* in 1929. Jack Cuthbert appears to have deserved every word of this praise.

Born in Kingussie, Scotland, in 1894 (where he took up golf at the age of nine), Jack Cuthbert came to Canada in 1911. He worked as a clerk with the Canadian Bank of Commerce from 1911 to 1922, mostly in Winnipeg, but also in Moose Jaw, Saskatchewan. He then appears to have joined a brokerage firm in Winnipeg.

He was golf editor of the *Free Press* for a number of years until his firm moved him to Edmonton in the late 1920s. During his later years in Winnipeg, he was the secretary of the Manitoba Golf Association.

Jack Cuthbert won the club championship of the original Winnipeg Golf Club (or Norwood) in the year he joined, 1912, at the age of eighteen. This was the first of many club, provincial, and Western Canada Golf

Jack Cuthbert as an amateur in 1924.

Association titles he was to acquire over the next twenty years, some of them not in the record books.

Cuthbert was slightly built and – as described in *Canadian Golfer* in 1929 – "a bundle of muscles and nerve." He then weighed only 118 pounds. When he reached the last eight in the Amateur at Jasper in 1929, he admitted that he did not have the physical strength to play 36 holes a day, six days on end.

His neat, crisp style, his fluid swing, was much admired and copied by Prairie golfers. It first came to national attention in 1920, when he was one of very few western golfers to attend the Amateur at Beaconsfield. In the third round he had a homeric struggle with Charles Grier, which Grier (the eventual champion) won at the 20th hole.

In 1930, Jack Cuthbert was picked from a list of thirty-five applicants to be the professional to Calgary G & CC. It was the beginning of a long friendship, during which he was to serve also as the club's manager. He retired in 1963, at the age of seventy.

Jack Cuthbert moved around the Prairies, from Manitoba to Saskatchewan to Alberta, so R. J. (Bobby) Reith might then be considered Manitoba's outstanding amateur golfer between the wars. He was also its most controversial figure in national golf.

Like Cuthbert, Bobby Reith was a Scot. He was the son of a professional golfer, the grandson of a professional golfer, brought up in a household where golf was life and livelihood. In Canada he became known as "the boy wonder." When barely seventeen, he won the Manitoba Amateur and the Manitoba Open championships. His stern, serious attitude to the game did not endear him to his fellow golfers. Some thought him a cocky young upstart. He was probably aware of their feelings, and let it affect his game.

In the 1936 Amateur at St. Charles, Winnipeg, Reith had the advantage of a home crowd. In the semi-finals, he rather easily put an end to a tired Stan Leonard ("I used up too many 20 foot putts getting this far," Leonard admitted). And so to the final against Fred Haas, of New Orleans.

Haas had just defeated the favourite, Sandy Somerville. Bobby Reith was only too aware of this. He seemed to be overwhelmed by the very idea that he might defeat the victor of the inimitable Sandy. Haas took the lead from the first hole, and Reith never looked like catching him. From the beginning, he played untypically cautious, tentative golf, as though merely trying to keep the deficit respectable. He missed putt after putt, many of them eminently makable. The "ohs" and "ahs" of the partisan Winnipeg gallery of several thousand echoed every miss.

Well-meaning spectators made matters worse by approaching him between holes, advising him to change putters. His face set and determined, Reith struggled on manfully, but his game did not respond. The championship went to Fred Haas by 8 and 7.

Reith was undoubtedly beaten by a flaw in his mental approach to the game. He turned professional, going to the Essex Golf and Country Club to replace Bob Gray Jr. when Gray moved to Scarboro. He continued to fight a bad attitude towards a game in which he had mastered the mechanics. But he never fulfilled the promise he had shown in his mid teens.

Daniel James (Bud) Donovan was a constant threat to Bobby Reith's supremacy in the amateur ranks of Manitoba golf. This lanky son of Justice Donovan burst into prominence in the early 1930s. Tall (six feet one inch) and lean (140 pounds), of Irish-Canadian extraction, Bud Donovan was the complete antithesis of Reith. He had an ideal golfing temperament, a quiet and unassuming manner, and an infectious smile.

Although he lifted the provincial Open title in 1933, Donovan was never able to seize the province's amateur championship from Reith. Nevertheless, the Manitoba Golf Association chose him to tour Britain with the Canadian team in 1935. While there, he fought his way to the fifth round of the British amateur championships, further than any other member of the Canadian contingent. Covering the fairways in long, slow strides, he made quite an impression with his fine swing and long hitting. The press called him "the last of the gallant Canadians" when he finally yielded at the last hole of round five.

This was probably Bud Donovan's finest achievement in amateur golf. But the out-

Bud Donovan after winning the Manitoba Junior in 1929, with a record 75.

standing performance of his golfing career came later that year. In the first General Brock Open at Lookout Point he was runner-up to the U.S. professional Tony Manero, finishing ahead of all the other top professionals from the U.S. and Canada.

By the end of the Second World War, in which he served as a naval officer, Bud Donovan had given up serious competitive golf and moved east, working latterly in the insurance business. As a member of Scarboro GC, he gave back to golf some of the obvious pleasure it had given him by working as publicity officer for the OGA in the 1950s. He was also a colour commentator for golf radio broadcasts over CFRB in Toronto and for CBC-TV.

The Maritime provinces produced only two players considered to be among the top in the country in the 1920s and 1930s. Nationally, Gerald Mielke was ranked number eight in 1924, and Pete Kelly number twelve in 1938.

After the Second World War, Pete Kelly was selected to play for Canada against the Americans. And there was one glorious year when the Maritimes had three of the fifteen ranked amateurs in Canada (Walter Reed, Pete Kelly, Tommy Stewart). But a Maritimer has never reached the semi-final of a Canadian Amateur.

The brothers Gerald and Frank Mielke (pronounced Milky) dominated golf in the Maritimes for the greater part of this twenty-year period. They both qualified for the 1923 Amateur, but got no further than the second round. Perhaps discouraged by this, they do not appear to have played again in a national event until Frank came to the 1939 Amateur as one of Nova Scotia's first Willingdon Cup teams.

It was left to Pete Kelly in the late 1930s to show that there was some fire in the Atlantic provinces. In the 1937 Canadian Amateur at Ottawa Hunt, the pride of Charlottetown (where Kelly was then living) came up with the most stunning victory of the tournament when he threw three birdies in the first six holes at the 1936 finalist, Bobby Reith, and blew him out

of the event. The powerful, red-haired Kelly not only hit the ball a long way, but that day sank 20-foot putts from all over the green. His putter matched his hair for several rounds, carrying him into the quarter-finals, further than any Maritimer before or since.

Pete Kelly was to win many titles in the Maritimes between 1937 and 1952. Perhaps the most remarkable feature of his golf is that it was his secondary sport. Peter Cameron Kelly, who was born in St. Vital, Manitoba, in 1912, and spent his teenage years in Montreal, played for the Detroit Red Wings when they won the Stanley Cup in 1936 and 1937. He was inducted into the New Brunswick Hall of Fame as an outstanding amateur and professional hockey player.

Gerald Mielke of Nova Scotia.

Gerry Kesselring (right) *being presented with the Buckingham Trophy at Quebec in 1948 by W.H. Budden, Director of the Tuckett Tobacco Co. Ltd., acting on behalf of Mr. C.H. Sclater, the donor.*

In 1938, Charles H. Sclater put up a trophy for the Junior Boys' Championship of Canada (in 1938, for those nineteen years and under). Mr. Sclater was president of the Tuckett Tobacco Company and a member of the Hamilton G & CC. He was to become president of the RCGA in 1942.

His Buckingham Trophy (named after a brand of cigarettes) is one of the most distinctive in Canadian golf. It has nine small pillars, each fluted with an enamelled crest bearing the coat of arms of a province.

At first, the contestants were only nine in number, the winners of each province's junior championship. Each junior accompanied his province's Willingdon Cup team, was a fifth man on that team, and even had a chance to get on a team if he was good enough. Mr. Sclater also underwrote the expenses of each junior. The Junior championship was played simultaneously with the Willingdon, over 36 holes of stroke play. For the record, the first winner was Jim Hogan, a strapping lad from Jasper.

In 1959, the format of the Junior was changed, the competition being opened to any boy in the country who qualified. At the same time, a junior interprovincial team match was introduced along the lines of the Willingdon Cup. This competition and the Junior were sponsored by Pepsi-Cola, who put up a new trophy. The old Buckingham Trophy was retired; it had, after all, only nine fluted pillars, and since Newfoundland's entry into Confederation in 1949, it had needed ten.

CHAPTER

AMATEUR INTERNATIONALS, 1898-1935

CANADA DID NOT ENGAGE IN REGULAR amateur international team matches until the 1950s. Matches against the British were just not on, given the state of the RCGA's finances. But matches against the United States could be arranged for no more than the cost of travelling to a Canadian Amateur championship in another province. Nonetheless, there were only five in fifty years, mainly because Canada could not raise a team capable of giving the best U.S. amateurs a run for their money, given only a tenth of the golfers to choose from.

Canada played two series of matches against the U.S., twenty years apart. In 1898–1900, we took on U.S. amateur teams three times. Canada lost all three matches, one by the whopping margin of 93 holes. In 1919 a U.S. team came up to play in Canada, and in 1920 we sent a team to the United States. We lost both matches, but were not disgraced. In fact, we had some notable singles victories over such

world-beaters as Bobby Jones and Francis Ouimet.

The genesis of the first series goes back to September 1897. A leading U.S. golfer by the name of H. P. Toler spent two weeks in Quebec City, played over Cove Fields, met a few officers of the RCGA, and – at their request – agreed to promote the idea of a contest between the amateurs of the two countries. When word came back that the Americans were interested, RCGA secretary Stewart Gordon wrote to the USGA, arranging a match for the fall of 1898.

The RCGA Annual Meeting that year was held at Toronto GC. The Canadian Amateur final was played on Thursday 29 September. A team of ten Americans arrived the same day, had a quick round of the course, and went out against the Canadians on the Friday.

The matches were singles over 36 holes, 18 in the morning, 18 in the afternoon. Each round had to be played to a finish since, as was custom-

The first international amateur match between Canada and the United States, 1898. Back row, left to right, *Jasper Lynch (U.S.), G. D. Fowle (U.S.), J. F. Curtis (U.S.), A. M. Coats (U.S.), D. R. Forgan (U.S.), H. M. Harriman (U.S.), G. G. Hubbard (U.S.); and Dr. F. C. Hood, F. G. H. Pattison, G. T. Brown, V. C. Brown, and J. P. Taylor (all of Canada).* Second row: *H. J. Whigham (U.S.), C. B. Macdonald (U.S.), Col. G. I. Sweny,* RCGA *President, A. W. Smith, George S. Lyon, W. A. H. Kerr.* Front row: *F. P. Keene (U.S.), R. B. Kerr,* USGA *Secretary, S. Gordon,* RCGA *Secretary, G. S. Gillespie, W. H. Blake.*

ary, the team match was decided on the basis of net holes won. The Canadians lost by 20 holes; only W. A. H. Kerr, F. G. H. Pattison, and Percy Taylor won more holes than they lost.

The loss of 7 matches to 3 proved to be just about the best we could hope to achieve in the next twenty years.

The return match against a much stronger U.S. team at the Morris County GC, New Jersey, in October 1899, was a disaster for Canada. "Our team might have shown a little mercy," said one American. "The Canadians were simply outclassed," said the president of the USGA. "With the exception of two or three men they are far below the calibre of the best golf talent in this country." Which may have been true, but it was not the kind of thing you expect to hear from the president of a national amateur body.

The Canadian team was beaten to the tune of 93 holes. In the twenty matches played – ten in the morning, ten in the afternoon – only A. W. Smith won, and this in the afternoon against the U.S. amateur champion. "The visiting members were royally entertained . . . but they did not remain long on the grounds after their heavy defeat," wrote the American reporter of the match, and one can understand why.

If the tail of the team let us down in 1899, it saved us in 1900. The U.S. won the international at Quebec City, but only by 5 holes.

The venue probably had something to do with Canada's improved performance. Cove Fields was a unique course. All the Canadian players had played it at least once. Canon Von Iffland of Royal Quebec was singled out as Canada's best player.

More significant than course knowledge, however, was the fact that the United States had obviously not sent its top amateurs to Quebec City, perhaps feeling that a B team would not humiliate Canada to the extent that an A team had in 1899. Not one member of this U.S. team was ever to reach the finals of the U.S. Amateur.

All that can be said for Canada's leading players is that Smith was past his prime, and a sick man, and George Lyon's best days were yet to come.

It is easy to understand why the USGA, or the RCGA, or both, decided to drop these international matches after 1900. However, in the spirit of good fellowship following the First World War, the Americans agreed to revive the amateur internationals, and the second series began.

In July 1919 the USGA sent a team of champions to Hamilton: the current Open and Amateur champion, Chick Evans; two former Open and Amateur champions, Ouimet and Travers; three former Amateur champions, Byers, Fownes, and Gardner; and regional or state champions, Bobby Jones, Marston, Guilford, and Kirkby. Jones was only seven-

teen at the time and by far the youngest member of either side.

The Canadian Amateur was held at Lambton three weeks before the International. This gave the selectors the chance to assess the current form of our players in this first Amateur after the war. The selectors also hoped to have a look at the members of Manitoba's interprovincial team.

In the event, the Winnipeg General Strike kept the westerners at home, so Canada's team came from clubs in Ontario and Quebec. It would probably have been strengthened by the inclusion of Tom Gillespie and Charlie Hague of Calgary and Jack Cuthbert of Winnipeg. But these players were virtually unknown in Central Canada in 1919.

The format was changed for the Hamilton international. Matches would count, not holes, with the teams playing four-ball best-ball in the morning, singles in the afternoon. In the end, the U.S. made a clean sweep of the four-balls, five matches to nil. It also won the singles, seven matches to three.

Canada		United States	
McLuckie and Thompson	lost to	Evans and Byers	1 down
George Lyon and Turpin	lost to	Ouimet and Anderson	3 & 2
Reith and McDougall	lost to	Travers and Kirkby	1 down
Martin and Seymour Lyon	lost to	Gardner and Marston	4 & 3
Hadden and Hoblitzel	lost to	Fownes and Jones	3 & 2
G. S. Lyon	lost to	Chick Evans	4 & 3
Wm. McLuckie	lost to	Francis Ouimet	2 down
G. H. Turpin	lost to	Oswald Kirkby	2 & 1
T. B. Reith	lost to	Max Marston	8 & 7
Fritz Martin	defeated	Robert Gardner	4 & 2
W. J. Thompson	defeated	Jerome Travers	3 & 2
Seymour Lyon	lost to	J. G. Anderson	3 & 2
John Hadden	lost to	Eben Byers	4 & 3
F. G. Hoblitzel	defeated	W. C. Fownes	2 & 1
E. S. McDougall	lost to	Robert T. Jones	5 & 3

Canada v. United States, at Hamilton, July 1919.

Thompson and McLuckie lost their four-ball when neither could sink a putt, one from four feet, one from three, on the last green. Poor putting on the eighteenth also cost Reith and McDougall their match, after being 2 up at the turn.

"The hopes of the Canadians were decidedly zero-tinged about this time," wrote Ralph Reville after the four-balls, in an uncharacteristic display of twentieth-century jargon.

In the singles, some of the matches were closer than the results suggest. The clash between McLuckie and Ouimet was in doubt up to the very end. Seymour Lyon's opponent shot the best round of the day, 69.

Bill Thompson's win over Travers (once Open, four times Amateur champion of the U.S.) had to be the highlight of the day. Fritz Martin, too, did well to dispose of a double U.S. Amateur winner in Gardner.

As a spectacle, the International was a great success. Spectators came from as far away as Winnipeg and Chicago. Hundreds of automobiles were parked in and around the course, by far the greatest number ever seen at a golfing event in Canada up to that time. Parking, of course, was free, as was access to the course. It is another sign of the times that the ladies of the Hamilton club invited all the spectators to tea in the clubhouse.

The teams stayed and dined at Hamilton's Royal Connaught Hotel. After the toasts, George Lyon was called upon and responded with "My Wild Irish Rose."

Canada sent a stronger team for the return match at the Engineers' Country Club, Roslyn, Long Island, in September 1920. Frank Thompson, Charles Grier, and Norman Scott replaced Reith, Hadden, and McDougall, to good effect. Once again, our team would have been strengthened by westerners Cuthbert, Hague, and Gillespie, who made it known they could not play.

The Canadian team travelled to Long Island with the memory of a 93-hole defeat in

Canada		United States	
Grier and Turpin	lost to	Evans and Gardner	5 & 4
G. S. Lyon and W. J. Thompson	lost to	Herron and Kirkby	6 & 4
Seymour Lyon and F. Thompson	lost to	Ouimet and Fownes	5 & 4
McLuckie and Martin	lost to	Jones and Anderson	2 & 1
Hoblitzel and Scott	defeated	Marston and White	2 & 1
C. B. Grier	lost to	D. S. Herron	4 & 3
W. McLuckie	defeated	Francis Ouimet	3 & 1
Geoff Turpin	lost to	Chick Evans	3 & 1
George Lyon	defeated	Bob Gardner	1 up
Frank Thompson	defeated	Bobby Jones	2 up
Bill Thompson	lost to	M. Marston	1 down
Seymour Lyon	halved	O. Kirkby	
F. G. Hoblitzel	lost to	G. White	1 down
Fritz Martin	lost to	J. Anderson	4 & 3
Norman Scott	lost to	W. Fownes	2 & 1

Canada v. United States, at Roslyn, Long Island, September 1920.

the last encounter played on U.S. soil. The Engineers' course had the reputation of being one of the toughest in the Metropolitan district; narrow fairways, small greens, some of them "bunkered up to the eyebrows." So it proved, in the practice round. To break 80, it was said at the time, would tax the very best amateur or professional.

Canada lost by 10 1/2 matches to 4 1/2, as good as could be expected against such a talented U.S. side. But the greatest satisfaction came in the defeat of three of America's finest – Ouimet, Jones, and Gardner.

The format was the same as at Hamilton; four-balls in the morning, singles in the afternoon.

Frank Thompson's win over Bobby Jones has to be one of the finest victories of the series, although McLuckie's 3 and 1 defeat of Ouimet runs it a close second. And what of George Lyon's win over Gardner?

Having played and lost to the Americans at Philadelphia in September 1924, the British Walker Cup team visited Canada. They played in a series of matches against club teams in Ontario and Quebec. They also played against two select teams, one from each of these provinces. Although not strictly internationals, these matches were the closest Canada ever came to playing against a British side until the Commonwealth team matches in the 1950s.

In Toronto, the British defeated an Ontario select by 6 1/2 to 2 1/2; in Montreal, they defeated a Quebec side 5 to 4.

The visit also introduced Canadian golfers and administrators to British attitudes to amateur golf. The RCGA secretary B. L. Anderson accompanied the British team from Philadelphia and stayed with it during its ten-day visit. In his words, he was "privileged to get at first hand some of the tradition and ideals which, for hundreds of years, have guided the destinies of Golf in the Motherland." He came away feeling that perhaps North Americans occupied themselves too much with winning; playing the game seemed more important to the British, who never made excuses for losing. Junior championships might not, after all, be the best thing for our young golfers; the British believed that team sports better developed character than individual sports like golf. The R & A would never permit amateur tournaments in Britain to be commercially sponsored. Sponsorship was all very well for professionals, but golf was, above all, a gentleman's sport and should not be subject to undue publicity any more than to undue rivalry.

This *Weltanschauung* came as something of a shock to Anderson. He was to reflect upon the British golfing philosophy for the rest of his life. At the time he wrote: "Let us hope this spirit may be infused into the Youth of this country, for I fear that in some of the more advanced of us, this sportsmanlike instinct comes too late."

There were dinners galore during the British visit. There was also much wishful thinking by Canadians that this visit might lead to regular internationals between the two countries. But that was not to be. Frankly, it is hard to see how the RCGA could have financed a team to Britain every two years, given its low income from member clubs. But the hope was never permitted to die. In 1935, it did result in the RCGA sending a Canadian team across the Atlantic to play British clubs and to compete in the British Amateur championship.

At its AGM in February 1935, the RCGA announced that it was sending a Canadian team to Britain in May of that year. The objective of this Goodwill Tour was to promote Canadian golf in the Old Country, by having the team play against well-known British clubs – the R & A had sanctioned the visit, and would make all the arrangements for it, but had ruled out Canada's suggestion of international matches.

The press on both sides of the Atlantic at first treated the announcement with some cynicism; they saw it primarily as a scheme for sending the cream of Canada's amateurs to

The Goodwill Tour of Britain in 1935: left to right, *Bud Donovan, Dick Moore, Sandy Somerville, Robert Jacob (RCGA vice-president), Phil Farley, Gordon B. Taylor, Ken Black.*

the British Amateur championships at no expense to the players. The RCGA hotly denied any such subterfuge. This was not a backed invasion, no pot-hunting expedition. The players would be financed only for team matches and would be responsible for their own costs if they entered for the British Amateur. The RCGA did admit, however, that the timing of the visit had been quite deliberate. It would give team members the chance of entering for the world's greatest amateur golf tournament.

The RCGA wanted the team of eight players to be selected from the cream of golfers in the top golfing provinces. But it also insisted that "the team should equally represent the Dominion as young Canadian manhood and gentlemen." Sandy Somerville was appointed captain. Phil Farley was an automatic choice for Ontario, which added Fred Hoblitzel, not only as an able player but as an elder statesman. Quebec nominated Gordon B. Taylor and Ed Innes.

The other three were to be chosen from the West, out of an outstanding bunch that included Ken Black, Dick Moore, and Stan Leonard of B.C., Bud Donovan and Bobby Reith of Manitoba, and Stew Vickers of Alberta. In the end, Black and Moore represented B.C. Manitoba insisted on choosing its representative by holding a play-off, which was won by Donovan, the RCGA's "suggested" nominee.

At the eleventh hour, Jack Nash of London Hunt joined the Canadian team, his father paying his expenses. In England, D. O'Donald Higgins (one of two well-known golfing brothers of Prescott, Ontario) joined the entourage. The team was accompanied by Robert Jacob of Winnipeg, a vice-president of the RCGA.

Before these ambassadors of goodwill left on the *Empress of Australia,* they were gathered at Lambton for a "bon voyage" party and put through their paces by playing with and against a number of old hands such as George Lyon and Robert M. Gray.

The Canadian team arrived in London via Southampton at the beginning of May, in time for King George V's Jubilee celebrations.

Their first match against the Royal St. George's club at Sandwich was tied, an excellent result against a team that included several world-class players. They returned to Sandwich a few days later, to play in the Royal St. George's Challenge Cup, one of *the* events in Britain. Here they ran up against a true British seaside course in true British seaside weather. The strong, gusty winds blew away any chance they had of breaking 80, although Nash did so once in returning a 159, only five strokes behind the winner.

Over the next few weeks they played against many teams, notably Royal Liverpool and the Honourable Company at Muirfield (who gave them a hard day). The format was usually the same; foursomes in the morning, four-balls in the afternoon. The highlight was a visit to the Old Course at St. Andrews. "Not that it was the best course," Jack Nash later recalled, "but because of all the traditions that lay behind it."

Halfway through the tour, the team went to Royal Lytham and St. Anne's, to compete in the British Amateur championship. Royal Lytham is another links course, treeless, with rolling greens, thick rough, and winds that always seem to blow towards the bunkers. In the end, the title was won by a man used to none of this – the American Lawson Little, then at the height of his amateur career.

Sandy Somerville went out in the first round, losing to the Lancashire champion, Halliwell, 2 and 1. This was a bitter blow to Canada as well as to Somerville. Phil Farley put out a Scottish internationalist, Sam McKinley, in round two. On the third day, all the Canadians but Bud Donovan were eliminated, Gordon Taylor by long-hitting Cyril Tolley. Dick Moore went out after a fight that lasted twenty-one holes.

The last of the gallant Canadians – as the press called Donovan – struggled through round four. In the afternoon of the same day, however, he met J. Morton Dykes in the fifth round and put on a fine exhibition of fighting golf, only to lose at the last hole.

If nothing else, the Goodwill Tour gave our top Canadian amateurs a taste of seaside golf, and a more sympathetic understanding of why British championships are often won by what seem like – on this side of the Atlantic – extraordinarily high scores. The tour accomplished much of what it had set out to do. A Canadian did not win the British Amateur, but the good press given the Canadians everywhere they played, the way in which they accepted defeat and victory, epitomized the British approach to golf that B. L. Anderson had found so intriguing ten years earlier.

21
CHAPTER

WITH THE PROFESSIONALS: THE OLD GUARD AND NEW

DURING THE WAR, THE CPGA HAD BEEN kept alive by the members of the old guard who organized it in 1911, but their two main tournaments, the Canadian Open and the CPGA championship, had been cancelled for the duration.

The CPGA's secretary-treasurer, Karl Keffer, was overseas with the army for the last two years of the war. Within a few months of his return, he had revived the CPGA championships, which had been first held in 1912. These were now on a grander scale. Whereas only fourteen players had competed in 1912, over four times that number – including assistants – made up the field in 1921. The professionals played for the P. D. Ross Cup, for a gold medal put up each year by the Dunlop Tire and Rubber Company, and for the prize money. The purse varied from year to year, depending on the generosity of the host club and other sponsors. In a good year, the winner might take home $250, the tenth man $3.33.

The year 1924 was particularly lucrative. The Macdonald Company (cigarette manufacturers) put up $500; A. G. Spalding and Bros., $150; Beaconsfield GC, $100; the CPGA's honorary president, J. D. Montgomery, $100; the Canada Golf Ball Co., $50; and a member of Beaconsfield, $50. This brought the purse to $950, or $200 more than the prize money at that year's Canadian Open. Canadian professionals were, by and large, respected as a hardworking, sober group of men, and clubs liked to show their appreciation whenever they could.

The assistant professionals played for a much smaller purse and, from 1928, on a different date.

The professionals had also organized the CPGA "to protect the mutual interest of members." Among other things, this meant looking after a brother professional who was down on his luck. There is plenty of evidence that this spirit of brotherhood went beyond mere words. When Arthur Woodward died suddenly in 1922 the CPGA held its championships that year at his Country Club of Montreal, organized a pro-am tournament at nearby Beaconsfield, and raised over three thousand dollars (a lot of money in those days) for Woodward's family.

For seven years after the war, the leading Canadians in the Open and the CPGA championship continued to be members of the old guard: George Cumming, Charlie and Albert Murray, Davie Black, Karl Keffer, Percy Barrett, Nicol Thompson.

The CPGA events clearly belonged to that chunky, good-natured Scot, Davie Black. This man was never to finish higher than second in a Canadian Open, yet he lifted four CPGA titles in six attempts, the first two when playing out of Ottawa's Rivermead club, before he moved in 1920 to Shaughnessy Heights. In August of that year he hopped on a train to come back east to defend his title at Royal Montreal. In an era when breaking 70 was news, he reeled off hole after hole in par or birdie, with machine-like precision, following a 68 with a 67, to win by the grand margin of ten strokes.

Davie Black played in his last CPGA championship at Lambton in 1921. He was heading for a six-stroke victory over a field of forty-four, when he fell foul of an enthusiastic photographer. The fellow with the camera asked Black to pose as he was about to putt on the sixteenth green. Not content with this, he snapped Davie as he was driving from the seventeenth and eighteenth tees. Black dropped a stroke at each of these three holes. So far as I know, this is the first recorded instance in Canadian golf of a golfer succumbing to the scourge of all players, the click of an amateur's shutter. But Black held on to his championship by the safe margin of three strokes. With a string of three successive victories, he was awarded a full-size replica of the P. D. Ross Cup.

In July 1922, Davie Black had to undergo an operation on his back and so could not

When the British Ryder Cup team played an unofficial match against Canadian professionals in 1927, Davie Black, left, *was top Canadian and took second money. He is seen here with Britain's Archie Compston.*

Charlie Murray, right, *and Britain's Ted Ray, the captains in the international match, in a sketch by LeMessurier.*

defend his title. In later years, the burden of time and money was too great to justify his coming all the way from Vancouver to the national championships. But he came east in 1927 to play for Canada against the British Ryder Cup team. He took second place and was leading Canadian. This apart, Davie Black had to content himself with the B.C. Open and the Pacific Northwest championships.

Karl Keffer defended his Open championship in 1919 (having won in 1914) but did well to share second place. After having lost two years of his golfing career when serving in France, he had fallen victim to the influenza epidemic that swept post-war Britain. In January 1919, he lay near death in a Liverpool hospital. Yet in the Canadian Open seven months later he proved himself a match for the British professional Jim Barnes and the rising young star from Atlanta, Bobby Jones. These three tied for second place.

Charlie Murray went one better in 1920, losing in a three-way play-off for first place. The well-built, genial, and exuberant Murray was the most outgoing of Canada's professionals. In the winter months, he was professional to the Gulf Stream Country Club, Del Ray, Florida, where he was as much loved and respected as he was at Royal Montreal. (In 1922 it was reported that Charlie had been offered twelve thousand dollars a year to be the private instructor to a wealthy Washington businessman. When he declined, the job went to the American Leo Diegel.) In his time he golfed with governors general, presidents Taft and Harding, and the Prince of Wales. Among his prized possessions were a pin given him by the Prince of Wales and a piece of plate presented to him by the members of Royal Montreal, when he and Charles Grier beat Harry Vardon and Ted Ray in an exhibition match in 1920. Charlie Murray died suddenly after an operation in 1938, when only fifty-six. Hundreds attended his funeral at Montreal's Christ Church Cathedral; club members, fellow professionals, leaders of the city's business community. "It is like losing a brother," said Colonel English, secretary of Royal Montreal.

Charlie's brother Albert won his only CPGA title in 1924. This was a good year to win; the

Albert Murray in 1930.

first-place cash was five hundred dollars, thanks to a few generous sponsors.

The dean of the profession, George Cumming, played in every Open until 1942. He was still swinging the club as sweetly as ever.

Percy Barrett had become paunchy between 1907, when he was Open champion, and 1923 and 1925, the years he won the CPGA title. He was the last of the old guard to put his name on a national trophy.

Although he was unquestionably one of the finest golfers in Canada for some twenty years, Nicol Thompson of Hamilton won only a single national title. In 1922, he led the field in both rounds of the CPGA championship, to win by a stroke. This was one of the CPGA's least rewarding years: Thompson took home only one hundred dollars in cash.

By 1926, most of the old guard were past their best as players. For a year or so, a new generation of professionals had been threatening their supremacy. The years before the Second World War clearly belonged to the newcomers.

As we have seen, golf surged in popularity after the First World War, leading to an unprecedented demand for skilled professionals, as teachers, clubmakers, and greenkeepers. The number of head professionals in Canada went up from around sixty in 1919, to over three hundred by the early 1930s. The number then levelled off, as the years of depression and drought hit the economy of the country and the wealth of clubs.

The demand for skilled teachers and clubmakers could not be met from within Canada, or from the United States, which was also experiencing a boom. Canadian clubs went to the only other source of supply, to Britain, and especially to Scotland. Canada continued to attract British professionals, for the same reasons as in the early years of the century: the move usually meant promotion, higher wages, better working and living conditions, fewer class barriers. When the manager of Rosedale went to Scotland in the early 1920s

in search of a professional, he came back with the names of thirteen applicants.

When we come to assess who were the leading playing professionals in Canada between the wars, the main criterion has to be a player's performance in the country's two national professional events, the Canadian Open and the CPGA Championship. In those years, all CPGA championships and all but one Open were held at clubs in Central Canada. Only a handful of professionals came from the West or the Maritimes to compete, so in the years between the wars our leading playing professionals came from clubs in Ontario or Quebec.

From 1926 through 1935, four Canadians (all immigrant Scots) stood out in national championships: Willie Lamb, five times a CPGA champion; Andy Kay, CPGA champion in 1931, five times the leading Canadian in the Open; Jimmy Johnstone, twice a CPGA champion; Lex Robson, the CPGA champion in 1932, twice the leading Canadian in the Open.

Andy Kay and Willie Lamb arrived in Canada within a year of each other. Kay came from a well-known family of Scottish professionals but had been working for several years at the Newcastle Golf Club in England. Lambton brought him over in 1923 to replace one of the old guard, Willie Freeman.

Kay had won the championship of the British PGA's northern section so, not surprisingly, he was an instant success in Canada. Within a few months he had won the inaugural Ontario Open. In the 1925 Canadian Open, Kay had several chances to take the lead, but he was poorly served by his putter and had to be content with tying Walter Hagen for third place.

The Open was played over 72 holes, which suited Kay. In the 36-hole CPGA championship he never did so well. His solitary win came in 1931, when he shot a 30 over the front nine at Rosedale.

In the 1920s, the supply of British professionals could not keep up with the North

One of the old guard, one of the new: Nicol Thompson of Hamilton, left, *and Andy Kay of Lambton.*

American demand. As a result, some of those who came to professional jobs in Canada had been amateurs in Britain, low handicap players at artisan or working-men's clubs who had picked up many of the skills of the professional. Willie Lamb was one such amateur when he came to Canada.

In 1923, the Secretary of Toronto GC spent a weekend at Scotland's Turnberry golf course, and mentioned to the local professional, Tom Fernie, that he was looking for a young man to assist George Cumming. Fernie recommended Willie Lamb, a twenty-one-year-old amateur golfer in Montrose. A stylish golfer, long off the tee, Willie played off a plus 2 handicap. Toronto eventually chose Lamb from a large number of applicants and installed him as an assistant to Cumming at the beginning of the 1924 season.

Willie was a quiet, unassuming golfer, of few words. He took his golf very seriously and was seldom seen to smile on the golf course,

Willie Lamb.

no matter how well he was doing. Fred Lyon recalled that he and George Lyon played with Willie shortly after his arrival. Willie shot a fine round, but uttered nothing more than a monosyllable in eighteen holes of golf. After sinking his putt on the home green, he touched the peak of his cap as a sign of respect, mumbled something like "thank you, sir" in his broad Scottish accent, and made off for the workshop.

Willie Lamb served as assistant to George Cumming for five seasons, honing his skills of clubmaking and greenkeeping. During this time he found himself a well-paying winter post at a club in Mexico and won the Mexican Open Championship. By 1927 he had lowered the course record at Toronto to 66, and had won prize money in the CPGA assistants' championship.

At the CPGA annual meeting in 1928, Willie was elected to full professional privileges, although he was still an assistant to Cumming. He went out the next day and shot two rounds of 73, good enough to earn him his first CPGA title, the $250 that went with it, and the gold medal from Dunlop.

Four more CPGA titles were to follow in the next seven years. Some brought him more rewards than prize money and medals. His first win in 1928 led to his appointment as the professional at Toronto's Uplands club. In 1929, his $250 share of the purse was supplemented by a $500 cheque from the Avon Indian Rubber Company, since he had won with an Avon ball. And after his fourth championship in 1933, he was selected by Lambton to replace his friend Andy Kay, who had left to join a U.S. club. Lamb served Lambton for many years.

The third of this group of Scots, Jimmy Johnstone, came to Canada by a more circuitous route, having left his home club in Dunbar for South Africa, in 1922. While the professional at the Pretoria GC he won the Open championship of the Orange Free State and Basutoland and was runner-up in the South African PGA. Back in Dunbar for the winter of 1923–24, he answered an advertisement and was chosen to be professional to the River View Golf & Country Club in Galt, Ontario.

Jimmy Johnstone.

At Galt, Johnstone quickly established a reputation as a patient teacher, a skilled clubmaker, and especially as a top-notch player. Rosedale coaxed him into leaving Galt after two years. He was to serve this club for twenty-six years and to become one of the most respected professionals in the country.

Jimmy Johnstone's first CPGA title came in 1926, when he shot 70 69–139 over Montreal's Summerlea course, to win by eight strokes. He successfully defended his title in 1927. Much respected by his fellow professionals, Johnstone was elected to be the first vice-captain of the newly formed Ontario PGA.

Alexander (Lex) Robson, like Willie Lamb, had been a Scottish amateur, but from a well-to-do, middle-class family in Blackhall, Midlothian, where he headed the golf team at Stewart's College. For three years he won the gold medal of the Bruntsfield Links Golfing Society, capturing also the Coronation Cup, which came with the championship of the Braid Hills golf course in Edinburgh.

Robson came to Canada as the secretary to Toronto's Weston Club in 1925, having been recommended by no less than R. T. Boothby, a former captain of the R & A. At Weston, he served for a time as both professional and man-

ager-secretary. He accomplished little in national golf until 1930, when he was appointed professional to the nearby club at Islington. Thereafter, Robson was frequently in the money at CPGA championships, but his only win came in 1932. Some brilliant putting helped him shoot a 33 in the back nine at Rivermead, good enough to beat Andy Kay in a play-off.

Lex Robson reserved his finest performances for the Canadian Open, tying for second place in 1933 and for third a year later.

Lex Robson and Jimmy Johnstone also dominated what came to be known as the "Canadian Professional Championship for the Millar Trophy." Melville ("Cap") Millar, secretary of the Islington Golf club, and Mrs.

P. D. Ross, Ottawa newspaper publisher, member of a distinguished golfing family, and donor of the CPGA's championship cup.

Captain Melville Millar.

Lex Robson.

At the Millar Trophy in 1940: left to right, *Bill Kerr (Toronto Hunt), Bob Burns (Weston), Stan Horne (Islesmere), Willie Lamb (Lambton), Bob Gray (Scarboro).*

Millar put up this trophy for competition in 1928. (Incidentally, Millar had as romantic a life as you could wish for, having fought alongside Buffalo Bill and been a U.S. cavalryman in the Sitting Bull uprising and in the Mexican revolution. He was later to make his mark in golf course construction.) At first, entry to the Millar was restricted to members of the Ontario PGA. From 1940, the tournament was opened up to professionals from Quebec, and from 1943 to all Canadian professionals. The Millar was the professionals' match-play championship. But until well into the Second World War it was a provincial event.

Kay, Lamb, Johnstone, and Robson were products of the Scottish school of golf, and had technically fine swings, with Lamb the most stylish of the four. They were modest men, and quiet-living. Only Johnstone could be charac-terized as gregarious, perhaps because he had travelled more widely than the others. They were not dashing golfers or extroverts in the style of a Charlie Murray. They came to North America at a time when a new breed of professional golfer was emerging – the tournament player. None of them could match consistently the top tournament players from the United States. Playing for money was only a minor part of their jobs. Their first duty, after all, was to the members of their clubs.

Many other British professionals came to Central Canada in the years between the wars. They may not have won much in the way of prize money, but the anecdotal evidence is that many of them won a close place in the hearts of club members.

John (Jock) Brown, a huge, rough-cut Scot with a soft soothing burr, made his name as a teacher at Montreal's Summerlea. He turned out provincial and national champion Gordon B. Taylor and Bill Taylor, two of the finest stylists the game has seen, as well as Yolande Moisan and Doris Taylor Rudel.

Bob Cunningham Sr., a tall, well-built Scot, was reckoned to be one of the longest hitters in North America. "Keep yer heid still, laddie," the older members of St. George's will tell you, in imitation of their one-time professional.

Arthur Hulbert, professional at Toronto's Thornhill until his untimely death in 1945, was top Canadian in the 1931 Open.

Big Bob Burns served Montreal's Hampstead and Toronto's Weston clubs and won the CPGA title in 1942.

Ernie Wakelam, latterly at Royal Quebec, frequently won prize money in the CPGA championships.

Ulsterman Tommy McGrath went from Hamilton's Glendale to Moose Jaw (where he won the 1928 Western Canada Open) before settling in at Dundas Valley.

Bobby Alston did not arrive until 1931. Latterly he was with Ottawa's Chaudière club. In the period 1932–39 he only once failed to make prize money at CPGA championships.

Hugh Logan of Rosedale and Cobourg (where his son also worked) was probably related to Arthur Logan, a Toronto GC assistant in the late 1890s. The George Elder who came to Whitlock GC, Hudson Heights, was probably related to the professional of the same name who was at nearby Beaconsfield twenty years earlier.

Jack Young (assistant to Royal Montreal, 1919–69) was joined by brother Nelson in the 1920s.

The three Ayton brothers came from Scotland to work for a few years in Canada; George at Regina, Alec at Senneville CC, David at Vancouver's Point Grey.

Fred, Sid, and Arthur Hunt worked at clubs in Ontario; Fred was professional to Brantford GC for over thirty years.

Some professionals came and left with mixed reputations. There is anecdotal evidence that Davie Spittal and his brother Willie had been clubmakers in the St. Andrews workshop of Old Tom Morris. Davie was the better known in Canada, having first come to Lambton in the early teens of the century as a youthful clubmaker. He seldom stayed at a club for long. Before the First World War he moved from Lambton to Sarnia to Halifax to Scarboro. After the war he developed a reputation as a fast-talking, fast-living, fast-swinging professional, with a weakness for whisky uplifters. His last job was at the Idylwylde G & CC, Sudbury. He died there, suddenly, in December 1938, at the age of fifty. Although he probably visited too many liquid hazards, Davie was a good enough golfer to win the Ontario Open in 1929 and 1931 and to be runner-up in the CPGA championship of 1925.

The flow of immigrant professionals virtually dried up as we entered the 1930s. The game temporarily stopped growing and spreading, and supply could be met from a new generation of home-bred professionals emerging from the ranks of caddies. Their careers had a common pattern. They came from families that could not afford to join private golf clubs, so they would start out by caddying at a city club, picking up the game by hitting balls with an old mashie donated by a club member. They would win a caddie tournament and be encouraged to take a job in the professional's workshop. If they lived in a city with a municipal golf course – and these were becoming widespread in the 1920s – they would join the municipal club and compete in tournaments. Canada's first generation of home-bred professionals had started in much the same way, but without the advantage of public courses.

In the first few years of its existence, Toronto's municipal Humber Valley club turned out eight professionals. Roy Bronsdon won the caddie tournament at Scarboro in 1921, was Humber Valley champion a year later, and went back to Scarboro as an assistant professional in 1927. He later landed a plum job with the Brae Burn club in Boston.

Two other Scarboro caddies, Jack Littler and Frank Revel, went straight into the club's workshop to learn their trade, later becoming fully fledged professionals in Ottawa and Barrie.

In those days, few top-class amateurs turned professional. But Redvers (Red) Mackenzie turned professional with Montreal's Marlborough club a year after reaching the final of the Canadian Amateur. Red was another of the sportsmen who could play both first-class hockey and first-class golf.

A young businessman, Hugh Borthwick, was the sensation of the 1927 Ontario Amateur, taking Somerville to the last hole in the final. Hugh turned professional at about the same time as brother Dick.

But in Central Canada, as elsewhere, such instances were rare in the 1920s and 1930s. Most of the new generation of home-bred professionals had never won provincial or national honours as amateurs.

The domination of the Scottish quartet of Kay, Lamb, Johnstone, and Robson was finally broken in 1934. A young French-Canadian professional, Jules Huot, won the CPGA championship at the Country Club of Montreal, by a margin of six strokes over Lex Robson. It is true that Willie Lamb took the title away from Huot in the following year, but that was the last victory of the Scots.

In 1936 another Canadian-bred player, Stan Horne, snatched the title from Lamb in a tight last round. Between them, Huot and Horne were to capture five of the six CPGA titles that immediately preceded the Second World War.

Jules Huot was the first French-Canadian golfer to become a national figure. He was born in January 1908, at Boischatel, Quebec, and by the time he was strong enough to carry a set of golf clubs, Royal Quebec had fortuitously moved from Cove Fields to Montmorency, literally across the road from his home. Jules picked up the game as a caddie, as did three of his seven brothers.

Frank Locke, the professional at Royal Quebec in those days, thought enough of his young

Jules Huot, the first top-ranking French-Canadian professional.

Rodolphe Huot in his shop.

assistant's ability to enter his name for the 1924 Quebec Open. Jules did well for a sixteen-year-old. Five years later he moved to the assistant's job at nearby Kent GC, and was soon its head professional.

In his first CPGA championship in 1933, Jules Huot finished ninth. But in the following year's tournament – the first played over 72 holes – he started as one of the favourites, having just won the Quebec Open. His fine form did not leave him. He opened with a 68, which gave him a two-stroke lead. With 18 holes to go, he was only one stroke ahead of Lex Robson. Paired together for the last round, their tussle became virtually a match-play final. Huot generally outdrove and outputted Robson. His 29 for the front nine, six under par, was one of the most remarkable displays of golf ever seen in Canada, and gave him an unassailable lead. His 68 won him the title with a margin of six strokes.

"Le petit Jules," as he was affectionately called – he stood five feet five inches and weighed about 130 pounds – repeated his win in 1939. The professionals' championship was played over his own course at Kent GC that year, so he was obviously the man to beat. At the time, some suggested that the psychological pressure of "home-course advantage" is often a disadvantage. But when Jules Huot shot a 65 in the opening round, the field more or less capitulated. During the next three rounds the other players at least had the satisfaction of viewing the splendours of the Montmorency Falls.

Canadian-born professionals took the first six places in this championship, a first in its twenty-year history. What is even more astonishing is that the brothers Huot took three of the first five places. Roland Huot, professional at Royal Quebec, tied for second place. Rodolphe Huot, his assistant, came fifth.

Jules Huot's day of glory was, as we shall see, at the General Brock Open in 1937, when he defeated a strong field of Americans.

Stan Horne was the most successful Ontario-bred professional between the wars. Golf was in his blood. Born in England in 1912, by the

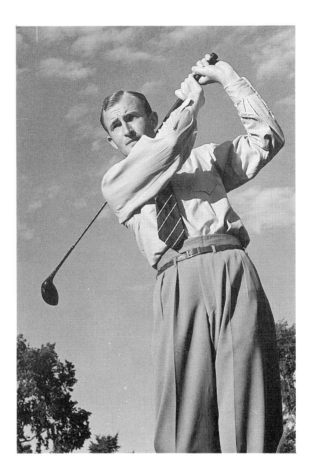

Stan Horne driving.

time he was old enough to caddie he was living in Fonthill, Ontario. The newly opened Lookout Point GC had hired Stan's father, Arthur, to be its greenkeeper. During his teenage years, Stan Horne not only caddied but also frequented the workshop of the club's professional, Art Keeling, who was renowned as a golf teacher. This led to a four-year stint as Keeling's assistant, before promotion to head professional at Ottawa Hunt. Thereafter, success followed success. In the 1936 CPGA championship over a heavily bunkered, rain-soaked course at Cataraqui G & CC, Stan Horne opened poorly with a 78. At the halfway mark he was six strokes behind Willie Lamb. But on the heavy turf and tricky greens everyone but Stan Horne faded. Two rounds of 72 gave him victory by four strokes over Lamb and Dick Borthwick.

The next year Stan Horne successfully defended his title over his own course. A lean and lanky 145 pounds, he was hitting the ball prodigious distances. On these two days he was also unbeatable around the greens.

His third successive title came at the scene of his first, Cataraqui. Willie Lamb did not play in 1938, standing down in favour of his assistant, his brother Bob (after all, someone had to look after the shop at Lambton). And Bob Lamb showed his gratitude by firing a 69–70 to lead Gordie Brydson by a stroke. But these two collapsed on the second day, and Stan Horne, Bob Gray Jr., and Jules Huot all caught them. Horne's closing 68 was just good enough to win.

The CPGA introduced a 36-hole championship for senior professionals that year. Art Keeling won, which was only fitting.

This was only the beginning of Stan Horne's long friendship with the game of golf and its tournaments. Although he was never to recover the form of 1937–40, when he was ranked as Canada's top professional, he still had two national titles to come. Playing out of Montreal's Islesmere club, Stan Horne won the Millar Trophy in 1946 and 1948, in a tournament by then open to all members of the CPGA.

The 1930s saw the emergence of a number of Canadian professionals in Central Canada who were eventually to win national titles. But their successes came mostly after the Second World War, when their names became familiar in golfing households: Bob Gray Jr., Gordie Brydson, Bill Kerr, Dick Borthwick.

In 1939, former newspaperman C. W. (Baldy) MacQueen – at the time publicity manager to the RCGA – came out with this personal ranking, in descending order, of Canada's professionals: Dick Borthwick, Stan Horne, Bob Gray Jr., Lex Robson, Bobby Alston, Arthur Hulbert, Gordie Brydson, Willie Lamb, Jules Huot, Bill Kerr.

MacQueen's top pick, Dick Borthwick, had done well that year, but in provincial championships – he won the Quebec Open and Ontario's Millar Trophy. It is noteworthy that no golfer from outside Central Canada had made the list. As MacQueen pointed out: "No pros from Western Canada nor the Maritimes competed in events along with their brothers of Quebec and Ontario and so for this [ranking] one has to decide who are the leading pros in the two central provinces."

But all that was about to change. Two professionals from British Columbia, Freddie Wood and Stan Leonard, were about to make nonsense of Baldy MacQueen's national rankings.

"Professional golf today is undoubtedly on a totally different footing to what it was some years ago. It holds out great possibilities and inducements to any energetic young player of ability. The financial returns are a very long way ahead of an ordinary clerkship or, for that matter, a managership in a bank or a financial institution." The words are those of Ralph Reville, written in 1921. His remarks were occasioned by J. Munro Hunter's appointment as professional to Calgary's St. Andrews Golf Club.

The Edmonton golfer was the first of Canada's leading amateurs to join the professional ranks, so his was a historic conversion. The six-feet-five Hunter had learned his game in Edinburgh. Unbeaten in the Alberta Amateur Championship between 1913 and 1920, he had also placed second in the Alberta Open. He was perhaps the longest hitter of a ball in the country. In 1955, the *Edmonton Journal* carried this storied evidence of his great length, in the reminiscences of Tommy Morrison, a local professional:

> . . . the inimitable Gene Sarazen . . . watched Hunter drive three balls in a long-driving event. Sarazen was approaching the tee when he saw Hunter hitting. "Do you know what I did," said Sarazen. "I just put my three balls back in my bag."

A few others followed Hunter's example in the West. At about the time Hunter was leav-

A number of British professionals immigrated to the Prairies between the wars. The Scot Eric Bannister came from the Sandy Lodge club to Winnipeg's St. Charles CC and was its professional for some twenty-seven years.

The name Fletcher is inextricably bound to the story of golf in Saskatchewan. Hugh came to Canada in 1912, working for half a dozen clubs in Winnipeg before finally settling down at the Citizens club in Moose Jaw. His brother Fred is perhaps better known. He came from

J. Munro Hunter of Edmonton (right), *four times amateur champion of Alberta, seen with Harry Black in 1920, before Hunter turned professional.*

ing Canada for a more lucrative job in Milwaukee, another distinguished amateur turned professional, Arthur Cruttenden (or "Crutty"), had immigrated to Alberta just before the First World War. An amateur in Britain, he appears to have joined Calgary Golf and Country Club as its professional in 1914 but to have resigned after a few months. As an amateur, he won the Alberta Open in 1919; three years later he turned professional with Calgary Bowness. Cruttenden later moved to Toronto's Summit GC and was runner-up in the CPGA championship held there in 1928.

We have already met Bobby Reith of Manitoba, another amateur turned professional. It is worth noting that he and Redvers Mackenzie were the only Canadian Amateur finalists to turn professional in the years before 1948.

Fred Fletcher of Moose Jaw in 1928, defending his Saskatchewan Open.

Cheshire to be Hugh's assistant in 1919 and followed him around for several years. In 1925 he joined Bill Brinkworth at Wascana CC. The families were old friends (Hugh had been at school with Brinkworth in their native Scotland) and became united when Fred Fletcher married Bill's daughter Daisy. They had four children, appropriately named Par, Stymie, Dormie, and Birdie.

Fred Fletcher had several seasons as a professional at Moose Jaw before returning to the Wascana club, where he was professional or greenkeeper at various times over the next thirty years. He was an excellent tournament golfer. Slightly built, weighing around 115 pounds, with one leg withered from childhood polio, Fred Fletcher was still one of the longest hitters in the Prairies. When he won the Regina Open in 1926, *Canadian Golfer* noted that he was "a likeable, unassuming player, entirely free from the affectations which afflict some of the pros." In the following year he lifted three titles: the Saskatchewan Open, the Western Canada Open, and the Western Canada Professional Championship. A charter member of the Canadian Golf Course Superintendents' Association, Fred was still playing golf in 1983, while living in a retirement home with Daisy.

We have already met that legendary figure of prairie golf, Bill ("Brink") Brinkworth, who became "The Squire of Jasper" in 1936. In 1920, Brink's wife had persuaded her brother Hubert Cooke to come out from England to help in the workshop at Wascana.

Cooke was only nineteen at the time, and did not, apparently, have any previous experience in the world of golf. But two years with Brink, followed by two as an assistant to Ernest Penfold at Winnipeg GC, prepared him for the professional's job at Prince Albert GC. He was there for forty-one years. In that time the course expanded from nine to eighteen holes and became the "Cooke Municipal Golf Course." As the professional-manager at Prince Rupert, Cooke instituted perhaps the largest and finest junior section in the province.

Tommy Ross, another Scot, established an enviable record in Saskatchewan tournament golf between the wars. He took Brinkworth's place at Wascana. During the years of depression and drought he moved to the Regina club, where he stayed for over thirty years.

Bill Kinnear was never given the title "The Squire of Saskatoon," but he deserved it. This Scottish carpenter, who was hired in 1910 to lay out a new course for Saskatoon GC, remained as a professional in the city till 1946.

The trio of Davie Black, Jimmy Huish, and Alex Duthie was as well-known and as respected in B.C. golf as was any group of professionals in the East. They were only three of several immigrants who did much by their teaching and example to raise the status of golf in the province between the wars.

In 1921, Victoria GC brought over thirty-one-year-old Phil Taylor from Wanstead Park in Essex. He had often been well-placed in

Phil Taylor, shortly after his arrival at Oak Bay in 1921.

British tournaments, but was probably best remembered for his sensational 71 in the British Open of 1914. Such scores were rare before the First World War. When he left Britain for Canada, some English followers of the game thought him the best player to emigrate.

Taylor was a quiet, unassuming fellow. His neat, orthodox style came with an ideal temperament for golf. He was to prove a perfect fit for the quiet, dignified club at Victoria, of which he was to become such an essential part until his retirement in 1960. Renowned as a patient and far-sighted teacher, Phil Taylor also did well in West Coast tournaments. He won the B.C. Open three times, the Pacific Northwest Open at least once.

Bill Heyworth, essentially a clubmaker and teacher, had been an assistant to Tom Vardon before coming to Canada in the early 1920s. He later joined Vancouver's Hastings Park municipal course.

Alex Marling came from Royal Aberdeen in 1921 to replace George Ayton at Regina GC. After three seasons he took the place of Willie Black at Royal Colwood. Marling had been the Scottish professional champion in 1913, but a war injury had impaired his great talent as a player.

Then we have the Sutherlands, Duncan and Don. Both hailed from the northeast of Scotland, but they were not related. Don came from Dornoch, that small but prolific golf breeding-ground north of Inverness, where the Sutherland clan abound; Dunc, from Tain, on the other side of the Dornoch Firth. The Edmonton G & CC engaged Dunc in 1920, to be its professional and manager. He later moved to Vancouver's Point Grey and over something like thirty years became an institution in B.C. golf.

Born in 1900, Don Sutherland was thirty when he joined Vancouver GC. Like his compatriot, he proved himself as a craftsman and teacher rather than as a tournament player. After moving around several clubs in the province, Don Sutherland retired. He also applied for and was granted reinstatement as an amateur, so that he could return to his native Dornoch and play tournament golf there. He was then eighty-three years of age. (I played over Dornoch in the summer of 1984 and, just before leaving, noticed an elderly gentleman on the practice fairway, swinging a club so smoothly I had to ask the hotel manager if he knew him. "Don Sutherland. He recently came back from being a professional in America." I went back to the practice ground, hoping for an interview. But Don Sutherland had gone, no doubt satisfied he was in good enough shape for his first amateur tournament in half a century.)

As in the east, the flow of immigrant professionals to the west all but dried up in the 1930s. The boom days were over. A new club needing a professional might seek a young man from the growing ranks of Canadian-bred assistants.

There was at least one notable exception to this. When the new Capilano club was looking

Dunc Sutherland, when at Edmonton G & CC.

Jock McKinnon of Capilano.

for its first professional in 1937, it considered offering the job to "the young man who is so popular . . . the highly regarded and colorful Point Grey professional, Dunc Sutherland." (The quote is from the club's history.) But the job went to John (Jock) McKinnon, a twenty-two-year-old Scot who was brought over from Monifeith, near Carnoustie.

Jock McKinnon had been a Scottish internationalist at the age of seventeen, and had won the Scottish assistants' championship in 1935. Capilano wanted an outstanding young golfer, preferably from Scotland, and that is what it got. In British Columbia, Jock McKinnon was to take over the role of "the grand auld Scot"

from the beloved Davie Black. Jock stayed with Capilano until 1979. At his farewell dinner, members recalled his arrival and long years of service:

> He was heatherish and handsome, with rolling R's and A's as heavy as Highland porridge . . . He had a straightforward, clear, fearless-looking eye and impeccable manners . . . That was forty-two years ago . . . He still addresses each and every member by his or her surname. As a distinguished representative of the Royal and Ancient game, he was never off the fairway.

George Cumming would have been proud of him.

The two most celebrated names to rise from the ranks of the province's caddies became professionals in the 1930s. The rise of Wood and Leonard to become the top professionals in the country will be examined later.

The Maritime clubs did not have a playing professional of national stature until Jimmy Rimmer joined Halifax G & CC (Ashburn) in 1934. He was to win four out of the last six Maritime professional championships before the Second World War. Rimmer had come out from Britain around 1925 to be professional at Jasper Park.

In New Brunswick a new face appeared in the 1930s – Archie Skinner. Born in St. Andrews, Scotland, in 1913, he was brought as a boy to Galt, Ontario, where his father, James, worked as the greenkeeper/professional to the Waterloo County G & CC. In 1920, James Skinner moved to be greenkeeper at the Algonquin club in St. Andrews, New Brunswick. Archie became the club's professional when John Peacock retired in the late 1930s.

Archie Skinner won his first N.B./P.E.I. Open title in 1934, and went on to capture two fistfuls of championships in the Maritimes over the next twenty years. Strangely, he did

Kas Zabowski, a leading Maritime professional in the 1940s and 1950s.

Sam Foley of Gorsebrook, winning the Maritime Open Championship in 1928.

not do well in the 1939 Canadian Open held at a course he knew well – Riverside, Saint John.

Kasmir Zabowski had been a professional in Winnipeg for ten years before coming to Halifax G & CC in the early years of the Second World War. Having placed well in CPGA events, he had been ranked number seven in the country in 1939. He was to be the most successful playing professional in the Maritimes over the next fifteen years.

Between the wars, our professionals always had a hankering after a regular series of international matches against the Americans or British or both, along the lines of the Ryder Cup. The nearest they came to an international was a competition against the British Ryder Cup team on its way back home in 1927. When the British let it be known that they were prepared to play in a 72-hole competition, 36 each in Toronto and Montreal, for some three thousand dollars' prize money, the RCGA promptly took them up on the offer. It selected a team made up of a mixture of the old guard and new: Charlie Murray (captain), Phil Taylor, Davie Black, Jimmy Rimmer, Jimmy Johnstone, Andy Kay, Nicol Thompson, Albert Murray, Davie Spittal; reserves were Jock Brown and George Cumming.

This team did better than expected against a British team obviously tired by its sojourn in the United States. After the first 36 holes at Toronto GC, Jasper's Jimmy Rimmer lead with 145, and Davie Black was second with 147. The nearest Brit, Arthur Havers, lay in fourth place with 149.

The British were back on form for the second leg at Royal Montreal, Havers winning the 72-hole competition from Davie Black by a stroke (296 to 297) with Andy Kay third. Canadians took three of the first six places.

Just before the 1937 Open at the St. Andrews club in Toronto, a team of Canadian profes- sionals took on a team from the visiting Americans. The team of Bob Gray Jr., Bobby Alston, Ernie Wakelam, Bobby Burns, Gordie Brydson, Stan Horne, Roland Huot, Jules Huot, and Bill Kerr played eight singles in the morning, four four-balls in the afternoon. The Americans won, eight matches to four.

Gray, Alston, and Wakelam won their sin- gles, Gray's win being an exceptionally fine one against the U.S. Open champion, Ralph Guldahl. Alston and Burns won their four-ball.

The match was marred by controversy; Willie Lamb, Jimmy Johnstone, Lex Robson, and Dick Borthwick were selected but did not play. They objected to the Americans being paid sev- enty-five dollars, whereas the Canadians were not offered a cent.

22
CHAPTER

AMERICANS INVADE THE OPEN

URING THE 1935 CANADIAN OPEN, eighteen competitors were asked to complete a questionnaire. One question: "Where does the Canadian Open rank among the important tournaments of the world?" And another: "What would you suggest to improve the Canadian Open?"

The thirteen Americans who answered ranked the Canadian Open anywhere from fourth to tenth. To most it came after the U.S. Open, the British Open, the PGA Championship, and the Western Open. To some, it ranked lower than other events hardly known in Canada. (The Masters, remember, was then in its infancy.)

Canadians were disillusioned. For years, the American winners of the Canadian Open had been telling them that it was the number-two tournament in North America. In fact, Tommy Armour had further inflated the Canadian ego. In 1929, he thought it "the second greatest championship in the world." What had happened, then, to lower its prestige so drastically between 1929 and 1935?

The answer, of course, was nothing. The Canadian Open had probably never ranked high-er than fourth or fifth in the minds of U.S. professionals. In his *Fifty Years of American Golf* (1936), H. B. Martin includes the Canadian Open in his list of minor championships. But having just won our Open, no U.S. professional was going to play down his success. And our visitors were, for the most part, well-meaning and courteous. They told us what we wanted to hear. As for Tommy Armour – well, his remark was probably a sly dig at his old adversary, Walter Hagen, who had won the British Open four times but never the Canadian.

The response to the second question – how to improve the Canadian Open – was unanimous. Increase the prize money! The point was well made. Canada's Open would not consistently attract the top U.S. players so long as the purse was a miserly $1,465. There were events on the PGA Tour with purses of $10,000, one with $15,000. The big names in U.S. golf would have to be enticed north by higher prize money, or they would desert the Canadian Open, and its ranking would be lower still.

This put the RCGA on the spot. The Open had never had a commercial sponsor. The prize money came from the competitors' entry fees and from receipts at the gate. The higher the prize money, the less left over to help amateur golf in Canada, which was the *raison d'être* of the RCGA's existence. But if the RCGA did not increase the prize money, the Open would attract fewer stars from the United States. This in turn would bring out fewer spectators, the gate receipts would go down, and there would be less money for amateur golf. The RCGA was caught in a catch-22.

The solution was commercial sponsorship. But this was anathema to the traditionalists within the RCGA, who claimed the game would be cheapened. The British Open, they pointed out, had no sponsor, yet it attracted many of the top U.S. professionals, all willing to incur the high cost of travelling to Britain for the chance of winning a slice of only $2,500. Which was true, but a *non sequitur*. The British Open had seventy years of tradition behind it. The championship had always been fiercely fought for by the finest golfers in the world. To have one's name engraved on the championship trophy below the names of Willie Park, Harry Vardon, Ted Ray, Bobby Jones was worth much more – in endorsements and exhibition fees – than the prize money. When Walter Hagen won the British Open in 1922, he gave his $500 prize money to his caddie. Back in America, with the British Open title to his credit, he and Joe Kirkwood (the Australian trick-shot artist) went on a coast-to-coast tour. In his book, H. B. Martin called it "the greatest golfing pilgrimage for financial gain ever known."

With no such tradition to sell, the Canadian Open could attract American stars only by increasing the purse with commercial backing. More than a little reluctantly, the RCGA took this step in 1936. Joseph E. Seagram Ltd. put up a magnificent gold cup and a hefty chunk of cash. The Canadian Open purse was increased to $3,000, with another $600 going to the leading Canadian professionals.

That year, entries jumped to an all-time high, and by 1938 gate receipts had more than doubled. Many in Canada congratulated them-

selves on having made the Canadian Open once again the third-most important championship in the world. Wisely, perhaps, they did not seek to test their judgement by sending out another questionnaire . . .

The foregoing illustrates that by the 1930s the success of the Canadian Open was being measured by the number of leading U.S. professionals it attracted. This state of affairs had come about gradually over the years following the First World War.

For a start, the number of entrants nearly tripled, from 32 in 1914, to 88 in 1919. The field kept increasing. When held at a venue near golf-rich Toronto, the Open attracted many more, including more Americans. In 1923, when a field of 139 played at Toronto's Lakeview, the late starters had to finish by the light of automobiles, and players pleaded for a qualifying round. For the first time, in 1924 at Mount Bruno, a 36-hole cut was made, only those players within 20 strokes of the leader going on to play the last two rounds. And a year later, when 160 played at Lambton, the Open was stretched over three days. This became the accepted format, so that only about seventy players competed in the final two rounds on the third day.

Until 1930, the entries of all professionals were accepted, as well as of all amateurs with a handicap of 6 or less. The entrance fee of five dollars did not deter the many who had not the slightest hope of getting this back (all the prize money went to the top ten). From 1930, applicants had to provide evidence of their performance in recent tournaments before they would be accepted.

Spectators were charged one dollar for the first time in 1923. Boy Scouts were used to "police" the course, and may also have sold tickets, as they were to do at Mount Bruno a year later. In both these years, spectators contributed only about $1,500, so two-thirds of those present must have been there as guests. The money was split four ways: 30 per cent to the RCGA, 30 per cent to Open prize money, 20 per cent to the club, and 20 per cent to the PGA.

The popularity of the Open as a spectacle increased steadily throughout the 1920s and 1930s. The American stars became household names in Canada, rivalling the likes of amateurs Somerville, Farley, and Black. The largest galleries were probably at the Opens held over the public course in Toronto, St. Andrews, in 1936 and 1937, when the final day attracted some 10,000.

The Americans only gradually took over the Open.

In 1919, the field was predominantly Canadian, but a few British professionals entered from the U.S., including Big Jim Barnes and J. Douglas Edgar. They were joined by the American professional Leo Diegel, only twenty at the time, and by the American amateur Bobby Jones, who was three years younger but well on his way to everlasting fame as the world's finest golfer of his generation.

The visitors took three of the first four places. J. Douglas Edgar won, and the best Karl Keffer could do to salvage Canada's honour was to tie Jones and Barnes for second place. Still, Canadians did occupy five of the top ten places.

At the last moment, the RCGA doubled the purse because of the good entry, but that brought it up to only $430, with $200 plus a gold medal going to the winner. The next year, in 1920, when J. Douglas Edgar successfully defended his title at Ottawa's Rivermead, the purse was advertised as $265. Although the club generously brought it up to the same as offered in 1919, the prospects of so little cash, and the longer distance to travel, reduced the entry by a quarter, and only two U.S.-based professionals entered. Charlie Murray tied with Edgar and the Scottish amateur Tommy Armour, but lost in a play-off.

In 1921, the official prize money was doubled to $450. Six U.S.-based professionals entered, as well as the visiting Australian Joe Kirkwood. Between them they took the top three places. But five Canadians were in the top ten.

Charlie Murray, our most successful professional in the Opens right after the First World War.

Twice as many professionals came from the U.S. to Mount Bruno in 1922, but the big-name players had crossed the Atlantic to compete in the British Open. At Mount Bruno, two Canadians tied for third place, Eric Bannister of Winnipeg's St. Charles and Albert Murray of the nearby Country Club of Montreal. Four Canadians were in the top ten, so things didn't look bad at all.

Next year the Open returned to Toronto, a venue the U.S. players preferred because of lower travelling expenses. Fourteen entered from the U.S. and no less than nine finished in the top ten. Although Hagen and Macdonald Smith were at the British Open, this was the classiest field yet, including as it did Gene Sarazen, Johnny Farrell, Jock Hutchison, and the winner, Clarence Hackney. Andy Kay of Lambton finished sixth.

It is fair to say that here, at Lakeview, U.S. professionals clearly dominated the Canadian Open for the first time. Thereafter, the success of Canadian professionals in their own major championship depended very much on how many leading players came up from the United States. Which, in turn, depended on what other tournaments were being held at the same time, offering more money.

For the first time, at the 1923 Open, the RCGA had made spectators pay a one-dollar admission, so in 1924 it had the funds to increase the prize money to $750. This enticed thirty entries from the U.S. to Mount Bruno. The only Canadian to make the top ten was again Andy Kay.

The pattern became familiar. In 1925, Kay tied Hagen for third, and our amateur, Bill Thompson, finished tenth.

In 1926, Charlie Murray fought the rain at Royal Montreal to take fifth place, with Andy Kay eighth.

Canada's Diamond Jubilee Open, with a purse of $1,320, attracted all the U.S. giants to Toronto, with the exception of Bobby Jones, Bill Melhorn, and Jim Barnes. Tommy Armour won. Americans took the first eight spots. Our Andy Kay was ninth.

In 1928, we had to be content with sharing thirteenth place (Arthur Hulbert). The next

Eight of the Open invaders: left to right, top: *Tommy Armour, Horton Smith, Percy Alliss (British), Johnny Farrell;* bottom, *Billie Burke, Leo Diegel, Macdonald Smith, Harry Cooper.*

year, the amateur Sandy Somerville was our best, but fourteenth. We had two places in the first ten in 1930; a solitary seventh place, Jules Huot, in 1931. Andy Kay tied for tenth in 1932.

Then came one of those periodic spikes of optimism, when there is talk of a revival, a rebirth. In 1933, Lex Robson tied for second place, and Bobby Alston for ninth. Never mind that four top U.S. players had withdrawn; Robson finished ahead of Sarazen, Diegel, Farrell, and Horton Smith.

Robson rescued us again in 1934, this time in a tie for third place. But hope receded in the following two years, when we finished no higher than eighth.

When Bob Gray Jr. took ninth place in 1936, he did have the distinction of having his name engraved on the Rivermead Cup. This cup had been put up in 1920 for the winner of the Open. From 1936, when Seagram started to sponsor the Open, the winner of the Open had his name inscribed on the Seagram Gold Cup, and the Rivermead Cup then went to the leading Canadian.

We fared little better at Toronto's St. Andrews in 1937, when Stan Horne and Bobby Alston shared sixth place. (The purse was now up to $3,000 – not counting the special $600 for leading Canadians – and went to the top fifteen.) Robson again made money in 1938, but only by squeaking into tenth place.

In 1939, the Open was held in the Maritimes for the first time, at Saint John's Riverside. The venue kept many of the Americans away. The cost of travel also deterred many Canadians, and the number of entries fell by half. This should have been Canada's year, but Jug McSpaden won, and four Americans went home with the top money. Still, we had four in the top ten, including Somerville, who tied for fifth.

In 1940, Stan Horne took seventh place, tying Scarboro's Bob Gray Jr. Mark that second name.

Many Canadians probably prayed for the 1941 Open to be washed out after the second round. Had there been a snowstorm on August 9, Bob Gray Jr. would have been the first Canadian champion in twenty-seven years. As it was, Sam Snead shot a closing 66 to force Gray into second place. Gordie Brydson was fourth, Bill Kerr fifth. Three places in the first five was our best showing since 1914. But missing from the field were U.S. stars Ben Hogan, Byron Nelson, Jimmy Thompson, Ralph Guldahl, and Craig Wood. They would not compete in a tournament offering less than $5,000 to the general field. And many of the Americans who *did* show in 1941, including Sarazen, Snead, Bulla, the Mangrums, and Horton Smith, had their expenses paid by sports equipment companies, to whom they were under contract.

In 1942, it was back to bread and water. The top Canadian, Gordie Brydson, could finish no better than fifteenth. The stage was set for the future.

Marshalls were used to control crowds, but not always effectively. In 1935, when Gene Kunes won at Montreal's Summerlea club, the *Toronto Daily Star* carried this account of the finish:

> So keen was the barging to reach the new champion that one hurrying woman stumbled at the top of the green and rolled happily into the sand trap. She was up again like [boxer] Jack Doyle going down. She replaced no divots of sand, but charged furiously into the mob to snatch a brief instant of intimacy with today's hero.

The Rivermead Cup.

Marshalls were so thick on the course, they were tumbling over one another. One man figured every member of Summerlea must be a marshall for the day. Armed with limber bamboo rods, they fled before the rushes of the trampling herd and effectively blocked them off. Kunes was forced to play a chip shot from the edge of the green with humans packed so closely around him a full swing would have torn some eager peeper's ear off.

This, then, is the factual evidence of the growth of the Canadian Open and of the growing success of the U.S. invasion. How and why this came about requires a closer look at the changing state of professional golf between the wars.

At the same time as American golfers were dominating Canadians, they were increasingly doing the same to the British. Golfers from the U.S. took all but one of the British Open titles in the years 1921 to 1933. Walter Hagen won four British titles, Bobby Jones three. Of the six Ryder Cup matches played between the wars – they started in 1927 – the American professionals won four, the British two. This supremacy in international golf was to last for half a century. How did it come about? What magic elixir suddenly made U.S. tournament golfers the finest in the world?

The answer has something to do with the economic theory of supply and demand, and with the Darwinian concept of the survival of the fittest. As the ever-increasing supply of prize money created a demand for tournament competitors, so more and more professionals gave up their jobs at clubs to concentrate on tournament golf. Of the thousands who tried to make a living this way, only the finest survived. The rest fell by the way and went back to being club professionals. The few who rose to the top did so by studying the game, by practising the game assiduously, and by playing the game competitively, with a frequency, determination, and thoroughness never

before seen in the world of golf. Tournaments became their business.

The supremacy of the U.S. professional was confined to a small, select group of men, perhaps fifty out of three or four thousand. These were the tournament professionals, the forerunners of today's PGA Tour. Most of them were attached to golf clubs but derived little of their income from routine duties at the club. They made a living of sorts by playing in tournaments around the country, by giving exhibition matches, and by endorsing golf equipment.

Even before the First World War, the U.S. had many more professional tournaments than Canada. Mostly, these were held in the winter golf resorts of the south. Increasingly, they gave the U.S. professional a competitive edge over British as well as Canadian professionals. In the 1920s, the Americans overtook the British, then outclassed them.

G. A. Philpott came over to the United States in 1927 as manager of the British Ryder Cup team, which failed dismally in its objective of winning the cup and the U.S. Open. The American approach to golf surprised and dismayed Philpott. He wrote in *Canadian Golfer:*

> . . . What did give me a shock was their mental attitude towards the game, which amounts to this: Golf is not a game; it is just a business. A tragic discovery this, to one schooled in the British convention. [This leaves our professionals] with an awkward choice. Either they must fight the opposition with their own weapons, or be prepared to suffer eclipse. . . .
>
> The American professionals . . . are all in the same line of business, manufacturers of "pars," "birdies," and "eagles," and there are so many first-class players, business is exceptionally keen . . . In America you must win or you are quickly forgotten . . .
>
> [The] American professionals have come to the obvious conclusion that the best way lies in saving as many strokes as possible round and on the greens. And it is here they are concentrating the whole of their efforts . . . They have made an intense study

of putting, and have reached a point where they try to hole out in one putt, whatever the distance. They have trained themselves to be satisfied with nothing else.

[The members of the U.S. Ryder Cup team] do not worry about the niceties of style, conventional methods, or traditions or reputations; all they seek is to become mechanical swingers of clubs – highly developed pieces of machinery, for the production of par figures or better . . . Practice naturally enters largely into the scheme of things – stern, relentless, practice. They cheerfully . . . spend laborious hours either at the practice teeing-ground or upon the practice putting green . . . because of the great financial rewards which await the "topnotchers" in that country.

The financial rewards of which Philpott wrote had increased steadily in the 1920s, largely through the efforts of the United States Professional Golfers' Association (the PGA) founded in 1916. The PGA put together what later became known as the PGA Tour. The Canadian Open, in time, became a regular event on the Tour, and many Canadian professionals sought hard to join it.

The PGA Tour, or circuit of tournaments, had its modest beginnings in the years following the First World War. It eased itself into existence, and grew from there. A PGA officer once selected 1922 as its birthday.

The idea that spectators would pay money at the gate to see experts play golf was planted in the minds of professionals during the First World War. They would compete against each other, sometimes paired with leading amateurs. Spectators would be charged a dollar to watch them, the money going to the Red Cross.

In 1921, the PGA asked clubs organizing tournaments to charge spectators, the money to go to a PGA benevolent fund, and most of the clubs complied. The USGA did likewise for the 1922 U.S. Open, the money going to amateur golf. In later years, sponsors would put up the prize money, but would often keep the gate receipts to recoup some of their costs.

The swashbuckling, charismatic Walter Hagen ("I never wanted to be a millionaire . . . I just wanted to live like one") was perhaps the first to realize that golf professionals could make good money as entertainers. As winner of the 1914 U.S. Open, he had been much in demand for war-time exhibition matches. After the war, spectators came to be attracted as much by the man as by his golf. In dress and manner, he stood out from his fellow professionals. He wore expensive suits, if somewhat flamboyant. When visiting a club, he had the parvenu insolence to enter the members' clubhouse; the caddie shack or the professional's workshop was not for Walter Hagen. He had a name for keeping his opponents or partners waiting on the first tee, as much to discomfit his opponents as anything, and when he did arrive, it might be in a chauffeur-driven automobile.

Such is the legend surrounding the man. Some were amused by golf's first showman; others labelled him a truculent boor and a poor sportsman. "Hagen may be one of the greatest, if not the greatest, professional golfer in the world, but he is certainly not by any means one of the most popular. He is altogether too swanky, both on and off the links." So wrote Ralph Reville, in 1927. He recalled that Hagen had turned up late for the 1925 Canadian Open at Lambton. "An old trick of Hagen's . . . which should call for prompt disqualification."

When Hagen told British professionals that they were "too gosh darned lazy" to win, the New York *Herald Tribune* chastised him for being a loud-mouthed braggart.

But, in the end, even Ralph Reville came to admire the man, and to realize that in Hagen's own way he had forced professional golfers to realize their own worth and given them a new dignity. More than any other man, "The Haig," or "Sir Walter," opened to professionals the doors of the private clubhouse.

Hagen soon found he could make much more money in exhibition matches, in tournaments, and by sponsoring golf equipment than he could as a club professional. Winning a tournament was important not so much for its prize money as for the publicity it gave him. The British Open title in 1922 brought him only $500 in prize money but probably more than a hundred times that amount in exhibition fees and endorsements, now that he could add "British Open Champion" to his list of successes. Other professionals, notably Gene Sarazen, followed Hagen's example, although many kept some association with a golf club.

The circuit of tournaments in which Hagen, Sarazen, and others competed, started as a winter circuit in the southeast and southwest states. Some competitors came from clubs in the northern, snow-bound states, and from Canada. In the summer, the tournament players would come north for the U.S. Open and the PGA Championship. They might even play in the Canadian Open if it did not clash with a more lucrative event elsewhere.

As the 1920s progressed, a few cities in the northern states took to sponsoring their own Open golf tournaments. The PGA naturally did all it could to encourage them. It persuaded some chambers of commerce that organizing a professional tournament and giving it the name of, say, "The Bugsville Open," would bring Bugsville lots of good publicity and attract investment. As soon as one city did this, others followed, adding perhaps $1,000 to the prize money. Just before the Depression, the Agua Caliente Open at Tijuana, Mexico, was offering prize money of as much as $25,000.

Organizing tournaments became an increasingly onerous task for the PGA. It was only one of the many services it offered its two-thousand-odd members, the vast majority of whom did not play in tournaments. So, in 1929, the PGA established a tournament committee, the work of which was soon taken over by a newly formed Tournament Bureau of the PGA. In 1930, the PGA hired Bob Harlow to run this bureau. A former newspaperman who was also Hagen's manager, Harlow formalized the structure of a tournament, laying out what was expected of the sponsors and of the committees running it. He tried to ensure that professional tournaments were being run in a professional way. Look at the organization behind a tournament today and you will find it based on Harlow's formula.

All Harlow's committees were staffed by volunteer labour. The financial success of golf tournaments to this day is underwritten by the willingness of hundreds of volunteers to give of their time and energy for the privilege of working alongside top professionals or amateurs. Some who volunteer see very little of the play.

Before the Second World War, PGA tournaments were usually self-supporting. The money paid at the gate would normally cover the cost of organizing the event (say $1,000) and the prize money ($5,000). But advance ticket sales were hard to make. Since bad weather could keep spectators away, a sponsor was needed to insure against this, such as a chamber of commerce, or a local company that could charge the shortfall to advertising.

The Depression put an end to the PGA's plans of adding a northern, summer tour, to the winter tour of the southeast and the southwest states, so it was not until the 1950s that the PGA Tour operated year-round (or nearly so).

The Canadian Open was seldom part of the "official" PGA tournament circuit before 1936. Its low prize money of some $1,400 put it in a class with several other unofficial tournaments in the U.S. While touring professionals might play in these unofficial tournaments, there was nothing to stop the PGA Tournament Bureau from coming up with a conflicting but better-playing event elsewhere.

"Official" tournaments attracted a better field for reasons other than the prize money. U.S. professionals were selected for the Ryder Cup on the basis of points awarded in official tournaments. Also, from 1937, the professional with the lowest scoring average in official tournaments was awarded the Vardon Trophy; this prestige award meant more money in endorsements.

One of the chronic problems that troubled the PGA Tournament Bureau and the sponsors was ensuring that the big-name professionals would turn up. In the 1930s, some professionals were guaranteed $100 appearance money, but their demands quickly escalated and this incentive was dropped. The Canadian Open was to be plagued by the problem of professionals who promised to appear and then didn't.

The PGA circuit of tournaments developed a new breed of professionals, who brought with them a new breed of problems. Their competitive edge was honed regularly by playing against each other. Only a few made a decent living. They virtually monopolized the Canadian Open in the years between the wars.

But the first man to win the Open after the First World War was not an American, but an Englishman.

Only four golfers have successfully defended our Open title, by winning back to back: J. Douglas Edgar (1919, 1920), Leo Diegel (1924, 1925 and 1928, 1929), Sam Snead (1940, 1941), and Jim Ferrier (1950, 1951).

The first to do so, Edgar, won his first title by a margin of sixteen strokes, a record that has never looked like being equalled. Within a year of winning for the second time, he was killed in circumstances that have never been fully explained. As we shall see, his death led to a further tragedy.

J. Douglas Edgar was thirty-four when he came to Canada in 1919, a British-born professional who had joined a U.S. club after the war. His only previous claim to fame had been a modest one – victory in the French Open of 1914. The British magazine *Golf Monthly* did not even have his photograph and had to cable Canada for one to be sent.

Edgar played with an unusually heavy bulger driver, one weighing close to seventeen ounces and with a whippy shaft. He also putted with a cleek putter, in a stabbing motion, with no follow-through. He hit high shots to the green, with plenty of backspin.

Edgar's total of 278 at Hamilton's Ancaster course (made up of 72 71 69 66) was a record for a national Open championship in Britain and North America. What is more, no com-

petitor in a national championship had ever broken 70 twice in the one day. (The Open was then a two-day affair, 36 holes a day.)

The unwatered fairways of Ancaster were playing exceptionally short during those hot August days of 1919. Bobby Jones was one of several who drove the 330-yard second hole. Hugh Reid, a Lambton amateur, drove to the fringe of the ninth green, on a hole measuring 425 yards. All of which explains the low scoring, but not the huge margin of victory.

There is really no explanation for that except to say that Edgar, on the second day, sustained for 36 holes the high state of grace that most golfers experience from time to time for perhaps two holes in a row. He could do nothing wrong. He was skilled at the push shot, and was using it effectively. And all the putts that were makable, he made. How else can you explain his run of 3, 4, 2, 3, 3 in the final round?

Edgar retained his title at Ottawa's Rivermead club. But he had lost the divine touch of Ancaster and was a mere mortal. He won only

J. Douglas Edgar, triumph and tragedy.

after a play-off with Charlie Murray and the Scottish amateur Tommy Armour.

This was a championship remembered as much for its sad errors and dramatic changes of fortune as for its brilliant play. George Ayton went into the final round with a two-stroke lead over Armour, and a five-stroke lead over Edgar and Murray. The leaders did not go out last as they do now, but in more or less random order, depending on the draw. Ayton was out early. His machine-like golf of the first three rounds broke down completely. He shot an 82 and was out of the race. This Scottish-born professional played out of the Regina GC, so the hopes of the West went with him.

The fickle crowd had soon abandoned Ayton and turned to Edgar and Murray. When these two finished with scores of 298, the focus turned to Armour. There he was, out in 35, several strokes ahead, with the championship seemingly in his grasp. Then his game soured. A 5 on the 255-yard tenth; a 6 on the next, a par four. He came to the sixteenth needing three pars for victory. After a fine drive, his second to the green hit overhead branches and fell into the sloping bank of a ditch. He played out, but found another ditch near the green. Then came one of those seemingly miraculous recoveries that were to mark Armour as a player who did not choke in adversity. He picked the ball cleanly with his niblick, made the green, and sank a 10-foot putt for a bogey. He scrambled again at the seventeenth, and again at the last hole, but made the pars he needed to tie.

In those days, the rules of the Open called for an 18-hole play-off on the following day (a Saturday). It turned into a contest bristling with tense moments, dazzling play, and surprising switches of fortune. Armour again seemed a sure winner, but at the seventeenth hooked two tee-shots out of bounds, enabling Edgar to hold on to his title by the smallest of margins. The most splendid feature was Charlie Murray's fighting recovery. After being four strokes behind after seven holes, Charlie Murray caught Armour and beat him for second place on the eighteenth green.

One unusual feature of this Open at River-mead was the use of local Boy Scouts as caddies. Their costume added a touch of the picturesque to the scene. The RCGA accounts show that they were paid a total of $35 for their efforts. One good deed . . .

J. Douglas Edgar did not turn up for the 1921 Open, held in July. Some U.S. professionals said he had taken his family back to England. Which turned out to be true, in part. Edgar had since returned to Atlanta to finish the season at his club, but had not come to Canada because of ill health.

Then came the news of his death. On the night of 8 August 1921, Edgar bled to death in front of his home in Atlanta. Some suspected a hit-and-run driver; others, that he had been waylaid and stabbed to death. His club offered a reward of $5,000 to anyone who could bring forward information, but the mystery was never solved.

Tragedy compounded tragedy. A few months later, Edgar's close friend Louis Tellier committed suicide. The popular French professional to the Brae Burn club in Boston had taken to heart the death of his pal Douglas. Depressed and in poor health, he hanged himself.

J. Douglas Edgar's legacy to us is his book of golf instruction entitled *The Gate to Golf*, published in 1920. This is a short book of only fifty pages, long out of print. The "Gate" Edgar described was a mechanical device he had invented, two strips of wood laid out facing the line of flight, with the ball in between. "During the whole of the downward swing [the golfer's] mind should be concentrated on swinging the clubhead through The Gate." In this way, the golfer forgot about hitting the ball and was more intent on swinging the clubhead. For Edgar had come to the conclusion that "it was the ball that worried [golfers] and beat them. I found that so long as their minds were concentrated on the swing and the *movement*, the ball did not seem to worry them at all."

Many of Edgar's theories were considered radical at the time, but have since been accepted. Bobby Jones once recalled a conversation with Edgar at Ancaster, when Edgar told him that his "hands felt thin," a sign that he was going to play well. (Jones also gave Edgar the credit for introducing him to the concept of what we now call "the inside-out swing.") A controversial book when it first came out, it was, according to Tommy Armour, the best book ever written on golf. In an article in *Golf* magazine in 1960, Armour wrote:

> Douglas Edgar was the father – pioneer – of the present-day method of hitting the ball – called from "inside-out." His book is built on that method of hitting. He is one of the many great players I took lessons from, but he was undoubtedly the greatest of them and taught me the most.

Between the wars, all the top U.S. professionals played in the Canadian Open at least once. Most of them won, some more than once. This team of Open champions could have given a mulligan to any other team you care to name: Walter Hagen (1931), Tommy Armour (1927, 1930, 1934), Sam Snead (1938, 1940, 1941), Leo Diegel (1924, 1925, 1928, 1929), Harry Cooper (1932, 1937), Lawson Little (1936), Craig Wood (1942), Macdonald Smith (1926).

Of those who tried and failed, the most illustrious have to be the amateur Robert Tyre (Bobby) Jones and the professionals Gene Sarazen and Horton Smith. Jones was only seventeen when he tied for second place in 1919. Sarazen and Smith had several unsuccessful tilts at our title. The careers of two youngsters, Byron Nelson and Ben Hogan, were still in the ascendancy when they played. Nelson was to win at the end of the Second World War.

Four of the above team – Snead, Diegel, Mac Smith, and Cooper – had ten victories between them. Yet not one of them ever landed the U.S. Open. For three of them – Diegel, Smith, and Cooper – the Canadian was the only national title they won.

Bernard Darwin wrote of Leo Diegel that he was "the greatest golfing genius I have ever seen." From Bernard Darwin – who had seen the finest in the world – this was praise indeed.

Diegel still has the finest record of any golfer in the eighty-six-year history of the Canadian Open. He won it four times, twice back-to-back, and was runner-up once. Yet his first victory at Mount Bruno in 1924 could as easily have been a disaster.

In the fourth and final round at Bruno, Diegel made the turn in 33. He was then five strokes ahead of Gene Sarazen. On the deceivingly simple short tenth hole, he missed the green and lost a stroke. On the long twelfth, he lost another. And another on the thirteenth, and yet another on the fifteenth. Four strokes gone like fluff in the wind.

Diegel had blown the 1920 U.S. Open in much the same way. But he was now four years older. He dug deep and found some semblance of his game again. And when word came filtering across the fairways that Sarazen, too, had run into trouble, Diegel took enough inspiration from the news to salvage two pars and a bogey. This proved good enough for a two-stroke victory.

Leo Diegel was far from being a stylish golfer. Small of stature and build, he tended to sway into the ball. But he was long and straight off the tee, and had made himself into a successful, if eccentric, putter. To putt, he stooped over the ball, his arms out like chicken wings, forearms parallel to the ground, left elbow pointing to the hole. Bernard Darwin called it "diegeling" and conjugated the verb "I diegel, you diegel, he and she diegels." But it was eminently successful, and thousands who witnessed his putting went away to diegel for themselves.

Gene Sarazen's second place at Mount Bruno was, by the way, the closest he came to winning our championship.

When Diegel won again in the following year at Lambton, it was Hagen who let him off the hook.

On the opening day, Hagen had arrived by car from Buffalo at five in the morning. He had never seen the Lambton course before, yet he shot a par round. Then he went straight to bed.

Leo Diegel in 1920.

Diegel diegeling.

With eighteen holes to go, Diegel was four strokes ahead of the man he most feared. Hagen was a notoriously strong finisher. To make matters worse for Diegel, the two were paired together. Hagen's easy, nonchalant attitude to the game was the very antithesis of that of the nervous, fidgety Diegel, who could not stand still for more than ten seconds when waiting his turn to play.

The spectators, naturally, concentrated around this pair. Which suited Sir Walter. He liked playing to the crowd. Onto the first tee he stepped, this prince of professionals, without a care in the world. Crack! went his drive. The ball soared in a long, high, sliced parabola, to finish out of bounds. Minutes later, he put his fourth shot into a greenside bunker. On this par-four, 365-yard hole, the great Walter Hagen took an 8.

Diegel needed this cushion, for he threw away stroke after stroke in this final round, to finish only two ahead of Brady, the only one of the leading group not to crack.

At Rosedale in 1928, Hagen did even worse when facing Diegel. This time their positions were reversed, with Hagen three strokes ahead of him going into the final round, but only one ahead of Britain's giant Archie Compston.

With none of the pressure that comes from leading, Diegel went boldly for everything. He fired a 4-under-par round of 68, for a total of 282. Several holes back, Hagen and Compston were hemmed in by a record crowd. In those days, spectators wandered freely over the fairways, getting as close to the players and the attendant risks of swinging clubs and flying balls as they dared. Hampered by the mob and a heavy crosswind, Hagen fell by the way. Compston shot birdies to reach the turn in 32. Then he too collapsed, managing no better than 40 coming home. So it was Diegel again by two, with Compston, Hagen, and Macdonald Smith all tied for second.

Leo Diegel, "he of the springy step and jerky swing," won his fourth and final championship at Kanawaki in the following year.

And he did so with rounds of 70 67 71 66, for a record-breaking 274. Canadian professionals failed miserably that year. It was some small consolation that Somerville's 293 was a record for an amateur in the Open.

This was Diegel's finest win, given the strain of leading, then being caught by Armour. On the last nine holes he knew what he had to do, and he did it. He may never have appeared at ease with himself, but at least he did not choke. "Looking all over like a bundle of nerves, especially on the putting green," he stood on Kanawaki's superb 420-yard finishing hole, needing only a 6 to win. A 280-yard drive and a mashie left him safely on the elevated green. He just missed a birdie.

When accepting the runner-up's cheque, Armour made what was described as "a clever

Diegel winning his fourth Open at Kanawaki, 1929.

Runner-up Tommy Armour putting; note the bamboo poles used for crowd control.

little speech." The Canadian Open, he claimed, was not the third- but the second-greatest championship in the world. He ranked it next to the U.S. Open – which he had won – and above the British Open – which had eluded him.

Hagen had come to Kanawaki as a four-time winner of the British Open. He left Kanawaki without a cent in prize money. If he heard Armour's clever little speech from his seat in the members' bar, he probably took the cigar from his mouth and smiled: "That sonovabitch."

Armour's words could not have been better timed, for *he* was to become the next Canadian Open champion. In 1930, at Hamilton's Ancaster course, he defeated Diegel in a play-off.

This was a cliff-hanging, record-breaking, suspense-ridden championship. But the spectators on that hot, sunny Saturday afternoon at Ancaster must have suffered from acute anticlimax. If there are still traditionalists who abhor sudden-death play-offs, let them study what happened at Ancaster sixty years ago:

The neat, handsome Johnny Farrell (he won $1,000 for being the best-dressed professional in the U.S.) shoots a final 3 under par 69 and is in the clubhouse with 278. He is already being hailed as the winner. The RCGA had sold the radio broadcasting rights for $300, and listeners are being told that Johnny is the new Canadian Open champion. Farrell hears this and is worried. "Wait till they're all in," he cautions, with what is taken to be an excess of modesty.

But Johnny Farrell is right. Way out on the course, under a blazing sun, Armour and Diegel have not heard the broadcast. Which is just as well. For Armour is six under par for the round and making a mockery of the difficult Ancaster course. Not to be outdone, Diegel is three under, and playing the game of his life.

The jungle telegraph carries the news to the crowds around the clubhouse. The spectators who had abandoned Armour when he bogeyed the first hole rush to the sixteenth in disbelief. The pair of them come to the 500-yard seventeenth, both needing two pars to beat Farrell by a stroke. They get these with ease. At eigh-

teen they play safe, are on in 2, and just miss birdie putts. Their totals of 277 push Farrell into third place. Shoot the radio broadcaster!

Tommy Armour's 64 was hailed as "the lowest score in a major championship." For sure, nobody had ever shot a 64 in the U.S. or British Opens.

After such a finish, a sudden-death play-off on that Saturday afternoon between Armour and Diegel would have sent the four thousand spectators home satisfied and exhilarated. But the rules of the Open called for a 36-hole play-off. Tournament golf was prohibited on Sundays. On Monday, Armour had to play in Detroit to qualify for the PGA championship. (He shot two 75s and failed.) So it was Wednesday before Armour and Diegel met at Ancaster.

After 18 holes they were tied at 69. In the afternoon, the scores were still level coming to the eleventh (or 29th). This tricky dog-leg had cost Farrell the title, when he had hooked his drive into a bush and taken a double-bogey. Now Diegel made the same mistake off the tee. His ball finished in the trees to the left. He took two to get out, and finished with a double-bogey 7. Three strokes down, he never recovered. So Tommy Armour won what he claimed was the second-most important golf title in the world.

In the excitement of the Armour–Diegel battle, the earlier achievement of home professional Nicol Thompson tended to be overlooked. In the opening round, he shot a 66 to take the lead. Ironically, his partner, Armour, was eight strokes worse. "Such is the Kingdom of Golf," as Ralph Reville was wont to say.

Thompson held on to his lead through the second round with a 71. A 74 71 finish gave him the seventh-place cheque of $50.

There were no fewer than eighteen rounds in the 60s at Ancaster. By 1930, the steel shaft and the long-flying ball had made a 69 common. Admittedly, Ancaster was playing short in 1930. As in 1919, a long hot summer had baked its fairways. Drives of 300 yards were common. Players were using mashie-niblicks where they had once needed woods. But Tommy Armour's 64 was still a score to make George Lyon shake his head in disbelief.

Armour's was a popular win. This former Scottish amateur was a favourite with the spectators. He had picked up golf as a boy, on the public Braid Hills course in Edinburgh. In his younger days he was also an accomplished musician, and he earned his first money playing violin in an Edinburgh theatre orchestra.

In the First World War, Armour served with distinction in the Royal Scots, and he came out of the war as a major. He had been wounded in the war, virtually losing the sight in one eye, and the injury made this high-cheekboned Scot look older than he was. He came to Canada and the U.S. in 1920, an amateur golfer working for the North British Rubber Company, the manufacturer of golf balls and bags. He was subsequently appointed secretary-manager of the Westchester–Biltmore hotel in Rye, New York. In 1925, he turned professional.

The 1930 Open was his fourth appearance in our championship, and the second of his three victories. His first win came three years earlier, in 1927. This Open at the Toronto Golf Club did not have the sensational finish witnessed at Ancaster three years later, but it was not without its dramatic swings of fortune over the closing holes.

Coming to the long thirteenth, Armour needed to cover the last six holes in one under par to tie Macdonald Smith, the leader in the clubhouse.

At this 524-yard par five hole he was halfway to the green with his drive. He used his driver again from the fairway, and the cheers of the spectators probably told him he had not only hit the green but was near the pin. Down went his putt for an eagle 3. When he also eagled the 500-yard sixteenth, the roar of the crowd was heard in the clubhouse. "Greater golf than this has never been witnessed on any course," was Ralph Reville's verdict at the time.

So Armour came to the par-three seventeenth hole with a seemingly safe cushion of three strokes.

This hole at Toronto Golf Club has changed little in the last sixty years. For the 1927 Open it measured 222 yards. The fairway is narrow. It is bounded on the right by trees. On the left is a nasty, downward-sloping bank, fringed with bushes and scrub. The green is well guarded by traps. From the tee, it is a patch of green at the end of a tunnel. A hook or a slice, and the ball can be lost forever. A push or a fade, and you face a triple bogey. The hole is named The Graveyard.

Armour was acknowledged to be the finest iron player in the world. All week his irons had served him well. So the gallery was surprised when he whipped out his spoon, or 4-wood. He may have imagined himself impregnable, protected by the same divine force that had guided his ball to a brace of eagles. Every golfer has at some time experienced that ephemeral state of grace. To some, it comes from no more than sinking a couple of six-foot putts.

Armour's ball left his spoon and crashed down the slope to the left. Here was a jungle of wild growth beyond where the fairway stopped: trees, bushes, thickets, vines, all hard to penetrate. Somebody found Armour's ball, probably a spectator. His first attempt to get it out failed, although he advanced it up the slope. At the second attempt, he somehow squirted it through a gap visible only to him. The ball landed on the green. His double bogey 5 removed all the padding from his cushion and left his supporters limp. But all he needed to take the lead was a par at the eighteenth. He got it.

There was a remote chance that Hagen, playing behind, might catch him. But Hagen three-putted sixteen, bogeyed The Graveyard, and double-bogeyed the last hole. So Armour won his second national Open within the space of a month or so, having come to Toronto as the U.S. Open title-holder. He was the first to win the U.S. and Canadian Opens in the same year.

Although Armour survived it, many championship hopes are buried in The Graveyard. In the 1921 Open, the American Mike Brady

The Armour swing around 1930.

Hagen in swing, 1929.

needed only pars at the two finishing holes to win by a stroke. A treacherous crosswind carried his tee-shot at The Graveyard into the bushes and scrub. He took a triple bogey and lost to Trovinger (the first American-born professional to win our Open).

Frank Thompson would probably have been leading Canadian that year had he not broken his favourite mashie-niblick trying to extricate his ball from the same scrub. A year later, Alexa Stirling would probably have beaten Mrs. Gavin for the Canadian Ladies' Open Championship had her ball not been swallowed by The Graveyard's bushes.

In that 1927 Open, Armour had needed ten strokes at The Graveyard in the last two rounds, as against eight at the par-five thirteenth. That year, *Canadian Golfer* reported that a survey of all the championships at Toronto GC revealed the astonishing fact that the

highest average score at *any* hole, including the par fives, was at this par-three seventeenth.

The man who came to be known as the Silver Scot won his third Canadian title at Toronto's Lakeview in 1934. By now, the silver was showing in his hair – he was, after all, close to forty. But his iron shots were still as crisp and as pin-splitting as ever. Three strokes ahead of "Wild Bill" Melhorn at the halfway mark, two ahead with a round to go, Armour was not to be caught. His long irons to the par-five sixteenth hole gave him birdies in both rounds, and that was his margin of victory.

This Open was notable for the collapse of tour-toughened golfers who had been expected to give Armour a fight for it. Leo Diegel opened with a 65, then followed with an 82. Hagen shot a sloppy 81 and a third round of 65. Melhorn's challenge to Armour was bogeyed to death, and he finished with an 81.

Having won the Canadian Open in 1930, Armour lost his title to Walter Hagen at Mississaugua in 1931.

On his record alone, Hagen was a deserving winner of the Canadian Open. Already the holder of the U.S. title (twice) and the British title (four times), he had been trying for twenty years to win the Canadian. He had been the favourite to win for years. No Open field was quite complete without him. So in any other year – given that a Canadian was not in the running – the gallery would have warmly welcomed a win by The Haig.

In 1931, however, he was upstaged by a young British professional, Percy Alliss. Hagen beat him in the end, in a 36-hole play-off. But it was Alliss who thrilled the crowds with some of the finest come-from-behind golf ever seen in Canada. It was Alliss, not Hagen, who captured their hearts, when their minds told them that Hagen was the logical winner.

Percy Alliss was the professional to the Wannasee club in Berlin, Germany. (His son Peter, today's television commentator, was born in Germany in 1931.) Percy had come to North America to get a taste of what golf was like on this continent. Although he had won the German Open several times, as well as the Welsh professional championship, he was not considered good enough for the British Ryder Cup team visiting North America that year. Ironically, he clearly outperformed those members of the team who played in the Canadian Open, including Henry Cotton and Archie Compston.

This was the first of six Opens to be played at Mississaugua. Its course had been lengthened and upgraded by Stanley Thompson and now stretched over 6,500 yards. Many of its fairways had a watering system by 1931, so the hot dry winds of that summer had not reduced its playing length. As best as we can judge from contemporary reports, Mississaugua was as manicured, picturesque, and hospitable a setting for the 1931 Open as it is today.

In the opening round, the spectators naturally followed the American favourites. They saw Hagen and Armour come in with 68s, Farrell

Percy Alliss drives as Walter Hagen, right, *watches, at Mississaugua, 1931.*

a stroke behind. The few who followed the unknown Alliss were rewarded by an exhibition of superb putting and a 67. The fancied British Ryder Cup team stars failed as dismally as they had in the U.S. Open, and were written off after the second round. Better than any member of this team was a new young French-Canadian, Jules Huot, with 70.

In the second round, Hagen duplicated his 68 to lead the field at 136. At the end of the third round it was a three-man race: Hagen 208, Farrell 210, Alliss 211.

The weather at Mississaugua had so far been conducive to low scoring – warm, sunny, with not enough wind to test the judgement. All that changed in the space of a few hours on Saturday afternoon, in the middle of the final round. A heavy rain and high wind swept down the Credit Valley. The water could not drain quickly enough from the fairways and greens. Puddles formed.

Hagen was out ahead of Alliss and Farrell. On the outward nine he shot a 36, one stroke better than in the morning. But on the rain and windswept inward nine he lost three strokes to finish with a 74. Given the state of the weather, his 282 looked safe. All the more so when word reached the clubhouse that Alliss had lost three strokes to him with a 39, and that Farrell was also over par.

Out on the course, Alliss started getting strokes back from the tenth, and by the fifteenth he knew what he had to do – cover the last four holes in 13 strokes to tie Hagen. This was not only six less blows than Hagen had needed, but called for three birdies out of four.

Alliss did it. We don't know exactly how. Perhaps the reporters who had been following him sought refuge in the bar, giving him up as a certain loser. From an old film of the 1931 Open, we know that rain-soaked spectators formed a circle of umbrellas around the eighteenth green as Alliss and Farrell came up the fairway. We also know that Walter Hagen watched from an upstairs window. And *he* knew that Alliss and Farrell had been playing miraculous golf in the rain. So much so that when they landed their second shots on the green, they both needed birdie putts to catch the man looking down at them.

Farrell's putt on the sodden green came up short. Alliss, from 12 feet, took no chances. Hagen, himself one of the most daring of putters, saw the ball hit the back of the cup and fall in.

Percy Alliss, in the wind and rain, had fired a 4 under par 32 over the back nine. "Unquestionably the greatest golf ever uncorked in the Canadian Open or, for that matter, in any other Open," Ralph Reville enthused.

The 36-hole play-off on the following Tuesday (both players had other commitments on the Monday) was notable for a remarkable display of aggressive putting by Alliss. But Hagen's superior approach shots

left him with few long putts for his 68 in the afternoon, and victory by a stroke.

In this round, Hagen had that snatch of good fortune all champions need. At the fifteenth, from a new tee built for the Open, his drive failed to make the 210-yard carry over the creek. But it landed on a rock and bounced out to the fairway.

Some four thousand came to see the play-off, bringing the total attendance up to fifteen thousand, at the time a record for the Open.

And what of Jules Huot? He came in with a 291, for seventh place and fifty dollars. He was the leading Canadian. Ontario spectators got their first look at this young professional. They were to see a lot more of him over the next thirty years.

Sam Snead also won his first Canadian Open at Mississaugua, in 1938. Hagen had not played in the previous year's Open, and was on a world tour in the spring of 1938 when he learned that the Open was returning to Mississaugua. He cabled to say he would be there.

Hagen was one of a strong entry from the U.S.: Harry Cooper, the title-holder; Lawson Little, Jimmy Thompson, Horton Smith, Paul Runyan, Ed (Porky) Oliver, and, of course, Samuel Jackson Snead.

Young Snead was a controversial figure in 1938. Although he early acquired a reputation for parsimony, no one questioned his ability. His fluid, rhythmic swing has probably never been matched. As early as 1935, when Snead was twenty-three, Gene Sarazen had said of him: "He's the greatest natural golfer of modern times. The fellow can outhit any of us by thirty yards, and can putt as well as Hagen. His irons are more accurate than Jones! All he needs is seasoning to be the best golfer who ever lived." Sarazen was not the one to give undue praise to a fellow professional.

But Snead ran into problems in his first big tournament at Pinehurst. After talk of his disqualification, he withdrew when the other players would not overlook his misdemeanours. Other incidents followed, in other tournaments, which Hilles Pickens attributed to Snead being "seemingly too anxious to secure his place among the stars." He withdrew from a tournament because he wasn't playing well, and was chastised by the PGA. But when he could control his temper, he showed that he could win. Coming to Mississaugua for the 1938 Canadian Open, he was that year's leading money-winner.

Sam Snead won at Mississaugua with a score of 277. This was fifteen strokes fewer than Hagen in 1931. Yet, if anything, the course was tougher than it had been in 1931. The weather was kinder in the final round, but that accounted for perhaps three or four strokes at the most. So it seems that the lower scoring was just a reflection of both the keener competition in the United States and the better equipment. Even Walter Hagen came in six strokes lower than in 1931, although in 1938 this was only good enough for seventh place.

After 54 holes, the 1938 Open became a tournament for Cooper, Snead, and Runyan, in a three-way tie.

In the final round, Cooper had the championship won, then threw it away. At the first hole, his 70-yard pitch went in for an eagle 2. To Snead and Runyan, last off the tee, this must have seemed like an omen. For most of that round, the pair scrambled. At the turn, Snead was one over par for the round, Runyan two over. Early in the inward half, Runyan hit a string of poor shots and was out of the race. On the fourteenth hole, Snead was two over par; up ahead, Cooper was going to the eighteenth, with a five-shot lead.

Within minutes, there was a dramatic swing in their fortunes. Cooper was normally one of the world's most accurate and steady shotmakers. But on this last, critical hole, he hit a long, hooked drive, which finished out of bounds on the road. Lying 3 after his second drive, he pulled his approach shot into the spectators. A chip and two putts later, Lighthorse Harry stumbled into the clubhouse having finished with a triple-bogey 7 and an even par round of 72. He shook his head: "That won't stand."

He was right. The news of Cooper's disaster came to Sam Snead as he stood on the fifteenth tee. A minute earlier, his task had been virtually impossible. But now, birdies on two of the last four holes would give him a tie. He birdied the fifteenth. Another birdie at the sixteenth. A 10-foot putt at the seventeenth took a bad break and he had to settle for a par. At the last hole he, too, almost blew his chances. His drive took a bad kick to finish with a poor lie in a gully. His 5-iron did not allow enough for the wind in the golfer's face and finished in the crowd, short and left of the green. This left him with a difficult up and down from 30 yards. With something like five thousand spectators jostling for a view, Snead chipped the ball dead. Mississaugua was faced with another play-off, but one mercifully reduced to 18 holes – or intended to last only 18 holes.

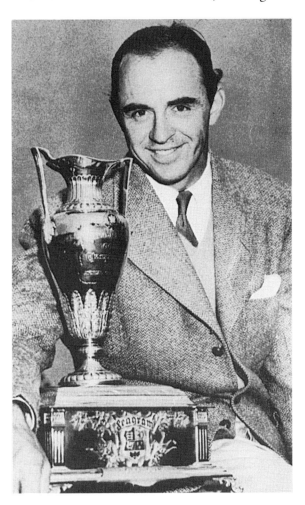

Sam Snead first won the Seagram Cup in 1938.

Winning the Open meant more to Snead than to the veteran Cooper, who already had his name on the Seagram Cup; winning again would add little to what his agent could ask for in endorsements. That may explain why Cooper did not rest on the Sunday before the Monday play-off. He had previously scheduled an exhibition match at Brantford for Sunday and he went ahead with it. That made Monday his fifth straight day of golf. His mental and physical exhaustion began to show by the afternoon. In the morning round, "Slammin' Sam" lived up to this early nickname, but his short game was off. An eagle 3 at the twelfth (the hole known as the Big Chief) helped him equal Cooper's 69. In the 9-hole continuation of the play-off, Cooper was obviously weary. Bogey followed bogey, leaving Snead the winner by five strokes.

Sam Snead did not defend his title in 1939, when Jug McSpaden became the Open champion at Saint John's Riverside club.

Although not strictly "Opens between the wars," the story of the 1940 and 1941 Opens is still the story of Snead.

In 1940, he arrived in Toronto, with his bride of a few days, planning to attempt to regain the title over Scarboro. Snead again had to face the holder in a play-off.

By 1940, he had acquired a reputation as a choker. In the 1939 U.S. Open, a par 5 at the final hole would have given him the title. Shaky and nervous on the 72nd tee, he had hooked the ball into the rough, pushed the next into a bunker, needed two to get out, and three-putted for a triple bogey 8. The memory was to haunt him.

Snead appeared to be running away with the 1940 Canadian Open. He started with rounds of 67 68–135, seven under par. Ray Mangrum was five shots back, McSpaden six. After a shaky opening nine, Snead's game had been faultless. His great length off the tee was well under control, leaving him with second shots of short irons or wedges on the par fours. On the par fives, his long irons to the greens left him close enough for a realistic chance at

eagles. Some of his 15- and 20-foot putts were dropping. He was playing loosely, at ease with the world. Had there been six rounds and not four, Snead would probably have played as aggressively in rounds three and four.

At Scarboro, he may have had visions of blowing this tournament as he had the U.S. Open. Whatever the reason, the free-hitting golfer of Thursday and Friday became a conservative plodder on Saturday. Many have said that the best way to preserve a lead is to increase it. But Samuel Jackson did what was foreign to his nature. He tried to preserve his lead by nursing it. Having witnessed Snead's third round of 75, Hilles Pickens wrote: "It is a saddening thing to see such a strictly effusive golfer trying to play carefully."

Snead started to steer the ball, as we all tend to do when trying to play safely. His putting stroke became tense and tentative, making him miss a couple of three-footers. His hands shook perceptibly. He survived only because those chasing him failed to take advantage of his fall. McSpaden, with a third round of 74, narrowed the gap by only a stroke; Mangrum, with a 73, by two strokes.

In the final round, McSpaden was out first. As Snead continued to make bogeys, McSpaden caught him, then went ahead. He finished with a 69, for a total of 281, three under par.

As McSpaden walked off the last green, Snead was starting the fifteenth. He had already lost three strokes to par and needed to cover the last four holes in one under, just to tie. Given his form on that Saturday, the odds were against him. But now that he was behind for the first time, Snead had no reason to play conservatively. For him, the fifteenth hole in the final round was the most critical of the tournament. It is a short uphill par-four. The elevated, sloping green is guarded on the left by a deep bunker. Snead's drive was 30 yards short of the green. His direct line to the flag was over the edge of the bunker. His pitch shot was on line, but he cut the ball too much in an attempt to stop it close to the flag. It landed on the edge of the green, stopped, then trickled back into the bunker.

His next shot from the sand could have been as disastrous as his first bunker shot in the U.S. Open. But Snead was now fighting from behind and mentally a different man. The ball came out first time, finishing 15 feet short of the pin. He confidently rolled it in for his par.

The birdie he needed came at the seventeenth. His approach finished six feet from the hole, and down went the putt for a 3. At the last hole, he almost snatched the tournament from under McSpaden's nose, but left his 15-foot putt six inches short. So, for the second time in twenty-four months, Sam Snead played off for the Canadian Open.

Harold (Jug) McSpaden had this 18-hole play-off won, threw it away, had a chance to tie, then threw that away as well.

McSpaden's swing was not as mechanical as Snead's and was liable to let him down in a crisis. He relied on strong wrist action to give him length, flicking at the ball in the manner of many of the players of the time. His swing failed him at the sixth hole of the play-off, when he was two strokes ahead of Snead. His drive went into the creek and he took 6 to Snead's 4. The two were even. Nevertheless, McSpaden held on until the eighteenth. Both were on in two. Snead got his par. McSpaden's first putt of 30 feet finished a yard away. His downhill putt for a half slipped past the hole, and Snead was the winner.

In the years around 1940, no other Canadian professional quite caught the imagination of the golfing public in the way Bob Gray Jr. of Scarboro did. For over twenty-five years, the Canadian golf fan had watched the national title go south. CPGA champions had come and gone. None had been able to sustain his best golf for the four rounds of the Open. Unlike the Americans who captured the title, they never seemed able to raise the level of their game when they had to, by the margin needed to win. Bob Gray appeared to be Canada's best hope in years.

Robert Trail Gray Jr. was born in Fraserburgh, Scotland, in 1909. His father brought

Bob Gray Jr.

the family to Canada when Bob was four and became the professional to the club at St. Thomas, Ontario, in the early years of the First World War. By the time Bob Junior was making a name for himself, his father was the greenkeeper at Essex County G & CC, near Windsor. Young Bob became an assistant to John Burns at Essex and two years later was appointed professional at Chatham.

Here he worked diligently on his game and, within a year, had broken the record of this nine-hole course. The years 1929 to 1933 he spent at two clubs in Michigan. Still only twenty-five, but with ten years of club experience under his belt and obvious skills as a player and teacher, he landed the plum job at Essex County, where he had started his career. But his playing skills did not fully mature until he moved to Scarboro G & CC in 1938. It is as Bob Gray of Scarboro that he is most often remembered.

Bob Gray was tall and slender, with huge hands and long, powerful arms. In 1940 there was no questioning his tremendous length off the tee, but it was being said of him that he had too much power for his own good: he would have bursts of low scoring, but he lacked the control he needed to score well consistently. Long hours of practice at Scarboro had made him perhaps the finest sand player in Canada and one as accurate as any on the green.

His record in the CPGA championships was good but not outstanding. He finished second to Stan Horne in 1937 and 1938, the closest he was ever to get to this title. Better control of his length in 1940 led to a win in the Millar match play, and again gave him the Rivermead Cup for low Canadian professional in the Open.

In the last two rounds of the 1940 Open, Gray had been paired with Sam Snead. He showed he could all but match Snead's booming drives and, on this day at least, could match him in accuracy. Although he outscored Snead by five shots in these two rounds, it was by no means enough to catch him.

Bob Gray went to the 1941 Open at his peak. By popular acclaim he was now the best controlled power-hitter in the country. That in itself would have been enough to assure him a gallery. But by now he had acquired that aura of crowd-appeal that clings to some golfers and not to others. Exciting golf was expected of Bob Gray, and exciting golf came out of Bob Gray. Not quite good enough to win the Open, but enough to stamp him with a fleeting greatness.

"Somebody will shoot a 65 in the Open at Lambton, and I'll bet money on it," he told reporters a week before the event. There were no takers.

He did it himself, in the second round on that memorable Friday afternoon in August. Out in 32, with birdies at one, three, and eight, he came home in 33. Added to an opening round of 70, this gave Bob Gray a lead of two strokes over Johnny Bulla at the halfway mark.

Sarazen and Horton Smith were a stroke further back. The defending champion, Snead – reportedly suffering from a bad back – was four behind Gray.

Bob Gray's golf had been flawless, except for a three-putt at the seventh hole, for his only bogey. Hilles Pickens gives us a feeling of the times:

> Friday was Bob Gray's day. It seemed as if all golfing Toronto was there, cheering him on. Radio men carried his every action to the ether; reporters buzzed around him on the course and in the club house. It is doubtful if any Canadian has had a greater day unless it was Ken Black at Shaughnessy Heights back in 1936, when he shot a 63 to win the $5000 Vancouver Open.

For the final two rounds on the Saturday, Gray was paired with Horton Smith, the U.S. Ryder Cup player and two-time Masters champion. And Bob became the first Canadian in many years to take the galleries away from an American star. In their rush to view Gray's next shot, the crowd paid scant attention to the unfortunate Smith.

In the third round, Gray shot a 70, after a shaky start. This was not good enough to ward off Sam Snead. With a 66, the second-best of the week, Snead tied Gray with a round to go.

In the afternoon, Sam Snead teed off some eight holes ahead of Bob Gray. Snead used his great length to good advantage. On the par-five tenth hole, he powered his tee-shot some 375 yards, needing only a 7-iron to the green. A four-foot putt gave him his eagle.

When Snead posted a 69, Gray knew he needed the same to tie. In retrospect, he was seen to have lost his chance at the sixth hole. His 320-yard drive left him with a short pitch and putt for a birdie. But the pitch went astray, leading to a bogey. After that, his fight was all uphill. Still, he came to the par-three eighteenth at Lambton needing a deuce to tie. He took 4. And that was that. Snead had won his third Canadian Open. But not in twenty years, since Charlie Murray lost in a play-off to Edgar, had a Canadian come closer, or so re-awakened hope.

Snead used the smaller British ball at Lambton. ("But don't quote me. I work for an American firm that makes the large ball.") Did his sore back bother him? "No, but my feet gave me a lot of trouble. My right leg is three-quarters of an inch shorter than the left, and I have to wear a pad in my shoe. That gave me more trouble than my back."

This early promise of Bob Gray was never fulfilled. He was to win the Millar three more times, but he never again challenged for the Open. He remained, outwardly at least, as charming as ever. But much of the money earned at his club, and from his brief essay on the PGA Tour, went on high living. He died in 1966, at the age of fifty-seven.

Overshadowed by the electrics of Gray's 70 65 on the first two days of the 1941 Open was the equally fine 68 67 on the last day by another Canadian. This was good enough to give Gordie Brydson fourth place.

Brydson was one of several Canadian professionals who had combined golf with hockey. In the period 1924–38, he played for a number of teams in the Canadian Professional Hockey League and the American Hockey League, including the Toronto Maple Leafs. Earlier, while still in his teens, he had played football for the Toronto Argonauts. In 1928, he went to work for George Cumming at the Toronto Golf Club, and a year later he was promoted from caddiemaster to assistant, replacing Willie Lamb. After winning the Ontario Open in 1930, he joined Toronto's new Willowdale club as its professional. The year 1932 saw him begin a forty-year association with Mississaugua.

In the CPGA championships between 1932 and 1942, Gordie Brydson usually finished somewhere in the top ten. He lost in 1942 after a play-off with Bob Burns, but won the Rivermead Cup that year for low Canadian in the Open. The CPGA title was eventually his, in 1944 and 1948, as was the Millar – by now a national event – in 1953. As we shall see, he very nearly won the 1954 Open, but had to settle for a share of second place.

A neat, tidy man, and always a snappy dresser, Brydson was a smooth swinger of the club, with

Bob Gray Jr. and Stan Horne watch Ben Hogan drive at Mississaugua in 1942.

no single outstanding feature as a player. He became one of the most popular club and playing professionals in Canada, and president of the CPGA.

The small, bespectacled "Lighthorse" Harry Cooper (he galloped round the course) won the Canadian Open in 1932 and 1937, and twice was runner-up when defending his title. He won his first Canadian Open because of the misfortune of others.

The Ottawa Hunt course in 1932 was one of the toughest tests in Canada. Its par was a difficult 73, its fairways narrow (but not in the best of condition for the Open), its greens small, most of them heavily bunkered and some with severe undulations. On the final day, many of the pins were placed in almost impossible positions. Given those features, and the gusty winds of Saturday, it is not surprising that the final-round scores were very high. Cooper was the only player to break 70 in the three days of play.

Walter Hagen was, as usual, the favourite to win. Typically, he arrived four hours late for his starting time. (Some accounts have him well-liquored and having to be fortified with strong coffee.) Hagen then proceeded to sink a 70-foot chip shot for an eagle 2 at the first hole. The accomplishment is probably a record to this day.

This was really the Open that Al Watrous tossed away. The stylish veteran – he had won our Open in 1922 – needed only a one-over par final round of 74 to beat Cooper. A mixture of nerves and high winds blew him off course, and he took 44 for the first nine holes. Under the circumstances, his inward half of 34, or two under par, was brilliant. It was also too late. Cooper won by a margin of three.

Harry Cooper was born in 1904, in Leatherhead, England, where his father was a professional. Before Harry was in his teens, the Coopers immigrated to Canada, the father working for a time in the clubhouse at Hamilton G & CC before moving to Texas.

In 1933, Cooper came second when defending his title. At Toronto's Royal York (St. George's),

Joe Kirkwood never looked like being caught after round three and won by 8 strokes.

The weather had no pity for the golfers in 1937, when Cooper won his second Canadian title. A cold wet wind and rain blew dozens of hopes away at Toronto's first pay-as-you-play course, St. Andrews. Cooper's winning score of 285 over the rain-soaked fairways and greens was 14 strokes more than Lawson Little's one year earlier. Young Ben Hogan, appearing in his first Canadian Open, could do no better than 71 83. On the other hand, little Jules Huot improved his score on that miserable Saturday. His 72 71 was the lowest of the day.

The sandy-haired Jug McSpaden, a brilliant but erratic golfer, was probably the finest iron player after Tommy Armour. Although he tried many times for the Canadian Open, his only victory came a few weeks before the outbreak of the Second World War.

The 1939 Open is the only one ever held in the Maritimes. It was a great local success. Frank Robertson of Saint John, a governor of the RCGA (its president in 1948), had pushed to have the national Open on the East Coast, so when it was awarded to his home club, Riverside G & CC, he set about proving that Opens could be successful at venues outside Ontario and Quebec.

Only about a third of the top American professionals in the previous two Opens turned up at Riverside, for a number of reasons. Saint John was a long way off their beaten tracks, and by 1939 tournament sponsors in the U.S. were putting up purses of at least $5,000 for three-day events, against the Canadian Open's $3,000. Although the PGA had given its blessing to a mid-August date, a dozen U.S. star players did not show up. Not one champion of the 1930s competed; Sam Snead was ill, Harry Cooper and Lawson Little had decided to skip the summer tour to be at their clubs. Leo Diegel was there, but a twitching shadow of the Diegel of the 1920s.

The course at Riverside, or, to be more precise, the way that the course was set up for the last two rounds, defeated many golfers.

Jug McSpaden, winner in 1939.

Riverside had started to expand its nine-hole layout to eighteen back in 1920. This took several years to complete. In the 1930s, a local businessman, Percy W. Thomson (brother of former Ladies' champion Mabel Thomson) took a keen interest in improving the course, largely at his own expense. He called upon Donald Ross for advice, and the exchange led to new greens, new traps, new trees, and a new watering system. Riverside had always been a fine venue for golf – well manicured, with holes that tested all the shots and, standing on the banks of the majestic Kennebecasis river, one of the most scenic landscapes in the country. Now it was a championship course, or nearly so, being on the short side at 6,250 yards, with a par of 70.

Over such a course, you might expect the scores in the Canadian Open to be low. There was a 67 in the first round, nothing out of the ordinary. Perhaps fearful that the professionals would humiliate the course with a bunch of 64s, making a mockery of their layout, the organizing committee decided to make the course more difficult by placing the pins in inaccessible positions, hiding them behind bunkers, or placing them on the very front of greens.

The eighteenth hole at Riverside, 1939.

This was a well-intentioned but regrettable step – or, rather, steps, for the committee found progressively more fiendish places for the pins as the tournament went from the second to the third to the fourth round. Holes were hidden so close to bunkers that even the most daring of golfers went for the flag at his peril. The inability to stop the ball near the hole left players frustrated. The winner, McSpaden, covered the first two rounds in 136. He needed 10 more strokes for the last two.

At the halfway mark, the leaders were Jug McSpaden 136, Ralph Guldahl 139, and Stan Horne 141. Guldahl (playing with a sore left side) lost this championship to McSpaden (287 to 282) at Riverside's fourth hole. This par five bends to the right from the tee. Stretching 500 yards, it can be reached in two if the drive is long enough and not cut off by the trees on the right. McSpaden birdied it in the third round, parred it in the fourth. On his last two attempts, Guldahl needed five strokes more. In round three, striving for distance, he hooked his drive, then pushed his second, to finish with a 7. In the last round he pushed his second into trouble, for another double bogey. The five shots he lost to McSpaden on this one hole were the five he needed to tie.

Not everybody found Saturday's pin placings an excuse for higher scoring. Sandy Somerville, for one, shot two of the lowest rounds of the day – 71 72, or five strokes lower than the winner. This lifted him to a tie for fifth place with Stan Horne, the best showing by a Canadian amateur since before the First World War.

This Open in New Brunswick went a long way to achieving its aim; it helped stir up interest in golf in the Maritimes. For a week, Saint John was firmly in the centre of the national golfing map. One observer noted the keen interest on the faces of the high school caddies, most of them seeing the big names in Canadian and U.S. golf for the first time. (One of these caddies was Ralph Costello, who was to become president of the RCGA in 1981; he recounts his experience that day in *The First Fifty Years: The Story of the New Brunswick Golf Association*, 1987.) But, as Guldahl point-

ed out, the publicity would have been much greater if the course had not been protected from a possible record score by impossible pin placings. Record low scores were nothing to be ashamed of and would have caught the interest of every newspaper in the country.

Lawson Little. Here was a slugger if ever there was one. The bull-necked, barrel-chested Little put a frightful amount of energy into propelling a golf ball. On his day, he could also match distance with astonishing accuracy.

Little had won the U.S. and British Amateur championships twice before turning professional in 1936. By winning the Canadian Open that year, Lawson Little became the first to have his name inscribed on the Seagram Gold Cup. Too, the 1936 Open was the first held over a pay-as-you-play course – St. Andrews, Toronto. And yet another record was set that year, for Little won with the then lowest score of 271.

This Open became a slugging match between Little and the only man longer off the tee, Jimmy Thompson. These two were the pre-tournament favourites, and when paired together in the last two rounds, they attracted 90 per cent of the gallery, said to be the largest in the history of the Open.

After 36 holes, the only man who seemed to have a chance of catching Little's start of 67 66–133 was Paul Runyan ("he of the magic putter and sartorial perfection") who was four strokes behind at 72 65–137. He had needed only 25 putts in his second round. But Friday night brought heavy rain and wind. The prophets for once were right when they said good-bye to Runyan's chances on such a heavy course. In the third round he lost four strokes to par, and to Little, on the first five holes.

Paired with Little, and ten strokes behind at the beginning of the third round, Jimmy Thompson went for everything. His 320-yard drives were followed by deadly pitches and a putter that worked a magic of its own. At one point, five straight birdies brought him to within four. But Little rallied and went into the last round with an eight-stroke margin.

Although Thompson brought the margin back to three with a string of birdies in the first three holes of the afternoon, Little fought back. A birdie at the last hole gave him back the eight-stroke margin he had started with. His 271 had never been equalled in the Canadian Open.

Lawson Little's spectacular display of low scoring was accepted at the time by the most discriminating of critics as the finest they had ever witnessed. "The most dazzling finish in the history of golf anywhere" were the words used to describe it by Hilles Pickens.

And what of the rest of the field? They were, to quote a writer at the time, "strung out behind like the tail of a kite, waving in the futile ten and twelve stroke wake of the leader."

Lawson Little defended his title over the same course in 1937. He needed 26 more strokes, finished in a tie for sixteenth place, and went home with fifteen dollars. Thompson was only one stroke better. That was the year of Lighthorse Harry Cooper.

There were other champions, at other courses.

Macdonald Smith was a Carnoustie man. His upbringing probably helped this stylish Scot (he modelled his game on Vardon) survive the downpour at Royal Montreal in 1926. Accompanied by Charlie Murray, he struggled through the rain to make up three shots on Sarazen, and to beat him by three.

When Al Watrous of Michigan won at Mount Bruno in 1922, a topic of conversation was the scoreboard. The club's secretary, R. J. R. Stokes, "had installed a particularly clever system of scoring, whereby the leader's figures were posted conspicuously the moment the cards were checked over." We tend to forget that spectators in the years between the wars had little idea of who was leading the Open at any one time, and by how many.

Before the 1923 Open, it was freely predicted that nobody could break 300 at Toronto's tough Lakeview course. Well, Clarence Hackney of Carnoustie and Atlantic City did, by five strokes, although he was the only one. When Armour won over the same course in 1934, some twenty players did what had seemed impossible twelve years earlier. Such is progress.

23

EARLY COURSES
AND ARCHITECTS

WE HAVE ALREADY SEEN HOW PRIMI-
tive were the golf courses of Canada
a hundred years ago.

The subtleties and aesthetics of golf course
design were beyond the country's neophyte
golfers. Thirty acres of common or farm land
could be transformed into a nine-holer in a
day. Someone who knew how golf was played
would hammer a stake into the ground to
mark the tee and another to mark the green,
both on as flat a piece of ground as could be
found. And so on round the course. To fit
nine holes into the land, one fairway might
have to cross another. If a few natural hazards
happened to lie between the tee and the green,
then so much the better. But the art of getting
the ball to the green was difficult enough
without erecting bunkers, even if this were
permitted on public or grazing land.

A hired man with a hand mower might be
given a day to cut the grass on tees and greens
and to pull a roller over the greens to flatten
the worst of the lumps. The course was then
ready for play.

The hole on the green was of no fixed size
and had no liner. It would be at least as big as

today's 4 1/4-inch hole, and probably bigger.
Golfers used to scoop earth from the hole to
make a tee; when this hole was too big another would be dug a few feet away.

In 1940, when reminiscing on his early
days at Toronto GC, the Honourable C. A.
Masten wrote in *Canadian Golfer*: "We laid
out the course as we went along, digging the
holes with our jack knives." As for a new
course laid out in 1894: "I recall with wonder
and amazement the bold way in which we,
like pioneers of old, cut down trees and laid
out the course without any professional assistance whatever . . . Flags were not necessary,
and would in any case have been stolen on
public ground. A three-foot stick sufficed to
mark the position of the green."

The first courses at Royal Montreal were in
a public park, complete with the hazards of
nannies and perambulators. The first of Royal
Quebec "ran over and across the old French
forts and earth works, the hazards being deep
precipices, old fortifications, gullies, moats,
rocks, swamps, and bogs."

The two courses at Niagara were on com-
mons used in the summer months for a militia

348

This earth tee of the early 1900s was apparently scooped out of the course.

An artificial tee at Victoria's Oak Bay, 1930.

training camp. The second course had "a railway cutting, dry moat, dykes, numerous roads, trails, rifle pits, and long grass."

The first Kingston course on Barriefield Common had "marshes, stony ground, roads, heights and hollows," and Toronto GC's had "gullies, sand roads, sand banks, swamps, bogs, fences, and hills." The Rosedale links of 1904 had the fairway of the fifth hole crossing the fairways of the fourth, twelfth, and fourteenth; the fairways of holes nine and eleven were intersecting; and that of hole fifteen cut across the middle of a cricket field.

The first course at Vancouver (in 1892) was on the seashore.

When we talk today of "hazards," we mean bunkers or water hazards. In the Victorian years, a hazard was all-inclusive   anything and everything that was hazardous to the clean striking of the ball. Clubs boasted of the fiendish nature of their hazards.

In the 1890s, the provision of hazards was not left entirely to nature, historic ruins, or the whims of farmers. Where hazards did not exist in the "right" places, clubs wishing to conform to the current philosophy of design, installed them.

This photo appeared in a Toronto newspaper in 1896 with the caption "Rosedale Golf Club – a Bad Lie."

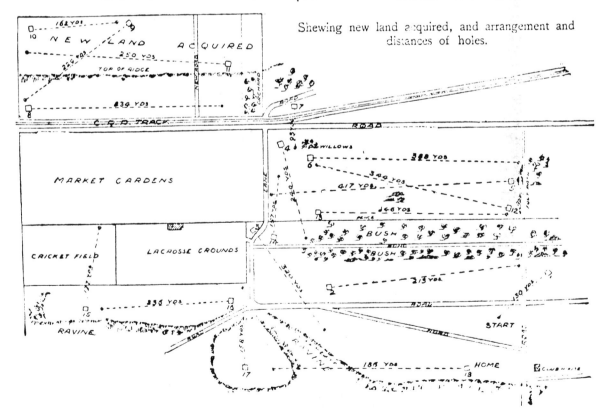

The crossing fairways on the Rosedale course, 1904.

Just as the late-Victorian child was punished for being errant, so too was the late-Victorian golfer. Some golf holes came to resemble steeplechase courses, with cross-bunkers replacing hedges, stretching from one side of the fairway to the other. "If a man is to get into a hazard, let it be a bad one," wrote an amateur golf architect of the time.

The green was often protected by yet another cross-bunker. Since this was intended to catch poor *second* shots, some clubs permitted long-hitters to lift out without penalty if this second bunker caught their drives.

Small wonder that this type of course came to be known as being of *penal* design.

These purely functional courses, with their penal bunkers and almost dead flat greens, square or circular, were slow to vanish in Canada. In Britain and the United States, golf course design became an art and a business in the fourteen years before the First World War. A few top U.S. amateur golfers studied British courses and incorporated the layout of holes in new courses then being built in the United States.

Canada had no one of their ilk, and it was left to outsiders to change our ideas of what constituted a proper test of golf until our own Stanley Thompson came along after the First World War.

The American architect Robert Trent Jones, then in partnership with Stanley Thompson, wrote an article for *Canadian Golfer* in 1936

Cross bunkers on the Edmonton golf course around the turn of the century.

A square green at the Murray Bay golf course around 1915, typical of Canada's early courses.

And a square "brown" at Waterton Lakes Park, Alberta, in 1928.

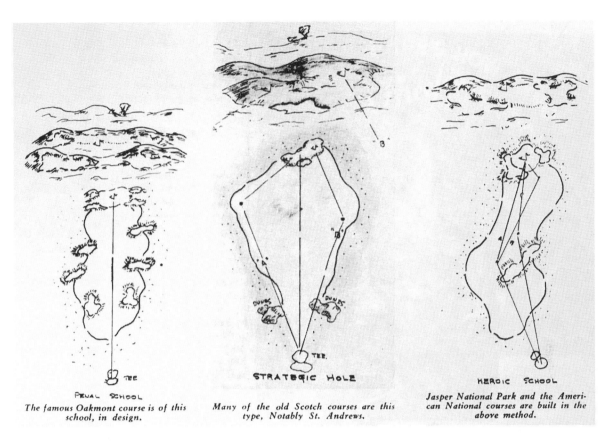

PENAL SCHOOL
The famous Oakmont course is of this school, in design.

STRATEGIC HOLE
Many of the old Scotch courses are this type, Notably St. Andrews.

HEROIC SCHOOL
Jasper National Park and the American National courses are built in the above method.

The layouts of a penal, a strategic, and a heroic hole, as envisioned by Robert Trent Jones in 1936.

which illustrated how the philosophy of golf course design had changed in the first thirty years of this century.

In 1932 he had overheard a conversation about Sandy Somerville having "all the shots in the bag." Jones came to understand that "we, as architects, in part contribute the guiding hand in shot development by the designs which we create." Golfers assiduously practise to play the type of shot demanded by their hoodoo holes. These holes demand shots not "in the bag." Accompanying this article was a sketch of three types of golf hole: the penal, the strategic, and the heroic.

The St. Andrews golfer, Jones pointed out, was prone to swing in a "free and lusty style, maliciously intent upon distance . . . For the design of St. Andrews is of the strategic school, devoid of numerous traps, but such as they are, ingeniously placed, demanding as much canniness as one can muster. . . ."

On the other hand, golfers at Pinehurst tended to be timid, with a tendency to steer the ball on this penal course, which bristles with traps.

The *heroic* type of architecture then coming into vogue was a mixture of the penal and the strategic. It was developing a heroic golfer who was prepared to consider the varying degrees of penalty associated with the diagonal hazard and to bite off as much of it as was in his (or her) bag. Jones goes on to say:

> Collectively all three types of architecture produce every shot known in the realm of golf. Individually each requires shots characteristic to its own school. It would therefore seem logical that the ideal golf course should be a combination of all three. With two or three holes of the spine quivering penal: three or four holes of the mind developing strategic: the remainder of them the popular heroic.

Stanley Thompson's course at Jasper was one of only two courses in North America that Jones considered based on this conception. To play Jasper, he believed, a golfer needed "all the shots in the bag."

The modern golf architect is in some respects like the golf writer, with moments of sustained emotion. But unlike the writer he can not readily go back and redo what he has done if he does not like the structure of his work.

Before this modern breed of architect came to Canada, two British artisans had laid out a number of courses here around the turn of the century: Willie Dunn and Tom Bendelow.

Willie Dunn came from Musselburgh. He had worked as a professional and greenkeeper, and had some experience at laying out facilities in Britain and France before coming to make his fame and fortune in the United States, in 1893. Many of his early courses in the U.S. were probably no more than stake-and-hammer jobs.

His first job in Canada was for Royal Montreal. Having moved to a new site at Dixie in 1896, the club hired Willie Dunn in 1900 to reroute its twelve-hole course and to add another six. But the land available was barely sufficient and the course was cramped. Two years later the club acquired more acreage and brought Willie back to try again. He designed another layout but the members were never happy with the new Willie Dunn course, completed in 1903.

Willie Dunn's greatest gift to Canada should have been Lambton. This new club hired Willie to design its first course, and on its completion in 1903 he spoke enthusiastically of the result: "Gentlemen, I have laid out more than one hundred golf courses all over America, and I must take off my hat to Lambton as the finest I ever saw."

The New York correspondent of the British magazine *Golf Illustrated* reported Lambton's coming in January 1903: "Willie Dunn has just laid out an eighteen-hole course of 6350 yards for the Lambton Country Club, of Toronto, Canada. One of the holes is 750 yards long . . . The bogey for the hole is 6 . . . The seventeenth hole is 325 yards."

When the Lambton course was officially opened in June of that year, the 750-yard hole had mysteriously disappeared, as had the 325-yard seventeenth, which was now the longest hole at 550 yards. So Willie's layout had obviously been tampered with. What is more, the routing of the holes had been completely changed in 1906, for the first Lambton tournament.

". . . the Lambton course was well laid out, a fact possibly due to the guiding hand of our old friend, George Lyon," wrote a visiting British golfer Harold Hilton in 1912, perhaps unaware of Willie Dunn's work.

Two years later, British golf writer Henry Leach had equally fine praise: "The fourth hole is one of the jewels of Canadian golf. The teeing ground is on a height, and below it is a series of descending plateaux, like giant's steps until the level is reached. When he has made a very passable drive, the player is called upon with a very proper second to carry Black Creek which guards the green and is coiled like a snake about it . . ."

Today, the fourth hole is still as Leach described it. How much we have to thank Willie Dunn for it, and how much George Lyon, will no doubt one day be determined by the historian of Lambton.

The 750-yard hole at Lambton may have reflected a tendency of the times to manufacture tests of stamina. A few years later, members (probably helped by club professional Arthur Russell) laid out the first course at Toronto's Lakeview. In an (undated) article in *Outdoor Canada*, the secretary boasts of their 750-yard ninth hole ("the longest in Canada"), and the 650-yard sixteenth, both par sevens.

Tom Bendelow, a prolific Scottish-born architect, also came up from the United States in the early 1900s to leave his mark on a few sites in Canada, including the courses of Royal Ottawa, Montreal's Victoria, Rosedale, Winnipeg Golf Club Limited, and Winnipeg's Pine Ridge. These courses were later revamped by more accomplished architects, so probably nothing remains of the old Bendelow layouts.

In 1915, *Canadian Golfer* recorded that, a few years earlier, Bendelow had laid out a course for the Calgary Golf and Country Club.

In *The Golf Course* (1981), the authors show Bendelow as the architect of Calgary's municipal course. *Fraser's Golf Directory and Year Book* for 1923 attributes this course to the Banff professional, William Thomson. The opening of the links in 1915 was recorded in *Canadian Golfer*, which credited the design to a local man, Fred Searson, who is said to have struggled for a month to fit eighteen holes into the available land.

The matter of who laid out Calgary's municipal course illustrates how difficult it can be to establish the architect responsible for a course some seventy years after the event. Before the First World War, golf writers paid scant attention to golf course design. Golf architects became newsworthy in the 1920s.

The Golf Course was written by a noted Canadian golf architect, Geoffrey S. Cornish, and an American lawyer, Ronald E. Whitten. It is one of the classics of golf literature. Robert Trent Jones aptly described it as "a monumental achievement." Amongst other things, the book lists the architects of over ten thousand golf courses. The authors attributed a course to an architect only when they were satisfied that the evidence was reliable. Naturally, the earlier the course and the less important the architect, the more difficult it was to unearth reliable facts about his work.

Another problem facing the researcher is the transient nature of a golf course. When a club constructs a new course, or changes its existing course – and it may do this several times over the years – it is under no obligation to publish the facts. These may be recorded in the minutes of the club, but never broadcast.

Take the Toronto Hunt course, usually credited to architect Willie Park. The club's minute-books and contemporary newspapers reveal that the course has a long history of change. The first nine holes were laid out in 1897, *north* of the Kingston Road, by unrecorded hands. Charlie Murray and George Cumming made changes over the years, and

by 1910 four holes had been moved to south of the Kingston Road. In 1918 Willie Park remodelled the course, and relaid most, if not all, of the greens. It then became a Willie Park course. The club acquired more land and hired George Cumming to produce a layout with all the holes south of the Kingston Road. This meant abandoning the five Willie Park holes north of the Kingston Road, and rerouting the other four. This work was completed in 1943. If this was then anyone's course, it had to be George Cumming's.

In the pages that follow, I attribute courses to certain architects. In most instances, the facts were taken from newspapers or other periodicals published about the time the courses were being built or modified. I have not attempted to follow the courses' subsequent history beyond the early 1930s.

The pioneer of modern golf course architecture was the Scot Willie Park of Musselburgh, who was later to leave his indelible mark on Canada.

Willie Park was one of the most articulate of Scottish golf professionals. His *The Game of Golf* (1896) is the first book to devote a chap-

Willie Park Jr., the first of the new breed of architect.

ter to golf course architecture. He entitled it "Laying Out and Keeping Golf-Links." Most of his advice is old hat today. ("If possible, avoid making the line of play to one hole cross the line of play to another.") But you will find courses today where this other piece of advice has been ignored: "The first two or three holes should, if possible, be fairly long ones, and should be, comparatively speaking, easy to play. Holes of a good length permit the players to get away without congesting the links . . ."

Willie also admits his fondness of large greens, but as the finest putter of his day he may have been prejudiced. In 1920 he came out with his other book, *The Art of Putting.*

Willie took to laying out new, inland courses, with large greens having sinuous undulations, some of them two-tiered, guarded by subtly placed bunkers. Bunkers, not traps. Willie was careful to distinguish between the two. In his 1896 book he wrote: "A bunker that is not visible to the player is always more or less of a 'trap'." This is, I believe, the earliest recorded use of the word *trap.* Nowadays, the words *trap* and *bunker* are treated as synonyms, which would not have pleased Willie one whit.

Some of Park's contemporaries in Britain – Colt, Mackenzie, Strong – we will meet later, as well as the Scottish-American Donald Ross. To score well, the golfer had to think his way around their courses. On every hole there was no longer a single target, the green, but a number of targets, the green being the last. Of the several routes to the flag, the golfer had to choose the one best suited to his ability, judgement, and nerve. Bunkers might be laid out in heroic couplets (no pun intended) daring the player to try carrying one, if not the other. Matches could be won or lost according to the player's chosen strategy.

The United States was quick to follow, and often led, in this new brand of *strategic* golf architecture. Canadians, most of them ignorant of this changing world, were still playing over courses designed in a candlelit world.

Although Willie Park visited Canada off and on for only a few years between 1917 and 1923,

he worked on some twenty sites. In 1920, he wrote, ". . . the American knows what a golf course should be, and now he does not accept anything. A great part of my work concerned the reconstruction of links, which had been ruined by bad designing." Some of this reconstruction work was in Canada. He appears to have done such extensive work at Dartmouth's Brightwood GC and at the Calgary G & CC that these were virtually new courses.

Canadian golfers were first made aware of Willie's presence in Canada in 1917, when he met with his friend Andrew Forgan. At seven o'clock of a November evening, the two of them spent an hour in Montreal's Windsor Hotel, next to the station. Willie had to catch the 8:05 train for New York, where he had his office. Andrew Forgan, white-bearded and in his early seventies, had come to Montreal to visit his daughter, and had been caught by the outbreak of war. (He was to die there in 1925, the same year as Willie.)

Willie was in Montreal laying out a new course, Mount Bruno. He always had a soft spot for this course. "One of the biggest and finest links I have had to deal with," he wrote in 1920. It remains one of the most challenging and picturesque in Central Canada.

Rumour had it that Willie Park was going to stay on as the professional at Bruno. But if he had ever seriously considered this, he had second thoughts. Instead, he installed his sister's son, Frank Park Glass. A few years later, Frank's brother Charlie was installed as an assistant at the club in Senneville, near Montreal, another Willie Park remodelling.

Mount Bruno had the largest greens in Canada. Their enormous area and rolling character made them difficult and costly to maintain with the equipment then available. But the RCGA thought so highly of the course that it awarded Mount Bruno the Open championships of 1922 and 1924.

Willie Park was too busy chasing around the country to attend the first of these Opens, and too near death to attend the second. How much the strain of overwork had to do with his early demise – he was only sixty-one – is problematical. But between 1918 and 1923, he seemed to be everywhere in Canada, at a time when he was also laying out or remodelling some forty to fifty sites in the United States.

Willie Park opened an office in Toronto's King Street East, in 1919. That same year, he remodelled the Toronto Hunt course, and the course at Brightwood, where he added a second nine. He also submitted plans for expanding the Whitlock course near Montreal from nine to twelve holes. (Within a year or so, the club had decided on eighteen.)

In July, he was out in Winnipeg, going over the course of The Winnipeg GC Ltd. at Bird's Hill (the club wanted it brought up to championship standard). He sent them plans on how to lengthen it to 6,400 yards, adding new bunkers and greens. The first RCGA Annual Meeting west of Ontario was played over the remodelled course in 1921. Ralph Reville wrote of the Willie Park greens: "The monotonous flat green is nowhere in evidence. Instead, there are rolling greens and angle greens – greens, in fact, of almost every variety."

On the same visit, Willie met with the directors of the new Southwood club and gave them a layout for an eighteen-hole course.

Montreal's Beaconsfield GC was slated to house the Open in 1920. It hired Willie to toughen its course. He added length, three new tees, thirteen bunkers (removing at the same time six walled bunkers), and reconstructed eight greens. In the same year, he started work on a new eighteen-hole course for Laval-sur-le-Lac. That winter, he went back to Scotland for a rest.

The Mount Bruno course was being completed in 1920, when Royal Montreal held a general meeting in the Windsor hotel to agree a costly expansion at Dixie; a new eighteen-hole course, improvements to the existing eighteen (Willie Dunn's), and a new clubhouse. It would be the first club in Canada to have two eighteen-hole courses, one 6,204 yards, the other 6,300 yards; the clubhouse alone would cost a quarter of a million dollars. In their post-war enthusiasm for golf, the members endorsed the project in its entirety. Another job for Willie

Park, who at that moment was working on a project at Atlantic City.

Later the same year, he got the nod from Weston. It wanted a new, modern, full-sized course. And around this time, Ottawa Hunt and Motor Club decided that it, too, needed a 6,500-yard layout from Willie Park, to replace the one-year-old course designed by Davie Black.

Willie's biggest job came in 1922: twenty-seven holes for the new Montreal club of Summerlea, then situated near Dixie station. In May of that year he was out in Calgary, revamping the courses of three clubs: the Calgary G & CC, Bowness, and St. Andrews. The Country Club job was almost a completely new course, including a new watering system for fairways and greens, one of the first in North America. Willie Park's work on Royal Quebec's new eighteen-hole course at Boischatel was also commissioned around 1922. The club moved to this site three years later.

In the fall of 1923, Willie Park fell ill and left New York to spend the winter in Musselburgh. He had to relinquish several important contracts in Canada, including the revamping of the courses of Scarboro and of Hamilton's Glendale. His condition got progressively worse, and he died in Edinburgh in the spring of 1925.

Willie Park is remembered in the clubhouse at Mount Bruno, where there is a Willie Park room. Weston showed its appreciation by organizing an annual tournament for the Willie Park Trophy, inscribed on which you'll find most of the big names in amateur golf in Central Canada. The trophy stands on one side of the bar in the Willie Park lounge, his photo on the other side. Willie would have liked that.

The Toronto GC had been the first in Canada to bring over from Britain one of this modern breed of golf architect, in 1911. Its course in the east end of Toronto was being enveloped by an expanding city and had to be sold. A

club committee and George Cumming came up with a new site, 260 acres on the banks of the Etobicoke River. Around this time, Cumming was designing facilities for other clubs in Ontario. But his own club was obviously determined to have an experienced British architect work on its new site. It settled on H. S. Colt.

Harry Colt was then in his early forties. By the time he came to Toronto, Colt was firmly established as one of the leading architects of his day.

Cornish and Whitten point out that Colt can claim a number of firsts. "He was the first designer not to have been a professional golfer; he was the first real 'international' designer, although Willie Park Jr. rivalled him; he was the first to prepare tree-planting plans for his layouts; and he was the first to use the drawing board consistently." Colt did not believe in holes of over 500 yards.

The club spent $220,000 on its new course and clubhouse. At the time this was the greatest amount ever spent on a golfing facility in Canada. It drew breathless admiration from Britain's Henry Leach, then visiting Canada. In *The Happy Golfer* he devotes several pages to Toronto GC, under the heading "A Masterpiece."

Many parts of the world were laid under tribute for the making of this new course . . . In order to give a grass to the course that would stand the rigours of the climate better than the ordinary grasses with which the courses of North America are generally sown, seeds were obtained from Finland. Then nearly all the rough work of construction was done by Bulgarians and Roumanians, these immigrants being splendid for work of this kind. They were paid at the rate of about seven shillings a day, and they lived in huts which they made on the ground, and saved the greater part of the money that they earned. A little over . . . 80,000 dollars were paid for the land, and about the same amount was spent on its preparation and completion as a course; while . . . 100,000 dollars were spent on the building and equip-

ment of a splendid club-house, embracing the utmost comfort and convenience, with about fifty bedrooms . . . British golfers must surely pause with wonder when they hear of a place like Toronto spending [$220,000] on a new golf course.

When the club moved to its new location in 1913, its course was soon accepted as one of the finest in North America, the clubhouse as one of the most charming. Although lengthened and modified over the years, with some of the greens rebuilt and bunkers added, the layout remains much as Colt envisaged it in 1911.

Harry Colt had no sooner finished at Toronto GC than he was asked to submit a design for Ancaster, the new home of the Hamilton G & CC. Again, Colt's work has been modified over the years, but Ancaster has always ranked as one of the finest tests of golf in Canada. In a 1988 poll, it was the oldest course to rank in the top five in the country.

Alistair Mackenzie, another Cambridge graduate (in medicine), collaborated with Harry Colt in some of his layouts and also designed many of his own. In 1919, he outlined in *Canadian Golfer* the concepts he tried to follow in golf course design, showing how far we had come from the days of the old penal type of course. He incorporated an almost identical list of ideal features in his book *Golf Architecture* (1920), which was to influence all future architects.

In Canada, Mackenzie laid out a new nine-hole course for the St. Charles CC, Winnipeg, in 1929.

Another of Colt's university acquaintances went into partnership with him. Captain Alison – as he then was – designed Toronto's York Downs course, opened in 1922. The members of this club were recruited largely from Toronto GC and Toronto Hunt. They decided against an elaborate clubhouse, preferring instead to sink their money into a fine course in the city's Don Valley. Captain Alison also supervised the construction of the course, using as contractors the new firm of Thompson, Cumming and Thompson. An expanding city eventually took over the Colt–Alison course, forcing York Downs to move further out.

In 1929, the firm of Colt, Alison and Morrison designed and supervised the enlargement and improvement of the Forest Hills facility in Montreal. This club no longer exists.

During the boom that followed the First World War, a number of Canadian clubs brought in the Scottish-American architect Donald Ross to upgrade their courses. He also laid out a number of new sites, or rebuilt courses to such an extent that these can be considered his designs. Donald Ross of Pinehurst ranked as one of the world's leading golf architects.

Ross made at least one trip to Canada before the war. In 1912, Royal Ottawa had an eighteen-hole and a nine-hole course, which between them had only thirteen artificial bunkers, as against the forty-seven in Toronto's

layout by Harry Colt. So, in May of that year, the club invited Donald Ross to upgrade its main course, which he did, adding bunkers and remodelling some of the greens. When Henry Leach visited the club in 1913, he rated the course as one of the four best he had seen in North America.

In 1919, Mississaugua hired Ross to bring its course up to championship standard. He rebuilt eight greens and twelve tees, stretching the course to 6,300 yards. While in Toronto, he virtually rebuilt what remained of the old Bendelow course at Rosedale (which had since been changed by the club's professional, Frank Freeman). Ross gave Rosedale eleven new greens and three modified greens, all well bunkered. At Lambton, he modified five holes. He was also called upon to alter some of the greens at Montreal's Kanawaki, which had been criticized as being too flat and uninteresting.

In 1919 and 1920 Ross was also busy reshaping three courses in Winnipeg (at the

Donald Ross in front of his first golf shop at Pinehurst, twenty-nine years later, in 1929–30.

same time as Willie Park was working on two other courses in the same city). In the spring of 1919, Pine Ridge invited him to have a look at its Bendelow course at Bird's Hill, and while he was there he visited St. Charles CC and Elmhurst. As a result of his visit, St. Charles rebuilt its eighteen-hole course in 1920.

There is no public record of exactly how he changed the layout at Elmhurst, but it has since been considered a Donald Ross course and one often highly praised.

Like Colt, Donald Ross did not believe in holes of over 500 yards but insisted on a well-balanced course, scientifically bunkered. At Elmhurst, his longest hole was 461 yards.

In 1922, CPR hired Donald Ross to remodel its Algonquin Hotel golf course, at St. Andrews, New Brunswick. (Ross was a friend of the local professional, John Peacock, who spent his winters at Pinehurst as an assistant. Ross may have had a hand in expanding Algonquin to eighteen holes early in the century.) The eighteen-hole course at Algonquin probably plays today much as he left it, a gem of a layout overlooking Passamaquoddy Bay. Algonquin is by no means a course fit for the Open, but it has that hard-to-define quality that makes it easy to recall after an acquaintance of only one round.

When Essex County Golf and Country Club in Ontario moved to a new site in 1927, it hired Donald Ross to lay out its course at Sandwich, near Windsor. The area was heavily wooded. Some 20,000 stumps and trees had to be dynamited, over 30,000 cubic yards of dirt hauled in to build up the greens, the fairways disced and harrowed eight or ten times before seeding. But when completed, the course soon ranked among the best in Canada, with its superb tree-lined fairways and large, undulating greens.

In 1920, Toronto's Lakeview GC brought in Herbert Strong to remodel its course. Strong was another English professional who had found designing courses in North America more lucrative. He rebuilt Lakeview into one of the toughest tests of golf in Canada.

But Strong's masterpiece in Canada is the Manoir Richelieu hotel course at Murray Bay, Quebec, situated on the north shore of the St. Lawrence and owned and operated by Canada Steamship Lines Company. He wrote later: "The scenery surrounding the Manoir Richelieu Golf Course at Murray Bay is the most

Herbert Strong's Manoir Richelieu course at Murray Bay.

impressive setting for a links of which I have knowledge. The chief task I faced, was to build this natural beauty into every possible feature of the play. No designer could have more varied or lavish material to work with."

The course is spread out on a ledge of the Laurentian Hills that rise sharply from the St. Lawrence. Its clubhouse is eight hundred feet above the river. Thomas H. Uzzell's *Golf in the World's Oldest Mountains* (1926) gives a hole-by-hole description of this magnificent layout, which has changed little over the years: "Views of sky, water, and mountain forests unsurpassed; eighteen holes of golf, varied, intriguingly dramatic; putting greens among the best in Canada . . ."

The work on the course began in June 1924. U.S. President Taft drove the first ball when nine holes were opened for play in July of the following year. The second nine were completed a year later.

Around 1930, Herbert Strong started on a nine-hole course in the old-world village of

St. Andrews East, Quebec, on the north shore of the St. Lawrence just west of Montreal. This course was given rave notices when it was completed in 1931.

The first Canadian golf course architect to make a name for himself internationally was Stanley Thompson, in the 1920s. Some would claim that he outclassed even Colt, Mackenzie, Ross, and Strong. But long before 1920, when Thompson came on the scene, a number of Canadian professionals had taken to laying out courses.

When Royal Ottawa was organized in 1891, it called on Royal Montreal's professional, William Davis, to lay out its first nine-hole course. Davis was also the first professional to lay out a course in the United States. The new Shinnecock Hills club in Long Island asked Royal Montreal for his services in the same year, 1891. But his layout at Shinnecock was soon abandoned in favour of another site.

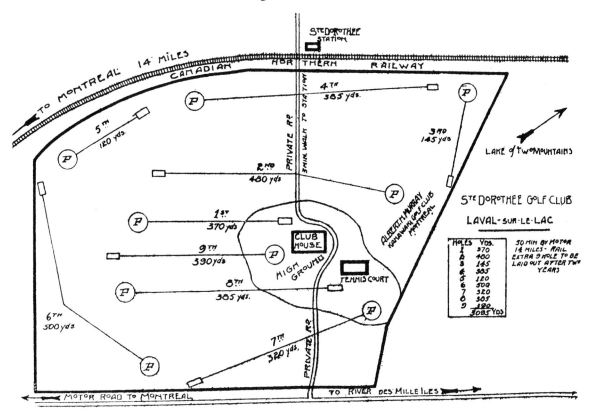

Albert Murray's plan for Laval's first course, 1916.

From the early 1900s, Canadian professionals were often pressed into service as course designers, clubs assuming that a man who taught the game for a living must necessarily be an expert on how to lay out a course. The records of who was responsible for what are fragmentary and often contradictory. In any event, although a few of these sites may still be golf courses, they will all have been remodelled, most of them completely rebuilt.

Only a few early courses can be traced to Charlie Murray, but his brother Albert became a prolific architect. Among his early designs in Quebec were those at Val Morin, Grand' Mère, Laval-sur-le-Lac (later rebuilt by others), the Hermitage Club, Magog, Knowlton, St. Patrick, Rivière du Loup, and Boule Rock. He had revamped the Cove Fields course for Royal Quebec in 1906, and when the club had to move from Cove Fields after the 1915 season, he laid out their new course at Montmorency Falls. Before the end of the First World War, he had also laid out a few courses in New York state.

Albert Murray did most of his golf architecture after the Second World War, when he retired as a club professional. His scrapbook in the RCGA library names some thirty-three courses that he laid out, another thirteen that he modified, but he dates only a few of these.

In the Canadian West, four architects were kept especially busy: Bob Smith, Alex Duthie, William Thomson, and A. Vernon Macan.

Bob Smith, a Scot who had worked for Spalding, came to Canada after the First World War and laid out at least ten courses in Saskatchewan, Alberta, and British Columbia, at a time when he was professional to four western clubs.

The long-time professional at Vancouver's Jericho CC (1910–42), Alex Duthie, revamped this old nine-hole course in 1924. He designed eleven new holes, linking these up with seven old holes to give Jericho a new eighteen-hole layout on the Point Grey promontory. The course was a mixture of seaside links and parkland, and was a much-admired facility until the club closed.

After Penticton GC reorganized in 1923, it hired Duthie to design a new nine-hole course. He laid this out on a series of flat bench lands on the side of a mountain. It opened for play in 1926.

Duthie's finest piece of work was probably at Kelowna GC. When this opened in 1926, it was the first eighteen-hole course in B.C.'s interior. Located among rolling, wooded hills, overlooking the valley of Glenmore and the town of Kelowna, with the Okanagan Lake in the distance, this was one of the most picturesque courses of its day.

William E. Thomson, a short, stocky Scot, laid out only a handful of courses in Canada. But three of these were in the national parks of Banff, Waterton Lake, and Jasper, and they attracted a lot of attention from visitors to the West. His name has been overlooked by those who have written of golf at Banff and Jasper.

William Thomson came from Scotland in 1907, to serve as a club professional, first in Winnipeg, then at Banff. The town of Banff lay within the Rocky Mountains Park Reserve. Centred around the local hot springs, it had attracted many visitors since the opening of the CPR's Banff Springs Hotel in 1888. Visitors to the hotel had been playing golf on a makeshift course with sand greens since the turn of the century. CPR hired Thomson in 1910 to lay out a proper nine-hole course. Within a few years, he was being looked upon as something of a wizard, having transformed acres of waste ground into what was described at the time as a gem of a course, one of the finest in the West. It was laid out in a triangle, with the apex at the clubhouse below the hotel, and the other two points on Mount Rundle and the river. Its new, large, turfed greens were watered from a system that supplied the whole course. The course was intended mainly for visitors to Banff hotels, but members of a local golf club were allowed to play.

In 1917, the Dominion government took over the nine-hole Banff Golf Course (no

A view of William Thomson's Waterton Lakes Park golf course, 1932.

longer Banff Springs), which then became the responsibility of the Rocky Mountains Park of Canada. Thomson was commissioned to lay out an additional nine holes, and was given prisoners-of-war to help clear away rocks and cut down trees for the new fairways. At the same time, they cleared the space for a new road and carpark; an increasing number of visitors were coming to Banff by automobile.

His success at Banff led to Thomson designing another two courses for the Parks Branch. In 1921, he laid out in Waterton Lakes Park a nine-hole course of 2,790 yards, located between the Blaikiston River and the town of Waterton, overlooking Waterton Lake. It opened for play that summer. As at Banff, its fairways were set amidst some of the grandest vistas in the Rockies: slopes clad with flowers and forest, snow-peaked mountains, mirror-like lakes.

In 1921, when the Parks Branch was set to construct a third golf course, this time at Jasper Park, it engaged Thomson to look for a good location near the town of Jasper.

He was not the first to search this area for the ideal site for a golf course. In 1914, Sir Arthur Conan Doyle had visited Jasper during a lecture tour of Canada and had plumped for a site near Lake Pyramid, on the west side of the river, about a mile from town. Before the area could be cleared, the war came along and put an end to the project. (Yes, the creator of Sherlock Holmes very nearly created a golf course in Canada. He was a keen but humble golfer. "I played in Egypt until they told me that excavators had to pay a special tax. I inaugurated a private course in Vermont also, and the Yankee farmer asked us what we were boring for.")

Thomson had a look at the Conan Doyle site. The cost of clearing trees and rocks he judged to be too great. But on the east side of the river, he found a plateau along the margin of Lake Beauvert, extensive enough for nine holes plus another nine if these were ever needed. The well-drained, sandy loam was ideal for a golf course.

Thomson planned his layout in 1922. All nine holes were to be set in an amphitheatre of some of the grandest scenery in the Canadian Rockies, with Mount Signal rising to a height of 8,000 feet on the southeast side, lakes Beauvert, Trefoil, Annette, and Edith in the west. The CNR had already erected a number of lodges for summer visitors adjacent to the proposed new course.

The Parks Branch did not proceed with Thomson's plan. Ironically, William Thomson's two national park courses, and his site at Jasper, were later to be taken over by another of the same clan, Stanley Thompson. Evidence of Thomson's creation virtually disappeared and, sadly, his name is no longer associated with the development of golf at these three sites.

A. Vernon Macan.

William Thomson stayed on as professional at Banff to see it modified by Donald Ross, then rebuilt by Stanley Thompson in 1927.

We met Vernon Macan as one of B.C.'s leading amateur golfers, but his greatest contribution to golf was the string of courses he laid out along the Pacific coast over a period of some fifty years. Cornish and Whitten list a dozen or so of these, some in the United States.

Before the First World War he had a hand in the design of Royal Colwood's magnificent course in Victoria, which he later modified. Marine Drive (1923) was amongst the earliest of his post-war courses. The club's board also retained him in 1926 to ensure that he agreed to the changes it was then contemplating.

When CPR decided to build its new championship course in South Vancouver, it went to Macan. The Langara Golf Links, overlooking the delta of the Fraser River, opened in 1926. At the time it was unrivalled in public courses along the Pacific coast, and Macan considered it his *pièce de résistance*.

Having remodelled the old Shaughnessy Heights, he was asked to build the new Shaughnessy course, when the club moved from the heights. His other courses in those years included Nanaimo and Penticton (also attributed to Duthie). He also remodelled the course of Victoria GC.

During his fifty years as professional to the Toronto GC, George Cumming performed so nobly as a player, teacher, and accepted dean of Canada's early professionals that his work as a golf architect has been largely overlooked. In an autobiographical note written in the 1940s, he makes no mention of it. But in the 1920s he advertised himself as a course designer, and in these boom years he laid out or remodelled some twenty courses. I have not been able to trace more than a few of his earlier works.

One of his first jobs on arriving at Toronto Golf Club was to put the club's course into decent shape. This course, remember, had been the site of the 1898 Amateur, and of the first international match with the United States. In an article published in 1914, a Toronto golf writer, J. Lewis (Lew) Brown, recalled how George improved it:

> . . . To attempt to break and harrow those fields into a good golfing turf, to re-arrange the holes and to make new greens, was the task before him . . . One of the first things he did was to remove the three great stones at the first hole in the middle of the field of play, which were always an eyesore to every golfer who saw them. At the second, he added bunkers of the new style . . . [the third] hole was nothing more than a verita-

ble Sahara, mixed with cinders, which blew over from the passing trains . . . He changed the fourth hole, which was nothing but a piece of twitch grass, and straightened it out parallel with the third. At the eighth, he cleared the swamp of undergrowth . . . The old Brown house and the Ambrose and Miller residences were removed . . . leaving a clear field of play. The punch bowl was another of his achievements . . . Likewise on all other holes he added changes wherever he saw fit . . . Up till two years ago . . . there was not a course in Canada to touch it. . . .

In 1912, with the help of George S. Lyon, he laid out the first course for the new Summit GC, Toronto. The course was not opened until after the war. In 1913, on laying out a new course at Mississaugua, he met with the board of directors, "for the purpose of explaining his plan of play and scheme of trapping and bunkering." (Note that he distinguished between traps and bunkers.) In 1915, he was called in by London Hunt, when the club decided to build itself a new eighteen-hole course.

He laid out the Humber Valley and Windermere courses when a partner in Thompson, Cumming and Thompson, and this company supervised the construction. His later courses, from the new course for Bayview in 1928, were laid out in partnership with Captain Melville Millar (of Millar Trophy fame), who was noted for his painstaking and economical methods of course construction.

No golfer has more indelibly left his stamp on Canada than Stanley Thompson. Between 1920 and 1953, this Canadian amateur golfer turned golf architect sculpted out of farmland, heath, forest, and mountain some of the finest and most scenic golf courses in the world. A handful of the sites he worked on in the 1920s and 1930s have fallen to developers – such as St. Andrews, and part of Uplands, in Toronto. But so long as his much-bruited Banff and Jasper remain – to say nothing of Capilano, St. George's, Cape Breton Highlands, and

Digby Pines – his legacy to us will be both admired and enjoyed.

Some of his public links tend to be overplayed and at times have the appearance of a dowager fallen on hard times. But, there again, it is a fine thing that these links are public, so that everyone may share in the pleasure of walking their fairways.

It has been widely written that Stanley Thompson had a hand in the design of some two hundred courses. Whoever first came up with this figure may have been stretching the facts, as Stanley Thompson himself was wont to do, mischievously, when being interviewed. It is hard to discover the names of more than about 125 courses, 25 of these outside Canada. Cornish and Whitten list most of these in *The Golf Course*. Robert Moote has published a revised list in *Score* magazine (1981).

Stanley Thompson was very much like his creations – larger than life; a man with noble images and great clarity of mind; flamboyant, eccentric, a man whose story has fact and fable too finely intertwined to be easily distinguished. Did he have as little disregard for money as legend would have us believe? Or as much addiction to cigars, steaks, and whisky? Yes and no, those who worked for him will

Stanley Thompson, right, *looking over the site of the Seigniory course with Cal Taylor, the club's professional, in 1931.*

tell you. And those who worked for him are as much his legacy to us as his links. For they, in turn, have given us many gems of courses, some in the Thompson style, some in their own. The great Robert Trent Jones learned his art at Thompson's side in the early 1930s. So did Canadians C. E. "Robbie" Robinson and Howard Watson, who joined Thompson in 1929, as did Geoffrey Cornish and Robert and David Moote a few years later.

As we have seen, Stanley Thompson was one of five Thompson brothers, all of whom were to make a name for themselves as golfers in the first quarter of this century: William, Stanley, Mat, and Frank as amateurs, Nicol as a professional. Born in 1893, in what is now the east end of Toronto, Stanley caddied under George Cumming at the Toronto Golf Club. As a boy, he went to a school near the village of Norway, and later attended Malvern Collegiate. He is also said to have taken a course at the Ontario Agricultural College at Guelph.

In a note written after Stanley Thompson's death, one of his former associates, Howard Watson, said: ". . . the need to further his ambition led to his first professional course design at Newton Bay, Ontario, at the age of seventeen, and an early association with George Cumming and his brother Nicol." So while some of Cumming's caddies went on to make a name for themselves as professional golfers, Stanley Thompson appears to have shown an early interest in Cumming's other activity, golf course architecture.

In October 1915, this paragraph appeared in the pages of *Canadian Golfer*:

> Stanley Thompson, who was for several years at the Norway Point Golf Club, at the Wawa Hotel, Muskoka, is at present in England with the Second Regiment, being attached to the Fourth Brigade, and his younger brother Frank, who was at Niagara-on-the-Lake last year, has enlisted with the Medical Corps.

This suggests that Stanley Thompson had been the professional at Norway Point. (Frank may also have been the professional at Niagara, but more probably this refers to him attending the militia camp at Niagara.) George Cumming was in the habit of farming out his young assistants to resort courses, to give them experience in running a professional's shop. But if he did work as a professional before the war, Stanley Thompson's war service was long and distinguished enough to absolve him from this crime, and he came back from the war as an amateur. Rising from the ranks to become a commissioned officer, he had been mentioned in dispatches for gallantry in the field while serving with the Royal Canadian Artillery in France. He returned from overseas service in 1919.

By February 1920, Stanley Thompson was part of a new company, Thompson, Cumming and Thompson, headquartered at 24 King Street West, Toronto. Nicol Thompson was advertised as the popular Hamilton professional and golf architect, George Cumming as the celebrated Toronto professional and golf architect, and Stanley Thompson as the young amateur recently returned from overseas. Young Stanley's speciality (the advertisement said) was landscape gardening – he had taken courses in this profession.

Everybody in Canadian golf had heard of George Cumming and Nicol Thompson. In addition to his successes as a player, Nicol had laid out courses at Midland and at Niagara Falls, New York. Few had heard of Stanley Thompson. He had still to make a name for himself in national amateur golf. So young Stanley, whether by accident or design, did a first class job of promoting himself, by linking his name with two highly respected professionals.

The firm of Thompson, Cumming and Thompson (TCT) took over the jobs that George Cumming and Nicol Thompson had initiated when working for themselves. The company was inundated with work. Many clubs had postponed improvements to their courses because of the war, so 1920 would have been a busy year for architects even without the flood of new clubs, all wanting new courses.

Stanley Thompson was advertising in 1923.

The heavy workload of TCT was obviously too much for Cumming and Nicol Thompson. Their first responsibility was, after all, to their clubs. In April 1921 TCT announced that, owing to stress of business, it had sold its interests to Lewis and Thompson Inc. (L & T), with offices in New York, Philadelphia, and 24 King Street West, Toronto. Lewis was a U.S. contractor engaged in constructing golf courses, among other things. The managing director of L & T, Stanley Thompson, was reported to have a number of golf course construction contracts in hand. His brother Frank also moved to L & T.

L & T lasted for less than a year. With more business than he could handle, Stanley Thompson set up his own company in January 1922.

Stanley Thompson and Company Limited of Toronto, Montreal, and Cleveland, was capitalized at $75,000, with Stanley Thompson as president, Frank as secretary-treasurer, and Ken Walton as chief engineer. The company undertook not only to design and construct golf courses, bowling greens, tennis courts, polo grounds, and city parks, but also to maintain these facilities. On its payroll were such specialists as landscape architects, plant pathologists, a soil chemist, a tree surgeon, and a town planner. A visitor to the company's head office in King Street in January 1922 came away with the impression that "every city, town and village in the country has come under the strange spell of the game [golf] and is taking it up eagerly."

His excitement is easy to understand. In its first year, the company got away to a flying start. The company had taken over the uncompleted and new work of TCT and L & T and within a few months was working on facilities for the new Thornhill and Lake Shore clubs in Toronto, and for the Royal Muskoka Hotel. Before mid-summer, it had acquired the contract for constructing the course at York Downs (designed by Captain Alison of Alison, Colt, and Mackenzie). It was busy on links for the clubs at Cedar Brook, Toronto; Burlington; Elgin G & CC; and Halifax G & CC, at Ashburn. The contracts for courses at Toronto's Uplands and at Lingan CC, Sydney, appear to have been agreed a few months later.

The speed with which the company could turn farmland into golf courses so impressed the visiting Arthur Field of the Cleveland *News-Leader* that he wrote in October of that year:

> When it comes to turning farms into golf courses, you have to hand it to Ontario. In April, the Longstaff estate and surrounding farm at Thornhill was just that. Today, there is a nice little general club house, a ladies' club house, the old two-storey stable has been transformed into a dandy locker-room for men, there is a caddie house, and thirteen holes have been made good enough for golf. That is hustling, brothers! Indeed, they tell me that April saw the first work on the Thornhill Golf and Country Club Ltd., and May 24th saw golfers manhandling the elusive pill on a few rough holes. If anyone can beat that for speed, I would like to hear of it.

Early in 1924, CNR asked Thompson to look at its Rocky Mountain resort of Jasper, with a view to giving it an eighteen-hole golf course. The company's Jasper Park Lodge could already accommodate 350 guests. When company president and chairman Sir Henry Thornton had visited the lodge, he – as a keen golfer – had concluded that it needed a first-class course if it was to continue to attract first-class patrons.

Stanley Thompson first visited Jasper in May 1924. He chose a site with outstanding views. But in a *Canadian Golfer* article on Jasper published in 1924 he made it clear that beautiful scenery did not necessarily make it a magnificent golf course: ". . . the principle observed in planning the course has been that the golf should be sufficiently high-class to justify itself apart altogether from the extraordinary setting in which the course is being placed. While there are peaks of great height and extraordinary grandeur in the distance surrounding the entire course, yet the terrain actually utilized for the course construction is only such as is proper for good golf."

The route chosen by Thompson was more or less circular, with very little paralleling. Many holes cut through forest; three were flanked by Lake Beauvert. Special attention was given to the contouring of the greens; as far as possible, the natural slopes were preserved. The plan for bunkering made it a stiff course for the scratch player, but there was always a way around for the shorter hitter who could place his shots.

Clearing the site of timber and boulders took up all the summer of 1924, requiring fifty teams of horses and five hundred men. The first nine holes were opened by Field Marshal Earl Haig in July 1925, the full eighteen in the summer of the following year.

The magnificent Jasper, no matter how much it cost, made Stanley Thompson an architect of international repute. Its seal of approval as a championship course was given in 1929, when the RCGA chose it as the venue for the Canadian Amateur Championship. This was the first time that the association had selected a course west of Winnipeg. CNR ran a special train for the event, bringing to Jasper a large contingent of the Eastern press, as well as golfers, to marvel at the grandeur of this layout in the Rockies.

Banff followed, two years later. In June 1927, CPR commissioned Stanley Thompson to look over the links at its Banff Springs Hotel ("the course on top of the world"), which it had recently taken over from the Dominion government. This course had been laid out by William Thomson, and upgraded by Donald Ross in 1919. CPR wanted an eighteen-hole

Four of Stanley Thompson's courses

The par-three "Cauldron" hole at Banff Springs.

The first hole at Royal York GC (St. George's G & CC) shortly after it opened, in 1930.

Digby Pines Hotel Golf Course, Nova Scotia.

Capilano Golf Club, Vancouver.

layout that would outclass all other resorts in North America.

Thompson laid out a new course with three sets of tees: the longest, 6,640 yards for scratch golfers, the shortest, 6,045 yards, for ladies. The bunkering and tees were arranged so as to give, in effect, three different courses. The fairways were doubly wide, to give two distinct routes to each hole; for the bold, a short route harassed by bunkers, with the reward a birdie; for the short hitter, a longer route free from bunkers, with the reward a par.

As a golf course, Banff was as fine a test as you would find anywhere in the 1920s. Like Jasper, its setting in the Canadian Rockies made it superb. The cost of the course alone was reportedly some half a million dollars, since large quantities of rock had to be blasted away, to convert mountains into molehills. This staggering sum made Banff the most expensive course ever built, anywhere.

It opened for play in 1929 and was soon acclaimed as Thompson's masterpiece. In the high-altitude, rarified air of Jasper and Banff, golfers found that a well-struck ball might go anywhere from 5 to 10 per cent farther than at sea-level. But to counter this, the mountains caused optical illusions, and distances often looked much less than they were.

CPR was obviously happy with Thompson's work at Banff. In 1929, it commissioned him to construct the course for Toronto's Royal York Hotel (St. George's G & CC). Today this course ranks in Canada's top ten. In the same year, CPR had him design a course at Digby, to go with its New Pines Hotel. He laid this out sloping towards a stream in the centre, so that almost the entire course could be seen from each individual fairway. The stream also provided a source of artificial lakes.

Other Stanley Thompson gems were still to come, notably Vancouver's Capilano in the late 1930s. But his genius surfaced and flourished in the 1920s. After Jasper and Banff, he was arguably the world's number-one architect.

Clinton "Robbie" Robinson and Howard Watson joined Thompson's firm in 1929, in the midst of the Depression, at a time when

C. E. (Robbie) Robinson, one of several noted architects who worked for Stanley Thompson.

Guelph graduates were eager for any kind of work. But Depression or no, 1929 was still a busy year for the company.

The country had also been seized by a craze for miniature, or Tom Thumb, golf courses, and Thompson was then busy on several of these, including one at the Old Mill, Bloor Street, Toronto. Another, on Yonge Street, close to the heart of downtown Toronto, had holes ranging from 20 to 65 yards.

The owners of these courses simply coined money. "Even the picture houses are seriously feeling the competition . . . enthusiasts are especially evident in the evening and for that matter well onto midnight and even after that hour. Not since the days of ping pong has any game so caught the popular fancy," said *Canadian Golfer* in August 1930. The craze was to die as swiftly as it had been born.

It was about this time that a young Cornell University graduate by the name of Robert Trent Jones joined the firm. Early in 1932, Stanley Thompson and Company Limited reorganized under the name of Thompson,

A Tom Thumb course on the roof of Montreal's Mount Royal Hotel, 1929.

Jones and Thompson, the second Thompson being Stanley's elder brother, William J. (Bill).

While in Toronto, Jones wrote an article on the artificial watering of courses, something we now take for granted:

> It really is a bit embarrassing to a designer of a high-class golf course to see a player like Sarazen get home with a drive and a spade on a hole 450 yards long. Furthermore, it is not conclusive proof that the winner would necessarily be the best under normal circumstances. After playing over the Royal York [St. George's] in the Canadian Open Championship of 1933, Gene Sarazen said to me, "This would be one of the hardest tests of high-class golf in the world if it had a fairway irrigation system." Who is in a better position to utter such a pungent statement?

In North America at least, we take it for granted nowadays that the course used for a national championship will have a watering system on its fairways. Today the weather has much less influence on how a course will play, wind and not rain being the main factor that can alter its effective length.

These two men of genius, Stanley Thompson and Robert Trent Jones, worked together for only a few short years. Jones then went out into the world to put into practice under his own name all that he had learned from his master and all that he had been teaching his master. Writing in *The New Yorker* in 1951, Herbert Warren Wind selected Thompson, Jones, and Alistair Mackenzie as those who "have taken a lead in the effort to keep golf course design pure and to preserve the integrity, the strategic challenges, and the natural looks of the best holes of the best Scottish links."

In 1940, Stanley Thompson and a Toronto syndicate headed by Fred Hoblitzel purchased the Cutten Fields Country Club at Guelph. Frank Thompson was installed as manager and Stanley came to live there in his Dormie House. (Legend has it he believed a large sum of money had been hidden in a wall by a previous owner.) Nicol Thompson Jr. became the club's professional. Later, Stanley Thompson's widowed sister moved to Cutten and became the manager of the club.

We tend to forget that Stanley Thompson was still playing competitive golf in the 1930s; in 1934 he reached the semi-finals of the Ontario Amateur.

On 4 January 1953, at the age of fifty-nine, Stanley Thompson had a heart attack at the Royal York Hotel on his way to lay out golf courses in South America. He died the same day in the Toronto Western Hospital. Hilles Pickens wrote of his passing in *Canadian Sport Monthly*:

> Scion of the greatest golfing family in Canadian history, Stan was unchallenged for a number of years as the finest golf architect in the world. His courses, some 200 of them, stand as living memorials to his ability. Stanley was the debonair gentleman in good times and bad . . . an exponent of the grand manner in life, capable of re-couping lost fortunes with the magnificent flourish of a fictional character. Yet there was a shyness about him that was in marked contrast to his great zeal for his work and his mode of living. He bore the mark of genius; gave much to life and left us, who remember and loved him, the lifelong thrill of taking mashie in hand and duelling with his unmistable [sic] artistry for the rest of our days. His courses, like his friendship, only become more intriguing and mellower, with

the passing of time, yet his twinkle and spark will be missed as long as a single golfer who knew him continues to play the game.

Pickens's word to describe Stanley Thompson's unmistakable artistry came out in print as *unmistable*. Stanley Thompson's vision, his artistry, was indeed unmistable, in the sense that his legacies to us continue to shine, undimmed by time.

The new expensive courses of the 1920s brought to a head the problem of how to keep turf in good shape in a country where turfgrass is subjected to extremes of temperature.

The RCGA tried to instill a cross-country interest through its Green Section, which was set up in 1924 but did little after its first two years because of a lack of funds. It was left to provincial golf associations as well as to associations of greenkeepers to carry on. The Golf Greenkeepers Association of Ontario, the first such association, was also formed in 1924. Much of its practical work was done in conjunction with the Ontario Agricultural College (now the University of Guelph).

The care of the golf course in Canada was not institutionalized nationally until after the Second World War. The RCGA's Green Section was revived in 1949, and had soon started to organize annual turfgrass conferences, one of the benefits of the Dollar-a-Year Plan. In 1966, the newly formed Canadian Golf Course Superintendents Association (CGSA) took a hand in running these conferences, and from 1975 it took over the responsibility entirely. The CGSA also set up the Canadian Turfgrass Research Foundation, run jointly with the RCGA.

CHAPTER

SECOND GEAR: WHAT WE WORE ON THE LINKS

He bought two gaudy scarlet coats
Brass-buttoned with green collars
His knickerbockers made the bill
Close to $100.

– *Orillia Times*, 1899.

THE EARLIEST ENGRAVINGS OF GOLFERS in Britain suggest that they played in their everyday clothes, from the shoes up. With the formation of the first clubs in the eighteenth century, members – all men, of course – started to wear uniforms, usually red frock-coats with white hose. The red coats were only partly ceremonial. The uniform did serve to distinguish them from the general public, but it also served to warn pedestrians on the common to look out for flying golf balls.

By the middle of the nineteenth century, customs had changed. Reminiscing in 1898, an old St. Andrews golfer noted that "very few of the ancients [of the mid-century] wore red coats . . .

the great majority elected to play in what must have been the oldest and most cherished garments from their wardrobes. Consequently, a medal day at St. Andrews, or Musselburgh, did not reveal much sartorial trump."

In the British Amateur championship of 1892, there was not a single red-coated competitor. The British magazine *Golf* saw this as just one more example of how standards had lowered since the game in Scotland had become democratic and spread to the middle classes; it was no longer a pastime belonging to "the landed gentry, the advocates, the highly placed Government officials, and the well-to-do professional classes." The red coat, after all, added a couple of pounds to the annual cost of playing golf. By and large, male golfers in Britain had taken to wearing just about anything else by the 1890s.

When the Scots brought the game to Canada in the 1870s, they revived the old custom of playing in a red coat, with a heavy pair of walk-

373

These eighteenth-century golf clothes in Britain were just what you wore every day.

ing shoes, usually with tackets on the sole. They wore the coat with trousers, rather than hose and breeches (it also served the useful purpose of alerting the public walking on Fletcher's Field or Cove Fields to the presence of flying golf balls). A newspaper report of the match between Royal Montreal and Royal Quebec in October 1893 describes the scene:

> When the players were scattered over the side of the old Mount Royal, they presented a pretty sight, for the bright scarlet coats of the golfers were in pleasant harmony with the bright autumnal tints of the leaves, so soon to fall and be buried under a mantle of snow.

That was all very well for Canada in October. There is evidence that the coats came off in the summer months, tradition or no.

Golfers were still wearing the red (or hunting pink) coat at the turn of the century, and on many courses it appears to have persisted until the First World War. This note on the latest sartorial fashions comes from *Saturday Night* in 1900:

> The fashion in men's golfing costumes has undergone some change. Not long ago the knickerbockers, or "golfies," as the uninitiated call them, were the correct things to wear when playing the royal and ancient game. To-day these are superseded to a great extent by the long flannel trousers and gay-colored half-hose. The regulation pink coat and grey crush hat, with particolored band, lend an additional dash of color to the make-up. The latest novelty in neckwear is a large silk scarf folded as if for a sash, caught at the neckband in front, crossed at the back, and the ends knotted in front, this being found a most comfortable and effective neckdress.

The courses shown on these pages are a sampling of the work of some early golf course architects.

Calgary Golf and Country Club, designed by Willie Park.   PHOTO BY MICHAEL FRENCH.

Rosedale Golf Club, Toronto, a Bendelow course rebuilt by Donald Ross. PHOTO BY MICHAEL FRENCH.

Summit Golf and Country Club, Toronto, designed by George Cumming and George Lyon, modified by Stanley Thompson. PHOTO BY MICHAEL FRENCH.

Essex Golf and Country Club, Ontario, designed by Donald Ross. PHOTO BY MICHAEL FRENCH.

Royal Colwood Golf Club, B. C., designed by A. Vernon Macan. PHOTO BY MICHAEL FRENCH.

Jasper Park Lodge Golf Course, designed by Stanley Thompson. PHOTO BY MICHAEL FRENCH.

Banff Springs Golf Course, designed by William Thomson, rebuilt by Stanley Thompson. PHOTO BY MICHAEL FRENCH.

Royal Ottawa Golf Club, a Bendelow course modified by Donald Ross. PHOTO BY MICHAEL FRENCH.

The silk scarf replaced the tie, but it was a passing fad.

The "golfies" were much more sensible than the trouser in wet grass, but some golfers complained that the cuff at the knee restricted their freedom of action. Too, insects could bite through their hose. So those who still preferred the knickerbockers over trousers took to wearing leggings, or long spats, with them. Effective perhaps, but not too elegant.

With the knickerbockers they might wear a Norfolk jacket, a popular item in Canada until the late 1920s. Its large patch pockets held tee-moulds, balls, pipes, and tobacco. In the summer, the jacket, but not the tie, was discarded, and men played in long-sleeved white shirts, ties, and linen trousers or white linen knickerbockers.

The peaked tweed cap had become popular in the 1890s, although some men wore deerstalkers or straw hats. Again, these would be discarded for light linen hats in the summer.

The important difference between the British and the North American golfer in the way of dress was that a coat, or jacket, was a *sine qua non* of British golf until the 1930s. No matter the temperature of the day, the British male golfer was not to be seen on the links without jacket and tie.

British golfers visiting Canada were reluctant to discard their jackets, even in the summer. The governor general the Duke of Connaught obviously did not believe that the British convention need be followed in Canada, since he was often to be seen golfing over Royal Ottawa in his shirtsleeves.

A growing concern to clubs in the 1920s was the damage being done to greens and to

The golfing coat was de rigueur *in 1915.*

Geoffrey Turpin (Amateur champion in 1913) in a Norfolk suit, in 1922.

clubhouse floors by golf spikes, now longer and sharper. Several manufacturers brought out golf shoes with rubber or leather studs, but these never caught on.

The knickerbocker, in the form of "plus-fours," soon became popular again, although some golfers had never discarded them for the trouser. Harry Vardon wore them when he came to Canada in 1900 and 1913 – he was said to be the first professional to do so – and that was good enough for many golfers. By 1929, Walter Hagen considered them a necessity. ("When one goes back to long trousers after playing golf in knickers he feels as if something were radically wrong, and it is, as long trousers flapping in the wind are not a help to one's game.")

In the 1930s, a few Canadian golfers started to appear in shorts. Jack Cameron played in shorts for some years. In the West, particularly in Winnipeg, shorts became a (short-lived) fad.

In the late 1930s, Hilles Pickens devoted more than one editorial in *Canadian Golfer* to complaints about the growing sloppiness of men's wear on the links:

> The fact that players of every sort and class can win a place on an Interprovincial team is a grand democratic thing which opens the

portals of a splendid association to some slightly less fortunate. But when such players arrive to represent their provinces . . . they then have a responsibility to the game and to this association they have gained, *in their appearances.* This year, we noted what struck many as TOO MUCH NONCHALANCE IN THE DRESS of many competitors . . . Those appearing in such gards [sic] as sleeveless sweaters *without shirts* have no place, we at least feel, in Canada's Amateur classic. Golf is a gentleman's game – with this goes neatness of appearance.

By the end of the Second World War, the tie had been abandoned on Canadian links. The introduction of the T-shirt did not sit well with many. Here is Pickens again, still complaining about the sartorial habits at the Amateur:

> One fellow showed up wearing braces. One came on the tee with dirty old shorts, hardly respectable in length. Short, unlaundered socks, unshined shoes and a hat so battered it defies accurate description. On top of this his T-shirt was dirty and ragged – hanging out of his trousers all around . . .

We had come a long way.

By the time golf became all the craze in the early 1890s, the bicycle had already liberated many North American women from the strictures of Victorianism and three layers of petticoats.

Newspapers and magazines had carried photographs of British women golfers. These showed Lady Margaret Scott in full, unhampered swing, with a silk blouse wrapped about her figure, a corduroy skirt, sailor hat, and heavy shoes. "It is evident, also, that this lady wears no stays," wrote New York's *Cosmopolitan* magazine approvingly, in 1896. It went on to advise its women readers what to wear for golf:

> A brown cloth skirt, with gaiters and knickerbockers, a blouse or shirt of flannel, silk, or

Jack Cameron invariably wore shorts, and on this one day in 1933 was copied by three friends. Left to right, *Eddie Innes, Phil Farley, Jack Cameron, Gordon B. Taylor.*

The earliest dresses came down over the ankles.

any wash material to suit the weather and the season, with an easily adjustable coat like a Norfolk jacket, and a close hat of felt or straw without flowers – these are the wearable and advisable elements of a golf toilet. A golf skirt should be of heavy material, and should come to the ankles. A shorter length is both undesirable and unnecessary. A red coat as a uniform is attractive, and would look well with the linen skirts which one wears in the summer.

Photographs of the 1890s show this ensemble to be popular attire in Canada. The bottom of the skirt was trimmed with leather to prevent wear. The skirt had at least two drawbacks. In wet weather it soaked up moisture and dragged in the mud. In windy weather, its movements distracted the player while she was playing her shot. So women took to wearing a device known as a "Miss Higgins." This was a band of elastic webbing, which the golfer slipped down over her knees when addressing the ball. It acted as a flexible strait-

jacket, which might seem a contradiction in terms, but which best describes its function.

In the colder months, Canadian women golfers, like most of the men, wore red coats or jackets. "It was . . . comforting to see the scarlet coats of the players scattered over the course," wrote *Saturday Night* of the Rosedale– High Park ladies' interclub match in 1898. At least one of the players wore a black and scarlet tam. Again, at the 1902 ladies' championships, held in the fall, "All the players wore the traditional red coats and natty walking skirts."

In her book, *Ladies' Golf* (1904), May Hezlet advises British women golfers to wear "a short skirt - really short, not simply a couple of inches off the ground." Which meant three or four inches at the most. Canadian women golfers wore skirts of about that length.

Some wore knitted jerseys or cardigans in colder weather, and golf capes; others, scarlet waistcoats. The straw boater for ladies gave way to other fashions. Here, *Saturday Night* in the summer of 1899:

Miss Linton of Royal Montreal in 1900 wore a red jacket, grey skirt, high-collared shirt, and used woods with spliced (oval) necks.

This Canadian Miss of 1904 wore a reddish sweater, an off-white skirt, and a high-necked shirt and tie.

The picturesque poke bonnets are the fashion – dainty things of white and shaded organdie with ruckings around the edge and wide strings under their chins – the picturesque pokes of our grandmothers . . .

And the same magazine a year later:

Fashions for golfing women have not changed very much since the fall. The skirt and jacket are of reversible cloth, the plain side forming the collar and cuffs of the jacket, and sometimes the narrow hem of the skirt. . . .

The skirt is made with a little more fullness on account of the box pleat, which now relieves the flat effect that was so noticeable at the back of last year's skirts. The opening is at one side only. . . . The broad cowboy hat is replaced by a neat "Alpine" of felt to match the frock, or of skirt material. . . .

The long quills that were so popular have given way to silk pompoms of color to match the hat.

Some ladies switched to the tam–o'-shanter, which was not considered *de rigueur*.

With skirts shortened, the shoe became visible. In spite of the advice given to lady golfers that heels should be broad and flat, photographs show that many still wore semi-high heels, which must have wrought havoc with wet greens. The soles had tackets, or hobnails, making the shoes heavy. One enterprising manufacturer made a slip-on rubber sole with rubber studs, which proved popular with men and women.

The First World War brought a shorter skirt, "a really short skirt, providing one's ankles and feet will permit it, of course," according to one authority. Really short, then, meant showing perhaps eight inches of leg. The war also brought more colourful blouses. Some

An example of the headgear of the 1890s.

The **"Kylemore"**
(Registered No...)

Rainproof Sporting Overcoat.

PERFECT FREEDOM
IN
ANY POSITION.

Price £4 4s.

For Walking,
Driving,
Golfing,
Fishing,
Motoring,
& all Outdoor Sports.

GUARANTEED
WATERPROOF.

Weight 2½ lbs.

A popular form of waterproof around 1900.

THREE NEW GOLF HATS

A sampling of golf hats at the turn of the century.

Slip-on golf shoes of 1900.

professional shops began selling brightly coloured silk, or artificial silk, sweaters.

In the early 1920s, there was a movement to get women out of flapping skirts and into knickerbockers, but it met with limited success. In 1923, many prominent lady golfers in Winnipeg appeared on the links in knickerbockers, and the same costume was seen on at least one Ontario course. But the craze did not catch on. Instead, the multiple petticoat disappeared, skirts moved up something like an inch a year and became lighter, so that by the mid 1920s there was no further need for "Miss Higgins."

The British woman golfer was as much tied to tradition as the man. When Cecil Leitch came to Canada in 1920 to play in our championships, she remarked on the fact that she was playing in a heavy, button-up woollen sweater and a dark woollen skirt, when all around her were dressed for a Canadian summer: "It was a most attractive sight to see dozens of women in

. . . and shorter. A cartoon by Paul Goold of 1917: "all dressed up in her golfing clothes."

Mrs. Glassco of Beaconsfield just before the First World War, when skirts were getting shorter . . .

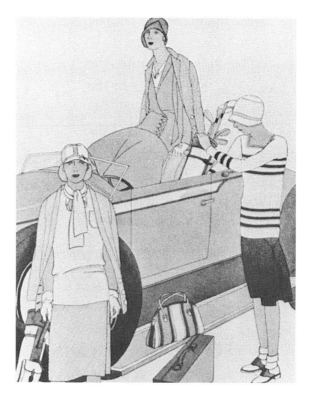

And shorter still. The Flapper age of the 1920s.

white skirts and thin sweaters (or jumpers, as we would call them) with the turn-down collar and turn-back cuffs of a light blouse, and a narrow waist belt completing a truly becoming outfit."

GOLF KNICKERS

"CROWN" GOLF KNICKERS are made to answer every outdoor requirement.

Golf knickers for ladies, as advertised in Canada in 1923, never caught on.

Left: *Ada Mackenzie,* right, *and Mrs. Murdoch of Humber Valley, in the 1924 championships, before Ada had her sportswear shop.*

Above: *Ada had more sensible wear in 1933.*

The all-knit dress or sports suit – sweater and skirt – of the mid-1920s, the skirt perhaps three inches below the knee, was all very well so long as the weather was fine. In rain, it might absorb moisture with disastrous consequences. In 1925, Ada Mackenzie was playing in the U.S. Ladies' championships at St. Louis. A U.S. publication carried this rather unkind report of her match:

The most comical incident of the week was in the Mackenzie–Collett match. Mackenzie wore a two-piece knitted dress, and the more it rained, the more the dress stretched. Mackenzie, extremely tall and thin, looked taller and thinner as the match neared the eighteenth green, with her skirt hanging down to her heels. But to make it funnier, she had a friend, a short chubby woman, who followed the match the whole way. This friend was also wearing a knitted frock similar to Mackenzie's, but it was evident that the two dresses did not come out of the same factory, nor from the same country, for the

friend's dress began to shrink with the rain, and it shrank and shrank until the cuffs were drawn well above her elbows, and the skirt diminished in about the same proportion, but she was loyal to her friend, the Canadian champion, until the last putt dropped.

It was experiences such as this that persuaded Ada Mackenzie to open her own quality sportswear store in Toronto.

In 1933, a Gloria Minoprio turned up for the English ladies' championships wearing a pair of tight-fitting dark flannel trousers, which today hang in the Women Golfers' Museum in Edinburgh. Her outfit caused quite a stir in golfing circles, but there was nothing in the rules to prevent her wearing a bathing suit if she wanted. The lady was eccentric in other ways – she played with only one club.

A year later, a Miss Barron turned out to play for Wales in grey flannel trousers, a pullover sweater, and a beret. Apparently she had been playing in such a garb for some time. The view in Canada was that her example would not

The cloche hat was popular in 1928, when these four CLGU *members travelled to Alberta:* left to right, *Mrs. K. C. Allen (Manitoba champion), Helen Paget (Quebec champion), Mrs. R. K. Bearisto (six times the Manitoba champion), and Evelyn Mills of Ontario.*

Nora Combe Paterson of Victoria also wore fancy hose in 1929 when winning the Empress Hotel Ladies' championship.

lead to a general adoption of the ensemble. But within a year or so, trousers were to be seen on most courses, although still not common or particularly popular with the members. Their adoption was probably hastened by the increasing use of waterproof trousers as rainwear. Women golfers had tried waterproof capes and coats and found them wanting, and umbrellas protected only part of the figure.

In the mid-1930s, the young lady of the links might wear a frock of white silk crêpe with a polka-dot trim, a belt to match, a lightweight panama hat, square-toed walking shoes with spikes, and one or two doeskin gloves. Holt Renfrew sold a "Caddie Pocket" dress in striped chambray for $18.75.

The increasing use of synthetic fabrics quickly changed fashions after the Second World War. In the 1950 Ontario Junior Girls' championships the costumes came in for as much comment as the play (". . . entries wore rainbow ensembles, including perky hats, jazzy sweaters, and what not"). The colour was a jolt to Ada Mackenzie, particularly the flamboyant plaid cap, brilliant yellow sweater, and blue skirt of the girl who came second, Marlene Stewart. For the first time, women started to appear on the course without stockings.

By the 1960s, culottes were said to be running a close second to Bermuda shorts. And we now had the "See-Thru," a golfing umbrella with a transparent plastic window. Miss Higgins would have been surprised to discover that the outfit could now be paid for with another piece of plastic.

Marlene Stewart and Roma Neundorf were forbidden by the Ontario Ladies' Golf Association to wear Bermuda shorts at Weston G & CC in 1957.

25

DEPRESSION, DROUGHT, AND THE SECOND WORLD WAR

BY 1930, GOLF'S YEARS OF GROWTH AND expansion had come to an end. The boom was over. The world had been plunged into an economic depression – the Great Depression – the worst in living memory.

No sport escaped its effects, but golf appears to have survived better than most. In 1933, the editor of *Golf and Sports Illustrated* congratulated the golfing fraternity on having come through with few fatalities:

> Up to the time of writing this article, the most encouraging phase of the situation is that we have not been notified of the actual closing down of one golf club. . . . It is doubtful if there is any other business, or any other organization in Canada, that can show such a marvellous record as this, and it certainly speaks volumes for the game of golf, those who play it, and those who manage it.

Alas, he was out of touch with reality. Perhaps none of the well-known city clubs had to close, but it was a different story with the small rural clubs in the Prairies. To make matters worse for Canada's wheat belt, the early 1930s were years of prolonged drought. Farms and communities disappeared. The years 1931–41 saw a net migration of a quarter of a million people from the Prairie provinces. Canada's per capita income went down by about 50 per cent, that of Alberta fell by 60 per cent, that of Saskatchewan by more than 70 per cent.

In 1932, the same magazine had made a plea for lower caddie fees, unchanged for some years at 65¢ to 75¢ a round. It pointed out that a food basket of eggs, bacon, butter, and bread, which cost $1.86 a few years earlier, cost only 60¢ in 1932. These figures, better than words, illustrate how the Depression had hit the farmer.

As a result, many prairie golf clubs went to the wall. How many is hard to say, since we have no reliable count of the number of clubs in Canada between 1931 and 1954. When the RCGA and the provincial associations did a head count of clubs in 1954 (in other words, after the Depression, the drought, and the Second World War), Saskatchewan had only half the number of clubs it had in 1931, Alberta and Manitoba about two-thirds. Most of these probably disappeared in the 1930s.

All clubs were affected in one way or another. The stock market crash hit many large city clubs. Since the First World War, some of them had acquired the trappings of luxury hotels, and now they had to readjust to severely reduced budgets.

Club committees everywhere started to take a greater interest in the finances of their clubs, applying the same budgetary controls as in their own businesses.

All but a few clubs in the East and on the West Coast appear to have survived the Dirty Thirties. But they lost many members, although they reduced or eliminated entrance fees and cut annual dues, staff, and clubhouse services.

By early 1933, Dundas Valley G & CC had reduced annual dues from $40 to $25; Sarnia, having lost money in 1932, was requiring its professional to work without a salary, to make what he could from coaching; Winnipeg's public courses could not attract enough golfers even at fifty cents a round; its Pine Ridge club was being helped by the sale of bent clippings from its course; Victoria GC had reduced its green fees from $2.00 to $1.50, its entrance fees from $200 to $100; Halifax was managing without a reduction in fees, but only as a result of a successful drive for new members; Lambton had cut out entrance fees entirely.

For some people, life went on much as before. The troubles seemed to flow around them. Provincial and national championships were held, although the Mielke brothers could not attend the Maritime championships in 1931 "because of business conditions." This is one of the few reported instances of the economy of the country intruding into the world of championship golf.

Regardless of the economy, new golf clubs continued to appear. In Toronto, the Woodbine and Cliffside courses were laid out in 1932, and York Downs, Lambton, and Toronto Hunt spent money on improving their courses. General Electric opened a new eighteen-hole course at Peterborough; a new club was formed at St. Mary's. These works were all a boon to the unemployed.

The rest of the 1930s saw a slow recovery in the growth of the game. Then came the war, and clubs had to learn all over again how to deal with falling memberships and shortages.

On the outbreak of the First World War, just about every form of sport had been abandoned and organized sport more or less obliterated. This had not been government policy. The politicians believed that men and women on war work needed some form of relaxation and had a duty to keep fit. But in 1914 there were few sports organizations to see to it that the government's policies were followed. The decision was left up to individuals, and many abstained. Somehow it did not seem right to be playing games when young men and women were dying. Too, people did not want to be branded as unpatriotic.

As evidence of the importance the federal government placed on keeping fit in the Second World War, the National Physical Fitness Act was passed in 1944, and a National Physical Fitness Council was created. Through this council, the government started to give grants to the provinces so they could sponsor sport and health facilities.

From the beginning, sports organizations had made it clear they would not permit sport to die out as it had in 1914. Early in the war, the RCGA came out with a firm policy on wartime golf. The game had to be kept alive. Clubs were urged to give servicemen and servicewomen full playing privileges. Tournaments that required much time, travel, and expense would be cancelled, including the Canadian Amateur and the Junior and the Willingdon Cup. On the other hand, the Canadian Open would go on as usual. Only the leading professionals and a few top amateurs competed in this.

The Open would help to retain interest in the game. It would also serve to demonstrate that playing golf in wartime was officially blessed and that clubs should somehow do their best to keep things going.

Men's provincial golf associations followed this lead. They kept tournaments going so long as there were sufficient entries, a means of transportation, and a supply of golf balls.

The Open championship did become a victim of the war in 1943 and 1944, but only because the PGA severely reduced its tournament schedule. Too many U.S. players were on war work or in the services, and gasoline needed for travel had been rationed.

As in the First World War, golf tournaments raised money for war charities all across Canada. After the 1942 Open, the RCGA sent a cheque to the Red Cross for $1,500, not much by today's standards perhaps, but equal to one-third of the prize money. The B.C. Golf Association outdid all others that year. Vancouver golfers sponsored a Lions Gate Open, raising $7,500 for the RCAF Benevolent Fund, the most successful fund-raising tournament in the country.

As it had in the First World War, the CLGU set an example for the other golf associations in Canada. It decided to postpone all national and provincial championships and to use golf as a means of raising money for the war effort. In 1941, it sent a cheque for $40,000 to the Wings for Britain Fund, money raised by ladies' branches across the country. British newspapers carried a photograph of Spitfire "W" with a note that "this Spitfire was donated by the Canadian Ladies' Golf Union."

After its success with the Spitfire, the CLGU opened The Canadian Ladies' Golf Union War Service Fund. This was as successful as the Madge Neill-Fraser fund had been in the First World War. In all, the CLGU raised more than $81,000 during the war years. And CLGU sewing rooms turned out thousands of garments for war-stricken people.

The CPGA kept its national championship going, except in 1943, and made the Millar match-play tournament a national event. Professionals who were not in the services or on war work organized exhibition matches for war charities, carrying on the tradition of George Cumming and friends in the First World War.

The Spitfire donated by the CLGU.

With few exceptions, golf clubs were severely pinched by the war. An article published at the time said that more than 85 per cent of them managed to keep operating, suggesting that nearly 15 per cent had closed down.

Some clubhouses were requisitioned by the government, but information on which ones was not always made public. In others, the number of staff was cut in half, meal and accommodation services cut out. The older professionals served also as greenkeepers and club managers, often in their time off from war work. Courses were kept open, long grass or no. Hardest hit were clubs some distance from metropolitan centres, since their members had limited transportation.

A few clubs in the West did surprisingly well. After the United States entered the war, Americans stationed at training centres in Alberta helped to give some clubs there a wholesome boost in revenue.

The Second World War did something to reduce the elitist image of golf and golf clubs, by widening the social gates of membership. In 1943, the secretary of the RCGA, B. L. Anderson, saw this as a post-war problem:

> Less fortunate clubs have tried to keep their heads above water by taking in new members whom they might not accept in normal times. These clubs may require years to return to normal status: some, in fact, will never regain normalcy. Thus, a question in management which arises is: "Would it be better to close up for a year or two rather than lower the standard of membership?" . . .

USE THE NEW HITLER RE-PAINTS FOR LONGER DRIVES—EVERY BALL GUARANTEED TO GO FURTHER. UNTIL YOU'VE USED A HITLER RE-PAINT YOU DON'T KNOW YOUR OWN STRENGTH.

Hilter repaints in the Second World War.

What will the standard be after the war? New conditions of equality of men and women and standards of living and society will come into being all over the world.

For many golfers who carried on playing, an uncut golf ball became a treasure. In 1944, a dozen pre-war balls fetched $77 at a Scarboro raffle. A shortage of rubber meant that manufacturers soon stopped making new balls and concentrated on reprocessing old ones, giving them new covers. Reconditioned golf balls were graded, 1 to 4, according to quality. Many golf balls sent for reconditioning were in such a poor state that they were fit only for grades 3 and 4, the cheapest and most plentiful. Grades 1 and 2 were very scarce and established their own black market.

The Province of Quebec Golf Association was typical of many bodies that organized major hunts for golf balls. Its program included: recovery of balls from homes where golfers were no longer active; local Boy Scout contests, with prizes to the Scout group that could find the greatest numbers of golf balls; posters in clubs and department stores, and the use of stores as depots for returned balls; and direct advertising in the press. Just how successful the Quebec Old Ball Committee was has not been recorded publicly.

The manufacture of golf clubs and equipment in Canada ceased in October 1942. Stocks were sold out within a few months. But people could play with old clubs, and the shortage of new clubs was never a problem – except to those who made a living by selling them.

PART FIVE

GOLF INTERNATIONAL 1945 - 1974

(Over) *Marlene Stewart, wearing her Stewart tartan tammy, after winning the Ontario Ladies' Championship in 1951.*

26

THE TIDE OF COMMERCIALISM

THE FORTY-FIVE YEARS SINCE THE END of the Second World War have witnessed a number of remarkable events in the world of golf. George Lyon would be astonished to learn that a man had hit a 6-iron on the moon. He would also be impressed to hear that by pushing a couple of buttons on a box in the corner of the living room he could watch, live, the British Open. He would not believe that a professional golfer who had not won a tournament in years could be the highest-paid sporting figure in the world.

The world of golf has become much bigger since he last saw it in the 1930s. In other ways, it has become much smaller. In his day, an international team of Canadians going overseas had to reckon on being away a month. Sending golfers abroad was quite an event. Today, Canada flies teams all over the world, men and women, all the time. You can now jet a golfer from New Zealand to Canada in a shorter time than it took Robert Bethune to transport members of his Ontario team from Brantford to Quebec in the 1880s.

But if commercial jet travel, commercial television broadcasts, and commercial endorse-ments have helped to commercialize the game since the Second World War, they have also made it grow and undergo great social change.

Although golf boomed immediately after the First World War, there was no such phenomenon after the Second. During the late 1940s and early 1950s, the number of golf facilities in Canada appears to have climbed slowly to reach the six hundred mark, but that is where it had been before the years of depression and drought.

The post-war boom in golf got under way in the second half of the 1950s, but for a year or so growth barely kept pace with population. In the 1960s, however, we added something like three hundred new courses, and by 1970 we had close to one thousand.

Since 1984, the Canadian Golf Foundation or CGF (an offshoot of the RCGA and other ruling bodies) has been compiling statistics on the number of golf courses in Canada. Its figures for 1989 show that there were 1,571 courses in the country. Of these, 902 were public courses and 669 were private or semi-private courses. (Semi-private courses have members, but also allow the public to play at certain times and under certain conditions.) The CGF's figures suggest that semi-private courses outnumbered private courses by nearly two to one, although some courses could not be strictly categorized.

The significance of these figures lies in the number of courses where a golfer can walk in off the street and play by paying only a green fee. In the 1920s these probably comprised only some 20 per cent of the courses in Canada; today they comprise close to 80 per cent. The CGF did not at the same time do a survey on the number of golfers in this country, or on how many play at the different types of facility. In the early 1980s, the American-based National Golf Foundation made public such figures for the United States. These figures enable us, by comparison, to arrive at a round figure of about two million golfers in this country in 1989. Probably some 80 per cent of these golfers play over public or semi-private courses.

This did not happen by chance. Right after the war, the RCGA and other associations lobbied for more municipal courses with such bodies as the Canadian Federation of Mayors and Municipalities. In Toronto, to take one city, the fight was long and strenuous. The city did not have any municipal courses in 1949 when lawyer Roy Caldwell set up his Toronto Municipal Golf Association, recruiting such directors as newspaperman Gordon Sinclair and our old professional friend Launcelot Cressy Servos as secretary. Backed by the RCGA and the Ontario Golf Association, they eventually persuaded the Toronto parks department and council that a city with twenty-six private courses needed at least one municipal course for budding young golfers. Thanks to them, the municipal Don Valley course was built in 1951. Later, they were instrumental in converting Lakeview at Port Credit from a private course to a municipal course in Mississauga.

The social pendulum of golf in Canada has thus taken a remarkable swing since the First World War, when golf was played almost exclusively at private clubs.

The public course has made golf affordable. But even this great expansion in public golf facilities has been inadequate to meet the demand. In 1990, private clubs in metropolitan areas such as Toronto had long waiting lists; entrance fees had gone up tenfold in as many years. Public courses are jammed, but around cities where they are needed new ones are not being buil Land is costly, and new courses and clubs ave increasingly been linked to private housing developments. Some sell equity memberships at around $40,000. Golfers who can afford it see this as a quicker and more economically sensible way of getting an assured game of golf than waiting in a five year queue to put up, say, $30,000 as an entrance fee to an established city club. It enables them to sell their memberships at the going rate should they give up golf or leave the city, or should their course be taken over for development.

The periodic spurts of growth in Canadian golf now appear to be more closely linked to the boom periods in the country's economy. But Canada is a large country, and the golf boom has not been evenly distributed, just as the periods of economic boom have not been evenly distributed. At a time when Central Canada was entering an economic and golfing boom, having got over the shock of the high oil prices of the previous ten years, oil-producing Alberta was facing a slump, for the same reason. Under the headline of: "Local golf 'bogeyed' by economic hard times," Allen Panzeri wrote in the *Edmonton Journal* of 13 May 1985:

> Unlike jogging, golf is not recession-proof. It is ... expendable in bad economic times. Which is precisely what happened in Edmonton over the last three years . . . most golf clubs in and around the city, private and public, have suffered, some worse than others.
>
> Private clubs have had to hustle to attract golfers – with offers of reduced fees for new members . . . [one club] has reduced initiation fees for new members to $500 from $2,500.

The growth of golf in Canada, as elsewhere, was fuelled by a number of social changes. Reduced working hours in industry and commerce gave more people the Saturday free for sport. Improvements in real salaries and wages gave them more disposable income. People are living longer, retiring younger, have better pensions, better health, are keener on fitness. These were the same factors that contributed to growth after the First World War. After the Second World War, however, a new joker entered the pack – television.

"Every age has a keyhole to which its eye is pasted," wrote Mary McCarthy. The post-war age of golf has had its eye pasted firmly to the little square box of television.

When president Eisenhower played golf on television, he probably was as influential in popularizing the game as Arthur James Balfour had been in late-Victorian Britain. But it was the televising of major golf tournaments that did the trick in Canada, as in the United States.

The belief that golf had enough appeal as a spectator sport to attract a television audience was slow to take root in North America.

Bing Crosby was a winner of our Jasper Totem Pole in 1947.

Cynics pooh-poohed the idea. The logistics were against it. How, they asked, could you cover eighteen holes spread over several square miles? It would be like trying to cover, simultaneously, eighteen games of football. So it was ten years after the Second World War before anyone tried it seriously. At first it flopped. Then along came a young American professional, Arnold Palmer. The sight of this young man chasing the pack at a U.S. Open, attacking the ball and the course with a seemingly reckless abandon, fired the imagination. Too, he was as American as apple pie, handsome in a rugged way, with a disarming smile that captured the heart. On the course, Arnold let us share his agonies as well as his joys – not for him the stoic suffering of a Willie Park, nourishing ulcers. His face was the barometer of his success. It winced and grimaced and sighed and smiled, just like that of any 24-handicapper. The spectators at the course and on the box suffered and rejoiced with him. Television's first golfing hero took over the stage, and the viewers shouted encore.

Encores they have been given, ever since. The Canadian and U.S. Opens are now only two of many tournaments on the men's and ladies' professional tours beamed to our homes throughout the year. Golfers now pay weekly homage to the seventy or so professionals who make the cut into the final two rounds. Seventy golfers, out of the twenty million or so who play the game in North America! And even that overstates the nmber, since we see only the few leaders of the pack who tee-off last.

Some of these leaders have been Canadians, but few have stirred the passions. We watched television just the same. The ongoing competition between Arnold Palmer and Jack Nicklaus to be the number-one golfer of the second half of the twentieth century has excited viewers in Canada and Britain as much as it has viewers in the United States. The tele-apotheosis of Palmer and Nicklaus will be studied as a phenomenon of the century, when golf historians come to look back.

Through television, professional golf and amateur golf have nourished each other. The screen has popularized the game, attracting new amateurs. As their numbers have increased, so has the number of viewers. As the number of viewers has increased, so has the amount of money corporations are willing to spend sponsoring professional events and advertising their goods on television. To the playing professional this has meant higher purses. Take the Canadian Open. The prize money has shot up in the last thirty years, from $25,000 in 1960, to $1.2 million in 1990. The RCGA ploughs part of its profits on the Open into the ever-widening field of amateur golf. It now runs many more tournaments than before the days of television, including a mid-Amateur for those too old to compete with college boys, too young to be Seniors.

Corporations have taken over from chambers of commerce as the sponsors of most tour events. The Bugsville Open has become the Swiftcut Razor Bugsville Open. Next year it could be the Softsoap Bugsville Open. No matter who sponsors it, Bugsville will help organize the tournament, and some local charity will benefit.

The Canadian Open had to take on its first sponsor in 1936, and has had only two in fifty-four years. This could be a record for a sponsored event in any sport and speaks well for the sponsor and the RCGA.

Golf on television has nothing like as many viewers as hockey, football, or baseball. But since it appeals to a more affluent audience, viewers are assailed by ads for Cadillacs instead of Chevies, for investment houses instead of cut-price furniture. Television sells more golf clubs than baseball bats; golfers continue to be suckers for promises. Seeking to buy perfection, hard-headed businessmen never ask for a forecast rate of return before forking out a couple of thousand dollars on clubs made of exotic new metals or plastics, guaranteed – in a loose sort of way – to give extra yards off the tee, or to keep the ball straight.

The money from television has meant increased purses. But television has been good to playing professionals in other ways. The mythical image conjured up of the playing professional of the 1920s, with imputations of reckless living, is all but forgotten. The playing professionals on television project a good clean image, are well-dressed, are reasonably articulate and well-behaved, never haggle over million-dollar contracts, never argue with the referee like tennis players, never get into fights like hockey players, never spit like baseball players, and never rough up the opponent like football players. Professional golfers have ". . . some of the highest standards in sports. There are *no* histrionics." This according to no less a figure than Britain's Margaret Thatcher. Top golfers with astute managers like Mark McCormack (at one time the manager for the world's three top players, Palmer, Nicklaus, and Player) were soon earning top money by endorsing products on television, more money than they were making by playing golf. They endorsed not only golf equipment, but promoted all sorts of totally unrelated products, from candy bars to insurance companies to laundry and maid services.

This new supply of wealth in professional golf has resulted in many more playing professionals around the world, competing on circuits other than the PGA Tour. British playing professionals have recovered some of the status they lost to the Americans in the 1920s, and now compete in a European Tour alongside a new breed of playing professional that emerged in Europe. The Americans no longer dominate the game as they did until well into the 1970s.

Only one Canadian – Pat Fletcher in 1954 – has won the Canadian Open in the last seventy-six years. And since no Canadian has won the British or U.S. Open, our professionals have had to be content with less lucrative endorsements, mainly for golf equipment. Yet we have had in Stan Leonard and Al Balding, later in George Knudson, golfers who have won against fields just about as tough as any in the Canadian Open. More recently, our Dave Barr has come within a whisker of winning the U.S. Open. So it can be done, and it will be done.

Our own Gordie Brydson endorsing a golf shirt.

The post-war years saw the start of a U.S. Ladies' Professional Golf Association (LPGA). Now, when not watching the PGA Tour on television, we might watch the LPGA Tour. Our women professional golfers on tour have been about as successful as our men. In Sandra Post we had a world-beater who did win major U.S. events and many others. But women's golf has never been as lucrative, either in prize money or in endorsements, as men's golf. The television audiences are smaller, the sponsors harder to get.

The Canadian professional tour, in spite of occasional outbursts of optimism, has not managed to keep pace, lacking as it does the television personalities of the PGA or European tours. It has less appeal to viewers and hence to sponsors. But in 1990 players competed for purses totalling a million dollars, ten times the figure of a decade ago.

In amateur golf, we have produced several world-class players, men and women. In the 1950s and 1960s, Canada's Marlene Stewart Streit was the finest woman amateur in the world, winner of the Canadian, British, United States, and Australian titles. And in Weslock and Cowan we had two amateurs who could hold their own in any amateur field. Cowan did, twice winning the U.S. Amateur title.

Looking over the fairways of the average golf club, George Lyon would notice one change in our golfing habits – the virtual disappearance of the caddie. When the caddie disappeared, so did the traditional breeding ground for our top golfers.

At one time, just about all the top amateur and professional players in the country had learned their skills caddying. But after the Second World War, summer caddie camps for schoolboys disappeared, and there are few clubs in Canada still holding caddie competitions. Whereas once the ambition of every Canadian schoolboy golfer was to win the caddie competition, it is now to win a golf scholarship to a U.S. college, and to proceed to the PGA Tour.

The rise of college golf was a phenomenon of the 1960s. College golf is almost full-time golf; academic studies are secondary. College golfers are forced on like rhubarb, as Priestley once observed of actors. To take the analogy one step further, it is also true that you can hardly tell one stick from another, so mechanically alike are their swings. All but a handful of the twenty Canadian Amateur Championships between 1971 and 1990 went to players attending (or who had attended) U.S. colleges on scholarships. In these same years, many of the Canadian professionals on the PGA Tour were players who had been through the grindmill of college golf, as are all the Canadian women now on the LPGA Tour.

George Lyon would have noticed that the wheel had replaced the caddie, bringing about

Almost as tall as the ball-washer.

Not all boys . . . The caddiemaster at Royal Montreal in 1920 with one of her caddies.

Note the badges on the caddies of the Halifax GC at the turn of the century.

one of the most noticeable changes in club golf since the Second World War. If the pull-cart reduced the ranks of schoolboy caddies, the motorized golf car all but exterminated them as a species.

Golfers had been experimenting with placing the golf bag on wheels since the turn of the century. But the pull-cart was not commercialized until after the war, and it was an instant success.

Motorized golf cars, fuelled by gasoline or electric batteries, were slower to take hold.

They did not properly begin their gradual growth to popularity until the 1960s. Now there are few private clubs in North America without them, just as there are few in Britain with them. They carry one or two golfers and anything from one to four bags.

Many look upon the motorized golf car as a blessing, a few think it is an abomination. To the club or the club's professional, it has become a lucrative new source of income. More important – and this fully justifies its existence

Caddies were largely replaced by the modern pull-cart, shown here with its Vancouver inventors, Jock Irvine and Clay Puett.

– it has extended the playing career of many old and infirm golfers. But when used by those of sound limb, it has become a source of irritation to traditionalists who insist that golf is a walking game. They cite the use of golf cars as symptomatic of the cheapening of the game in this commercial age.

That is only one of the beefs of many an old golfer. Having seen what has happened to golf since the Second World War, some look back with nostalgia and argue that golf has become too big and impersonal. Many who lived through the 1920s and 1930s will tell you that golf between the wars was simple and beautiful, the pursuit of innocent pleasure. To them, it seems that clubs do not have the same clubbiness; that the flood of commercialism has swept away the true spirit of the game, and many of its traditions. They will insist that golf was never better than before the war; then, with the logic of Alice, they will refer to these years as "the Dirty Thirties," and remind you that the decade was haunted by ghosts of the needy, who could not afford food, never mind golf.

Again paradoxically, these same people will complain that golf has also become too small, that we pay too much attention to an elite few on television and disregard the essential golfer, the amateur.

It is true that the amateur golfer has gradually been forgotten (except by the manufacturer trying to sell him, or her, the latest in implements) or so it would appear on the surface. But the country's golf associations still have thousands of officers and volunteers dedicated to organizing amateur golf tournaments, which are more prolific than ever. Only the spectators and the media have abandoned amateur golf, the one because of the other. And it is probably true that none of this would have happened without the power of that little square box. At least, so argue the sentimentalists. But is the game really that much worse off?

There are those who will argue that golf has *improved* since the war: that the rise of the public golfer has democratized the game; that change will always spell degeneracy to a nostalgic few; that those who golfed before the First World War probably had similar beefs about the brash new world of the 1920s. But those who look back to the good old days are not all petulant and crusty old men and women, and there is probably more than a smidgin of truth to their argument. If you have lived in a village that has become a town or worked for a family firm that has been bought out by a conglomerate, you will have some idea of how these golfers feel, and of what they mean when they say something has been lost in the name of progress.

27

THE AMATEUR GOES WEST

BEFORE THE OUTBREAK OF WAR, THE RCGA had awarded the 1940 Amateur championship to Edmonton's Mayfair G & CC. Mayfair's course in the valley of the North Saskatchewan River is one of the finest tests of golf in the Prairies.

Dr. A. W. (Whit) Matthews of Mayfair chaired the club's committees, under the general supervision of the RCGA's secretary, B. L. Anderson. Everything pointed to an outstanding tournament.

Then, quite suddenly, things went sour in Europe. The "phoney" war became a real war. The RCGA cancelled the Amateur Championship. The committees at Mayfair stood down. All national golf in Canada was suspended. There were to be no national amateur championships for a long and desperate six years.

When the RCGA re-instituted its tournaments after the war, it naturally awarded the Amateur to Edmonton's Mayfair. In 1946, Whit Matthews's plans were dusted off, although he was no longer chairman of the club's committees. (In 1944 he had served as the RCGA's president.) With B. L. Anderson retired, the RCGA's new secretary, Bill Taylor, was now the official in charge.

In any six-year period of a national championship you can expect to see many old faces gradually yield to newcomers emerging from their early teens. The six years of war hastened this process. Coming back to civilian life, some players had to forget about championship golf and concentrate on earning a living. Major Sandy Somerville retired from competition and did not play at Mayfair. Major Gordon B. Taylor, still recovering from a war wound on his left arm, competed for a few more years. Some old faces were absent. Ontario's Joe Thompson had been shot down over Africa. Alberta's Bob Proctor, an artillery officer, had died in Europe.

In the end, and somewhat remarkably, two pre-war favourites fought their way through the field. Witnesses of the 1939 final must have experienced a sense of *déja vu* as Ken Black and Henry Martell once again squared off in 1946, almost seven years to the day after they had met at Mount Bruno. But this time their roles were reversed. Martell, Edmonton's curly-haired golfing policeman, was to have his revenge on perhaps the finest match player in the country, whose job in a Vancouver war plant had left him with little time for anything other than weekend golf.

Henry Martell, the man they called "Hammering Hank," won with an astonishing burst of low scoring in the second round of the 36-hole final, shooting six under par for five holes, including a hole-in-one.

At thirty-four, Henry Martell could go no further in amateur golf. Within a year of his victory at Mayfair, he became the first winner of the Canadian Amateur to turn professional. Ken Black retired from tournament golf to concentrate on business.

Although we could not have guessed it at the time, Martell was the last of the pre-war players to win the Amateur. Thereafter, it went to one of a new breed.

The emergence of new faces in amateur golf during the war years is recorded in the rankings of Canada's top players. From 1935, Hilles Pickens had ranked the top fifteen players in the country. He did this every year until 1956, skipping the years 1940–45, for obvious reasons. His rankings reflected current form.

Five of the top fifteen amateurs of 1939 were still ranked in the top fifteen in 1946. Henry Martell and Ken Black were obvious choices. Phil Farley and Jack Nash had long been in the running for provincial and national titles. Quebec's Rolland Brault had won the provincial title in 1939.

Of the newcomers, the most notable was Nick Weslock, ranked number two. Weslock was to prove himself the country's finest amateur over the next twenty years or so.

Rising stars Rudy Horvath and Bill Ezinicki were promoted to first and second place in the 1947 rankings.

As a sergeant-pilot in the RCAF, Horvath, of Windsor, had won the Western Ontario Championship in 1944, and in 1946 he had reached the quarter finals of the U.S. Public Course Tournament. A year later, he was to win the Ontario Amateur and have the lowest score in the Willingdon Cup matches. Rudy

Horvath turned professional and was among the first Canadians to go on the PGA Tour.

An NHL player, Bill Ezinicki was yet another enthusiast of both hockey and golf. In 1946, by virtue of his daily routine of thirty-six holes plus an hour or so of practice, he earned the sobriquet of "The Horse." He reached the semi-finals of the Amateur, only to be defeated by Ken Black. Short of stature, compact, strong, and superbly conditioned – the result of his NHL training – Ezinicki was reckoned to be the most improved amateur golfer of the year.

Phil Farley was the most resilient of the pre-war amateurs. He had made the rankings when these were re-introduced in 1935 and he remained a ranked amateur until 1954. This fine amateur golfer and golf administrator then gave up the fight for the Canadian Amateur, a title that had eluded him for over twenty years.

After the war, Farley was never to come closer to winning than in 1949, at Riverside, Saint John. Knocking out many of the rising stars, he came to the last hurdle, the American Walker Cup player and U.S. and British champion Dick Chapman.

On the 29th tee at Riverside, it looked as though his home club of Scarboro was in for a long night of celebration, for Farley was 4 up with 8 to go. Although Chapman fought back, Farley was still dormie 2.

At the 35th hole, Farley was on the fringe in two, about 25 feet from the cup. He fretted over the next shot, changing from a 9-iron, to a 7-iron, to a putter. Predictably, he did not leave the ball dead. Nevertheless, a putt of four to five feet would have given him a half and the title. He studied the line for thirty seconds, changed his grip, and putted. His ball did not even touch the hole. Dormie 1. At the 36th, he again took three from the back of the green. The match was all-square.

The sudden-death play-off between Farley and Chapman was never more appropriately named. "One could almost smell the taint of tragedy in the air," one witness recalled. At the second extra hole, Farley heeled his drive, and failed to reach the green with his next. His pitch was 10 feet past. He jabbed at the equalizer, missed it to the right, and conceded. Wrapped in silence and despondency, this normally cheerful man made his way back to the clubhouse.

After this defeat, some writers referred to Phil Farley as "the ageing veteran," forgetting that although he seemed to have been around forever he was only thirty-seven. This made him the same age as George S. Lyon when George took up golf. They forgot, too, that the young veteran Farley was a fighter. It was not in the nature of the man to give up.

Phil Farley's gallant struggle in the 1951 Amateur at Royal Ottawa was to be as fitting a memorial to him as any victory. Everything pointed to this being *his* year. But in the final he met a young Walter McElroy, carrying the hopes of Vancouver.

A party of supporters from Scarboro left at 5:00 a.m. to see Phil win – they hoped – his first Amateur title. They arrived at the end of the morning round, to find him 8 down, but still full of spirit. Some of them debated whether to stay for the afternoon's round or drown their sorrows elsewhere. They stayed, and watched a historic fight-back.

In the afternoon, Phil Farley made one of the greatest recoveries ever seen in the Amateur. Taking hole after hole, he was only 1 down coming to the seventeenth (or 35th). Here, McElroy sunk a 35-foot putt, just when he needed it most. That was good enough to win the hole, and the match by 2 and 1.

The governor general, Viscount Alexander of Tunis, presented the trophies. With McElroy's permission – a generous gesture, this – he first congratulated not the winner, but Phil Farley, for his "magnificent fighting comeback."

This was Phil Farley's last fling. He never again looked like winning the title he had sought for twenty years. It is hard to think of any other Canadian golfer – unless it be Tom Reith in the early years of the century – who has a better claim to be the finest amateur never to win the national title.

Phil Farley was a first-class badminton player. For many years he was also a top contender for curling honours. His keen eye served him as well as a skip on Ontario's rinks as it did on its links. In the 1960s, he had a heart attack. His only concession to his illness was to stop curling for two years.

An RCGA governor for twenty-five years, its president in 1967, several times a CSGA Senior champion, this gentle man still had a lot to give to Canadian golf. He died in 1974, after a short illness, at the age of sixty-two. Rightfully, Phil Farley found his place in the Canadian Golf Hall of Fame. In the world of amateur golf, winning national titles is not everything.

Walter McElroy's win in 1951 was the second consecutive Amateur title to go to a B.C. golfer. Bill Mawhinney had won in 1950. Since only one B.C. golfer, Ken Black, had previously been successful, the victories of Mawhinney and McElroy might suggest that there had been a sudden upsurge in the golfing standards of the West Coast. But, in fact, B.C. had been challenging Ontario's domination for eight years before the Second World War. The province would have had more national amateur titles if its two finest players, Freddie Wood and Stan Leonard, had not turned professional.

The rise of B.C. as a power in amateur golf is reflected by its performance in the Willingdon Cup. From 1931, B.C. entered a team, along with other provinces. The original and ulterior motive for reviving these team matches was soon forgotten; they had very soon stopped being a jolly get-together, a friendly prelude to the Amateur, and had taken on a life of their own.

The Willingdon Cup came to be the most stimulating and testing amateur golf event in the country. The rivalry between provinces became intense. To be selected for a provincial team became a much-coveted honour. The provinces came to plan their internal tournaments around finding the right men for the team. Players who had any hope of being selected turned out for tournaments they might otherwise have passed up, so that local events took on a new importance.

Until 1973, each player in the team of four played two 18-hole rounds, making eight rounds in all. The Willingdon Cup went to the province with the lowest aggregate. One bad round by one player could destroy a team's chances. This made the competition even more intense. A player knew that three other team-mates – to say nothing of the other golfers in his province – were breathing down his neck. All of which brought an excitement and tension to the matches, making them as much a test of mental reserve as of technical ability. For all these reasons, it can be said the Willingdon Cup has done more than any other event to raise the standard of men's amateur golf in this country.

A Willingdon Cup team is made up of the four finest male amateur golfers in a province, so the results of the Cup matches over the years are a more reliable guide to a province's ranking in national golf than is the number of national champions it has produced.

On this basis, the rise of B.C. as a force in national golf clearly goes back to the early 1930s, when it started to come second to Ontario. Since the war, B.C. and Ontario teams have had about the same number of wins in the Willingdon Cup matches.

Ontario has always been the province to beat. It holds just over a third of the nation's

The Ontario team, winners in 1949, left to right, *George Eluck, Phil Farley, Gerry Kesselring, Don Varey.*

population, but proportionally more of the nation's golfers. British Columbia, with less than a third of Ontario's population, does have the advantage that its golfers on the coastal plains can play the year round.

In the years 1947 through 1961, B.C. teams won the Willingdon Cup seven times, and had six second places. For the first few of these years the teams were anchored by Amateur champions Walter McElroy and Bill Mawhinney, in

B.C.'s Willingdon Cup team set a record low score in 1948. Left to right, *Walter McElroy, Bill Mawhinney, J. D. Robertson, Percy Clogg, Hugh Morrison. McElroy and Mawhinney were to win the Amateur.*

One of B.C.'s Golf Schools for Juniors, 1965; the enthusiasm of these professionals was behind B.C.'s successes after the Second World War. Left to right, standing, *Jock McKinnon, Sid Dahl, Roy Gleig, Doug McAlpine, Ken McBride, pupil Jim Russell, and Lyle Crawford.* In front, *Mel White, Roy Hiesler, Ron Fitch, and Al Nelson.*

later years by another Amateur champion, John Johnston. But on their day, other members of B.C. teams were quite capable of winning the national Amateur, notably Bob Kidd, Doug Bajus, Bert Ticehurst, Bob Fleming, Hugh Morrison, and Ron Willey. In the same years, B.C. was also turning out winners of the Canadian Junior, in Mawhinney, Laurie Roland, Gordon MacKenzie, Bill Wakeham, Alan Kennedy, and Terry Campbell, products of B.C.'s long-standing commitment to Junior golf.

Walter McElroy was something of an enigma. He first came to national attention in 1946, as runner-up in the national Junior. Standing five feet ten inches, weighing about 120 pounds, the slender, curly-haired McElroy impressed all who saw him strike a golf ball.

In 1948, at the age of twenty-one, McElroy was ranked number one in the country, having been low amateur in the Canadian Open. But the B.C. and the national amateur titles eluded him. After being heavily defeated by young Mawhinney in *The Vancouver Province*'s Match Play Open, he was criticized by some sports writers as not being able to take it. Soon after, he announced his retirement from tournament golf, saying he wanted to devote his time to his business.

Walter McElroy came from a well-to-do family. As a boy, he had lived next door to Shaughnessy Heights, and he started playing at the age of eight. His family put him in the hands of a fine teacher, Benny Colk of the Langara club. By the time Walter was sixteen, he was sweeping local junior tournaments. Then came six years of problems with a foot ailment, which caused much discomfort, and it, as much as anything, was the cause of his giving up serious golf in 1949.

His story, fortunately, has a happy ending. In 1950, following an operation on his foot, he took up competitive golf again. Spurred on by the urge to prove he was far from through, he went back to serious practice under the guidance of Benny Colk (who was also his brother-in-law). By winning the 1951 Amateur from

Phil Farley, Walter McElroy proved his point. He was to play in B.C. teams until 1954.

Bill Mawhinney, too, overcame obstacles to go on to great triumph. He overcame polio to become such a fine golfer that he won both the national Junior and Amateur. He made an early entry into big-time golf. As the Junior

B.C.'s Mawhinney winning the Junior in 1948.

champion, he found himself at the age of nineteen playing in the 1948 Canadian Open at Shaughnessy Heights. A year later, this tall, slender, serious-looking Westerner took Stan Leonard to the 36th hole of *The Vancouver Province*'s Match Play Open. In 1950, he played in several PGA tournaments.

All this experience helped Mawhinney in his Amateur final that year against a formidable Nick Weslock. Playing the better golf, Mawhinney took the first few holes, was 7 up at lunch, and went on to win by 6 and 4. (At twenty-one, Mawhinney was not the youngest to win the Amateur, as some newspapers reported at the time; Don Carrick still holds that distinction, having won at the age of eighteen.) Bill Mawhinney turned professional in 1952.

British Columbia produced another sensational youngster in Laurie Roland, of Marine Drive. In 1949, only sixteen, he became the B.C. Junior champion, and played in that year's Amateur at Saint John. In the quarter-finals, he disposed of Ernie Crowell, the pride of the Maritimes, a win that made him the youngest golfer ever to reach the semi-finals. He almost caused a sensation when he met the seasoned American, Dick Chapman, but lost on the last hole. "One of the toughest matches in my life," admitted the man who had once held the U.S. and British titles.

In spite of this brilliant debut, Laurie Roland needed three attempts before he finally won the national Junior in 1951. In that year, he was ranked number seven in Canada. But things went sour for this temperamental young man. He reached the semi-finals of the Amateur once again, in 1951, to be squeezed out by Phil Farley. In the same year, he was selected for the Canadian team that played against the U.S. Walker Cup team at Saucon Valley.

Subsequently, Roland played little competitive golf. He was killed in 1957 when a Pacific Western Airline DC-3, which he was co-piloting, crashed at Port Hardy on Vancouver Island.

For seven years after Walter McElroy's win in 1951, the Canadian Amateur went to an Ontario or U.S. golfer. Johnny Johnston brought it back to B.C. in 1959.

Johnston was no golfing prodigy. A highly articulate real-estate salesman, married with three children, Johnston was thirty-four when he won the Amateur, his first major win. It was not that he was a late developer, but rather that he was a man who had decided to focus his efforts on making a living and raising a family before turning to serious golf. He had worked on his game for a year before the Amateur, and had been in B.C.'s Willingdon Cup team in 1958.

Johnny Johnston wins for B.C. in 1959.

In 1959, the Amateur was held at Johnston's home club, Vancouver's Marine Drive. One of those fancied to win was his clubmate, Bob Kidd, playing in B.C.'s Willingdon Cup team for the fifth time, so it came as no surprise when Kidd led the qualifiers with a pair of 69s. Again, when Johnston and Kidd met in the semi-final, the knowledgeable money was on Kidd. But Johnston prevailed handily, by 6 and 5, and went on to meet Ontario's Gary Cowan in the final.

Some fourteen years younger than Johnston, Cowan was then only starting on a long and brilliant career. He was already challenging Nick Weslock in Ontario, and had come out of his first Willingdon Cup as the low individual scorer.

Like so many 36-hole finals of the Amateur, this one developed into two quite separate matches. Johnny Johnston took 68 strokes in his morning round, five fewer than Gary Cowan, and went to lunch 5 holes up.

By the end of the thirteenth in the afternoon, Cowan had won them all back with birdies. The fourteenth hole was pivotal. Having lost a five-hole lead, Johnston could not afford to suffer the psychological blow of fighting from behind. But Cowan helped him by firing an 8-iron over the green at this 147-yard par three, and he helped himself by firing his tee-shot only two feet from the pin.

With Cowan needing to win the eighteenth to keep the match alive, both players were on in two, Johnston some 20 feet away, Cowan just inside. Johnston lagged his putt to within 14 inches. He relaxed, took off his glove, and watched Cowan try for the birdie he needed to survive. Cowan missed by inches. Still, he made Johnny Johnston sink that short putt for the championship. Golf being what it is, who can blame him?

There were other fine B.C. Willingdon Cup players who could not produce their best golf in the Canadian Amateur. Vancouver's tall, lanky Doug Bajus started golf as a boy caddie and never took a lesson in his life. In 1954, when he tied for fourth place in the Canadian Open, he was ranked as the country's top amateur.

Lyle Crawford was runner-up to Ontario's Moe Norman in the 1955 Amateur, defeated at the 39th hole. That year, the Willingdon Cup team of Bajus, Crawford, Kidd, and McCall lopped 17 strokes off the previous record as they walked away with the cup. Their score of 561 has never been equalled.

The rise of B.C. to become a force in national golf was mirrored by Alberta's performance in the 1960s. Until then, this province had never been able to produce a team good enough to finish better than third in the Willingdon Cup.

Alberta did have a sprinkling of the country's finest amateurs right after the First World War and, in the 1930s, produced some fine players in Bob Proctor, Duane Barr, Whit Matthews, and Stew Vickers, as well as the first winner of the Canadian Junior, Jimmy Hogan. When

Henry Martell turned professional, his brother Burns and others such as Vern Mohs, Glenn Gray, and Bud Loftus all played well for Alberta in the years following the war. But they were never consistently good enough to do much for Alberta in the Willingdon Cup.

Alberta's golden years started in the mid-1950s. In the 1960s, the province won four Willingdon Cups, the only time the domination of Ontario and B.C. has been challenged successfully for a whole decade. During these years, the Alberta team was anchored by three outstanding golfers who also played for Canada in many international matches: Keith Alexander, Bob Wylie, and Doug Silverberg.

Robert (Bob) Wylie, from Lamont, Alberta, had been a prominent amateur in the early 1950s but then turned professional. When reinstated as an amateur in 1960, he joined the province's team as a thirty-year-old with a wealth of experience. After playing for Canada in the Americas Cup team tournament in Mexico in 1961, Wylie stayed on to win the Mexican Amateur title.

Bob never got as far as expected in the Canadian Amateur. He was still playing for Canada in the 1980s, at a time when he was also winning the national Senior championship.

Douglas H. (Doug) Silverberg of Red Deer was something of a golfing prodigy in Alberta. At the age of sixteen he became the Alberta Junior champion, a title he held for another two years. He and Laurie Roland had to play-off for the Canadian Junior title in 1950 and 1951, each winning it once from the other.

For some twenty years, the six-feet-one-inch easygoing Silverberg was eminently successful in provincial and international golf. But he never did as well as expected in national golf. He was to represent Canada in twelve international teams, a performance recognized in 1988 when he was elected to the Canadian Golf Hall of Fame.

The third of the Alberta trio (and another elected to the Hall of Fame) was the most successful. Born in 1930 in Vulcan, R. Keith Alexander attended the University of Colorado on a golf scholarship, and came out with a degree in journalism. He is the first Canadian to come out of a U.S. college golf team and win the Canadian Amateur, which he did in 1960.

From the mid - 1950s to the early 1980s, Keith Alexander's name comes up repeatedly as Alberta's champion, Amateur and Open. He was to represent his province twenty-six times in the Willingdon Cup, a record equalled only by Nick Weslock.

Standing five feet six inches, weighing only 140 pounds, Alexander is a quiet, solemn figure on the golf course. (He is also lean. Phil Farley likened him yawning to a darning needle. His walk and demeanor are also reminiscent of the *Spy* cartoon of Johnny Ball, a storied figure in English golf around the turn of the century.) His smooth, silky swing reminded many of Montreal's Gordon B. Taylor.

Based on his strong provincial showing, the RCGA chose Alexander for the 1960 Americas Cup team matches at the Ottawa Hunt Club. Usually a consistent, steady player, he was not at his best against the Americans and Mexicans. But in the Willingdon Cup matches and the Canadian Amateur held at the same venue, his game improved as the week progressed.

In the final against Gary Cowan, Keith Alexander got away to a fine start. His 3 up at the ninth was as much due to Cowan's lackadaisical beginning as to anything. Confronted with deliberate, steady play, Cowan did well to tie the match on the eighteenth green.

In the afternoon, it looked like being the same story. Out in a steady if not spectacular 37 strokes, Alexander found this good enough to be again 3 up at the turn. This time he did not allow Cowan to recover, and went on to win by 4 and 3.

Alexander played in all but a few of Canada's internationals over the next twenty years.

From the time of the very first interprovincial team matches in 1882, right through to the end of the 1950s, only Ontario, Quebec, and British Columbia had emerged as winners. In 1960, Alberta broke this monopoly. For the record, the winning Alberta team consisted of the quiet, precise Alexander; the newly recruited Wylie; Ed Schwartz, a stocky, twenty-three-year-old star from Lethbridge; and Edmonton's Neil Green.

The event was not without drama. After the regulation 36 holes, Alberta and B.C. were tied.

Keith Alexander, Alberta's second winner of the Amateur in 1960.

Alberta won the Willingdon Cup for the third time in four years in 1966 with, left to right, *Bob Wylie, Keith Alexander, Ed Thomas (non-playing captain), Doug Silverberg, and Ray Rhoades.*

This was a rare happening. Only once before, in 1938, had two teams finished level in the Willingdon Cup. The officials decided that a sudden-death play-off (or a short 5-hole play-off, the format used in 1938) was out of the question. For one thing, several players, including Alexander and Wylie, had played 108 holes in three days, including the Americas Cup. So, after a day of rest on the Sunday, the two teams played another 18 holes. Alberta won decisively, 294 to 310.

For the rest of the 1960s, Alberta was anchored by Alexander, Silverberg, and Wylie, and had the finest record of any province.

Saskatchewan (in 1964) and Manitoba (in 1974) have each won the Willingdon Cup once. Home advantage meant something to both teams, since Saskatchewan won at Saskatoon, Manitoba at Winnipeg.

The Saskatchewan team comprised Ernie Greenley, Keith Rever, Ed Ross, and Jim Scissons, none of whom was to make his mark in national golf as a player. Yet at Saskatoon's Riverside club, Rever and Ross both had individual scores better than those of the much-fancied Weslock, Cowan, and Alexander.

The Manitoba team, ten years later, comprised Steve Bannatyne, Barry McKenzie, Ted Homenuik, and Gavin Spiers. Of these, Ted Homenuik was the only figure of national ranking.

The Homenuiks of Saskatchewan, later of Manitoba, were nearly as prolific as the Huots of Quebec, who preceded them by some twenty years. Rudy, Wilf, Ted, and Stan always seemed to be winning something in Saskatchewan juvenile, junior, and amateur golf, in the early 1950s, one of them often the runner-up to another. There is no evidence that they conspired to carve up the province's golfing honours and share them around the family, but that's the way it turned out. Some of the boys moved away from Saskatchewan. Ted and Wilf went on to repeat in Manitoba golf what they had done back home.

Saskatchewan's winning Willingdon Cup team of 1964, left to right, *Alex Bland (non-playing captain), Keith Rever, Ernie Greenley, Ed Ross, Jim Scissons.*

Ted Homenuik, centre, *joint runner-up in the 1953 Junior, with the winner, Gordon Mackenzie*, right, *and joint runner-up David Pemberton-Smith.*

Lea Windsor of Halifax GC (Ashburn), Junior Champion of 1952.

The Homenuiks were born on a farm near Veregin, some thirty miles from Yorkton. John and Mary Homenuik moved to Yorkton to be near schools, and it was at Yorkton's Deer Park Golf Club, with its sand greens, that the boys started to caddie and to play golf. In seven of the twelve years between 1950 and 1961, a Homenuik was either a winner or a runner-up in the Saskatchewan Junior boys' championship.

Playing out of clubs in Winnipeg, Ted Homenuik was one of Manitoba's top amateurs until the late 1970s. Small and dark – he was given the sobriquet of The Little Brown Man – he made up in accuracy around the greens what he lacked in distance. Nick Weslock overwhelmed him when they met in the 1957 Canadian Amateur final. Four years later, he gave Gary Cowan a rare fight in the final, only to lose at the last hole. In that year, 1961, Ted played for Canada in the Americas Cup.

Although some say that Ted was the better golfer, it was Wilf who went furthest in the game. Small (five feet seven inches, 140 pounds), wiry and nervous, he looked all set as a youth

Jim Doyle of Winnipeg, winner of The Amateur in 1968.

Winnipeg's Wilf Homenuik, winner of the CPGA championship in 1965 and 1971.

to make his name in hockey. But Wilf reckoned he had more of a future in golf. After winning the Manitoba Amateur in 1956 and 1957 – once from Ted – he turned professional. Over the next ten years, he won a number of provincial Opens in the Prairies. His most successful stretch in national golf was 1965 to 1971, when he won the CPGA championship twice and the last two Millar tournaments before this event was discontinued. He went on the PGA Tour in 1966, but won only $230 in official money that year. Although he was never to win a PGA event, he did win two on the Caribbean Tour and a PGA satellite event at Shreveport in 1971.

WESLOCK, COWAN, AND THE QUINTESSENTIAL STRIKER

THE 1947 CANADIAN OPEN WAS PLAYED at the Scarboro G & CC. In the third round, the U.S. professional Clayton Heafner was paired with a twenty-nine-year-old Canadian amateur named Nick Weslock. And Heafner found it hard to believe what he was seeing. Time after time, Weslock's high approaches or recoveries would bite into the green and spin back to within birdie distance.

When Weslock came in with the lowest score of the day, a 65, Heafner registered a protest: Weslock's wedge must surely have illegal grooves to grip the ball the way it did.

That year, the PGA had found several professionals carrying clubs with grooves filed too deep. So the RCGA Rules of Golf Committee got out its callipers and measured Weslock's wedge. No, it told Heafner, the club was quite legal. Weslock's magic wedge shots were being manufactured by the skill of the player, not by the grooves of his clubface.

Nick Weslock went on to use the club as effectively in the fourth round. He took third place in the Open, four strokes behind South Africa's Bobby Locke. No Canadian amateur had come so close to winning the Open since George Lyon's second place in 1910. No Canadian amateur, and only one or two professionals, has come so close since.

This incident was probably the genesis of Nick Weslock's sobriquet "The Wedge." Even *he* does not remember when the name was first pinned to him; it had certainly stuck by 1950.

Jimmy Demaret had also witnessed Weslock's display in 1947 and thought him one of the three best wedge players in the world.

But a golfer does not live by wedge alone. Weslock was an extremely good long-iron player, and could outdrive most amateurs, although his tee-shots were always the most erratic feature of his game. He was an outstanding putter. Professionals having difficulty with their putting stroke have been known to come to Weslock for help.

When Nick Weslock was at his peak, in the 1960s, some rated him the best amateur Canadian golf had ever produced. Phil Farley had admired his skills years earlier. "He is the greatest amateur medal player in the country right now, and possibly the best ever," he said of Weslock in 1949. He was certainly one of the most powerful, standing five feet ten inches, weighing a muscular 180 pounds, strong in arm and thigh, with a body kept fit by daily exercise.

Nick was – is – a professional amateur; a perfectionist. Golf is his life, next to his family. But he does not let that spoil his enjoyment of the game or his sense of humour. He believes that golf should be fun. He has a sharp wit. In competition he could hum, whistle, and tease his way round a golf course, without losing his ability to concentrate on his shot when he needed to. Banter is not always what is opponent or fellow competitor wanted; it has been suggested there was a touch of gamesmanship in Weslock's style. ("He might have won the tournament if he hadn't spent so much time trying to heckle Moe Norman out of the running," a provincial paper once wrote of him. It was a

Four-time Amateur champion Nick Weslock.

wasted effort. Norman won.) He was outspoken, opinionated, and made good copy. The press loved him, although they were not always kind to him.

Weslock is by nature a neat and tidy man. Above all, he is meticulous about the state of his golf clubs. "Every grove on the clubface of my irons has to be absolutely free of dirt or I'm uncomfortable," he admits. His clubs are made to order. If not satisfied with one of them, he will adjust it in his basement workshop.

He is equally meticulous about his clothes. In an age when amateurs played in white shirts and grey slacks, Weslock was easily recognizable on the golf course in his rainbow outfits, which he often changed between rounds. He was to wear a red, white, and blue chequered cap long after others thought it had gone out of style. As for his golf bag, Jack Marks of *The Globe and Mail* once wrote that "it looks like a neat little drug store, with his bottles of Geritol and elixirs." As soon as he could afford to, Weslock travelled in a Cadillac. A former president of the RCGA admits to having seen twelve pairs of golf shoes in its trunk, "every one polished so it gleams."

Nick Weslock had not been raised in a world of Cadillacs and fancy wardrobes. He was born in Winnipeg, in 1917, the son of a cabinet-maker. When he was seven, his family moved to Windsor, Ontario. He went straight from school into an auto plant, to learn the skills of a toolmaker. Early in the war, he was drafted to work in a Hamilton arsenal.

In 1947, he moved to Detroit with a valve company, as its Ontario representative. At the same time, he applied for U.S. citizenship. It was then that he changed his name from Wisnock to Weslock, as the rest of the family had done.

But things did not work out, and he was back in Canada by 1951. After a spell as the Ontario field engineer for a Detroit valve company, he set up in business for himself, in Burlington, Ontario. He became firmly established as a self-taught consulting engineer and partner of a company that made parts for the automotive industry.

This, then, was the setting in which Nick Weslock played golf, and his career in amateur golf has to be seen in this context. His championships came late in life. By the time he had won his second, third, and fourth Canadian Amateurs, he was in his late forties. By then, his business career was settled and he had no money problems. Only his commitment to his family restricted his hours of practice and his days away at tournaments.

Like all top-class amateurs, Weslock was tempted to turn professional. "You'd be crazy," the American professional Al Watrous told him, when he learned of Weslock's income from his business. So he continued to play as an amateur, and no one has had more enjoyment from the game. But then, few have put so much study and hard work into winning four Canadian Amateurs (1957, 1963, 1964, 1966) and six Canadian Seniors.

Nick Weslock was a member of seventeen Canadian amateur international teams between 1952 and 1978, and of twenty-six Ontario Willingdon Cup teams (a record shared with Alberta's Keith Alexander), and was leading Canadian amateur in the Open at least thirteen times – a record that no one has come close to equalling.

Six years of frustration followed his return to this country in 1951. National and provincial titles eluded him. The Canadian Amateur was still settled by match play, a format he did not then care for. ("He is a flopperoo in match play, but a bearcat in medal play," summed up the *Sudbury Daily Star*.) In the head-to-head combat of match play, he had not learned to ignore his opponent and to compete against the course.

In 1957, the Amateur returned to the St. Charles CC in Winnipeg. By now the stymie rule had been abandoned, and Weslock was adapting his mind to playing the course. The British Walker Cup team, on their way to the U.S. championships, stopped over in Winnipeg. The question was, did Canada have anyone capable of stopping them?

As the match-play rounds progressed, Nick Weslock was seen to be the man to beat. In

the first round, he disposed of England's Bonallack, and, in the quarter-finals, another Walker Cupper, Scrutton.

This brought him face to face with Vancouver's Bob Kidd. As it turned out, this was where the championship was settled. The B.C. champion was a solid hitter and noted as a sterling match player. In a round of the Amateur two years earlier, he had come from 2 down with 3 to play to defeat Weslock after four extra, nail-biting holes. Now, in 1957, the two of them had been contemplating a showdown all week. Both had been playing virtually unbeatable golf. Weslock had managed to control his power off the tee, with little or no loss of distance. This single fact gave him just the extra confidence he needed. He flew into Kidd, jumped his man with a birdie at the third, shot 34 in the first nine, and found himself 4 holes up. And that's the way it was after the morning round.

In the afternoon, Weslock held on grimly. His margin looked insurmountable to all but Kidd. From the tenth (or 28th) hole, Kidd's putter took on a magic of its own. He shot three birdies in four holes, cutting Weslock's margin to 1. Some looked for signs of Weslock cracking. The opposite happened. At the 517-yard, dog-leg fourteenth (32nd) Kidd was ten yards behind off the tee. In trying to fade a 3-iron over the corner of trees and into the opening of the green, he shanked. The ball scuttled into the right rough. The best he could manage was a 6. Weslock won the next two holes and the match, 4 and 2.

Winnipeg's Ted Homenuik had shot his bolt in defeating the Walker Cup player Thirwell in the other semi-final. He was no match for Weslock and went down by 9 and 8.

Winning the 1957 Canadian Amateur was something of a watershed in Weslock's life. He looked upon his victory over Kidd as the highlight of his years at the game.

Twenty-three years earlier, he had been a seventeen-year-old caddie at the Essex County Golf and Country Club, Windsor. In 1936 he captured the Essex–Kent Amateur title, and he held on to this for another two years, playing out of Roseland GC. Even then, he was making a name for himself as a long hitter. The opposition was tough in that corner of Ontario. He had to meet such players as a youthful Rudy Horvath, Shin Neal, and Jimmy Hogan. Weslock defeated just about everyone in 1940, to take the Essex–Kent title for the fourth time in five years. Then came his move to the war plant in Hamilton and membership in the Burlington G & CC.

During the war years he made the step up to provincial tournaments and was quickly recognized as a force in national golf when he won an Ontario Amateur and just missed another two. His third-place finish in the Canadian Open of 1947 was seen as the harbinger of many national amateur titles. Few people imagined that it would take Nick Weslock another ten years to win his first. Which brings us back to Winnipeg.

Having proved himself, Weslock now talked of taking things easy, perhaps dropping the Willingdon Cup matches in the future. But he *was* looking forward to the Masters (the Canadian Amateur champion was usually invited). Well, he did play in the Masters, and he did cut down his competitive golf. But not for long. The trophies from five Ontario championships – Amateurs and Opens – were added to his shelves over the next five years.

In 1962 and 1963, he earned the first two of four consecutive medals for being low amateur in the Open. He also started on volume seven of what came to be known as "Weslock's Little Black Book."

He had started to fill volume one back in 1939, after playing with an old Scottish professional, Bobby Cruickshank. Cruickshank told him how to play chip shots from just off the fringe. That night, he wrote down the hint on the first page of a five-inch loose-leaf notebook with black covers. Over the years, he collected hundreds of such tips, each of them catalogued by departments – driver, long irons, short irons, wedges, putters – with a note of who had provided the tip, and where and when. He carried the books in his golf bag for ready reference. "Over the years, they've helped me in just about every tournament I've played in."

Six of these little black books were in his bag for the 1963 Amateur at Saint John's Riverside club. He came to Riverside in a particularly confident mood, after a fine showing in the Canadian Open.

He was one of those fancied to win the Amateur, along with the title-holder, Tom Draper of Detroit; Bert Ticehurst of B.C., low scorer in the Willingdon Cup for the third time in five years; and team-mate Gary Cowan.

At the time, Cowan was the unofficial world amateur champion, having been low individual in the World Amateur Team Championship in 1962. The title made Weslock mad. "I personally like Gary very much and admire his golf," he said at the time. "However, I get hot under the collar every time some of these Toronto writers refer to him as the amateur golf champion of the world."

There was no seeding in the Amateur. So the luck of the draw brought Weslock and Cowan together for the third straight year, this time in the third round. The intense silent rivalry between these two had created many a keenly fought battle in the past, but none better than the one to be seen in 1963. Weslock, at forty-five, was twenty years the senior. Against anyone else, Cowan would have had an important psychological edge. Each had one victory over the other in their last two encounters in the Amateur. So this was the rubber. And the older man won, but not as easily as the score of 4 and 3 would suggest.

The match was virtually decided on the 285-yard thirteenth hole, where Weslock stood on the tee 3 up. He meant to lay up with a 3-wood but finished in a greenside trap. With a chance to get one back, Cowan went for the green with a driver. His shot carried the traps and ended 15 feet behind the pin. This gave him a sure 3 and a possible birdie. Weslock exploded out, but was still 12 feet away. Cowan missed his birdie. Weslock stroked the ball in for a half. A discouraged Cowan lost the next hole and the match.

Weslock almost threw away his semi-final against the holder, Draper. Two up at the turn, he had to get down in two from 30 yards to win. Typically, his wedge shot left the ball looking into the hole.

In the final, Weslock overpowered Ticehurst as he had young Ted Homenuik six years earlier. He shot a 66 in the morning. When he followed this with a 34 going out in the afternoon, he was 8 up. Three pars later, the match was over. Weslock had won his second Canadian Amateur by 7 and 6.

The sobriquet of "Nick the Wedge" has characterized Weslock for so many years that we are inclined to overlook his skills with the putter. And, in particular, with "The Glider," a centre-shafted model he made in his workshop and perfected in the early 1940s. Jug McSpaden saw Weslock perform with it during an Open and advised him to patent it. He did, giving the rights to Spalding, which then had a plant in Brantford. But as an amateur he could not make money from it.

As we have seen, Weslock is a perfectionist. His approach to attacking the enemy, the golf course, led him to chart courses, years before this was a commonplace. He was doing this before the war. A newspaper article by Andy Lytle in 1946 reports that:

> [Weslock] is a meticulous player, who some time ago formed the habit of giving himself private publicity on courses he expected to play. He is a better than average draughtsman. So, because he considers what's worth doing is worth doing well, Nick would play this course or that one, and, as he did, would chart fairways and greens, make notes of hazards, mental or actual, which hole was ringed by trees or bad traps which might leap out and snap at the unwary . . . He had pretty well charted the Ontario courses, and was looking further afield when war interrupted all games.

His charting included measuring distances from objects (such as bunkers or trees) to the green. This is a common practice today, but Weslock must have been among the first to do it.

None of this was of any use to him when he won his third Amateur on an unfamiliar course, at Saskatoon's Riverside Country Club. Here, in 1964, he and Gary Cowan met in an Amateur final for the first time.

Weslock came to Saskatoon having won seven of his last nine tournaments, including the Ontario Open. His game had been off earlier in the year. A lesson from Gordie Brydson had quickly corrected his driving, and just before Saskatoon he went to George Knudson who straightened out his irons.

Despite three-putting seven times, Weslock was never behind in this final. At the fifteenth, he holed out from 70 feet for a birdie. Three up after the morning round, Weslock gave them all back by the middle of the afternoon. The match was virtually decided on the 35th hole, a par three. Cowan's 8-iron was caught by the wind and rolled back down the hill in front of the green. Weslock hit a 9-iron to within four feet. Cowan chipped about 20 feet past the hole and missed the return. Weslock had an easy 3.

Cowan needed to sink a 15-foot putt on the last green to save the match, but rimmed the cup.

Weslock and Cowan after the 1964 final.

Having won three Amateurs, the forty-six-year-old Weslock was asked the perennial question: would he now retire? "When I start to miss it, I'll retire," he responded. Presumably, he meant the ball.

In the ninety or so years that the Canadian Amateur Championship has been played, there has been no more bizarre final than at Summerlea G & CC, Quebec, in 1966, when Nick Weslock won his fourth and last title.

The other finalist, Bill Brew, was a husky, thirty-year-old college professor from Connecticut. He had behaved quite rationally all week, until the final. Relatively unknown outside New England, he had also played well beyond himself. In the semi-finals, Brew was too good for the exciting young South African Bobby Cole, holder of the British title.

Weslock had survived another duel with Cowan, but only after one particularly lucky shot. (When Weslock won with a half at the eighteenth, Cowan went to the scoreboard and changed the name to Wesluck.)

If the two thousand spectators thought that the Weslock–Brew final would be something of an anti-climax, even dull, they were in for a surprise. The morning round went smoothly enough. Neither player was at his best. They exchanged ten holes, shot two-over-par 74s, and went to lunch all square.

On the way to the clubhouse, Brew asked Weslock if they could have a quick tomato juice and play on. Weslock explained he had a migraine and had just taken a painkiller. He thought the hour's break would do him good. Brew then appealed to the RCGA officials, who insisted that he stick to the normal one-hour rest.

After lunch, Brew was in a petulant and irritable mood. He was also in a hurry. To one observer, "He broke from the gate like a high-strung horse." On the first hole, he skulled his tee-shot about eighty-five yards, hit the next into a trap, barely got it on the green, and three-putted. But that was only the beginning. In the first five holes, three of his drives went no further than 100 yards. His two double-bogeys put him two holes down. He was playing at a speed that would have outpaced Moe Norman. Too, his grumpiness and obscene comments were visibly upsetting Weslock.

Jim Gaquin, executive director of the RCGA, was a fellow New Englander. He spoke to Brew. "I told him this was the Canadian championship, and that he should not make light of it. With a display like this, he was embarrassing himself as well as the RCGA." Brew's excuse was that he was in a hurry to get home; he had not expected to reach the finals.

After this, Brew regained his composure and played some remarkable recovery shots. He squared the match at the twelfth (or 30th). But when he hit two shots into the trees at the fourteenth (32nd) Weslock recovered the lead and never lost it. He won by 1 up.

When questioned by the press, Brew denied that anyone had spoken to him about his conduct, and stomped from the room. The explanation of his eccentric behaviour came later. He had entered for the qualifying rounds of the U.S. Amateur, to be played at Westchester, New York, starting on the day after the final of the Canadian Amateur. With a seven-hour drive ahead of him, Brew wanted to finish the match with Weslock as soon as possible.

As for Weslock, he was ecstatic about his fourth Canadian title. For he, too, had his eyes on the U.S. Amateur. "The best part about my win is that, as the Canadian champion, I will automatically qualify for the U.S. championship next year . . . I've always wanted to play in it."

Ironically, the U.S. Amateur title that Bill Brew and Weslock wanted went to Weslock's greatest rival in Canada, Gary Cowan.

The scene is the Merion Golf Club, in Ardmore, Pennsylvania, just outside Philadelphia. The East Course at Merion had been the setting for Ben Hogan's memorable struggle to win the U.S. Open in 1950, and for the amateur Jack Nicklaus's record-breaking total of 269 in the World Amateur Team Championship of 1960. It is not a long course by championship standards – a mere 6,500 yards – but it has some of the toughest finishing holes in golf.

The year is 1966; the time, late in the afternoon of a warm September Saturday. Deane Beman, a twenty-eight-year-old insurance executive from Bethesda, Maryland, appears to be heading for his third U.S. Amateur title. With one hole to play, he needs only a par four to win by two strokes from the surprise, come-from-behind leader in the clubhouse. That leader happens to be Gary Cowan, of Kitchener, Ontario. Cowan stands six feet, weighs 170 pounds, is wavy-haired and handsome. He is a year younger than Beman and is also in the insurance business. He is one of golf's longest hitters, a good wedge player, and, on occasions, an excellent putter.

Going into the final round, Gary Cowan had been four strokes behind Beman, with a bunch of other U.S. stars separating him from the leader. Largely unnoticed, playing before a small gallery of friends, Cowan had overtaken all but Beman by birdying four of the last seven holes, for an inward half of 32. His 67 was the lowest round of the day. As Lincoln Werden of *The New York Times* saw it, Cowan had used every bit of strategy he knew to tame the course's creeks and hazards.

Despite his good scoring, Cowan was disgruntled at having missed an eight-foot putt for his par on the eighteenth (or 72nd) hole. His friends commiserated with him as he sat in the clubhouse, sipping beer, watching Beman on television. When Beman hit a good drive at the last hole, Cowan put on his coat, ready to receive the prize for second place at the closing ceremonies.

Then the unexpected happened, and Gary Cowan's world was changed forever. Beman opened what William Safire has termed "a window of vulnerability." The eighteenth at Merion is a tough 455-yard par four. In 1950, Hogan had hit the most celebrated 1-iron shot in history to its undulating green. What club Beman used has not been recorded, but his ball finished in the right bunker. With his next shot, he skulled the ball clean over the green and into the rough. His next, a chip, went only five yards. He had played four and was not yet on the putting surface. Winning was no longer

on his mind. His problem was how to survive. He chipped again, and this time the ball rolled to within a foot of the hole. He tapped in for a double-bogey 6. His total was 285, the same as Gary Cowan's. Cowan was still alive. He and Beman faced an eighteen-hole play-off the next day, Sunday afternoon.

Gary Cowan and Deane Beman were old friends and rivals. In 1964, they had tied for leading amateur medal in the Masters. They had been in opposing teams at the Americas Cup and at the World Amateur Team Championships.

Their eighteen-hole play-off on the Sunday was anti-climactic. The golf was mediocre. Again, the drama was saved for the closing holes. Coming to the sixteenth, Cowan led by 2 strokes, having birdied the fifteenth to Beman's bogey. The 430-yard sixteenth is one of Merion's "quarry holes." The second shot has to carry a menacing old quarry, largely overgrown by Scottish broom and brush. Cowan's drive hit a tree and was deflected into a pot bunker. He played out, but his ball dropped down into the quarry. His third shot from the quarry went far to the left of the green, finishing on a narrow footpath. He recovered well with a wedge, but the ball flew over the green into the gallery. He chipped from long grass, but failed to reach the green. Another chip, and he lay six feet from the cup. He holed out for a triple bogey 7.

Throwing away a two-stroke lead with only two holes to go is often enough to throw away a match. Cowan later admitted what everyone knew, that the triple bogey made him sick. Only his inner reserves of strength and concentration were to save him. And what of Beman? Cowan's disaster had given him an unexpected opportunity to go ahead. But after lying on the edge of the green in two, he took three more to get down. The match was all square. For perhaps the first time that day, the spectators were excited, sensing that the play-off might go to sudden-death.

The seventeenth at Merion is a 224-yard par three, set among trees and flanked by bunkers. Both players reached the green safely, with Cowan 20 feet from the pin. He lagged up, and tapped in for his par. Beman was only 12 feet away, so had a good chance of a birdie. His first putt was 30 inches short. Then, catastrophe. His second putt failed to drop. He could not believe it, and stepped back from the ball in amazement, examining the line again. But the ball was still there, sitting on the edge, and he had to settle for a 4.

With a stroke in hand, Cowan only needed to halve the last hole. Having played 2, both players were about six paces from the hole. But Cowan was off the putting surface, and his ball had settled in a cuppy lie. Beman just missed his first putt, so could do no better than 4. Cowan decided to use his putter from the fringe. The ball jumped out of the indentation and rolled out and stopped some eight feet from the cup. This for the championship. Cowan stroked the ball firmly, and in it went. He had shot a 75 to Beman's 76. He had won what was arguably the most prestigious event in amateur golf, the U.S. championship.

Gary Cowan's win was only the third by a foreigner in the sixty-six years of the U.S. Amateur. England's Harold Hilton had won in 1911, Canada's Sandy Somerville in 1932.

The win pleased Gary Cowan for a number or reasons, not the least of which was that "this should get some people off my back." The people were those who had criticized his repeated failure to win the Ontario Open or to repeat his solitary win in the Ontario Amateur. The fact that he had won the Canadian Amateur in 1961 (and had tied for low amateur in the Masters in 1964) was apparently not good enough.

Looking back on Gary Cowan's career, there is a temptation to conclude that he is as good an example as any of a player who revelled in stroke play, but who was never at his best in the head-to-head combat of match play. In the 1962 World Amateur Team Championship in Japan, his play was faultless. His long, accurate driving was a feature of the tournament. His score of 280 won him the unofficial title of World Amateur Champion.

Yet this same man won the Canadian Amateur title only once, despite having reached the semi-finals of this match-play event no less than six times, the final five times.

Gary Cowan would readily admit to a preference for stroke play (as would Nick Weslock), but to conclude that he was a poor match player would be to fly in the face of the facts. His achievements in international match-play are second to none. From 1958, he played for Canada nineteen times (a record for any Canadian) and for ten of these nineteen times he was playing in the match-play events of the Americas Cup or the Commonwealth Team Matches. In singles matches against the best amateurs from the United States and Mexico and from the Commonwealth countries, Gary Cowan's record is the finest of any Canadian. Between 1958 and 1961, he went undefeated for a string of thirteen matches, winning ten and tying three. Those who fell to his flashes of unbeatable golf included the former British and American titleholder, Harvey Ward (by 3 and 2, in 1958); another U.S. champion, Charlie Coe, and a U.S. Walker Cup player, Bill Hyndman, both in 1960.

In 1961, Cowan took on the world's finest amateur, Jack Nicklaus, in match play, and tied him, shooting a 71 to Nicklaus's 72. The greater the challenge, the better Gary Cowan seemed to play. Referring again to his critics, he once said, "What they don't realize is that I've got to be charged up to play, and I get charged up when I'm out of the country." By "out of the country" he meant playing in international golf. His wins against Coe and Hyndman were over the course of the Ottawa Hunt Club.

Gary Cowan was born in Kitchener, Ontario, in October 1938. As a ten-year-old, he caddied at the nearby Rockway Golf Club, a public course a few blocks from his house. The professional, Lloyd Tucker, let him play eighteen holes a day if he helped weed the course and pick up trash. He coaxed lessons out of Tucker by standing in front of his shop, swinging a club, knowing that Lloyd would want to come out and correct him. Like Gerry Kesselring and Moe Norman, products of the same club and the same professional, Gary Cowan lived for golf and its practice, for as long as he could afford to. In the winter months he would work as a bellhop in the southern states so that he could play the year round.

As a lanky, blond youth of seventeen, he made quite an impression in the 1955 Ontario Amateur. Hilles Pickens observed that "great interest was shown in the play of Gary Cowan of the Rockway Club. He defeated three strong players . . . and was only defeated by Nick Weslock in the fourth round, by 1 up."

Gary Cowan went on to win the Canadian Junior title in 1956. Brought into Ontario's Willingdon Cup team that same year, he immediately set a new individual record of 66 70–136, one that was to stand for twenty-five years. It seemed only a matter of a very short time before this maturing young man would capture his first of a string of national titles.

Cowan's assault on the Amateur ended with a victory in 1961. By now, he had a string of international victories to his credit. Yet he still had to fight for every hole to defeat Winnipeg's Ted Homenuik. When the six-feet tall, slashing lad from Kitchener met the five-feet-six-inch Homenuik, it was a case of broadsword versus rapier. Neither player was in the habit of showing his emotions on the course, although Hilles Pickens observed of Cowan that "poor play causes him to look like an angry Norseman lacking only the double-headed axe and spun gold beard." Slow to warm up, Cowan let his opponent gallop away to a three-hole lead before he switched into second gear (if Norsemen ever changed gear). By the eighteenth, he had pulled back the deficit to a single hole.

Ted Homenuik had collapsed against Weslock in 1957. But now, four years later, he was a much more experienced and confident player. In the afternoon, Cowan's booming drives soon squared the match. But these were not always on line, and he often had to scramble for a half. The two were all square going to the 550-yard, slightly downhill seventeenth (or 35th). Here Cowan used his length to good advantage. He was on the green with a drive and a 3-iron. Homenuik was short after two

woods and his chip went 25 feet past the pin. He had to settle for a 5 to Cowan's birdie 4. Needing only a half at the last hole, Cowan got it comfortably, to win 1 up.

At the 1970 Canadian Open, Cowan played some of the best golf of his life. After three straight rounds of 70 at London Hunt, he was only three strokes behind the leader. Properly psyched up for the final round – as anyone could tell from the fiercely determined face – he checked in at the starter's table. There, a television commentator asked him, "Gary, have you ever thought of turning pro?" He had been asked this question a hundred times, but never at a moment like this. The incident snapped his concentration. He hooked his tee-shot into the water, took a triple bogey, and finished with a 79.

When Gary Cowan won the U.S. Amateur in 1966, at least one American periodical belittled his victory by implying he had won by default. *Sports Illustrated* published Deane Beman's account of the championship under the title of "How I lost the U.S. Amateur." Cowan's fourth round of 67 was overlooked, although it was the lowest of the day. The words hurt Cowan. There was one sure way of easing their sting, and that was by winning the U.S. Amateur again, this time from the front. That is precisely what Cowan did.

In the fall of 1971, in the space of forty-five glorious days, Gary Cowan asserted his claim – made by others on his behalf – to the title of the greatest amateur golfer of his day.

Let us look at the second victory first. He went to New Zealand in October, as one of a Canadian team competing in the special Commonwealth Tournament marking the centennial of New Zealand. As an added event, the organizers ran a 36-hole stroke-play competition for all competitors. Britain's team included five who had wrested the Walker Cup from the Americans that summer. So the competition was as tough as could be found anywhere outside of the United States. And Gary Cowan won. His score of 141 was one less than that of England's Michael Bonallack.

Gary Cowan in quest of the U.S. Amateur

On his way to the title in 1966.

"I've just won it!" in 1966.

"Look! I've done it again" in 1971.

Cowan, the uncrowned "Commonwealth Champion," had gone to New Zealand as the U.S. Amateur champion. Some six weeks earlier he had taken on the best amateurs in America and had won the U.S. title for the second time.

In the years between 1966 and 1971, Cowan had placed three times in the top ten of the North–South Amateur at Pinehurst, and had won in 1970, thereby establishing quite a reputation in the United States. But the 1971 season had started badly. He had shot 83 75 in the Masters, then missed the cut in the Canadian Open. One of his partners in the Open had played with him before and noticed he was standing too close to the ball. Cowan corrected his stance and his golf immediately improved. He set a new course record in taking third place in the Canadian Amateur, and walked away with the Ontario Amateur, leaving Weslock behind to the tune of 10 strokes, a margin of victory that is still a record. He had also mellowed somewhat over the years, and was acting less aloof and more open with the press now that he was no longer playing in Weslock's shadow. When he came to the U.S. Amateur at Wilmington Country Club,

Delaware, in September, he was a player to be reckoned with.

The cream of U.S. amateur talent was at Wilmington, including Ben Crenshaw (the NCAA champion from the University of Texas) and Vinnie Giles, a three-time runner-up. Canada's Nick Weslock was there too. In winning his second U.S. Amateur, Gary Cowan did it the hard way. He started the final round with a one-stroke lead to defend. As with Beman in 1966, the drama came at the last hole.

It is doubtful if any U.S. Amateur championship has had a more startling finish. Coming to the eighteenth (or 72nd), Cowan needed a par 4 to give him victory by one stroke over Eddie Pearce. Pearce had already completed his round and was sitting by the last green.

Cowan hooked his drive into the rough, some 135 yards from the green. Pearce later said, "I thought there was going to be a play-off. I didn't think Cowan was going to make his par, but [that he'd] make bogey for sure." On television, commentator Byron Nelson also thought it probable that Cowan and Pearce were heading for a play-off. But Gary Cowan's lie was not as bad as it appeared from a distance. He had been lucky. The ball had bounced out of a bunker at the corner of the dog-leg. Another foot and he would have been blocked out by a tree and forced to play sideways to the fairway.

The rough at a USGA championship is always demanding. Cowan could see his ball, and he knew he could get his clubhead to it. But he also knew there would be little stop on the ball when it landed on the green. At the same time, he did want to get the ball to the putting surface. He had been close to this same spot in the second round, and his wedge had left him short. So he knew the club he needed – a 9-iron.

Gary Cowan had come to this hole thinking he had a two-stroke lead over Pearce. He was unaware that Pearce had birdied the last hole to cut his lead in half. Having found his ball, Cowan asked USGA president Phil Strubling for permission to walk up to check the scoreboard near the eighteenth green. "He told me I couldn't, because it would delay play," Cowan

said later. (Cowan's group was the last of the day, so Phil Strubling probably had in mind the play of the others in the group.) Cowan accepted the ruling. "I said to myself, what the heck, you know what you have to do." Out came his 9-iron. He fired the ball at the green, where the pin was tucked in the back right.

When he saw the ball hit the green, Cowan thought it was going to roll past the hole. "Then I heard the people. I knew they weren't going to clap like that if it hadn't gone in." The ball had rolled up the incline. It then did what Byron Nelson had forecast one second sooner. "It's going in the hole!" Gary Cowan had finished with an eagle 2, "the greatest shot of my life." He had won the U.S. Amateur Championship by three strokes. He had won it for a second time, a feat which no foreigner had achieved before or has achieved since. Each of his four rounds of 70 71 69 70 matched par or better. His total of 280, or four under par, was three ahead of Pearce, four ahead of Giles, and six ahead of Crenshaw, who tied for sixth place.

Gary Cowan found his second U.S. title much more gratifying than his first. The stigma of having won by Beman's default had been erased. (Of the *Sports Illustrated* reporter, he asked, "Who are you going to say lost it this time?") He had early established himself as the man to beat, and he had kept himself just ahead of the pack.

But the time had come in his life when he felt he should be devoting more time to his family and to earning a living. (After a few years as a salesman in the golf business he had become an agent with an insurance company.) "Anybody can win one U.S. Open," Trevino once said, "but when you win two, you must be a great player." The same can be said of any man who wins two U.S. Amateurs. Gary Cowan had little more to prove. When talking of Canadian amateur golf, people now spoke of "Cowan and Weslock" rather than "Weslock and Cowan."

A happy postscript. In September 1990, just before his fifty-second birthday, Gary Cowan gave up the game of selling insurance and embarked on a new career. Having played with Arnold Palmer in the U.S. Senior Open a few months earlier, and having tied for twenty-sixth place when Palmer missed the cut, he was encouraged enough to try for the U.S. Senior PGA Tour. In November he tied for sixth in the qualifying school. A new professional was born. Given the determination and ability of the man, few doubt he will succeed.

The galleries at the Canadian Amateur championships in the early 1950s witnessed good golf, sometimes spectacular golf. But apart from Phil Farley and Jack Nash, there were few sentimental favourites, and none in the mould of a Somerville or Lyon.

In 1954, a new young star fought his way to the quarter-finals. From the very first round, he captivated an audience that grew larger by the day. His name was Murray Norman, but he was better known as Moe. Canadian galleries had never seen anything quite like him. This twenty-four-year-old ex-caddie from Kitchener stood five feet seven inches, was slightly built but with sinews of steel and whipcord. On the course, he entertained the crowd with his speed of play, his genius at shot-making, and his acting the part of court jester.

Moe Norman played with a rapidity unparalleled in first-class golf. In one motion, he would shuffle into his stiff, upright stance with arms outstretched, reaching for the ball, snatch a look down the fairway, lower his head slightly, swing the clubhead, and follow through with straight arms directing the ball to its target. And having done great violence to the ball, he would set out after it, pounding his way down the fairway, bag slung over his shoulder, as if hoping to give the ball a second swipe before it had quite recovered from the first.

His speed of play was combined with such a pure, clean, striking of the ball, and with such accuracy, that he both astonished and frustrated the spectators. Could a golf ball really be struck as well with so little preparation? What

about the sacred tenets of lining up the feet, checking the position of the ball, loosening up with a practice swing or two, getting set with the waggle? What innate skills did this upstart have that he could dispense with all the preliminaries?

For his long and accurate driving, the gallery christened him "Pipeline Moe." But that was not all that attracted the crowds to this smiling, rather cheeky-looking young fellow. He clowned his way round the golf course, joking with the gallery, entertaining them by driving the ball off oversized tees – some of them eight inches high – in the manner of a Joe Kirkwood. Looking back, we can see in Moe Norman a blend of Lee Trevino and Huckleberry Finn.

During his short, turbulent, chimerical career as an amateur, Moe Norman was to turn Canadian golf upside down. In his long and equally enigmatic career as a professional, he was to enthrall us, disappoint us, make us laugh and sometimes want to cry, but always he entertained us. There has been no more colourful character in Canadian golf. No one has been the subject of more legend and anecdote, much of it spun from a fickle memory. At the same time, there are knowledgeable observers of the game who will tell you that he is the finest striker of a golf ball we have ever produced.

Few of the spectators who watched him play in the Canadian Amateurs of 1954, 1955, and 1956 knew the serious side of Moe Norman, or of the abyss of insecurity below that smiling exterior.

Moe Norman's skills at manoeuvring a golf ball had not come intuitively but were the result of hours, days, weeks, months of practice, practice, and still more practice. When Moe Norman was not playing competitive golf, he would be playing a practice round or, more likely, hitting balls by the hundred, until it was too dark to see. After years of this, he no longer had to think consciously about how to swing a golf club.

In the 1955 Amateur at Calgary G & CC – which he won – he shot a morning round of 65 against Doug Bajus in the semi-final, and went on to win by 6 and 5. He spent the rest of the afternoon on the practice fairway, honing his game. This obsession with practice nearly cost him the title. By the time he met Vancouver's Lyle Crawford in the final, he had played fourteen rounds of competitive golf in nine days and had practised continuously when not playing. After a brilliant start against Crawford, which had Moe 3 up after four holes, physical and mental fatigue set in. Crawford was almost as distressed. Calgary's hot and rarefied atmosphere added to their discomfort. Moe Norman won in the end, but not until the thirty-ninth hole, by which time his legs were jelly.

Moe Norman, left, wins the Amateur from Lyle Crawford, 1955.

This final brought out the destructive features of Norman's fast play. As an amateur, he was never more than an average putter, spending nothing like the time on the practice green that he spent on the practice tee. But he putted with the same speed and impatience. At the seventh hole of the final, he should have gone 4 up, but in rushing an 18-inch putt, he missed it. When putting for the match at the thirty-fifth he again missed by playing too hastily. Nevertheless, it was a quickly struck seven-footer on the 39th hole that gave him a birdie and victory.

In the year following his win of the Amateur title, Moe Norman became obsessed by the need to retain it. He had to show the world that 1955 was no fluke. Self-doubt made him practise all the harder. He went to the 1956 championships in Edmundston as confident

as he would ever be. The Canadian Open champion was there, Doug Sanders, the only amateur ever to win the title. So were another two dozen Americans.

Jerry Magee of Lambton was the giant-killer at Edmundston, defeating Sanders at the eighteenth hole in the quarter-finals. In the same round Moe Norman was up to his old tricks again. Five up on Bob Fleming, he took to entertaining the gallery with a running commentary as he drove from an outsize tee. In the semi-finals, he shot a 64 in the morning round to go 9 up on the luckless American John Miles. Hilles Pickens described it as one of the most memorable rounds ever witnessed in the Amateur, and wrote: "The American contingent agreed Moe could have beaten any golfer in the world with the calibre of golf he displayed during the whole week. . . ."

In the final, Moe Norman never looked like losing, although Jerry Magee played superlative golf. The two of them finished the first eighteen holes in two hours and two minutes, which must surely be a record for an Amateur final in the second half of this century. But there was never any suggestion that Jerry Magee was stampeded into defeat. Moe Norman never let his desire to play quickly hurry his partners or opponents. For the week of the Amateur, Moe Norman was 31 under par. By now he had the galleries eating out of his hand. They felt themselves at one with this easygoing, smiling, underprivileged young man who entertained them.

Moe Norman was a product of the Rockway Golf Club in Kitchener, and of its professional, Lloyd Tucker. Gerry Kesselring had come out of the same stable and was one of Moe's early heroes. The same club was to produce Gary Cowan, hard on the heels of Norman. But as a striker of a golf ball, Moe Norman was the finest of the three.

As a young boy, he had recovered quickly from an injury that could have been disabling. The family car had backed into him, one of its tires injuring his head. He took to caddying and golfing in the summer, pin-setting at a bowling alley in the winter. In 1954, after tying Al Balding, Gordie Brydson, and Murray Tucker for second place in the Ontario Open, he was selected to play for Canada in the Americas Cup. Reputations then meant nothing to Moe Norman. Far from over-awed, he met and defeated America's Bill Campbell, one of the top amateurs in the world. In the Willingdon Cup matches which followed, he picked up the largest gallery by wisecracking his way around the course as though he were playing in a weekend game at Rockway.

In the Willingdon Cup a year later, the crowd encouraged him to try out his eight-inch tee. "Nope," he replied. "Nick Weslock made me promise not to use it." But he added with a grin, "How about a 6-inch tee, folks? The Captain said nothing about using *it.*"

In those years, Moe Norman was a cheerful, kindly young man, lacking in both the self-confidence and the social graces expected of a Canadian Amateur champion. Living on soda pop, candy bars, and spaghetti, carrying only his golf bag and a spare towel, he would hitchhike his way to tournaments, often sleeping in the open beside his clubs. He was at a loss for words in the social milieu of the clubhouse. After the morning round of the final against Lyle Crawford, he and a caddie chum from Kitchener let the others go to lunch in the clubhouse grillroom, while they took off their shoes and socks and dangled their feet in the Elbow River. When he had won, he hid in the bushes to avoid having to make an acceptance speech. In later years, when a winning professional, Moe Norman taught himself to overcome this self-consciousness. He would force himself to stand before an audience and make a speech which would be as gracious as the best of them.

As a young amateur, Moe Norman's income from pin-setting at a bowling alley was barely enough to live on. It did not allow him to play all the tournament golf he wanted to play. His need for more money to meet his travelling expenses was to be his undoing. In 1956, he was again selected to play for Canada in the Americas Cup matches. Canadian fans were looking forward to his clash with the U.S. Amateur champion, Harvey Ward. During the summer of that year, rumours had been circulating about Moe Norman selling his amateur medals and accepting money for travelling expenses to tournaments (tournament organizers knew he was a great draw). The president of the RCGA, Jim Anglin, tried to get in touch with Norman to have him deny these rumours, but Norman refused to return his telephone calls. When Anglin went to Kitchener, Norman went into hiding. The RCGA had no alternative but to drop him from the Americas Cup team.

Hilles Pickens did manage to get in touch with Norman by telephone. Norman admitted that he had, indeed, taken money, but in the form of loans totalling $390. Moreover, he had repaid some of the loans (he had cancelled cheques to prove it) and intended to repay them all.

In January 1957, Moe Norman let it be known he was turning professional. This, before the RCGA had time to consider his status as an amateur. But his action probably anticipated what would have become a necessity.

As we shall see, even as a professional, there was within Moe Norman a propensity to self-destruct.

There was an ironic twist to the Moe Norman affair. Only a few months later, in the spring of 1957, U.S. Amateur champion Harvey Ward admitted to receiving a loan of $11,000 for expenses. The loan was repaid. But Harvey being the darling, golden-haired boy of U.S. amateur golf, the USGA did not strip him of his amateur status, and he continued to play for U.S. teams.

TRAVELS WITH AN AMATEUR

GIVEN ITS HIGHER INCOME after the Second World War, the RCGA started to look again at promoting amateur international matches. It had been rather put out when Britain and America had started competing for the Walker Cup in 1922. Some covert hints to the USGA and R & A that Canada would like to make the Walker Cup a tripartite affair had fallen on deaf ears.

In 1949, the members of the British Walker Cup team passed through Toronto on their way home from Winged Foot, New York. (The Americans had walloped them to the tune of 10–2.) A Canadian team was hastily put together, comprising Phil Farley (Captain), Nick Weslock, Jack Nash, Gerry Kesselring, Don Varey, all of Ontario; Tom Hunter, Tom Riddell, of Quebec; and Alan Boes of Manitoba. The match was played at Toronto GC. The result, 6–6, surprised the British, or so they generously said.

In the chit-chat that followed the match, a British golf writer travelling with the team pointed out that the Walker Cup was a challenge affair, like the America's Cup in yacht racing. What is more, the writer said, Mr. Walker

had it in mind that Canada might be one of the countries to challenge for his cup. Sure enough, it was there in black and white, in earlier editions of the *Golfer's Handbook*: "The cup is not intended for competition solely between Great Britain and the U.S.A. France, Canada, Australia, the Argentine, or any other nation could submit a challenge which might be accepted."

When the RCGA's Colin Rankin next met with the R & A and the USGA, he brought up the matter of Canada's willingness to challenge. But nothing came of this. With nearly thirty years of tradition on their side, the British and Americans were not going to change the format. So the RCGA focused instead on organizing matches with the USGA.

As we have seen, there had been two series of Canada–U.S. amateur internationals, the first at the turn of the century, the second after the First World War.

Charlie Watson, a member of the RCGA's tournament committee for a number of years,

424

was the association's president in 1950. With his keen sense of promotion, he took up the matter of an international match with the USGA, and found it receptive. A Canadian team played the Americans just before the U.S. Amateur championships at the Saucon Valley G & CC, near Bethlehem, Pennsylvania, in 1951.

The Canadian team, selected by the RCGA, was made up of the players it considered to be the top eight in the country. At the end of that year, Hilles Pickens also ranked them, and his rankings are shown in parentheses: Walter McElroy (1), Gerry Kesselring (2), Nick Weslock (3), Phil Farley (4), Bill Mawhinney (5), Don Doe (6), Laurie Roland (7), Alan Boes (14). Sandy Somerville was the team's non-playing captain. The format of the Walker Cup was used; foursomes on the first day, singles on the second, with a point for victory, and a half point for a halved match. Canada did not do as well as expected, losing the foursomes 3 to 1, the singles, 7 to 1. The Canadian team did not seem to play with the confidence or the grim determination required to defeat the Americans – such was the conclusion of the savants at the time.

This match with the U.S. appeared to act as a catalyst. In the following year, the golf associations of Canada, Mexico, and the United States instituted the first of a series of team matches for the Americas Cup. Within a few years, Canadian amateur teams were flying to international team tournaments all over the world. A series of Commonwealth team matches was started in 1954. Every four years, the RCGA sent a team to Australia, or New Zealand, or South Africa, or Britain, or it hosted the matches in Canada. The series was abandoned after 1975. The biennial World Amateur Team Championship, for the Eisenhower Trophy, started in 1958. Over thirty nations sent teams of four to such exotic spots as Kawana, Japan, Algarve, Portugal, and Rome, to say nothing of St. Andrews. Canadian amateur teams travelled to tournaments in Brazil, the Dominican Republic, France, Columbia, and Morocco.

The Canadian amateurs who were good enough to be selected also played golf in other countries on their way to these tournaments. They played on types of courses not found in Canada, on strange turfs, and in climates never experienced at home. But more importantly, they established new friendships amongst themselves, and with the golfers of other countries, which is the whole purpose of international amateur golf. In Canada's international golfers learned much about golf in other countries, Canada also learned much about its international golfers. Some matured into world-class sportsmen. The challenge brought out the best in them. Some had their finest hours competing in other countries. But their individual accomplishments have been buried in the anonymity of the team results in the record books. We shall look at a few who deserve particular mention for their performance in Canadian teams.

A Chicago sportsman, J. G. Bowers, president of the U.S. Western Golf Association in 1952, put up the Americas Cup for biennial competition between amateur golf teams from the United States, Canada, and Mexico. Considering that the Asociacion Mexicana de Golf only had some twenty to thirty clubs from which to put together a team, it did well whenever it could make the matches a true, three-cornered fight, as was the case in 1956, when Mexico finished ahead of Canada.

The matches were played over two days. On the first day, the six competitors from each country played in three groups of foursomes, the two players from each country hitting alternate shots. On the second day, they played in six groups of three, one from each country, so that a Canadian was playing simultaneously against an American and a Mexican. In 1952 and 1954, the matches were played over thirty-six holes, with a total of 27 points at stake (9 for foursomes, 18 for singles). From 1956 to 1965, the matches were reduced to eighteen holes, so that each competitor played in two sixsomes and two foursomes. The points at stake doubled to 54.

The Americas Cup matches were played every second year between 1952 and 1960 and again between 1961 and 1967, each country hosting them in turn. By 1967, the three countries were sending teams to the World Amateur Team Championships, and Canada was going to the Commonwealth Team Matches. The burden of time and money became too great, so the Americas Cup matches were allowed to die.

| Year | Points | | | Venue |
	U.S.	Canada	Mexico	
1952	12	10	5	U.S.
1954	14	13	0	Canada
1956	29 ½	11 ½	13	Mexico
1958	30	17	7	U.S.
1960	21 ½	20	12 ½	Canada
1961	29	14	11	Mexico
1963	26 ½	19 ½	8	U.S.
1965	19 ½	22	12 ½	Canada
1967	23 ½	17 ½	13	Mexico

The only Canadian team to win the Americas Cup, 1965. Standing, left to right: *Keith Alexander, Doug Silverberg, Nick Weslock, Johnny Johnston, Bert Ticehurst, Gary Cowan.* Kneeling: *non-playing captain Bruce Forbes, Bill Pidlaski.*

Canada knocked the U.S. out of first place only once, in 1965, at the St. Charles CC, Winnipeg. The core of the team that year was made up of four who were to play for Canada between eleven and nineteen times each, and who played together as a group seven times: Weslock, Cowan, Alexander, and Silverberg. In 1965, the other team members were Johnny Johnston (playing in his sixth international), Bert Ticehurst, and Bill Pidlaski. Keith Alexander had the only unbeaten record in the singles matches that year, winning two and tying two. In the foursomes, Silverberg and Pidlaski won all four. Had there been a prize for the most spectacular burst of golf, it would have gone to the young American player Mark Hopkins. He shot eight birdies in eleven holes. And that is how Weslock came to lose by 5 and 4.

Over the years, Canadian amateurs were to have many notable wins in the Americas Cup. In 1952, Walter McElroy brought down Frank

Stranahan to the tune of 4 and 3, by keeping the ball in play on the fairway and by deadly putting. Gerry Kesselring defeated Harvey Ward at the thirty-eighth, and Weslock beat Charlie Coe, 3 and 2. Bill Mawhinney had back trouble and could not play that year.

Two years later, Doug Silverberg had a great victory over Harvey Ward (who was about to win the Canadian Amateur). The Canadians that year put on an unprecedented display against an American team. Silverberg, Don Doe, and Norman won both their singles, and our team lost by the margin of only one point.

George Knudson played in 1956 and went through his matches unbeaten.

In 1958, Gary Cowan appeared in his first Americas Cup, and he was to play in all the subsequent series. That first year, he won all four singles matches, including one against Harvey Ward. His record in the Americas Cup was second to none.

In 1960, at Ottawa, Cowan was Canada's only winner in the singles, triumphing over Charlie Coe and Bill Hyndman. Jack Nicklaus was then making the first of two appearances in the series. Ron Willey and Johnny Johnston took on and defeated Nicklaus and Beman, not once, but twice.

At the Club Campestre Monterrey in 1961, both Weslock and Cowan held Nicklaus to a half. In the Weslock–Nicklaus–Farias match, a fluke nearly robbed Weslock in his fight with Nicklaus. He had hit a fine shot to the twelfth green and expected to find himself within birdie range. But his ball had landed on Farias's ball and scuttled thirty feet away. Justice and equity were served when his long putt dropped, to give him the hole needed to square the match.

The Americas Cup was discontinued in 1967.

The Royal and Ancient Golf Club of St. Andrews was two hundred years old in 1954. To celebrate its bicentenary, it invited teams of six amateur golfers from each of Canada, Australia, New Zealand, and South Africa to compete in a round-robin tournament with a team from the British Isles (Great Britain and Ireland). The St. Andrews' bicentennial tournament was perpetuated in the form of Commonwealth Team Matches, held every four years from 1959 to 1975. Golfers all over the Commonwealth expressed the view that these matches were the best thing that had happened to the amateur game.

Political problems prevented South Africa in 1971 and Australia in 1975 from taking part. Canada won the tournament in 1971 and 1975.

Our winning team in the Commonwealth Team Matches, on the way to New Zealand, 1971, 1971. Left to right, RCGA president Patrick C. Osler, Gary Cowan, Doug Roxburgh, Nick Weslock, Stu Hamilton, Bruce Forbes.

Canada beat Great Britain and New Zealand in 1954; beat New Zealand and tied with Australia in 1963; beat New Zealand and South Africa in 1967; beat Great Britain, Australia, and New Zealand in 1971; and beat Great Britain and New Zealand in 1975.

The matches took the format of the Walker Cup, each country playing foursomes and singles against every other country, with a point for a win and a half point for a halved match. After four unsuccessful attempts to win a series, Canada finally did so at the Auckland GC, New Zealand, in 1971. Not for the first time, political problems arose which altered the face of the tournament. South Africa was no longer a member of the Commonwealth but had been invited to send a team. This led to anti-apartheid demonstrations in New Zealand, with the threat of

more if South Africa did not withdraw. It did withdraw, and the tournament was subsequently linked not to the Commonwealth but to New Zealand's centennial celebrations.

The core of the winning Canadian team was again its four stalwarts, Weslock, Cowan, Alexander, and Silverberg. To these were added Stu Hamilton and Doug Roxburgh. Roxburgh, only twenty and playing his first international, was the youngest competitor. But then Weslock, at fifty-four, was by far the oldest. The New Zealand tournament was held in October, a time of year that suited Canada, since it was the end of our playing season.

The team of Dave Webber, Ken Tamke, Jim Nelford, Doug Roxburgh, Cec Ferguson, and Robbie Jackson went to Durban in 1975. After losing to South Africa, this team made a

Our winning team in the 1975 Commonwealth Team Matches. Left to right, *Dave Webber, Ken Tamke, Jim Nelford, R. Bruce Forbes (team captain), Doug Roxburgh, Cec Ferguson, Robbie Jackson.*

great comeback, beating the favoured British team and retaining the Commonwealth Trophy.

In 1958, a World Amateur Golf Council was established. Its purpose was "to promote friendship and sportsmanship among people of the world." It organized the first World Amateur Team Championship that same year. These championships have been held at two-year intervals ever since, some thirty nations sending teams of four to a venue in some golf-playing country, to compete for the Eisenhower Trophy.

With so many nations taking part, match play is out of the question, so each members of a team plays four 18-hole rounds over four days. At the end of each day, a team discards the highest score of its four. The team with the lowest four-day aggregate is the winner.

The concept of selecting only three out of a team's four scores each day was frowned upon by the purists. But it made good sense. A team was able to continue if one of its members fell ill during the tournament.

There was initially some talk of recognizing the lowest individual scorer as "World Amateur Champion." But this was also frowned upon by the top brass, who did not want to destroy the image of the tournament as a team event.

Although Canada was not to win the Eisenhower Trophy until 1986, we did better in the early years of this tournament than in the Commonwealth matches. This may have had something to do with the fact that the World team matches did not feature foursomes, a format rarely used in Canada. Whatever the reason, Canada came second to the United States in 1962 (Cowan, Wakeham, Weslock, and Wylie) and second to Great Britain in

The flag-raising ceremony at the World Amateur Team Championship, Japan, 1962.

1964 (Cowan, Weslock, Silverberg, and Alexander). In these and other years, we saw good performances from Canadian players.

In 1962, Canada's Gary Cowan had the lowest individual score and was recognized by the press (if not officially by the organizers) as "World Amateur Champion." But for some inspired putting by the Americans on the last day, Canada would have won this tournament.

In 1964, in Rome, Britain's Leonard Crawley wrote of Keith Alexander's final round: "In the Annals of International Golf there has been no more outstanding performance." Alexander was last to play that day, and needed a par 72 to give Canada a tie with Britain. At the end of the twelfth hole he was 5 over par, and all looked lost. Then came his finest hour. On the thirteenth, he scrambled a par four by getting down in two from a bunker. His tee-shot at the 160-yard fourteenth was 18 inches from the cup. Two fine woods on the 480-yard fifteenth left him with 15 feet for an eagle, which he just missed. A beautiful iron on the difficult 190-yard sixteenth was 10 feet away, good enough for his third birdie in a row. He made it four with a chip and a six-foot putt, and needed a birdie at the last hole to tie Britain. He hit a good tee-shot on eighteen, and as he played his second, the gallery watched in stunned silence. But he pulled the shot slightly, found a trap in front of the green, and took bogey. So Canada had to be content with second place, just two strokes behind.

In 1966, Canada sent what was probably its strongest team ever to a world tournament: the fearsome foursome of Weslock, Cowan, Alexander, and Silverberg. But they could do nothing with the greens in Mexico City. Cowan broke his putter when he banged it against his shoe, and consequently had to putt with a 2-iron; Silverberg chewed his cigars to bits; Alexander admitted to being all knotted up inside; Weslock threw his hands to the heavens: "The texture of these greens is incredible!"

Playing internationally has its moments. In 1972, at Buenos Aires, the team of Dave Barr, Roxburgh, Weslock, and Alexander, accompanied by the RCGA's Bruce Forbes, had their hotel rocked by a bomb, which killed several people. On the war to the airport, their bus caught on fire and they had to escape through a window.

Alexander continued to play internationally for Canada until 1977, Cowan until 1981. By then, a new crop of youngsters was coming to the front. But many of them disappeared into the professional ranks just as we looked set to win out first World championship. Doug Roxburgh was one of those who remained an amateur. He has played a dozen times for Canada. In 1978, when we came second to the U.S., Roxburgh came second in the individual scoring.

The federal government's policy on South Africa stopped us playing in 1982. The RCGA complied, reluctantly: "It should not be construed from our action that members of the Executive Committee and Governors of this Association necessarily agree with the position of our Government."

In 1986, Canada went to Caracas and won the World Amateur for the first time. The team of Mark Brewer, Jack Kay Jr., Warren Sye, and Brent Franklin went into the last round three strokes behind the Americans. They finished three strokes up. Mark Brewer's 70 69 69 69–217 tied for second individual place. It would be nice to report that the same team defended in 1988. But of the four, only Warren Sye remains an amateur. He had his reward in 1990, when he won the Canadian Amateur.

CHAPTER

THE RCGA: CATCHING UP WITH THE TWENTIETH CENTURY

THE RCGA had neither a permanent staff nor a permanent office until 1920, when it appointed a part-time secretary-treasurer.

Before that, by custom, an honorary secretary-treasurer had been elected at the AGM, usually from the club chosen to host the next Amateur championship. For a year, his business office or his home became the office of the RCGA. The association reimbursed him for his expenses and gave him an honorarium of one hundred dollars.

At the AGM of 1912, members had voted to have a permanent secretary-treasurer. But the post was not filled. Either the right man could not be found or the salary of two hundred dollars a year plus expenses was not attractive enough.

When the honorary secretary of the RCGA enlisted during the First World War, B. L. Anderson, a member of Lambton G & CC, took his place. With the second post-war Amateur to be held in Beaconsfield, Anderson handed over the duties of secretary to the secretary of that club in June 1919.

At the AGM a year later, it was unanimously agreed to elect a permanent secretary-treasurer. A motion that B. L. Anderson be appointed was seconded and received with enthusiasm. So began a relationship that was to last for a quarter of a century.

We often say of a man that he has become an institution in his own lifetime, meaning that he has become such a part of the established order of things, such a familiar and respected figure, that his society never seems quite the same without him. Old Tom Morris was an institution at St. Andrews; George S. Lyon was an institution in Canadian golf for the first three decades of this century. A man need not be a Morris or a Lyon to become an institution, but he should at least be as much respected.

Long before his death in 1946, B. L. Anderson came close to being an institution in

431

B. L. Anderson, the RCGA's first impresario.

Canadian golf. All through the 1920s and 1930s and up to the end of the Second World War, B. L. ran the affairs of the RCGA. In his time as secretary, he witnessed many changes. Canadian golfers increased their number tenfold, changed from hickory to steel and from sand tees to wood, standardized the ball, upped the Open prize money from $500 to $10,000, and elected twenty-five presidents of the RCGA. And B. L. Anderson did more than witness these changes – he had a modest hand in their shaping.

Custom required that he be given the title of "Secretary-Treasurer." But that title diminishes his role. His duties were those of executive director, tournament manager, public relations officer, editor of the RCGA's *Annual Golf Review*, comptroller, and secretary to at least three committees. What seems just as astonishing as the breadth of his job with the RCGA is the fact that he performed it with the help of only a part-time secretary and while managing the affairs of his own insurance company. For twenty-five years, the office of the RCGA was the office of the president of B. L. Anderson Limited.

All of this was only possible, of course, because Anderson had the time to spare, and because the world of golf, before the Second World War, was a smaller and more leisurely one. Golf was still very much a game for amateurs. At the end of Anderson's stewardship, commercial sponsors were beginning to make it a business, but it was to be some years before television turned golf into big business.

The RCGA had been established in 1895 to run national championships, and it did little else until after the Second World War. In 1945, its annual revenue was only $4,000. It had eighteen governors (or directors, as they were then called). Its membership was less than a quarter of what it is today. Apart from the executive committee, it had only one permanent standing committee, on the rules of golf.

If that puts the role of B. L. Anderson into some sort of perspective, it might also discount unfairly his contribution to the RCGA and to golf. For over a quarter of a century, he *was* the RCGA to golfers across Canada. Year after year, president after president would pay glowing tribute to B. L., thanking him for his untiring efforts, his diligence, his support.

Former RCGA governors Fred Lyon and Bill Taylor – Taylor took over from Anderson – remember him as a respected, hard-working man of strong convictions, dedicated to the game, but of an introverted nature; a man who was at times dogmatic and autocratic, and – as one of them put it – "a bit of a loner." Well-known amateurs who remember him as he was in the 1940s recall that he was always respected but not always liked.

B. L. Anderson was probably aware of how he was perceived for he wrote of himself in 1937: "In such a position [secretary-treasurer of the RCGA] it is very nearly impossible to be popular. One has to be the 'No man' to too many simple requests. The best one can hope for is to be fair."

Burrett Lyman Anderson (known to his friends as Burt, and to the golfing world as B. L.) was born in Phelps, in the state of New York, in 1877, and was educated at the University of

Rochester. When he came to Toronto in 1904, he worked for a short time in the advertising department of the *Toronto Daily Star*. But he soon switched to become business manager for *Industrial Canada*, the organ of the Canadian Manufacturers' Association. Three years later, he moved up to become assistant manager of the CMA's insurance department. This led him to purchase an interest in an insurance agency, which he bought out in 1916, renaming it B. L. Anderson Limited.

In his younger days, B. L. had been a keen tennis player. In Toronto, he took up golf. His name appears in newspaper notices about Toronto's High Park GC, and in 1912 he attended the RCGA's AGM as a delegate of this club. About then, or earlier, he also joined Lambton,

where he remained a member until his death in 1946.

As legend grew around the man, myth often became confused with fact. "He fostered and visualized the Interprovincial team championships," Hilles Pickens wrote of him, which may not have been strictly true. He advocated paying the expenses of leading amateurs from each province to attend the national Amateur. But the idea of reinstituting the interprovincial matches was first raised at the RCGA's AGM in 1926 by George S. Lyon and W. J. Thompson of the Ontario Golf Association.

B. L. Anderson's contribution to Canadian golf was well defined by Hilles Pickens in 1945, when B. L. retired:

B. L. (second from left) in 1942 discussing plans for that year's Open with, to his right, Bradford Ellison, and, to his left, Joe Rothschild and Merle Schneckenburger of Seagram.

Canadian golf owes to the energy, zeal, and judgement of B. L. Anderson, the kind of leadership and care which is seldom the privilege of a sport to obtain from a single individual; the kind that few, very few, individuals have the ability, tenacity and love of the game to give.

There is little doubt that the governors of the RCGA would have considered B. L. Anderson for the Canadian Golf Hall of Fame, had there been one in 1946. However, this honour was eventually bestowed on the woman who had been Anderson's long-time assistant.

In 1934, Marion Torpey (later Mrs. Doherty) came to work in Anderson's insurance office. By 1936, she was doing most of the secretarial work on RCGA affairs, and in 1945 she was appointed the assistant secretary of the RCGA. This "foundation of knowledge and guiding light" gave forty years of service to the RCGA, before retiring in 1976.

When B. L. Anderson resigned because of ill-health in 1945 (he died a year later), William D. Taylor took over as honorary secretary-treasurer.

Bill Taylor was widely known in the field of sport, both as an expert skier and as a golfer of national repute. Born in Montreal in 1907, he and brother Gordon had started golfing at the Summerlea Club as boys. Like Gordon, he had several times been a member of Quebec's Willingdon Cup teams, and some consider Bill as fine a player. He had also served as the honorary secretary-treasurer of Quebec's golf association (PQGA). His great personal charm and his ability as a golf administrator were qualities well-known to his friends, including Jack Fuller, also of Montreal and the president of the RCGA in 1946.

In 1931, Bill Taylor had joined the advertising department of the Montreal publication *Golf and Sports Illustrated*, then the property of Hilles Pickens Sr. He became advertising manager in the following year. He had come to

Bill Taylor: golfer, administrator.

know Ralph Reville of *Canadian Golfer*, so he acted as the negotiator when Pickens took over *Canadian Golfer*, in 1933. After the takeover, Bill Taylor found himself general manager of the magazine. But he left in 1940, to join the Toronto office of the Montreal Standard Publishing Company. The move put him conveniently in the right city when RCGA governor Jack Fuller talked him into taking over from B. L. Anderson at the RCGA, in addition to his job at Standard.

B. L. Anderson was somewhat surprised at the RCGA's choice to succeed him. "He was not very happy that a young whippersnapper like me was taking over," Taylor recalled, some forty years later.

In the few years that he acted as the RCGA's secretary-treasurer, Bill Taylor managed to bring the association into the twentieth century. The RCGA had been running the national championships for fifty years, and running them very well. Apart from the service provided by its Rules of Golf Committee, however, it had done precious little for golf clubs in Canada.

The association wanted to give member clubs more for their money but constantly ran up against the same problem – a shortage of funds. After hiring a man in 1925 to run a Green Section as service to clubs, the RCGA found that his salary ate up twice their income from memberships. So the Green Section had to be discontinued after a year or so. The RCGA's promise of a national handicapping system had remained just a promise, for the same reason. The RCGA governors were mostly businessmen, who would have known that an underfunded operation cannot be successful.

At the same time, there is no evidence that golfers in Canada were crying out for better service, no evidence that the RCGA was ever accused of being unsuccessful. It met the needs of the 1930s, and that was an end to it. But after Bill Taylor had shown the RCGA how to quadruple its income, many recognized (with the benefit of hindsight) that underfunding had been chronic. Here is Charlie Watson, RCGA governor, in 1948: "It requires no accountant's acumen to see that for years the RCGA had been unsoundly and inadequately financed. If we have a week of bad weather during the Open, our slender reserves would vanish."

In 1928, the concept of having two classes of membership, allied and associate, had been dropped. A club now had to pay an annual membership fee from ten to forty dollars, depending on its number of male members, excluding juniors. Membership of the RCGA reached a peak of 161 clubs in 1930, when the income from clubs' subscriptions amounted to about half of the RCGA's total income of $6,000. During the Depression years, membership and revenue fell drastically. In 1934, some forty clubs were one or more years in arrears on their annual fees.

During most of its existence, the RCGA had had to compete with provincial golf associations for members. In Canada as a whole, about twice as many clubs joined provincial associations as joined the RCGA. But this average disguises wide variations between regions. In the West, four to five times as many clubs joined provincial associations as joined the RCGA; in the East, perhaps one and a half times as many. The reasons are not difficult to find. In the West and in the Maritimes, the RCGA was perceived as serving an elite in Quebec and Ontario. Clubs had more loyalty to their provinces. Provincial championships were open to golfers of higher handicap, so more could enter, from more clubs. The cost of travelling to a provincial championship was less, unless you happened to live in Quebec or Ontario, where the national championships were invariable held.

For all these reasons, only about one-third of the golf clubs in Canada were members of the RCGA in 1937. In that year, seeking new ways to increase membership and income, the RCGA recruited the provincial associations as affiliate members. Clubs now subscribed only to their provincial association, but automatically became members of the RCGA. The intention was to try this out for a year or so, to determine how much clubs should pay in membership fees to give the provincial associations *and* the RCGA enough money to do their jobs. In the meantime, the provincial associations guaranteed to pass on to the RCGA a portion of each club's subscription, so that the RGGA would have no less income from subscriptions than the $2,300 or so it had received on average over the previous five years.

The Second World War was to prolong this temporary arrangement so that it lasted for nine years. The change meant that the RCGA's membership had automatically increased from 123 in 1936, to 275 in 1939, a reflection of the greater number of clubs belonging to the provincial associations.

With Seagram sponsoring the Open from 1936, the income from the open (entry fees and the gate) became the RCGA's other main source of funds. But this was by no means a secure income. In a good year, the Open might net $4,000; in a bad year, $200. It all depended on the weather and the venue.

The state of the RCGA's finances when Taylor took over from Anderson at the end of 1945 was such that the association could afford to spend only about $2,500 a year on salaries and wages.

Taylor's greatest contribution to the RCGA in the few years he was there was his conception and introduction of a new method of funding. It came to be known as the Dollar-a-Year Plan. The concept was simple. The sum of one dollar was added to the annual dues of each senior male member of clubs that belonged to a provincial golf association (and hence to the RCGA). This dollar was split fifty/fifty between the provincial association and the RCGA. Whereas the RCGA might have received (or begged for) a $25-a-year donation from a club with a senior male membership of 50, it now received $125 a year, *none of which came out of the club's existing revenues*. So the club, the provincial association, and the RCGA all stood to benefit.

Encouraged by the support of president Jack Fuller, Taylor introduced the concept to the RCGA governors in November 1946. The Dollar-a-Year Plan became part of the RCGA's new constitution, adopted in November 1947.

To help him sell the idea to provincial associations and to clubs, Taylor recruited E. Harold Banks to be his full-time assistant. More affectionately known as Banksie, this extroverted ex-rubber planter and ex-newspaperman had great personal charm and wit. He had played golf in many countries around the world. Retired from the CPR with a modest pension, Banks came along at the right time for Taylor and the RCGA. He had worked for the Ontario Golf Association, and now took on the additional responsibilities of assistant to Taylor.

The Dollar-a-Year Plan had this advantage over the old method of billing clubs for an annual membership fee: the club members, and not the club, now forked out the money. A dollar a year added to his annual subscription would never be missed by a golfer, might not even be noticed on his account. Nevertheless, some clubs, as well as some provincial associations, did not readily accept the change. But Taylor had wisely sought and obtained the support of the influential Ontario Golf Association.

To some extent, the concept was sold to the West by Harold Banks's visit to golf associations and clubs, and by the lobbying of the RCGA governors from the western provinces. The majority of the Calgary clubs had in mind rejecting the plan, but Banks spoke to them in Calgary for two hours, persuading them it was in their best interests.

The PQGA was the most difficult to convince. The RCGA was headquartered in Toronto. Quebec golfers had the usual misgivings about anything that came out of Ontario, an extension of the rivalry that existed between the two provinces on the golf course. But the Quebec association had also been for many years the best financed in the country. It had a large and enthusiastic club membership (thanks to the hard work of former secretaries such as Taylor!). By the end of 1948, only twenty-five clubs in Quebec out of sixty had accepted the plan and were billing their members. Four years after the plan had been put into effect, Quebec was still reporting opposition by member clubs.

On the other hand, the Ontario Golf Association had never been very strong financially and now found its income greatly increased. In general, the same can be said of the other provincial associations.

Under the new RCGA constitution of November 1947, clubs belonging to a provincial association automatically became members of the RCGA. The RCGA's executive committee was replaced by a board of governors, which was in fact as much a change of substance as of name. The provinces still had the same proportional representation on the board, but there were now places for five past presidents as governors, and five additional governors could be appointed by the board at any meeting.

Within a few years, these governors were required to chair an increasing number of RCGA committees and activities, made possible by the Dollar-a-Year Plan.

The income of the RCGA increased dramatically in the years following the introduction of the plan. Income from member clubs shot up from $2,400 in 1947, to $16,000 in 1949, the first full year of the plan, and to $20,000 in 1953.

Within four years of the plan's implementation, the RCGA was doing what it had promised to do. It had put in place a national handicapping system, organized the first of a series of amateur team matches against the United States, run several turf clinics, paid the full expenses of the Willingdon Cup teams, and, perhaps most important of all, had made a start on what came to be known as Junior Development.

In 1947, the RCGA had three committees: one on the Rules of Golf, another on the Open, and a third that looked after the Amateur and the Junior championships. In 1948, it added a committee on Handicapping and Course Rating; in 1949 it re-established its Green Section, which had been defunct for twenty years, a year later, it had a committee working on Junior Development and Golf Week. By the middle of the 1960s it had separate committees on Finance, National Tournaments, Canadian Open Study, Open Championship, Amateur Championship, Senior Championship, Junior Championship, Amateur Tournaments Study, Amateur Status and Reinstatement, Handicap and Course Rating, Junior Promotion and National Golf Week, Rules of Golf, Long Range Planning, Nominating, Green Section Study, Membership and Public Relations, Liaison with Canadian PGA, Liaison with Fitness and Amateur Sports Directorate, Television, Selection, Golf House Project, and Editorial Board.

These were the visible benefits from Bill Taylor's brainchild. But by the end of 1948, the pressure of business had forced him to give up his post as honorary secretary to the RCGA.

Charlie Watson, RCGA president in 1950, a promoter of Junior Development, with a protégé.

Bill Taylor was elected a governor of the RCGA. This modest and talented man, with the voice of a Hal Halbrook, went on to become an enthusiastic member of the Canadian Seniors' Golf Association, and to captain the Seniors in internationals against the United States. To take over from him at the RCGA he recruited his friend Bill Hamilton, the first full-time secretary in the association's history.

A 2-handicap golfer, W. T. (Bill) Hamilton came from his own business, Hamilton Brothers, to be the secretary-treasurer to the RCGA in 1948.

Born in Toronto in 1914, Hamilton had taken up golf at the age of eighteen, at the public course Humber Valley. From there he moved to Lakeview (then a private club) and later to Mississaugua, where he became acquainted with Bill Taylor. Having golfed with Hamilton, Taylor knew him to have both a great affection for the game and an engaging personality. Taylor's recommendations that the association needed a full-time manager and

Bill Hamilton, administrator and professional.

National Golf Day to raise money for junior golf. In 1954, he added the title of Manager to his secretaryship of the RCGA. By this time, the organization of the junior and men's national championships, the Willingdon Cup matches, the Open, and the Americas Cup matches. had become too big a job to be handled by an RCGA tournament committee of businessmen. So Bill Hamilton took over the full direction of the association's tournaments. He proved himself so successful at this that the PGA (of America) offered him the position of tournament director. But his family did not want to move, which was a blessing for Canadian golf.

By the time Bill Hamilton left the RCGA in 1956 – to become the professional at Toronto's Oakdale club – the RCGA was established on a firm course to reasonable prosperity. After the steep climb it had taken under the direction of Taylor and Hamilton, it was to make a slower but steady progress until the next dramatic change in its fortunes, the move to Glen Abbey, twenty years later.

One of the men to guide the RCGA along the path to Glen Abbey was R. Bruce Forbes. He became executive director of the RCGA in 1970, after a succession of managers or executive directors had followed Bill Hamilton: course architect C. E. "Robbie" Robinson (1956–60), L. V. Kavanagh (1961–65), James F. Gaquin (1966–68), and L. V. Kavanagh again (1969).

In Bruce Forbes, the RCGA found itself once more with a man possessing a deep and abiding passion for the game of golf. "Golf has really been my life. I eat, sleep and drink the game," this tall, handsome, affable man was quoted as saying early in 1970. He was then an RCGA governor, having been its president in 1965. He came up the hard way, through the ranks, the way of most RCGA presidents between 1921 (when the honour was first made elective) and the early 1980s.

Bruce Forbes was born in Chatham, Ontario, but when he was three – some seventy

that Hamilton was the man for the job were accepted by the RCGA governors.

Hamilton knew little about the RCGA's affairs and had no previous experience in running a golf association. He was, in the words of Charlie Watson, "green as the grass on which we play this great game." But that was offset by his desire and willingness to learn from Taylor, from the association's other governors in the Toronto area, and from such as Harold Banks and Marion Doherty. He was – again in Watson's words – "sharp enough and astute enough to gather the crumbs which fell from their table and apply them to his own use."

Hamilton's first term with the RCGA lasted eight years. In this time he made himself into a professional golf administrator, a figure known, respected, and liked throughout Canada, as well as by the USGA and the PGA. To his credit goes the organizing of schools for golf course superintendents, and the concept and promotion of a years ago – his father started what is now the Forbes Brothers car dealership in Brantford. Bruce Forbes is therefore a Brantford man, through and through. He was schooled at the local collegiate and at the Ontario agricultural College (now the University of Guelph). After the Second World War – he was a Staff Captain in the Fourth Brigade HQ – he went into the family business. His father had been president of Brantford Golf Club, so there was never much doubt about his son's choice of sport or club.

At Brantford GC, Bruce Forbes soon played to a handicap of 1. But he admits that early in his career he knew that his contribution to golf would never be as Ontario champion. So began his interest in the affairs of his club. In 1952 he was club president. In 1956 he became a director of the Ontario Golf Association, and he headed the association in 1962.

Having been elected a governor of the RCGA in 1958, he worked his way through several committees, before being elected president in 1965. In the period 1965–70, he chaired the Green Section, and proved to have a green thumb for the job, promoting the first Turf Grass Conferences and hiring a full-time agronomist. He also became involved in the Open, chairing its rules committee for several years, and doing as much as anyone to attract the top American players to Canada.

International amateur team golf was just hitting its stride as Bruce Forbes became an RCGA governor. His natural aptitude for getting on with people made him a natural choice as Canada's non-playing captain. Over the next twenty-odd years he travelled with Canadian teams all over the world. He was, in effect, Canada's golfing ambassador, a post he relished and which brought him friends in just about every golfing nation in the world. Three times he returned with a winning team: he was there when Canada won the Americas Cup at Winnipeg in 1965, the New Zealand Centennial Tournament in 1971, and, four years later, the Commonwealth Tournament in South Africa.

Bruce Forbes was persuaded to take on the job of running the RCGA in 1970. He was to

A meeting of the world's rulesmakers at the R & A clubhouse. Second row, second from right, *W. Arthur Johnston, president of the RCGA in 1964;* fourth row, second from left, *Bruce Forbes, a vice-president of the RCGA.*

be its executive director for eight years. The 1970s were tumultuous years, in which the association lost one sponsor for the Open and found another, and moved its headquarters from Toronto's Bay Street to Oakville's Glen Abbey. From a handful in 1970, the RCGA's executive office staff increased to nearer twenty. Bill Hamilton came back in 1973 to be Manager and Tournament Co-ordinator. But, with a view to the future, the RCGA also acquired two young men who were to serve it well when Bruce Forbes retired – Geordie Hilton, executive director until 1989, and Stephen Ross, who took over that year.

Bruce Forbes had more than a little to do with the move to Glen Abbey, as we shall see in a later chapter. He was inducted into the Canadian Golf Hall of Fame in 1987.

In 1954, having established a new basis for membership fees, the RCGA started a drive for new members. In that year, a survey identified 498 clubs in the country (a figure almost certainly on the low side) of which 316 were RCGA members. In 1989, the number of clubs had grown to 1,571, and membership, to 1,287.

During this same period, the RCGA's income from member clubs increased from $20,000 to $565,000. By 1989, the dollar-a-year had been increased over fourfold just to cover inflation. In real terms, the RCGA's income per club had probably gone up by about 30 per cent, a measure of how the male membership of clubs has increased over the same years.

The RCGA's other main source of income, before the move to Glen Abbey, was the Canadian Open. But in the years 1948 to 1973, the Open provided only about a quarter to a third as much income as membership fees.

The higher income from the Open started in 1974; the television rights jumped from $23,000 to $52,000 when a U.S. network televised the Open from Mississaugua.

And where did the money go? The RCGA is a non-profit organization. The money made from membership dues and from professional golf (the Open) is ploughed back into amateur golf and into providing a service to members clubs. The RCGA has to meet an ever-increasing bill for running its national headquarters. It is expected to be a source of information on the game in Canada, including the rules, and to have at its fingertips an encyclopaedic knowledge of golf in this and other countries. Golf knows no bounds; neither do the responsibilities of the national bodies running golf in this country.

31
CHAPTER

SPONSORS, THE OPEN, AND GOLF ON THE AIRWAVES

ALMOST BY DEFINITION, EVERY GOLF tournament must have a sponsor. Without it, the tournament would not take place. But this chapter is about commercial sponsors, business organizations that help meet the cost of putting on a golf tournament by donating a trophy and money. In return, the organization has its name linked to the tournament and gets its money back in increased sales. That, at least, is the economic theory behind commercial sponsorship. It is a form of advertising.

Hiram Walker donated a trophy for the Niagara International Tournament in 1896. And Mr. Chipman of the Hudson's Bay Company put up the trophy for the Southern Alberta Golf Championship at about the same time. Commercial sponsorship, therefore, is as old as our oldest tournaments, but it made a significant breakthrough when Seagram came to sponsor the Canadian Open, and it became pervasive with the advent of television after the Second World War.

For forty years, commercial sponsorship was anathema to the RCGA. Back in 1896, when Hiram Walker had offered to put up a trophy for the Canadian Amateur Championship, he had been politely refused (". . . the Walker Cup should not be accepted by the Association for competition, nor should any prize be allowed that is merely an advertising medium," was the opinion of Royal Montreal's executive).

By 1936, the RCGA had little choice but to accept commercial sponsorship. The prize money for the Open had fallen far behind that of other less notable events in the United States. If the Open was to attract the top American professionals, the RCGA needed to double (at least) the $1,465 purse it offered in 1935.

Strangely, it was another distiller who came to the rescue. After much soul-searching, the RCGA approached the Joseph E. Seagram Company Limited. The company agreed to put up a handsome trophy for the Open – the Seagram Gold Cup – along with a hefty chunk of cash.

This was the beginning of a happy, and mostly prosperous, thirty-four-year relationship between Seagram and the Canadian Open. Even the conservatives within the RCGA had to admit that the marriage was a howling success.

By 1936, the RCGA's stiff opposition to commercial sponsorship had already been softened by the financial and aesthetic success of another commercially sponsored Canadian tournament held for the first time a year earlier. This was the General Brock Open. The general had helped save the roots of Canada back in 1812; the General Brock was to be as beneficial for the Canadian Open 124 years later.

In 1935, a Canadian hotelier co-sponsored a professional golf tournament that offered the biggest purse ever seen in Canada. The General Brock Open, with its prize money of between four and five thousand dollars, survived for three years. It attracted the top tournament players from the United States and was rated an outstanding success by players and spectators alike. The success of the General Brock gave the RCGA the final push into commercial sponsorship of the Canadian Open.

Vernon G. Cardy ran a group of hotels which at one time or another included the Mount Royal in Montreal, the Royal Connaught in Hamilton, the Prince Edward in Windsor, the Bigwin Inn in Muskoka, and the Alpine Inn in the Laurentians. He took up golf in the 1920s. Not particularly long off the tee, he was especially accurate with a small, gold-headed putter. But we honour him more as our first big-time commercial sponsor. Others may have recognized the commercial possibility of golf in Canada, but he was the first to bet his money on it.

In 1935, Cardy had just acquired something of a white elephant, the General Brock hotel in Niagara Falls, Ontario. As a means to making its name better known, Cardy conceived the idea of sponsoring a golf tournament with the same name as the hotel. He bought a gold trophy and talked Seagram into taking it over and co-sponsoring a tournament with a prize money of $4,000.

The General Brock Open was held at the Lookout Point Golf Club, Fonthill, Ontario, twelve miles from the General Brock hotel. In 1935 this course, it was said, stretched over 6,900 yards, making it one of the longest in North America. Its par of 74 had rarely been broken.

Filming the General Brock Open, 1935.

The size of the purse ensured the event a spot on the PGA summer tour, so the field was one of the strongest to visit Canada. The top five placers in the U.S. Open were there. So was a young man making a vivid impression on the U.S. scene, Byron Nelson. A Japanese golf team touring North America was invited. All but a few of Canada's top professionals entered, as did a few top amateurs.

The hills and valleys of Lookout Point had earned it the reputation of being a killer course. To survive seventy-two holes in three days you had to be in the pink of condition. That, at least, was the consensus before the players teed off. The surprising winner was Tony Manero, of Greensboro, North Carolina. Surprising, because this was his first tournament after a two-year illness. His 74 72 74 71–291 was achieved by playing within himself and by hoarding his reserves of strength.

But the big surprise of the 1935 General Brock was the performance of a twenty-year-old tall, lanky Winnipeg amateur. Daniel James "Bud" Donovan went into the final round seven strokes behind the leader, Byron Nelson. He caught Nelson with a 70, tying him for sec-

ond place at 292. He might easily have caught Manero had he not tried to back-hand a putt into the hole, only to whiff it. At the time, his performance at the General Brock was the best ever by an amateur in Canada playing against the might of U.S. professionals.

Bud Donovan (who nearly stole the show) with Vernon Cardy, left.

Walter Hagen accepting the Seagram Gold Cup on behalf of the U.S. team from Cleland of Seagram in 1935.

In 1936, the General Brock was again on the PGA summer tour. Strangely, the winner was again a semi-invalid. Craig Wood sprained his back early in the third round. (If you have ever seen this man take a swipe at a ball, you will understand why!) At lunchtime, he suffered such intense pain that he was on the point of withdrawing. But a pain-killing drug came to his aid. He went on to shatter par in the afternoon, winning by two strokes over the defending champion, Manero (who was by this time the U.S. Open titleholder).

Canada's top professionals had been out-golfed in the first two General Brocks. In 1937, all was forgiven. Jules Huot, the twenty-nine-year-old, 140-pound, French-Canadian professional, not only won the first prize of $750, but also shot a 280, to better the tournament record by five strokes. In the third round he set a course record with an astonishing 66.

The Americans – including Ben Hogan, Jimmy Thompson, Harry Cooper, Bill Melhorn – were never ahead at any stage of the tournament. Bob Gray Jr., then at Essex G & CC, led for the first two rounds, Jules Huot for the last two. Here was a field as strong as any you would find in a Canadian Open, and a Canadian had won by two strokes. The only disappointment of the day was Bob Gray slipping to eighth place.

Jules Huot's win in the 1937 General Brock was not the first by a Canadian in a PGA Tour event, since young Ken Black had put flight to the American challengers at Vancouver a year earlier.

The success of the General Brock Open in 1935 helped to coax a reluctant RCGA into seeking commercial sponsorship of the Canadian Open.

When Vernon Cardy first conceived the notion of an international golf tournament, he approached his friend Bill Taylor, then secretary of the PQ Golf Association. Would Taylor and Hilles Pickens run the General Brock Open? Fifty years later, Bill Taylor still remembers the reaction the idea generated in Toronto. "When word of this reached the RCGA offices in Bay Street, there was more than a little bristling. What did these Montreal upstarts think they were doing, coming to Ontario and organizing a tournament under our noses, giving out more prize money than the Canadian Open!"

But when Cardy brought in Seagram as co-sponsors, Seagram wanted the fellow with the most experience in organizing major tournaments. That fellow was B. L. Anderson, the RCGA secretary, who had been responsible for the Canadian Open for fifteen years. His first General Brock was a great success, confirming to Seagram that the RCGA knew its business.

The association's president, E. C. (Eddie) Gould, was the guest of Seagram's vice-president, William B. Cleland, at the 1935 General Brock. Gould was coming off a memorable year. "He's tiny, but he's wise, he's a terror for his size," someone wrote of him when he became president. (This all-star Ontario hockey player had turned to golf in 1919. In one month in 1930 he reached the final of two club championships, Hamilton and Brantford.) Other people had talked about sending a team of Canadian amateurs to tour Britain, he did something about it in 1935. Now he was convinced by all he saw at the General Brock that a

Ed Gould, president of the RCGA in 1935.

commercially sponsored tournament could be run with good taste and without forfeiting the dignity of the royal and ancient game. More than any other person, he was responsible for persuading the RCGA executive that commercial sponsorship was not the ogre some imagined, and for bringing in Seagram as sponsor of the Open.

The RCGA agreement with Seagram was signed in April 1936. The company would donate $25,000 over five years. Their $5,000 a year was to be allocated in this way: $3,000 to be the Open prize money; $300 to be prize money for the leading Canadian professionals, to which the RCGA would add another $300; $1,200 to be used by the RCGA in publicizing the Open; and $500 to compensate the RCGA secretary for the extra work entailed in running a sponsored tournament.

The agreement permitted Seagram to spend further sums in advertising its interest in the Open. The company also put up a new Seagram Gold Cup, which became the property of the RCGA for so long as it was used as the Open trophy. (It rests in the RCGA museum.)

Cleland negotiated the deal for Seagram. Although more interested in racing thoroughbreds than in playing golf, William Cleland – like those who succeeded him, notably Merle Schneckenburger – became an avid supporter and trusted friend of the RCGA.

The president of Seagram at the time, E. Frowde Seagram, had been smitten by golf at an early age and was a member of several clubs, but he died in 1937. In later years, Charles Bronfman was to be president of Seagram at a time when the company had to put up ever-increasing amounts of cash, and in him the RCGA found another loyal supporter and friend. (In fact, the Bronfman family were involved with the RCGA from the beginning, having acquired through their Distillers Corporation a controlling interest in Seagram, in 1927.)

The contract between Seagram and the RCGA started on a tentative, even suspicious, note. The RCGA had examined very carefully the clauses of the proposed agreement. Take the $1,200 for publicity. The funds were condi-

The Seagram Gold Cup for the Canadian Open.

tional on "suitable reference" being made to Seagram's participation in the Open. Not an unreasonable request. The incoming RCGA president wrote to B. L. Anderson, asking him to have this clause made clearer. ("The fears expressed by some [RCGA directors] was the possibility of our Association being exploited in this matter, [so] the words 'suitable reference' should be very clearly defined.")

Again, Seagram sought to have the RCGA agree that the $5,000 a year could be reduced to $3,300 (the prize money only) if B. L. Anderson should ever leave the RCGA. The RCGA president was already at odds with the clause in the proposed agreement which gave Anderson $500 ("not but what the Association might of their own free will recognize additional service on your behalf"), and found this further stipulation quite unacceptable. It was dropped.

Other details of the agreement were soon agreed and a happy marriage, which was to last for thirty-four years, began. Seagram was to sponsor the Open from 1936 to 1970. No other commercial sponsor has remained so faithful for so long in the history of the sponsorship of golf, perhaps in the sponsorship of any sport.

Very early in the marriage the two parties discovered they had more in common than they suspected. The RCGA directors found themselves dealing with men to whom the good name of the Open was as important as it was to themselves. Seagram found itself dealing with businessmen who could well under-

Charles Bronfman signs a Seagram-RCGA contract watched by Bruce Forbes and Phil Farley.

stand the company's problems of justifying the ever-increasing cost of sponsorship, manifest in the burgeoning Open prize money over the Seagram years:

1936–42	$3,000
1943–44	no tournament
1945–50	$10,000
1951–56	$15,000
1957–60	$25,000
1961–62	$30,000
1963–64	$50,000
1965–67	$100,000
1968–70	$125,000

In 1945 and 1946, the RCGA put up half of the $10,000.

In 1967, the city of Montreal put up an additional $100,000 for this Centennial Open.

From 1965, Seagram put up the prize money but received a rebate ranging from $9,000 to $42,000 a year, depending on the income from the Open.

Seagram's donation to the prize money was only the tip of an iceberg. The company would spend at least as much again on advertising, receptions, film production, uniforms for volunteers and caddies, scoreboards, and a host of other items.

In 1936, Seagram had no doubt convinced itself that its $5,000 would be recouped through the increased market share of its products. But in later years, when barred by federal legislation on liquor advertising from sponsoring its own telecast, the company's expenditures on the Open hardly seemed sound business practice. Its officers were aware, however, of the kudos that had accrued to the company because of its close association with the Open. They were also aware of the commitment and dedication of the RCGA governors to making the Open a success, and of the part the Open played in financing amateur golf in Canada. By then, they could not look at the company's marriage with the RCGA purely as a business venture. The Open had become the company's, and the RCGA's, joint creation. "The relationship between these two organizations is of the highest order," a Seagram officer wrote in 1963. "Each basks in the reflected glory of the other, and each writhes in the reflected criticism of the other." Those who believe that there is no place for altruism in the business world should examine the record of Seagram's support of the Canadian Open and, in general, of sport and the arts in Canada.

After the Second World War, the Open prize money had to be increased at an ever-increasing rate to keep up with tournaments in the United States. On top of this, the company continued to pay for advertising and publicity, plus a host of other items never taken into the reckoning by the average spectator. It had engaged Larry O'Brien as co-ordinator of its golfing commitments and was producing a film of the Canadian Open for distribution to golf clubs.

This long and cordial relationship weathered some nasty storms. Seagram and the RCGA fought a constant battle to retain the prestige of the Open. This was waged against the star players, those who attracted the crowds and hence the publicity, but who were often in two minds as to whether to compete. Arnold Palmer snubbed the Open for seven years between 1958 and 1965, when he and others attended the British Open.

In 1969, things came to a head when internal squabbling between the PGA and its tournament players led to a breakaway group of players forming the American Professional Golfers association (APG). There were anxious meetings attended by the Seagram president, Charles Bronfman, and the RCGA president, Ray Getliffe. Because of all their efforts, the 1969 Open at Montreal's Pinegrove was a reasonable success, although with a weakened field.

In February 1970, Charles Bronfman announced that his company would be pulling out of its sponsorship of the Open after 1972. The company could no longer justify the ever-increasing prize money at a time when it was trying to maintain its donations to so many other organizations. At the same time, by pulling out early, Charles Bronfman was living up to a promise made in 1964: "Our affection for the Open is so deep that if we thought for one minute that our sponsorship was having a deleterious effect on the Open, we would far sooner give it up in favour of any sponsor rather than hold on ourselves and impede its progress."

The Canadian Open was only one of Seagram's ventures into golf sponsorship, albeit the most important. After the Second World War, the company put up money and trophies for a host of others, among them:

– the Caribbean Tour. Supervised and administered by the PGA and Seagram's Larry O'Brien, this winter tour gave professionals five competitive rounds each week.

– the CPGA championship for the Seagram Shield.

– the Blind Golfers Championship. Seagram put up the first trophy for Canada's blind golfers in 1954, bringing in such personalities as Bob Hope to give it some publicity. (The company also made an excellent film on blind golf entitled "A Feel for the Game.")

In 1970, Seagram worked with the RCGA in search of a new sponsor. "I know a sponsor will be found," said Charles Bronfman. "We are assisting the RCGA . . . because golf enjoys national interest and the new sponsor, whoever it may be, undoubtedly will be able to use television and other promotional activities in support of the Canadian Open."

When Imperial Tobacco took over the sponsorship of the Open in 1971, it was its first venture into national golf. But the company was big in the promotion of other sports. "We have spent many thousands of dollars over the last few years in motor sport in Canada," the company spokesperson admitted, "and we cannot prove that we have ever sold a single cigarette because of it."

Claude Pattemore, left, many times Canadian champion, with Bob Hope at a Seagram-sponsored blind golfers' tournament.

The company was to sponsor golf through the name of one of its brands, Peter Jackson or du Maurier. Its chief executives were then Paul Paré, president of the holding company, Imasco, and Edmond Ricard, president of Imperial Tobacco. Paré and Ricard had concluded that someone had to take on the responsibility of keeping the Open alive, and they were soon to become as firm and loyal supporters of the Open as Seagram and Bronfman had been.

In 1971, Imperial put up $135,000 of the prize money for the Open. At the same time, it put another $79,000 into prize money for the CPGA's Peter Jackson Tour. In total, it was reckoned that the company's outlay would be close to half a million dollars a year on golf, since Imperial believed in heavily promoting the events it sponsored and in keeping alive the Seagram custom of making a film of the Open. As promotional consultant it hired Mark McCormack, the man who had improved the net worths of Arnold Palmer, Gary Player, and Jack Nicklaus.

Through its subsidiaries Peter Jackson or du Maurier, Imperial has sponsored a number of other golf events. The du Maurier Classic is just that – a classic Canadian event on the LPGA Tour. The du Maurier Order of Merit recognizes the most successful golfers on the Canadian TPD tour. The du Maurier Ltd. Series, introduced in 1990, is a four-tournament event for Canada's women professional golfers.

The company is still sponsoring the Open, twenty years later. It has seen the prize money grow from $150,000 to a figure eight times as much. It has faced many of the problems that Seagram faced and now confronts another which may force it out of all forms of sponsorship. In 1989, the federal government introduced Bill C-51, which along with other restrictions on tobacco, prohibits all forms of direct and indirect advertising by tobacco companies. If the Bill becomes law in its present form, Imperial may still sponsor the Canadian Open but will not be allowed to advertise the fact.

Other companies had sponsored golf in the 1930s. For amateur golf, CPR ran its first Empress Hotel mid-winter tournament at Oak Bay, Victoria, in 1929, and introduced the Prince of Wales Trophy to sponsor its Banff hotel. CNR put up the Jasper Totem Pole; Canada Steamship Lines, the Manoir Richelieu Shield. Hiram Walker ran a massive golf tournament over Toronto's Lakeview club for several years. About six hundred amateurs competed in the Hiram Walker in 1938.

After the Second World War, sponsorship took off, even before the days of golf on television. For a few years, we seemed to be flooded with sponsored tournaments.

A group of Quebec businessmen sponsored a new CPGA Open, in 1945, which was held just before the first post-war Canadian Open and attracted as strong a field.

Gilbert Ayres, owner of a textile and blanket company, and a director of the CPGA, sponsored the Lachute Open.

The Labatt Open, first held in 1953 over Montreal's Summerlea, had a prize money of $25,000, almost double that of the Canadian Open and the third largest in the world.

Dow Brewery sponsored several events during the 1950s, including the then fast-declining Millar match-play tournament.

Carling Brewery sponsored an International Pro-Am from 1957, between Canada and the U.S. Then, in 1964, it introduced the Carling World Open. This raised the jackpot to an unprecedented $200,000. Entrants had to qualify in one of several zones.

Amateur golf was also becoming dependent on commercial sponsors. In 1959, Pepsi-Cola started sponsoring national Junior interprovincial team matches. And here is an extract from the 1964 annual report of the Ontario Golf Association:

Without the generous sponsorship of Henry Birks and Sons in the Amateur; Wiser's Distillery in the Southpaw; North American

In 1957, Dow sponsored four events.

Life Assurance Co. in the Parent and Child Classic; Labatt's Brewery in the Public Course contest; Hiram Walkers in the Seniors' Tournament; and the Toronto Telegram in the Junior Championship, some of our championships would not be held.

Around the time that Seagram pulled out of the Canadian Open, other sponsors took a second look at the extent and wisdom of their commitment. Some people questioned whether companies were right to squander money on sport. Were they in fact able to justify the expenditure on sponsorship, as opposed to other forms of advertising?

Molson's Brewery decided no, and cut out a four-day golf festival in Quebec. Labatt had already pulled out of its Open. It had concluded that the promotional impact had been dissipated in a week. It still supported some CPGA events,

but "more as a contribution," a suggestion of altruism. Carling pulled out of the World Open, reckoning its impact on sales had not been as great as the company had forecast.

More and more, the sponsors of major golf tournaments came to justify their outlays on sponsorship in the increased sales brought about as the result of their event, and hence their name, being televised. Which brings us to golf on the airwaves.

Golf came over the airwaves a few years after the first commercial radio broadcast in Canada. In 1926, CNR sponsored a series of broadcasts (presumably golf instruction) over CNVR by Captain C. H. Perkins, professional at the Vancouver G & CC.

In 1930, Dunlop sponsored talks by Toronto GC's George Cumming over station CKCL ("Don't worry too much about keeping your head still," advised George, trying to destroy one of the shibboleths that has since been dispensed with).

A commentary on the Canadian Open was broadcast over local radio from at least 1930, when Armour won at Hamilton. The RCGA received a few hundred dollars for the broadcast rights, which were sold to local advertisers. In the 1930s, CBC also ran a commentary on the Canadian Amateur; Norman Lucas held the mike, his partner humped about the transmitter and batteries.

The Second World War brought the "walkie-talkie," enabling one man to both carry the transmitter and do the broadcasting. The problem was that he could only be in one place at any one time. An anchorman was needed in the clubhouse to keep track of the scores.

Broadcasting in wartime had its problems. Roy Dilworth was doing a play-by-play over a Canadian network, standing on a stool near one of the greens. When it started to rain, he could not say so, since wartime radio regulations forbade mention of the weather.

The surge of interest in golf after the war was recognized by radio broadcasters. In 1945,

Walkie-Talkie: Norman Lucas, right, *of the CBC, broadcasting the Canadian Amateur from London Hunt in 1938.*

the Open, the CPGA championship, the Millar, and the Ontario Open were all broadcast live on CBC Radio.

Golf on radio became a game for specialists. Hilles Pickens was often heard over the airwaves, broadcasting on the state of play at major championships and interviewing players. So were Doug Smith of Montreal, Bill Good of Vancouver, and Wes McKnight of Toronto's CFRB. They all knew the game, its vocabulary, and the dangers of banal commentary. They also knew the dangers of "dead air."

Television had been on the air for some years before it was recognized as a way of bringing golf to millions. Back in 1953, someone tried to sell the idea to NBC that golf and national television had a great future together. The director of sports at NBC thought it over and concluded that golf just wasn't a spectator sport and would never attract TV viewers regularly.

CBC radio broadcasts of golf in 1950.

Bobby Locke, being interviewed by Wes McKnight, after winning the Canadian Open in 1947.

NBC did try to televise the 1954 U.S. Open, but the results were pretty pathetic. The two announcers were perched on top of the clubhouse, couldn't see the eighteenth green because of trees, and had to rely on their monitor. But the sun threw so many shadows that they couldn't make out from the screen who was coming down the fairway, and they often got the names wrong. On the last day, just as Ed Furgol holed out to win the championship, they broke for a commercial and missed it.

Their performance was not much better in 1955. When Ben Hogan putted out at eighteen, he seemed a sure winner. Gene Sarazen was NBC's colour commentator, although they didn't call him that in those days. He went down and congratulated Hogan on camera for winning his fifth Open. Minutes after NBC had gone off the air, Jack Fleck came in to tie Hogan, and then beat him in a play-off.

Within ten years, the picture had changed dramatically, both literally and figuratively. From three fixed cameras and a handful of technicians, NBC and its competitors had gone to a dozen fixed cameras plus portables, mobile and stationary platforms, dozens of directors, and hundreds of technicians. More than six million homes were watching the Masters, the PGA, and the U.S. Open, and about as many switched on to see Palmer, Nicklaus, and Player in an exhibition labelled the World Series of Golf.

Arnold Palmer had much to do with the success of golf on television. "Ever since Arnold came from behind and won the 1960 Masters on the last hole with millions watching it on TV, this thing [golf on television] has been skyrocketing." So spoke one who should know – Mark McCormack. "The future of golf and the future of golf on TV are both unlimited." (He has been proved right, so far.)

In 1960, Texaco sponsored "Golf with Stan Leonard," an instructional series televised by CBC stations across Canada.

In the winter of 1963–64, an estimated half million Canadians watched weekly "Shell's Wonderful World of Golf" on CTV. By the mid-1960s every major PGA Tour event was coming live to the U.S. and Canada, in colour. Nicklaus and Palmer were as much TV heroes as the then current stars of baseball and football. Non-golfers watched, and many became hooked and took up the game. Golf and televised golf nourished each other, the growth of one helping to feed the other.

By a happy coincidence, the very first Canadian Open to be televised coast-to-coast by CBC-TV was in 1955, the year Arnold Palmer won at Weston. It took the producer, George Retzlaff, three days to get his team of two dozen in place. He had three cameras to cover action at the seventeenth and eighteenth holes plus the presentation area. The CBC used three commentators to provide coverage, in English only, and only on the last day of the Open. In 1956, the CBC gave us the Open from Beaconsfield in English and French.

Within ten years, the CBC was televising live the final two days, in both languages. It now started organizing for an Open a year before the event. The installation of twelve camera towers and telephone and hydro lines was taking up to ten days. The crew was now four times the size and included half a dozen commentators in English, the same number in French. At the 1964 Open at Pinegrove CC, the last six greens and the last five fairways were covered by cameras and commentators. Hand-held cameras with more powerful lenses were giving viewers close-ups, so that it seemed to the viewers that they were standing not a dozen steps behind the player. Contestants were now being identified by name tags worn by their caddies.

The next ten years saw increased coverage, and the use of slow motion and video playbacks. There were few courses where it was practicable (which means economical) to cover play at all holes, except by hand-held

camera. Stringing the miles of cable over eighteen holes would have been a lengthy and costly business. The CBC usually broadcast the last two hours of the third and last round, timed so that the leaders would then be coming into view. Occasionally, this meant that an exciting charge by someone well down the field – and hence out early in the day – could not be shown live. (In the 1973 Open at Richelieu Valley, South Africa's Bobby Cole started shooting the lights out over the last nine holes, an hour before the CBC was due to go on the air.)

The cost of televising the Open has to be recovered from commercial advertisers. The RCGA sells the Canadian television rights to the CBC-TV or CTV, who in turn sell the commercial slots between the shots.

The U.S. television rights of all PGA Tour events are controlled by the Tour, which sells the rights to a major U.S. network. As an event on the Tour, the Open, whether televised or not, gets a share of the Tour's total revenue from television, a share that is greater if the Open is televised and that increases with the purse. This is another incentive to increase the Open prize money.

Television has this further catch for the Open and its sponsor. If the sponsor of a U.S. golf tournament is prepared to buy network time for advertising or to sell it to others (and U.S. television has a much bigger market), the U.S. sponsor can often outbid the sponsor of the Canadian Open and Canadian advertisers. In return, the U.S. sponsor can choose to hold its tournament in prime golf-viewing time in July, the traditional date for the Open, bumping the Open to September.

By 1977, the Open had moved to its permanent site (more or less) at Glen Abbey, which had been designed as a spectator course, both for those attending and for those watching on television. Permanent television cables were laid underground so that just about all parts of the course could be covered by camera.

Showing a golf championship on television is *not* like trying to cover simultaneously eighteen games of football. On the last two days there might be no more than three or four groups in contention. The rest of the players might as well not be there. Many have finished their round by the time the game is broadcast live. Having said that, some recent Opens have been broadcast live almost in their entirety, for four days, so that we have also seen many of the early finishers. Too, video feedback now means that spectacular shots not shown live can be aired minutes after the event or even later.

"There's nothing more complicated, more nerve-racking, or more difficult than announcing a golf tournament," NBC's experienced Chris Shenkel found out twenty years ago. The late Henry Longhurst had mastered the art of commentating on golf. He showed that a word of explanation here, a keen observation there, was quite enough. Like Macauley, he had some brilliant flashes of silence.

Canada's Jim Nelford has also shown himself to be a first-class colour commentator; knowledgeable, articulate, able to select what matters and to tell you in a soft, fluid voice.

But few commentators have learned anything from the master, Longhurst, so their problems are of their own making. In observing the tenet that there should be no periods of silence, or "black air," they allow their commentaries to become word-floods. Yet silence is what the informed viewer often wants. Complain, and they will tell you to turn down the sound on your television set. But the noise of heavy breathing, the hushed whispers of the crowd, the whistling of the wind in the microphone, bring the viewer the urgency of the moment. This is the time for a stiff upper lip, and for a stiff lower lip.

32
CHAPTER

ONCE A SENIOR, ALWAYS A SENIOR, SOMETIMES VENERABLE, BUT NEVER AGED

IN SPITE OF THE GAME'S REJUVENATING powers, many golfers find the concentration and stamina needed for serious competition too hard to maintain after the age of fifty-five. Instead they start to enjoy the game in other ways. No golfer savours more than the senior the sheer pleasure of playing and of enjoying good fellowship. Youth may walk more briskly down the fairway, may stride longer between each shot, but youth is also more easily tormented by a poor lie or a balky putter. The senior golfer has been through all this before. Que sera, sera. Such misfortunes are nothing compared to the greater good fortune of being out on a fine green, with three other fine fellows (or girls) for companionship, playing a one-dollar Nassau. Thousands are alive today who would have withered away on retirement had it not been for the physical exercise and stimulating challenge of golf.

The invigorating effects of golf were recognized and written about by the British before the turn of the century, when youth and veteran competed against each other. But the British were the last to do anything about organizing tournaments solely for seniors, and the North Americans were the first.

For once, Canada lagged behind the United States. Horace L. Hotchkiss of the Apawamis club in Rye, New York, dreaded the thought of retirement. The idea of playing with golfers of his own age and interests so appealed to him that he organized a "Seniors' Tournament" (discarding the title "Old Men's Tournament"). The event was so successful, the spirit of good will so obvious, that the Apawamis tournament came to be held annually, attended by seniors from other clubs in the Eastern United States and Canada.

By 1917, the popularity of the tournament and the demands on the Apawamis club had grown to such a degree that the seniors decided to form their own association to run the event. They organized the United States Seniors' Golf

454

Association (USSGA), with a membership limited at first to four hundred, and with Hotchkiss as honorary president.

Several Canadian seniors had been going to Apawamis for years before the First World

Hands Across the Border

The cover of the dinner menu at the first Canadian–U.S. seniors' golf association team match, Apawamis, 1919.

War. Ralph Reville knew this. Sensing that a Canadian seniors' organization would be a success, he urged its formation in a December 1917 editorial in *Canadian Golfer*. Years later, he told of the response when he wrote a brief history of the association:

> The Editor, Mr. Reville, was both surprised and delighted a few days later to receive, amongst numerous other letters of approval, a communication from Mr. W. R. Baker, C.V.O., then President of The Royal Montreal Golf Club, stating that he had recently returned from a trip to New York, and, while there, had visited the Apawamis Golf Club, Rye, N.Y., the home of the American Seniors, where he met Mr. Horace L. Hotchkiss, Founder of the U.S. Seniors, and

had discussed with him the advisability of forming a similar organization in Canada. Mr. Hotchkiss and the other U.S. Seniors were enthusiastic about Canada entering the Senior field. Mr. Baker, in a subsequent letter, stated that he had consulted the Directors of The Royal Montreal Golf Club about sponsoring such an organization, and being the oldest golf club on the Continent, they considered they were particularly qualified to "father" such a desirable Association and unanimously decided to do so.

In March 1918, Walter R. Baker wrote to the leading golf clubs in Canada, calling for a meeting of interested seniors at Royal Montreal in May. About twenty attended this inaugural meeting, only one from outside Central Canada. But numerous letters of support were received from clubs across Canada. The Right Honourable Lord Shaughnessy was elected honorary president, Baker was elected president, and Reville, honorary secretary-treasurer, of the Canadian Seniors' Golf Association (CSGA). In anticipation of the first meet, and of matches against U.S. seniors, George Lyon was elected chairman of the tournament committee.

On the first Board of Governors of the CSGA were some familiar names:

– Walter Baker had been private secretary and comptroller to the governor general. When we first ran across him, he was executive agent for CPR in Winnipeg and helping Winnipeg Golf Club find land for its course. He was to be president of the CSGA until 1927.

– Clarence Bogert was another general manager of the Dominion Bank to become president of the Toronto Golf Club. He was to preside over the RCGA in 1926.

– Major Hume Cronyn's family had helped organize the first golf club in London, Ontario.

– John Dick of Lambton is best remembered as the man who introduced George Lyon to golf (or golf to George Lyon).

– Sir Jean George Garneau was one of the first French-Canadian members of Royal Quebec, and its president in 1920.

– P. D. Ross, editor and proprietor of the *Ottawa Journal*, had been president of Royal Ottawa in 1909–10. A member of an illustrious sporting family of Montreal, P. D.'s name is perpetuated on the CPGA's P. D. Ross Cup.

– George Lyon needs no introduction, and we have met before J. J. Morrison of Hamilton, Ralph Reville, and Frank Rolph of Lambton, who was president of the RCGA throughout the war years.

The membership limit of 250 was very quickly reached, and the age limit increased from fifty to fifty-five. The first tournament for the Shaughnessy Cup was played over Royal Montreal's Dixie course in September 1918. Since the war was not yet over, it was given the title of "The Patriotic Tournament of the Seniors." About eighty competed in the main event. Not surprisingly, George S. Lyon won by the grand margin of fifteen strokes over 36 holes.

The weather was kind to this first tournament of seniors. Or, as Ralph Reville wrote at the time: "Even old Jupiter Pluvius was considerate of the Seniors. Each night he visited the course and bestowed his bountiful baptism, but until the last ball of the tournament proper had been putted he refrained from visiting the participants with his aqueous attentions." One note of sadness impinged on an otherwise happy week. The news came to two competitors that their sons had been killed in the war.

George Lyon went on to win the Shaughnessy Cup in 1919–23, 1925, 1926, 1928, and 1930. Fritz Martin of Hamilton won in 1927, after a play-off with George L. Robinson of Lambton. Strangely, Lyon and Martin were the only two former Canadian Amateur champions to win the Seniors' until Sandy Somerville's victory in 1960.

In 1934, Robert M. Gray of Rosedale beat B. L. Anderson of Lambton in the final. This was the first of five victories for this fine Rosedale player, who would probably have been a force in the Canadian Amateur had it not been for the First World War. He may have won more as a senior if the Second World War had not put a temporary end to the tournament.

Over the years, many who met in the Canadian Amateur were to renew their rivalry as members of the CSGA. Sandy Somerville won the Shaughnessy Cup twice in the 1960s, and was twice the joint winner, once with Gordon B. Taylor, who was to win outright in 1968. In these years and later, he played against such other old friends and rivals as Jack Cameron, Bill Taylor (whom he defeated in the final), and Phil Farley and Jack Nash (both multiple winners).

Ed Ervasti of the London Hunt Club went through the tournament undefeated for five years (1976–80), and his record in the event, in terms of wins and second places, is second only to that of George S. Lyon.

Four members of the USSGA were made honorary members of the CSGA on its formation in May 1918. "All this is most agreeable," said Horace L. Hotchkiss, to the *Chronicle* in Rye, New York, adding, "it prepares the way for international competitions between the two associations."

Hotchkiss and two other honorary members were invited to the first CSGA championships at Royal Montreal. But the first international team match in 1923 was arranged almost at the last moment. "It is on the cards that an international match may possibly be arranged," Ralph Reville wrote, only a month before the tournament. But there was sufficient notice for CSGA president Baker to approach the governor general, the Duke of Devonshire, and have him put up the Devonshire Cup as an international trophy.

Canada won this first seniors' international, but by the narrow margin of 23 points to 19 (on the Nassau system). The result would probably have been different if the U.S. seniors had not generously waved aside the suggestion that they play a practice round in the morning. In the true spirit of seniors, they opted for the international in the morning, and friendly four-balls in the afternoon.

At the time, Ralph Reville called this first meeting of U.S. and Canadian seniors "the most notable golfing event ever staged in Canada."

The CSGA meet at Weston G & CC in 1959. Left to right, *Robert M. Gray (80), J. L. M. Thomson (83), T. E. Bennett (72), S. B. Playfair (82). These are their ages, not their scores. Gray was ranked fifteenth amateur in Canada in 1915.*

He probably foresaw from the spirit pervading Dixie that week a long and happy future for this international match; that the CSGA had succeeded in inaugurating a regular series of international matches, where the RCGA had failed.

After this first international, the captains decided to limit future teams to ten a side. But they were obviously overruled by their teammates, since the return match at Apawamis, and most matches thereafter, had teams of fifteen. Over the next eighty years, Canada was to win only a handful of matches against the U.S. But for the seniors, winning has never been as important as taking part.

Canada has provided several winners of the individual international trophy, including George S. Lyon (1923, 1930, 1931, 1932),

Robert M. Gray (1937 joint winner; 1938), Dr. G. F. Laing (1949; 1957 joint winner), Sandy Somerville (1964; 1966 joint winner), and Gordon B. Taylor (1968).

Within a few years the British had also organized a seniors' association. This led to the institution of a series of matches between Canadian, American, and British seniors. The first Canadian team in these triangular matches – half of the members coming from Lambton – sailed for Britain in June 1927, under the captaincy of George Lyon.

Singles and foursomes were played at Sunningdale, near London. The points scored were Britain 36, U.S. 23, Canada 19.

Canada has never won this triangular team match. It has been second many times, and just as many times has come close or been heavily defeated. But only the Second World War prevented this happy triangle from forming every year until 1938, then every two years from 1949. We have had some consolation in seeing several Canadians win the Individual Champions Founders Cup, including Robert M. Gray of Rosedale (1935, 1938) and Gordon B. Taylor (1969, in a four-way tie).

The CSGA championships have only twice been held outside Central Canada (in 1921 and 1925, when they went to St. Andrews, New Brunswick). As a result, seniors' associations have flourished in the other provinces. What is more, two regional associations have stood the test of time, one on the west coast, the other on the east.

The seniors of the West Coast who wished to join the CSGA were faced with the same problem as were amateurs who wished to enter the national championships: the geography of their

country was against them. So, in 1923, they formed a seniors' equivalent of the Pacific Northwest Golf Association.

Senator G. H. Barnard of Victoria GC was the prime mover behind the association, and he was to become its first president. In July, he called a meeting of senior members of Victoria GC and Royal Colwood. A committee of five was formed to approach other clubs in the Canadian and U.S. Northwest, inviting them to send representatives to a meeting and dinner in the Union Club, Victoria. The response was overwhelming. The members organized themselves into "The Seniors North West Golf Association," adopting a constitution based on that of the CSGA.

The first tournament was held at Victoria's Oak Bay, in November. The competitors were drawn from the clubs at Victoria, Vancouver, New Westminster, Seattle, Portland, and Tacoma.

As in the east, the SNWGA tournaments led to a renewal of old and friendly rivalries between golfers who had played in the Pacific North-

The Pacific Northwest Seniors' team, which tied the first match against American seniors in 1923. Left to right, F. P. Criddle, R. W. Gibson, W. B. Ferrie, J. Ogilvie (in rear), J. E. Wilson, C. S. Battle, J. A. Sayward, L. A. Lewis, C. B. McNeill, Phil Taylor (professional at Victoria GC), W. A. Ward (captain), Senator G. H. Barnard, L. H. Hardie, J. Caven, Judge Lampman, and J. W. Waghorn. Lewis of New Westminster won the individual championship.

west tournaments ten to twenty years earlier. You see appearing again such names as Ogilvie, Ward, Wilson, and Waghorn – the tournament came too late for Harvey Combe.

A seniors' international became part of the proceedings. For the record only – since results are not important to seniors – the first international in 1923 was tied. Last man in for Canada, Senator Barnard, won his singles to save the day.

In *Golf Gleanings Old and New* (1953), Frank N. Robertson has given us a fairly full history of Canada's only other national or regional seniors' golf association for men, the Maritime Seniors' Golf Association.

This was established in August 1925, after an informal meeting in April of six gentlemen from the Moncton, Sackville, and Saint John clubs. One of those present came to be looked upon as the "father" of the organization – A. C. Currie, honorary secretary-treasurer of the association until he retired in 1937. About sixty members from fourteen clubs in the Maritimes joined in that first year, mainly from clubs in New Brunswick.

It took some years for the association to reach its membership limit of two hundred. But it has many fewer clubs to draw on than the Canadian or the Pacific associations. Over the years it has been just as dedicated to preserving the spirit of community in golf for those on the shady side of fifty-five.

The winner of the CSGA's Shaughnessy Cup was for many years looked upon as the Senior Champion of Canada. But the championship was not open to all senior golfers; you had to be a member of the CSGA to compete, and this association had a limited membership.

The RCGA had felt for some time that a truly national tournament for seniors should be developed, but it did nothing until 1962. A former president, Colin Rankin, and his brothers put up the Rankin Memorial Trophy (in memory of their father, another former president, John I. Rankin). The RCGA organized the first national senior tournament at the St. Charles CC, Winnipeg.

For the first two years, this was a match-play tournament. Since 1964, it has been determined by 54 holes of stroke play.

The first Senior Championship of Canada went, appropriately enough, to another former RCGA president, the popular George Hevenor of Toronto's Summit club, who was to repeat his win two years later in 1964 and again in 1965. Just as in the CGSA tournaments, we have seen old rivalries renewed between Phil Farley (two wins) and Jack Nash (one). But the first to come up with a string of victories was a Canadian Amateur champion of the post-war years. Nick Weslock came out on top six times between 1973 and 1983, years in which he had one, then the other, hip joint replaced. Since then, Bob Wylie of Alberta has just about monopolized the event.

Colin Rankin, right, *presents the Rankin Memorial Trophy in 1962 to its first winner, George Hevenor.*

When the ladies decided to recognize the call of senior golf, they named their association "The Women's Senior Golf Association." They may have dropped the "Canadian" inadvertently. Or perhaps there simply seemed no need to include it, since as yet there was no equivalent

U.S. organization. They had beaten the U.S. women to the punch (although the British women had formed an association a year or so previously, long before the British men). Whatever, the Canadian organization eventually became the Canadian Women's Senior Golf Association (CWSGA).

The organizing meeting was held during the ladies' Close at Lambton GC in September 1922. With an initial age limit of forty, a number who had played in the national championships pre-First World War were eligible, and joined. Among these were Elizabeth Cleghorn Mussen of Royal Montreal (the first president of the CWSGA, an aunt of hockey stars Odie and

Sprague Cleghorn, and affectionately known as "Billie"), Mrs. A. E. Whitehead, Florence Greene of Royal Montreal (the oldest, or at least earliest, golfer present), Mrs. A. F. Rodger of Lambton, Mrs. W. C. Stikeman of Rosedale, and Mrs. Hamilton Burns of Rosedale, the last-named the honorary secretary. Membership was limited at first to fifty.

The senior women held an impromptu competition during that week at Lambton, won by Mrs. Rodger. She was named by at least one writer as "the first lady Senior Champion of America," but since the CWSGA did not recognize this as an official tournament, the honour properly went to Mrs. Sydney Jones of Toronto

"Billie" Mussen, first president of the CWSGA in 1922.

Mrs. Sydney Jones, left, a six-time winner of the CWSGA championship, seen after her fourth win, in 1929, with Mrs. Garth Thompson, runner-up, and the winner in 1933.

GC. Playing over the Royal Montreal course in September 1923, against a field of over thirty seniors, she shot a 97 to win the first CWSGA title, after a four-way play-off. (*The Canadian and Provincial Golf Records* show Mrs. Jones winning with a total of 192, which was her combined score in the seniors' and in the qualifying round of the Close championship, played the same week. Beginning the following year, the seniors' championship was over 36 holes.)

To the senior women, as to the men, the dinner after the event became an event in itself. The guests at the first dinner included Edith Leitch of England (whose singing was one of the features of the evening's entertainment) and Mrs. Gavin, also of England. Toasts were drunk to just about every past lady champion, and also to George S. Lyon as "the daddy of them all." But the main toast was to "the indestructible spirit of Youth."

The senior women soon had their own song, which would be heard at every dinner until singing – perhaps unfortunately, perhaps not – went out of fashion. (The chorus: "Happy days, golfing days/Over all too soon/Oh, what fun since we've begun/Up in Tillie's room/Oh – happy days, golfing days/Friendships we'll prolong/Billie's Babies, on your feet/And sing our Senior song." I do not know who Tillie was, unless it is a reference to Mrs. Tilley of Lambton, which hosted the organizing meeting. Mr. Tilley put up the cup for the seniors' championship.)

Innocent and happy days, for Billie's Babies. Mrs. Mussen was to serve as president of the CWSGA until 1936, just two years before her death in 1938, which occurred a day or so after returning from an annual seniors' meeting. No builder of golf in Canada has been more highly respected.

Some multiple winners of the CWSGA title over the years have been Mrs. Sydney Jones of Lambton (six times); Mrs. Agar of York Downs (in five consecutive years); Ada Mackenzie of the Ladies' GC of Toronto (eight times); and Mrs. Lockwood of Rosedale (five times).

The CWSGA seldom makes the news today. It appears to be restricted to members of clubs in Central Canada and New Brunswick.

The Canadian Ladies' Senior Golf Championship (also called the National Seniors' Championship) was first held by the CLGA in

Mrs. J.H. Todd of B.C., Canadian Ladies' Senior champion in 1976.

1971, when it was organized by the Ontario branch under its president Aileen Salter. The winner of these "over fifty" golfers has her name inscribed on the Ada Mackenzie Trophy.

The ladies' national, like the men's, has reunited on the friendly field of battle many former adversaries. But for some reason, it has produced fewer winners who had once held the Ladies' Open or Close titles – in fact, the first and only one of these is Marlene Stewart Streit, who first won in 1985.

33
CHAPTER

FLETCHER, PALMER, AND THE CANADIAN OPEN

AFTER FORTY YEARS OF TRYING, Canada finally reclaimed its Open Championship.

Pat Fletcher's win in 1954 should not have been any surprise. He arrived at Vancouver's Point Grey G & CC with impressive credentials. He had won the Saskatchewan Open three times, the CPGA championship in 1952. More significantly, he had put on a fighting show when the Open was held at Scarboro in 1953, finishing only four strokes behind the winner. Of all the PGA Tour players, only three had finished ahead of him, and trailing along behind were several former Open winners.

Neither Seagram nor most RCGA governors were at all enthused over the idea of holding the Open in Vancouver in 1954. The site was too far from the PGA circuit to ensure a first-class field. Holding the Open in British Columbia a year later would have made much more sense, they pointed out, since it would then have followed the U.S. Open and Western Open, both

scheduled to be held on the U.S. west coast. But the western governors of the RCGA were vociferous and won the day. They wanted the Open to be part of the celebration of the British Empire Games being held in Vancouver in 1954. (What golf had to do with the Empire Games was never made clear.) The Canadian Open could surely survive without the PGA Tour, they argued. In spite of the competition of the Empire Games, advance ticket sales at Point Grey went well. Some eight-thousand dollars' worth had been sold a week before the Open, and the club needed only another one thousand dollars to cover its costs.

The Canadian Open at Point Grey, then, was the first in some years not to be an official PGA event. The competing $25,000 Manakiki Open in Cleveland kept all but four PGA Tour regulars away. But these four included a former Open winner, Lawson Little (admittedly past his best), and Shelley Mayfield, a Texan who had been in the running for the U.S. Open that

462

year. The up and coming Bob Rosburg was also in the field. But Mayfield was considered the main challenger, for many the favourite.

It was not only local sentiment in Canada that favoured Stan Leonard to win the 1954 Open. He was accepted by East and West as Canada's finest professional of the post-war years, and many felt that justice would be served if he now crowned his CPGA successes by winning the national Open. Leonard was one of the game's longest hitters. Point Grey was a short course by Open standards, measuring only 6,405 yards. It favoured the accurate rather than the long hitter. Its narrow, tree-lined fairways were fringed by a clutching rough, its small greens guarded by deep and unforgiving bunkers.

When Pat Fletcher finished early with a 65 in the opening round, he looked a certain leader. But news came that Bob Rosburg was doing well, and spectators rushed to catch him at the tenth. This did nothing but encourage Bob, for he proceeded to fire a string of birdies and finish with a 63.

Stan Leonard more or less shot himself out of the running on that very first day. Only by birdying three of the last four holes did he manage a 74. Mayfield was even worse, with 76.

Mississaugua's Gordie Brydson was seen lurking there, three strokes behind Fletcher, and some recalled that he had won the CPGA title over this very course in 1948.

Fletcher fired a 70 to catch Rosburg in the second round. But he missed two very short putts on the seventh and ninth, bogeying both holes. Brydson fell another stroke behind Fletcher, with a 71. Rosburg's irons were not as crisp, and he missed too many greens. Others fell to the optical illusion created by Point Grey's tunnel-like fairways, which made it difficult to judge distance.

Canadian pundits had been saying for years that the country would never develop a winner of the Open until some of our younger men had been tempered in the fires of the PGA circuit. But at the end of the third round, a forty-year-old Canadian led the field: Gordie Brydson fired another round of three under par 68.

This was good enough to overtake both Fletcher (74) and Rosburg (75), who had wretched days, and to take the lead by two strokes. The fight was narrowed to Brydson (207), Fletcher (209), Rosburg, and Bruce Cudd, an American amateur, (210).

Brydson was driving as straight as Fletcher, but longer. He was off-line only once, at the sixteenth, but hit a sensational iron through the trees to get his par. This jaunty, natty dresser chainsmoked – or chewed – eight cigars on his way to a clutch of three straight birdies in the homeward nine. His manner was relaxed, as befits a man who had come to the coast with no real expectation of winning. At the eighteenth, he drove his ball into a greenside trap. As he made to sandwedge it out, a photographer nuzzled close to snap the shot. When an official asked him to leave, Brydson said not to worry, the man was only doing his job.

On the other hand, Pat Fletcher was obviously tense, showing none of the confidence of the first two days. Rosburg's temper had frayed at the edges as he ballooned to a 75. Brydson and Fletcher were judged to be the straightest off the tee, and their lead was attributed as much to this fact as anything.

There was little thought given to poor Rosburg in the evening before the final round of the Point Grey Open. Canada was confident it was about to have its first champion since Karl Keffer, forty years earlier. Fletcher or Brydson, it made no difference. Both were home-bred, and that was all that mattered. As he emerges from forty years in the wilderness, a man does not debate his chances of going back in, nor does he question who leads him out.

Brydson appeared to be that leader. Oozing confidence, replete with a pocketful of cigars, he strode majestically over the opening holes of the final round at Point Grey like a man who knows he is making history. He opened birdie, birdie. His lead was now three over Fletcher, playing ahead.

Gordie Brydson's problems started at the eighth, where he three-putted. This seemed to unnerve him, for his nightmare started at the next hole. Like most holes on this course,

Pat Fletcher with the Seagram Gold Cup, after bringing us in from the cold.

Gordie Brydson, who nearly took his place.

the ninth fairway is flanked by bushes and trees. Brydson hooked his drive, and the ball stopped under a tree. He tried both to extract it and to go for the green. The ball hit trees. He had little choice but to try to roll his next through a bunker. It stayed in the sand. He wedged out, but missed the seven-foot putt. Double bogey. At the tenth, things got worse. His approach shot hit the flagstick, rebounding 50 feet away. He chipped on, but not close enough, and needed two putts to get down. The triple bogey 7 wiped out his lead. What was worse, it ruined his concentration and confidence.

As Fletcher was playing the twelfth hole, he heard that Brydson had triple-bogeyed the tenth. He admitted later that he had been ready to jump in the river after his first half of 39. Instead, after nearly throwing away the twelfth, he sank a six-footer for a birdie.

As Brydson went on his sorrowing way to three more bogeys and one birdie, Pat Fletcher played like a man possessed. He shot a second

half of 32 for a total of 71. His four under par 280 made him Canadian Open champion by a margin of four strokes. With Rosburg and others frittering away strokes, Bill Welch of Washington tied Gordie Brydson for second place.

It was left to the Vancouver amateur, Doug Bajus, to salvage British Columbia's pride. His total of 285 was good enough to tie Bruce Cudd and Ontario's Rudy Horvath for fourth place.

With the possible exception of Brydson, there could have been no more popular winner than Pat Fletcher. This quiet, unassuming, and rather shy man was to carry his title with great dignity. Only after he had won did we have a close look at his record and realize that his time was overdue. At the Scarboro Open in 1953 he had finished top Canadian and ahead of four previous Open winners. If he could finish ahead of them in 1953, he could have done the same in 1954. The fact that they did not show up was not his fault.

Born in Clacton-on-Sea, England, in 1916, the son of a dentist, Pat Fletcher had been brought to Canada when he was only four. During the Depression in the West, he caddied at Victoria, where he lived with his widowed mother. He had started to play golf at Oak Bay at the age of nine and had progressed in the usual way through the caddie ranks to become a professional. He worked for three clubs in Edmonton before the war. After the war, he took over from Bill Kinnear at Saskatoon G & CC, becoming that club's second professional since 1907.

Fate played a part in his win at Point Grey. He had not intended entering for the Open, but his friend Stan Leonard had bribed him with the promise of good fishing on the Pacific Coast.

Pat Fletcher was not a long hitter of the ball, but he seldom strayed from the fairway. His strength was his short game. Many considered him the finest wedge player in Canada. Hilles Pickens thought him the finest he had ever seen and he had seen every good wedge player on this side of the Atlantic, Weslock included. When Pat came to Point Grey he was thirty-eight, and had filled out his six-foot frame to just under two hundred pounds.

Pat Fletcher went on to become the long-serving professional to Royal Montreal, and the president of the CPGA, 1962–65. He was a frequent visitor to the Canadian Open, even after his retirement to his home in Victoria, where it had all started for him.

It is a great pity that illness prevented him from defending his title in 1955. Instinct tells you he would have put up a stout fight to keep what was his. Too, he might have changed the course of golfing history by denying Arnold Palmer his first win on the PGA Tour. . . .

The 1955 Canadian Open at Toronto's Weston club was held in the third week of August.

The Open field was as strong as any in the history of the event. Slammin' Sam was there, a three-time winner in the past; so was smiling Ed (Porky) Oliver, doing his bit to perpetuate the myth that fat men are jolly; and Tommy (Thunder) Bolt, noted for his club-throwing tantrums; the blond Art Wall, who was destined to win and lose Canadian Opens in the future; the stringbean Dave Douglas, winner in 1953; Jack Burke, whose father had come so close to winning in 1913; Ted Kroll and Doug Ford, another two winners in the future; and a youthful Billy Casper, carrying only half the weight of the fellow now on the Senior Tour.

The Canadian Open – for the moment at least – was an official event on the PGA Tour, hence the large turnout of top American professionals. They had all been in Chicago the week before, for George S. May's extravaganza, the Tam O'Shanter Open. Toronto was within easy motoring distance of Chicago. Of course, you had to finish in the top ten at Weston to be sure of winning $300.

Canadian hopes rested on its two members of the PGA Tour, Stan Leonard and Al Balding.

Weston is an attractive parkland course. It then measured around 6,400 yards, with friendly bunkers and little in the way of rough. "Too open for an Open, too easy for a national championship," in the opinion of some. The greatest hazard that week was the hot, humid weather.

In the first round, a pleasant-looking strong young athlete with a watermelon smile came in with a 64, eight under the par of 72. His name was Arnold Palmer. Right after winning the U.S. Amateur ten months earlier, he had turned professional. He had been in the army before he joined the tour, and at twenty-five years of age he was old for a rookie.

At Weston, Arnold Palmer was an unknown. Caddies had their pick of who they wanted to carry for. If they picked the winner, they stood to benefit from a share of the prize money. Arnold Palmer was near the bottom of their list.

Palmer fully expected that his 64 would give him the first round lead. But Charlie Sifford came in with a 63. Charlie had held the title of U.S. National Negro Champion.

After shooting a 67 in the second round to go 13 under par, Palmer never looked like losing. Sifford collapsed into the 70s. Jack Burke added a 66 to his 67 and was two behind; Jerry Barber, Tommy Bolt, and Canada's Stan Leonard were a stroke or so further back still.

In the third round, we saw on parade for the first time a platoon of what was to grow into "Arnie's Army." By the second day, Canadian spectators had taken this smiling young man to their hearts. They followed him everywhere, lining his fairways. Three of his shots were heading for the rough when they bounced off the bodies of the first Palmer Platoon, rebounding to the short-cut grass. Hilles Pickens – who had no way of knowing he was witnessing an event of great historical importance – reported with some surprise: "One chap, with a dent right between his eyes from a Palmer shot, brushed the injury aside, and utilized the occasion to request Palmer's autograph when the latter rushed up to enquire his condition."

If this chap still has that dent between the eyes, let him wear it proudly, for it contributed to the making of golf history. This ricochet helped Palmer come in with another 64 and to sit in the clubhouse with a score of 195 for 54 holes. Some had visions of new records. How could this young man fail to better the 263 turned in by Johnny Palmer (no relation) at St. Charles CC three years earlier?

Very easily, as it turned out. In the final round, Arnold Palmer could manage only a 70, to win by the margin of four strokes.

It would be ludicrous to ask of anyone who shoots 23 under par what went wrong during the last round. But for the record, his driver turned erratic, his putter cooled off. Indeed, at one point Fred Hawkins came within two strokes of catching him.

When interviewed immediately after the Open, Arnold Palmer claimed that he won the championship at the fifth hole of the final round, when he hooked his drive into the trees, put his second into a stand of pines, yet

managed to sink a six-foot putt for a bogey. Had he double-bogeyed, he said, he would probably have blown wide open.

Twenty years later, in an interview with Bob Drum, reported in *Golf Canada*, Arnold Palmer recalled that he had made one slip about halfway through his final round. He was probably thinking of this fifth hole when he said:

> Only once during the last round was I in trouble: I had been traveling with Tommy Bolt, who had taken a liking to me, and, as luck would have it, we were paired together in the final round.
>
> I had hooked my ball in the trees somewhere in the middle of the round, and was debating what to do. Faced with a tough situation and with a good lead, I was trying to figure out how to play the next shot.
>
> It was at this point that Bolt said: "Just chip it out into the fairway." I was well aware that getting advice from anyone but your caddie was a two-stroke penalty. I had already made up my mind to play safe, but after Tommy had told me what to do, I was forced to go for the green. That way, I felt confident that I had not received any help from him.

Going for the green meant manoeuvring the ball through a ten-foot gap in the trees. (In 1990, when playing in a skins game at Weston, Palmer hooked his ball into the same trees. Did he remember?)

In this way, Arnold Palmer won his first of over seventy tournaments, and was on his way to becoming the world's most popular golfer. No man did more for the game, the growth of prize money, or the esteem and the net worth of the playing professional.

The CBC may have had some prescient sense that this was history in the making. For the first time ever, CBC-TV broadcast the Canadian Open coast to coast.

And how did the Canadian press see Arnold Palmer at the time? "This Palmer is a cool, able golfer. His swing is relatively orthodox . . . He is a healthy hitter, but not the longest. His winning edge came about more or less as per-

Arnold Palmer's reward after his first win on Tour.

centages born of a solid swing, a hot putter, and Arnold's strength and condition to take almost unbelievably humid heat that was featured by Toronto for these four days . . ." "A fine lad, and obviously a coming player."

Of Palmer's last round of 70, one reporter wrote: "This tragedy should be inscribed on a scrap of paper, thrust in an old bottle, and dropped in mid-Atlantic for posterity."

Tommy Bolt said: "This kid is good. He has the power of concentration. Do you know, he didn't ask me how he stood until we were on the 17th. My, that's concentration!"

Stan Leonard finished fourth, seven shots behind. No other Canadian was close.

And Sam Snead? After fighting the greens on his way to a third round score of 76, he blamed the implement. A newspaper photograph shows Snead's caddie holding the several parts of a broken putter. And Tommy Bolt? In the third round, his caddie could stand him no longer and quit.

The Open at Weston attracted most of the top U.S. professionals, and the course was in such fine and fair condition that the players came up with no newsworthy complaints.

All post-war Canadian Opens have not been so fortunate. They continued to be plagued by the endemic problems of all PGA events, and a few extra because of the importance of the Open to Canada: how to ensure a date around the prime time of early July, without losing players to the British Open; how to ensure that top U.S. players turn up as promised; how to stop the chronic gripers from criticizing the state of the course, or in other ways antagonizing the host club, the volunteers, and the sponsor. In all these respects the Canadian Open was, and still is, no different from other events on the PGA tour. (In 1990, the course used for the Tournament Players' Championship was severely criticized by the players, whose course it is!)

In an attempt to improve the image of its tournament players, the PGA tried the stick-

and-carrot approach. Tour players were fined for failing to compete after entering a tournament or for failing to complete a round after qualifying. Fines were assessed for "conduct unbecoming a Tournament Player," such as the use of abusive or profane language to officials, spectators, club members, the press, or caddies. Breaking clubs was also punishable. Accepting undercover payments from sponsors could lead to disqualification.

Over the years, the innate good business sense and fair-mindedness of the overwhelming number of Tour professionals probably did more to improve matters than any carrot or stick. The problems are people problems and will never completely go away. But the image of the touring professional has improved at a time when the image of other professional sportspeople has been deteriorating.

The purse continued to be a problem. The RCGA and the sponsors have had difficulty in keeping the Open both attractive and affordable. After the war, sponsors and television bid up the prize money for professional golf tournaments at an incredible rate. In percentage terms, the purse needed to attract a PGA tournament went up faster in the 1950s and 1960s than at any time before or since. Arnold Palmer's first prize in 1955 was $2,400. Had he won in 1965, he would have collected $20,000. And the winner in 1965 has Arnold Palmer to thank for much of this increase.

The growing popularity of golf on television has led to sponsors of other tournaments offering the PGA Tour a more attractive package for a spot in July, thus bumping the Canadian Open to September.

These problems of the Canadian Open were ones common to tournament golf. In Canada, they were of concern to more than the RCGA. As commercial sponsor, Seagram had a financial interest in the success of the Open and therefore an interest in ensuring that the field was of the highest quality. No person worked harder at this than the Seagram Director of Public Relations and Tournament Co-ordinator, Larry O'Brien. If his title is a challenge, so were his responsibilities.

O'Brien was Seagram's tournament co-ordinator for ten years. His job took him everywhere, and often tried the patience of this warm and polished administrator. Charlie Boire of the *Montreal Star* (where O'Brien had started as a cub reporter) labelled him "golf's perpetual man in motion." Seagram sponsored the Canadian Open, the CPGA championship, the Mexican Open, the Caribbean Tour, and a Far East tour, so O'Brien was constantly hopping on a plane for some distant corner of the world.

All the top U.S. golf tournaments were on his schedule, for it was there that he met the Tour's top players. His job: to convince them that playing in the Canadian Open was essential to their future happiness. He knew them all by name and reputation. He was quoted as saying of them:

> Some of the players are very fussy. Besides, you have to worry about travel plans, train times, flight schedules, and hotel and motel rates. Some players even want to know what's on the menus at the hotels and golf club. In addition to these things, we have the players' wives to consider. We try to arrange fashion shows, sightseeing tours and other arrangements.

Perhaps his greatest feat was saving the 1969 Open from being an unmitigated disaster. The PGA had split its ranks, and it appeared as though all the big names would play in the competing American Golf Classic. Helped by the RCGA's Bruce Forbes, O'Brien flew everywhere, making use of the warm personal relationships he had established over the years, reminding players of favours owed, twisting arms, promising everything but appearance money. In the end, he recruited four former champions in Bob Charles, Billy Casper, Sam Snead, and Doug Sanders, to say nothing of Roberto de Vincenzo, British champion Tony Jacklin, and the eventual winner Tommy Aaron.

When he left Canada for Palm Beach late in 1969, to become vice-president of the management firm of J. Edwin Carter (where he would oversee eight major tournaments),

Larry O'Brien remained as a consultant to our Open. In 1969, *Golf Canada* made him its first "Golf Personality of the Year."

Hagen, Snead, and Armour, Canadian Open winners in the years between the wars, were among the world's finest crowd-pleasers. Just by their presence they brought an excitement and a prestige to the Open that was seldom experienced in the two decades after the Second World War. What is more, two of the outstanding characters who won the Open in the period 1945–65, Byron Nelson and Bobby Locke, appeared to have no interest in coming back to defend their titles. If Arnold Palmer's magnetism was already apparent in 1955, it had no record of success to sustain it. To be a crowd-pleaser, you needed more than personal charm. Palmer did not win the U.S. Open until 1960.

Byron Nelson, also known as "Mr. Golf" and "Lord Byron," walked through the field at Thornhill's course in 1945, to win the first Open after the war. He won more easily than his four-stroke margin suggests. This was Nelson's eleventh straight tournament victory, an unequalled feat made somewhat easier by the absence of so many professionals on war service.

Nelson had appeared once before in a Canadian Open. As a struggling young rookie, he had won $42.50 for finishing tenth in 1936. In 1945, this sum was mentioned with much derision, just as we would now look upon his winner's cheque in 1945, of $2,000. A reporter who was there saw Nelson finish "standing majestically on the towering 72nd tee, and smacking a mighty drive far out to the right, into the rough near a large tree. With 5,000 storming in his wake, he pitched the ball safely over a creek . . . to rest 30 feet from the flag. With a final artistic gesture, tall, slender Lord Byron sent his putt straight to the back of the cup. . . ." Fine stuff, indeed!

Byron Nelson did not come back to defend his title, or to play in another Canadian Open.

In 1947, Canada got its first glimpse of Bobby Locke of South Africa. Arthur D'Arcy Locke was then just short of his thirtieth birthday. Having won everything there was to win in his home country, he had come to the U.S. in 1946 as the runner-up in the British Open. In his first year on the PGA Tour, he won tournament after tournament, taking a lot of money from the pockets of U.S. professionals. He finished by lifting their Vardon Trophy for the lowest average score of the year.

Locke did all this dressed in baggy knickerbockers and swinging a club in a most un-American way. His putting stroke, in which he hooked the ball to the hole, made him the deadliest of performers. He blasted the illusion that nobody could beat the American professional on the green. Moreover, he did so by wielding a rusty old putter given him by his father when he was a boy of nine. His caddie was under strict orders never, but never, to polish it.

Byron Nelson and his caddie, practising at Thornhill, 1946.

Spectators at the Scarboro Open of 1947 watch winner Bobby Locke, with Clayton Heafner and Stan Leonard, at the 18th hole.

Locke also blasted the concept that because tournament golf was big business, it required so much concentration that it could no longer be enjoyed. He never became upset if he missed a putt – which he seldom did; he raised his cap to spectators, he acknowledged their cheers with a relaxed, friendly wave and a smile. He was mild but serious in his criticism of the mechanical style and the grim attitude of the modern professional golfer. All this did nothing to endear him to his fellow professionals. When he came to Canada for the Open, he was at first thought to be rather odd. But he was to make many friends in this country and to play for Canada in team matches against the United States.

At Toronto's Scarboro club in July 1947, Bobby Locke fired four rounds in the 60s, to finish at 16 under par. This won the Canadian Open, by two strokes, from Porky Oliver. The spectators had been looking forward to a duel between the world's finest putter and one of the worst, Sam Snead. Locke did not turn up for a practice round on the Monday, and Snead did not turn up at all.

Apart from Locke's win, and Porky Oliver's 63 on the second day ("the fattest man was the hottest man"), the outstanding feature of this Open was the play of the Canadian amateur, Nick Weslock. He had rounds of 67 70 65 70, to take third place away from a bunch of U.S. professionals and Scarboro's Bob Gray. In the final round, Weslock played with Locke and Herman Kaiser. They were followed by a crowd of several thousand. The marshalls had difficulty in keeping the spectators away from the players, notwithstanding the organizers' proud boast that over a mile of rope was being used on the course. To shoot a 70 under such circumstances was surely one of Weslock's finest achievements.

Since the war, until Glen Abbey became the permanent home of the Open, the event has been held most frequently at Royal Montreal, Mississaugua, St. George's, and Scarboro, each of which hosted the event three times.

Nicklaus, Palmer (runner-up), and Knudson at the 1964 Open at Pinegrove CC, Quebec.

The scoreboard at the 1966 Open at Shaughnessy G & CC, Vancouver.

As the Open grew in size and complexity, other clubs refused to be the host; some did not have a course sufficiently challenging; others did not have the parking space for automobiles.

It has often been said of national championships that certain courses always produce worthy champions. It is not that others are poor courses, merely that some layouts have holes that test the brave and the nerveless, forcing the golfer to decide what is an acceptable, and what an unacceptable, risk. These courses are as much a test of the golfer's mental attitude as they are of his skill as a striker of a golf ball. Such courses invariably produce champions who have been tempered in the fires of tournament golf for some years.

Royal Montreal gave up its old course at Dixie and moved to Ile Bizard in 1958. Of the other three courses it can be fairly said, I think, that they have produced worthy champions over the years. Mississaugua probably has an edge over the other two, having given us Walter Hagen (1931), Sam Snead (1938), Craig Wood (1942), Jim Ferrier (1951), Gene Littler (1965), and Bobby Nichols (1974), all of them winners of at least one of the three major U.S. championships of Open, Masters, and PGA.

Jim Ferrier of Australia, back-to-back winner 1950–51.

The only man to defend his title successfully since the war, Jim Ferrier, won his first title over Royal Montreal's Dixie course in 1950, and went on to keep it over Mississaugua.

Big Jim had been on the PGA Tour for several years and had won the PGA championship. He was thirty-eight when he came to Montreal, a well-built, deliberate, careful, unexciting golfer, but one with bags of confidence.

He was never really challenged for the Canadian title in 1950, except by our own Stan Leonard in the first two rounds. The three former champions in the field – Snead, Little, and Kunes – were never a threat, although at the time Snead was the leading money-winner on the Tour.

Lennie Harman, professional of a nine-hole course at Knowlton, Quebec, had a brief day of glory when he shot a 67 in the first round. Leonard's opening rounds of 68 66 were to prove equally as fleeting, although they did send a surge of hope through the galleries. But thereafter it was all Ferrier. Even with a closing round of 70, he finished three strokes ahead of newcomer Ted Kroll.

Ferrier's defence of his title was a more exciting affair. Mississaugua is not a long course. It demands a premium on accuracy, not on length. The long-hitter off the tee who is not accurate will find himself stymied by a tree or in tight rough. The greens are small, some of them devilishly contoured. Holes eleven through fourteen are particularly testing. Championships have been won and lost at the long twelfth, the "Big Chief."

In 1951, gusty winds, torrential rain, scorching sun, and lung-clogging humidity found Ferrier a match for all. He came to Mississaugua as the leader of the Tour, just ahead of Hogan, Snead, and Mangrum, none of whom ventured north. Ferrier led with an opening 65, but was literally blown from his lead in the second round, when he could manage only a 72. Jack Burke went ahead with 66 66. Burke still led after the third round but went to pieces in the fourth.

Porky Oliver looked as though he might come in with a 65 to tie Ferrier when he dared the odds at Mississaugua's two long testing holes, the twelfth and thirteenth, and went birdie eagle. But the hot streak left him and he finished second, two behind Ferrier.

If any Canadian Open set the stage for the extravaganzas of the 1970s and 1980s, then it was probably the Open at Mississaugua, in 1965. The prize money had been doubled to $100,000, attracting a field of all the top players on the Tour. As an experiment, a Pro-Am was held as a prelude to the Open. The attendance was close to 60,000, easily a record. (The spectators consumed 40,000 hot dogs, probably another record.)

For the first of many times, Jack Nicklaus very nearly won but had to settle for runner-up.

The tournament chairman at Mississaugua was Richard H. (Dick) Grimm, who was to leave his family business and take over the running of the RCGA's professional tournaments in 1983. The show he put on in 1965 could not have been better orchestrated.

Going into the final round, Australia's Bruce Devlin, five under par, led by two strokes from Palmer, Nicklaus, and Littler. But Devlin quickly fell from grace. He had been hit by a shoulder injury on the opening day and this probably contributed to his collapse.

The battle was engaged between Palmer, Nicklaus, and Little, but not for long. Palmer started badly and was soon out of the race.

Gene Littler, being presented with the trophy in 1965 by Charles Bronfman of Seagram, with RCGA president Bruce Forbes.

Nicklaus took the lead at the seventh, where he was four under par for the tournament, one ahead of Littler.

The tide turned in Littler's favour at the Big Chief. Nicklaus drove 297 yards, leaving himself 240 yards to the flag. Palmer was about as

long, but chose to lay up. The spectators cheered when Nicklaus reached for a wood.

The green at the twelfth is a narrow shelf protected by the creek in front and by two big elm trees on the right. With the wind in his face, Nicklaus took an almighty smack at the

Jack Nicklaus meets the Big Chief: (i) puts his ball in the water, (ii) finds his ball, (iii) plays out.

ball. It cleared the creek, hit the bank on the far side and rebounded, finishing three inches under water. Another few feet to the right and he would have made the green. Standing with one foot on a rock, Nicklaus wedged the ball out of the water, over the green, and into the gallery. His return chip finished four feet from the flag, but he missed the putt and had to settle for a bogey. The Big Chief had claimed another victim.

Playing right behind Nicklaus, Littler could see what had happened. For the first time that week he did not try to carry the creek in two ("If Nicklaus couldn't make it, I couldn't"). He laid up, pitched on to the green, and got his birdie to go one ahead.

Jack Nicklaus fought back with birdies on fourteen and sixteen, which Littler matched, so that Nicklaus came to the seventeenth still one stroke back. This hole is a 323-yard dog-leg to the right. Nicklaus drove over the trees, to within 80 feet of the pin. Some witnesses say a spectator coughed as Jack was about to wedge to the flag. But he later admitted to lifting his head. Whatever the reason, he flubbed the shot and had to settle for a par. On the final hole, he missed an eight-foot putt for the birdie needed to draw level.

In the second round of this Open, Ernie Nerlich, the professional at Richmond Hill GC, took fourteen strokes at the eighteenth hole. After driving two out of bounds, he was five off the tee. He shanked his sixth into the undergrowth, took five more to extract it, another to get it on the green, two putts to sink it. Ernie laughed it off. ("I met Dr. Livingstone in the jungle.") For a time, a 7 on any hole at Mississaugua was known as a half-Nerlich.

The same hole destroyed George Knudson's chances in the third round, when his drive went into the same ravine. "I was thinking about Ernie," he admitted later, "and hoping I wasn't going to break his record." He didn't, but his triple bogey 7 put an end to any hopes he had of catching the leaders.

The Big Chief knifed Nicklaus again when the Open was next played at Mississaugua, in 1974. Bobby Nichols, 38, a former PGA champion, led by a shot going into the last round. But he had in Lee Trevino (three strokes back) and Nicklaus (five back) only two of a bunch who would take chances on a course offering the choice of eagles or disaster. Nicklaus started his last round with three birdies in the first five holes. He came to his nemesis, the twelfth, with every chance of catching Nichols. His 1-iron to the green was thin, his ball falling into the rocks of the riverbank. This time he took three strokes to rescue it, finishing with a 7. Trevino never looked like catching the leader.

In the end, Nichols won quite handily with a four-stroke margin. "The Big Chief was the turning point for me," he admitted. "I'd got through the first nine without too much trouble. I got careless on the tenth and eleventh, and bogeyed them both. I was quite nervous coming to the twelfth. I decided to go for the green, playing for the gallery to carom the shot if I had to. Everybody does that when there's a big crowd. It worked, and I got a birdie."

Bobby Nichols owed his victory in part to Canada's Gary Cowan. The American professional had been in a putting slump and had placed no better than fortieth in recent tournaments. During a practice round, Cowan advised him to pause after taking the head of the putter back. It worked. In the final round, Nichols's putting saved three pars at a time when Nicklaus looked to be catching him.

The state of the golf course raised many hackles at this Mississaugua Open. The amount of effort and money spent by members in preparing their course illustrates why clubs are so often reluctant to offer their facilities for national championships.

The course had been perfect going into the winter of 1973–74. In the late winter, a storm ravaged many of the greens, tees, and fairways and washed away bridge supports. Hard work had repaired much of the damage by the middle of May, when another storm undid the repairs. Early in July, a drought stunted growth on the fairways and rough.

For the first two rounds of the Open, the PGA officials set up the course with many of the tees forward, fearing the forecasts of imminent thunderstorms. The forward tees and the short rough made the course too easy, charged many of the players, Nicklaus, Palmer, Trevino, and Weiskopf among them. "Make your course as tough as you can, and forget weather forecasts," Nicklaus advised. But by Sunday rain had helped restore most of Mississaugua's lost bite.

St. George's was hard, dry, and dusty, the weather hot and humid, for this club's first post-war championship in 1949 (when the club was still called Royal York). U.S. professionals Demaret, Snead, Middlecoff, and South Africa's Bobby Cole did not show up as expected. To make matters worse, several of the advertised players in an RCGA clinic did not appear, so the RCGA refused to pay the fee demanded by the PGA.

Bob Gray's record for the course, 68, was broken no fewer than thirteen times during this Open, the first time by the winner, Dutch Harrison. After two rounds there was virtually no contest, this ambling giant from Arkansas coming in with 17 under par to win by four strokes. The leading Canadian, Bill Kerr, tied for third place, his best-ever showing in the championship.

St. George's greens are larger than Mississaugua's, but few have anything like a straight putt to the hole. On many of the fairways, too, the drive has to be placed perfectly if the player is to avoid an uphill, downhill, or sidehill lie. The twelfth through sixteenth are the testing holes. The fourteenth, a 445-yard par four, could be characterized as the Little Chief. As at Mississaugua, a creek runs diagonally across the fairway in front of the green. But here the fairway slopes down towards the creek, so that the shot to the green may have to be played from a downhill lie.

In the 1960 Open, winner Art Wall had his only final-round hiccup at the fourteenth. He left his approach short, and the ball plugged in mud. He managed to extract it and walked away with only a bogey. As it happened, his challengers came to grief, and he finished six strokes ahead.

If this was not the most exciting of Opens, it was because Art Wall was not the most exciting of players. Although Masters champion and Golfer of the Year in 1959, his "stoical perfection" – as somebody described it – attracted few spectators at St. George's until his closing round. If he was not a charismatic winner, he was at least a worthy winner of the Open, having previously tied for fourth place (1958) and second place (1959).

This Open did have its moments. In the first round, Al Balding set a new course record of 64, and at the halfway mark was only one behind Wall's 133. But a third round of 77 put paid to any hopes of a Canadian win.

Sam Snead was tied for third place with a round to go, four behind Wall. But Snead made a poor start. Then came a cloudburst that threatened to wash away the course, and play had to be suspended. Snead complained that he had other commitments and wanted to

see the tournament finished that day. Play was resumed after a two-hour delay, and Snead tied for ninth.

Art Wall's winning score of 269 was 19 under. This led to complaints that such low scoring was a blow to the prestige of the Open and the club, and that something had to be done to toughen one of Stanley Thompson's masterpieces. Before the next Open at St. George's, the course was lengthened by about 100 yards. Two of the short par fives were made into par fours, two very fine par fours stretched to par fives.

When Bob Charles won the Open at St. George's in 1968, he did so with a score of 274, five more than Art Wall had needed, but only six under the new par for the course.

This Open set a number of records. The final round was held on a Sunday, the first time the Open had breached the sabbath in Ontario. A record number of spectators (estimated at 35,000, but this must be an exaggeration) turned out on the final day. The Open was won for the first time by a left-handed golfer. A record number of stars failed to make the cut, including Palmer, Peter Thompson, Ken Venturi, Wall, and Ford. The last hour would probably have set a new record for excitement, had there been any way of measuring this.

No fewer than eleven players went into that final round with a good chance of winning. The top seven: at 208, Knudson and Charles; at 209, Nicklaus, Weiskopf, Aaron, Casper, and Sikes. These seven golfers had got to this position by remarkably different routes. Great things had been expected of Knudson, then having his best year yet on the PGA Tour; no player was under greater pressure to win. At St. George's, he had the feeling he could not put his feet on the ground. And that was *before* the starter called his name and told him how much was expected of him.

The burden of Canada's expectations bore down on poor George. He shot a 75 in the first round and was in danger of not qualifying. After the round he was nowhere to be found, having sought refuge in Lloyd Percival's Fitness Club. He felt badly about letting us down.

In 1968 at St. George's, winner Bob Charles's ball lies inches from the pin for a birdie at the 72nd hole, while Nicklaus plays to the green.

On the second day, Knudson came back with a 69, including a hole in one at the short sixth. (The ball dropped two feet in front of the hole, hopped five feet past, and rolled back in. The TV cameraman ran out of film seconds before the ball went into the hole.) But it was Knudson's third round of 64 that electrified the crowd. This round was *not* vintage Knudson – he was sinking putts that day in a manner quite unlike the real George.

For him and for our hopes, the last round was a tragedy. His putting was wretched, and a few bogeys soon put him out of the running.

(He always maintained that he played as good golf, tee to green, in his closing 73, as in his 64.)

Knudson was playing in the last group, behind Charles and Nicklaus, with Charles leading by one coming to the 457-yard final hole. Needing a birdie to force a play-off, Nicklaus drove all of 300 yards. First away, Charles hesitated between a 7 and an 8-iron, and was talked into a 7 by his astute caddie. His ball finished ten inches from the pin. For the second time, Jack Nicklaus was to be the bridesmaid.

Scarboro has a Tillinghast course, or mostly so. The original eighteen holes were laid out in 1914, but ten years later the club hired the American golf architect A. W. Tillinghast to remodel eleven of the eighteen holes. A creek winds its way through the course and comes into play over a dozen times. In fourteen through sixteen, the course has an unusual string of three holes measuring (for the 1953 Open) 222 yards (par three), 295 yards (an uphill par four), and 264 yards (par four), all well guarded but the latter two obviously birdieable.

After being the scene of Bobby Locke's triumph in 1947, Scarboro was next the battlefield for the "Photo-finish Open" of 1953.

The dramatic turnaround in this Open came at the fifteenth hole of the final round. Wally Ulrich, an ex-Marine veteran of Korea, drove from the tee with a three-shot lead and was seemingly coasting home. He played his second out of a rut, leaving it eight feet above the hole on this sloping green. His putt went rolling downhill, had a quick look at the cup, decided it didn't like the view, and continued on its merry way until stopped by a bunker. Ulrich exploded out to within eight feet and two-putted for a heartbreaking double bogey.

The fickle gallery deserted the poor fellow to watch Dave Douglas perform miracles over the closing holes. A tall stringbean of a man, the thirty-five-year-old quiet-mannered, conservative Douglas – someone observed of him that he looked more like a bank teller than a professional – had been a steady money-winner but seldom a winner. Now only a single stroke behind Ulrich, he proceeded to birdie the last three holes. Whereupon Ulrich dug down deep, found there was still a patron saint of golf, and proceeded to birdie the sixteenth himself. Had there been any justice, his putt for a birdie on eighteen would surely have dropped. But it died on the lip, and the stringbean Douglas had won.

The same four finishing holes were to determine the winner at Scarboro in 1963. Six ahead with a round to go, Doug Ford found out on the fifteenth tee that twenty-five-year-old Al Geiburger was sitting in the clubhouse with a 65 under his belt. To win, Ford needed a birdie. This did not make him play any the more cautiously or slow down his pace. (He was once described as "the guy who always looks as though he's playing through the group he's playing with.") He got his birdie at the seventeenth, by sinking an 18-foot putt. Geiburger, trying his best not to watch on television, was heard to say that no one could birdie that hole from where Ford had been.

Courses like St. George's and Scarboro were fast becoming too cramped by residential development to be considered for the Open in the 1970s. And it is hard to see where you would now park the automobiles at Mississauga. But these old clubs put on some fine shows for us when asked, and their members worked hard to make their Opens a success.

Arnold Palmer's victory in 1955 was his first on the PGA Tour. The same can be said of the winners in the next three years.

Palmer defended his title at Beaconsfield in 1956, but not successfully. In the face of atrocious weather for the first two days, the scoring was remarkably good, with Doug Sanders of Miami Beach one stroke behind at the halfway mark.

This twenty-three-year-old amateur had won the 1951 International Junior Championship and in 1953 the Southeastern title. In Canada, he went on to succeed where the amateurs Bobby Jones (in 1919) and Tommy Armour (in 1920) had failed – he won the Canadian Open championship. He did this in a sudden-death play-off, the first time the RCGA had used this way of settling a tie.

Don Finsterwald was rather annoyed at being beaten by an amateur, but he had no need to be. Doug Sanders almost immediately turned professional and became a very successful and

Doug Sanders in 1956, the only amateur to win the Open, with J. E. Frowde Seagram.

flamboyant member of the Tour, noted for his rainbow-coloured attire, as well as for his short back-swing.

The 1957 Open was held at Kitchener's Westmount club, to tie in with Seagram's centennial. For the opening round, the fairways were not cut short enough for the professionals' liking; the grass between the clubhead and ball made it hard to get backspin. Too, the aprons were hard, the greens bouncy. The RCGA had put the pins in the front centre of the greens, which was not the best spot under the circumstances. The Tour players complained loudly and openly. The worst offenders were Bob Rosburg, Art Wall, and George Bayer, but Stan Leonard and Pat Fletcher were among those quoted as saying "The worse course ever to hold the Open." Jack Fleck and the brothers Boros pulled out of the event.

Rex MacLeod of *The Globe and Mail* put their complaints into some sort of perspective:

As is customary in most preliminaries, there was unanimous caterwauling about the condition of the fairways and greens. Ignorant laymen, who inspected the course meticulously from a host of score cards, adjudged the layout to be close to perfection, but the pro shooter greeted their findings with derision. [Some of the professionals] suggested that it might be tough to go round this course in five or six under par . . . In other words, it looks like any other tournament.

After the first round, the fairways were cut with a verti-cutter and the aprons watered. Some professionals then complained that the RCGA had made the course too easy. "All the cry babies should be happy today," said Doug Ford who, a day earlier, had threatened to thump a spectator for criticizing him. "They've made it a ladies' course," said Arnold Palmer, who would be much more tactful today.

The RCGA asked the PGA to take punitive action against the worst of the complainers.

The six-feet-five-inch 240-pound George Bayer was the largest man ever to play the PGA Tour when he won at Westmount. The longest hitter on the Tour had been struggling to win for three years but did not need his length for Westmount. He just played good, steady golf, with one brilliant 64 in the all-important third round. By this time, his own scores were making a mockery of his earlier criticism of the course. He had the good sense to admit this when accepting the Seagram Gold Cup.

A twenty-six-year-old raw-boned rangy Texan named Wes Ellis seemed to come from nowhere to win the 1958 Open at Edmonton's Mayfair, when the handsome Jay Hebert appeared to have the title all sewn up.

It is true he had only a two-stroke lead over Ellis going into the final round, but nobody was paying much attention to Ellis. Canadian eyes were on Leonard and Balding, at three back. Could one of them catch Hebert and repatriate the Gold Cup? Well, we know the answer. But while we were watching them try, young Ellis snuck in with a 66, to steal the championship by a stroke.

Doug Ford ended the run of new boys by winning the championship in 1959, at Islesmere. He was an old friend of Canada, and Canada had been generous to him. Since turning professional in 1949, he had improved his bank balance just about every year by playing the Canadian Open, his best finish being third. This ice-cold, U.S. Ryder Cup player with the looped swing had won the PGA Championship in 1955, the Masters two years later. He liked to play golf at the gallop, in the manner of Scotland's George Duncan and Canada's Moe Norman.

Former U.S. Open champion Jack Fleck did not see Doug Ford being presented with his trophy. After a mediocre second round, Fleck drove to the club for the third, could not find a parking space in the players' enclosure, and drove off, never to return. The PGA fined him $100. As we have seen, Ford was to win again, at Scarboro in 1963.

The 1962 Open at Laval-sur-le-Lac was historic in that it brought together two golfers who were to be the finest in their own countries, George Knudson and Jack Nicklaus. They were paired together for the final round and attracted the largest gallery. Knudson had led the field after the first day with a 67, but was never in the hunt after that. Nicklaus was obviously jaded after the recent PGA Championship, but he did recover in the last two rounds to tie for fifth place.

Canada's young Wilf Homenuik met with a double misfortune in the 1962 Open. He had a hole in one. At most tournaments, this would have won him anything from an automobile to $50,000, but at Laval there was no special prize. He also finished as the leading Canadian professional. But the RCGA had decided that year to discontinue the award of the Rivermead Cup and the prize money that went with it.

Montreal's Expo of 1967 was all part of Canada's centennial celebrations. So it was fitting that the 1967 Open should be held in that city.

The city fathers had two years to do something about the image and reality of its municipal Yellow Course, where the Open was to be played. They gave it a complete facelift, adding a new watering system, fifteen new tees, two new greens. They also remodelled the other sixteen greens, and added two thousand trees. "It's one of the finest public courses in North America," said Jack Tuthill, field director of the PGA, and the man responsible for seeing that the course measured up to PGA standards.

But Tuthill's enthusiasm was not shared by everyone. The course was variously described as "the skid row section of the Gaza strip," and "an arid waste, fit only for caravans."

The city of Montreal doubled the prize money to $200,000, enough to attract the finest on the Tour, including Palmer, Nicklaus, and Casper. There were 288 entries, the largest ever to that date, so that 163 of the non-exempt players had to play-off at Pinegrove G & CC for thirty-one spots.

Art Wall went into the final round with a two-stroke lead. Nicklaus, four behind, looked likely to catch him when he covered the front nine in 32, but he then had a string of bogeys. Coming to the par-five final hole, Art Wall seemed a certain winner, still two strokes ahead. Unaccountably, he proceeded to hit three consecutive poor shots, then three putts, the last from five feet. (This from one of the world's finest putters.) Billy Casper, playing in the same group, sank a 12-foot birdie putt to catch him.

The crucial hole for Casper in this round had been the par-five seventh. He pushed his ball out of bounds, but still made par.

The eighteen-hole play-off on the Monday between two of the world's greatest putters was described at the time as an exhibition of dull proficiency. It produced a remarkable exhibition of scoring, mostly the result of long putts sunk. Casper (at that time a svelte 180 pounds and thriving on a new diet of buffalo steaks and religion) set a course record of 65, to win by four strokes.

Canada's three top professionals – Knudson, Balding, and Norman – failed to make the cut in the 1967 Open. Young, handsome Adrian Bigras put them all to shame. He, Wilf Homenuik, and amateur Nick Weslock were the only Canadians to make the cut. Bigras finished with a 69 to take fifteenth place (worth $2,714).

Tom Weiskopf had been on the PGA Tour for nine years when he won his first Canadian Open in 1973 at Richelieu Valley, thirty miles southeast of Montreal.

The six-feet-three-inch, well-built Weiskopf seemed to have everything going for him. He could outswing Nicklaus in the purity of his action, even outdrive him in distance. But he could not outgolf him, golf being so much a game of the mind. For Weiskopf was a victim of his own bad temper, childish pouting, and petulance.

In a way, fate had not been kind to him. "The worst thing that happened to Weiskopf was to emerge from Jack Nicklaus' home town, via

Tom Weiskopf, right, *winner in 1973 and 1975.*

Nicklaus' alma mater, Ohio State, with a magnificent natural golf swing and power," Ken McKee observed in 1973. Rivals for many years, these two did not clash at Richelieu Valley; Barbara Nicklaus was giving birth to a son and Jack was at her side.

Weiskopf came to the 1973 Canadian Open on a roll, and as the player of the year. He was then thirty years of age, and recovering from the loss of his father, whose death seemed to have had a cathartic effect on him. A new Tom Weiskopf appeared, one determined to take his golf seriously, to control his outbursts, to do less fishing and hunting, and to practise his game. Having won only five tournaments in his first nine years on tour, he suddenly had four wins in seven starts. More important, ten days before coming to Canada he had won the British Open at Old Troon, a course he was not predisposed to like. The new Weiskopf seemed to be promising to deliver what the old Weiskopf had lost somewhere along the way.

With Nicklaus and Casper the only top U.S. players absent, this was a strong field at Richelieu. Heavy rain waterlogged the greens and delayed the start. The soggy greens produced what Trevino called "a forest of spike-marks," frustrating the better putters in the field.

But if anything the rain made the course easier. In the first round, Hale Irwin set a new course record of 65, to lead Weiskopf, Forrest Fezler, and Hubert Green by two strokes.

For the second round, the wind and rain turned the 6,900-yard course into a tiger. Only three players broke the magic 70. Putting had become even more of a nightmare; because of the rain, the greens could not be cut for two days.

Weiskopf had mastered the course and himself and went into the final round with a one-stroke lead over Fezler. Bobby Cole of South Africa, seven strokes behind, opened with five consecutive birdies and looked capable of shooting another five. But the great God of Equity fingered him, and Weiskopf won from Fezler by two.

Weiskopf won his second Open at Royal Montreal, two years later. This was the sixth Open run by this club and the RCGA, but the first at the club's new headquarters.

Some questioned the wisdom of holding the 1975 Open at such an inaccessible site as Ile Bizard. There was no public transport, and the traffic to the island had to pass over a narrow bridge. But the doubters need not have worried. Well over sixty thousand witnessed a classic Canadian Open.

The event was played over Royal Montreal's Blue course, usually rated in Canada's top ten. Not overly long, it demands good second shots, since the rough around the greens is deep and tough. Some of the greens are long, with narrow entrances, so that the shot to the hole can vary by two clubs, depending on the placing of the pin.

Weiskopf had a strong field to contend with. Of the then top fifty money-winners on the PGA Tour, all but five came north, including the leading money-winner, Nicklaus.

Should Jack Nicklaus never win the Canadian Open title and one day look back over his near misses, he will probably rank the 1975 Open as the one he threw away through lack of information. Consider what happened on the closing holes on that Sunday afternoon.

Weiskopf had started the day a stroke behind the leaders, Nicklaus and Brewer, both at four under par. He was playing in the final group of the day, with Brewer and Gilbert. Nicklaus was one group ahead. The lead seesawed throughout the afternoon, but with never more than a stroke in it. Nicklaus, Weiskopf, and Brewer shared the lead at six under after the fourteenth.

At the fifteenth, Nicklaus sank a seven-foot putt for a birdie and a one-stroke lead. He made his pars at the next two holes and came to the eighteenth believing he still had only a one-stroke lead. But behind him both Weiskopf and Brewer had run into trouble at the sixteenth and made bogeys. Unaware of this, Nicklaus felt he needed to birdie the eighteenth to give himself an unassailable two-stroke margin. So, instead of playing a safe 3-wood shot away from the water on the left of the eighteenth fairway, Jack went with his driver from the tee. The ball hooked into the hazard, and he did well to salvage a bogey 5.

Still, this looked as though it might be good enough, till Weiskopf birdied the short seventeenth, which tied him for the lead.

Weiskopf played well away from the water at the eighteenth. His second shot at this demanding 448-yard par four finished in the rough, but he made a fine recovery shot and sank his putt for a tie.

The play-off lasted only one hole, the 414-yard fifteenth. Weiskopf outdrove Nicklaus by a few feet. Nicklaus put a 7-iron some nine feet from the pin. With the same club, Weiskopf finished less than three feet away, a winning shot if ever there was one. If Nicklaus knew instinctively that he had lost, he never showed it as he walked to the green.

34
CHAPTER

THE CPGA: YEARS OF EXPANSION

THE SECOND PHASE IN THE DEVELOP-
ment of the Canadian Professional
Golfers' Association – its consolidation
and its acquisition of major sponsors – began
in the early 1940s, under the presidency of
Gordie Brydson. From the time the CPGA had
incorporated in 1938, he and his committee of
directors had been working towards bringing
into the CPGA fold the various district associations that had sprung up across the country.
Their aim was to have the CPGA accepted as
the central body.

Taking a leaf from the book of its American
cousin, the association remodelled itself after the
fashion of the PGA. It established five CPGA
zones: the Maritimes, Quebec, Ontario, the
Prairies, and British Columbia. Each zone had
its own executive, and each sent a representative
to sit on the executive board of the parent CPGA,
headquartered in Toronto. (Gradually over the
years a further four zones have been added; the
Prairie zone has been split into Manitoba,
Alberta, and Saskatchewan; and there are now
zones for Ottawa Valley and Northern Ontario,
a reflection of the great increase in the number
of clubs in these areas. Too, the Maritimes zone

has been renamed Atlantic, and now includes
Newfoundland.)

At a meeting in Montreal in 1944, the CPGA
executive passed a resolution that "all professional golf associations throughout Canada are
to be under the jurisdiction of the CPGA . . .
and only members of the CPGA can participate
in any tournament whatever, in whatever zone
professional tournaments are to be held."

Guiding the CPGA was its new honorary
president, J. P. Emile Collette. His appointment was to have far-reaching consequences
for the CPGA and for golf in Canada. Here was
a self-made and successful businessman, president of Associated Textiles of Canada, headquartered in Montreal. Small of stature, large
in spirit, and a keen golfer, Emile Collette was
among the first to realize that the world of
golf would change beyond recognition after
the war. Professional golf would require sponsors, and sponsors could be attracted to professional golf. The game would become international, and Canada could be in the forefront
of making it so.

In all of this, Collette's aim was altruistic.
He was out to help Canadian professionals

fulfil their long-standing objective of boost-ing Canadian golf in stature as well as in size. This would, coincidentally, bolster the professionals' own businesses. During the war years, he was restricted to restructuring the CPGA and to arranging professional tournaments that raised money for war charities. In August 1943, as president of the Seigniory Club of Montebello, Quebec, he organized a match at the club between the professionals of Quebec and Ontario, the proceeds to go to the Red Cross. Again, in 1944, he was instrumental in reviving the CPGA championship at the same club. Wartime conditions restricted the members to some thirty professionals from Quebec and Ontario. So it is perhaps unfair to the Maritime and western professionals to label this a Canadian championship, as the record book does.

At the end of the war, Emile Collette saw to it that the CPGA took advantage of the new general affluence and the upsurge in interest in spectator sports. In 1945, he persuaded a group of Montreal businessmen to sponsor a CPGA Open Championship, with a purse of $10,000, a record purse for Canada. This move upstaged the RCGA, which had not yet decided where and when to hold the Canadian Open.

The 1945 CPGA Open was held at the Isles-mere G & CC, in June. The prize money attract-ed many of the leading U.S. professionals. Collette had the unique distinction of also being an honorary director of the PGA, and a friend of its tournament director, Fred Corcoran. When Corcoran asked if Bing Crosby could play at Islesmere, the CPGA had no diffi-culty in saying yes. His presence helped swell the number of spectators, many of whom were witnessing golf for the first time. (One was overheard to say: "You see when they pick up the ball on the green and put down money? Well, that's how they gamble on golf.")

In spite of some administrative problems, the CPGA Open was declared a great success. Byron Nelson won, and was to go on to win the Canadian Open two months later. Bing Crosby shot a 77, and left after two rounds. The prize for the top Canadian amateur went to Nick Weslock, then establishing himself as the country's finest. The event was also a finan-cial success. It was the first four-day national tournament to be held over a Thursday to Sunday and it attracted some 20,000 specta-tors. It generated $14,000, which more than offset the prize money.

The tournament also gave the CPGA and its capable tournament director, Earl Morris, some hard-earned experience in handling a major event. Hard-earned, because quite a number of spectators got in without paying; too, someone had forgotten to publish the starting times in English-language newspa-pers; and nobody seemed to know exactly how the prize money was to be divided.

In 1946, Emile Collette persuaded Gerhard Kennedy of the Northern Shirt Company, Winnipeg, to sponsor the second – and, as it turned out, the last – CPGA Open.

This $10,000 CPGA Open was played over the Niakwa GC, again attracting about 20,000 over four days. Spectators came to see the likes of Ben Hogan (the winner), Jimmy Demaret, Jimmy Thompson, Lawson Little, Sam Snead, and Canada's Stan Leonard. For the first time in Canadian golf, a walkie-talkie system was used to flash the standings back to the main scoreboard, hole by hole.

The net proceeds from these two Opens gave the CPGA some money in the kitty, which was Collette's main purpose in staging them.

In 1949, Gerhard Kennedy was elected to the new honorary post of Western President of the CPGA. This move helped stifle the com-plaints of the western professionals, particular-ly those in British Columbia, that the CPGA had an eastern bias. In 1949, the dates of the CPGA championship and the Canadian Open had become separated, so that western entries would have had to make two trips to the East if they wanted to play in both. B.C. profes-sionals, led by Jock McKinnon, talked of breaking away from the CPGA and joining the PGA. But when the facts were explained to them, when it was demonstrated that the two events could not be scheduled closer together, the mutiny subsided. Having a western repre-

Emile Collette.

Ben Hogan winning the CPGA Open in 1946.

Earl Morris, the CPGA's tournament manager after the Second World War.

sentative of the stature of Gerhard Kennedy helped to achieve what we would now call "better communications."

Emile Collette was also a governor of the RCGA. He used his influence with the PGA to convince this body (at least temporarily) that the Canadian Open should be recognized as an official PGA tournament.

Collette also pressured the PGA into agreeing to a series of international matches between the professionals of the two countries. Canadian professionals had never quite given up the hope that the Ryder Cup matches between Britain and the U.S. could be extended to include Canada. But that was rather a forlorn hope, and all but abandoned by 1950, when Emile Collette and CPGA president Ken Murray attended the PGA annual dinner in Chicago. They took up the matter of international matches with the PGA officers. Somewhat to the Canadians' surprise, the Americans liked the idea.

Collette was on the board of Canadair Limited, a subsidiary of the General Dynamics Corporation. He persuaded John Jay Hopkins, the chairman of both these companies, to put up a trophy that would serve as the equivalent of the Ryder Cup.

The first of the series of international matches for the Hopkins Trophy was held at the Beaconsfield G & CC, in August 1952. It was sponsored by Canadair, who put up $15,000 in prize money for each of three annu-

al matches. These were played along the lines of the Ryder Cup: the teams of six, plus one spare, played four-balls on the first day, singles on the second day. The Canadian team of Pat Fletcher, Stan Horne, Jules Huot, Stan Leonard, Gordie Brydson, Bill Kerr, and Bobby Locke was defeated 20 1/2 points to 6 1/2, by a strong U.S. team. Why did the Canadian team include Bobby Locke of South Africa? A frequent visitor to Canada and an honorary member of the CPGA, he was included to give the team strength, although some people with a strict sense of nationalism objected.

The series of Hopkins Trophy matches was the culmination of Emile Collette's long-standing dream for Canadian professionals. The matches were played for five years. John Jay Hopkins went on to organize the International Golf Association (IGA) with Collette as one of its directors. The IGA was a non-profit organization dedicated to the furthering of international goodwill between Canada and the rest of the free world, by conducting international golf matches. In 1953, it held the first multi-national professional team tournament for the Canada Cup, now known as the World Cup.

The CPGA had moved into international golf during the presidency of Ken Murray. This tall, affable, fast-talking professional had suc-

The CPGA executive, 1950: every one a legend.

ceeded his father at Royal Montreal, when Charlie died suddenly in 1938. He had been selected for the CPGA's top job in 1949.

Ken Murray was essentially a businessman professional, and one of the most popular men in the game. He did much to cement relations between the CPGA and the PGA of America, and he shared Emile Collette's dream of international golf matches for Canadians.

During this period, the CPGA started to perform a new function. With the increased interest in the sponsoring of golf tournaments, many would-be sponsors turned to the CPGA for advice and assistance. Seagram, John Labatt Ltd., Jay Hopkins and the IGA, Bradings Breweries, and Dow Kingsbeer Breweries were among those who invited the CPGA to work with them in organizing professional tournaments.

The CPGA itself had taken on a new sponsor for its annual championship. From 1947 to 1953, the event had been sponsored by Cohama, a division of Associated Textiles. Emile Collette put up the Cohama Trophy for the winner, and the P. D. Ross trophy was retired.

In 1954, the event was taken over by the House of Seagram, so the Seagram Shield now replaced the Cohama Trophy. By 1958 Seagram had increased the prize money from $3,000 to $5,000. In 1962, in recognition of the jubilee of the CPGA championship, the company doubled the purse to $10,000. In the same period, the purse for the Canadian Open went up from $10,000 to $30,000. The CPGA's sponsor – who was also the Open's sponsor – was recognizing the general trend towards higher purses for professional events.

Left to right: *George Clifton, George Dulmage, Bob Cunningham, Bob Gray, at the Dow championship in 1953.*

Program for the Labatt Open, 1955.

In the 1950s, the CPGA was predominantly an organization for club professionals. Canada had nothing to compare with the PGA Tour. A handful of Canadian professionals had tried their hand on the American circuit, none of them with any great success. More young Canadian professionals would have gone south given the right financial backing. But backers were hard to find, given the high standard of golf on the American circuit.

The CPGA knew that a few Canadian successes in the world of Ben Hogan and Sam Snead would be a shot in the arm for golf in Canada. When the concept of bursaries for professionals was mooted, the CPGA was quick to support it.

In the fall of 1952, Frank and Harry Doughty of British & American Motors came forward with the idea of the British & American Motors Bursary Tournament. It was open to Canadian professionals aged thirty or younger. The prize money of $4,000 was divided equally between the top three golfers. They would be expected to spend ten weeks on the PGA winter tour, with the prize money to support them. (The winner also got the B & A Trophy; the three of them, expensive golf bags.)

The first playing of the B & A Bursary took place at the Islington GC. The short-swinging Rudy Hovarth of Windsor won the trophy, the tall, handsome Jack Kay, and Johnny Henrick, both of Montreal, sharing with him the $4,000 prize money.

Among the future winners of the bursary were Al Balding and Moe Norman. When the B & A was replaced by the MacNaughton–Brooks Bursary (put up by Toronto businessmen Mac MacNaughton and John S. Brooks) George Knudson was also to become a beneficiary. Over the years, many young professionals were to use bursary winnings to stake them on the PGA Tour (and its satellite tours), but only Balding and Knudson were to win often enough, or finish high enough, to make a living.

As we have seen, the Millar match-play tournament started as an Ontario PGA event and later was opened to professionals first from Quebec, then from the rest of Canada, during the Second World War. But in practice it remained, with few exceptions, an event for professionals in Ontario, where it was always held. The original intention had been to play this tournament at the course of the previous year's winner, but after 1931 it was held mainly at the Islington Golf Club, whose Cap Millar had put up the trophy.

Golf started as a match-play game, so the Millar had tradition on its side. It soon had a record for excitement equalled by few stroke-play tournaments. To radio listeners, it will always be linked to Wes McKnight of CFRB in Toronto, who gave a live commentary, helped by colour commentators such as Islington professional Les Franks.

Lex Robson had won the Millar six times before the war; from 1940, Bob Gray and Bill Kerr were each to win it four times. In 1945, Kerr beat Gray in the final "as far from the clubhouse as possible, and in rain to end all

rains," complained a very wet McKnight. Four years later, the Gray–Kerr duel lasted 25 holes: Gray won after hurdling a stymie, as fitting a finish as you could ask for. In 1948, Stan Horne won after smashing the ball to the green with a 4-iron, from an underwater lie. Then in 1952, Islington's own Al Balding had the first of his four victories in the Millar. His winnings helped finance him on the PGA Tour, and he was on his way to establishing himself as one of the finest professionals we have produced.

Al also reached the final in 1956 and 1957, to be beaten by two of the very few Westerners ever to play in the Millar – Stan Leonard and Bill Mawhinney. Mawhinney was something like 35 under par for his six rounds of match play.

The Millar would probably never have become a truly national match-play championship. A professional is going to think twice about flying from the West Coast to Ontario, given that he could well find himself out of the tournament after 18 holes. In 1965, the format was changed to 72 holes of stroke play (reduced to 54 a year later). But that killed the whole spirit of the Millar, and it effectively died, mourned by many. It was discontinued after 1968, leaving Wilf Homenuik to go down in history as the undefeated champion.

In 1962, Dick Borthwick, president of the CPGA, and Merle Schneckenburger, of Seagram, put their names to a new agreement which would give further aid to the CPGA's playing professionals. Seagram was sponsoring a Caribbean and a Far East Tour and a few entries to the Mexican Open. A player could qualify by coming up with a good performance in the CPGA championships.

The Caribbean Tour gave professionals five weeks with five competitive rounds each week. It was supervised and administered by the PGA, which arranged flights, hotels, and visas for the entire group. The publicity was in the hands of Larry O'Brien of Montreal, who had joined Seagram a year or so earlier. The tour comprised five tournaments: the

Opens of Panama City, Maracaibo, Venezuela, Puerto Rico, and Jamaica.

Many an aspiring professional was to cut his teeth on the Caribbean Tour. Our own George Knudson led the entire circuit in 1963, against such fine PGA players as Jim Ferree, Charlie Sifford, and Art Wall.

Administering the CPGA right after the war was the job of the president and his executive, working out of their homes or professional shops, but they were soon to be joined by tournament manager E. D. (Marsh) Marshall. A year after the association's jubilee in 1961, president Dick Borthwick opened a permanent CPGA office in Toronto's Bay Street and engaged a full-time secretary, Betty Graybeil. Membership was then about 350, which is what it had been ten years earlier. But the CPGA's services had grown. A new pension plan for members had been introduced in 1960, and a new insurance plan against loss of income, a year later.

In the late 1960s, the CPGA appointed its first paid full-time executive director. Bill Hamilton we have already met, as the secretary-treasurer of the RCGA who had turned to professional golf with Toronto's Oakdale club. Hamilton was a natural choice to be on the CPGA executive committee. And when the association could afford a paid manager in 1967, he was also a natural choice for this post.

Under Hamilton, the CPGA started a series of annual business schools for its members. Being a professional golfer in the 1960s called for much more than a sound swing and an ability to teach. The new professional had to project the image of a businessman; he had to

CPGA's Bill Hamilton mops up during the 1967 championship at St. Catharines G & CC, Ontario.

dress well but not overdress, had to be courteous without being subservient. In the words of professional Murray Tucker, a speaker at these training seminars, the club professional had to be player, teacher, businessman, accountant, personnel director, cart and club repairman, tournament director, arbiter, public relations man, and psychologist. Over a hundred professionals and assistants attended these week-long annual schools.

When the federal government introduced legislation limiting the advertising of liquor, Seagram could no longer be identified as the sponsor of cultural and sporting events in a manner which gave the company some return on the large amounts it was spending. Reluctantly, it felt forced to withdraw from the sponsorship of the CPGA's championship, just as it was later to withdraw from sponsoring the Canadian Open.

In 1967, Labatt took over as sponsor of the CPGA championship, putting up $13,500 prize money, upping it to $20,000 a year later. The CBC was now televising the last two days of the event, giving wider recognition to both players and sponsor.

In 1971, a new and powerful sponsor was found for a CPGA dream of many years, a Canadian professional tour. Imasco had just taken on sponsorship of the Open. Through its subsidiary, Peter Jackson, Imasco now offered to put up $79,000 in prize money for a series of professional tournaments in Canada, to be run with the help of the CPGA. The objective was to give to tournament experience to young Canadian professionals.

In its first year, 1971, the Peter Jackson Tour was made up of seven events: a new event, the Atlantic Open (with a purse of $5,500), and the long-established Opens of Quebec, Ontario, and British Columbia (each purse $16,000), of Manitoba and Alberta (each purse $8,500), and of Saskatchewan (a $7,500 purse). There were to be no half measures with Peter Jackson. Having appointed Al Balding as its tour coordinator, it brought in Mark McCormack as a promotional consultant.

Bill Hamilton, too, needed help. He hired David Zink, a twenty-eight-year-old club professional to be, among other things, the CPGA's director of the Peter Jackson Tour.

The Peter Jackson Tour was a success while it lasted. But the parent company had many commitments as a sponsor, not the least of which was to a Canadian Open requiring more and more prize money. So it stopped sponsoring the CPGA's tour in 1977, and the tour had to be discontinued, not to be revived until well into the 1980s.

Labatt continued to sponsor the CPGA championship, but under the name of the Labatt International; a number of PGA stars were persuaded to enter – among them Palmer, Trevino, Ray Floyd – a move which gave the company larger gates and almost guaranteed it a live showing on Canadian television. But these stars had to be persuaded with appearance money. This did not sit well with at least one Canadian professional on the PGA Tour, Jim Nelford, who had supported the CPGA championship partly out of a sense of loyalty. Nelford criticized Labatt's paying as much as $30,000 to bring in U.S. professionals – famous or not – while refusing to do the same for Canadians like himself. In future he would forget his national pride in the CPGA championship and compete only if the money was right. But his protests came too late. The championship at Quebec City in 1983 was not broadcast. Labatt pulled out of national sponsorship of golf, saying that it wanted to put its money into local and provincial events.

All of this was a sign of the times. The marketability of the CPGA championship – indeed, of all Canadian golf tournaments with the exception of the Open – was not what it had been. The world of golf had become increasingly more "Hollywood." Audiences were no longer being attracted by the quality of the performance, but by personalities. When trying to promote larger gates at CPGA events, the editor of a Canadian golf magazine asked: "Is it not true that good golf is as exciting regardless of who swings the club?" His question was rhetorical, but it deserves an answer. No, it is probably not true. People probably do not go to the Canadian Open hoping to see better golf than they would see at a CPGA championship. They go to see personalities, the icons of the little square box, no matter how they are scoring.

With no Canadian tour after 1977, Canadian playing professionals headed for other fields. Some went to Europe, Australia, Asia. But many had no medium in which to play competitive golf for a living, and the game languished – this at a time when the PGA Tour and others were prospering. The inactivity fed itself; the longer it lasted, the longer it was liable to last. To get a sponsor, you need a tour. To get a tour, you need a sponsor.

By 1984, the picture looked much brighter. A newly formed Tournament Players Division (TPD) of the CPGA had taken its first tentative steps under the presidency of professional Ken Tarling. The TPD acted much like its counterpart in the PGA. For tournaments, it was soon to have its own mobile field office, its own field force to look after player registration, the selection of courses, pin placements, and the like, leaving local committees to handle other matters.

At first Tarling had no tour to organize. Some provincial Open championships were still being held, but were not part of any single, structured, entity. The total prize money amounted to only $100,000. In 1984, Timex agreed to sponsor the CPGA championship in place of Labatt. By 1985, the prize money for tournaments had been raised to nearly half a million. Labatt had agreed to put up $25,000 for the Labatt Order of Merit, to go to the leading professionals on the TPD tour.

A Canadian Professional Golf Tour began to take shape. Executive director Bob Beauchemin had his own vision of how it should be run, having experienced the PGA Tour firsthand. His aim was fifteen tournaments, incorporating the provincial Opens, including a CPGA and a TPD championship, all with purses of at least $100,000.

This PGA tour-in-miniature appears to be flying five years later. In 1990, there were ten events (including provincial Opens) each with a sponsor; the total prize money was some $1 million, double what it had been five years earlier. Du Maurier have also taken over as sponsor of the Order of Merit. The tour has been seen as a breeding ground for young Canadian and American professionals hoping to qualify for the PGA Tour. So it competes with tours in other parts of the world and, more recently, with the Ben Hogan Tour in the U.S.

The Canadian tour has little television time, although to the average spectator the standard of golf is probably indistinguishable from that of the Canadian Open. The big names of U.S. golf might be missing, but Canadian professionals on the PGA Tour invariably support the CPGA and TPD championship. You do not have to be a golf aficionado to be caught up in the excitement of the moment, to find out that a CPGA event can be every bit as gripping as an Open.

For the past few years, the CPGA has also organized a championship for its women professionals; by 1990, entries had grown to over thirty. In 1990, du Maurier created its own tour for women – the du Maurier Ltd. Series, comprising four events.

In the late 1970s, the CPGA became the owner of its own golf club. The Royal Oak course had been laid out a year or so earlier as part of a residential development in Titusville, Florida. It was intended for a market that never materialized, so the project turned sour. A group of Toronto businessmen took it over and offered to sell the course and clubhouse to the CPGA for next to nothing if the CPGA would take on the job of selling the residential lots. The idea of a CPGA course had gleamed in the eye of many a president, so the offer was accepted.

The professionals worked hard at disposing of these residential lots. Most of the lots went to the members of their clubs, and they went quickly enough to satisfy the property owners. In 1978, the Royal Oak Golf Club became the CPGA's own. It hired a professional and elected a CPGA committee to manage the affairs of the club.

Not all CPGA members were enthused, and some were incensed. Those in clubs west of Winnipeg would have preferred a CPGA course nearer home. If it had to be in the United States, they would have chosen California. Feelings ran high. The East versus West schism re-opened.

But time – and the realization that Royal Oak is now an asset worth many millions – had healed these differences. The CPGA uses the club for recreation and training, sending apprentices there for winter schooling, to learn the skills of Moe Norman. It runs a series of Royal Oak tournaments, a sort of stationary mini-tour for its members who winter there.

Royal Oak was a success, but not because of the CPGA's business acumen in the 1970s. Far from it. The association had taken on a heavy burden in that decade. It had grown in size and complexity. It had lost an experienced manager in Bill Hamilton, who returned to the RCGA to manage its national tournaments. Like many a small business that expands quickly, its costs had increased faster than its income. Its budgetary controls were inadequate. In 1981, things came to a head. The CPGA, $80,000 in debt, had to find someone to sort out and manage its affairs. The president, Garry Maue, turned to the CPGA's education consultant.

Back in 1969, Robert H. (Tex) Noble had been running a business course at Toronto's Humber College, when Bill Hamilton asked him to develop training and educational programs for the CPGA. He had been a consultant to the CPGA ever since.

But what does an education consultant know about the problems of professional golf? Quite a lot, as it happens. When Tex Noble was in his early teens, his parents emigrated from Scotland, settling in Calgary. In the 1920s,

his aunt was a member of the Calgary G & CC, and young Tex caddied for her. Smitten by the game, he got a job in professional Jack Cuthbert's shop. When Jack's assistant (Bill Leonard) left in 1932, Tex took his place. He spent his summers in Calgary, his winters teaching at a club in California or Texas (hence the nickname, Tex).

In 1936, Noble went back to Britain, hoping to make his fortune playing hockey for the Wembley Lions or the Brighton Tigers. But his Canadian style of hockey was too robust for English tastes. Instead, he found himself recruited as a management trainee by the Canadian department store chain Zellers, then expanding into Britain. The war came along to interrupt what could have been an exciting career in business. But it brought new challenges. He rose from a private with the Royal Edmonton Regiment to a major in the Intelligence services. He stayed in the army after the war and did stints in Germany as a Political Intelligence Officer before retiring in 1966. The Dean of Business at Humber College asked him to develop and run a business course, which led to his meeting with Bill Hamilton.

Tex Noble had not lost his love for golf. In 1955, the RCGA reinstated him as an amateur. He dabbled in golf course architecture (helping to lay out Camp Borden's Circle Pine course) and was president of the Commonwealth Golfing Society.

So, as a former professional golfer, trained as a businessman, experienced as an army officer, just retired from teaching people how to manage, Tex Noble took on the task of managing the CPGA and its tournaments, while putting its affairs in order. The job took him two years. In that time, he halved the number of directors to ten and doubled members' dues, which had remained much the same throughout the 1970s. He put the association back on its feet and back in the black.

35
CHAPTER

LEONARD, BALDING, AND THE GOLD TRAIL

THE YEAR IS 1930. WILLIE LAMB IS WINning his third consecutive CPGA championship, at the Burlington GC, Ontario. Just about every leading professional golfer in Central Canada is there, including Arthur Riley of Sudbury's Idylwylde GC, the most westerly club represented. There are no entries from Manitoba, Saskatchewan, Alberta, or British Columbia, none from the Maritimes.

Ralph Reville notes their absence, sadly. And he makes the prophecy:

> It will only be a very short time now when the airplane will make even Vancouver and Victoria a couple of days' jaunt from Toronto or Montreal, and then the championship of the professionals will become truly Canadian.

This "very short time" was ten years away. In the fall of 1940, an airplane brought a twenty-five-year-old professional to Toronto, on his way to the CPGA championships. Born and bred in Vancouver, Stan Leonard was the assistant professional to Jack Cuthbert at the Calgary G & CC. He had only recently joined the CPGA, and this was his first CPGA championship.

Leonard was virtually unknown in the East. A few remembered him as the slim youth with the slashing swing who had taken Sandy Somerville to the 37th hole in the semi-finals of the 1935 Amateur. By 1940, he had only partly overcome his slashing swing, but he had filled out his five-feet-eight-inch frame to a lean and muscular 150 pounds.

Stan Horne, Bob Gray, and Jules Huot were the ones fancied to win the 1940 CPGA title, although some had their money on Gordie Brydson, others on Bill Kerr.

The Cedar Brae course was new to Stan Leonard, and he was tired from his long journey. On the first day he shot 73 72, which left him seven behind Huot and six behind Horne. Next morning, his third-round 70 moved him up into the top ten.

493

Then came the afternoon, and the face of Canadian professional golf would never be quite the same thereafter. Leonard's long driving had been the outstanding feature of his first three rounds. In the final round, he also found the pace of the greens. His putter was an old Schenectady, bought for two dollars in a second-hand store in Calgary. On that Tuesday in August 1940, he wielded it with deadly accuracy. Out in 33, he came back in 32, to set a new course record. His total of 280 vaulted him into a tie for first place with Bill Kerr. Next day, he outshot Kerr in the play-off, 69 to 72. The CPGA championship had been won by a player from outside Central Canada for the first time since Davie Black's win in 1921.

Stan Leonard's win should have served as a warning to the pundits in the East that a new force had arrived in Canadian golf. But his last round was looked upon as something of a fluke, his win as a victory unlikely to be repeated. Why, they asked, should a young man who had failed in several attempts at the Amateur champi-

onship suddenly become good enough to win the professional title?

For a month or so, it looked as though they might be right. Back home again, Stan Leonard lost two tournaments in short order to Freddie Wood. When the quiet Wood trimmed him in the 1940 Western Open, there was no doubt in the minds of B.C. golfers. Freddie was the best in the West and arguably the finest in Canada.

Come 1941, however, the honours started to swing the other way. Stan Leonard outgolfed Freddie Wood in just about every tournament they played. The question in B.C. was no longer who was the better golfer, but rather who in Canada could match this pair of western professionals. This led to a challenge, East versus West.

Sponsored by the Kinsmen Club of Vancouver, the proceeds to go to the Red Cross, the Leonard/Wood versus Horne/Huot matches began at Victoria's Oak Bay, in July 1941. Fresh off the plane, the eastern pair were defeated 2 down over 18 holes, best ball.

Stan Leonard..

Freddie Wood.

In the second encounter over 36 holes at Freddie Wood's Quilchena course, Vancouver, the western pair was 5 up on Horne and Huot after 18 holes. But Leonard then turned wild off the tee, and only Wood's fine play saw them through by 4 and 2.

Stan Leonard travelled with the eastern pair to Edmonton, picked up a new partner, Henry Martell, and walloped Horne and Huot by 6 and 5.

The next stop was Calgary, where the two-some of Leonard and Jack Cuthbert gave the West its fourth win, by 3 and 1.

The final meeting of the original four took place in Montreal. Playing on the toughest course yet – Laval – Horne and Huot recorded their only win, but by the barest of margins, 1 up. They were never ahead in any of these matches until the sixteenth hole in Montreal.

Stan Leonard played slashing, go-for-every-thing golf throughout the series. But there was now no need for him to defend his style to the purists. Only two days before the encounter at Laval, he had successfully defended his CPGA title, giving the West its second major profes-sional title since the days of Davie Black.

The 1941 CPGA championship was held at Islesmere G & CC, a typically tough eastern course, with none of the lush fairways Leonard and Wood had been used to in B.C. Moreover, it had some long, tight holes, and Leonard was known to be a sprayer. Stan Horne was the pro-fessional at Islesmere, so, to retain his title, Leonard not only had to control his driving, he had to beard the lion in his den.

Arriving on the eve of the tournament, he had time for only one practice round, played in driving rain. But that was enough. On both days he played like the champion he was and never looked like losing. (Not even when he stepped back to look at his ball, and fell into the pond at the fourth hole of the final round.) He won by three strokes, with Stan Horne sec-ond, Freddie Wood fourth.

Stan Leonard owed this second title to his length off the tee and his deadly putting. If there was any weakness in his game, it was his approach shot to the flag. His drives were so close to the greens on the par fours that he could get no bite on his second shots, so that the ball invariably finished on the back fringe.

Born in Vancouver in February 1915, the son of a plasterer, Stan Leonard was a product of B.C. golf between the wars. The province was then a leader in the promotion of juniors. Its amateur and professional golf associations were behind clubs that supported caddie and school-boy golf. Stan Leonard was about ten when he started caddying at Vancouver's Shaughnessy Heights, playing a few holes at sundown when the members were in the clubhouse. (Shaugh-nessy was ahead of most clubs in its encourage-ment of juniors, building them their own club-house, complete with showers and lockers.) At about the same age, he and his friends laid out their own golf course at Little Mountain (he has referred to it as the smallest goat-track he has ever played). As his game improved, he won several caddie tournaments. In 1929, when only fourteen, he won with a 73, and the club re-warded this feat with a junior membership. In the following year he repaid the members by lifting their club championship. When he left school, he continued to caddie at Shaughnessy but joined the Glen Oaks GC, which played over the public Langara course. At sixteen, he began his apprenticeship under Dave McLeod, a renowned Scottish clubmaker.

We have already looked at his career as an amateur, from the time in 1932 when he entered and won his first B.C. championship, stealing it from such favourites as Dick Moore and Ken Black. Having won, he had to satisfy the offi-cials that he was only seventeen, since caddy-ing at the age of eighteen would have made him a professional.

When he gave Somerville a hard fight in the 1935 Amateur, a few observers recognized in him one of the finest prospects to come out of the West. But his slashing drive was seen to be both his greatest strength and his greatest weak-ness. At that time, he threw himself at the ball with all the exuberance of youth. His full pivot and whipcord wrist action sent the ball enor-mous distances. But if the ball flew far, it also flew far off line often enough to ruin his scores.

He continued to win city and provincial tournaments, but it was not until he defeated amateurs and professionals alike in the 1937 Pacific Northwest Open that he decided to try his hand at professional golf. He became an assistant to Bill Heyworth at Vancouver's public course in Hastings Park. Heyworth never made headlines as a player, but he knew a lot about the golf swing and had a sound system of instruction. He was among the earliest of professionals to use the movie camera to demonstrate their errors to his pupils. In 1940, Stan Leonard moved to Calgary G & CC, as a playing professional and the assistant to another great teacher, Jack Cuthbert. But the war years did not permit a club the luxury of two professionals, nor did it permit all professionals the choice of staying at their clubs. In 1942, now a two-time CPGA champion, Stan Leonard went into a machine shop in Vancouver, where he worked for the rest of the war. In that same year, he was named professional to Vancouver's prestigious Marine Drive, taking the place of Jimmy Huish.

During the later war years, Leonard played little competitive golf. His weekends were given over to exhibition matches for war charities and to his duties at his club, his evenings to practice. In those years, he slowly came to master his swing and to combine great length with reasonable accuracy.

Stan Leonard's long hours of practice, his perseverance, his dedication to his game, were to bear full fruit after the war. In the years 1945 to 1963, he established in Canadian national professional tournaments a record that has never been equalled. The major wins in his career as a professional were:

CPGA championship	1940, 1941, 1950, 1951, 1954, 1957, 1959, 1961.
Millar match-play championship	1956
Rivermead Cup	1945, 1946, 1950, 1951, 1952, 1955, 1958, 1959, 1961.
Canada Cup/World Cup	Individual champion in 1954, 1959.
PGA Tour wins	Three, one in each of 1957, 1958, 1960.

Stan Leonard has said that his first win on the PGA Tour, the 1957 Greater Greensboro Open, brought him his biggest thrill. He has also rated as his best round of golf one of the 69s he shot in the 1959 Masters at Augusta. That year he and Palmer led the Masters after 54 holes, but Leonard finished in a tie for fourth.

His string of victories in the CPGA championships probably did most to boost the spirits of golfers on the West Coast. To them he was simply "Stan the Man," an epithet as popular in B.C. as any of the nicknames given to Ben Hogan in the U.S. Only once did Leonard have the advantage of playing a CPGA championship on B.C. turf – in 1948 – and then, ironically, the title went to Toronto's Gordie Brydson.

The venue of the national championships continued to be a sore point with western professionals. When elected president of the B.C. PGA in 1945, Stan Leonard made this point. "You Easterners have to count us in more . . . the last big RCGA tournament held in B.C. was the Canadian Amateur in 1933 . . . Keeping the Canadian Open in the East is an item about which Westerners are none too pleased."

Pat Fletcher, CPGA champion in 1952.

Henry Martell, CPGA champion, 1953, 1958.

He claimed his third CPGA title in 1950, at Montreal's Summerlea, with rounds of 74 69 69–212, two ahead of Bill Kerr and Jules Huot. He then crossed the road to Royal Montreal, and shot rounds of 68 66, to lead the Canadian Open by a stroke. In the third round, his 71 left him 4 behind Jim Ferrier of Australia. There was much speculation that Leonard could still win by shooting another round in the mid 60s. But three consecutive bogeys soon put an end to that. He finished fourth.

When he successfully defended his CPGA crown at Hamilton's Ancaster course in 1951, he did so in dramatic fashion. Throughout the 54-hole tournament he fought a bad cold caught at the Open. In the oppressive heat, his cold became a fever. At some holes it literally brought him to his knees, and at one point he blacked out. "Perhaps the Gods took compassion," Hilles Pickens noted at the time. "Even as his eyes and his swing seemed to turn to water, they granted him a magic touch on the greens which offset his temporarily wayward strokes."

On the second and last day, his fever was at its peak. In the morning's first five holes he shot three bogeys and two birdies. Having birdied the eighth hole, he collapsed on the ninth. From here until the eighteenth, he committed an endless series of errors on the fairway, only to recoup his losses by sinking long putts. He somehow finished with a 70, and was only two strokes off the lead.

The lunch break seemed to help him. After a shaky start in the final round, he went from strength to strength. The tournament soon became a rout. Eleven putts in nine holes gave him birdies at the third, fourth, and eighth. He holed putts of six feet at the tenth, of 20 feet at the thirteenth, and seemed all set to match Tommy Armour's course record of 64. Dead-tired and happy, he had to be content with a 65. Nobody seriously challenged him, and he won by five strokes.

For many years, Stan Leonard looked upon his second round of 70 at Ancaster as his finest in competition, and one can understand why.

When a man wins a championship by nine strokes, he expects to monopolize the headlines. Stan Leonard ran away with his seventh CPGA title in 1959. But it was Ernie Wakelam's performance that stood out in bold print and was the talk of the spectators. This sixty-one-year-old five-feet-four-inch 120-pounder had been a threat to Willie Lamb and company thirty years earlier. But at sixty-one? Yet there he was, shooting only six more than his age. One behind Leonard after the first round, he clung there after the second. The crowd loved him. It was never a question of who was going to win, but rather of whether Ernie could hold on to second place. In the intense heat of that July afternoon, he played his heart out, never wilting, joking with the crowd. Although – in the words of one observer – "he chipped and putted the course to death," the best he could do was an 80. That left him in eighth place, but earned for him the title of Canadian Senior Professional Champion.

And what of Stan Leonard? His total of 204 was 12 under par, good enough to win by nine strokes.

In 1961, twenty-one years after he won his first CPGA championship, Stan Leonard won his eighth and last. Some say it was his greatest. He had no fever to fight, as in 1951, but he had a youthful pack of hungry young tigers chasing him, let by Al Balding. He simply ran away from them all, and almost from the start. His 67 67 69–203 set a record for the championship and gave him a seven-stroke margin over Balding. Yet his final 69 was not without adventure. On his five bogeys, eight birdies, his only comment was: "Some days the ball just seems to want to roll in. It's nice."

Stan Leonard had long since left Marine Drive. In 1955, at the age of forty, he had broken his leg and spent months just chipping and putting. He then resigned his post to take a crack at selected tournaments on the PGA Tour, something he had always wanted to do. With characteristic thoroughness, he became one of the first two Canadians to make a living from the Tour.

Over the years, Stan Leonard had played in some of the PGA's West Coast tournaments, as had other Canadian professionals. But the "U.S.

Leonard, middle, *with Gene Sarazen and Art Wall, in "Shell's Wonderful World of Golf."*

Gold Trail" was a tough road on which to make a living. No Canadian professional had ever been near the top frequently enough to consider staying on tour and making a career as a tournament professional.

By 1955, Leonard reckoned he had saved enough money to finance himself on the PGA Tour for two years without having to finish consistently in the top ten just to survive. He was also buoyed by his successes in the Canada Cup (now the World Cup). In 1953, he and Bill Kerr had taken second place as a team, and he had the second best individual score. In 1954 he had gone one better and taken the individual honours. If he was good enough to beat the top professionals from twenty countries, he was surely good enough to survive on the American circuit.

So, at the age of forty, Stan Leonard made this remarkable bid for recognition in the toughest golf league in the world. For the next seven years he was to play down south in the winter months, returning to Canada for the summer. Once on the Tour, he quickly established a reputation as a professional professional, one to be respected as a player and as a person. (He also acquired the nickname "Popeye," because of his strong forearms.)

Leonard was tough and determined to the point of being mean, all good attributes on the Tour. "You have to have a little meanness in you to win," he once admitted. He made a fine start in his new career by nearly winning a Tour event in Canada.

The $10,000 Labatt Open at Montreal was an official PGA event in 1955, and it attracted a strong field of U.S. professionals. Stan Leonard shot a closing 65 over Summerlea, to tie Gene Littler. Their sudden-death play-off was something of a letdown, Leonard taking a bogey 6 to Littler's 5.

That was the closest Leonard was to get to victory until his first win in 1957. On the long, wet Sedgefield course in North Carolina, he shot 276 to win $2,000 and the Greater Greensboro Open by three strokes from Mike Souchak. His win was important for more than the money. Several times in the past he had thrown away tournaments in the final round. In the Greensboro, it was Souchak who faltered coming in, and Leonard who held off his challenge, shooting four birdies in the first five holes of the final round. All this in the face of a somewhat hostile gallery, rooting for Souchak. But Leonard did not complain, a sign of his maturity.

He made money in all but one of the dozen or so events he played in 1956, and again in 1957, although his annual total winnings were, respectively, only $9,000 and $13,000.

In 1958, he put together four sterling rounds of 69 69 69 68–275, to win the Champion of Champions at Las Vegas. This time he won when Billy Casper put his ball into the water at the 71st hole. (Stan Leonard's $10,000 was said to have been more than doubled by a grateful punter who held his ticket in the Calcutta.) That year, in the twelve rounds he played in the Canadian Open, the Masters, and the Champion of Champions, he averaged 69.3 strokes.

He did not win any Tour events in 1959 but had the satisfaction of being made honorary professional for life by his old club, Marine Drive. He was also given the title of "Vancouver's Goodwill Ambassador" for carrying the city's flag so successfully in Australia, which he visited for the Canada Cup matches. He defeated that country's Peter Thompson for low individual honours.

His third and last win on the Tour came in 1960. The Western Open was played one week after the Canadian Open and with virtually the same field. Art Wall had won the Open, whereas Stan Leonard had tied for an inglorious thirty-first spot. Yet at Detroit, only a few days later, he and Wall came out on top together, after Leonard had made up a six-stroke deficit in the last round. Their sudden-death play-off finished on the first hole, with Leonard's birdie.

In the Masters, Stan Leonard came closest to winning a major U.S. tournament. In 1958, he finished tied for fourth place, only two strokes behind Arnold Palmer. In 1959, he and Palmer were tied for the lead after the third round. But they both blew their chances, and Leonard again had to be satisfied with a tie for fourth.

For seven seasons, 1955 through 1961, Stan Leonard had been a highly successful part-time competitor on the Tour. Then, inexplicably, his game left him. In 1962, he missed two cuts in a row, took a horrendous 81 in the Doral Open, and failed to survive the cut in the Masters. He left the Tour and went fishing, hoping to recover his lost form. But when he rejoined the Tour in the summer, he could not once finish in the top ten. He was the first to admit that the nomadic life, and his forty-seven years, probably had something to do with his slump ("But a guy doesn't grow too old overnight"). Whatever the cause, the magic of these seven years was never to be recaptured. He left the PGA Tour a richer, more satisfied, and more respected golfer, having accomplished what he had set out to do. The last word to Sam Snead: "I am glad Leonard didn't come on the circuit until he was forty years of age."

In the three tournaments he won on the American circuit, Stan Leonard met and defeated fields as strong as any in the Canadian Opens in which he played. He twice won the International Trophy as the leading scorer in the Canada (World) Cup. Yet, like some of the world's finest golfers – including Sarazen, Hogan, Nicklaus – he never won the Canadian Open. There is no question but that the added strain of playing for their national Open keeps many Canadian golfers from producing their best form in Canada's major championship. But it is also true that the odds are against them winning this one simply because they want to win it more than any other. Having said that, Stan Leonard's record for consistency in the Canadian Open is the finest of any Canadian since the First World War. He won the Rivermead Cup nine times between 1945 and 1961, by finishing as follows:

1945 — 11	1955 — 4
1946 — T-3	1958 — T-4
1950 — T-4	1959 — T-11
1951 — T-6	1961 — T-9
1952 — T-12	

His best chances of winning came in 1946. This Open at Beaconsfield was the first to be held over four days, Thursday through Sunday. Although some top U.S. players were in Britain for the oldest Open, the field was a strong one, including a Lloyd Mangrum fresh from winning the U.S. title.

After birdying the eleventh in the final round, Leonard was tied with George Fazio, the leader in the clubhouse. But misfortune dogged him on the inward half. He ran into trouble at the short thirteenth and took a bogey. He missed a six-foot putt for his birdie at the fifteenth. At sixteen, a horrible hook off the tee left him behind a stone house. He had to play sideways and took another bogey. To tie Fazio, he now needed to birdie the last two holes. At the par-three seventeenth, his tee-shot was 14 feet away. His next putt was costly, "a $10,000 putt," one observer called it. Unaccountably, he left it two feet short. He got his birdie at the last hole, but it came too late. Stan Leonard tied for third, only one stroke away from a play-off for first place. (Dick Metz caught Fazio, but lost the play-off.)

Allan George Balding emerged late in life, and from obscurity, to challenge Stan Leonard for the throne of Canada's top professional golfer. Once upon a time, he was called "Canada's modern Cinderella Man of professional golf."

It is hard to name any other Canadian professional who made his way to the top, but who did not work his way up from the caddie shop, or switch to golf from our other national sport of hockey, or graduate through the ranks of first-class amateur golf. Al Balding came by none of these routes. It is true that as a youth in the 1930s, he caddied at the nearby Islington GC, in Toronto's west end, and skipped over the fence to play golf with other caddies. But he was never very good at the game, and he certainly never had it in mind to make golf his chosen profession.

He was fifteen when the war came along. When he was old enough he enlisted, to serve overseas as a private in the 13th Field Battery. After the war, he took a number of jobs, working with the Goodyear Tire Company, driving a truck for Carling O'Keefe. These were manual jobs, and they helped develop his arm and shoulder muscles. Then, in 1948, he won a company golf tournament, with a score of less than 80. But it was not wholly this that headed him towards professional golf. He suffered a shoulder injury in an accident that made heavy labour prohibitive. So, a year later, at the age of twenty-five, he turned professional by getting a job as summer starter at Toronto's Oakdale club. Only then did he think of golf as a profession, and only then did he start to practise seriously.

Al Balding did not have as much natural golfing ability as Stan Leonard. Indeed, the two have been likened to Ben Hogan and Sam Snead in their relationship to each other. Leonard had something of Snead's natural ability, Balding something of Hogan's will to make himself perfect by hard work. But in physique and in style, the similarities were reversed. Balding is six-feet-two-inches tall; and Hogan once said of him that he had the finest swing next to Sam Snead.

Balding's hard work paid off quickly. In 1950, he won the Ontario assistant championship. The next two years were critical to his education as a golfer. In 1951 and 1952 he served as an assistant to Les Franks at Islington. Les was something of a father figure to the young Balding. Franks was also a fine teacher of the golf swing and a firm believer in practice and still more practice. In 1952, Balding came to the attention of the golfing public for the first time, by winning the Quebec Open and a hard-fought battle for the Millar Trophy.

Financial help from friends and winnings from the B & A Bursary competition in 1953 and 1954 allowed him to play in a number of events on the PGA winter tour, but there he won little but experience. On his return from the Tour in the winter of 1953–54, he did land the job of professional to Toronto's Credit Valley GC, which at least gave him an assured income.

Al Balding's breakthrough year was 1955. In the summer, at Ancaster, he won his first CPGA championship, with a clear five-stroke victory over Rosedale's Murray Tucker. In November of the same year, he became the first Canadian to win *in the United States* an event on the PGA Tour.

We often overlook the fact that B.C.'s amateur, Ken Black, had won the Vancouver Jubilee tournament back in 1935, and that Jules Huot had won the General Brock Open in 1937, another official PGA event. But no Canadian had ever gone down to the United States and "stolen" a PGA tournament from the American professionals in their own backyard. The psychological effect of this on Canadian golf could be likened to the effect of the first four-minute mile on athletics. If it could be done once, it could be done again. And again. And it was.

Al Balding was travelling on a limited budget. Now over the age of thirty, he was no longer eligible for the B & A Bursary. When he arrived at Sanford, Florida, to play in the Mayfair Open, he was running out of funds and would probably have left the winter tour had he not won.

The scoring was low over this 6,200-yard driver and putter course. After firing 69 66 66, Al Balding was lucky to be tied with Porky Oliver for first place with a round to go. Nerves threatened to take charge of him in the fourth round. An eagle 3 at the second hole did much to relieve his tension, but he was still only 1 under for the round at the turn. Ahead of him, Oliver bogeyed the sixteenth, to give Balding a two-stroke cushion coming to the last hole. He needed all of it, so close did he come to disaster. Perhaps it was only when he hit the last green in the regulation two strokes that Balding realized the enormity of what he was about to do. Needing to sink an eight-foot putt for a birdie, he missed. Needing to sink an 18-inch putt for his par, he missed again. This was a moment of sheer terror for watching Canadians, and for Balding too. But the ball needed only a tap, and he gave it just that, dispelling any fears

that he might get an attack of the yips and be unable to move the clubhead.

For winning the Mayfair Open, Al Balding was given the sum of $2,400. This was perhaps the most important win of his life, for the money gave him the means, and the win gave him the courage, to continue on the Tour. He earned $9,000 in 1956 and was fiftieth on the PGA's money list.

Early in 1957 he gave up his post at Credit Valley to concentrate on the American circuit. Along with this decision came his second win, in a satellite event. For edging out Chick Harbert by a stroke in the Miami Beach Open, Balding improved his bank balance by only $1,200. But he made money on thirty-one of the tournaments he played that season, finishing in sixth place in the PGA's money list, the highest ever by a Canadian. Some of the money came from wins in two other satellite events, the Havana Open and the West Palm Beach Open. Most of that year's earnings of $30,000 came from prize money.

But 1957 was very nearly an even more extraordinary year for this tall, cigar-chomping professional. In the so-called World Championship Tournament at the Tam O'Shanter club in Chicago, which had by far the highest prize money of the year, he missed an eight-foot curling putt that would have earned him a play-off for the first prize of $100,000. Too often in the future he was to be referred to as "the man who barely missed winning $100,000." In fact, Balding had many chances to win this tournament. But second prize was worth $7,500, and as he himself wrote in his account of the tournament, "After all, I'm only out of pocket $92,500. Look at the income tax I saved."

Al Balding was to make a living out of the Tour until the 1970s, when a recurrence of his shoulder injury limited his ability to play. By this time, his victories for Canada in the World Cup had assured him of his place in international golf.

Back home, in the years 1952 through 1970, Al Balding established a record in national professional golf second only to Stan Leonard's. In this period, he was to win four CPGA champi-

Al Balding, conducting a Junior Golf Clinic during National Golf Week, 1967.

onships and to take first or second place in eight out of nineteen years. Similarly, in the Millar tournament he was to win four of his six finals. His best showing in the Canadian Open was in 1969, when he tied for fifth place, seven stokes behind the winner, Tommy Aaron.

Balding came to the 1956 CPGA championship as the defending champion. Torrential rains washed out the first round at Toronto's Downsview course, so the title had to be settled over 36 holes. Balding's 69 69–136 was good enough for a win by two strokes over his partner on the PGA Tour, Leonard.

By 1963, when he won his third CPGA title, Al Balding had been through lean and despondent years. In 1960, he had lost a play-off for the Rivermead Trophy. That was bad enough, since he had never won this national token.

But in 1960, a win would have brought him automatic selection for the Canada Cup and a place in the Masters. Three strokes ahead with only a few holes to go, he blew his chances with a horrendous hooking 7. Some felt that this loss knocked a lot of the stuffing out of Balding. There had been tears in his eyes when he asked, "Why does this always have to happen to me?"

Whatever had been knocked out of Al Balding, it was not his ability to win. In the 1963 CPGA Championship, he played as a man possessed. The fight became a two-man duel between Balding and Leonard. Having missed an 18-inch putt on the last hole of the second round, Balding was two strokes behind with a round to go. All steamed up, he spoke of what he needed to win – a round of 66. Playing as

Balding (right) *was also the individual low scorer when he and Knudson won the World Cup in 1969.*

determinedly as he'd ever played, he did one better. His brilliant 65 defeated Leonard by two strokes. Balding's 202 was then a record for the championship.

We saw a lot of Al Balding in later years, in spite of several shoulder operations between 1966 and 1977. From the mid-1970s, the Al Balding Golf Week raised money for Easter Seals. He has played on the U.S. Seniors' Tour off and on over the years, never with much success. Back to a trim and fit 180 pounds since 1990, still chomping on a cigar, he may yet surprise us.

Having turned professional in 1957, Moe Norman never settled down but led the life of an itinerant player for prize money. Over the years, our clown prince of golf became attached to a number of golfing centres: a driving range at Don Mills, the De Haviland Golf Centre, the Pleasure Park – all in Toronto – and the Golf Haven of Gilford, Ontario. He would spend his winters in Florida, picking up prize money where he could, and his summers in Canada, playing in provincial Opens or on the CPGA tour – in any tournament that offered him the chance to make some cash. For fees of a few hundred dollars, he would put on exhibitions of his ball control, firing hooks, slices, high shots, and low shots, driving balls from the top of outsize tees or pop bottles.

For twenty years or so, he was a force to be reckoned with in Canadian professional golf. He won the CPGA championship twice, in 1966 and 1974, and the Millar match-play tournament in 1964. In 1971, when the Peter Jackson Tour was inaugurated, he led the money winners with $7,000.

More recently, Moe Norman has had a virtual stranglehold on the title of CPGA Senior champion, including a winning streak of seven years in a row between 1979 and 1985. In all this time, he has never stopped being an enigma and a source of controversy. In the same way, he has never ceased to astonish us with his striking powers or to be liked by many and worried about by those who care for his well-being.

His entry into professional golf was anything but smooth. The CPGA withheld mem-

Moe Norman as a young professional, playing off a high tee.

bership – he had incurred the wrath of his fellow professionals by selling golf equipment at cut-rate prices to members of clubs that had CPGA professionals.

In August 1957, he came third in the B & A Bursary. This paid his expenses for the PGA winter tour of 1957–58.

Back in 1956, Moe Norman had been asked why he never played well in the Canadian Open, against professionals. His answer: "I don't have anything to play for in these tournaments. If I turn pro, and the bucks were on the line, it would be a different thing."

But in PGA Tour events, it was not a different thing. He seldom played well. The slow play, he said, put him off; galleries made him nervous. Too, his reputation in the U.S. had preceded him. Invited to play in the 1956 Masters, he had walked off after nine holes of the second round, his thumbs swollen from too much practice. This had not endeared him to players or to officials, who did not know his reasons.

In two PGA events in 1958, he did not help his cause by fooling around on the course, using a pop bottle as a tee. When asked later about the PGA Tour, Norman said: "That's work! And after you get all through, all you have is the inside of a donut. The inside of a donut, that's what I got during my time down there. The inside of a donut." (Moe is in the habit of repeating phrases, as if savouring them.)

The Tour events merely served to lower his self-confidence and perhaps made him afraid of winning, since winning meant speeches and having to face the press. But U.S. professionals who have played with him have been unanimous and unstinted in their praise of his skill as a shotmaker.

Calgary was always good for what modest ego he had. He had won his first Amateur at Calgary G & CC. Calgary's Willow Park GC proved that self-confidence was all he needed to win. Here it was that he won his two CPGA championships, in 1966 and 1974. Moe Norman was *confident* he could play well in Calgary and at Willow Park, and that made all the difference.

At Willow Park in 1974, Norman was heralded as "The Fastest Shot in the West." Chattering away to the spectators, or to himself, he was likened by Mike Bartlett to "the magpies which occasionally descended on the course." He awed those who witnessed his control of the ball. "Nothing to it, nothing to it," he would shout as he curved the ball around a tree, or blasted it stiff from a bunker.

By and large, CPGA professionals held Moe Norman in high regard as a shotmaker and as a person of integrity. Bob Panasiuk praised him as one of the better playing partners. "You can always play well with Moe. He gives you straight answers, and he'll never let you take the wrong club." Never known for his diplomacy, Moe Norman also had a mean side that would often be rude to innocents.

Later in life he came to weigh 200 pounds and to look lumpy and blowzy. He tried working with teaching professional Irv Schloss. "He's given me sixteen pages to study, and I've memorized seven of them," said Norman. "He's the greatest on the mental side of the game. It's all in the mind. It's so simple, really." Simple, but for him unattainable.

As a shotmaker, Moe Norman was, and still is, the finest we have ever produced, say many who should know. He is also a shrewd observer of the strengths and weaknesses of others. His flaws are those of the mind. The aspirations of the man were never clear, even to himself. Did the court jester ever really want to be king? But if Trollope is correct, and ambition is the last infirmity of the noble mind, then Moe Norman is well off without it. In Canadian golf he is a legend; to some, a hero. Not all our heroes need be made of the stuff of greatness.

Bob Panasiuk came to us as a very junior golfer in the mid-1950s and stayed a long time on the national scene. He never rose to the heights of a Weslock or a Cowan in his brief career as an amateur, or to the stature of a Leonard or a Balding as a professional. Many felt that he was too busy enjoying his golf to succeed as they did, too fun-loving; playing golf was more important to him than winning, especially if winning meant long hours of practice.

He came out of the Essex–Kent nursery, the birthplace of champions. When he was fifteen, he had a taste of international golf as a member of the Ontario Junior team which gave battle with the boys of Washington for the Robert Simpson Cup. He played in the first junior interprovincial team match in 1958, as the Canadian Junior champion. What endeared him to the purists was the beauty of his swing. "Of all the previous Buckingham Trophy winners, has there ever been one who swung the club better than 16-year-old Bob Panasiuk of Windsor?" asked Hilles Pickens.

When still at high school, Panasiuk stood six feet and was defeating the likes of Weslock and Cowan in the Ontario Amateur. When he won this title in 1959, at eighteen, he was the youngest ever. He was then undecided about turning professional. He made the move two years later. Our hopes were high. He was saluted as one of the country's great players of the future.

But somewhere along the way, the lanky "Panny" just missed following in the footsteps of Leonard and Balding. In 1973, Ken McKee was already calling him "one of these overnight

Bob Panasiuk, CPGA champion in 1972 and 1973.

sensations who has been laboring for years to achieve 'instant' success." He showed flashes of the golfing genius expected of him in winning back-to-back CPGA championships, in 1972 and 1973, and a handful of provincial titles. The French Canadian press named him "Le Cogneur" or "The Hammer" after seeing him attack the ball while he was winning the CPGA title over the course of Rivermead Golf Club. He also won two bursaries for the PGA Tour, where he had little to show for his appearances. But then, he was never fooled into thinking that happiness could only be achieved south of the border.

Panny gave the impression that he was quite content with what he had. On the few occasions he felt inclined to prove himself, he did. His first CPGA title might have been a fluke; to show it was not, he determined to hold it for a second year, and did. Many felt that given a continuous incentive to prove himself, he would have fulfilled the promise of his youth.

36

SIR GEORGE

FROM SAN DIEGO, ACROSS THE DESERT and the Santa Cruz, the Knudson gang rode to the shoot-out at Phoenix, new irons at George's side. He had no premonition that he was about to make two kills in a row.

The February weather cheered him. Afternoons, the sun never got high enough to scale the rim of his smoked glasses. Since early January, when he, Shirley, and the two boys had motored west, they'd only had two poor days. But the kids were getting restless. He'd promised to have them home by early March. He could afford to take a few weeks off. In the five opening tournaments of the 1968 PGA Tour, he had earned $10,000, about half of this in "official" earnings. (Had it not been for his chronically poor putting, it would have been much more.)

In 1968 George Knudson was experimenting with aluminum-shafted clubs, convinced, like many others at the time, that they were helping his game. By mid-February, when he arrived in Phoenix, he had reshafted his driver and short irons in aluminum and meant to do the others in March. He had found the driver much easier to swing. The aluminum shaft was giving him better control.

The Phoenix Country Club course was tougher than most on the PGA Tour. After six days of rain, the fairways were playing long. But George Knudson was at his best on tough courses, since they demanded good iron play and had less premium on putting.

The field at the Phoenix Open was average for a Tour event. Jack Nicklaus was there, but Arnold Palmer was taking a week off before defending his title at Tucson.

In the opening round, Frank Boynton shot a 66 to lead George Knudson and three others by a stroke. Knudson's 31–36 included seven birdies.

On the Friday, Knudson and his putter played every hole together. He had been experimenting with a more upright putting stance, his shoulders more square to the ball, the ball nearer the left foot. He had needed only 27 putts in the first round, and now took the same in the second. He felt as comfortable there with a putter in his hand as he was ever to feel. On holes one, two, and three, he fired three straight birdies. On the 147-yard third, his tee-shot hit the cup, and he was left with only a two-footer for his deuce. He almost

507

Sir George in 1985, at the time of his election to the Canadian Golf Hall of Fame.

made eight birdies in a row – seven in the inward nine – but had to settle for six. At the end of the day, George Knudson had shot a 64, to lead the field by two strokes. His 131, or 13 under par, was the lowest 36-hole total he was ever to shoot in competitive golf.

On the third day, his putter betrayed him. But a 70 preserved his lead, and his 54-hole score of 204 was the lowest on the Tour that year.

On the final day, George Knudson was made to fight. He might as well have putted with an ice cube. His two bogeys in the first six holes lost him the lead to Tom Shaw. Then Shaw fell apart, and the chase was taken up by Sam Carmichael. When Knudson's tee-shot on the par-three fifteenth hole went into the lake, and Carmichael got his birdie, it looked as though the lead might change again. But Knudson salvaged a bogey by sinking a four-foot putt, and the two were tied. ("The most important shot of the tournament," he said of

it later.) As it happened, Carmichael also collapsed with a brace of bogeys. When a tense but confident Knudson birdied the last hole to finish at 272, or 12 under par, he was 3 ahead of the field. He picked up a $20,000 cheque out of a purse of $100,000.

In his last two rounds, Knudson had needed 34 and 31 putts, a total of eleven more than in his opening rounds. This tells the story of the tournament, and the story of George's life.

The next stop on the PGA Tour was the Tucson Open. After winning, a golfer will often be on such an emotional high as to be mentally frayed by the end of the same week. Knudson considered Tucson with mixed emotions. For the first two days at Phoenix, confidence had flowed down the shaft of his putter. By the third day, its chronic ills had returned. But the rest of his clubs were doing exactly as he bade them, and it seemed a pity to pass up the chance of another cheque. So the Knudson gang headed southeast.

After three rounds of the Tucson Open, George Knudson was 4 behind the leaders. Four behind, but remarkably exuberant. For a time during Saturday's third round, he had felt like cracking. There were moments when he had wanted to walk off the course, the tension was so great. Yet he managed to hold on. When he survived Saturday, he knew he could win, and told his caddie so. If he could be so tired and so tense, and still be in the running, he felt he could win for a second straight week.

In the final round, George Knudson's destruction of this 7,200-yard, par 72 course, started on the eleventh hole with a tap-in birdie 3. A 10-foot putt went in on twelve; a curling, 35-footer on thirteen; a short one on fifteen; an even shorter one, less than a foot, on seventeen. Seven birdies, no bogeys, and a round of 65. "Under the circumstances, coming from behind, the greatest round of my career, in ten years on the Tour," he later described it.

Knudson had finished forty-five minutes ahead of Frank Beard, who was tied coming to the last two holes. When word reached Knudson, sitting in the clubhouse, that Beard had bogeyed the seventeenth, he compared his position to blackjack, one of his favourite card games. "This is like sitting on 17 and not knowing whether to draw."

Beard needed a birdie at eighteen to tie. He failed to get it. George Knudson had won $20,000 for the second successive week. With official earnings of $43,600, he shot to the top of the PGA money list.

The news of George Knudson's duplex win on the PGA Tour came as the climax of a memorable month for Canada. Nancy Greene had been winning gold medals at the Grenoble Winter Olympics. But George now stole the headlines. After his win at Phoenix, his photograph had appeared on the front page of some of the nation's newspapers. On the Monday following Tucson, the half-inch headline was as near the top of the sports page as newspaper titles would permit. He had also etched his name on the tablets of golf history. The nearest any non-U.S. citizen had come to Knudson's feat of back-to-back wins on the Tour had been in 1961, when Gary Player won two out of three.

George Knudson went on to accumulate $71,000 in official prize money in 1968, and to finish in seventeenth place on the PGA money list.

A cocky lad from Winnipeg, George Knudson made himself into Canada's finest male golfer of the 1960s and 1970s. Some would argue he was the best we have ever produced. Certainly, no Canadian has ever come close to matching his success in the toughest test of all, the PGA Tour: eight wins in twelve years, the first in 1961, the last in 1972. He came very close to winning one of the four majors in 1969, when he tied for second place in the Masters, one stroke behind the winner.

The PGA Tour kept Knudson pretty busy during his best years as a professional. But he still found the time to win five CPGA championships between 1964 and 1977, in itself a record rare enough to earn him his place in the Canadian Golf Hall of Fame.

This grinning, spare-looking lad let his crew-cut grow and find its natural wave. Then he filled out his scrawny frame with muscle, to become a handsome figure on the fairways, easily identified by his dark glasses and his graceful, cat-like walk. It was more the stride of a sprinter, or of a ballet dancer, than of a golfer. Invariably, his lips would be open, a cigarette between his teeth. Or he would walk with his right arm at his side, a cigarette cupped in his hand. Two, three packs a day. "It's just a lousy habit, and I wish I didn't have it." George battled the cigarette as he battled the putter. In the end, both defeated him.

George Knudson's eyes had always been so sensitive to sunlight that he golfed behind glare-cutting glasses. "Without them I squint. With them, I can keep my eyes open. I'm more aware of what's going on." He also needed sunscreens, or blockers, for his skin. "I've always had trouble with it . . . I got red blotches on my face and hands from the sun. The skin of my face used to peel off once a week. I

George Knudson receiving the Buckingham Trophy from G. E. Miquelon as winner of the Canadian Junior Championship, 1955.

dreaded the thought of having to shave, because my skin was so tender after a game of golf." But the sun-blocking creams were not wholly effective, for in 1976 he developed skin cancer.

George Knudson's cockiness as a youth was bred of confidence, not of ego. As he matured, he retained a confidence in himself to a degree rarely found in a Canadian golfer. He also came to know his limitations and sought to subvert them. First, his physical structure and strength. Second, his chronic failure with his putter. In 1966, when he was twenty-nine, he stood five feet ten inches, but weighed only 140 pounds. He was not physically strong enough to play full out for 72 holes. Physical exhaustion quickly led to mental exhaustion. What is more, his lack of strength cost him distance off the tee. This he overcame to some extent by the quality of his swing, the purity with which he struck the ball. But he knew he was being outdriven by inferior swingers who had more muscle. In 1966, he took his problems to Lloyd Percival of Toronto's Fitness Institute.

Percival's slogan was "Nobody ever drowned in sweat." He made Knudson sweat his way to a 25 per cent increase in strength, using weight-lifting and running exercises, each one designed to strengthen a muscle he needed in golf. "How many golfers do you know who could lift 525 pounds?" Knudson asked, a year or so later. Percival also worked on Knudson's putting, making him swing forty-pound weights with a putting stroke. He taught him how to relax tension on the course. This included a simple exercise called the monkey slump. (During the second of his back-to-back wins in Arizona, Knudson felt the tension within his body in the third round, and went into his monkey slump, by leaning over, resting his arms on his thighs, and letting his body hang loose.)

When George Knudson appeared on the PGA Tour in 1968, players noticed his improved physique, his greater thrust with the right side, and the extra distance he was able to squeeze out of a club. Arnold Palmer looked at the iron

Knudson had used to make a shot and observed: "Either you're getting stronger, or I'm getting older."

In the first five tournaments of 1968, his improved conditioning helped him score better. And when the Phoenix and Tucson Opens fell to him, Knudson became one of Percival's most ardent disciples.

Given his two wins on the PGA Tour, George Knudson came to the 1968 Canadian Open as Canada's favourite. The spectators were to witness him at his worst – and also at his superlative best. The old George Knudson would have been emotionally destroyed by an opening round of 75, five over par. It was a measure of his new-found strength that he was able to shrug it off and follow with 69, 64. He philosophically summed up his feelings: "I didn't win the golf tournament, but I feel that I probably lived as much in that one week as I've lived in my entire lifetime. The experiences, the frustrations, the pleasures – it was all these things . . . Maybe I tried too hard. But being able to live it and accept it – that was the most important thing."

The year 1968 was to end as it had started, on a note of triumph. George Knudson had previously won the individual honours in the Canada Cup in 1966. In 1968, Knudson and Balding went to the same tournament (since renamed the World Cup) in Rome, and won. Knudson was 7 over par, the victim again of a balky putter. But his 295, coupled with Balding's 274, gave Canada the cup by two strokes. The individual title went to Balding.

George Knudson was born in Winnipeg in June 1937. His mother recalled that he was very thin as a boy and a light eater. At school he played baseball and rugby, but his first love was skiing. And skiing was to remain his main form of relaxation, and another form of expression, once golf became his vocation. As a boy, he was a bundle of nervous energy: "At 13, I couldn't sit down and eat with the family. I had to eat by myself. I was too highly strung."

When he was about ten, he found himself a summer job as a caddie at the St. Charles Country Club. In time, he was promoted to boot-boy in the clubhouse. ("You may not know this, but I have cleaned your shoes," I heard him tell Marlene Stewart Streit, to her amusement. The shoe-cleaning would have been during the CLGA championships at St. Charles, in 1950, when George was thirteen.)

Golf quickly captured him. As a caddie, he was allowed to play Friday mornings on the St. Charles course. But he was free to hit balls every day, and he did. Golf for him became 95 per cent practice, 5 per cent play. In 1954, he won the Manitoba Junior championship with a 36-hole total of 142, seven strokes lower than the 1953 winner over the same course.

Knudson was then a scraggy youth, a month or so past his seventeenth birthday. He had already decided that he wanted to be a professional golfer. He had also settled on his hero. At thirteen, he had discovered Ben Hogan's *Power Golf*, and was often to ascribe much of his success to that book, especially to its photographs. He modelled himself on Hogan.

His penchant for practice and more practice – another Hogan trait – paid off in the Canadian Junior of 1955. By now playing under a visored cap and behind smoked-glass spectacles, he set a new Canadian Junior Championship record over the Calgary G & CC, shooting 71 69–140.

In 1956 and 1957, Knudson played for Manitoba in the Willingdon Cup matches. The second year saw him runner-up to Gary Cowan in the individual scoring. In the qualifying rounds of the Amateur, he was the leading Canadian. But his temperament was not suited to match play, and he never got far in the Amateur. By 1958, he was ready to turn professional. He knew that if he stayed in Manitoba, he would be far from the action in the world of professional golf. So he went east, to become an assistant to Bill Hamilton, at that time the professional to Toronto's Oakdale club.

From the beginning of his career in the money ranks, George Knudson's aim was to make his name and fortune by playing on the PGA Tour. Bill Hamilton and the members of Oakdale were aware of that and afforded him all the time he needed for practice. And practise he did. Artist Peter Swan once depicted him holding a club with bleeding hands, and George acknowledged that, yes, he sometimes practised until his hands bled. He just enjoyed hitting a golf ball.

This investment soon paid dividends. In 1958, he won his first championship as a professional, the Manitoba Open. He also won the MacNaughton–Brooks Bursary. This entitled him to a third of the $4,500 prize money, designed to cover his expenses on the PGA winter tour. He made the grand sum of $100 in his first year on the Tour, in the early months of 1959.

In the following two years, money from the bursary and from wins in provincial tournaments helped to finance further trips south. In 1960, he made $240 on the Tour. The following year was only a little better. Then, quite unexpectedly, he won his first PGA event.

George Knudson's first win on the PGA Tour, in December 1961, came as something of a surprise. He had opened well at the Coral Gables Open, Florida, and after two rounds was tied for the lead. Sixteen players, among them Gay Brewer, were within two strokes.

Brewer, two strokes behind going into the last round, started playing "like a man whose pockets were empty and the rent due." Knudson was so concentrating on his game that he did not know he was in a position to win until he left the fifteenth (or 69th) green. Al Balding walked over to tell him that Brewer had finished with a 65. George could win with a 66. For that, he needed one more birdie. It came on the seventeenth.

From the total purse of $20,000, George Knudson collected $2,800. He also got a kiss from his redheaded wife, Shirley, who was to prove such a strength in his life.

Knudson had played well all that week. But it had been some inspired putting that gave him his win. What encouraged Knudson and his supporters at Coral Gables was his ability not only to sink these vital putts, but to keep his cool concentration when faced with Brewer's challenge.

Over the next eleven years, George Knudson was to win another seven PGA tournaments, plus four on a PGA satellite tour in the Caribbean. This record of his money winnings is taken from the PGA's *The Tour Book* (the Caribbean wins are shown in italics):

the children for long stretches. But there was a limit to the number of weeks his family could be dragged from one event to the next. During the 1968–69 winter he tried touring as a bachelor, but it didn't work.

Typically, after winning the Greater New Orleans Open in 1967, Knudson left the Tour for five weeks. He spent June visiting the Montreal Expo with his family, practising and playing weekend golf. As a result, his game was not

	Tour Wins	Prize Money	Place in Money List
1959		$100	T-212
1960		$240	T-193
1961	Coral Gables Open	$5,682	70
1962	*Maracaibo* and *Puerto Rico Opens*	$14,664	45
1963	Portland and *Panama* Opens	$18,531	44
1964	Fresno and *Caracas* Opens	$18,782	41
1965		$39,793	22
1966		$23,522	41
1967	Greater New Orleans Open	$40,832	29
1968	Phoenix and Tucson Opens	$71,360	17
1969		$43,964	43
1970	Robinson Open	$46,571	50
1971		$41,634	60
1972	Kaiser International Open	$74,366	30
1973		$28,160	93
1974		$10,166	142

He continued to make money on the PGA Tour over the next several years, to bring his total official earnings up to $532,000.

George Knudson did not play regularly on the PGA Tour until 1962. However, to him "regularly" meant from twenty-five to thirty tournaments a year, out of some forty-five. He often admitted that he would have liked to play in only fifteen or twenty events of his own choosing, assuming, of course, that he could make enough in official prize money to finish in the top sixty, and so be exempt from having to qualify for the following year's Tour.

There were a number of reasons for his skipping so many tournaments. The more successive weeks he played, the more the tension got to him. He was in essence a family man, and could not stand being away from Shirley and

sharp in that year's Canadian Open at the Montreal Municipal. He never challenged, finishing well down the field.

At New Orleans, he had played some of the finest golf of his life in taking his fourth PGA event. He won by a stroke from Jack Nicklaus. Ironically, it was Nicklaus who was suffering from a streak of wretched putting. Years later, Knudson was to recall that at New Orleans he had played "the best ever series of consecutive shots, a dozen in a row, I've ever hit. I was pinpointing everything in that stretch." At one hole he sliced a 2-iron around a tree, and got down in two more for his birdie. ("I didn't know I had the shot in my bag.")

It was his ability as a shotmaker, and not as a low scorer, that he savoured most. He once went round in 72 in the U.S. Open and was absolutely elated with the way he had played. Next day, he was much less enthused over a 69.

In his very last win on the PGA Tour, in 1972, he had one of his finest tournaments. His 66 69 66 70–271 included 26 birdies. It also included two double bogeys on the last nine. But by then he was so far ahead of the field it didn't matter. That week, at the Kaiser International, he felt close to omnipotence. He saw no reason why his rounds in the 60s could not have been reduced to the 50s.

George Knudson was a perfectionist consumed by inner fires when he did not play as well as he was capable of playing. Some players get rid of their feelings by throwing clubs in public. A dignified man, George did most of his suffering in the privacy of his home.

George Knudson never read Willie Park's *The Art of Putting* (1920). But in the 1960s he came to realize what Willie meant eighty years earlier when he wrote: "No player who putts indifferently can ever hope to excel."

Willie Park also understood the importance of confidence: "The art of putting lies to a great extent in the player having confidence in himself. If he goes up to his ball in the full belief that he can and will hole his putt, he has a better chance of doing so than if he is troubled with doubts about this and that rough place his ball has to cross, and if his vision is obscured by the dread of a missed putt."

Jack Nicklaus once said of George Knudson that he was "a million-dollar player with a ten-cent putter." And George agreed, admitting that he was short in both practice and in confidence. "I can putt as well as the next guy, but I've given 95 per cent of my game to striking the ball . . . You have to feel good about your stroke to sink them. I'm working on this."

The story of his life is that of one of the world's finest strikers of a golf ball being humbled by his putter on the greens. In a poll to name an all-star team in 1966, Knudson's colleagues on the Tour picked him as the most perfect man with fairway woods. Statistics compiled by IBM that year show that, tee to green, George Knudson was second to Jack Nicklaus in accuracy, and was the second top man in driving accuracy, hitting the fairway 79.8 per cent of the time. But he averaged 31.6 putts a round, which placed him in a lowly 120th place. If this measures just how wretched was his putting, it also measures just how brilliant was the rest of his game, since he consistently made the top sixty qualifiers on the PGA Tour.

Every major championship has its legends of "ifs." If George Knudson had not been paired with Gary Middlecoff in the second round of the 1969 Masters . . . if he had not putted so desperately poorly on the first and second day. As it was, he finished in a tie for second place, a stroke behind George Archer.

Knudson had been invited to the Masters in 1966, had shared the lead after 65 holes and then choked. One of the delights of winning his back-to-back events in 1968 was the prospect of being given another chance at the Masters in 1969. He came to Augusta superbly fit and with high hopes. But after two rounds his chances looked slim. Playing magnificently from tee to green, his 70 73 included no putts of any length and left him six strokes behind the leader.

The 73 had required immense concentration. He had been paired with the slowest player on the Tour, Dr. Gary Middlecoff. Ken McKee of the *Toronto Daily Star* noted that Middlecoff took eight minutes to 4-putt the fifth green. And on the eleventh tee, Knudson opened a soft drink, drank it, lit a cigarette, and Middlecoff still had not hit his drive. Stan Leonard had the same problem in 1958. Leading the Masters with a round to go, he had been paired with the slow Dr. Middlecoff and had blown his chances with a 75. This was not a way of snuffing the Canadian challenge. Tradition required visiting foreigners to be paired with former Masters winners, and Knudson and Leonard happened to draw the wrong man.

When his round with Middlecoff was over, Knudson went to the practice green. He found he had been gripping his putter too tightly. In Saturday's third round, his putting was greatly improved. But although he shot a three under par 69, he was far from happy with his play from tee to green. Still, he had pulled to within four shots of the leader.

In the final round, George Knudson was still three behind with four holes to go. At the fifteenth he stroked in a 10-foot putt for a birdie; a 30-footer went in for another birdie at the sixteenth. One stroke back coming to the last hole, he knew he had a chance. His putt for a third birdie came within two inches. His 70 was the lowest score of the five leaders, and was good enough to tie for second place.

The mechanics of the golf swing always had a fascination for George Knudson. Keeping a golf ball under control, striking it and making it go exactly where he wanted it to go, gave him more satisfaction than scoring well in tournaments. But how was this to be achieved, consistently?

As we have seen, his own swing was modelled on Ben Hogan's, or so George believed, having studied the illustrations in Hogan's book. As a young professional on the Tour, he would drop everything to watch Hogan practise. He once played eleven rounds with Hogan in three weeks, at the Carling World and PGA championships, and spent a lot of time studying how Hogan set himself up for the act of striking the ball. He once had the rare privilege (his words) of sharing a sandwich with Hogan, who seldom spoke to anyone on the Tour.

When he left the PGA Tour in the mid-1970s, George Knudson started to teach golf, latterly at Buttonworth GC golf school. His ideas on how to swing a golf club hardened into beliefs, which he found hard to articulate.

When George came to express his doctrines, he enlisted the help of golf writer Lorne Rubenstein. They jointly authored *The Natural Golf Swing* (1988). Knudson's precepts are sim-

Knudson always said "Ben Hogan's way is my way."

ple: golf involves a swing motion directed towards a target; it is a whole-body movement; we don't hit at the ball, but swing a *unit* – hands, arms, club, the whole body – *through* the ball towards the target. The ball merely gets in the way. All this, while the golfer remains *in balance*.

The book was to be George Knudson's last gift to us. In 1987, as he was preparing to launch himself on the Senior Tour, he was discovered to have lung cancer. Never daunted, he underwent radiation and chemotherapy treatment, lost his hair, and went back to the Fitness Institute to get himself in shape. But Sir George could not slay this dragon. Fighting to the end, he died in January 1989, at the age of fifty-one.

37
CHAPTER

MARLENE COMES TO TOWN

IN 1950, WOMEN'S GOLF IN CANADA HAD little to cheer about. Since the revival of our Ladies' Open championship after the war, American women had walked away with the title every year. The powerful, long-hitting Grace Lenczyk of Connecticut had won our title twice and was semi-finalist in 1950. Grace DeMoss of Oregon beat another American, Mrs. Joseph Herron, in the 1949 final and was runner-up to California's Dorothy Kielty in 1950. In that year, only one Canadian reached the semi-finals. Our Ladies' Open had become an all-American affair, as it had been for most of the 1920s.

Equally as alarming was the apparent lack of new talent. Toronto's Sydney Pepler Mulqueen had been the only Canadian to reach a post-war final, in 1947. And she was a veteran. She had held the title throughout the war years, having won in 1938. Her victories in the Ladies' Close went back to 1923. All through the war she had been much too busy for any serious golf, and she came to the 1947 championships having played only one full round of golf in six years.

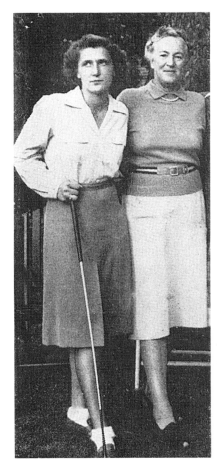

America's Grace Lenczyk, left, winner of our Ladies' Open in 1947 and 1948, with Ada Mackenzie.

515

Ada Mackenzie did everything that could be expected of her. She reached the semi-finals in 1947 and 1948, only to be defeated by Grace Lenczyk, who was half her age. We had looked to Ada to stop the British in 1913. It was asking too much to expect her to halt the Americans thirty-five years later. But she, Cecil Smith Gooderham, and Sydney Pepler Mulqueen still ruled women's golf in Ontario. They had been friends and opponents for over twenty years.

The younger women were not quite good enough. Quebec's British-born and raised Mrs. Graeme Pyke, and home-bred Daintry Chisholm; British Columbia's Mrs. Margaret Todd and Babs Davies (twice a semi-finalist); Mrs. Edey of Winnipeg: they all looked likely winners of the Open when playing against each other in the Close. But they were outclassed by Americans in the Open.

The CLGU was blamed for the failure of Canada's young girls. Why was it not sponsoring junior golf, nationally? Why was there for girls no equivalent of the Buckingham Trophy, which had done so much to breed competitiveness in the male youth of the country? Why did the CLGU's branches in the provinces arrange the qualifying rounds of the inter-provincial team matches so that only well-to-do matrons, or wives with no young children, could afford the time and money to play, and young mothers and working women were not given the chance?

The CLGU had a good defence, although it seldom tried to defend itself. In Canada, eight years of national championships had been given up for the war, as against only four in the United States. For six years, the CLGU had devoted its entire efforts to war charities. Some of those now criticizing the CLGU were forgetting that a few years earlier they had been writing such words as: "When the final reckoning of work in connection with raising War Funds is made, the name of Mrs. Edwin Crockett, of Toronto [president of the CLGU] will surely stand out in bold relief."

In 1948, two Americans met in the final of the Ladies' Open at Riverside, Saint John. "Something must be done to improve the class of golf in the women's division in this country," thundered Hilles Pickens.

As he wrote these words, a fourteen-year-old girl, standing all of four feet ten inches, was striking balls down the middle of the practice fairway at Lookout Point GC, near Fonthill, Ontario. Under the care of the club's professional, Gord McInnis, the shaping of Marlene Stewart had begun.

A few years later, Pickens was at Burlington G & CC, when a member pointed out to him a diminutive girl playing golf with a youth. Even from a distance, his practised eye saw great promise in her swing. "But here," he reminded himself years later, "here was a mere infant!"

When this mere infant of sixteen played in the Ontario Junior girls' championship of 1950, her handicap was down to 10, her height up to four feet eleven inches. Although she shot a 90 to be runner-up, her costume, not her golf,

Marlene Stewart, at sixteen, after defeating Ada Mackenzie in the Ladies' Open at St. Charles CC, Winnipeg, 1950.

captivated the press. "Girls in Fonthill don't wear latest creations from Paris. But Marlene startled officials with a flamboyant plaid cap, brilliant yellow sweater and blue skirt. She had the pep to go with it."

A month later, the girl in the gay plaid cap ran up against Ada Mackenzie in the second round of the Ladies' Open. What she wore was no longer of any consequence. All eyes were on her golf. At times it approached greatness. She beat Ada, the first favourite to go out, by 4 and 3.

The swiftness with which Marlene Stewart thereafter rose from obscurity to adulation is without equal in Canadian golf. These 1951 headlines tell the story:

MARLENE STEWART SWEEPS OPEN AND CLOSE
SEVENTEEN-YEAR-OLD ASTOUNDS GOLFDOM
HER STRAIGHT GAME AND REMARKABLE SPIRIT

The scene of her greatest triumph that year was the course at Laval-sur-le-Lac. Hilles Pickens wrote this of the girl he had first seen in Burlington, now playing in the final of the Ladies' Open:

Some 2000 stood at the 33rd tee a little stunned, fingers crossed, wondering if it were possible that Canada could have developed such a prodigy. The mighty Grace Lenczyk, of Newington, Conn., who in 1948 held the Canadian Open, the U.S.A. Open, the U.S.A. Intercollegiate and the Tam O'Shanter "World title," was facing defeat at the hands of this amazing little girl from Fonthill, Ontario. . . . Marlene, wearing a cunning little tartan cap, had played coldly determined golf to capitalize upon every opening. By lunch she was leading, 2-up.

[Marlene was three up with four to go, as they stood on the 33rd tee.]

It was from here to the end that the startling confidence and control of the young Canadian star showed in brightest relief, for Miss Lenczyk, throwing caution and worry over her swing to the winds, whipped back into the picture with a magnificent eagle three at the 33rd, and followed this with a

supreme pitch at the 34th to net her another birdie three!

Now Marlene was facing stark disaster, with her once-safe lead reduced to a single hole with two left to play. At the 218-yard 35th, Grace once more hooked badly, 30 yards to the left of the green, and Marlene, for the first time, strayed to the right. Her ball struck high in a tree, 90 yards from the green, and dropped to the ground. Her second, a 7-iron pitch, was 17 feet above the hole, leaving her a downhill, sidehill, putt. Grace Lenczyk made a phenomenal chip to a point five feet below the cup.

As Marlene, almost bursting with excitement now, addressed her treacherous putt, a Toronto Telegram photographer appeared, far inside the ropes, directly behind the hole *in her line*. . . . As the angry crowd saw the situation they howled, "Get out of there." He moved a little then settled down again, practically in her line once more. This time the entire 2,000 fans shouted the poor, zealous fellow clean outside the ropes where he belonged. But what effect had all this on Marlene's nerves? This was the crucial moment. Gauging her stroke with almost miraculous coolness, Marlene borrowed a full eight inches and holed that very impossible-looking putt. The crowd went mad with delight and amazement.

The rest was anti-climactic. The Canadian girl holed a two-foot putt for a half at the 36th, to win by 1 up.

So ended the long winter for women's golf in Canada. So began the long career of the greatest woman golfer this country has produced. Over the next twenty-five years, she was to win every major women's amateur golf championship in the world, while setting a national record never yet equalled by any Canadian.

Marlene Stewart Streit was born in March 1934 in Cereal, Alberta, on a farm – although her father, Harold Stewart, was an electrician by trade. Drought forced the Stewarts to move further south. Then, in 1940, when Harold

Stewart was turned down for the armed forces, he brought his wife and daughter to Fonthill, Ontario, where Marlene Stewart grew up.

Her friend and neighbour, Anne Sharpe, some four years her senior, started caddying at Lookout Point GC and in 1946 persuaded Marlene to do the same. Marlene was then twelve, and not much taller than some of the bags she toted. But a dollar was a dollar. "If you happened to get one of the big spenders, you might get as much as $1.50, or even $2.50," she recalled.

Monday was caddies' day, when the girls were free to play the course. Anne had already taken up the game and under Gord McInnis had quickly developed into a fine provincial player. McInnis had watched Marlene with a club in her hand and had seen the makings of another champion. She caddied and shagged balls for him, studying his swing, learning by imitation. She could relate to McInnis, for he, too, was short in stature.

When she was fourteen, Marlene bought Anne Sharpe's old clubs with her caddie money and joined Lookout Point as a junior. She spent that summer on the practice tee, or on the course, going to McInnis for advice. From him she learned the fundamentals: grip, stance, posture, alignment and balance, and – in her swing – smoothness and rhythm. She made phenomenal progress. For one thing, she was a natural athlete. (In spite of her four feet eleven inches, she was a good basketball player.) But above all, she had an overpowering ambition to succeed through hard work.

Watch Marlene Stewart Streit today, and you will see that ability to shut everything out but the task at hand. For her, practice is a special kind of joy. She sees in the club an instrument for control of the ball. As she picks it up, the door to the outside world is closed. The eyes look at the target, then at the ball. The memory selects the movements needed to get the ball to the hole, the mind's eye visualizing the ball in flight. All negative thoughts are purged. This is not the time to think consciously about the stated tenets of good golf, like keeping the head still, or not cocking the wrists too much, or not swaying into the ball. These should all come automatically, having been built into the memory on the practice tee. She concentrates on how the hole should be played, on exactly where she wants the ball to go, and on making sure she is lined up to the intended line of flight. This is not the time for fear or self-doubt. Marlene is supremely confident that this shot, practised a hundred thousand times, will be as near perfection as anyone can make it. Concentrate, concentrate, concentrate. Believe that only perfection is acceptable. She swings the clubhead smoothly, but strikes the ball with all the power that a five-feet-one-inch body can muster. The ball flies close to the arc of flight she had seen in her mind's eye, rolls close to where she had expected it to roll. The breath had been exhaled as the clubhead made contact with the ball. She nods in quiet satisfaction. On the practice tee, this will be only the beginning. The ritual will be repeated and repeated until the mind's-eye flight of the ball, and the real flight of the ball, are indistinguishable. But with perfection her goal, she knows that practice on concentration will be needed forever.

In the beginning, it was not always so easy. "When I was young, I had a hot temper," she once wrote, "a hot temper that hurt my concentration. But Gord put an end to that by threatening me with suspension unless I stopped carrying on. I learned to channel my anger by concentrating on each shot, by keeping my mind in the present, an ability I've tried to maintain over the years."

The hours of practice led quickly to success. In her first tournament she took third place in the Ontario Junior Girls' with a score of 104. In 1950, a 90 gave her second place. Then a few weeks later came that astonishing win over Ada Mackenzie in the Canadian Ladies' Open. Ada said afterwards: "It was the only time in my life I have been six holes down after playing six holes. That unbelievable child was four under fours . . . She played the first six holes in twenty strokes." She added, prophetically: "You'll be hearing from her for a long time."

She was right. Within a few years Marlene Stewart was to become the best-known and most highly respected competitor in women's international golf. Americans visiting Canada soon had a healthy regard for her skill and determination. The British were to sample it in 1953.

Canadian Ladies' Close:	1951, '52, '53, '54, '55, '56, '57, '63, '68.
Canadian Ladies' Open:	1951, '54, '55, '56, '58, '59, '63, '68, '69, '72, '73.
British Ladies':	1953
United States Ladies':	1956
Australian Ladies':	1963
Canadian Ladies' Senior:	1985, '87, '88
U.S. Women's Senior:	1985

In 1953, Marlene was one of a Canadian team sent over by the CLGU to tour Britain and to play in the British championships.

That year, the British Ladies' was played in June, over the links at Porthcawl, Wales. A Canadian had never reached the finals of this event, although Violet Pooley and Ada Mackenzie had reached the semi-finals. At Porthcawl, five Canadians got past the second round. All but Marlene Stewart were out by the third or fourth. In the quarter-finals, she put on a superb display of power golf to beat Elizabeth Price of England by 6 and 4. That afternoon, she defeated the Scottish champion, Jean Donald, by making a brilliant recovery from a bunker at the eighteenth. When her four-foot putt went down for a win, she performed a jig in relief and jubilation. (She was, remember, only nineteen at the time.)

In the final, Marlene met the experienced Philomena Garvey. One of those fancied to win, Miss Garvey had twice been Irish champion and wanted badly to add the British title. But Marlene Stewart took the lead at the seventh hole of the 36-hole final, and was not to be caught. She won the last five holes before lunch, to complete the first round in 72, for a

six-hole lead. An iron to the heart of the short fourth hole (or 22nd) put her 7 up. Thereafter, they battled stroke for stroke, until Philomena Garvey ran out of holes. Marlene Stewart had won the much-coveted British title by 7 and 6, the most decisive margin of victory in more than twenty years.

Her brilliant play throughout the championship drew unstinted praise from the British press. With a touch of awe, bordering on disbelief, they tried to sum up what they had witnessed from this small frecklefaced nineteen-year-old.

"We walked in dazed procession," wrote Desmond Hackett of the *Daily Express*, "wondering how so young a girl could know so much wonderful golf. Apart from the immortal Babe Didrickson Zaharias, I have never seen anything so coldly calculated and correct as this child. We have seen a girl who will surely become the greatest-ever woman golfer."

The more circumspect and revered golf writer Pat Ward-Thomas called her "clearly one of the world's finest players today." The even more circumspect *Times* had to admit to having witnessed "quite exceptional golf." "The smallest and certainly one of the greatest women champions in the world," quoth the *Herald*. "She played like a giant," wrote the *News Chronicle*. "Machine-like," said the *Daily Telegraph*.

They dubbed her "Little Miss Robot," or "Little Ben" (after Ben Hogan), or "Golf's Little Mo," after the American tennis prodigy, Maureen (little Mo) Connolly.

And what did Marlene Stewart have to say? "I'm thrilled. It was a great match to win." She had felt confident of reaching the semi-finals, she said, but that was about as far as she had expected to go.

Ada Mackenzie had the last word. "Marlene just does not make mistakes."

It was one thing to prove herself in Britain. It was quite another to do the same thing in the new arena for women's golf, the United States.

Since the inauguration in 1932 of the women's amateur team matches between Britain and the U.S. for the Curtis Cup, the American ladies had established a clear superiority. The British title may have been considered the pinnacle of achievement in the 1920s, but by the 1950s, to be ranked number one a woman amateur golfer had to win the U.S. Ladies'. In 1936, the British champion, Pam Barton, had gone to America and had lifted this title. Twenty years later, Canada's Marlene Stewart went to the Meridian Hills Country Club, Indianapolis, and did the same.

The year 1956 had been exceptional for Marlene, even before Meridian Hills. She held the U.S. intercollegiate title, and had won the Ontario Ladies' as well as the Canadian Ladies' Open and Close. She was also the U. S. North and South champion and winner of the Jasper Totem Pole.

The field at Meridian Hills was particularly strong, including three former U.S. champions. The girl fancied, however, was nineteen-

Marlene on her way to the U.S. Ladies' title in 1956.

year-old Wiffi Smith, fresh from securing the national titles of Britain and France.

In the first three rounds, all the former champions, and Wiffi Smith, fell like ninepins. The holder, Pat Lesser, was defeated by a home-town girl, JoAnne Gunderson, a seventeen-year-old high school senior who had held the national junior title. She went on to reach the final.

In the other half of the draw, Marlene Stewart had one squeaky close match, but in her semi-final she was just too much for her opponent. Marlene was unbelievably steady about the greens; the other wasn't.

The final between Stewart and Gunderson was a match between extremes. Even at seventeen, the blonde girl they now call "Big Momma" (JoAnne Gunderson Carner) stood five feet seven inches and weighed 150 pounds. Marlene was giving her seven inches, forty pounds, and a lead of some fifty yards off the tee; for JoAnne's swaying, whiplash swing could boom the ball all of 280. But championships are seldom won off the tee. Marlene Stewart had learned to counter length with accuracy. Few could match her short game. No one could match her dogged persistence, her tremendous competitive fire.

After trailing by a single hole at lunch, Marlene's short game for once let her down. She lost three in a row. When JoAnne chipped in from 50 feet on the twenty-fourth, "she made me mad," Marlene admitted later. Counterattacking, she won the twenty-sixth by chipping to within four inches of the pin, the twenty-seventh with a 45-foot putt that hit the stick and stopped (quite legal in 1956). The loss of two quick holes is bad for the nervous system. The American girl lost another in the rough at the twenty-ninth, a fourth when she three-putted the thirtieth.

You can not make errors like that against a veteran of twenty-two whose nicknames included "The Comeback Kid." Marlene Stewart played steady, irreproachable golf and let her opponent make the mistakes. A straying wood and a scuffed chip at the thirty-second, and Marlene was ahead. The next two holes were halved. Then came the thirty-fifth. Marlene

was 11 1/2 feet from the hole, JoAnne, 10 1/2 feet. (The referee had to measure.) Marlene stepped up, studied the line, and rolled the ball into the hole. JoAnne tried to follow her, but left it short. The Comeback Kid had done it again. By winning six of the last ten holes, she had added the U.S. title to her list of championships.

This was the zenith of a remarkable career. Marlene Stewart had reached the goal she had set herself in 1949, which was to become the best amateur woman golfer in the world. What more proof was needed, now that she had won four Canadian Open and six Canadian Close championships, plus the British and the United States titles, all in the space of six years?

In 1956, at a loss for superlatives that had not already been used, we resorted to quoting statistics. For the second time – the first being in 1951 – she was awarded the Lou Marsh Trophy as Canada's outstanding athlete. Her name had been posted as the winner thirty-four consecutive times; she had gone through the entire season, including eight major tournaments, without a single loss; no one had ever won the U.S. intercollegiate and the U.S. national title in the one year; Alexa Stirling Fraser was the only other golfer to win the Canadian and the U.S. titles in the same year. (We obviously overlooked Dorothy Campbell, who did it in 1910.) It was as if we were praising a child prodigy whose talents were about to disappear.

The subject of all this said, after her win at Meridian Hills: "I don't care if I never win anything again. This is the one I wanted to win most of all. It's the biggest thrill of my life, and I was glad to do it for Canada." And the future? "I'm going to start work in a couple of weeks or so in Toronto. I don't want to play golf all my life – I want to get married."

Ten years later, when Marlene Stewart Streit and JoAnne Gunderson Carner met for the second time in the final of the U.S. championship, both were married, and Marlene had two girls. In these ten years JoAnne had won the U.S. national title three times. Marlene was in a slump; she had not won a Canadian championship in three years.

For a time, history seemed about to repeat itself. Twice, Marlene was three holes down in their final, and twice she recovered to square the match. The short game was clearly hers in 1966, as it had been in 1956. But her opponent was still outdriving her by up to fifty yards. Despite the stakes, the two conceded each other putts all day, some as long as two feet. Still tied at the thirty-sixth, they sent the championship into sudden death for the first time in its history.

Marlene made clutch putts on the first four holes. At the 41st, her luck ran out. For only the second time that day, she hit a poor drive off the tee. It finished in the left rough, among trees. She caught a branch on the way out, and her ball skittered into a bunker. She blasted out, leaving herself with an eighteen-footer for any chance of a half. She missed, and that was

it. Both players were near exhaustion. Their marathon match is the longest ever in the championship.

Reaching these three national finals – the British in 1953, the U.S. in 1956 and 1966 – were Marlene Stewart Streit's finest accomplishments. But we have marched ahead of ourselves. In terms of her career in national golf, we are at about the ninth green, having skipped a number of holes. We will now go back to the second tee.

Marlene Stewart won her first Canadian title in 1951, her most recent in 1973, not counting the Seniors. About half-way through, she took three years off to start a family. So her career conveniently divides itself into the two phases – before 1960, and after 1962. Conveniently, because while she was away for these three sea-

After winning the British championship in 1953.

A

DINNER

to

Honour

MISS MARLENE STEWART

First Canadian ever to win

THE UNITED STATES
WOMEN'S AMATEUR GOLF CHAMPIONSHIP

ROYAL YORK HOTEL, TORONTO
OCTOBER 19TH 1956

After winning the U. S. championship in 1956.

sons, one set of challengers was yielding to a new set. Mary Gay, Betty Stanhope, Rae Milligan, Mrs. Graeme Pyke, and Roma Neundorf were among those who tried to stop her during the first phase. Judy Darling, Gail Harvey, Gayle Hitchens, Mary Ellen Driscoll, Jocelyne Bourassa, Sandra Post, Marilyn Palmer, Barbara Turnbull, and Helene Gagnon were slightly more successful later.

Her assets of deadly accuracy and indomitable fighting spirit gave Marlene Stewart Streit an authority over her competitors which she never relinquished. Like all great champions, she carried with her an aura of invincibility. Canada had many fine women golfers unfortunate enough to be contemporaries of Marlene Stewart Streit, yet fortunate enough to be her friend. Tall, capable Mary Gay of Kitchener, later of Calgary, would have made a deserving national champion. But in many bids for a national title she took second place to Marlene no less than six times. Their meeting in the La-

Marlene and Rae Milligan at the Daks tournament in Britain, 1959.

dies' Open of 1954 set the pattern. A solid hitter of the ball, Mary Gay yet found herself 8 down after eighteen holes, and lost by 9 and 8. "She succumbed early to the complex that seems now to paralyze Canadian ladies when playing against Marlene," Hilles Pickens concluded.

Mary Gay did knock Marlene out in the quarter finals of the 1957 Ladies' Open, but her game unravelled in the final against Betty Stanhope.

Marlene Stewart Streit thrives on match play. If ever a golfer was made for head-to-head combat, it was she. (In her early years, she would shake hands with her opponent and explain that she preferred to play in silence, to keep her thoughts focused on the job at hand.) With her opponent at her side, she knows exactly what she has to do to win. Her fighting recoveries are legend. Take the second round of the 1953 Ladies' Open, where she was three down with three to go against Pat O'Sullivan of Connecticut. Marlene won the last three holes, then rolled in an eighteen-foot putt at the nineteenth to win. In the semi-finals, three down with four to go, she took the last four holes in a row from Pat Lesser, in a finish nothing short of sensational.

Her preference for match play did not prevent her from running up some huge winning margins in the Close, a 54-hole stroke-play event since its revival after the Second World War. In her seven straight wins between 1951 and 1957 (the Close was suspended for 1958 and 1959) she won by margins of 2, 15, 10, 9, 15, 5, and 8.

In the years 1954 through 1956, Marlene Stewart attended Rollins College, Florida, where she could golf all the year round. Having graduated, won the intercollegiate and the U.S. titles, and been honoured at a dinner in Toronto attended by His Worship Mayor Nathan Phillips and four hundred other golfers and dignitaries (French Canadian soup, English roast beef, Canadian browned potatoes, Swiss Roll, American coffee), Marlene went to work for J. Bradley Streit, a Toronto businessman who had helped finance her education. Early in

1957, she married his nephew J. Douglas Streit, a geologist and engineer, and a partner in his uncle's investment and mining firm.

Playing her best golf since winning the British title, Marlene Stewart Streit captured her fifth Open title at Saskatoon in 1958. In the final, Mary Gay held her to a one-hole lead in the morning round. The fireworks came after lunch. Marlene's 9-iron, wedge, and putter helped her birdie five of the first nine holes. Mary Gay was only two over par for the holes played, when she lost by 8 and 6.

The following year brought a major disappointment. The CLGU sent a team of six to compete in the first Commonwealth Tournament and in the British championships. Marlene won the first tournament played in Britain, the Daks Ladies' International. This was a handicap event. Giving Australian champion Margaret Master four strokes, Marlene defeated her 2 up. And in the final, she gave Canada's Rae Milligan five strokes, yet won by 2 and 1. In six matches, she had to concede her opponents 62 strokes. This left her, by her own admission, "dog tired

Betty Stanhope of Edmonton, after winning the Ladies' Open in 1957.

. . . Golf is the last thing I want to think about for a few days."

The Canadian team went straight to Ascot, Berkshire, for the British championship. Still drained by her efforts, Marlene Stewart Streit was disposed of by 4 and 3 in the very first round.

Some in Canada were critical: she should not have exhausted herself in a handicap event. But what was she to do? Not compete? Ease up, and let herself be beaten? Those who complained did not understand the nature of the woman. She competed to WIN. The competitive spirit could not be turned off and on like a light. She did what she had to do, in the true spirit of amateur golf.

In the Commonwealth matches that followed the British championship, Marlene went through her singles undefeated and was acknowledged to be the outstanding player of the series. She defeated the newly crowned British champion, Elizabeth Price, 3 and 1.

Her sixth Canadian Open title came to her that summer. The first phase of her golfing career was over. Time now to start a family.

Mary Gay was not the only outstanding player overshadowed by Marlene in the 1950s, but she was exceptionally unlucky not to have won a national championship. No golfer in Canada has ever done so well in national golf without a title to show for it. She was runner-up in the Open or Close nine times between 1952 and 1965. A member of the team to tour Britain in 1953, Mary Gay was also in Canada's first Commonwealth team in 1959. The flu kept this tall, powerful player from showing off her best talents at St. Andrews.

Also in the 1959 team was Rae Milligan of Jasper and Calgary. When she came to Burlington in 1955 to knock local favourite Marlene Stewart out of the Ontario championships, Rae Milligan's long woods and pinpoint irons earned her the title of "Boom-boom." (For the record, Marlene had just been through a harrowing experience when her plane made a forced landing.) Rae Milligan reached the Open semi-finals three times and

Judy Darling of Quebec, Open winner in 1960 and 1961.

Gayle Hitchens of B.C., Ladies' Open winner in 1962.

was runner-up in 1962. She twice came second to Marlene at the Close.

Another Alberta girl should have been in the 1959 Commonwealth team. In 1957, Betty Stanhope quit her job with an Edmonton oil company to concentrate on golf. That year, she won the national Open. This tall, relaxed girl was not exceptionally long off the tee but was a fine match player under pressure. She knocked out a strong American and went on to overwhelm Mary Gay in an all-Albertan final.

There was an understandable outcry in the West in 1958, when the newly married Betty Stanhope Cole was not selected for the team to visit Britain in the following spring. "She married recently, and needs some time to herself," the CLGU selection committee claimed, rather lamely.

But Mrs. Cole's day was only just beginning. This fine athlete – she was also a provincial curler – was the Close runner-up in 1962 and 1964, before winning this national title in 1967. When she temporarily gave up national competitive golf in 1980 to devote her spare time to the CLGA, she had one of the finest records of those who were contemporaries of Marlene Stewart Streit: a winner of the Canadian Junior; of the Open and Close; five times an internationalist; twenty-five times a member of an interprovincial team; fourteen times the Alberta champion between 1957 and 1980; and ranked the number one player in Canada in 1974 and 1976.

In the more than twenty years between 1937 and 1960, the Ladies' Open went almost exclusively to Marlene Stewart Streit or to an American. To find a winner from Quebec, you had to go back to 1936, when Whitlock's Dora Virtue Darling defeated Margery Kirkham at Royal Montreal.

In 1960, Judy Darling of Whitlock did what her mother had done twenty-four years earlier. In the Open final, this petite twenty-two-year-old blonde holed a six-foot putt on the last green to defeat America's Anne Stranahan, 1 up. She then burst into tears in the arms of her mother, who had flown to Saint John for the final.

Judy Darling had earned her title. She came to Saint John as a three-time champion of Quebec (she won again in 1960 and 1961) and a former national Junior champion. In the Open, she led the qualifiers with a 72, a women's course record. Her toughest match was against her team-mate, the smooth-swinging Dulcie Lyle, who stood a head taller than Judy. Both were under par when Judy won.

The other finalist, the powerful redheaded Anne Stranahan, was married to America's Frank Stranahan, twice winner of the Canadian Amateur. By then a professional, Frank was there to walk the course with his wife. He saw her make a fine recovery in the last nine holes, to square the match at the thirty-fifth. A bogey at the last hole put paid to her chances. But Judy still had to make that pressure putt of six feet.

Judy Darling held on to her Open title in 1961. At Vancouver's Point Grey she defeated seventeen-year-old Gayle Hitchens of Capilano. This final had everything: good golf, a great comeback, a tight, tense finish at the 36th hole. At lunch it had looked all over. Playing straight, steady golf, Judy was 4 up. When she won the first two holes in the afternoon, it seemed for Gayle Hitchens more a question of staving off a débâcle than of snatching a victory. But just as it looked all over, this final suddenly came to life. Gayle won four in a row and just missed a deuce to bring the deficit to one. Her 30-foot putt at the 35th did go in, and this battle looked as though it might go to sudden death. But Judy pitched a 9-iron to within five feet of the last hole, giving her a birdie and a win by 2 up.

Although still a grade-twelve student, Gayle Hitchens had twice been runner-up in the national Junior, before winning this in 1961. What marked her as a girl with a future was

The Comeback Kid after winning the Ladies' Open in 1959.

her display in the semi-finals of that year's Open. Against a highly ranked American, Miss Burns, she was not given a ghost of a chance. Sheer determination and skill saw her win by 3 and 1.

Gayle Hitchens was to win the Open in 1962, at the age of eighteen. Over a wet and soggy course in Winnipeg, and "playing like a pretty little machine," she gave holes away at the beginning of both rounds of the final but recovered to beat Rae Milligan by 5 and 3.

Few golf champions can give up the game for three seasons and return to play with as sharp a competitive edge. When Marlene Stewart Streit returned to tournament play in 1963, she was the mother of two girls. For three years, her mind had been focused on other interests. New champions had come on stage, other players had been honing their skills. So the 1963 championships were an acid test, even for a woman of Marlene's calibre.

It is all very well for us now, with the advantage of hindsight, to wonder how we could ever have doubted her resilience. Here she is, nearly thirty years later, and still capable of winning any women's tournament in the country. But in 1963 she had been on the national scene for only thirteen years and had already reached her goal of winning the world's major titles.

In the first round of the 1963 Close, Marlene shot an 81, the highest score of Ontario's interprovincial team of four. There may have been doubters who nodded "There, I told you." But if so, they would have been laughed off the course the next day. Marlene came in with a second round 73. Only Betty Stanhope Cole was able to match this, and no other player came within 3. Marlene went into the third and final round with a one-stroke lead. With only two holes to go, she had increased this to three over Gail Harvey, playing just behind. A double bogey at the seventeenth, coupled with Gail's birdie at the sixteenth, saw her lead disappear like a straw in the wind. At the final hole, the spectators witnessed Marlene Streit at her most unforgiving. She fired a 6-iron to within 12 feet of the flag. Taking her time over the putt, she rolled in a birdie. After a three-year lay-off, Marlene Stewart Streit was back where she belonged.

The Close turned out to be a preview of the Open. Marlene broke the course record to lead the qualifiers. In match play, nobody ever looked like stopping her. Drives went down the middle, irons straight and true, long and crucial putts consistently found the cup. Anne Stranahan fell to her in the semi-finals, Gail Harvey in the final. For the seventh time in ten attempts, Marlene was Ladies' Open champion.

Within a month she was in Australia with the Canadian team competing in the Commonwealth tournament. While there, she won the Australian Ladies' Championship, taking on the best from the Commonwealth countries. In the final she defeated Mrs. Porter of Great Britain by a decisive 8 and 7. So three national titles had come her way within the space of four weeks.

Some comeback!

Marlene was to win the last Close championship before it was discontinued, in 1968. Over a rain-soaked course at Montreal's Elm Ridge, she again took the title from Gail Harvey Moore.

She was to win the Open title four more times: in 1968 from Jocelyne Bourassa; in 1969 from Barbara Turnbull, of Saskatoon. That was the end of match play in the Open. From 1970, it was decided by 72 holes of stroke play. That did not stop Marlene from chalking up two more wins. In 1972, a final round of 72 gave her a seven-stroke margin. In the following year, she only just scraped home by a stroke, and was nearly caught by Marilyn Palmer.

Marlene Stewart Streit played twice in "Shell's Wonderful World Of Golf," a series made for television. She was the only North American amateur to compete. In 1965, in Oslo, she defeated LPGA Tour player, Marilynn Smith, to win $7,000. A year later, at Toronto Golf Club, she won $3,000 as runner-up to the great Mickey Wright. Her performance in these events dispelled any doubts there may have been about whether she could have succeeded in professional golf had she chosen to try.

As an amateur, Marlene could not accept the prize money but donated it to the Ontario Ladies' Golf Association. The Marlene Streit Awards Fund, designed to finance junior golf in Canada, has helped to send some of our girls to championships in the U.S. and Britain.

Her eleventh Open title in 1973 was to be her last. She came second in the Open five times, most recently in 1982, some thirty-two years after the girl in the plaid cap first won our hearts.

Just as George S. Lyon, Sandy Somerville, and Ada Mackenzie started on new careers as Senior golfers, so is Marlene Streit. She won her first Canadian Senior title in 1985. But that is not to say that she had made her last threat in non-Senior golf. In 1985 she competed in the British Ladies', for the first time in twenty-six years. No one dared suggest she was too old to capture the title she had won thirty-two years earlier. She qualified handily, with a round of

77. (This should have been a 76; for the first time in her life she signed a wrong score card. "This makes me look a doddery old woman.") In match play, she reached the quarter-finals.

Later that year she went down to the Sheraton Savannah Resort and CC to win the U.S. Senior Women's Amateur, her first appearance in this event. Having been runner-up for the same title three times, she tied in 1990, but lost in a play-off. She still goes to Gord McInnis for lessons. Not for her swing, but to learn again how to concentrate. Yes, there is a lot of golf left in Canada's first lady of the fairways. She has never *stopped* competing.

Marlene Stewart Streit came to Canadian golf at a time when Ada Mackenzie was past her best in the game. Women's golf in this country had fallen on hard times. American girls were taking our championship south, regularly. Marlene put a stop to all of that. By 1953, she had placed Canada firmly on the map of international golf. By 1956, she had become the world's finest woman player, feared and respected by opponents in Canada, Britain, and the United States. No Canadian golfer, man or woman, not even

Gail Harvey Moore, winner of the Close in 1964 and 1965 and of the Open in 1970.

Sue Hilton of London Hunt & CC, winner of the Canadian Junior and Close championships in 1962.

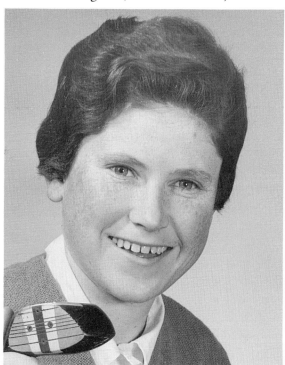

Cathy Galusha of Red Deer G & CC, Alberta, winner of the Canadian Junior Girls' Championship, 1963.

the legendary George Lyon, won so many national titles, or dominated national golf for so long, and by such a margin. A Member of the Order of Canada and one of the first members of the Canadian Golf Hall of Fame, Marlene Streit gives back to golf her greatest gift: the inspiration she is to the junior golfers with whom she plays. No person has been a better ambassador of Canadian golf. It would be rash to predict there will never be the likes of her again. Who knows what future millenniums might bring?

Gail Harvey was a pupil of Scarboro professional Bob Gray in the late 1950s, and developed into one of the most stylish of the young girls then coming on the scene. Three successive national junior titles came her way, the first when she was only sixteen.

Gail went on to win three national titles: the Open in 1970, the Close in 1964 and 1965. In this period, she had more success than the others who challenged the dominance of Marlene Stewart Streit.

She first ran up against Marlene in the 1963 Close and lost when Marlene birdied the last hole. Her revenge came a year later, when a final round of 71 gave her victory over Betty Stanhope Cole. Her 54-hole total of 215 was to remain a record in the Close.

She successfully defended her title in 1965, over the tough Westmount course in Kitchener. Her win came as no surprise and was uneventful. In the second round she fired a 71, three under the women's course record, virtually to end the competition. She went into the third and final round with an eight-stroke lead over Mary Gay, increasing it to nine by the end of the day.

In October 1969, Gail Harvey Moore (now married and living in B.C.) was involved in an automobile accident. For six weeks she lay in hospital with a fracture of the pelvis. "I never thought about whether or not I'd be able to play again," she said. "I was more concerned about getting to the stage where I could go to the washroom!" But back she went to the golf course, and within months she had captured the B.C. Ladies' title.

In 1970, Gail Harvey Moore and Marlene Stewart Streit met in what was to become a thrilling shoot-out for the Ladies' Open. For the first time, the championship was determined by 72 holes of stroke play. Gail's back had also been injured in the accident and was still giving her problems, but out on the course the pain was forgotten, and it had no noticeable effect on a swing that was as smooth as ever.

Marlene led by a stroke after 54 holes, but Gail caught her in the final round. As in their 1963 encounter in the Close, Marlene needed to birdie the last hole to win. But unlike 1963, she failed. So the two set out on sudden-death. The first two holes were halved. Marlene's display at the third, a 140-yard par three, was completely out of character. Her tee-shot went over the green and settled in a spot near the out-of-bounds fence. She had to chip over a mound to make the green, which sloped away from her, so her ball finished on the far fringe. Her third shot went five feet past the flag. With Gail only a foot away in two, she conceded.

Marilyn Palmer O'Connor, that fine B.C. player with the whimsical smile, came on the national scene in 1963, when she was runner-up in the Canadian Junior girls' championship. Three years later she was to win the Close, after a sudden-death play-off that went to the twenty-first hole.

Cliffhangers became routine in her long career in national golf. In 1967 she lost the Open to Bridget Jackson of England at the thirty-seventh hole; a year later, in the semi-finals, she held on to Jocelyne Bourassa until the nineteenth; in the next year's semis, she lost on the last green. In the 1973 Open, Marlene Stewart Streit took the title from her by a stroke.

Marilyn has been chosen to play for Canada ten times in the years 1967–86. She excelled and revelled in the head-to-head combat of the Commonwealth match-play tournament. In 1971, the British champion, Mickey Walker, threw eagles and birdies at her. Unperturbed, she fought back to win by 2 and 1, Canada's only victory against the British. The referee said she had never witnessed a better display of golf.

38

CHAPTER

TWO GIRLS ON TOUR: SANDRA POST AND JOCELYNE BOURASSA

I T IS FEBRUARY 1960. AT FLORIDA'S PORT Charlotte Country Club, America's Kathy Whitworth has just given her first golf clinic after turning professional. She and fellow tour-player Mary Ann Reynolds are playing an exhibition match against two sisters from Oakville, Ontario.

Suzanne and Sandra Post are both amateurs. Suzanne, at seventeen, is a sturdy girl who strikes the ball crisply. But it is Sandra who catches the crowd's fancy. For this blue-eyed blonde is not yet twelve years of age, and several inches short of five feet. But her poise, balance, style, and confidence are those of a girl twice her age. Her cut-down clubs are held in two small hands growing stronger by the day from constant practice. Her swing mimics the professionals. The clubhead goes back over her right shoulder, just beyond the horizontal. Then forward it comes, swishing the air with all the force a seventy-pound body can muster. Away goes the ball, straight

as an arrow. The clubhead comes up over the left shoulder, till the shaft points to the ground, and the girl's body is facing the line of flight, hands high in the air. The ball flies 165, sometimes 175, yards off the tee. The spectators applaud. Around the greens, Sandra Post has already developed a touch of genius: pitch shots dead to the pin; putts near or in the cup. The spectators applaud. Mary Ann Reynolds and Kathy Whitworth smile at the young girl's earnestness and mark her down as a champion of the future.

The next eight years are generous to Kathy Whitworth. By 1968, she has won over forty tournaments and a lot of money on the LPGA Tour. She is ranked number one in the United States, which means number one in the world. A year earlier she had won the LPGA championship. Now, at Pleasant Valley Country Club in Sutton, Massachusetts, she is in danger of losing this title. A precocious twenty-year-old from Oakville, Ontario, a rookie on the LPGA Tour, a professional for only four months, is running away with the championship. Sandra Post had stunned a crowd of 15,000 on Saturday by tying with the great Kathy Whitworth in this premier professional event. Now, on the Sunday, the two of them are fighting it out head-to-head in an eighteen-hole play-off.

For the first eleven holes of play, Kathy Whitworth is three under par – good enough to lead anyone, you might imagine, especially a nervous young rookie. But if this young rookie has nerves, she does not show them. For the first eleven holes she is five under par, two strokes in the lead.

Sandra on her way to the LPGA championship, 1968.

At the twelfth hole, Sandra Post is in trouble. She gets out of it by chipping the ball into the hole to go six under.

At the fifteenth hole, Sandra Post is in trouble again. But again she chips into the hole, and is now seven under.

"It was fantastic," Kathy Whitworth says later. "I was supposed to be the ogre picking on this little kid. You saw what happened. I

got a real tiger by the tail." At the seventeenth, Kathy Whitworth can hold the tiger no longer. Kathy's ball goes into the water and she takes an eight. Sandra Post wins the LPGA championship by seven strokes. She becomes the first foreigner and the first rookie ever to win this premier event. She has humbled the Pleasant Valley course, considered one of the toughest in America, by going round in 68, five strokes under par.

"It was my privilege to be here, just to see her play," says Kathy Whitworth, elegant in defeat. As an officer of the LPGA, she presents the winner's cheque of $3,000 to her victor.

Sandra Post's victory in the 1968 LPGA championship was no freak of circumstance. There are countless instances in the history of the game where players appear from out of nowhere to perform well above their ability for a few glorious days, only to return to limbo. However, Sandra Post had been playing well since coming on the LPGA Tour in February of that year. She had made money in all but one of her nine tournaments before Pleasant Valley.

In April, she had become the first woman professional to break 30 for nine holes in tournament play, in the Lady Carling Open at Atlanta. (Unfortunately, it didn't count. She called a 2-stroke penalty on herself after her caddie placed a hand on the green to get a feel for the grain.) In that season, she went on to win about $18,000 in prize money, including $3,500 for fifth place in the World Series of Golf. This made her eleventh in the official money list for 1968 and earned for her the award of Rookie of the Year. Endorsements probably doubled her income. Spalding came out with a Sandra Post line of women's clubs; she modelled sportswear for Susan Van Heusen and signed a contract with the Lido Golf Centre at Oakville for more than $5,000.

Over the next decade and a half, Sandra Post was to win another eight events on the LPGA Tour, earning more in prize money than any of our other professionals in the same period, male or female.

Such summary conceals the truth of those years. If 1968 was a flourish of trumpets, heralding a bright new future for Sandra Post, then the trumpeters played the wrong notes. The year is better likened to the top of a roller-coaster. In the next four years she was to ride the rough rails of illness, a divorce, and separation from the game she loved, before ascending to the joy of her second professional victory. Recovery from the personal tragedy of those years was slow in coming, and was never complete.

Sandra Post's instant success as a professional flies in the face of her mediocre record as an amateur. Outstanding as a junior, she was never to reach even the semi-finals of the Canadian Ladies' Open or to finish higher than third in the Close. The explanation lies in the nature of the girl. She never had the burning ambition needed to win. Her goal was higher, her horizon more distant. The Canadian title was a stepping stone she could afford to skip. Her goal had been set many years before, as a child. Which brings us back to how an eleven-year-old girl ever came to be playing in an exhibition match with Kathy Whitworth, in February, 1960. . . .

If any Canadian golfer has the right to be labelled a child prodigy, then that golfer has to be Sandra Post. She was helped by some inherited instinct for golf, since her father was a fine club player. Cliff Post, a successful fruit farmer from just outside Oakville, was good enough to play off a 4 handicap. He coached both his daughters in the game, instilling in Suzanne, then in Sandra, a burning desire to reach the top.

The Posts – father, mother, and two daughters – spent six weeks of winter at Boynton Beach, Florida. Here, at the age of six, Sandra Post found herself attracted to professional golfers in action. The women were the most interesting to watch. For one thing, they wore beautiful clothes. While other girls of her age showed an interest in dolls or movie stars, Sandra Post became infatuated with the world of women's golf. Her heroines, amateur and profes-

Sandra Post with Marlene Stewart Streit in 1961, at the Ontario Junior championship, Brantford.

sional, became Wiffi Smith, Barbara Romack, Patty Berg, Kathy Cornelius, Beverly Hanson, Mickey Wright, and Marilynn Smith. She envied Marlene Stewart Streit, who came to Florida each winter to compete against the American stars in such tournaments as the Helen Lee Doherty Invitational at Fort Lauderdale.

Sandra Post's father and sister first showed her how to swing a golf club. But she became a faithful mimic of those she watched. "That's the way Barbara Romack does it," she would tell Cliff Post when he found her swinging a club in their Florida home. By now she knew what she wanted to do with her life: "I want to be a professional golfer." How much this was inspired by love of the game, how much by the glamour of the tournament players and their "beautiful clothes" is of no consequence. The goal had been set, the means established. The means were practice, play, and more practice.

At the age of nine, Sandra played in her first tournament, Ontario's Father-Daughter, Mother-Son, foursomes. Cliff and Sandra Post did not win, but they stole the show. The slight, four-foot-one-inch girl of fifty-nine pounds was hitting the ball 125 yards and straight, with "the swing of a future champion" – or so thought George Laughlin of the *Toronto Telegram*. He also found her surprisingly keen and determined. The press photographers had a field day with this very junior miss. She swung a club for them, kneeled by her bag and trolley, and lined up a putt in the manner of Marilynn Smith (whom Sandra now referred to as her "buddy," and with whom she corresponded).

Children under the age of eleven were not allowed on the course at Oakville GC. So Cliff Post had to get special permission for his younger daughter to play nine holes a day and to practise endlessly. But she was able to join the nearby Trafalgar club, quickly becoming the star of its junior golf school. By the age of ten, her handicap was 25. In Florida she competed in the Women's South Atlantic Golf Tournament, confident, if a little nervous. No, she didn't expect to win, she answered in all seriousness, but she was getting experience for the future. That same year, she was the youngest competitor ever to play in the Ontario ladies' championships.

At twelve, she won the junior club title at Trafalgar, from her sister Suzanne. "The Babe of the Woods and Irons," the members called her affectionately.

In January 1962, at the age of thirteen, she shot an 88 at the Doherty Invitational in Florida, but just failed to qualify. By fourteen, her handicap was down to 6, the result of seven hours a day on the golf course. That year she made her way into the top sixteen qualifiers of the Ontario Ladies'. After leading the qualifiers in the provincial Junior championship, she was selected as one of a two-girl team to play in the national Junior at Winnipeg. In 1963, when fifteen, she had her first of three wins in the Ontario Junior. A year later, in the month she turned sixteen, Sandra Post took the Ontario ladies' title.

This win led to her first clash with the Ontario Ladies' Golf Association. The provincial junior and ladies' teams to play in the national team championships at Calgary were selected from the players who had accumulated the most points in certain designated tournaments. One designated tournament was the Ontario Junior, and Sandra had been knocked out in the semi-finals. The fact that she had won the Ontario Ladies' cut no ice with the selectors. So she was chosen for neither the junior nor the ladies' team.

By now it was a well-known fact that Sandra Post had set her sights on a golfing career after she finished school. "I'll go at it full-time," she announced after winning the Ontario title. Her stated intention to turn professional was sufficient grounds for taking away her amateur status. But it was lack of points, not of discretion, that lost her a place.

Bitter at her being dropped, Cliff Post was determined to have her play in the championships in Calgary, although this meant paying her own way. They were amply rewarded. Sandra Post ran away with the Canadian Junior Girls' Championship, winning by eight strokes over 54 holes. What is more, with rounds of 77 78 74–229, she came third to Gail Harvey and Betty Stanhope Cole in the Close, beating one of her idols, Marlene Stewart Streit. It was a further twist of the knife that she could now boast of being selected as a reserve for the Canadian team to play in the first Women's World Amateur Team Championship in France.

The next three years held little but disappointment. She twice defended successfully her national Junior title, but played poorly in the Open and Close, or ran up against a competitor playing better than normal. It was the same story in the United States. In the space of four weeks in 1967, she finished second in the Harder Hall Women's Invitation, and was defeated in the semi-final of the South Atlantic Women's Championship. In the Helen Lee Doherty Invitational, Alice Dye sank an impossible downhill putt to snatch victory from her at the thirty-eighth hole. Canadian critics arrived at a consensus which Joe Noble put succinctly in *Golf Canada*: "One reason Marlene Streit became great was she started to win early. It gave her confidence and she went on to great things. Unless Sandra gets a big win soon, she may lose her confidence and fade away."

The end of three frustrating years came in January 1968. In the final of the South Atlantic Women's Championship, Sandra had her revenge on Alice Dye, winning the final by 3 and 2. At a Press Day meeting she revealed that she was turning professional: "Guess I've always wanted to be a pro because I just love to play golf." It had never been a question of *if* for Sandra Post. Since the age of six, when she first saw those women professionals in their beautiful clothes, it had really been a question of *when*.

On reviewing Sandra Post's career as an amateur, we come back to the question of why, after an outstanding record as a junior, she did not do better in the ladies' national championships. Since she was barely out of the junior ranks when she turned professional, this may

be judging her too harshly. But she herself admits that the concentration and the spark needed to win were often not there. The minute she turned professional, her whole attitude to the game changed. "I threw away a lot when I was an amateur. Now [only a few months after turning] I *think* more, because it's my occupation, and errors cost me money."

Sandra Post was never a true amateur in spirit. She had little time for socializing after golf, but preferred to go home or to practise. Her relationship with the governing bodies of golf was sometimes less than harmonious. Her confidence in her own ability often came out as brashness. She did not like to lose and was not a good loser.

Sandra Post was not Canada's first woman professional golfer. In 1931, eighteen-year-old Verena Newton walked away with the handicap event at the Ladies' Close, playing off 18. A year later she took over the professional's duties at Lakeside GC, in the Muskokas,

Verena Newton, perhaps Canada's first woman professional golfer, seen here in 1932.

Cathan McWilliam Shoniker, the CPGA's only female member in 1959.

saying: "I can't just go on playing golf for fun because I can't afford it." Taught by Hugh Logan, the one-time professional at Rosedale, she reshafted and repaired clubs. Others followed her example. But Sandra was the first to join the LPGA Tour. To earn her LPGA card, she had to finish in the top 80 per cent of the field in three of her first four tournaments. She did this with lots to spare.

"Sandy" or "Postie" – as they called her on the Tour – took to her new life like a duck to its favourite pond. She already knew many of the players, and some had helped persuade her to join their ranks. Her initial success surprised no one, least of all herself. Fitted out with a Florida accent, effervescent and bubbly off the course, she appeared to be supremely in command of her emotions when playing. One observer commented:

> Sandra is a cool golfer. Most of the 50 women on the circuit have mannerisms to show pleasure, exasperation, or disappointment. Sandra looks as if she works to keep emotion out of her face. She rarely smiles, and when she makes a good shot, barely acknowledges the gallery's applause.

Sandra Post's successes as a professional on the LPGA circuit extended over fourteen seasons:

1968	LPGA Championship
1974	Colgate Far-East Open
1978	Colgate–Dinah Shore Winners Circle
	Lady Stroh's Open
1979	Colgate–Dinah Shore Winners Circle
	Lady Michelob
	ERA Kansas City Classic
1980	West Virginia Classic
1981	McDonald's Classic

The period of void – 1968 to 1974 – can be explained by the recurrence of an old injury, and other problems. In 1970 she married John Elliott Jr., a young American professional golfer just returned from a stint as a U.S. Marine in Viet Nam. The marriage was not a success. The competition between career and marriage – she was on her tour, he on his – handicapped them both from the start. In three seasons, Sandra Post played in only thirty-nine tournaments, winning a total of only $12,000.

Elliott lost his PGA card and joined the Canadian tour, where he was referred to as Sandra Post's husband, which he didn't like. Marci McDonald of *Maclean's* magazine reported him "in a series of tantrums with officials, ripping up his scorecard, screaming over rulings . . . chalking up a two-week suspension after a verbal set-to."

Sandra Post lost her marriage, fifteen pounds in weight, and ended up in the hospital, hemorrhaging from the stress. At some time in the middle of this nightmare, she also suffered from chest and back pains, a recurrence of an old injury sustained when thrown off a horse. For weeks she did not touch a golf club. Divorced and back on the LPGA circuit, she found the mental recovery to be slow. Several times in 1974 she was in a position to win on the last day but failed.

In December 1974, Sandra went to the $72,000 Colgate Far-East Open in Melbourne, Australia. She had a 1-shot lead going into the last round. This time she held on, edging out Australia's Margie Masters. It was a sign of a changed Sandra Post when she burst into tears on being presented with her $13,000 cheque: "It's not the money, it's the win. After seven years you have no idea what this win means."

In the years 1975 through 1977 she played well and seldom failed to take some prize money from a tournament. In those years, she ranked tenth, twelfth, and ninth in the LPGA money list, a record which any Canadian male professional golfer, then or since, would be happy to settle for.

Her two victories in 1978 earned her some $92,000, moving her up to seventh place in the LPGA rankings. And the next year saw her reach the top of her roller-coaster career. She won three LPGA events, came second in several others, and finished with $179,000 in official prize money. For the year, this left her second to Nancy Lopez. In effect, Sandra Post had become the number-two woman professional golfer in North America, and therefore in the world.

Her most important wins in these years were the back-to-back victories in the Colgate–Dinah Shore Winners Circle, at the Mission Hills club, Palm Springs. The Dinah Shore was – and is – one of the "majors" on the ladies' circuit, in prestige as well as in purse. Holding on to the title in 1979, after winning it in 1978, was an outstanding achievement for Sandra Post, one which tends to be overshadowed by her LPGA championship eleven years earlier. (It is equivalent to a man winning back-to-back Masters.) To retain the title was a supreme accomplishment; to win under the trying and controversial circumstances surrounding the 1979 Dinah Shore was a psychological triumph.

At the 1978 Dinah Shore, she had been suffering from injured tendons in her left hand and arm, although only her friends knew just how much. She made light of it at the time. (How can you say you're suffering, having shot a 65?) She was in pain during the winner's press conference, which was not a success. Ignorant of her pain, the press later characterized hers as "among the three worst interviews." That was in 1978, but the criticism still hurt a year later.

She arrived at Mission Hills to defend her title in high hopes, having altered her swing on the advice of professional Elmer Priestorn, and was striking the ball better than ever. On her arrival, her friends were quick to tell her she had been slighted in several ways: first, the photo of Nancy Lopez appeared on the cover of the program, when it should have been Sandra, as last year's winner; second, Nancy, and not Sandra, had been invited to play with Dinah Shore; third, Sandra had not been invited to the Dinah Shore talk show, and the holder was usually invited. Colgate later explained that its decision to use Nancy Lopez had been a marketing one. Nancy was then the hottest property in golf.

The media got hold of the story that Sandra was in a huff, and gave this as a reason for her not turning up at the Pro-Am dinner to receive a copy of her portrait as a past winner. In fact, no one had told her about the presentation. For the second year, the media seemed set on making her, and not her golf, newsworthy. The difference in 1979 was that all this was taking place before she had set foot on the first tee.

Ironically, perhaps inevitably, the battle for the 1979 Dinah Shore developed into a struggle between Sandra Post and Nancy Lopez. In the final round, Nancy Lopez went to the tenth hole with a two-stroke lead. Then Sandra Post made her charge. She just missed an eagle at the eleventh; chipped in for another birdie at the twelfth; birdied the sixteenth with a 30-foot putt that toppled in off the rim. When Nancy bogeyed the seventeenth, Sandra's lead stretched to two. But her opponent birdied the final hole, so she was to win by a margin of only a stroke. Her 276 was seven under the record for the tournament.

That was a good year. So were the next two or three. But the constant demand on the emotions, the tension of life on the circuit, was reducing the quality of life. In 1983 she called it quits. There was some truth in the excuse she gave at the time that she was experiencing aches and pains, and a numbness in her right thumb. But the reasons were perhaps more emotional than physical. After thirty years of competitive golf, she wanted peace of mind.

When she was a child, her family called her Jojo. Later, her friends called her Joce. To others on the LPGA Tour, this French-Canadian girl who joined them in 1972 was "Frenchy." Some of the less-informed members of the press referred to her as "the French girl."

Jocelyne Bourassa, a jaunty, dark-haired beauty of five feet five-and-a-half inches, with determined blue-grey eyes and an engaging smile, captured the hearts of many Canadians, golfers or not. Very much a product of Quebec – and oh! how it was proud of her – she had the Trevino-like quality of making golf seem fun while playing it with deadly earnestness.

When not talking to herself on the fairways, she was chatting to the spectators (this helped her relax). She attracted crowds everywhere. As a young amateur playing for Canada in New Zealand, she acquired her own faithful gallery. It took to wearing a red hat and a red shirt, as she did. You only had to look for this blaze of red on the fairway to find where Jocelyne Bourassa was playing. As a professional, she was voted the Most Colourful Personality by the others on the LPGA Tour.

Jocelyne in full swing.

Eighteen at the time, in 1965 she became only the third teenager to win the Canadian Ladies' Open. (The other two were Marlene Stewart and Gayle Hitchens.) She won the title again six years later. As a junior, she visited Britain with a team of four and came home with the Scottish Girls' Open Stroke Play title. She played for Canada twice as an amateur; in the Women's World Amateur Team Championship in Madrid, 1970, and a year later as a member of the team we sent to the Commonwealth tournament in New Zealand. Jocelyne was undefeated in the New Zealand series. She went on to do well in the New Zealand championships, lead-

ing the qualifiers and reaching the semi-finals of match play.

Jocelyne's success in 1972 persuaded a Montreal businessman, Jean-Louis Levesque, to sponsor her on the LPGA Tour. He also organized a Canadian Ladies' Professional Golf Association (CLPGA), with Montreal professional Luc Brien as its executive director. One of its objects was to establish an annual bursary fund to help young Canadian girls like Jocelyne go on the American circuit.

Levesque also decided to bring the LPGA Tour to Montreal by sponsoring an LPGA event. The newly chartered CLPGA announced a $50,000 tournament, La Canadienne, to be held in June 1973.

From the first mention of La Canadienne, sentiment, hoopla, and probably a fair chunk of cash favoured Jocelyne to win. Common sense told the pundits she did not stand a chance, given the pressure of the sentiment and the hoopla, to say nothing of her opponents, the finest women golfers in the world. ("I wouldn't have bet a plug nickel," Dick Irvin had the honesty to admit later.)

The year 1973 had not been kind to Jocelyne Bourassa. An operation on her left knee had restricted her to seven tournaments on the LPGA Tour, before the Tour came to Montreal's municipal course in the middle of June. In winning La Canadienne, Joce achieved something of a miracle. "One of the best examples of personal courage under fire I have ever encountered while covering sports," admitted the same Dick Irvin. "She sunk the putts when she had to sink them."

You could barely see these putts through chinks in a gallery twenty feet deep. Some newspaper accounts of the day capture the excitement of the moment, but not the effect on the nerves. This was a close thing, a very close thing. For a time it looked as though Jocelyne must surely go down, so great was the weight of our hopes on her shoulders.

On the first day, thanks to birdies at each of the last four holes, she led by two strokes. On every tee and fairway, she had to fight her way through several thousand admiring spectators.

Heavy rain delayed the second round for a day. When it was over, Jocelyne's lead was down to a stroke. On the third and last round, she fought herself all day. The groans of *ohs* and *ahs* from the six thousand people trying to follow her told the story to those who could not get close enough to see for themselves. She came to the eighteenth hole one stroke behind the veteran leaders in the clubhouse, Judy Rankin and Sandra Haynie.

The eighteenth at the Montreal Muni was a 490-yard par five. Jocelyne was long off the tee and hit a good second. After a deep intake of breath, she hit a wedge up, up, and away. But not away enough. The ball came down eighteen feet short of the hole. Some accounts said twenty-five feet. Whatever, it was hopelessly short of where millions of television viewers wished it. The only person not to lose heart was the owner of the ball. She read the break perfectly, stroked the ball perfectly, and in it went. The crowd went wild. Several went down on their hands and knees, crying with relief. Jocelyne Bourassa smiled. Someone shouted "le trou soixante, le trou soixante," and the spectators dashed to the sixteenth hole for the play-off.

Sudden death. All three parred the sixteenth. At the seventeenth, Judy Rankin three-putted and was out. There was no sign of strain on Jocelyne Bourassa's face as she came to the eighteenth tee for the second time that day. Then, so suddenly that the fact was slow to penetrate the mind, victory was hers. Sandra Haynie put her second into the water. The town of Shawinigan went on a binge.

What does she remember today of La Canadienne? "I was in an altered state all week. No time to myself. The only people I could bring myself to speak to were [brother] Gilles and my family. But I was confident. A little voice inside me kept saying 'Don't they know they cannot win? This is my tournament'." And the spectators? "I would never have got through that crowd without my two bouncers, who kept them away from me." And the 18-foot putt to tie? "I remember after hitting the shot to the green, I wanted to see Gilles. He told me later

that I had this dazed look on my face . . . When the putt went down, I started to shake all over. But I did not feel nervous, not until the play-off." And the play-off? "People clapped when Sandra's ball went in the water . . . I was so embarrassed. On the last green, I could not bring the putter back to hole that two-foot putt."

For Jocelyne Bourassa, winning La Canadienne was the highlight of a golfing career started in a humble way when she was thirteen. Her brother Gilles was the professional at Shawinigan, where the Bourassas lived. But she played too well for the ladies of the town, so she started golfing at Trois Rivières' Ki-8-Eb Country Club (pronounced kee weet eb). There she broke 80 when only fourteen, the result of her booming drives and deadly short game. They served her well when she won three Quebec Junior championships (1963, 1964, 1965), but let her down in the Canadian Junior which she never won. Only a few months beyond her sixteenth birthday, she took on the finest of Quebec's women golfers and became provincial champion. And two years later she won her first Canadian Ladies' Open.

The Open final between Jocelyne and New Brunswick's Mary Ellen Driscoll in 1965 was something of a letdown for the spectators. Playing over the tough, 6,433-yard course of the Westmount club, Kitchener, both girls were fatigued after nine days of golf (in the Close and Open). They sprayed tee-shots, missed greens, pulled putts, in a display of less than championship golf. Jocelyne won because she was longer off the tee and putted better.

For Mary Ellen Driscoll, this final had been a long time coming. In a dozen or so attempts, she had never got past the first round. Yet today her record in provincial golf is without equal in Canada: twenty-four New Brunswick or P.E.I.–New Brunswick titles, another four in the Nova Scotia championships; thirty-five interprovincial team matches. In addition, she has titles in Junior and Senior golf.

The win in 1965 made Jocelyne Bourassa a national figure. "The precocious pixie from

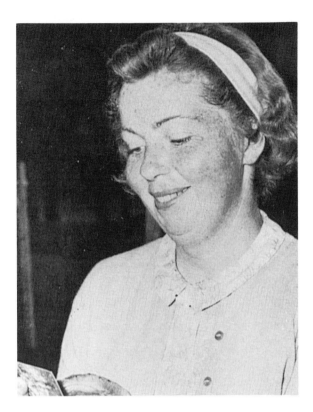

Mary Ellen Driscoll, runner-up to Jocelyne Bourassa in 1965.

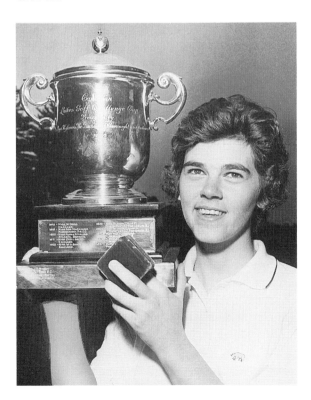

Jocelyne Bourassa holds the Duchess of Connaught Cup after winning the Ladies' Open in 1965.

Shawinigan," *The Globe and Mail*'s Jack Marks called this breezy firecracker with the charismatic smile. Her chipping got her out of many tough spots at Westmount. One spot had a hidden tree stump, which her clubhead found on the follow-through. She managed to make her shot, but finished the week with a bandage on her right wrist. "It stopped me from 'ooking," she responded in English. "I cannot turn my 'and ovair on de club." (Her opponents' French was much less fluent.)

In 1966, Ada Mackenzie saw a great future in this young French-Canadian girl: "She has that competitive fire that the great players all have." The fire burned steadily, but the results came slower than expected. In 1967, four of our juniors toured Great Britain and Ireland, and played in the Scottish Girls' Open Stroke Play Championship. This was held at Dunbar, a links course that calls for a variety of pitch-and-run shots seldom used in Canada. Playing under conditions foreign to her in every way, Jocelyne won by three strokes.

She had to wait another four years for her next national title. By 1971, the Ladies' Open was a 72-hole stroke-play event. Shooting steady golf over Capilano's testing layout, Jocelyne was still one stroke behind Marlene Streit coming to the last round. She caught Marlene, and needed a birdie to win on the par-five eighteenth. Few would relish a face-to-face play-off with Marlene Stewart Streit. So Jocelyne went for the green with a 3-wood. The ball flew long and straight, then bounced about forty yards onto the putting surface. Two putts later, the title was hers for the second time in six years.

This victory over Canada's greatest woman golfer made up for her loss to Marlene in the 1968 match-play final of the Open. It also made Jocelyne an automatic choice for the Canadian team sent to the Commonwealth tournament in New Zealand. There, she went through the singles undefeated. Later, in the New Zealand Ladies' Open Amateur, she was defeated in the semi-finals by Belle Robertson, the Scottish champion. But Jocelyne had already won two trophies, for leading at two stages of the stroke-play qualifying rounds.

Gotcha! Jocelyne sinks a 15-foot birdie putt against semi-finalist Carolyn McLure on her way to winning the 1965 Ladies' Open.

Jocelyne Bourassa attended the University of Montreal, 1965–69, graduating with a Bachelor of Science in physical education. With the help of a government grant, she went on to do graduate work on the sociology of sports, at the University of Wisconsin. She then became a physical education teacher, part-time sportswriter, and part-time golf instructor. Golf was her favourite of several sports; she excelled in just about everything she tried – basketball, volleyball, track, skiing. Her later fame brought with it many responsibilities as well as honours. She became a member of the National Advisory Council on Fitness and Amateur Sport, was the Canadian Woman Athlete of the Year in 1972, and was made a Member of the Order of Canada.

This was quite an accomplishment for a girl who had often been branded as something of a rebel when she first started playing provincial and national golf. She had several early brushes with the ladies who administered tournaments for the CLGA and its branches. This was partly the result of the language barrier (her

English was mediocre as a teenager), partly the result of the unfamiliar country club environment she found herself in. She soon discovered that there were certain protocols to be observed.

After New Zealand, Jocelyne Bourassa expected to go back to her job teaching physical education in high school, and to her work conducting golf classes for the YWCA. But suddenly she was given the chance to turn professional, when the Montreal businessman, Jean-Louis Levesque, became her sponsor, backing her to the extent of $10,000. Levesque and his wife became her close friends and faithful supporters.

Repaying his $10,000 became her target for her first year on the LPGA tour. ("The way Mr. Levesque helped me, I just had to play well," she recalls.) She met her target with something to spare. By the end of the 1972–73 season, she had finished in the top ten in half her twenty or so LPGA events, earning $16,000 and the title of Rookie of the Year.

Her bonhomie charmed the galleries in the United States. In Birmingham, Alabama, spectators were so taken by her extroverted good nature that they elected her to the roster of the Royal Order of Happy Faces. Although they were not to see her win, they were to see her come within a whisker and lose boldly, going for victory. By coincidence, her opponent in the play-off was Kathy Whitworth.

After winning La Canadienne, Jocelyne's future looked bright, but the recurrence of an old injury was to limit her performance on tour. Playing basketball at the University of Montreal she had sustained a cartilage injury to her left knee. This was to plague her throughout her career as a golfer. In 1976, she was forced to learn a whole new way of swinging a golf club, one which put less stress on her left side. But by 1979 she was running out of money and patience. The time had come to try something new, to divert her energies in other directions. She left the Tour. After a few months as the women's golf coach at Arizona State University, she joined the Houston Group. This led to her appointment as the Tournament Director for the Peter Jackson (now the du Maurier) Classic, the one Canadian stop on the LPGA Tour. So golf remains as much a part of her life as ever.

39

THE CLGA:
HOME AND AWAY

THE CLGU CHANGED ITS NAME IN 1966, explaining that "quite frequently the Canadian Ladies' Golf Union was confused with the various Trade Unions in this Country." So *Union* became *Association*. (In this and later chapters I shall refer to the association as the CLGA, whether dealing with matters before or after the adoption of the new title.) The change is understandable, but none the less regrettable. The CLGU had been formed with the help of the LGU of Britain, at a time when women were uniting to assert their rights in a sport dominated by men. Apparently, the LGU has never contemplated dropping "Union" from its name. The word has a fine ring to it, reminding us of the historical reasons for its use.

This was the least of the changes to the CLGA in the years after the Second World War. The association quickly grew in size, scope, complexity, and stature. The CLGA had been set up to organize national championships, to see that "pars" were up to date, and to solicit for members, and operated on a small annual budget of three or four thousand dollars. By the time it celebrated its seventy-fifth birthday

in 1988, it had grown to 960 clubs with a membership of 77,000 women golfers, and was being run like an international business.

At the end of the Second World War, the CLGA reorganized itself with the intention of becoming truly national. It faced up to the same problems that had bedevilled the RCGA. With few exceptions, its officers had been drawn from one of the city clubs in Ontario, usually Toronto. Only four of its championships had been held outside Central Canada (three in Winnipeg, one in Vancouver). The post-war aim was to rotate the championships throughout the provinces and to make the president and vice-president of the provincial branch hosting the championships automatically the president and vice-president of the CLGA.

Since it would have been impracticable to rotate the secretariat in the same way, it was agreed that it should stay where it had been since 1920, in Toronto. A new Administration Committee was set up in Toronto, the chairwoman to supervise all of the affairs of the association other than the running of the national championships.

This organizational structure seemed to work well from 1947 until 1970. The CLGA was then offered space in a new federal government building in Ottawa, the Administrative Centre for Sport and Recreation. As its name implies, this building was to house some fifty sports and recreation bodies. The financial savings such a move offered were too great to be ignored, so the association moved its national office to Ottawa and reorganized once again. The Administration Committee was eliminated. The vice-president now served for two years before moving up to become president for two years, giving the association some continuity of management. These posts could now be filled from any branch in Canada. The speed of travel by commercial airlines and the means to pay travelling expenses had further democratized the association.

The CLGA has been as fortunate as the RCGA in its choice of secretaries. In December 1951, Margaret Kathleen Rowe retired after twenty-five years of service, having guided the association's affairs through the difficult years of the Depression and the Second World War. Winifred Heath, then Peggi Walls, followed her.

In 1958, Monica Briggs came along to establish herself as another long-serving and much-respected secretary. She had to give up her post when the CLGA moved to Ottawa. The CLGA then hired Les Whamond, who had managed golf institutions in England before coming to Canada.

The financial health of the association improved gradually after the Second World War. Before then, its income traditionally came from member clubs and from the sale of yearbooks. Clubs paid a flat fee based on their size. This brought in revenue of only two or three thousand dollars a year. The sale of the year book might bring in about the same, giving the CLGA an annual revenue of approximately four thousand dollars.

Seeking to improve its bank balance, the CLGA went to a Dollar-a-Year Plan, similar to the RCGA's, starting in 1952. But it made the mistake of making the plan voluntary, and not

Kay Farrell of B.C., president of the CLGA in 1949 and 1955.

a condition of membership. The voluntary plan confused some clubs and was not a great success. In 1959, the Dollar-a-Year for each individual member became mandatory.

As with the RCGA, the effect on the finances of the CLGA was dramatic. Income from member clubs increased from about $3,000 a year in 1950, to $36,000 by 1962 (a dollar from each of 36,000 members). Since then, the dollar a year has had to be increased to keep up with inflation. The growth in real income of the CLGA has come from an increase in membership.

The setting of pars for golf courses had been one of the reasons for the CLGA's existence. In fact, it had a national handicapping system in place twenty years before the RCGA had one. But the method of determining pars became outdated. The parring of courses came to be replaced by the newer concept of course rating.

The CLGA followed the RCGA method of course rating, setting up its first national rating committee in 1960. The introduction of course rating caused some confusion among member clubs, which was not helped by such CLGA statements as "course rating seems to have become an established method of par- ring courses."

The CLGA went through the same gamut of experiments as the RCGA, trying out, for instance, Decimal Distance Rating, before dropping it for the current, more subjective, method.

Junior development – encouraging young girls to take up golf, and providing them with the incentive of their own championships – came with the money to fund it.

Always conscious of the need to keep with- in the bounds of amateur status, the CLGA could not pay the expenses of individual juniors to the Open and Close champi- onships. But it could pay the expenses of teams, and this it did. In 1953, an East versus West junior team match was arranged. Two years later, this was expanded to a junior

interprovincial match, in which teams of two competed for the Ada Mackenzie Challenge Trophy.

In the same year, taking advantage of the fact that the best golfers from each province were gathered together, the first Canadian Junior Girls' Championship was held as part of the Close.

The ladies' interprovincial team matches prospered. By 1955, the Maritime branch had split into separate branches for Nova Scotia, New Brunswick, and P.E.I./Newfoundland. Soon, Newfoundland was to form a fourth branch in the Atlantic provinces. At the CLGA's Golden Anniversary meet in 1963, all ten provinces entered teams for the first time.

Apart from wins by Quebec (1947, 1951) and B.C. (1955), Ontario dominated the team cham- pionships for the first dozen or so years after they resumed following the war. The first sign that this domination was over came in 1961, when Ontario was forced into third place by

The Quebec ladies' interprovincial team, 1949, with Bing Crosby. Left to right, Mrs. W. H. Smith, Daintry Chisholm, Mrs. J. C. Whitelaw, Mrs. Graeme Pyke.

B.C. and Manitoba, and in 1962, when Manitoba won for the first time.

From 1966, B.C. teams have clearly had the edge, originally anchored by a number of stalwart players who were making a name for themselves in national and international golf – Gayle Hitchens Borthwick, Marilyn Palmer O'Connor, Gail Harvey Moore, Dale Shaw. Vancouver's Marine Drive was turning out as many fine girls as it was boys. Alberta had its day in 1973, when it won for the first time; Betty Stanhope Cole, having played for Saskatchewan and Ontario, was back home.

More recently, there has been a high turnover of team members, as the best of the young players have left to join the LPGA Tour.

A Close championship had been felt necessary after the First World War, when the Canadian Ladies' championship was opened to outsiders and outsiders began to win regularly. But in 1958, having defeated in the Open the best players sent by the U.S. in five of the past seven years (thanks largely to Marlene Stewart Streit), the purpose of the Close seemed to have disappeared.

These same arguments had failed to have the Close permanently dropped in the 1930s, and they failed again twenty years later. For, having cancelled the Close in 1958, the CLGA brought it back in 1960.

Its demise was overdue by 1969, when it was finally discontinued. The reasons given by the CLGA were as valid then as they had been in 1938 and 1958: "A Tournament of two weeks' duration is a test of endurance for Committee members and players alike, and also for the host clubs."

In the CLGA's new format, the annual meet was reduced to five days. The Junior, the interprovincial team matches, and the qualifying rounds of the Open were played concurrently. Then, in 1970, the Junior was given its own date and venue. At the same time, the Open was made into a stroke-play event, which, together with the interprovincials, could be completed in four days. Like all championships that have given up match play, this one lost something in the process. Canada did so poorly in the foursome events at the Commonwealth tournaments that the CLGA introduced a foursomes championship in 1974, but it was discontinued after 1983.

The winning Manitoba team in the interprovincials, 1962. Left to right, *Susan Thompson, Marian Lawrence, Marlene Netterfield, Heather Lawrence, Marg Homenuik, Ann Taschan.*

Ever since the inauguration in 1932 of the team matches between the ladies of Britain and the United States for the Curtis Cup, Canada's ladies had hoped to make it a tripartite affair. After all, the Cup had been put up for competition by the Misses Curtis "for biennial competition between teams from the United States of America and the British Isles at present, in the hope that other countries will join the competition at some future date."

This future date was never to arrive.

Canadian ladies had played unofficial international matches against the United States in 1930, and against visiting British Curtis Cup teams in 1934, 1938, and 1950.

When the Cup was being played in the United States in 1950, Canadian ladies challenged the two participants to include a Canadian team. The answer was a polite No, since the challenge could not be accepted for one year only and the CLGA did not have the money to send teams to Britain. But by the time the money was there, it was clear that the ladies of both Britain and the United States were resolved to keep the Curtis Cup a bilateral affair, just as the men had been to keep Canada out of the Walker and Ryder Cups.

The voluntary Dollar-a-Year Plan helped finance a Canadian team to Britain in 1953, not to play in any official internationals, but to take part in a series of matches against district and regional teams. Ada Mackenzie, as captain, took a team of six to Britain in May of that year: Marlene Stewart, Mary Gay, Daintry Chisholm, Babs Davies, Mrs. Graeme Pyke, and Mrs. Margaret Todd. The highlight of the tour had to be Marlene Stewart's capture of the British Ladies' title.

On their way to the Curtis Cup matches in 1954, the British team visited Quebec and Montreal. Again, an unofficial international match was arranged between them and a Canadian team, played at Montreal's Beaconsfield.

This, then, was the not very satisfactory experience of the CLGA in trying to arrange international matches before 1959. In that year, everything changed – so much so that within a few years Canadian women seemed to be constantly on the move, playing matches in the most distant corners of the world.

But there was a price to pay. The CLGA had to rely on federal government grants to help finance its overseas ventures. In 1961, the government passed legislation to help the likes of the CLGA: "An Act to Encourage Fitness and Amateur Sport." An initial grant of ten thousand dollars in 1962 helped the CLGA pay the expenses of interprovincial teams and to plan a team for Australia in the following year. This made the association more susceptible to political pressure when problems arose with competing in South Africa, or alongside South African teams.

The men had held their first Commonwealth team matches at St. Andrews in 1954.

In 1959, a Women's Commonwealth Tournament was held on the same lines and at the same venue. Lady Astor and the LGU put up a trophy to be competed for every four years by a team of four. Canada sent over five players: Marlene Streit, Mary Gay, Roma Neundorf, Rae Milligan, Judy Darling, and a non-playing captain, Mrs. Mary Jane McCarter. They played as a team of four in round-robin matches, foursomes and singles, to finish second to Britain: Britain 4 wins, Canada 2 1/2, South Africa 2, Australia 1 1/2, New Zealand 0.

Marlene Streit registered our only win against Britain, defeating Elizabeth Price, who had just won the British title. Marlene was also deemed to be the outstanding player of the tournament. After the tournament, the Canadian team toured England and Wales, playing against a number of clubs.

For political reasons having to do with apartheid, South Africa did not compete after 1959. Canada has won twice, in 1979 and in 1987. The team of Marlene Stewart Streit (captain), Michèle Guilbault, Gail Harvey Moore, Marilyn Palmer O'Connor, and Stacey West went to Australia in 1979 and defeated each of the three other countries, in what was

The second ladies' team to go abroad, in 1959, placed second in the Commonwealth Team Matches. Left to right: Mrs. R. D. Staniforth and Mrs. John Shipley (CLGU officials), Mary Gay, Mrs. M. J. McCarter (captain), Marlene Stewart Streit, Roma Neundorf, Judy Darling, Rae Milligan, plus cheerleader Ada Mackenzie.

to be our best showing ever in women's internationals.

In 1987, the team of Gail Anderson, Audrey Bendick, Cathy Burton, Judy Medlicott, and

COMMONWEALTH TOURNAMENT 1963
Royal Melbourne Golf Club, Melbourne, Australia

CAPTAIN

MRS. J. H. TODD
Victoria Golf Club
Victoria, B.C.

MRS. J. D. STREIT
Lookout Point C.C.
Fonthill, Ontario

MRS. J. D. EVANS
Whitlock Golf Club
Hudson Heights, Quebec

COMMONWEALTH
TEAM
MEMBERS

MRS. G. COLE
Highlands Golf Club
Edmonton, Alberta

MISS RAE MILLIGAN
Calgary Golf & C.C.
Calgary, Alberta

MISS GAYLE HITCHENS
Capilano Golf & C.C.
West Vancouver, B.C.

The Canadian team in the 1963 Commonwealth Team Matches.

Jennifer Wyatt won in New Zealand, defeating two countries and tying the other.

In 1964, La Fédération Française de Golf proposed to the USGA that there be a match between French and American women golfers, after the Curtis Cup matches in Britain. The USGA agreed but went one step further in suggesting that teams from other countries be invited to play.

The Women's World Amateur Team Championship was first held in Paris, in October of that year. Twenty-five countries each sent a team of three. Each member played four rounds of eighteen holes over four days, but each day only a team's two best rounds counted. The winner was the team with the lowest aggregate for the seventy-two holes.

Canada decided in advance that its team would be made up of the three top players over four stroke-play rounds, being the three rounds of the Close and the qualifying round of the Open. So this team picked itself: Betty Stanhope Cole (captain), Joanne Goulet, and Gail Harvey. France won this first World championship, with the United States second, Britain third, and Canada fourth.

As with the Commonwealth tournament, the teams sent to compete in the World championships took part in many other local events. The outstanding feature of this visit to Europe was Joanne Goulet's performance in the British Ladies'. In the quarter finals, she was 5 down with five to go, but proceeded to win six in a row. In the semi-finals she took her opponent to the 20th hole before going down.

The Women's World Amateur Team Championship has been played every two years, the United States team winning all but three. Canada came second in 1966 and in 1978.

In 1966, when it was played in Mexico City, Marlene Stewart Streit was chosen to hit the first ball, a recognition of her standing in world golf. She confirmed this standing by turning in the lowest individual score of the tournament.

In 1978, when Canada again came second, our Cathy Graham Sherk was the lowest individual scorer, by four strokes.

When playing in other countries, Canadian women often found themselves at a disadvantage. If the tournament was held before June, it was too early in the season for the competitors from the Prairies and the East to give of their best. Too, the courses – meaning the turf and the layout – were often of a nature not found in Canada. After visiting France and Britain in 1964, Gail Harvey wrote:

> Prince's Golf Club, where we played in England, is a seaside course, with absolutely no similarity to any course I have ever played on in Canada. The fairways were burnt and brown, due to an exceptionally rainless summer, the greens were true, and the rough and bunkers provided hazards sometimes almost impossible to deal with. The thing which particularly amazed me was the terrain. The course was completely bare of trees, except for one enormous bush on the tenth hole. If you stood on any little rise and glanced back over the golf course, you had the impression of standing alone in the middle of an enormous hay field.

After the 1963 Commonwealth matches in Australia, non-playing captain Margaret Todd wrote that "the greens at Royal Melbourne

were disastrous for us. We had never seen such large and such fast ones."

When the Commonwealth matches were played in Australia or New Zealand, jet lag was more of a problem for Canada than for other countries. Here is Margaret Todd again: "Four days is not enough time in which to get ready for a tournament of that calibre, especially when it is held in a far-away country. All travel is very tiring, and it takes a few days to adjust to different climate, difference in time, and difference in general routine." She was not making excuses, merely warning the organizers of future visits.

She also wrote of our inexperience in foursomes: "Now that I have witnessed a Commonwealth Tournament, I realize how important the play of foursomes is in matches. In Canada, we never seriously play this type of game . . . I feel we should consider arranging a foursomes event in Canada." The CLGA took heed of her advice, in 1974.

Latterly, our teams played in a distinctive red outfit. They came to be known as "The Red Devils" or "The Ladies in Red" or – most complimentary of all – "The Happy Canadians."

The essence of these international meets was good fellowship through golf; the taking part was as important as the winning. With few exceptions, the CLGA chose its international teams with this in mind; players would be expected to represent Canada on and off the course.

To anchor its international teams, the CLGA came to rely on a few players, who always did us proud.

Marlene Stewart Streit played in five Commonwealth tournaments (1959, 1963, 1967, 1979, 1983) and three World Team tournaments (1966, 1970, 1972). She is the only one of these five players who also visited Britain with the Canadian team of 1953.

Marilyn Palmer O'Connor played in three Commonwealth tournaments (1967, 1971, 1979) and six World Team tournaments (1968, 1972, 1974, 1976, 1978, 1986). Marilyn also played in a special International Team Match, held in Australia in 1973. She was selected for

The Commonwealth team of 1973, left to right, *Marilyn Palmer, Mrs. Elizabeth Hoffman, Dale Shaw, Mrs. Barbara Turnbull, Mrs. Marion Minns (non-playing captain).*

Florence Harvey (above right) at the CLGA championships in Calgary, 1964 . . . and some unnamed celebrators at these championships.

the 1975 Commonwealth team, but took scarletina in Britain and could not play.

Gail Harvey Moore played in three Commonwealth tournaments (1967, 1971, 1979) and four World Team tournaments (1964, 1966, 1968, 1970). She also played in an International Ladies' tournament in 1979.

Gayle Hitchens Borthwick played in three Commonwealth tournaments (1963, 1967, 1971) and three World Team tournaments (1966, 1968, 1972).

Betty Stanhope Cole played in two Commonwealth tournaments (1963 and 1971) and three World Team tournaments (1964, 1974, 1976).

These five women still meet in provincial and national events, some as seniors. Now that our best young amateur golfers are bred in U.S. colleges to go on the LPGA Tour, we shall probably never see the likes of them again.

PART SIX

THE GLEN ABBEY YEARS 1975-1990

(Over) *Richard H. Grimm, Director of Professional Tournaments for the* RCGA.

CHAPTER

NOMADS AND COLLEGE GOLFERS

FUTURE HISTORIANS OF CANADIAN GOLF will probably look back and see the 1980s as a decade when Canadians who had gone to U.S. colleges on golf scholarships clinched their bid to be our leading players and winners of our national championships. They will also see the 1980s as the decade when many of our aspiring male professional golfers became globetrotters.

The takeover by ex-college players has been gradual over the last twenty years. Until the early 1980s, so was the rise in the number of Canadian professionals going overseas to compete on foreign tours. A Far East Tour had been launched in 1962, and a few pioneers had sampled it, notably Al Balding and Dan Halldorson. During the 1980s there was a surge in the number of young professionals going overseas, and by 1990 touring abroad had become commonplace, helped by a strengthening (through higher prize money) of the European Tour, Asian Tour, Japan Tour, and Australian/New Zealand tour. Look, for instance, at the experience of the young B.C. professional, Rick Gibson. In 1990, his sixth year on the

Asian golf circuit, he played in the Open championships of Hong Kong, the Philippines, Malaysia, Indonesia, India, Thailand, the Republic of China, and Korea. He placed third in the Asian Tour order of merit.

Gibson is one of the many who see these foreign tours as a stepping stone to the PGA Tour. Some have found that, PGA card aside, they are not immediately ready for the toughest golf tour in the world. By honing their game overseas, they hope to try again, whilst seeing the world and making a better living than they could as a professional playing only the CPGA Tour in the summer months.

The historian may also reflect on how well our women professionals have been doing on the LPGA Tour, not in wins perhaps, but in the number who now compete and who make the prize-money list. It is not unusual to see the names of six Canadians in an LPGA Tour event in the U.S., and to see four make the cut.

So we have entered the decade of the nineties with optimism. Some of our young nomadic professionals – Gibson, Mijovic, Franklin, Kay – are going to settle down some day and win honours on this continent. Some of our young ladies – and most of them on tour have yet to hit their best years of the thirties – will start to emulate the feats of Sandra Post. The breakthrough day is surely near for Dawn Coe, Lisa Walters, and company.

Most of our new young players, of both sexes, came to professional golf through the U.S. college system, which deserves a closer look.

In 1971, having just won the U.S. Amateur Championship for the second time, Gary Cowan seemed a little surprised by what he had achieved. He is quoted in *Golf Canada* as saying:

> Everywhere I looked, there was a fine college player. They just stand up to the ball and know it's going to go long and straight. They play so much competitive golf throughout the spring, they've gotten very tournament-tough by the time of the U.S. Amateur. They're so confident, because they do it every day. They're not worried about the rough – they pay no attention to it. They go out to the practice tee for hours. I hit it three times and that's enough for me.

Eddie Pearce came second to Cowan. Eddie was a nineteen-year-old student at Wake Forest University.

Jim McLean of the University of Houston was fourth.

One of the favourites finished sixth – a nineteen-year-old from the University of Texas named Ben Crenshaw, who was also the National Collegiate Athletic Association (NCAA) champion.

The point is *not* that these young men were attending college in the United States. Nor is it that they were playing golf there. A handful of young Canadians attended U.S. colleges at the turn of the century, played golf for their colleges, and were among the most promising amateurs in this country.

The point *is* that Pearce, McLean, and Crenshaw were attending college on a golf scholar-

ship. The cost of their college tuition, books, and room and board was being paid for them because they had been outstanding golfers at high school. Their life at college was very much taken up in playing golf, not just friendly rounds of golf, but tough, competitive golf, against teams from other colleges. Their aim was to graduate from college, yes. But it was also to make a name for themselves in NCAA golf, win the U.S. Amateur, turn professional, and make a good living on the PGA Tour.

In the last thirty years or so, the breeding ground of many of our playing professionals has changed. Once the caddie shack, it is now the college campus. Today, some 90 per cent of the top one hundred money winners on the PGA Tour have played golf at a U.S. college. And you'll find the same preponderance of college girls if you look at the winners of LPGA events.

U.S. colleges had golf teams back in the 1890s. But the game was low key until the 1950s; the number of scholarships in golf was nothing like the numbers in other sports.

Dave Williams, golf coach at the University of Houston, is usually credited with putting golf on the front pages of campus newspapers. He saw university golf as the ideal breeding ground for the professional circuit, since the earlier breeding ground, the caddie shack, was becoming extinct. Williams began building a championship team at Houston, using what little scholarship money he could squeeze out of the university budget. He expanded the Houston team's playing schedule to give them the experience of competing against the best colleges in the States. As a result, in 1956 Houston won the first of many NCAA golf titles.

Williams's success encouraged others. In 1958, the All-America Intercollegiate Tournament was first held, hosted by Houston. Paying spectators came in such numbers that college golf was able to put money back into other college sports. Jacky Cupit (1961) and Kermit Zarley (1970) are two members of these early Houston teams who went on to become playing professionals and winners of the Canadian Open.

Ohio State University had a double Open winner in Tom Weiskopf (1973, 1975), as well as the perennial runner-up in Jack Nicklaus.

By 1970, around six hundred U.S. universities and colleges had inter-collegiate golf programs. And an increasing number of Canadian boys and girls were being attracted to them by college recruiters eager to offer scholarships to youngsters whose golf showed promise.

In Canada, there was nothing to compare to intercollegiate golf and to golf scholarships. A few Canadian universities may have had golf teams for many years, but the game was a minor university sport.

The first Canadian to go on a golf scholarship to a U.S. college was Bud Donovan of Winnipeg, who entered Notre Dame in 1937. One of the first Canadians after the war to go to a U.S. college on a golf scholarship was Keith Alexander of Calgary. He entered the University of Colorado in 1953, played on the golf team until 1956, for a time as captain, and was selected to the All-American team in 1954 and 1955. Having graduated in journalism, Alexander gave no thought to turning professional. Of the college golf-grinders, he was the first Canadian to win our Amateur, in 1960.

Later in the 1960s, three of our national junior champions were recruited by U.S. colleges: Wayne Vollmer (1963) by Arizona State University – he later turned professional; Ian Thomas (1965) by Miami University in Ohio; Wayne McDonald (1966) by Indiana State University – an All-American, he went on to win our Amateur in 1969. They found the experience good for their golf. "The competition is stiff, and you learn to score better. It almost becomes a job, something you have to do every day, regardless of circumstances," said McDonald.

This set a pattern that has since been repeated with many of our national and provincial juniors, who have gone on to become playing professionals. But it was another college boy, our junior champion of 1970, who was to prove himself the most worthy successor to Lyon, Somerville, Weslock, and Cowan, as the

Wayne McDonald, Amateur champion in 1969, when at university in Indiana.

finest Canadian amateur golfer over the last two decades.

The 1972 Canadian Amateur was held at Calgary's Earl Grey club. The holder, America's Dick Siderowf, was there to defend the title he had won in 1971. (Siderowf was then hitting a peak. He was to win the British amateur championship in 1973 and 1976.) Other past winners were there, notably Keith Alexander and Nick Weslock. So was Canadian internationalist Bob Wylie, who had set the record for Point Grey ten years earlier. The course had since been tightened, and nobody expected to see any records broken in 1972.

But a twenty-year-old college student from Vancouver did just that in the second round. Doug Roxburgh's 65, six under par, had never been equalled on Point Grey, and it gave him the lead. Weslock's putter was not kind to him, but he was still in the hunt, as was Siderowf.

In the third round, the day-old record was beaten again. Another young B.C. amateur, Dave Barr, birdied eight holes, bogeyed one, and came in with a 64. This moved him up several notches, but not enough to catch Roxburgh, who drew even further ahead of his nearest challengers. In the final round, Roxburgh fought off Barr and others to win by four strokes, with a total of 276, or eight under par for the course. Barr was second, Siderowf third.

This tournament brought together for the first time as winner and challenger the two golfers who were to prove themselves the finest in Canada in the decades of the 1970s and 1980s, one as an amateur, the other as a professional.

Dave Barr as a student at Oral Roberts University.

Dave Barr was then virtually unknown in Canadian amateur circles, a twenty-year-old student from Kelowna, B.C., on a golf scholarship at Oral Roberts University.

Roxburgh was well-known and his win had been prophesied by many. Runner-up in the Canadian Junior in 1967, when only fifteen, he had won the title in 1970 by the clear margin of six strokes. This led to a golf scholarship at the University of Oregon (he left after two years to finish his studies in commerce at Simon Fraser). In 1971, he had lost in a play-off to Siderowf. His achievement in getting so far was made especially remarkable in that he was playing with borrowed clubs, his own having been lost in transit. This performance earned him a place in Canada's team at the New Zealand Centennial Tournament in 1971.

In British Columbia, Roxburgh was looked upon as a natural successor to Ken Black. He has since proved himself that. In the space of twenty years between 1969 and 1989, he has won the B.C. Amateur no less than ten times, beating an eighty-year-old record set by Harvey Combe.

He has represented Canada twelve times in international matches, including the World Amateur Team Championship (1972, 1974, 1976, 1978, 1988, 1990), and the Commonwealth matches (1971, 1975). He and Cowan won the International Team Championship in Venezuela in 1981. In 1972, he was Canada's selection to play in an international team of eight against South Africa.

His record of four wins in the Canadian Amateur is the equal of Weslock's, and is bettered only by that of Somerville and Lyon. What is as important for Canadian golf is that he is in every way – in terms of skill, bearing, mental attitude, and modesty – a worthy successor to these men. Roxburgh might well better their records in the Amateur, if we can judge from the way he won in 1988.

His second win in the Amateur came in 1974, over Winnipeg's relatively short Niakwa course of 6,154 yards, tougher than its length suggests. The competition was as impressive as it had been in 1972. Defending champion Andy Bean was soon to turn professional and make his name on the PGA Tour. Two-time U.S. Amateur winner, Gary Cowan, had just won the Ontario Amateur for the tenth time. Dick Siderowf was hoping to regain the Canadian trophy.

The first round was washed out by rain (no doubt to the chagrin of Gary Cowan, three under par at the fifteenth), so the competitors had to play thirty-six holes on the last day.

Playing over a spongy course on the first day, and in an early morning fog on the second, Roxburgh went into the third round with a 3-shot lead. If that lead looked safe, it no longer did during the round. Roxburgh's loose play lost him three strokes to par by the halfway mark. On his heels was a rejuvenated Cowan, on his way to a 67. At one point he caught Roxburgh, but the B.C. player found his normal, steady game in the inward half, and regained the three strokes he had lost.

A 3-stroke lead over Cowan is nothing. But in the event it proved to be three more than was needed. Roxburgh's 70 in the afternoon, for a four-under par total of 280, was a stroke better than Cowan could manage, and he finished at 284. For the fifth time, the Ontario player was runner-up.

Roxburgh's final hole of the tournament was noted with humour by *The Globe and Mail*'s James Christie:

> [Roxburgh] strode to the back of the green where he had cracked his second shot off a tree, drew out a wedge and flubbed the ball just to the fringe, but not on the green, with a 25-foot downhill putt to the flag. The two-time champion stood over the ball and turned to look at the leader board behind him. He did not need this putt, but the weary crowd did.
>
> Roxburgh stooped over the putter and gave the ball a smart rap that would seal the win. It ran, gaining momentum, directly into the cup.
>
> It was the circus type of putt one expects of pros under pressure, engaged in a duffers' dog fight for dollars. Here was Roxburgh, putting on the gallery-gladdening act for

free, in the name of amateurism, with nothing more at stake than a returnable $200 prize and a 79-year-old basin donated by the late Earl Grey.

Doug Roxburgh's father had been a member of Vancouver's Marine Drive G & CC for many years when his son took up golf. Doug grew up in a province and in a club committed to junior golf. Since 1951, Marine Drive had produced an unprecedented six national junior champions. When one club out of over a thousand in Canada produces seven junior champions in twenty years (including Roxburgh), it has to be doing something the others are not, or doing it better.

Being coached in a club with a tradition of winning is an undervalued asset. Stan Leonard, many times a winner, was the professional at Marine Drive until he chose to go on the Gold Trail. The string of victories in the National Junior also set Marine Drive youngsters a goal they knew was attainable. The Canadian Junior was theirs, if they chose to play and to practise. (A plaque in Marine Drive doesn't let you forget the champions the club has produced over the years.) Playing competitive golf against former national champions gives a youngster a standard to aim for.

All that is for nothing unless the club professional is a good teacher and committed to juniors. Marine Drive had several such professionals. Jack Westover was among the successors to Leonard at Marine Drive and did most to forge and hone Roxburgh's game. From Westover, Roxburgh learned the basics that make his swing one of the finest we have today. When Jack moved to other things, Doug would still seek his advice.

To Roxburgh, winning came with practice and the encouragement of a string of city and provincial titles. At the age of fifteen, he fought his way to the finals of the national Junior, then a match-play tournament. His putting let him down, and he lost 4 and 3. Three years later he won by a margin of six strokes.

Doug Roxburgh ("Roxy" to many) is a bespectacled, trim, 160-pounder, standing five feet seven inches. His quiet demeanour hides a fiercely competitive spirit. He is not a long hitter by today's standards, but is an excellent striker of the ball. His accuracy with irons is legend, a part of the game essential to good scoring at Marine Drive, which is tight and well trapped. He went through two years of the mill of U.S. college golf but was determined to stay an amateur. "I plan to remain an amateur forever," he was quoted as saying after winning the national title for the second time in 1974. "I've just no interest in turning professional." Then, in an untypical burst of immodesty: "Now that I've won it again, it's my goal to win it more than anyone else."

But like any true amateur, he also had to earn a living. His future essays into national golf were to be dictated largely by his finding the

time to practise. For several years he did not practise or play often enough, or well enough, to qualify for B.C.'s Willingdon Cup team.

His third and tightest win in the Amateur came in 1982. He had not been scoring well before coming to Kanawaki, which is not a long course, but one with a tough rough and many greens small, fast, and contoured. These, and a cold wind for August, made the scoring surprisingly high. A first round of 76 left Roxburgh eight strokes behind leader Rick Gibson, another Marine Drive boy. But his game progressed with each round. A 73 and a 70 left him only two behind the new leaders, the experienced Bob Wylie (at fifty-two playing in his first amateur since 1972) and Stu Hamilton.

In the final round, Roxburgh did what he had to do. Starting out with two early birdies,

RCGA Vice-President William A. Farlinger presents the Earl Grey Cup to Doug Roxburgh on winning his third of four Canadian Amateurs, 1982.

he fired a 68, the lowest score of the day. A par at the eighteenth would have given him an outright win, but anyone who needs a par at this demanding par 4 had better watch out. Of Bob Wylie's final round, no more need be said. But Stu Hamilton's closing 70 was good enough to tie, as was a 69 from B.C.'s Brian Christie.

Christie was bunkered at the first hole of sudden death and he dropped out. After both players had missed the green at the second, Hamilton also missed a six-foot putt for par, and that was that.

Roxburgh's fourth win in the Amateur came in 1988, at Gallaghers Canyon Golf Resort in Kelowna, B.C. He was determined to win that year on a course he knew and liked, so he had worked on his game.

As in 1974, the first round was washed out, this time by a record rainfall. Roxburgh set off in great form with a course record of 66, four ahead of the field. Although overtaken in the second round, he took a 1-stroke lead into the fourth and coasted home.

By winning the Amateur over a span of sixteen years (1972–88), Roxburgh equalled a record set by George Lyon (1898–1914). Like Lyon, Somerville, Weslock, and Cowan before him, Doug Roxburgh was elected to Canada's Golf Hall of Fame in 1989. He is already giving back to golf some of the pleasure it has given him. At Marine Drive, he is involved with the program for juniors, and at his induction luncheon he committed himself to a future in golf administration, in the tradition of Somerville, Gordon B. Taylor, and Farley. If Doug Roxburgh does *not* go on to equal Lyon's record of eight national Amateurs, he may be the spur for someone else who does.

Canada produced a crop of fine amateur golfers in the decades of the 1970s and 1980s. Of those who did not turn professional, Rod Spittle (1977, 1978) of Willow-Dell GC, Ontario, was the only other multiple winner of the Amateur.

Winning for the first time the men's World Amateur Team Championship in Caracas, Venezuela, made 1986 our best year. This was a fresh young team, with nothing to lose; only

Warren Sye had played for Canada before and then only once. As we have seen, only Sye has remained an amateur.

By 1990, Warren Sye was an old hand, having five internationals under his belt, but the Amateur had so far eluded him. In that year, it was played at his home club, Weston. He won, thanks largely to his experience and to an ability to withstand the strain of the closing holes. The experience showed both in his play and in his acceptance speech.

Stu Hamilton, a four-time runner-up in the Amateur, has represented Canada three times. Frustrated in his attempts to win the Amateur, Stu has recently been more successful in the RCGA's Mid-Amateur Championship. This event was introduced in 1987. It is designed for forty-year-olds and over – those in the twilight zone between college boys and Seniors. It recognizes that the Amateur has become an event on the U.S. college tour, is sought after by full-time college golfers, many of whom have no intention of staying amateur, and who conflict with the whole spirit of amateurism. The RCGA has also re-introduced match play; the top thirty-two players in stroke play go on to fight it out, head to head, as they did in the Amateur before 1969. Stu Hamilton won the Mid-Amateur in 1990.

The winner of the first two Mid-Amateurs (1987, 1988) was Graham Cooke, who has represented Canada four times. He is also one of the country's leading course architects.

The old-timers have not altogether disappeared. Bob Wylie, who first played for a Canadian team back in 1960, was chosen again in 1989, when a senior golfer. Here is another record for Doug Roxburgh to set his mind to.

During the same years, a number of Canadian winners of the Amateur, products of the U.S. college system, turned professional: Jim Nelford (1975, 1976); Greg Olson (1980); Richard Zokol (1981); Danny Mijovic (1983); and Brent Franklin (1985, 1986, 1987). Had they remained amateurs, any one of them might well have gone on to win the national title as many times as George Lyon. But it is just as possible that if Doug Roxburgh had turned professional, he, and not Dave Barr, would now be our most successful professional since Knudson.

The Dave Barr who pounded out 300-yard drives while shooting his 64 in the 1972 Canadian Amateur is unrecognizable from the professional we know today. It is not that his drives are shorter, but that his hair is. Dave Barr never did suit the hirsute fashions of the 1970s. He played for Canada that year in the World Amateur Team Championship, but you would be hard put to find him in the team photograph.

In the same way, Dave Barr has been changing his metaphorical image. For some years, galleries in Canada saw him only as a fast-swinging, fast-talking, short-tempered professional, often graceless in defeat. He made no concessions to the mood of the spectators, but had the habit of sticking pins into them as well as into himself, even into those who *wanted* to support him.

We misread his intolerance with himself as a disgust with society. He was – still is – one of those players who cannot quickly get rid of a bad round, but who needs twenty minutes alone to compose himself and find again the man who gives his time gratis to junior clinics. This Dave Barr often gets left in the locker-room.

He has been burdened, too, by our expectations, as was Knudson. At Canadian Opens we put him in a glass case, stripped of the anonymity that protects him in other Tour events. To see what this does to a man, we have only to look at 1990. The strain of leading, of staying among the frontrunners for sixty-two holes, of knowing that we were writing and saying that this year, surely, must be Canada's year – all this is too much weight to hump over the last ten tough holes of Glen Abbey.

We now know Dave Barr to be a sensitive and caring man, a person of high personal integrity, one of the most highly principled and most professional professionals we have

nurtured (or the PGA Tour has nurtured). Still, all attempts to make him a hero have been foiled by his apparent determination to remain humble. Does he enjoy playing golf? Do *you* enjoy being a dentist? Golf is his chosen profession. He has no illusions about the romance of its traditions.

Dave Barr turned professional in 1974. His record may not be impressive by the standard of George Knudson in that, so far, he has won only two events on the PGA Tour. But against this, Barr can point to a win in the World Cup of 1983, when he was the lowest individual scorer, and to a tie for second place in the U.S. Open. In 1988 he won some $291,000 in official PGA Tour events and finished thirty-third on the money list, admittedly at a time when the prize money was many times greater than in the days of Knudson and Balding.

Despite the high purses on the PGA Tour, he has continued to come back to Canada to play in CPGA fixtures. This is partly out of loyalty to a Canadian tour that gave him his first winnings. He also recognizes that his name can help attract CPGA sponsors. Not that he and the sponsors have always seen eye to eye. He spoke bitterly against one of them when he felt it was giving Canadian professionals a raw deal.

For the most part, his appearances on the Canadian tour have also been financially rewarding (although there is no saying what he might have won had he competed that week in the U.S.). He has less to show in the way of national titles. He won the CPGA championship in 1985, the TPD championship in 1988. He was not the only one to be disappointed in his performance in the Canadian Open before 1988, when he tied for third place, only two strokes behind the winner.

Dave Barr was born in 1952, into a working-class family in Kelowna, B.C. He caddied at the local golf club, picking up the game in the customary way, using clubs discarded by his aunt. At the age of twelve or so, he was good enough to play on the municipal course, and he later had a junior membership at Kelowna GC. By fifteen, he was down to a handicap of 3 and was discovering that practice can be a pleasure in itself. When he started scoring in the 60s in amateur tournaments, Dave Barr knew that he wanted to be a golf professional.

He had limited success as an amateur in provincial and national events, apart from his second place in the 1972 Amateur. But his record was good enough to earn him a full scholarship at Oral Roberts University. For three years he was top man on the university golf team and a second team All-American to boot. In 1973 he placed fifth in the NCAA championships and won the Oklahoma State title. He did not wait to graduate in 1974, but chose to go after his CPGA playing card. He succeeded, and the professional Dave Barr was launched.

The six-feet-one-inch 180-pound Dave Barr came on to the Canadian tour at a time when it was being sponsored by Peter Jackson, and he won five provincial Opens in five years. By the time Peter Jackson pulled out, Barr had qualified for the PGA Tour at his third attempt.

Life on the PGA Tour was not kind to him for the first few years, when his official winnings met only half his living expenses. But he did survive. Then, in July 1981, he went to the Quad Cities Open at Coal Valley, Illinois – an unprepossessing name, sounding more like a battleplace in the Civil War. Five strokes behind going into the last round, he shot a sizzling 66. The event went into a five-man play-off, two of them Canadians, Barr and Halldorson.

Dave Barr has been involved in a number of long play-offs in his time. (He and Halldorson were to set what is probably a CPGA record in 1985, when the two of them scrapped for eleven extra holes in the Quebec Open.) At Coal Valley, Halldorson fell out with two others at the first hole. Barr needed eight holes to dispose of the American, Blackburn. This was not the longest play-off in the history of the Tour, but it was very close to it.

Barr's first-place money of $36,000 probably saved his career. He admitted at the time that he might well have quit touring in the U.S. had 1981 been as bad as the first four years. The self-confidence he found that day, the sudden release from the pressure of trying and failing, was as valuable as the cash. He struggled on, having cleared the first hurdle. But 1982 was dismal, and it took Barr two more years to break through to the comfort zone of steady money.

His second win on the tour may not have been as cathartic as his first, but it was much more satisfactory – to us Canadians – than his first. During the Quad Cities Open, most of the big names had been playing in the British Open. In May 1987 he defeated a tougher field, to win the Atlanta Classic by four strokes from Masters champion Larry Mize. His putter obeyed him that day. One behind with a round to go, and tied with Mize on the front nine, he shot four consecutive birdies on the back.

Dave Barr went through the U.S. college school of golf, which usually turns out golfers with swings made from a pattern mould, many of them indistinguishable. That is perhaps as it should be, if we are looking for perfection. But the world of golf somehow seems a duller place.

But Dave Barr is not one of these clones. He has learned how to work his own vein. His swing is among the most individualistic on the Tour, a carryover from his youth. He acquired an education at Oral Roberts but would not let a scholarship tamper with the way he swung a golf club. Peter Alliss has described it as a "caddie swing," meaning that it is original in execution, as many swings were when caddies taught themselves by mimicking others.

Barr has a ten-fingered grip. He picks the club up quickly, has a seemingly short, quick upright back-swing, during which he cocks his wrists, a habit that has earned him the nickname of "Hands." (He "waggles with the wrists," someone once wrote of him.) The clubhead comes flashing through at an incredible speed. He is happiest when he can play at the same speed.

In recent years, he has shown that he can overcome the burden of a bad hole, just as he can isolate himself from the field around him. This was manifest in the way he handled himself in the 1985 U.S. Open.

In the final round at Oakland Hills Country Club, Barr had a two-stroke lead at the twelfth hole. But his lead came and went so quickly he was not aware of it, and so was never burdened by thinking of what he would say in his acceptance speech. If you watched this final round, you may remember it by the disaster that befell the unfortunate T. C. Chen of Taiwan, who self-destructed his lead by taking a quadruple bogey on the fifth hole. This gave an opening to Barr and others, notably Andy North.

After Barr had hit to the short seventeenth, he met North walking off the sixteenth. They were tied. The men exchanged smiles. This should not be happening, the smiles said. Who did Barr and North think they were, topping the U.S. Open leaderboard?

Barr had chosen a 3-iron to play this 206-yard hole. The tee was sheltered from a following wind, which he could not feel, so his ball went through the green into the rough. He played a flop shot rather than a pitch and run, to give the ball a chance of stopping near the flag, but the ball ran too far. He missed the putt. He also bogeyed the eighteenth when his drive found a fairway bunker. Still, his putt for a par skirted the hole.

Barr finished in second place to North and tied with Chen and the South African Denis Watson.

Some critics had Dave Barr "choking" on the last two holes; others blamed his swing. But there was never any evidence of him changing his routine, and his swing had won him second place in the U.S. Open, unprecedented for a Canadian.

The rapid changes of fortune in the last round of this U.S. Open had given us no time to savour Dave Barr's challenge. Not so in the Canadian Open three years later. In the final round he shot two bogeys, eight birdies, a brilliant 66 at Glen Abbey, to go 11 under par. Shortly after he finished, the rains came, and play was suspended for the day. Still out on the course at 15 under was Ken Green. But he had seven holes to go, and there was no saying how the rain would affect the course and the scoring.

By the time play was resumed on the Monday morning, the rain had stopped, but a cold,

gusty wind was blowing. When Green bogeyed the second hole of the morning, some thought that Barr's 11 under might be good enough. But others out on the course started firing birdies. In the event, Green steadied himself enough to hold on to a one-stroke lead. Dave Barr was only two strokes back and tied for third place. You have to go back to Pat Fletcher's win in 1954 to find a Canadian who finished higher.

As important to Dave Barr as his placing was his reception by the Glen Abbey gallery: "They've been fabulous all week. I had chills up my spine coming up the eighteenth." The same galleries had been pressuring him: "Win it for us, win it for us." He didn't need that kind of pressure, he reminded us.

Once the Canadian tour had found its feet again, Dave Barr would forfeit his chance of American dollars to support CPGA events. He had won the championship in 1985 and come north again in 1988, a favourite to repeat. He had just tied for the Greater Hartford Open after firing a closing round of 63, only to lose in the play-off.

At Emerald Hills, Ontario, he set a new course record on the first day. But this came to naught in the fourth round, when he put his ball into the water at the seventeenth, to lose by a stroke to young Brent Franklin. Disgusted with himself for such an unprofessional performance, Barr refused to talk to anyone and went off to catch his plane.

A few weeks later he was back, this time to make no such mistake in the TPD championship. He won in a play-off against Australian Mark Officer.

Dave Barr has represented Canada eight times in the World Cup. In 1983, he had the lowest individual score, which is like winning the world championship of golf. The other Canadian on the team that won the cup in 1985 was his friend and fellow tour player, Dan Halldorson.

When Dan Halldorson won the Pensacola Open in the fall of 1980, he ended his apprenticeship on the PGA Tour. With the benefit of hindsight, we can say that his win was predictable. He had finished second at the Tucson Open, had tied for sixth at the noted Memorial. "The low-keyed Canadian," the PGA Tour called him in its press release. "One of the game's rising talents."

A few weeks after Pensacola, Halldorson and Jim Nelford flew down to the El Rincon Golf Club in Bogota, Colombia. For the second time in twenty years, Canada won the World Cup. Canada had two rising talents.

So 1980 was a very good year for Dan Halldorson. He finished in thirty-sixth place in the PGA money list. No Canadian professional had performed so well on the tour since Knudson.

Dan Halldorson went on to play in a total of five World Cup teams. His wins with Jim Nelford in 1980 and with Dave Barr in 1985 make him the only Canadian ever to be on two winning teams. He also went on to lift the CPGA title (1986) as well as a number of events on the Canadian Tour.

Dan Halldorson came to the PGA Tour the hard way. Born in Winnipeg in 1952, he took up golf in the late 1950s, during a vacation at Sandy Hook, some sixty miles north. He shagged balls for Wilf Homenuik, the professional. His game quickly improved. As a junior, he represented Manitoba in 1969 and 1970, and won the Manitoba Junior in 1970 playing out of Brandon G & CC. But he was not to make a name for himself as a national amateur or to try for a golf scholarship. He turned professional when he was still in high school, and he had an early success when he won the Manitoba PGA title in 1971.

In spite of a Canadian tour rejuvenated under Peter Jackson, the attraction of the PGA Tour was greater. Halldorson qualified in the fall of 1974. In his first year he accumulated the grand total of $619 in official prize money and lost his playing privileges. He had not been helped by a viral infection but did not make excuses. ("I knew my game wasn't good enough for the Tour," he admitted later.) For three years Halldorson worked on his game at home, in Manitoba, running a small golf school at Brandon.

The year 1977 saw him on the Canadian tour. Having won the Manitoba and Saskatchewan Opens, he tried golfing in the Far East that winter. A second Manitoba Open win, and a high finish in the CPGA championship, led to his selection for the World Cup teams of 1978 and 1979. In the meantime, persuaded by the evidence of an improved game, he had tried again for his PGA Tour card. He qualified in the fall of 1978.

His first year was poor, but then came 1980. Dan Halldorson's first win on the Tour did as much for his confidence as it did for his bank balance. "I learned at Pensacola that I can play with these guys on the Tour; in fact, I won the tournament without playing all that well. I take a lot of pride in my ability to manage my game even when I'm not striking the ball that well." His great strength was his consistency, his ability to reach the green in regulation.

His second PGA win came in 1986. The Deposit Guaranty Golf Classic at Hattiesburg is traditionally held at the time of the Masters in Augusta, so it does not attract the top players. Halldorson shot only one bogey in four rounds, to win by two from Paul Azinger. His prize money ($36,000) was considered as official earnings, although his victory was not looked upon as an official PGA win.

Dan Halldorson's demeanour on the golf course has not always been as mild as it is today. He had to work at controlling a short fuse, just as he had to work on his game. Health problems have not made it easy for him to keep his PGA card. Like Barr, he comes back to play in Canada. Although only thirty-nine, he is looked upon as a kind of elder statesman, and he does what he can to promote the Canadian tour. This was recognized by his election to the presidency of the Tournament Players Division of the CPGA.

For a time it looked as though the third of our PGA Tour quartet, Nelford, might just be about the best golfer we had produced since Knudson. He could hardly have performed better as a young amateur. And within two years of joining the Tour, he and Halldorson went on to win the World Cup. But while Barr and Halldorson registered wins on tour, victory eluded Nelford.

As a person, he had most of what it takes to turn success on the course into money. He was athletic, handsome, articulate, and had a good knowledge of the game. As an amateur, he had confidence in himself, although at times this was taken for cockiness, even arrogance.

Having won the B.C. high school championship and the B.C. Junior title in 1973, he made an impressive first win in the Canadian Amateur in 1975, at the age of twenty. Back-to-back eagles on the last nine gave him a 4-stroke victory over clubmate Doug Roxburgh.

Nelford made another dramatic finish in 1976, to retain his Amateur title. Going into the back nine he was something like seven shots behind the leader, the young Mexican champion Rafael Alarcon. But while Alarcon went on to register three bogeys, Nelford exploded with four birdies to catch him. A scrambling Alarcon held on until the second hole of sudden death, where Nelford sunk a 15-foot putt to retain his title.

Nelford impressed those who saw him with the manner of his wins. This purposeful youngster had all the poise and confidence of a veteran. He could strike the ball well and was beginning to show he had a full repertoire of shots in his bag, no doubt the result of frequent competition as a member of the golf team at Brigham Young University, where he had a golf scholarship.

He came back in 1977 not only to attempt the defence of a title, but also to try for a record in the modern history of the Amateur. Not since George S. Lyon in 1907 had there been three consecutive wins.

At Hamilton's Ancaster course, Nelford shot a dazzling 64 in the second round, to equal the course record set by Armour in 1930. He opened with an eagle 2 and went on to shoot another eagle in a five under par outward nine of 30. His approaching and putting could not have been bettered. A player noted for his fine closing rounds, Nelford seemed to have the championship sewn up on that second day.

Four strokes ahead of Rod Spittle going into the last round, Nelford still seemed secure. But then things went sour. The golf course got its own back on this young upstart, as courses have a habit of doing. He started to play protective golf, trying to preserve his lead, something that was out of character. His closing 75 was two strokes too many; Spittle, with a 69, had spoiled the champion's dream.

Nelford had the satisfaction of being the leading amateur in the Open that year (the only one to make the cut), his first of several fine appearances at Glen Abbey. He also won the U.S. Western Amateur, and fought his way to the fifth round of the British Amateur, perhaps the finest achievement of all. He then turned professional.

Born in Vancouver in 1955, Jim Nelford had taken up golf as a boy of eight while on a visit to an aunt and uncle in Saskatchewan. Like many others, he had to choose between hockey and golf and concluded he was too small for hockey (five feet ten inches, 155 pounds, in his early twenties). He played on a local municipal course until his father bought him a junior membership at Pitt Meadows in Haney, B.C. He was then thirteen. By the age of eighteen he was down to scratch and had won his first provincial title, the B.C. Junior.

In 1974, he was awarded a part-scholarship to Brigham Young, and for four years he worked his way through college golf, becoming a regular member of the BYU team. Back in B.C. for vacations, he would play at that great West Coast nursery, Marine Drive, alongside some of the country's top amateurs like Roxburgh. When he turned professional, Jim Nelford had as good a blooding as could be wished for.

In 1984, Jim Nelford came out with a book, *Seasons in a Golfer's Life*, co-authored by golf writer Lorne Rubenstein. It tells of his life on the PGA Tour in the years 1978–83. In many respects, this is a sad book, but revealing. Nelford experimented with his swing until he injured himself. After qualifying for the Tour in his first attempt, in the fall of 1977, he lost all the confidence he should have had after such a fine career as an amateur. He looked around for reasons for his failure and, for a time at least, seemed to blame everyone but himself. He started to play what he calls "scared golf." He stopped thinking of success as winning on the Tour, but as finishing in the top 125 money-winners, so he would not have to qualify next year. His sour golf led to sour business deals. Sponsors, he alleged, let him down. The only highlight of his career was winning the World Cup with Halldorson in 1980.

By the end of 1983, Nelford thought his apprenticeship was over. That had been a good year. He had won enough in place money to finish fiftieth on the money list, by far his best season yet. But the next year saw him slip back.

In 1979, Nelford had played at Pebble Beach in what was then the Bing Crosby tournament, one of the top events after the majors. He had needed a birdie on the last hole to tie but drove into the rocks on the beach, double-bogeyed, and finished sixth.

In 1984, the positions were reversed. Nelford was the leader in the clubhouse, and the only man who could catch him, Hale Irwin, also needed a birdie to tie. Well, Irwin got his, but in a fashion that will long be remembered by those who saw it. He pulled the ball slightly, in trying to cut the corner, just as Nelford had done in 1979. But Irwin's ball hit a rock and rebounded onto the fairway. From there he made the green and sank his putt for the birdie he needed.

In the second hole of the sudden-death play-off, Irwin made another remarkable shot, but this time he relied on skill and not luck. His drive finished in a bunker, some 210 yards from the green. He hit an iron to within feet of the hole and sank his putt for a birdie. That was the closest Jim Nelford came to winning an official PGA Tournament.

In September 1985, while water-skiing at Lake Saguaro, near his home in Phoenix, Nelford was struck by a motorboat. The propeller ripped into his right side and arm. The arm was shattered, broken in nine places, the ulnar nerve severed. Nelford spent weeks in hospital and some five months resting before starting on a program of rehabilitation.

After months of frustration, he returned to the Tour in 1987. But his arm had lost about a third of its strength and feeling, and he lost his PGA playing card.

Nelford still shows great courage in the face of disaster and shattered hopes. He was thirty years old at the time, an age when a professional golfer could be reaching his best years. Although he was back playing the Tour in 1987 and 1988, all the dreams he had of winning the Canadian Open are probably for naught, and somehow he has to become reconciled to this. There is this small consolation, that he has proved himself to be one of the finest colour commentators of golf on television.

We will remember the young Jim Nelford who thrilled us at the Canadian Open in 1979. He was still a few days short of being twenty-four, and one of only two Canadians to make the cut. A newly formed Nelford's Navy (in competition with Arnie's Army) cheered his every shot. Self-possessed beyond his years, Jim Nelford had the world by the tail that week. He finished eighth, the best showing by a Canadian in years. The crowd rose to him at the eighteenth green on the last day. In those days, he still had confidence in himself. "I'll be back to try again next year," he said. "I can win it." Yes, that is how we shall remember him.

Richard Zokol is of more recent minting. We first cheered him home at Glen Abbey in the Open of 1984. There he was, twenty-five years of age, paired with the great Trevino in the final round. "Take it from me, that kid has all the equipment to be the best Canadian in this tournament, maybe even win it," Nick Weslock had warned us before the Open started. Well, Zokol did not win, but he put on the best showing of a Canadian in fifteen years, tying for fifth place. He kept his cool in that final round with Trevino, and outgolfed his companion by shooting a cool 70. His composure was impressive. As we shall see, he was to thrill us again in the 1988 Open.

Keeping his composure was important to Richard Zokol, but not always easy. "I'm not out there playing golf," he once said, "I'm playing mind games. When I'm successful, I will be able to control both the golf ball and myself."

Nobody has worked harder at controlling himself – meaning those extraneous thoughts that superheat the mind and, as J. Douglas Edgar might have put it, unhinge the gate to golf. In an effort to conquer the mental side of golf, Zokol has worn headphones on the course, playing FM music in his ears, earning him the sobriquet of Disco Dick. He has tried lining up his shot in a fixed routine, performing a new form of waggle, raising and lowering the club as he addresses the ball, as though engaged in some religious rite. (We don't really know why a golfer waggles any more than we know why a hen shakes its head, or why trains shunt in the night.) All this on the advice of a sports psychologist. It is all very well to say that Charlie Murray never needed a sports psychologist. Charlie was playing for perhaps a month's wages; Zokol is playing for his future. "I can not concentrate for four hours, I get negative thoughts," he explained. Somehow, he had to control his turbulent emotions during a tournament. These tactics seemed to work, for a time.

Richard Zokol was the youngest of the four Canadians who played on the PGA Tour for most of the 1980s. He was also another British Columbian, and another product of Marine Drive, playing golf since he was a boy of eleven and caddying until he was sixteen. Like Nelford before him, he attended Brigham Young University, although he did not get a golf scholarship until his second year. In 1981, he captained the BYU team that won the NCAA championships.

That was a very good year for Richard Zokol, for he also won the Canadian Amateur championship. Coming up through the same junior program at Marine Drive as Roxburgh and Nelford, the B.C. and Canadian Junior titles had somehow eluded him. And his Canadian title came only after a hard fight and a play-off. But many thought this bright, athletic young man – five feet nine inches, 155 pounds, he also played racquetball and soccer – might well be the first Marine Driver to bring the Open title to the club.

He qualified for the PGA Tour in 1981 but has had to requalify several times since. He came nearest to winning a PGA event in 1988 and 1990, when he placed second.

Jerry Anderson attended the University of Texas on a partial scholarship but quit after two years. He then earned his spurs by playing golf around the world. Off and on for about ten years, he has been a golfing globetrotter, playing on the European Tour (which included Tokyo) and also in Malaysia, Thailand, Australia, New Zealand, South Africa, and South America.

A native of Montreal, Anderson moved to Scarborough, Toronto, when he was fourteen. After a comparatively undistinguished career as an amateur, he turned professional in 1978, at the age of twenty-three. He earned his CPGA playing card that year and in the following year won several provincial Opens. He did not try to qualify for the PGA Tour. Having played in South America and Australia, he decided to hone his game in Europe and other golfing countries. The European Tour had several world-class golfers, including Seve Ballesteros of Spain and Bernhard Langer of Germany. Sponsors and television were then combining to raise purses. The increase in demand had also led to a revival of British professional golf and the emergence of world-class professionals such as Nick Faldo and Sandy Lyle, who helped to improve the stature of the game in Europe. The Ryder Cup was no longer a walk-over for the U.S. team, as it had been for many years with one or two exceptions.

Anderson spent several years as a golfing nomad in various parts of the world, winning barely enough to exist. But his game improved as he played against such up-and-coming stars as Greg Norman of Australia, on their home turf. In terms of tournament golf, he was becoming street-wise.

During one of his summer visits to Canada in 1982, he was leading Canadian in the Open. That was good enough to earn him a place in Canada's World Cup team in 1983.

But 1984 was his most successful season. He came second in the German Open, after

Four of the Canadian Women on the LPGA Tour

Barbara Bunkowsky. PHOTO BY DON VICKERY.

Dawn Coe. PHOTO BY DON VICKERY.

Tina Tombs Purtzer. PHOTO BY DON VICKERY.

Lisa Walters. PHOTO BY DON VICKERY.

The winning Canadian team in the 1979 Commonwealth Team Matches in Australia. Left to right, Marilyn Palmer O'Connor, Gail Harvey Moore, Marlene Stewart Streit, Stacey West, Michèle Guilbault. COURTESY CLGA.

Hurrah! I've won! Cathy Graham Sherk wins the U. S. Women's Amateur in 1978. COURTESY GOLF JOURNAL OF THE UNITED STATES GOLF ASSOCIATION.

Canada wins again, in New Zealand in 1987 with, left to right, Gail Anderson, Cathy Burton, Jennifer Wyatt, Audrey Bendick, Judy Medlicott, and Heather Alexander (non-playing captain). COURTESY CLGA.

Marilyn Palmer O'Connor, internationalist, and winner of the Canadian Ladies' Close in 1966, and of the Open in 1986. COURTESY CLGA.

Canada wins the World Amateur Team Championship for the first time in 1986, in Caracas, Venezuela. Left to right, Geordie Hilton (RCGA executive director), Mark Brewer, Dr. Douglas Brewer (captain, and president of the RCGA), Warren Sye, Jack Kay Jr., and Brent Franklin. COURTESY RCGA.

Jerry Anderson, the winner of the CPGA championship in 1987, with the P. D. Ross Cup. COURTESY CPGA.

Jim Rutledge, winner in 1984. COURTESY CPGA.

Dave Barr, winner in 1985. COURTESY CPGA.

Four Regular Guys on Tour in the 1980s

Dan Halldorson. PHOTO BY GEORGE ALKHAS.

Dave Barr. PHOTO BY DON VICKERY.

Jim Nelford. PHOTO BY DON VICKERY.

Richard Zokol. COURTESY *SCORE.*

Glen Abbey and the Open

PHOTO BY GEORGE ALKHAS.

*Once an Abbey, now Golf House, home of
the RCGA* (PHOTO BY MINORA MATUSHIGE) . . .

*. . . and housing the Canadian Golf Hall of
Fame* (PHOTO BY ERIK HEPPNER) . . .

. . . and a library. PHOTO BY ERIK
HEPPNER.

. . . others, around the green of the short but treacherous third hole (PHOTO BY GEORGE ALKHAS) *. . .*

Many congregate around the clubhouse overlooking the eighteenth green (PHOTO BY LISA LEIGHTON, COURTESY *SCORE*) *. . .*

Some of the many volunteers at the Open. COURTESY RCGA.

Others like the view from up top; a television camara aloft. PHOTO BY GEORGE ALKHAS.

Two Who Did Not Win at Glen Abbey

George Knudson . . . (COURTESY RCGA)

. . . and Jack Nicklaus (not yet). PHOTO BY GEORGE ALKHAS.

Nicklaus came closest when he lost in sudden death to Tom Weiskopf at Royal Montreal in 1975. COURTESY RCGA.

Bruce Lietzke, winner in 1978 and 1982, seen here in 1978 with, left to right, Edmond Ricard of Imperial Tobacco, RCGA *president Bruce Bailey, and Dick Grimm.* COURTESY RCGA.

Curtis Strange, winner in 1985 and 1987. COURTESY RCGA.

Greg Norman, winner in 1984, cannot believe what a golf ball will do . . . PHOTO BY GEORGE ALKHAS.

The second-oldest winner ever was Bob Murphy in 1986. PHOTO BY GEORGE ALKHAS.

One of the few recent Canadian Open winners to be bred in Britain, Peter Oosterhuis, receiving his cheque and Inuit carving from, left to right, tournament chairman Bill Farlinger, Edmond Ricard, and RCGA president Ralph Costello, in 1981. COURTESY RCGA.

shooting a final round of 63. A week later, he went to Valais, Switzerland, and with rounds of 63 66 66 66–261, won the European Masters by five strokes. Prize money of some $80,000 in two weeks lifted him to ninth place in the European Order of Merit. His win also gave him exempt status on the European Tour for several years.

Then came a slump. The mental side of the game was partly to blame, aggravated by back problems. For a year or two he seriously thought of quitting. But in 1987, temporarily back in Canada and playing on the CPGA Tour in summer, things started to improve. He won the CPGA championship and a place in his second World Cup team. In 1989 he qualified for the PGA Tour.

Anderson is still a world golfer, if not a world-class golfer. He was Canada's first, and for a time its sole, nomadic touring professional. Understandably, he lists one of his special interests as "jet lag."

Another Canadian with reasonable success in Europe and in Asia is Jim Rutledge of Victoria. Rutledge turned professional in 1978 when only eighteen, a year after he won the Canadian Junior. Playing on the CPGA Tour in the summer months, he has been consistently in the top ten, and he won the CPGA championship in 1984.

It has been said for years that it is only a matter of time before Jim Rutledge breaks through, since he appears to have all that is needed to succeed – a notorious length off the tee, a good short game, and a fine temperament. But while playing well and profitably in Europe, he has failed in more than half a dozen attempts to qualify for the PGA Tour. (Perhaps his most remarkable golfing feat was in 1983, when he was trying to qualify. Needing to make up seven strokes in the final round to go on to the next qualifying stage, he shot nine birdies in ten holes.)

Ray Stewart has replaced Nelford – at least temporarily – as the fourth Canadian professional on the PGA Tour. Born in Matsqui, B.C., in 1953, he did not take up golf until he was seventeen, and it was another six years before he took it up seriously. A graduate of the University of British Columbia, he took up golf too late to think of golf scholarships. He is an electrical

Ray Stewart practises under the eye of Jack McLaughlin.

contractor by profession, but his love of the game pushed him into professionalism in 1980.

Stewart played the Asian Tour from 1981 to 1983, when he won his PGA playing card. But he was not then ready for the Tour and has held his card intermittently since. A second try in 1989 has proved more successful, and he has retained his card into 1991.

In 1988, when twenty-two-year-old Brent Franklin won the CPGA championship in his first year on the Canadian Tour, he established something of a record. He had worked his way up through the ranks, undefeated, winning the Junior twice, the Amateur three times, and then the CPGA, in a string of six straight national titles.

Born in Barrie, Ontario, but playing most of his golf out of Vancouver or Calgary, Franklin won his two national Juniors by the whopping margins of nine and eleven strokes (1983, 1984). He then proceeded to do what only George S. Lyon has done before – win three Amateurs in a row. One needed a play-off against the experienced Stu Hamilton; another was by only a stroke over Jack Kay Jr. This even-tempered young man seems one of our best prospects in years. When he was attending Brigham Young University – Nelford's and Zokol's alma mater – Zokol fingered him as a much better prospect than either himself or Nelford.

Franklin is only one of a bunch of young Canadians getting experience on foreign tours. We have already met Rick Gibson, yet another Brigham Young scholarship player and another All American. He won the CPGA championship in 1990.

Danny Mijovic, Amateur champion in 1983, won the Mexican Open a year later. He tried several times to get his PGA Tour card but failed. In 1990, he finished second in the Asian Tour order of merit.

Jack Kay Jr., like Franklin, was a member of our winning team in the 1986 World Amateur Team Championship. He won his PGA card in 1989 but did not retain it. He has since been on the nomad's circuit in the Far East.

On these foreign tours, competitors play on courses that vary widely in architecture and condition and in a wide variety of climate. Once tournament-hardened, who knows what Opens may be won by Franklin, Mijovic, Gibson, and Jack Kay Jr.

When Sandra Post left the LPGA Tour in 1983, having played only perfunctorily for a year or so, it looked as though we had several candidates ready to fill her cleats, all having the technical skills needed to win tournaments and lacking only experience.

A record of seven Canadians went on the LPGA Tour in 1984. With one exception, they had gone through the grinder of U.S. college golf: Dawn Coe, Lynn Cooke, and Dawne Kortgaard at Lamar University in Texas; Barbara Bunkowsky and Lisa Young at Florida State in Tallahassee; Judy Ellis at Ohio State.

But the one exception, the oldest and the most experienced, held perhaps the highest promise of all. She had, after all, been coached by Gord McInnis, who had given us Marlene Stewart Streit. She had won our Ladies' Open twice. More impressively, that same year she had won the formidable U.S. women's amateur title – a feat equalled only by Marlene – just a year after being runner-up. And she had crowned this achievement by winning, in effect, the women's world amateur championship.

An all-round athlete, Cathy Graham (later Mrs. Sherk) excelled in volleyball, basketball, badminton, and hockey. She turned to golf after shagging balls for her older brother, to give herself something to do in the summer months. In 1966, sixteen years old, she golfed for a season at Beechwood, a public course in Niagara Falls, before moving to the semi-private Willow-Dell.

The game did not come naturally to her at an early age as it had to Marlene Streit. Her progress was steady but slow until 1972, when she had the good fortune to meet Gord McInnis at a golf school and land a job at Lookout Point. McInnis subjected her to the rigours of his keen but merciless eye and his few words, making her concentrate on the basics as he had made a young Marlene Stewart and Anne Sharpe concentrate twenty years earlier.

Married in January 1973, Cathy Sherk's progress was temporarily halted in 1974 when she became pregnant, and she played no competitive golf in 1975, when her son was born. In the following year, she was runner-up to Marlene in the Ontario championship. By now the ambition was firmly fixed in her mind to beat her friend Marlene, to prove her ability not just to Gord McInnis but to herself.

In 1977, Cathy Sherk had her first national success. She won the Canadian Ladies' Amateur in dramatic fashion, shooting a competitive course record in the final round.

This win was doubly important to her. Only a week before she had lost her bid for the U.S. Ladies' Amateur title, to former winner Beth Daniel, at the 35th hole of the final. She came to the Canadian championships tired, and no doubt dejected. That she managed to shrug off

the physical and mental fatigue and the disappointment of losing marked her as a worthy successor to her clubmate, and as another success for Gord McInnis.

If we expected great things from Cathy Sherk, she was not to disappoint us. She made 1978 *her* year in women's amateur golf in North America. She won the U.S. Ladies' Amateur Championship, and retained her Canadian title, to be ranked number one in both countries. In the Women's World Amateur Team Championship, she had the lowest individual score, making her, in effect, the world's finest woman amateur. And on top of this, she achieved that long-held ambition of forcing Marlene Streit into second place in the fight for the Ontario title.

In the U.S. championships at Sunnybrook GC, Pennsylvania, defending champion Beth Daniel was the favourite. But her putter let her down in the quarter-finals, and she lost to Cindy Hill, the winner in 1974. Cathy Graham Sherk played sub-par golf to dispose of her first four opponents in an astonishing 59 holes.

Stacey West after winning the Canadian Junior in 1976.

Heather Kuzmich won an unprecedented four Canadian Junior titles, 1981–84.

Gord McInnis flew down to see his prize pupil perform. There is no record of what he thought of her after nine holes of the semi-final against Ms. Hill, particularly of her bunker play. Both girls played poorly, halving only one of the first nine holes. The second nine was not much better, but Cathy Sherk managed somehow to take a 1-hole lead at the seventeenth, and to make a difficult downhill approach shot for a half – and the match – at the last hole.

In the final, she met U.S. Curtis Cup player, Judy Oliver, a tediously slow and fidgety player, who plays as if she were standing on hot coals. But this did not faze Cathy. A birdie at the first hole helped. Although caught, she was never behind in her match. Three up going to lunch, she won by 4 and 3.

Writing in the USGA's *Golf Journal*, Charles Brome tells us amusingly of Gord McInnis's reaction:

> Did Mrs. Sherk's triumph at Sunnybrook finally provoke her teacher into an exhibition of unrestrained delight? Well, McInnis did weaken to the extent of taking both her hands in his for a moment. He even admitted, speaking very low, so one had to strain very hard to hear, that this time she had played well. Perhaps very well. Except, of course, for going to sleep on the third hole

Cathy Graham Sherk and Gord McInnis put on a clinic for juniors.

during the afternoon . . . Then he paused, and his face clouded.

Here was his star pupil, who had just become the first to win the national championships of both Canada and the United States in the same year since Marlene Stewart in 1956. Surely no one could have done better than that?

"We should have sent you to the British Championship, too," McInnis muttered. And he stalked away.

Would she now turn professional? She would think about it. First there was the matter of the Women's World Amateur Team Championship, in Fiji.

As it turned out, this was a cliffhanger. Canada lost to Australia, but only by a stroke, having made up five in the final round. Cathy Sherk's 72 74 76 72–294 gave her a four-stroke victory over Australia's Jane Lock for the unofficial individual title.

Having shown herself to be the finest woman amateur golfer in the world, Cathy Sherk gave up her clerical and managerial duties at the Cherry Hill CC – where she had been working since 1974 – turned professional, and joined the LPGA Tour. This softly-spoken, somewhat shy golfer could hit a long ball, had a fine tempo, a sure touch around the greens, a calm temperament, and an ability to concentrate. In short, she seemed to have all the qualifications needed to be a successful touring professional. But success did not come. The magic ingredient, which enabled a Beth Daniel to convert from a top amateur to a top professional, was missing.

Looking back on her six years on the LPGA Tour, Cathy Sherk now admits she had set out with no clear image of what she wanted to achieve. As an amateur, her goal had always been clear – to beat Marlene and to make herself Canada's top amateur golfer. A professional goal was more elusive. Just being on tour and competing against named players seemed an end in itself. That is not to say she played badly or was disillusioned. She constantly made money. But the icing on the cake – that all-important first win – eluded her.

After half a dozen seasons, Cathy Graham Sherk quit the tour. In 1989 she opened the Sherkwood Golf School in St. Catharines.

She was still to write a few more lines in our golf history. In 1987, she became the first CPGA Ladies' champion, in an event attended by some sixteen women professionals from across Canada. In 1989, she became the first woman to compete in a TPD event, when she entered the Ontario Open, played over Lookout Point. "It was my home club," she explains. "I owed it to Gord. And to George Knudson." The event was a memorial to George, whom she had never met. A gracious touch, from a gracious lady.

The other Canadian girls on the LPGA Tour followed what has become the customary route to fame, if not to fortune – success in provincial, sometimes national, championships; playing for Canada in internationals; recruitment by a U.S. college; playing for a college team; graduation (not always); a long apprenticeship on the LPGA tour, or on the Futures Tour. None has looked like approaching the success of Sandra Post, just as no male professional has looked like equalling the success of George Knudson. The standard of play is higher than in Sandra's day, and the competition fiercer. But that can be the excuse of any new generation.

Having said that, it is too early in their playing careers to pass any sort of historical judgement on the Canadian women now on the LPGA Tour. A professional often does not reach his or her best form until over the age of thirty.

Dawn Coe, exactly at that magic age in 1990, has been our most consistent touring professional, post-Post, although she has yet to win. She joined the LPGA Tour in 1984. Her first tournament win has been predicted for years and seems only a matter of time.

Dawn Coe was born in Campbell River, a small community on Vancouver Island. She has been keen on many sports both as a player and a spectator. The nearby March Meadows Golf Club was opened at the right time for her. At the age of twelve, she now had a place to play golf and – perhaps more important – to

acquire the skills that come only with frequent practice. Although a reluctant entrant into B.C. junior golf, she very quickly became a winner of the provincial Junior (1978, 1979).

After one year of college in Canada, she went on a golf scholarship to Lamar University, Texas. There she became an All-American in 1983, her final year on the golf team, and ranked seventh amateur in the NCAA. After winning the B.C. Ladies' (1982, 1983), she went on to win, inevitably it seems, the Canadian Ladies' title in 1983, and to play for Canada in the Commonwealth Tournament and in an International Women's Team Championship in Colombia. Her strong performances that year led to her turning professional.

Her climb in the LPGA rankings has been sure but not always steady. The loss of her mother in 1987 was a harsh blow to overcome and was reflected in her play. In 1990, she finished eleventh on the money list and, with $240,000, won more than any other Canadian golfer, male or female. Nevertheless, that all-important first win on tour has proved elusive.

An early weakness in putting largely overcome, her strength is probably her length and accuracy off the tee and with the long iron.

On tour, in her golf and in her demeanour, Dawn Coe serves as a model for the growing number of Canadian women professionals now playing weekly in LPGA events.

Dawn Coe's closest friend on the Tour is Lisa Young Walters of Prince Rupert (she married coach Mike Walters in 1988), another product of B.C. golf. Winner of the B.C. Ladies' title in 1979, 1980, and 1981, she went on to a scholarship at Florida State and, like team-mate Bunkowsky, became an All-American.

In her early years, she was noted for a short temper. "She didn't want to learn, caused friction on the team," her university coach is quoted as saying. But at univerity she quickly learned how to be more relaxed. If Dawn Coe is not the next Canadian to win an LPGA tournament, Lisa Walters looks a reasonable second bet.

In May 1984, Barbara Bunkowsky, at the age of twenty-five, could look to the future with optimism. By winning the Chrysler–Plymouth Classic that month she did what no Canadian girl had done since Sandra Post – come out on top in an LPGA tournament. She shot a dazzling 66 to catch and pass the experienced Pat Bradley. In only her second year on tour, she finished twenty-fourth on the money list. The LPGA commissioner, John Laupheimer, also thought she had a future: "She shows a lot of maturity, she's a very attractive young lady, and she's going to do a lot out there."

She still had some maturing to do. Within months of her victory, she was criticized for firing her caddie in the middle of the du Maurier Classic, dumping him for another she was rumoured to be personally involved with. Since then, she has had no more wins, although she has occasionally shown flashes of her old brilliance.

Barbara was one of several Canadians in the Florida State University golf team of the early 1980s. (The others were Michèle Guilbault, and Lisa Young.) While there, she played for Canada in the Women's World Amateur Team Championship (1980) and the Sixth Women's International in Paris (1981). But her best performance was her joint runner-up place in the British Ladies' Open Amateur Stroke Play Championship (1982).

Barbara Bunkowsky was brought up on golf. Her father owns the Burlington Springs GC, Ontario, where he is also the professional. She is an experimenter – or was – having tried a number of teachers, including George Knudson and Gord McInnis ("She doesn't know how good she is," Gord has been quoted as saying).

Although she left Montreal for New Hampshire eighteen years ago at the age of ten, Tina Tombs Purtzer is still a Canadian, if not generally considered one of "the Canadian connection" on the LPGA Tour. After winning state championships, she attended Arizona State, where she was twice All-American and ranked as one of the top ten U.S. amateurs in 1984.

She joined the tour in 1988 but played only a few events in her second year. Then in July 1990 she birdied five of the first six holes in the final round of the Toledo Classic, to win by four strokes. Before her win, she was little known in Canada – or in the U.S., for that matter.

The Futures Tour – for those girls who do not get their card on the LPGA Tour – has been in place since 1989, and some new young Canadians are making it their testing ground. One graduate from this is a product also of the Canadian Golf Foundation's scholarship program. Gail Anderson Graham has now progressed to the LPGA Tour, and she must surely be reckoned one of our bright young hopes for the future.

CHAPTER

THE RCGA AND
GLEN ABBEY

THE IDEA THAT THE CANADIAN OPEN should stop its flitting around the country and be played over a golf course specifically designed to house it was not a new idea in 1972. Had you dug deep enough into the psyche of any RCGA president since the Second World War – especially those of Jack Bailey and Bruce Forbes – you would have discovered this craving for a national golf club.

In 1958, Hilles Pickens did a little digging into his own feelings:

> We think that the Royal Canadian Golf Association might consider a National Golf Club, subscribed by well-wishers, to which they could return for each major national championship every second year and thus have certainty of a first-class course for major events and also to take some of the strain off finding suitable clubs to house national tournaments.

The problem was not merely one of finding a suitable golf course, but of finding one with an enormous, if only temporary, carpark, close to a major city, not too far from the U.S. bor-

der, and, preferably, served by public transport. The Open had become a victim of its own success. Ticket sales had tripled since the Second World War. The appeal of Palmer, Nicklaus, and company was stronger in the flesh than on live television. TV, far from keeping spectators away, seemed to attract more every year, all eager to see in person the new icons of golf.

In 1972, the Canadian Open was held in Ontario at the Cherry Hill club. Rod McIsaac, of medium height, found he had difficulty in getting a clear view of the players making their shots.

Cherry Hill treated its spectators no worse than did other courses. Here is Trent Frayne of *The Globe and Mail*, writing in 1974 about the Open at Mississaugua:

> Even on the sunniest days, the [golf] tournament buff's lot is not much. He's rapped $3 for parking up to a mile from the course entrance and, once inside, he discovers that the superstars he's seeking have been swallowed up by their galleries. They probably can't be seen driving because the crowds form

573

a dense horseshoe around the tees, and they often can't be seen putting because waiting crowds are packed a dozen deep at the greens.

Rod McIsaac had more than a passing interest in golf. He was the president of Great Northern Capital Corporation Limited, a real estate planning and development company with more then $200 million in assets across Canada and the United States.

A couple of years earlier, a Great Northern subsidiary had bought several parcels of land near Oakville, totalling some 1,300 acres. These included the property of the semi-private Glen Abbey Golf Club. Great Northern's intention was to hold the land for future residential and commercial development.

On his return from the Open, McIsaac spoke to the manager of the club, Reg Acomb, of his disappointment at seeing so little of the play. The two also discussed a weekend article by *The Globe and Mail*'s Jim Vipond. This much-respected sports editor had been talking to

RCGA governor Dick Grimm, chairman of the Open, and to Bruce Forbes, the association's executive director. He wrote of their ambitions:

[Grimm] wants to make the Canadian Open the fifth-ranked tournament in the world behind the British and U.S. Opens, the Masters and the U.S. PGA. And in the making he is looking for the perfect course as a permanent home for Canada's No. 1 golf tournament.

He has visited many golf courses in the United States and abroad and has talked to touring golf professionals the world over. . . .

Golf executives in the United States and Canada think Grimm is the one man who can make his golf dreams come true. . . .

Grimm and Forbes think along the same lines when discussing the future of tournament golf in Canada . . . A good tournament course need not be overly long with half-acre greens. This type course makes golf a chore for the club member and is not appreciated by the touring pro. . . .

In Toronto, Acomb put the question to Grimm: Would the RCGA be interested in turning Glen Abbey into a permanent home for the Open? Grimm was lukewarm at first. But he listened, noting that the president of

Rod McIsaac, who planted the germ.

Larry O'Brien with Jack Nicklaus, the man who helped it grow.

Great Northern was behind the query and wanted to talk about it face to face.

This led to the first of several meetings between McIsaac, Acomb, Grimm, and Forbes. They considered a number of alternatives for restructuring the Glen Abbey course and had a golf architect draw up route plans for several courses. They eventually agreed that Great Northern would spend several million dollars turning Glen Abbey into a championship course, open to the public, designed for spectators, and that the RCGA would contract to use it for the Open for twenty years.

Great Northern would become the owner of a championship golf course, highly publicized and highly regarded. It might not recover its capital expenditure directly from increased membership and green fees. But if the company used the name of Glen Abbey when advertising and promoting the sale of its residential properties, it should at least improve the value of its other eleven hundred acres.

The RCGA governors supported the concept. As sponsor of the Open, Imperial Tobacco was not overjoyed. The Open would no longer be identified every few years with Quebec, where the company had a large share of the market. But Imperial could also see advantages in identifying the Open with a new championship course. It is doubtful if anyone at that stage foresaw just how close this identification would become, or how successful Glen Abbey.

There was a quick consensus that the name of Jack Nicklaus as architect would be another selling point. Nicklaus had been designing courses for several years, first in collaboration with Pete Dye, then with Desmond Muirhead.

Early in the summer of 1973, Grimm, Forbes, and McIsaac met with Nicklaus and Larry O'Brien (who was on the Board of a Nicklaus company, Golden Bear Inc., and assisting Nicklaus on corporate affairs and public relations).

In March 1974, Dick Grimm (appropriately, now the president of the RCGA) signed with Great Northern an agreement to make Glen Abbey the site of the Open for twenty years. At a press conference, presidents Grimm, McIsaac, Edmond Ricard of Imperial Tobacco, and Jack Nicklaus of Golforce Inc. announced to the world, "The Canadian Open Golf Championship is to have a permanent home on a golf course designed by Jack Nicklaus."

Work on the Glen Abbey course got under way early in the following year, with Reg Acomb as project manager. The cost of converting Glen Abbey into a championship course and giving it a modern clubhouse was to come close to four million dollars.

The property at Glen Abbey is split-level, with 80 acres (five holes) in the valley of Sixteen Mile Creek, and 160 acres (thirteen holes) on a plateau some two hundred feet higher.

On the upper level in particular, Nicklaus moved vast volumes of earth. The material from three artificial lakes provided the base of his viewing mounds for spectators. The once-flat fairways were given rolling hills and gentle swales, and new bunkers were filled with imported sand. A thousand trees were planted. Most holes had four teeing areas, so that it could be played from the back tees as a championship course of 7,200 yards, as a medium course of 6,200 to 6,500 yards, or as a short course of 5,600–5,900 yards.

In a 1975 interview with Andy O'Brien, sports editor of *Weekend Magazine*, Jack Nicklaus spoke of how he had put into Glen Abbey all that he had learned about the art of golf course design, and much that was new:

> . . . nowhere else in the world will you find a course so adapted to tournament play that 10 of the 18 holes may be clearly seen by spectators within the area of a football field – 10 holes plus bits of several others. But what pleases me more than those features is the concept of play that I have long wanted to express in a course . . .
>
> Glen Abbey expresses my belief that golf is basically a game of precision, not power. It places stress on strategic rather than punitive design. . . .
>
> The average player may find [Glen Abbey] a bit more difficult than he likes, but the low-handicapper will soon realize that

brains, guile and courage will produce lower scores than muscles. I designed it in line with my belief that every hole calls for one very good shot to score par, and a great shot to score a birdie. The greens are all small (they average 5,000 square feet) because I believe large greens detract from the finesse demanded in chips, pitches and sand shots. Finally, the larger the greens the slower the traffic; the longer the putt the longer a player spends over the putt.

Again with the spectator and green-fee player in mind, half a dozen holes had their greens close to the clubhouse. This is a purely functional building, pyramid-shaped. Its five-tiered roof has seventeen private viewing areas for spectators around the upper perimeter. It can provide food, sustenance, and good viewing for some two thousand. When it first opened, Glen Abbey had private and public parking for some twelve thousand cars within a hundred yards or so of the course. In all these ways, it could easily handle upward of thirty thousand spectators a day.

To mark the official opening of Glen Abbey, Jack Nicklaus played a round of golf with Tom Weiskopf on 1 June 1976. When he came across a tee, a tree, a bunker, or a swale not in keeping with his original concept, he pointed this out to the Golforce consultant accompanying him. He is still doing the same thing fifteen years later. The man is a perfectionist.

Under the terms of the deal struck in 1974, Great Northern leased to the RCGA the clubhouse of the *old* Glen Abbey club, for twenty years, at a rental of one dollar a year. After Great Northern had renovated the building, the RCGA took it over in September 1975. It has since served as the RCGA's Golf House. It includes offices for about twenty staff and rooms for the RCGA's golf library, museum, and the Canadian Golf Hall of Fame.

From 1976, for the first few years of its operation, Glen Abbey had one hundred members who paid an annual fee for the privilege of being able to tee-off at certain times of the day. The members of the 100 Club had the privi-

lege of a small clubhouse at one end of the Golf House building. (There was also a 200 Club, but these members had to use the public clubhouse.)

The history of the Golf House building is recorded in an RCGA brochure:

> Golf House was built in the late 1930's as a private estate for Andre Dorfman, a mining engineer. With its polo fields, gracious rooms and lush gardens nestled in a grove overlooking the sweeping valley through which a river quietly flowed, the property afforded an elegant life style to its residents and guests. In the early fifties, Dorfman turned the property over to the Jesuits, and for a few years the men of the Toronto and Hamilton Dioceses studied in their new retreat, which came to be known as the Abbey. But they too soon moved, feeling the need to settle in the city.

Andre Dorfman was as much a promoter as a mining engineer. He had – as we would now say – "a piece of the action." This piece was lucrative enough to finance homes in New York, on the Riviera, and in Switzerland. Having bought the 350-acre parcel of land near Oakville just before the Second World War, he built what is now the Abbey building, but which he named "Raydor" (a phonetic contraction of the last syllable of his first name and the first syllable of his surname).

In 1952, Dorfman sold the estate to the Society of Jesuits, who used "Raydor" as a retreat house. Locally it became better known as "the Abbey." Faced with the cost of upkeep of the land, the Jesuits sold out to a development corporation, which built a golf course on the property in 1965.

Local legend has the Abbey building haunted by the ghost of an old monk. (Having worked in the building for three years, I'd say the ghostly sounds came from old water pipes.) This was the source of the Glen Abbey logo – a ghostly monk swinging a golf club.

Its new headquarters saved the RCGA some $9,000 a year in rent, a figure not to be sniffed at by an organization chronically hard put to find the cash needed to run its amateur programs. But within a few years, this saving paled in comparison with the funds generated by Glen Abbey and its Opens.

While all these changes were taking place to the old Glen Abbey course, Great Northern had been amalgamated with another realty company and the running of Glen Abbey had been put into the hands of a subsidiary, Abbey Glen Corporation.

The golf course changed hands again in 1976, when Genstar Limited, a leading land developer and house builder in Canada, acquired Abbey Glen Corporation.

Finally, in 1981, Glen Abbey became the property of the Royal Canadian Golf Association. The RCGA had come a long way since 1928, when its secretary had to get board approval to buy a new minute-book. It had come a long way since 1946, when its net annual income would have been barely sufficient to buy a dozen weekly tickets to the 1990 Open.

The RCGA historically had relied on two main sources of income to fund its amateur programs and other activities: the subscriptions of male golfers in member clubs, and the net income from the Open.

By the time it came to look at the financing of the purchase of Glen Abbey, the RCGA had found new and substantial sources of income – sponsors for its amateur events. The Fitness and Amateur Sport Branch of Health and Welfare Canada had long been helping to fund the Willingdon Cup team matches and executive expenses, Pepsi-Cola Canada had long been the sponsor of the Junior interprovincial matches. Air Canada had started to sponsor the national Senior championships, and Crown Life, a Canadian Pro-Am championship. But even so, expenditure on the RCGA services went up at a faster rate than revenue. The deficit had to be met largely by net income from the Open.

The net income from the Open has increased from $25,000 in 1970 to $130,000 in 1980, and to $618,000 in 1990. This at a time when the prize money increased from $125,000 to nearly $1.2 million.

The revenue of the Open derives mainly from:
– Ticket sales. Vigorous marketing by the RCGA's Open committees and the added attraction of golf as a spectator sport has doubled attendance over the last twenty years. An Open is no sooner over than the marketing of the next Open begins.
– The contribution of Imperial Tobacco to the prize money. This has gone up from $105,000 to $641,000 in the same twenty years.
– Television rights. The television rights to the Open have been acquired more consistently by a U.S. network since the Open moved to Glen Abbey.
– The Pro-Am, and the sale of corporate tents. In 1981, the RCGA instituted a Pro-Am on the Wednesday preceding the Open. Since 1986, a second Pro-Am has been held on the Monday. In another essay, copied from the British Open, the RCGA started to sell the rights to corporate tents at Glen Abbey during the Open week.

By 1980, Genstar was ready to sell Glen Abbey. The company was in the real estate business; it was not set up to be the operator of a golf club, and had no wish to continue as one.

But Genstar was also bound by the terms of the RCGA–Great Northern agreement, under which it was obliged to provide a course and parking for the Open until 1995. That being so, by 1980 it was ready to dispose of Glen Abbey to the RCGA at considerably less than its book value.

The RCGA appeared to have everything to gain by making a bid for the Glen Abbey course and buildings. The purchase would fulfil its long-held ambition to be the owner of its own "home of the Canadian Open"; Genstar's priorities for Glen Abbey sometimes conflicted with the RCGA's; and by 1981 the Canadian Open was paying Genstar some $90,000 a year for the lease of the course. Finally, if any institution could make the Glen Abbey course profitable, surely it would be the RCGA, with a large pool of experts to call on, in the fields of business and golf.

Some RCGA governors were understandably sceptical. The Open's net income had improved very quickly, but the event had never produced anything like the income being projected by those in favour of buying. In the end, a deal was struck and approved by the RCGA executive. In February 1981, Genstar sold the property – course, buildings, equipment – for $3.0 million, or less than half the money it had put into the property over the years. The RCGA put $800,000 down and agreed to pay Genstar the balance of $2.2 million in March 1984, along with interest on the balance.

For a year or so, things went sour for the new owner of Glen Abbey. In 1982, the golf course, far from breaking even, suffered an operating loss, mainly the result of high maintenance costs. The greens had been ravaged by a mysterious disease. Labour and time was spent in overseeding, fertilizing, spraying, and irrigating. The problem was not corrected until the spring of 1983. Coming on top of a general economic recession, it caused revenue from green fees to fall in 1982, and the clubhouse lost money on food and drink.

Years like these are sent to try every corporation. The good companies survive, and in the process learn much about themselves. So it was with the RCGA. It tightened its controls and had a hard look at expenditures.

The operation of Glen Abbey – course and clubhouse – was quickly turned around. Within a year it was making an operating profit. In 1984, the RCGA was able to pay off some of its debt and to renegotiate a new mortgage. Over the next few years the facility contributed more than enough to finance its own capital expenditures on equipment and alterations, and the interest on its mortgage.

Changes in the management of Glen Abbey contributed to its financial success. A golf professional with a head for business, Alan Ogilvie, was appointed Director of Golf. He and the RCGA's Glen Abbey Committee came up with new marketing and promotional strategies. The course increasingly became a popular venue for corporate golf outings. There are few public courses in the Toronto area where a company can take its employees and customers and give them a championship course as well as a fine restaurant.

The conflict between the wishes of Glen Abbey members (individual and corporate) and the public golfer was settled by doing away with memberships. In 1986, the RCGA made Glen Abbey a fully public course, with no members. By 1988, starting times could be (and had to be) booked a month in advance by paying in advance. This gave visitors to Toronto a chance to play over a course they might have seen on television in, say, Victoria.

The Open gives Glen Abbey the finest television exposure of any public course in Canada, and pays it for this exposure. Seeing the Glen Abbey course live or on television during the Canadian Open has persuaded many golfers to try it.

The course and clubhouse soon became a major contributor to the RCGA's net income; in 1989 it contributed more than the Open, which explains how the RCGA was able to pay off its mortgage at the end of 1988.

In these ways, and in the space of only ten years, the RCGA became the owner of land with a *book* value of about $5.0 million, to say nothing of Golf House and a very fine clubhouse. If any ghost haunts Glen Abbey, it must surely be that of its first permanent secretary, B. L. Anderson. Looking down on today's affluence, he will remember that he had to run the association for twenty-five years on a pittance.

Jack Nicklaus did what he set out to do: he gave Canada one of the finest spectator courses in the world. Every year, Canadian and American spectators vote it a success with their feet. The first Open at Glen Abbey in 1977 drew some 85,000 spectators. By 1980, attendance was over 100,000.

Nicklaus also gave Canada a championship golf course ranked by a few as the best in the country, but by most as somewhere in the top ten. What is perhaps more questionable is the depth of its appeal to the average golfer, playing off the white tees set at 6,300 yards or the yellow tees at 5,600 yards. But there is no denying the figures: if green-fee players also vote with their feet, then Glen Abbey has also been a resounding success as a public course.

The present course is very much as Nicklaus first envisaged it in 1973. Since 1978, Glen Abbey has been set up for the Open at a length of 7,100 yards, give or take a few yards.

The four par fives – one on the front nine, three on the back – are all short enough (500 to 529 yards) to tempt the player to go for the green in two. (As Nelford astutely observed when commentating at the 1990 Open, the players almost feel embarrassed if they do *not* go for these greens in two.)

The spectators particularly like the 500-yard eighteenth. With a following prevailing wind, players have reached the green with a medium club for the second shot. The problem is not so much one of carrying the lake with the second, but of stopping the ball before it flies up the slope at the back, leaving a third shot from a downhill lie to a green which runs to the water.

The 529-yard thirteenth is short enough to be tempting, long enough to be devastating. The player who goes for it has to carry the creek directly in front of the green. If too long, the ball rolls down an incline at the back.

Of the four pars threes, the most deceiving is the third hole, nominally 156 yards, over water. The long green runs almost parallel to the line of flight. Moving the pin from the front to the back can convert it from an 8-iron to a 4 and halve the landing area. This hole has ruined the chances of many fine players. In one Open, Canada's Dave Barr missed the cut after taking a triple and a double bogey at this hole. Tom Watson saw his chance of winning an Open virtually disappear with a triple bogey in the final round.

The twelfth, the toughest par three, is nominally 188 yards, with the green just beyond Sixteen Mile Creek. In 1983, a new tee was set into the hillside on the right of the creek. This hillside is a jungle of trees and bushes ready to swallow a ball pushed too far to the right.

The par fours make Glen Abbey what it is, a long and tough course. They stretch from 414 to 458 yards. In 1984, six Glen Abbey holes were ranked amongst the 105 most difficult holes on the PGA Tour. The par 3 twelfth was one of these; the others were par fours.

Glen Abbey's 426-yard fourteenth was rated the fifth most difficult hole of the 105. The creek runs down the righthand side of the fairway, and has to be carried to reach the fairway, converting the hole into a righthand dog-leg. The heroic driver will bite off much of the creek, making the second shot to the green a short iron. The danger lies in trying to bite off too much and finishing in the creek or on its rocky beach. On the other hand, biting off too little of the creek with a long drive could put you right through the fairway. Here you flirt with water, sand, and trees. The green also has an eighteen-inch swale dividing it in two. In a typical Open, bogeys and worse will outnumber birdies by ten to one, giving the hole a stroke average of about 4.5.

The 429-yard seventeenth has fourteen bunkers, one of them protruding into the green. No hole has caused more frustration among Open contestants. The hole plays into the face of the prevailing wind, to a tight landing area, with little chance of par for the player off line. The second shot must be dead accurate to reach the right level of the green. "I think this is a hell of a hole. I really like it," said its designer, Jack Nicklaus. Everyone would agree with his first statement. Few would share his enthusiasm. In the first Open played at Glen Abbey, this hole had a stroke average of 4.47.

Some of the terror of the three finishing holes at Glen Abbey was reduced in 1984, when the 471-yard par 4 sixteenth was converted into a 516-yard par 5. But since this hole and the eighteenth can be reached in two, and a bogey or worse threatens at the seventeenth, a four-stroke lead coming to the sixteenth is by no means impregnable.

On the whole, the professionals who have played in the Glen Abbey Opens like the course. They like its excellent conditioning, its immaculate fairways; they like the trueness of its greens; they like the fine silica sand of its bunkers (still imported from Ohio), where a ball will not easily plug and which leaves no footprints.

The course is essentially a second-shot course. Its landing areas for tee-shots are generous and never as tight as on a course set up for a U.S. Open. But the shots to the green make up for this. Eight of the holes favour the player who fades the ball. Two such players, Trevino and Lietzke, have each won two Glen Abbey Opens.

"The 11th through 15th [in the valley] are the best anywhere. Nicklaus didn't have much to work with up top." Dan Halldorson's opinion is shared by many. The valley holes could be part of a different course. But Halldorson also likened playing Glen Abbey during the Open to playing the Canadian National Exhibition.

Knudson also preferred the valley holes; up top he found too much space, too little definition.

When the sixteenth was a par four, Weiskopf thought it and the seventeenth "the greatest back-to-back par fours I've ever played." Jack Nicklaus, always on the lookout for ways to improve the course, even considered playing the sixteenth and eighteenth two days as par fours, two days as par fives.

Some well-known names have never been too keen on coming to Glen Abbey, notably Tom Watson, Tom Kite, Calvin Peete, and Larry Nelson. They do not like its brute force.

At many of the Glen Abbey holes there is a long walk between the green and the next tee. This is partly the result of topography, partly the result of bringing so many holes back to the central clubhouse for the benefit of the spectator. Nicklaus also wanted to provide the spectator with a clear, uncongested viewing area around tees as well as greens, and so had to keep them apart.

The Canadian Open is a collection of disparate cogs that someone has to assemble into smooth, well-oiled machinery. Richard H. (Dick) Grimm has been head mechanic for most of the Glen Abbey Opens. He came along in time to make them spectaculars. But that is much like saying he came along in time to manage his own success, since he and Bruce Forbes were largely responsible for the RCGA's venture into the Abbey in 1974. Having been RCGA president that year, it was in every sense of the fitness of things that the RCGA appointed him Director of Professional Tournaments in 1983.

Dick Grimm is seen in many lights. Here he is, to James Fichette of *Score*:

> You need to attract the strongest field of 144 top professionals; you need a championship golf course in the best possible condition; you must cater to the needs of thousands of spectators who will roam the site each day of the tournament; you must work with the print, radio and television media . . . you need caddies, marshalls, scorers, leaderboards . . . people to look after accommodation, transportation, parking, hospitality, information, records, corporate pavilions, retail sales and the Pro-Am . . . [you need] to provide first aid to people with sunburn, pollen allergies, upset stomachs, twisted ankles . . . you need an army of volunteers and a truckload of money. It all seems a perfect prescription for ulcers and migraines for the organiser . . . This dirty task is the responsibility of Dick Grimm.

The game of golf does much to keep us all in a state of decent humility. To organize professional golf, we also require a certain virtuosity not commonly given to mortal man. Dick Grimm appears to have this, and in that sense is above the rest of us.

It is easy to compose anthems about Dick Grimm, but he would be the last to join in the singing. No doubt he has his own memories of achievement. There is no job in Canadian golf where the nature of the man is more important to his duties. Grimm is a genius not for what he does, but for what he is. He is all but irreplaceable as the organizer of the Open. But he will step down some day, and no doubt the next Director of Professional Tournaments for the RCGA will in time be reckoned to be every bit as skilled at his job as Dick Grimm.

His successor may succeed in different ways. But he will still need to learn how to handle people; how to cool tempers and warm enthusiasm with equal competence. He will have to establish the same rich bond of friendship and trust between the RCGA, the sponsor, the PGA, and the player. If he is like Dick Grimm, he will talk little of past disasters, but will often commune with his own soul when pacing the fairways with his walkie-talkie. He will find out this truth, that if life had no hazards, it would also lose much of its richness.

Two weeks before the Open, at a time when the course, the players, the volunteers, and the weather have not yet been properly joined to-gether, he may bring to mind the wisdom of Dr. Johnson: "When a man knows he is to be hanged in a fortnight, it concentrates his mind wonderfully." And after each Open he will sweep out the small misfortunes like cobwebs from a room, to start afresh, planning for the next. He will learn to be an optimist, and not let his mind dwell with unction on the broken promises of the world's finest professional golfers. He will find that the job, like golf itself, is as much a test of temper as of skill.

Whatever he is, he will not be another Dick Grimm. This unpretentious, unflappable man with the dry sense of humour and plodding step could be taken for a college professor or a friar of the Abbey.

The only other person to be linked to the Open so closely for so long was B. L. Anderson, the RCGA's secretary from 1919 to 1945. But B.L.'s Open was as much like Grimm's as B. L.'s prize money of $3,000 is like Grimm's $1.2 million. And Anderson's introverted nature was a far cry from Grimm's outgoing personality.

Coincidentally, both men were American. Dick Grimm was born in Chicago in 1923, was educated at Yale, and spent 1942–46 in the U.S. Marine Corps. He first came to Canada in 1948 to work in the family cement-block business. In 1982, two years after this business was taken over, he felt he had had enough and was ready for a change of profession.

Dick Grimm had golfed in New York and Illinois. A few years after coming to Canada, he joined Mississaugua, moving up through several club committees and becoming an RCGA governor.

When Mississaugua was awarded the 1965 Open, Grimm was tournament chairman. So his love affair with the Canadian Open goes back over a quarter of a century.

Grimm recognized it as a love affair in 1974 when, as president of the RCGA, he saw Mississaugua again awarded the Open. "My baby is the Canadian Open . . . because I can watch each Open grow and finish and improve each year, while many of the other RCGA officers and governors must spend hours doing jobs which never have a beginning and an end. I like completion."

During his years as an RCGA governor he began to visit major U.S. tournaments like the Open, the Masters, the PGA, and the Kemper and Doral Opens. The PGA officials and players got to know him. He studied their tournaments with a critical eye, collecting ideas to be tried out in Canada.

Dick Grimm was a natural choice to chair the RCGA's Open committee for the first Opens at Glen Abbey in 1977–79. And when the RCGA concluded in 1983 that it needed him as Director of Professional Tournaments, he gave up the cement business to do what he does best.

Not the least of the problems facing Grimm as 1977 approached was where to find the volunteers to run the first Glen Abbey Open. Something like a thousand were needed, including 350 marshalls.

Traditionally, volunteers to chair and fill Open committees had come from the host club.

Clubs like Mississaugua, Scarboro, St. George's, Royal Montreal, where the Open had been held several times, had a core of members experienced in running Open committees.

The Glen Abbey Golf Club, newly established and with a membership of only two or three hundred, could not provide sufficient experienced chairpeople. So Grimm went elsewhere. He drew on RCGA governors in the Toronto area, but mainly on members of his own club, Mississaugua. Five chairmen were drawn from Mississaugans who had worked in the 1974 Open. As in previous Opens, eighteen clubs were found willing to marshall a hole.

With each successive Open, the advantages of having a more or less permanent band of volunteers became more evident, reinforcing the case for a permanent site for the Open.

Turnover among volunteers had been less than 15 per cent. Without these men and women, the Open would run at a loss.

In 1977, Glen Abbey had parking for some 15,000 vehicles in fields within a hundred yards of the course, as well as internal parking lots. As the surrounding spaces have been taken over for housing, space for automobiles has become a problem. Today, Glen Abbey's own parking areas can cater to 2,500 vehicles, and there is room for another 6,500 close by. Several thousand spectators have to be bused to the course from more distant lots. Genstar has an obligation to provide space up to 1995. If anything will force the RCGA to leave Glen Abbey, it might well be the shortage of parking space after that date. The Open continues to be a victim of its own success!

42
CHAPTER

OPEN WINNERS
AT THE ABBEY

LEE TREVINO MADE HISTORY OF SORTS by winning the first Canadian Open held at Glen Abbey, in 1977. He won by leading from start to finish, and by the comfortable margin of four strokes.

There was something of a carnival atmosphere about Glen Abbey during that week of 18 July. All but a few of the 156 players and 85,000 spectators were seeing for the first time what Nicklaus had sculpted. The weather was hot and sultry, so the concession stands did a pretty good business. Those lucky enough to have a pass for the clubhouse watched in air-conditioned comfort and, if guests of Imperial Tobacco, sampled what was to become a Glen Abbey tradition – lunch and refreshments in the Jack Nicklaus lounge upstairs.

Nicklaus was the favourite coming into the 1977 Open. If a Canadian could not win – Knudson was no longer on the PGA tour, but still seemed our only hope – then everyone wanted it to be Jack. He already had four second places in the Open. He had built the course, and it somehow seemed fitting that the architect of this massive monument of turf, sand, and water should prove it could be mastered.

But Nicklaus was more than a sentimental favourite, since he was high up in the money list that year, second only to Tom Watson. Two weeks earlier, Watson had beaten him by a stroke for the British Open. With Watson not competing at Glen Abbey, Nicklaus was odds on to win. When he turned up for a practice round at twilight, he still drew hundreds of fans. And he was confident. "I'm tired of finishing second," he said, referring not only to the Canadian Opens of 1965, 1968, 1975, and 1976 and the British Open of two weeks earlier, but to the Pleasant Valley Classic played a week earlier.

Missing from the field with Watson were a few other stars – Hale Irwin, Johnny Miller, Hubert Green. Pleasant Valley was a designated event, so they had been forced to attend; the Canadian Open was not, so they took a rest. But Palmer was at Glen Abbey, and when he was paired with our own George, they drew the largest gallery of the day. The winner in 1950 and 1951, Jim Ferrier, now sixty-two, withdrew, saying the weather was too hot, the course too long.

Thunderstorms had been forecast for the first day of the Open, so the PGA set up the

Trevino and Palmer.

pins in relatively easy positions. As a result, scores were lost. Twenty-eight players equalled or bettered the par of 72. At the end of the day, one stroke ahead of Nicklaus, Tom Kite, and half a dozen others was Lee Trevino.

Admittedly, Trevino's 67 – then a record for the course – was probably five strokes better than it deserved to be, thanks to some remarkable putting. Trevino had reverted to his old way of lining up putts, with the club ahead of, not behind, the ball. Whether this improved his putting is not material – he believed it did.

The man was also well suited to the course. An adept hands player, Trevino stood with a very open stance, fading the ball to its target. While some criticized his swing as being too unorthodox, Hogan did not agree. He thought Trevino's movement through the ball the finest he had ever seen. "Super-Mex" was also a great scrambler.

The second day saw a sudden switch in wind direction and velocity, from northwest and light, to southwest and moderate. Those

out in the morning had the best of it, so nature was also on Trevino's side. Again, his total of 26 putts was the foundation of his 68. This gave Trevino a three-stroke lead at the end of round two, over Nicklaus and Kite.

The afternoon wind-change played havoc with scores. Sixteen of seventy-five late starters didn't break 80. Palmer shot 81 and quit, citing a bad knee. The cut was made at 150. Only two Canadians survived – Knudson at 143, and our twenty-two-year-old amateur champion, Jim Nelford, 147, making the first of several notable Glen Abbey appearances.

Trevino is accepted as one of the finest of wind players. On the third day, he was the only one of the top men to break par, with a 71, increasing his lead to six strokes. Ray Floyd joined Nicklaus and Kite in second place. Canada's hopes, such as they were, disappeared when Knudson quit smoking for the first two holes and bogeyed them. Jim Nelford, suffering from the aftereffects of a nosebleed, had a horrendous 85.

"Trevino is catchable," said Nicklaus, "especially on this course. It's the type of course where a leader can falter." But while we were all watching Nicklaus, Kite, and Floyd try to do the highly improbable on the Sunday, Britain's Peter Oosterhuis snuck in with a 70, to take second place away from Kite, and to push Nicklaus and Floyd into a tie with others for fourth. Oosterhuis needed only ten putts on the front nine.

Trevino's closing 74 is the highest ever to win the Open at Glen Abbey. The dried-out greens may have contributed to his 34 putts, but just as likely he found that the great god of greens can taketh away as quickly as he can bestow.

Trevino's 1977 victory at Glen Abbey was quite different from his first in the Canadian Open, six years earlier, when he was somewhat fortunate to catch Art Wall and to defeat him in a play-off.

The 1971 Open at Richelieu Valley, near Montreal, established two firsts. This was the first Open to be sponsored by Imperial Tobacco.

And within four weeks, Trevino was to become the first to win the Triple Crown – the U.S., Canadian, and British Opens in the one year.

Trevino came to Richelieu Valley as the winner of the first of these three titles, the U.S. Open, achieved two weeks earlier.

Nicklaus was over in Britain preparing for the British Open, as were a number of other stars, but the other two of the big four were at Richelieu Valley – Palmer and Player. The field included ten of the top twenty money winners on that year's Tour.

The wind blew at Richelieu Valley, and Trevino had a name as a good Texas wind player. ("If the wind blows, watch out for Trevino," Wilf Homenuik correctly forecast.) But there were no indications from his opening 73 that Trevino was going anywhere, wind or not. This did not stop the merry Mexican from his usual banter on the course. ("All those French girls in those hot pants are driving me crazy.")

But then came a run of 68, 67, 67. This was good enough to make up two strokes on Art Wall in the final round. Trevino caught Wall on the very first hole, when his sand-wedge shot went in for an eagle 2. To some extent, Trevino was fortunate. Wall missed a few putts coming home, including a seven-footer on the seventeenth green, and an even shorter one on the eighteenth.

The sudden-death play-off was just that. On the 400-yard fifteenth, Wall was over the green with his approach, Trevino on the green but 20 feet away. Wall's chip looked into the cup but did not drop. Trevino stroked in the putt for a 3, and victory. (I remember him throwing the ball into the crowd but was too far away to catch it.)

"I used this locker and I won – Lee Trevino." Some lucky member of Richelieu Valley should have found this note on the Monday morning; a rather nice gesture from

Trevino being presented with the Triple Crown in 1972 by Imperial Tobacco's Edmond Ricard.

a man who can be rather fun, especially when he is winning.

Trevino went straight from Montreal to Royal Birkdale, in England, his heart set on winning the British Open that year. And he did. "You could say that I stumbled over the U.S. and Canadian Opens on the way," he was quoted as saying later. "The Canadian Open is one of the world's oldest . . . I rate it among the top four in the world." As we have seen, winners have always been generous in their praise, since the time of Armour.

Some 56,000 spectators saw Trevino win at Richelieu Valley. Nearly double that number were at Glen Abbey in 1979, when he landed his third Canadian Open title.

The field in 1979 was among the strongest ever seen in Canada. All but two of that year's top twenty-five money winners on the PGA Tour were there, including top man Tom Watson. This was one of Watson's rare appearances in our Open. And for three rounds it looked as though he might win. But he proved vulnerable to one of those inexplicable falls from grace which injure even the best of us, and had to settle for third place. He also proved vulnerable to the subtleties of Glen Abbey's short third hole.

But if this was Trevino's and Watson's Open, it was also Jim Nelford's. Who will forget the standing ovation given him as he walked down the seventy-second fairway, about to take eighth place in his second year on the PGA Tour? Canadians had been given little to cheer about since Knudson's sixth place at Cherry Hill in 1972. Jim was a few days short of being twenty-four. If we were full of high hopes for him, we had every right to be. "Nelford's Navy" was launched that year at Glen Abbey.

The course played relatively easy on the Thursday. In the first round, Australia's Jack Newton shot a record 64 to lead Tom Watson by two, Trevino and Johnny Miller by three. Then the wind blew away low scoring, as it had in 1977. As the second day progressed, swirling breezes started to whip up whitecaps on the lakes. Newton soared to a 74. Of those out in the afternoon, Watson was the only one to break 71. By his reckoning, the course was now playing some four or five strokes harder. His 69 widened his lead to three over Trevino, Newton, and D. A. Weibring.

On the Saturday, the par-4 fourteenth played havoc with scores. There was only one birdie all day, and an average score of 4.67. Many made the green in two, only to find the two-tiered green impossible. ("Jack Nicklaus had to get his idea [for the green] from a miniature golf course," said a bitter Dave Stockton.) Watson, with a 72, held on to his three-stroke lead over Trevino.

"I'll need a 68 to give myself a chance," Trevino said before the start of that fatal final round. Well, he was three strokes off his target, and still won. Watson's game collapsed, mainly the victim of errant tee-shots. But it was the innocuous-looking par-3 third hole that put paid to his chances. His tee-shot went into the bullrushes beside the pond. His third off the tee went into the same bullrushes, but he managed to play the ball and make the green in 4. Two putts gave him a triple bogey, and his lead had vanished. This more or less set the tenor of his day. He finished with a 78, twelve strokes more than he had needed in the first round.

Trevino had his own minor escapades, notably on the seventeenth, where his ball caromed off a tree and he had to settle for a bogey. But by this time the contest was over. He won by three strokes from Ben Crenshaw, with a despairing Watson third.

Again, Trevino won the Open with his putter. He acquired the implement from a spectator on the practice green at Glen Abbey, just before the Open, and it must be the finest $75 investment he ever made.

Bruce Lietzke won the 1978 Glen Abbey Open after an opening round of 76, and you have to go back to 1922 to find a winner who had such a disastrous beginning. Which tells us two things: first, that Glen Abbey is a lot tougher than most of the courses used in the intervening years, making such a recovery possible; second, that Bruce Lietzke is a very fine golfer, with a mental approach to the game that would not accept defeat on Thursday evening. His relaxed approach to professional golf had already won him several events on the PGA Tour. Standing six feet two inches, weighing a muscular 200 pounds, Lietzke has the talent to go along with the strength. He hits a high, fading shot, and a fade is usually what's needed at Glen Abbey.

To show you that one round of golf does not settle a championship, we should also record that after the first round Lietzke was a stroke behind Bob Zender, who eventually took the seventieth and last place of those who made the cut.

Three Canadian professionals were in the field: Knudson, Nelford, and Barr, the latter two then in their first year on the PGA Tour. None made the cut.

Lietzke's high score in the first round was partly the result of the strong gusty winds. Players had difficulty in standing on the tees and over their putts on the valley holes. There was only one score in the 60s that day, and even good wind players such as defending champion Trevino were several over par. But Arnold Palmer conquered the conditions and shot 70.

On the Friday, Lietzke came in with a brilliant 67 to match the course record (since broken several times), one of only nine scores in the 60s. Crenshaw was heading for the second-round lead when he put his ball in the water at the eighteenth and took a 9.

Lietzke took the lead with another 67 in round three. But he had Pat McGowan, Trevino, and Crenshaw on his heels. On the Sunday, Trevino looked the most dangerous of his pursuers. He caught Lietzke briefly with an eagle on the fifth, and should have gone for another eagle on the thirteenth – he said so himself – but laid up from 240 yards. His third shot went into a greenside bunker. Failing to get out first time, he lost his temper and slashed at the sand with his club. Luckily, he escaped a penalty, but could do no better than bogey 6.

In the meantime, Lietzke had himself eagled the fifth, hitting a 4-iron to within five feet of the hole. This was to prove the winner. He finished at 283, one under par, to beat McGowan by a stroke, with Trevino and Crenshaw tied for third.

Lietzke had a much easier task in 1982. The Open was held a week before the PGA championship in August, and that kept some players away. (So too did the memory of the greens in the 1981 Open. The greens had not then recovered from a disease that had struck them a year earlier.)

The weather was kind to the Open that year, as was the course to Canada. Six Canadians made the cut, including our three on the PGA Tour, Nelford, Halldorson, and Barr, as well as Jerry Anderson, then playing on overseas tours. But Jack Nicklaus did not make the cut for the first time in fifteen appearances in the Open.

A struggling rookie with a famous name was making his first appearance in the Open. Tommy Armour III was much taller than his grandfather who had won over fifty years earlier. But it was another new young player who was tied for the lead after the first round, with a 67. Greg Norman of Queensland, Australia, then twenty-seven, was setting out on a career which had already won him championships in Australia, Hong Kong, and Sweden.

Lietzke, only a stroke behind, caught and passed him with a second round of 68. In the third round Lietzke shot 68 for the third time, showing an enviable consistency over a course as demanding as Glen Abbey. This gave him a lead of two strokes over Tommy Valentine, and four over another newcomer, Hal Sutton.

Norman, a stroke further back, was not destined to make one of his now famous last-day recoveries, but blew his chances with a string of bogeys. Only Valentine challenged Lietzke. But his chances faded when he bogeyed the fifteenth, and in the end he finished in a tie for third place.

When Lietzke put his second shot a foot from the flag at sixteen, the Open was as good as over. In spite of a bogey at the treacherous seventeenth, where his drive hit a spectator,

Lietzke won with a total of 277, two better than Sutton.

Bruce Lietzke's record in the Canadian Open supports the notion that Glen Abbey was made for his style of golf. In the five Opens 1978–82 he won twice and had a second and a fifth place.

By the time he won the 1984 Canadian Open, Greg Norman was firmly entrenched as The Great White Shark. The name came from his Australian home, his flock of sun-bleached blond hair, just off-white, his sharp features, and his manner of attacking the ball and the course. He had established himself as an aggressive golfer ("I'll go for the flag 90 percent of the time, no matter where they hide it. I don't know any other way"). He was a world golfer, the winner of some thirty tournaments spread over a number of continents. Many considered him the finest player anywhere, and certainly one of the most exhilarating to watch since Seve Ballesteros of Spain. This was his first full season on the PGA Tour. A few weeks before coming to Glen Abbey, he had won his first tour event, the Kemper Open. More important, the week before Glen Abbey he had tied for the U.S. Open, losing in an eighteen-hole play-off.

Norman was a friend and admirer of Jack Nicklaus. The 1984 Open developed into a struggle between these two friends, both looking for their first win in Canada.

After the first two rounds, a twenty-four-year-old South African, Nick Price, seemed set for a runaway win, his pair of 67s giving him the lead by six shots. He had been helped by a brace of eagles; on the first day, he holed out his second shot (a wedge) on the 417-yard fourth hole, and the next day he did the same on the 433-yard eighth.

Price was no newcomer to the lead in a major tournament. In 1982 he had led the British Open by what seemed like the safe margin of three strokes with six holes remaining, only to have Tom Watson catch him and defeat him in a play-off. But there would be no repeat of this in 1984, Price assured us. He had learned his lesson at Troon.

At this point in the Open there was hardly a mention of Norman (seven strokes behind) or Nicklaus (eight strokes). But on the third day – moving day, they call it on the Tour – Price's driving let him down. Having hooked his first tee-shot, he became defensive. Still, he seemed to be coming in with a reasonable score, when he put his 3-wood into the water at the eighteenth and bogeyed for a 73. This let both Nicklaus (69) and Norman (70) come to within four shots, along with defending champion, John Cook.

The last round quickly became a fight between the Golden Bear and the Great White Shark (as the headline writers would not let us forget). Along with Price, they made up the last threesome. Following the fight were 90 per cent of the 35,000 spectators – or so it seemed at the time. After two holes, Price's lead had been cut to two. Typical of his continued misfortunes was the fourth, where he hit his drive over the trees on the right, his second into the rough on the left, and barely scrambled a bogey.

By the turn, Nicklaus and Norman had caught and overtaken him, exchanging the lead between them. The crucial hole for Nicklaus was the fifteenth. He stood on the green one stroke behind, having visited a hazard on the fourteenth. Unaccountably, he three-putted, while Norman sank a putt for a birdie. Both birdied the sixteenth. Norman was in the parking lot at the seventeenth, and went to the final hole with his lead cut to two. Nicklaus supporters looking for a miracle saw him hook his drive at the last hole, and this effectively stopped him going for the green. So, it was the Shark by two, and Price had to settle for a tie for third.

Before the first day's play, Nick Weslock had told us to look out for young Richard Zokol. Well, the old maestro was right. Again. Dick Zokol led the Canadians from early on the first day. After three rounds of 69 74 71–214, two under par, he was seven behind Nick Price, but only three from second place. A fine round of 70 on the last day was good enough to tie him for fifth place with the defending champion Cook.

In 1985, it looked as though Greg Norman would win the Open for the second consecutive year, to become the first man to retain the title since Ferrier in 1951. At the end of the second round he led by three. But things went sour for Greg, and he did well to tie Jack Nicklaus for second place. The man who beat both of them, Curtis Strange, was to win the Open twice in the next three years.

This was the Open that Jack Nicklaus probably lost when he missed a three-foot putt at a crucial point in the final round, the sixteenth. He was one behind Strange coming to the hole. When Strange pulled his drive into the rough at this 516-yard par five, with Nicklaus long and down the middle, Jack seemed to have the edge. He still seemed to have the edge when Strange played a superb wood from the rough to just off the green, for Nicklaus was on the green and not more than thirty feet away. His chances of tying the lead looked even better when Curtis over-chipped to the back of the green. And even when Nicklaus, going for his eagle, ran the ball thirty-six inches past the hole (another observer said fifteen), he still seemed sure of tying for the lead. But, unaccountably, he missed the putt. He and Strange had to settle for pars.

Of anyone else but Jack Nicklaus, you might say that losing such a simple chance to tie would be unnerving. But that does not explain his errant drive at the seventeenth. This hole had put paid to his chances in 1981, when he came second to Peter Oosterhuis. In 1985, in trying to keep the ball away from the trees and traps on the right, he pulled it into the rough on the left. His shot to the green had a look at the cup on its way to the edge of a bunker at the back. He took great care over his third. Before making the shot, he may have been disturbed by green-side photographers. Whatever the reason, he left it six feet short and missed the putt, to go two strokes behind.

There was still a chance he might catch Strange at the eighteenth. But no. Having little choice but to go for the green, Nicklaus overshot, faced a dangerous downhill pitch to the green, and had to bale out into a bunker to prevent his ball running over the green to the water. He did well to finish with a par, to lose by two. When it was over, he accepted defeat ruefully: "After all, I did tie my best finish in this tournament, didn't I?"

Nicklaus, Norman, and Strange had been in the last group to tee off on that Sunday afternoon, having earned that right in three quite different ways. Norman had opened with 67 68–135, to lead by three from Strange's pair of 69s. At this stage, Jack Nicklaus was eight strokes off the lead. In the third round, we saw vintage Nicklaus. His 66 equalled the lowest score of the week, and left him three back of Strange, who had added a 68. Norman had an adventurous third round of 73, having had a fight with his putter, and was now two off the lead.

Since no Canadian had a hope of winning, the crowd was rooting for the sentimental favourite and the popular Australian. This might have fazed a lesser man than Curtis Strange, but this outwardly cool player appeared the least concerned of the three. When Nicklaus caught him at the eighth hole, he came right back with his own birdie at the ninth. When Norman charged him at the thirteenth and made up a stroke, Strange might have been playing in a weekend three-ball, if we were to judge his emotions from the whimsical expression on his face. The crowd greeted his best shots with polite applause. They waited for the presentation of his cheque and his Inuit carving, but their hearts were with the runners-up.

Curtis Strange in 1985 was not yet the back-to-back winner of the U.S. Open, so we did not know what a fine player he was, or what an articulate spokesman for golf. Nor had he been a faithful attender of our Open. He had played in the early 1980s when Glen Abbey was having problems with its turf and had been put off by the state of the course.

When Curtis Strange came back in 1987 to repeat his victory (knowing he had to do well to win a place on the U.S. Ryder Cup team) he was clearly more popular with the spectators. His win was well-received, but only after Richard Zokol fell out of contention in the final round.

This was Zokol's Open. He didn't win, but he put up the stoutest fight seen from a Canadian in years. On a cold, wet, windy day, he opened with a 70, to tie for third. The second round was underway when rain and lightning called a halt to the day's play, with half the competitors – Zokol among them – still waiting to start. That meant getting up at 5:00 a.m. on the Saturday and playing the gruelling Glen Abbey twice in one day. Zokol did. Perhaps because his mind was focused on just finishing the third round and getting some rest, he played the best golf of the day – a 68 69 for a total of 207 and a share of the lead.

The two others on 207 were Strange and Mike McCullough, both of whom had completed their second rounds before the storm.

For the first time on the PGA Tour, Richard Zokol found himself a co-leader with a round to go. A night's sleep gave him time to dream about the enormity of what he might do. He had not even made the cut in seven of fifteen events that year and stood well down the money list. Anywhere in the top five, and he would double his earnings for the year.

When Strange's par on the first hole of the final round was good enough to break the tie, and when he followed this with a birdie, Zokol's dream took on a darker tinge. He fought manfully on, but on that Sunday Richard Zokol never gave himself any makable birdie putts. Three over after the outward half of his round, he did well to par the last nine holes for a 75. But that was only good enough to tie him for seventh.

Strange won by three, from Nick Price, Jodie Mudd, and David Frost. You could not help but wonder if Richard Zokol would have done better if he'd had to struggle through thirty-six holes on the Sunday. When he said, "We're playing mind games out there," he said it all.

John Cook won the 1983 Open after a tense, six-hole play-off against Johnny Miller, making this the longest Open since sudden-death play-offs were introduced.

Cook was then twenty-four, a pleasant-looking lad with an engaging smile. He had once been the World Junior champion (1974) and the U.S. Amateur champion (1978), and an All-American from Ohio State University. This was only his second win on the PGA Tour.

The 1983 Open had been dubbed the No-Name Open, since nine of the top ten on the PGA Tour money list did not show up. (The PGA championship was being held the week after, in Los Angeles.) In any event, this Open had about as close and exciting a finish as you could hope for.

Only three Canadians made the cut – Zokol, Nelford, and the 1982 amateur champion, Roxburgh. When it became evident after the first two rounds that none of them had much of a chance, Jack Nicklaus, as always, became the sentimental favourite (although Ralph Landrum, a rookie on the Tour, ran him a close second in many hearts). Nicklaus (211 after three rounds, or two under par) told his caddie – who was also his son – that he would need a 66 to catch Landrum (207), Cook (209), and Miller (210). He was exactly right. Landrum was still a challenge until the fifteenth, but then faded. Nicklaus came to the last hole six under par and tied with Cook and Miller, playing behind him.

Jack had been driving well all week. But now at this reachable par five he was short off the tee. There was no question of his trying to carry the water, so he laid up. His pitch shot to the green left him with a very makable birdie putt of eight feet for the lead. Father and son read the line correctly, but father pulled what should have been a straight putt.

The chances of both Cook and Miller failing to birdie the last hole were slim – they both got their 4s. So, for the second time in three years, Jack Nicklaus had failed by a stroke.

In the Cook–Miller play-off, over holes 16, 17, and 18, the first five holes were halved, John Cook having twice lipped the cup for birdies. Johnny Miller came to the sixth extra hole, the eighteenth, knowing he had played it poorly four times out of five. He could only par the hole. Cook made no mistake with a 10-foot putt for birdie, and the title was his.

If John Cook will never forget this Open, neither will Andy Bean. On his way to a 75 on Saturday, he playfully putted a short one with the shaft end of his putter, and was penalized two strokes. In the final round, by way of atonement, he shot a remarkable 62, to tie the course record. That included six birdies in an outward half of 29, and birdies on eight of the first eleven holes. He finished the tournament two strokes behind Cook and Millar. Would he have shot that 62, and tied, if he had not been fooling around on the Saturday? We shall never know.

Of the other winners at Glen Abbey, Bob Murphy was perhaps the most surprised to find himself receiving the Inuit carving that Imperial Tobacco presents to the winner. He had not won a PGA event in eleven years. In 1986, at the age of forty-three and four months, he was not the oldest winner of the Canadian Open – Kel Nagle was about two months older when he won in 1964. Bob's was a popular win, sending many forty-year-old spectators home strangely rejuvenated.

POSTSCRIPT

That, then, is the story of Canadian golf. Like all stories, it had to end somewhere. It ended in 1990, in the midst of a few rather bleak years. Our men had soared to the heights in the World Amateur Team Matches of 1986, our women in the Commonwealth Team Tournament in 1987, our nomadic professionals were making money overseas, but our men and women on the PGA and LPGA tours seemed to be in a holding pattern.

Those who have studied the history of golf have learned not to lose heart and that history repeats itself; that just when things seem at their darkest along comes a George S. Lyon or a Mabel Thomson, a Sandy Somerville or an Ada Mackenzie, a George Knudson or a Marlene Stewart, a Leonard, a Balding, a Weslock, a Cowan, a Post, or a Bourassa. "New patriots are born, higher hopes bloom out like stars," a Miss Willard wrote of the state of the human race a hundred years ago. "Humanity emerges from the dark ages vastly ahead of what it was on entering that cave of gloom . . . Only those who have not studied history lose heart . . . there is nothing new under the sun."

Only shortsighted pessimists would have thought of the years around 1990 as a cave of gloom, but the light and the spirit of our golf had certainly dimmed. A number of good friends to golf in Canada had died. Geordie Hilton had been taken in what should have been the prime years of his life; we lost Jack McLaughlin (at fifty-seven), Sandy Somerville, Robbie Robinson, George Hevenor, more recently Pat Osler and Tex Noble.

An economic depression had more than decimated — in the true meaning of the word — the waiting lists at many clubs, and at least one of the new equity clubs had gone under.

Out on the fairways we emerged from this short dark age in the last weeks of February 1992, and things have been looking brighter ever since. First Lisa Walters, then her close friend, the aptly named Dawn Coe, made the sun shine for us again by winning events on the LPGA Tour. Within two months, Richard Zokol had taken top money in a PGA Tour event. And Richard had no sooner put the money in the bank when Jennifer Wyatt came along to become the third Canadian this year to win on the LPGA Tour.

We should have known that 1992 was to be Canada's year on the fairways, for it started with a piece of news that threw light on the darkest of winter days. In January, the Golf Writers Association of America recognized the gutsy fight Jim Nelford has been putting up these past five years to make himself fit to play again, by announcing that he had won the Ben Hogan award. (This is given annually to a golfer who has overcome a serious injury or disability.) The award was long overdue. Canadian golf writer Lorne Rubenstein has been pushing Nelford's case for years.

Then, on 22 February, after nine years on tour, Lisa Walters won the Itoki Hawaiian Ladies' Open by shooting a string of birdies in the last round, to come in with a course record and her lowest tour score ever, a 65 ("I feel like I won a gold medal at the Olympics").

One week later, Dawn Coe started the final round of the Women's Kemper Open a stroke

593

ahead, was overtaken several times in the last round, but shook off her challengers in the closing holes and held on to win. ("I wanted to win so much . . . just to know how it feels . . . It feels great"). Neither win came as any great surprise; Dawn had already been in a play-off, and both she and Lisa had been threatening for years.

Walters and Coe had paid their dues on the ladies' tour, a hard nine-year apprenticeship. Not so Jennifer Wyatt, who won after less that four years on tour. Jennifer had lifted the B.C. Junior and the B.C. Ladies' titles, and had been runner-up in the Canadian Ladies' in 1985. In 1987, she was a member of our winning team in the Commonwealth Tournament in New Zealand, and she went on to win the New Zealand Ladies' Championship. Shortly afterward, she turned professional, and qualified for the LPGA Tour in 1989. On 10 May 1992, at the age of twenty-six, she won the Crestar Farm Fresh Classic by "taming the winds that wrecked just about everyone else."

So, three B.C. women have helped lead us out of the cave of gloom.

In April, B.C. veteran Richard Zokol registered his first win on the PGA Tour. He did what Dan Halldorson had done eight years earlier. Still working hard to control his mental approach to golf, he took advantage of the absence of the big boys (away playing the Masters) to win the Deposit Guaranty Golf Classic. Now that he's done it once . . .

It was heartening news, too, that Dick Grimm will not be lost to golf when he retires from his post as Director of Professional Tournaments after the 1992 Open, but will take on a new challenge – running our own Canadian professional tour.

The victories of Walters and Coe were historic firsts. No two Canadian golfers had ever won back-to-back tournaments on the LPGA or PGA tours. That aside, we are no longer dealing with golf history, but with recording current events. Some day, golf historians may look back and select these wins, and the move of Dick Grimm, and tell us of their significance for Canadian golf.

It is a brave person who digs into the past to make historical selections like this. So much has to be examined that something of significance can easily be thrown away. I had to give up mining a number of promising veins, leaving many historical gems out there waiting to be unearthed. Take the matter of Central Canada's most promising woman golfer of the 1890s, Ethel White. She married the son of the Chief Justice of Ireland and left us for Dublin. A British golf magazine of the time tells us she became Mrs. Gerald Fitz-Gibbon. Could she be the Mrs. Fitzgibbon who was runner-up in the Irish Ladies' Championship in 1907? And was the Miss Fitzgibbon who was runner-up in 1921 her daughter?

A quick peek into the history of Irish golf did not answer that question, but raised another. Was the George Combe who was educated at an English public school, the organizer of The Golfing Union of Ireland in 1891, and the runner-up in the Irish Amateur of 1893, related to *our* Harvey Combe, also educated at an English public school, who helped to organize golf in Victoria in 1893? I never did find out.

And whatever became of Miss Whish of Barrie, who played for Ontario against Quebec in 1900 and "who will doubtless be reckoned among the best players in the Dominion with a little more experience"? Perhaps Miss Whish acquired this little more experience and is hidden in the record books, disguised by her husband's name.

And what happened to eighteen-year-old J. Hubert McCulloch of Beaconsfield, who knocked out George S. Lyon *and* Fritz Martin in the 1919 Canadian Amateur, and who had "all the earmarks of a golfer of the first class"? Did Ralph Reville misread the earmarks? Or did Hubert, too, move to another country? (He was too young to have eloped with Miss Whish.)

While searching for him, I came to believe that his father, James L. McCulloch, the secretary of Beaconsfield, was related to the John McCulloch of the North Berwick Golf Club in East Lothian, who published in 1892 (under the pseudonym J.A.C.K.) a book called *Golf in the Year 2000*.

Which in turn led me to survey just how wrong people have been who have dared to predict the future of golf. True, Mr. McCulloch did make some inspired guesses about golf in the year 2000. ("The caddie of the future is an ingenious invention [on wheels] . . . that follows the player around the course at a respectable distance of twelve feet." And St. Andrews, he predicted in 1892, would have 450-foot-high poles with "special mirrors" so that golfers could watch the Open while sitting in London.) But he also forecast that by the year 2000 men would be playing golf all day, leaving women to run the country . . . We should all hope that this forecast is nearer the truth than a cartoon, below, which appeared in the British *Golf Illustrated* of 11 January 1901, entitled "Golf in 2001."

In this book on the story of golf in Canada, I have tried to put flesh on some of the names that appear in the eighty pages of national and provincial golf records, and, in the words of a nineteenth-century historian: "simply to show how it really was." In doing so, I found much that was magnificent about some of our Canadian achievements. Over the past hundred and twenty years, this country has nurtured men and women who were among the finest in the game of golf, as players and as builders. If we are as fortunate over the next century or so as we have been over the last, then future golf historians will come to say of them: "They set us down on the right road."

June, 1992

GOLF IN 2001.

PHOTO CREDITS

for black and white photographs

Provincial Archives of Alberta: 72 top and bottom, Photo CPA-204/3, 351.

Author's collection: 35 (based on a sketch in the American magazine *Golf*, 1898); from *Fraser's Golf Directory and Year Book*: 219 left, 375 right, 381 top left; from the American magazine *Golf* (1904): 133 bottom; from *Golf and Club News*: 402 bottom, 419 top left, 447; from the British magazine *Golf Monthly*: 163; from *The Green Book of Golf* (1913): 187; from *Montreal Herald*: 8; from *Outdoor-South*: 248; from the magazine *American Golfer*: 248 right, 332 left and right, 336 right, 380 bottom right; source unknown: 9, 88, 220, 313, 345 top, 409 right, 469, 487 top; from prints: 222, 374, 377; from a water-colour by G. G. Wiedegreim: 378 right.

Belvedere Golf and Winter Club: 92.

Brant Historical Society: 25, 28, 29, 196 bottom.

British Columbia Archives and Records Service: Photo 8744, 83.

CLGA archives: photo by J. bland, 528 bottom right; 539 bottom, 540, all photos 549; *CLGA Year Book*: 462, 547 bottom, 569 left and right, 570.

Canadian Airlines International: 427.

Canapress Photo Service: 419 bottom left.

CPGA archives: 318, 341, 438, 498, 502; from *The Book of Sport*: 18, 31 left and right, 44, 49, 150, 182 left and right; from Charlie Murray's scrapbook: 136 bottom, 268 left is a cartoon by LeMessurier of *Montreal Star*; from *CPGA Yearbook*: 393, 395, 451, 485 left, centre, and

right, 486, 487 bottom, 534 right, 539 top, 544; from *CPGA Bulletin*: 567.

Aime Desjardins: 142.

The du Maurier Limited Golf Library: 537.

City of Edmonton Archives: 230.

Margaret Esson Elliott: 259.

Brian Freeman: 136 top.

Glenbow Museum, Calgary: Photo NA 1508–1, 68, Photo NA 3632–24, 75 right; Photo NA 2710–1, 224.

The Royal Montreal Golf Club: from the British magazine *Golf*: 9 bottom, 155, 156 top left, 160; from the British magazine *Golf Illustrated*: 4, 43 left, 60, 97, 112, 149, 154, 156 bottom left, and right, 157, 161 top, 169, 184, 198, 355, 379 top right, centre, and bottom, 595.

Golf Journal, the United States Golf Association: 419 top right.

The American magazine *Golf Illustrated*: 158, 207 left, 329.

The Golf Book of East Lothian, 105.

Richard H. Grimm: 551.

Journal of the Canadian Bankers' Association: 19.

Manitoba Provincial Archives: 65, 66, 409 left.

Metropolitan Toronto Reference Library archives: from *Athletic Life*: 41, 46 left, 96; *Canadian Illustrated News*: 24; *The Globe*: 56, 107, 109 top, 113, 350 top; *Mail and Empire*:

193; *Picturesque Canada*: 33; *Toronto Star*: 276, 109 bottom, 140; *Saturday Night:* 120 left, 175, 192; *Toronto News:* 46 right; *Canadian Magazine*: 111, 130, 171 top, 174, 396 bottom left.

National Archives of Canada: Photo PA 115221, 75 left; Photo PA–20682, 85 bottom left; Photo PA 121876, 93.

New Brunswick Provincial Archives: Photo P93–161, 345 bottom.

Niagara-on-the-Lake Golf Club: 36 right.

Notman Photographic Archives, McCord Museum of Canadian History: Photo 63,003:1, 1; Photo 18,906, 15; Photo 77552, 17; Photo 136,465, 99; Photo 136, 245, 378 left.

Public Archives of Nova Scotia, Photo N–1730, 90.

John M. Olman (from a painting by T. H. Hodge): 20.

Archives of Ontario: 349 top, 369 centre.

City of Ottawa Archives and Corporate Records, Sheila Stewart Collection: Photo CA 2185, 57.

Sandra Post: 532.

Robarts Library, University of Toronto, copied from *Saturday Night*: xvi.

RCGA Museum: 123 top, 161 bottom three.
RCGA archives: 34, 61, 133 top; 176, 194, 414, 428, 429, 439, 446, 471 bottom, 481, 508, 558. From the American magazine *Golf* (1898): 85 top left, 128, 297; *Canadian Annual Golf Review*: 235, 323, 396 top left, 402 top, 403, 404, 406 left and right, 407, 408 top and bottom, 419 top left, 426, 432, 437, 439, 445, 449, 450 bottom, 459, 472, 479, 496, 497, 509, 524, 525 left, 543; *Canadian Golf Review*: 473, 474, 525 right, 531; *Canadian Golfer*: 36 left, 43 right, 47, 50, 73, 74 bottom, 85 bottom right, 91, 120 right, 141, 143, 164, 165, 166, 168 all, 171 bottom, 189 left and right, 201, 202 top and bottom, 204, 205, 206 left and right, 207 right, 208, 211, 225, 226, 229, 231, 233 top and bottom, 244 left and bottom right, 248 left, 251 left and right, 253, 254, 255, 256, 257, 258, 260, 262, 265, 266, 268 right, 281, 283, 285 right, 286, 288, 290, 291, 292, 293, 294, 304 left and right, 307 top and bottom, 308, 309 top and bottom, 312 top, 315 left and right, 317, 319 left, 324, 325, 333 top and bottom, 336 left, 337, 339, 352 top and bottom, 353, 359, 361, 363, 367, 375 left, 376, 380 top right, 381 bottom left, and right, 382 left and right, 396 left, 434, 442, 443 top and bottom, 444, 450 top, 455, 457, 460 left and right; *Canadian Sport Monthly*: 209 right, 217, 218, 219 top, 277, 295, 312 bottom, 319 right, 360, 369 bottom left and right, 370, 386, 387, 397, 401, 422, 464 left and right, 467, 494 left and right, 515, 523, 526, 528 left, top and bottom, 545, 547 top; *Fraser's International Golf Year Book*: 167; *Golf Canada*: 77, 504, 505, 514, 556, 574 left and right, 585. *Golf and Social Sports*: 216, 219 bottom, 246, 305, 349 bottom, 371; *Golf and Sports Illustrated*: 196 top, 209 left, 244 bottom right, 252, 269, 272, 285 left, 309 left; *RCGA scrapbooks*: 103, 110, 120 centre, 123 bottom, 135, 180 top and bottom, 183, 350 bottom, 365, 379 top left, 380 left, 534 left.

RCMP Museum, Regina: 53, 69 left and right, 74 top.

St. Catharines *Standard*: Photo by John McTaggart, 489.

St. George's Golf and Country Club: 213.

Sixty Years of Canadian Cricket: 119.

Marlene Stewart Streit: 383, 389, 516, 520, 521 left and right.

Vancouver City Archives: 78 left and right, 227.

Victoria City Archives: 81, 82, 316.

Victoria Golf Club: 151, 364.

Nick Weslock: 441.

York University Archives, *Toronto Telegram* Collection: 310, 343, 433, 457, 470, 471 top, 477.

APPENDIX A

Chronology

1788 Philip Loch(e) of Montreal applies for membership in the Royal & Ancient Golf Club of St. Andrews.

1826 Scots advertise a game of golf to be held at Priests' Farm, Montreal, on Christmas and New Year's days.

1854 Scottish seaman William Doleman practises his golf on the Plains of Abraham, Quebec City.

1870-72 Golfers play on Logan's Farm and Fletcher's Field, Montreal.

1872 Alexander Dennistoun returns to Montreal from Britain, having won the Silver Cross and tied for the Gold Medal at Royal Liverpool Golf Club.

1873 Dennistoun helps form The Royal Montreal Golf Club, the first active golf club in North America.

1873 Scottish bank clerks James Darling, James Cran, and Alexander Robertson golf at Brantford, James Darling, James B. Forgan, and J. J. Morrison at Halifax.

1875 In July, James Hunter of St. Andrews, son-in-law of Old Tom Morris, arrives in Canada and helps form the Royal Quebec Golf Club.

1875 In October, Royal Quebec play a club tournament, the first to be recorded in North America, and won by James Hunter.

1876 On 24 May the first interclub golf match in North America takes place, between Royal Montreal and Royal Quebec, at Quebec City.

1876 James Lamond Smith and friends start golfing in Toronto.

1879 W. Lindsay Creighton arrives in Brantford.

1880 Formation of the first Brantford Golf Club.

1880 J. Geale Dickson and friends start golfing at Niagara-on-the-Lake.

1881 Formation of Toronto Golf Club and the first club at Niagara-on-the-Lake.

1881 In June, the first interclub match in Ontario is held, between Toronto GC and Brantford GC.

1881 William Davis, the first professional in North America, joins Royal Montreal.

1882 The first men's interprovincial match between Ontario and Quebec is won by Quebec, 37 holes to 19.

1884 The club at Niagara-on-the-Lake fails after this season.

1885 Smallpox in Montreal causes the interprovincial match to be cancelled.

1885 The club at Brantford fails after this season.

1886 Formation of the first Kingston Golf Club.

1888 Formation of the first permanent golf club in the United States, at Yonkers, New York.

1888 The club at Kingston fails after this season.

1889 Golfers play at Stony Mountain, Manitoba.

1891 Formation of the Royal Ottawa Golf Club and the second Kingston Golf Club.

1891 A woman is admitted to membership of Royal Montreal.

1892 Golf begins to boom and spread across Canada.

1892 Formation of the first Vancouver Golf Club.

1892 Formation of the first women's golf club in Canada, at Royal Montreal.

1893 With the formation of Rosedale Golf Club, Toronto becomes the first North American city to have two clubs.

1893 Formation of the Victoria Golf Club.

1893 Formation of a golf club in Virden, Manitoba.

1894 Formation of Winnipeg Golf Club.

1894 The first women's interclub match in North America, between Royal Montreal and Royal Quebec.

1895 Formation of the first clubs in Alberta (Calgary GC and Macleod GC), New Brunswick (Algonquin GC), and Nova Scotia (Sydney GC).

1895 Formation of the Royal Canadian Golf Association, and the playing of the first Canadian Amateur Championship.

1895 George S. Lyon takes up golf.

1895 Victoria GC opens the first 18-hole golf course in Canada.

1895 The first Niagara International Golf Tournament.

1895 Victoria GC play Tacoma GC, Washington, the first international interclub match in North America, perhaps anywhere.

1897 The first women's interprovincial golf match between Quebec and Ontario.

1898 The first men's amateur international match against the United States, at Toronto GC.

1898 George S. Lyon wins his first of eight Canadian Amateur championships.

1899 Formation of Regina Golf Club, the first in Saskatchewan.

1899 Formation of the Pacific Northwest Golf Association.

1899 Toronto GC first plays in the League of the Lower Lakes.

1899 The first Vancouver Golf Club fails after this season.

1900 There are now about fifty golf clubs in Canada.

1900 George Cumming arrives to become professional to Toronto GC.

1900 Harry Vardon golfs in Toronto and Montreal.

1901 The first Canadian Ladies' Close championship, and the first attempt to form a Canadian Ladies' Golf Association.

1901 The introduction of the modern, rubber-cored golf ball renders courses too short.

1902 Mabel Thomson wins her first of five Ladies' Close championships.

1902 Formation of Charlottetown GC, the first in P.E.I. The probable date of the formation of The Bally Haly Golf Club, the first in Newfoundland.

1904 John Oke wins the first Canadian Open and sixty dollars.

1904 George S. Lyon wins the gold medal for golf at the Olympics in St. Louis.

1906 Formation of Jericho Country Club, Vancouver.

1906 The first Lambton Invitational Tournament.

1911 Formation of the Canadian Professional Golfers' Association.

1912 Ada Mackenzie plays in her first Canadian Ladies' Close championship.

1912 Charlie Murray wins the first CPGA championship.

1913 The first Canadian Ladies' (Amateur) Open Championship.

1913 Formation of the Canadian Ladies' Golf Union.

1914 George S. Lyon wins his eighth and last Canadian Amateur Championship.

1914 Karl Keffer wins the Open, the last Canadian to win for forty years.

1914 The first public golf course in Canada opens in Edmonton.

1915 First issue of *Canadian Golfer* magazine.

1918 Formation of the Canadian Seniors' Golf Association.

1919 The post-war boom in golf begins. There are now about 115 golf clubs in Canada.

1919 The Peace Year Amateur Championship brings out double the pre-war entry.

1919 Ada Mackenzie wins her first of six Canadian Ladies' Close championships.

1920 Stanley Thompson embarks on a career in golf course architecture.

1921 The weight and the size of the golf ball are standardized.

1921 The Canadian Amateur Championship in Winnipeg is the first outside Central Canada.

1921 Teams from Manitoba and Alberta play for the first time in the men's interprovincial team matches. Manitoba wins.

1922 Formation of the Canadian Women's Senior Golf Association.

1922 Trovinger becomes the first American-born professional to win the Canadian Open.

1923 There are now over 300 golf clubs in Canada.

1923 Formation of the Western Canada Golf Association.

1923 Formation of the Seniors' Northwest Golf Association.

1923 Spectators pay for the first time to watch the Open.

1924 First championships of the Western Canada Golf Association.

1924 Women take over the running of the Ladies' Open championship.

1925 Ada Mackenzie wins her first of four Canadian Ladies' Open championships.

1925 Formation of the Maritime Seniors' Golf Association.

1925 The rules of golf in Canada now permit the use of steel shafts.

1926 Sandy Somerville wins his first of six Canadian Amateur championships.

1926 There are now over 500 golf clubs in Canada.

1927 The first men's interprovincial team matches for the Willingdon Cup.

1930 The number of golf clubs peaks at about 600, before the Great Depression and drought.

1932 Sandy Somerville wins the U.S. Amateur championship.

1935 Amateur Ken Black wins the Vancouver Jubilee Open, and so is the first Canadian to win an event on the PGA Tour.

1935 A Canadian men's amateur team tours Britain.

1936 Seagram becomes the first sponsor of the Canadian Open.

1937 Jules Huot wins the General Brock Open at Lookout Point GC, and so is the first Canadian professional to win an event on the PGA Tour.

1939 The Open is held for the first time outside Central Canada, at Riverside G & CC, Saint John.

1940 Stan Leonard wins his first of eight CPGA championships.

1943 The Canadian Ladies' Golf Union raises funds for a Spitfire for the RAF.

1945 The CPGA Open in Montreal is the first Canadian professional event to be held over four days, including Sunday.

1946 The Canadian Open at Beaconsfield is the first to be held over four days, including Sunday.

1951 Marlene Stewart wins her first of eleven Canadian Ladies' Open championships, and her first of nine Canadian Ladies' Close championships.

1952 The first Americas Cup amateur team matches between Canada, the U.S., and Mexico.

1953 Inauguration of the men's Commonwealth Team Matches.

1953 Inauguration of the international professional team match for the Canada Cup (later the World Cup) and the individual championship for the International Trophy.

1953 Marlene Stewart wins the British Ladies' Championship, when a Canadian ladies' team tours Britain.

1954 Stan Leonard has the lowest individual score in the Canada Cup (World Cup).

1954 Pat Fletcher is the first Canadian in forty years to win the Canadian Open.

1955 Arnold Palmer wins the Canadian Open, his first win on the PGA Tour. This is the first Open to be televised coast to coast.

1955 Stan Leonard goes on the PGA Tour at the age of forty.

1955 Al Balding is the first Canadian to win a PGA Tour event in the United States.

1956 Marlene Stewart wins the Ladies' championships of the United States, Canada, and Australia.

1957 Nick Weslock wins his first of four Canadian Amateur championships.

1959 Inauguration of the women's Commonwealth Team Matches.

1959 Stan Leonard has the lowest individual score in the Canada Cup (World Cup).

1961 Stan Leonard wins his eight and last CPGA championship.

1962 George Knudson wins his first of eight events on the PGA Tour.

1962 Gary Cowan is leading scorer in the men's World Amateur Team Matches.

1965 Jack Nicklaus is runner-up in the Open for the first time.

1966 George Knudson has the lowest individual score in the World Cup.

1966 Gary Cowan wins the first of two U.S. Amateur championships.

1968 Sandra Post wins the LPGA championship, her first of three major, and six other, events on the LPGA Tour.

1968 George Knudson wins back-to-back events on the PGA Tour.

1968 Al Balding and George Knudson win the World Cup, and Balding has the lowest individual score.

1971 Imperial Tobacco takes over as sponsor of the Canadian Open.

1971 Canada wins the men's Commonwealth Team Matches in Auckland, New Zealand.

1971 Gary Cowan wins his second U.S. Amateur championship.

1972 Jocelyne Bourassa wins La Canadienne, the first LPGA event to be held in Canada.

1972 Doug Roxburgh wins his first Canadian Amateur Championship.

1975 Canada wins the men's Commonwealth Team Matches, in Durban, South Africa.

1977 Trevino wins the first Canadian Open to be held at Glen Abbey.

1978 Cathy Graham Sherk wins the U.S. Ladies' Amateur championship after being runner-up in 1977.

1979 Canada wins the women's Commonwealth Team Matches at Lake Karrinyup, Australia.

1980 Dan Halldorson and Jim Nelford win the World Cup.

1983 Dave Barr has the lowest individual score in the World Cup.

1985 Dave Barr and Dan Halldorson win the World Cup.

1986 Canada wins the men's World Amateur Team Matches.

1987 Canada wins the women's Commonwealth Team Matches.

1992 Canadians Lisa Walters and Dawn Coe win back-to-back events on the LPGA Tour.

APPENDIX B

Members of the Canadian Golf Hall of Fame

	Year of induction
Keith Alexander (amateur golfer)	1986
Al Balding (professional golfer)	1985
Davie Black (professional golfer)	1972
Ken Black (amateur golfer)	1987
Gordie Brydson (professional golfer)	1982
Betty Stanhope Cole (amateur golfer)	1991
Gary Cowan (amateur golfer)	1972
George Cumming (professional golfer)	1971
Marion Doherty (golf administrator)	1981
Phil Farley (amateur golfer)	1979
Pat Fletcher (professional golfer)	1976
R. Bruce Forbes (golf administrator)	1987
Alexa Stirling Fraser (amateur golfer)	1986
Florence Harvey (amateur golfer/administrator)	1972
Jules Huot (professional golfer)	1977
Karl Keffer (professional golfer)	1986
George Knudson (professional golfer)	1985
Willie Lamb (professional golfer)	1986
Stan Leonard (professional golfer)	1972
George S. Lyon (amateur golfer)	1971
Ada Mackenzie (amateur golfer)	1971
Henry Martell (amateur/professional golfer)	1982
Fritz Martin (amateur golfer)	1974
Rod McIsaac (builder)	1983
Albert Murray (professional golfer)	1974
Charles Murray (professional golfer)	1971
Sandra Post (professional golfer)	1988
Ralph Reville (golf journalist)	1986
Doug Roxburgh (amateur golfer)	1990
Doug Silverberg (amateur golfer)	1989
C. Ross (Sandy) Somerville (amateur golfer)	1971
John Steel (golf superintendent)	1988
Marlene Stewart Streit (amateur golfer)	1971
Gordon B. Taylor (amateur golfer)	1986
Stanley Thompson (golf course architect)	1980
Mabel Thomson (amateur golfer)	1986
Nick Weslock (amateur golfer)	1972

APPENDIX C
Winners of Canadian National Championships

	Canadian Open	Canadian Amateur	CPGA	CPGA match play for Millar Trophy
1895		Tom M. Harley		
1896		Stuart Gillespie		
1897		W. A. H. Kerr		
1898		George S. Lyon		
1899		Vere C. Brown		
1900		George S. Lyon		
1901		W.A.H. Kerr		
1902		Fritz Martin		
1903		George S. Lyon		
1904	J.H. Oke	Percy Taylor		
1905	George Cumming	George S. Lyon		
1906	Charlie Murray	George S. Lyon		
1907	Percy Barrett	George S. Lyon		
1908	Albert Murray	Alec Wilson		
1909	Karl Keffer	Edward Legge		
1910	Daniel Kenny	Fritz Martin		
1911	Charlie Murray	George H. Hutton		
1912	George Sargent	George S. Lyon	Charlie Murray	
1913	Albert Murray	Geoff. H. Turpin	Davie Black	
1914	Karl Keffer	George S. Lyon	George Cumming	
1915-18	not held	not held	not held	
1919	J. Douglas Edgar	W. McLuckie	Davie Black	
1920	J. Douglas Edgar	Charles B. Grier	Davie Black	
1921	W.H. Trovinger	Frank Thompson	Davie Black	
1922	Al Watrous	C.C. Fraser	Nicol Thompson	
1923	C.W. Hackney	William J. Thompson	Percy Barrett	
1924	Leo Diegel	Frank Thompson	Albert Murray	
1925	Leo Diegel	Donald D. Carrick	Percy Barrett	
1926	Macdonald Smith	C. Ross Somerville	Jimmy Johnstone	
1927	Tommy Armour	Donald D. Carrick	Jimmy Johnstone	
1928	Leo Diegel	C. Ross Somerville	Willie Lamb	Jimmy Johnstone
1929	Leo Diegel	Eddie Held	Willie Lamb	Bob Cunningham Sr.
1930	Tommy Armour	C. Ross Somerville	Willie Lamb	Willie Lamb
1931	Walter Hagen	C. Ross Somerville	Andy Kay	Lex Robson
1932	Harry Cooper	Gordon B. Taylor	Lex Robson	Lex Robson
1933	Joe Kirkwood	Albert Campbell	Willie Lamb	Jimmy Johnstone
1934	Tommy Armour	Albert Campbell	Jules Huot	Lex Robson
1935	Genes Kunes	C. Ross Somerville	Willie Lamb	Lex Robson
1936	Lawson Little	Fred Haas	Stan Horne	Lex Robson
1937	Harry Cooper	C. Ross Somerville	Stan Horne	Gordie Brydson
1938	Sam Snead	Ted Adams	Stan Horne	Dick Borthwick

	Canadian Open	Canadian Amateur	CPGA	CPGA match play for Millar Trophy
1939	Harold McSpaden	Ken Black	Jules Huot	Lex Robson
1940	Sam Snead	not held	Stan Leonard	Bob Gray
1941	Sam Snead	not held	Stan Leonard	Sam Kerr
1942	Craig Wood	not held	Bob Burns	Bob Gray
1943	not held	not held	not held	Bob Gray
1944	not held	not held	Gordie Brydson	Bill Kerr
1945	Byron Nelson	not held	Bill Kerr	Bill Kerr
1946	George Fazio	Henry Martell	Jules Huot	Stan Horne
1947	Bobby Locke	Frank Stranahan	Rodolphe Huot	Bill Kerr
1948	C.W. Congdon	Frank Stranahan	Gordie Brydson	Stan Horne
1949	E.J. Harrison	R.D. Chapman	Dick Borthwick	Bob Gray
1950	Jim Ferrier	Bill Mawhinney	Stan Leonard	Bill Kerr
1951	Jim Ferrier	Walter McElroy	Stan Leonard	Norm Himes
1952	Johnny Palmer	Larry Boucher	Pat Fletcher	Al Balding
1953	Dave Douglas	Don Cherry	Henry Martell	Gordie Brydson
1954	Pat Fletcher	Harvey Ward	Stan Leonard	Al Balding
1955	Arnold Palmer	Moe Norman	Al Balding	Murray Tucker
1956	Doug Sanders	Moe Norman	Al Balding	Stan Leonard
1957	George Bayer	Nick Weslock	Stan Leonard	Bill Mawhinney
1958	Wes Ellis	Bruce Castator	Henry Martell	Al Balding
1959	Doug Ford	Johnny Johnston	Stan Leonard	Bob Cunningham Jr.
1960	Art Wall	Keith Alexander	Bill Kerr	Bill Thompson
1961	Jacky Cupit	Gary Cowan	Stan Leonard	Al Balding
1962	Ted Kroll	Reg Taylor	Alvie Thompson	Frank Whibley
1963	Doug Ford	Nick Weslock	Al Balding	Alvie Thompson
1964	Kel Nagle	Nick Weslock	George Knudson	Moe Norman
1965	Gene Littler	George Henry	Wilf Homenuik	Al Johnston
1966	Don Massengale	Nick Weslock	Moe Norman	George Knudson
1967	Billy Casper	Stuart Jones	George Knudson	Wilf Homenuik
1968	Bob Charles	Jim Doyle	George Knudson	Wilf Homenuik
1969	Tommy Aaron	Wayne McDonald	Bob Cox	discontinued
1970	Kermit Zarley	Allen Miller	Al Balding	From 1966 was
1971	Lee Trevino	Dick Siderowf	Wilf Homenuik	stroke play.
1972	Gay Brewer	Doug Roxburgh	Bob Panasiuk	
1973	Tom Weiskopf	George Burns	Bob Panasiuk	
1974	Bobby Nichols	Doug Roxburgh	Moe Norman	
1975	Tom Weiskopf	Jim Nelford	Bill Tape	
1976	Jerry Pate	Jim Nelford	George Knudson	
1977	Lee Trevino	Rod Spittle	George Knudson	
1978	Bruce Lietzke	Rod Spittle	Lanny Wadkins	
1979	Lee Trevino	Rafael Alarcon	Lee Trevino	
1980	Bob Gilder	Greg Olson	Arnold Palmer	
1981	Peter Oosterhuis	Richard Zokol	Ray Floyd	
1982	Bruce Lietzke	Doug Roxburgh	Jim Thorpe	
1983	John Cook	Danny Mijovic	Lee Trevino	
1984	Greg Norman	Bill Swartz	Jim Rutledge	
1985	Curtis Strange	Brent Franklin	Dave Barr	
1986	Bob Murphy	Brent Franklin	Dan Halldorson	
1987	Curtis Strange	Brent Franklin	Jerry Anderson	
1988	Ken Green	Doug Roxburgh	Brent Franklin	
1989	Steve Jones	Peter Major	Jean-Louis Lamarre	
1990	Wayne Levi	Warren Sye	Rick Gibson	
1991	Nick Price	Jeff Kraemer	Tom Harding	

Canadian Ladies' Amateur

	Open	Close
1901		Lillias Young
1902		Mabel Thomson
1903		Florence Harvey
1904		Florence Harvey
1905		Mabel Thomson
1906		Mabel Thomson
1907		Mabel Thomson
1908		Mabel Thomson
1909		Violet Henry-Anderson
1910		Dorothy Campbell
1911		Dorothy Campbell
1912		Dorothy Campbell
1913	Muriel Dodd	not held
1914-18	not held	not held
1919	not held	Ada Mackenzie
1920	Alexa Stirling	not held
1921	Cecil Leitch	not held
1922	Mrs. W. A. Gavin	Frances Scott Gibson
1923	Glenna Collett	Sydney Pepler
1924	Glenna Collett	Vera Ramsay Hutchings
1925	Ada Mackenzie	Helen Paget
1926	Ada Mackenzie	Ada Mackenzie
1927	Helen Payson	Ada Mackenzie
1928	Virginia Wilson	not held
1929	Helen Hicks	Ada Mackenzie
1930	Maureen Orcutt	Margery Kirkham
1931	Maureen Orcutt	Ada Mackenzie
1932	Margery Kirkham	not held
1933	Ada Mackenzie	Ada Mackenzie
1934	Alexa Stirling Fraser	Vera Ramsay Ford
1935	Ada Mackenzie	Irene Jolin Horne
1936	Dora Virtue Darling	Sydney Pepler Mulqueen
1937	Mrs. John Rogers	Heather Leslie
1938	Sydney Pepler Mulqueen	not held
1939-46	not held	not held
1947	Grace Lenczyk	not held
1948	Grace Lenczyk	not held
1949	Grace DeMoss	Babs Davies
1950	Dorothy Kielty	Mrs. Graeme Pyke
1951	Marlene Stewart	Marlene Stewart
1952	Edean Anderson	Marlene Stewart
1953	Barbara Romack	Marlene Stewart
1954	Marlene Stewart	Marlene Stewart
1955	Marlene Stewart	Marlene Stewart
1956	Marlene Stewart	Marlene Stewart
1957	Betty Stanhope	Marlene Stewart Streit
1958	Marlene Stewart Streit	not held
1959	Marlene Stewart Streit	not held
1960	Judy Darling	Mrs. Dulcie Lyle
1961	Judy Darling	Janet McWha
1962	Gayle Hitchens	Sue Hilton
1963	Marlene Stewart Streit	Marlene Stewart Streit
1964	Margaret Masters	Gail Harvey
1965	Jocelyne Bourassa	Gail Harvey

	Open	Close
1966	Helene Gagnon	Marilyn Palmer
1967	Bridget Jackson	Betty Stanhope Cole
1968	Marlene Stewart Streit	Marlene Stewart Streit
1969	Marlene Stewart Streit	discontinued
1970	Gail Harvey Moore	
1971	Jocelyne Bourassa	
1972	Marlene Stewart Streit	
1973	Marlene Stewart Streit	
1974	Debbie Massey	
1975	Debbie Massey	
1976	Debbie Massey	
1977	Cathy Graham Sherk	
1978	Cathy Graham Sherk	
1979	Stacey West	
1980	Edwina Kennedy	
1981	Jane Lock	
1982	Cindy Pleger	
1983	Dawn Coe	
1984	Kimberly Williams	
1985	Kimberly Williams	
1986	Marilyn Palmer O'Connor	
1987	Tracy Kerdyk	
1988	Michiko Hattori	
1989	Cheryll Damphouse	
1990	Sarah Lebrun Ingram	
1991	Adele Morre	

Canadian PGA

	Tournament Players' Division	CPGA Women's Championship
1984	Frank Edmonds	
1985	Greg Olson	
1986	Bob Panasiuk	
1987	Craig Parry	Cathy Graham Sherk
1988	Dave Barr	Gail Anderson
1989	Jerry Anderson	Sharon Smith-Cranmer
1990	Ernie Gonzalez	Cathy Graham Sherk
1991	Mark Wurtz	Jackie Twamley

BIBLIOGRAPHY

Canadian Golf

Balsillie, Robert Ness, ed. *Fraser's Golf Directory and Year Book*. Montreal: Fraser Publishing Co., 1923.

Batten, Jack. *The Toronto Golf Club, 1876–1976*. Toronto: The Toronto Golf Club, 1976.

The Beaconsfield Golf Club, Seventy-fifth Anniversary, 1904–1979. Beaconsfield Golf Club, 1979.

Boyle, Mickey. *Ninety Years of Golf, An Illustrated History of Golf in Saskatchewan*. Regina: Mickey Boyle, 1987.

Calgary Golf and Country Club, 1897–1972. Calgary: Calgary Golf and Country Club, 1972.

Canadian and Provincial Golf Records. Oakville: The Royal Canadian Golf Association, published every five years and updated annually.

Chandler, Leonard R. *A History of Essex Golf and Country Club, 1902–1983*. Windsor: Essex Golf and Country Club, 1983.

Le Club de Golf Royal Quebec, 1874–1974. By various authors. Quebec: Le Club de Golf Royal Quebec, 1974.

Cockfield, A.S. and H.B. McNally. *Mount Bruno Country Club: Some Historical Notes*. Montreal: 1978.

Costello, Ralph. *The First Fifty Years: The Story of the New Brunswick Golf Association*. New Ireland Press, 1987.

Cruickshank, F. D. *The History of Weston Golf and Country Club*. Weston: Weston Golf and Country Club, 1980.

Denis, Frank T. *The Kanawaki Golf Club, 1914–1964*. Caughnawaga: The Kanawaki Golf Club, 1964.

50 Years of Golf at Islesmere. Islesmere: Islesmere Golf and Country Club, 1969.

Jones, Lyndon. *The Cataraqui Golf and Country Club: The First Seventy Years, 1917–1987*. Kingston: Mika Publishing, 1987.

Kavanagh, L.V. *History of Golf in Canada*. Toronto: Fitzhenry and Whiteside, 1973.

MacCabe, Eddie. *The Ottawa Hunt Club, 75 Years of History, 1908–1983*. Ottawa: The Ottawa Hunt Club, 1983.

McClung, J. W. *Edmonton Country Club, The Early Years*. Edmonton: Edmonton Country Club, 1986.

Mississaugua Golf and Country Club, 1906–1981. Mississauga: Bettie Bradley, 1981.

Nelford, Jim, and Lorne Rubenstein. *Seasons in a Golfer's Life*. Toronto: Methuen, 1984.

Peden, J.D. *Uplands Golf Club, 1922–1982*. Victoria: Uplands Golf Club, 1982.

Putman, H.L., ed. *Whitlock: The First Seventy-five Years*. Hudson Heights: Whitlock Golf Club, 1987.

Reville, Ralph. *Golf in Canada*. Montreal: Canadian Pacific Railway, 1918.

The Royal Montreal Golf Club. Montreal: The Royal Montreal Golf Club, 1923.

The Royal Montreal Golf Club, 1873–1973. By various authors. Montreal: The Royal Montreal Golf Club, 1973.

Robertson, Frank N. *Golf Gleanings Old and New: The History of the Maritime Seniors' Golf Association*. Saint John: The Maritime Seniors' Golf Association, 1953.

St. Charles Country Club, 1905–1965. Winnipeg: St. Charles Country Club, n.d.

Schroeter, Reg. *Rivermead Golf Club: The First 75 Years*. Hull: Rivermead Golf Club, 1985.

Thompson, William J. *Commonsense Golf*. Toronto: Thomas Allen, 1923.

Uzzell, Thomas H. *Golf in the World's Oldest Mountains*. Murray Bay: The Manoir Richelieu, n.d.

Webling, W. Hastings. *Fore: The Call of the Links*. Boston: H. M. Caldwell, 1909.

Webling, W. Hastings. *Locker Room Ballads*. New York: Betrano's, 1925.

Weslock, Nick. *Your Golf Bag Pro: Nick Weslock's Little Black Book of Golf Secrets*. Edmonton: Hurtig Publishers, 1985.

Wolf, David. *Golf Courses of Saskatchewan*. Saskatoon: David Wolf, 1985.

Golf, General

Bauchope, C. Robertson. *The Golfing Annual, 1888–1889*. London: Horace Cox, 1889.

Browning, Robert H. K. *A History of Golf: The Royal and Ancient Game*. London: Dent, 1955.

Clark, Robert. *Golf: A Royal and Ancient Game*. Edinburgh: R. & R. Clark, 1875.

Clougher, T. R., ed. *Golf Clubs of the Empire: The Golfing Annual*. London: Clougher Corp., 1926.

Colville, James. *The Glasgow Golf Club, 1787–1907*. Glasgow: John Smith & Son, 1907.

Cornish, Geoffrey S., and Ronald E. Whitten. *The Golf Course*. New York: The Rutledge Press, 1981.

Crampsey, Robert A. *St. Mungo's Gowfers, The History of Glasgow Golf Club, 1787–1987*. Glasgow: Glasgow Golf Club, n.d.

Darwin, Bernard, and others. *A History of Golf in Britain*. London: Cassell, 1952.

Davies, Peter. *Davies' Dictionary of Golfing Terms*. New York: Simon and Schuster, 1980.

Dobereiner, Peter. *The Glorious World of Golf*. New York: McGraw-Hill Book Company, 1973.

Donovan, Richard E., and Joseph S.F. Murdoch. *The Game of Golf and the Printed Word, 1566–1985*. Endicott, N.Y.: Richard E. Donovan, 1988.

East Lothian Golf. Musselburgh: East Lothian District Council, n.d.

Edgar, J. Douglas. *The Gate to Golf*. Washington: J. Douglas Edgar, 1920.

Everard, H.S.C. *A History of the Royal and Ancient Golf Club, St. Andrews, from 1754–1900*. Edinburgh: William Blackwood, 1907.

Farrar, Guy B. *The Royal Liverpool Golf Club: A History, 1869–1932*. Birkenhead: Willmer Brothers, 1933.

The First Seventy-five Years of the United States Seniors' Golf Association, 1905–1980. United States Seniors' Golf Association, 1980.

Galbraith, William. *Prestwick St. Nicholas Golf Club*. Prestwick: Prestwick St. Nicholas Golf Club, 1950.

Gillon, Stair A. *The Honourable Company of Edinburgh Golfers at Muirfield, 1891–1914*. Edinburgh: The Honourable Company of Edinburgh Golfers, 1946.

Goodban, J.W.D., ed. *The Royal North Devon Golf Club, 1864–1964*. The Royal North Devon Golf Club, 1964.

Goodner, Ross. *The 75 Year History of Shinnecock Hills Golf Club*. Southhampton: Shinnecock Hills Golf Club, 1966.

Graffis, Herb. *The PGA*. New York: Thomas Y. Crowell Company, 1975.

Hamilton, David. *Early Aberdeen Golf*. Glasgow and Oxford: The Partick Press, 1985.

Hamilton, David. *Early Golf in Glasgow, 1589–1787*. Oxford: The Partick Press, 1985.

Haultain, Theodore Arnold. *The Mystery of Golf*. Boston and New York: Houghton Mifflin Company, 1908.

Heck, Margaret Seaton, and Walter J. Hagen. *The Walter Hagen Story*. New York: Simon & Schuster, 1956.

Henderson, Ian T., and David Stirk. *Golf in the Making*. Crawley: Henderson and Stirk Ltd., 1979.

Hutchinson, Horace, and others. *The Book of Golf and Golfers*. London: Longmans, Green, 1899.

Hutchinson, Horace, and others. *Golf*. The Badminton Library. London: Longmans, Green, 1890.

Hutchinson, Horace, and others. *Famous Golf Links*. London: Longmans, Green, 1891.

J.A.C.K. (pseudonym John McCulloch). *Golf in the Year 2000*. London: T. Fisher Unwin, 1892.

Kerr, Rev. John. *The Golf Book of East Lothian*. Edinburgh: T. and A. Constable, 1896.

Leach, Henry. *The Happy Golfer*. London: Macmillan, 1914.

Low, John L. *Nisbet's Golf Year Book*, edited by John Low, later by V.G. Harmsworth. London: James Nisbet, annually 1905 to 1914.

Macdonald, Charles Blair. *Scotland's Gift: Golf*. New York: Charles Scribner's Sons, 1928.

MacKenzie, Dr. A. *Golf Architecture*. London: Simpkin, Marshall, Hamilton & Kent, 1920.

Martin, Harry B. *Fifty Years of American Golf*. New York: Dodd, Mead, 1936.

Martin, Harry B., and Alexander B. Halliday. *St. Andrews (New York) Golf Club, 1888–1938*. New York: St. Andrews Golf Club, 1938.

Martin, John Stuart. *The Curious History of the Golf Ball*. New York: Horizon Press, 1968.

Mathieson, Donald Mackay, ed. *The Golfer's Handbook*, edited by a number of persons since its first publication as an annual in 1898. Glasgow and Edinburgh: The Golfer's Handbook.

Murdoch, Joseph S.F. *The Library of Golf, 1743–1966*. Detroit: Gale Research Company, 1968. Revisions and additions, 1967–1977.

Murdoch, Joseph S.F., and Janet Seagle. *Golf: A Guide to Information Sources*. Detroit: Gale Research Company, 1979.

Official PGA Tour Book. Ponta Verda: PGA Tour, various dates.

Park, Willie. *The Game of Golf*. London: Longmans, Green, 1896.

Peter, H. Thomas. *Reminiscences of Golf and Golfers*. Edinburgh: James Thin, 1890.

Pottinger, George. *Muirfield and the Honourable Company*. Edinburgh: Scottish Academic Press Ltd., 1972.

Price, Charles, ed. *The American Golfer*. New York: Random House, 1964.

Price, Charles. *The World of Golf*. New York: Random House, 1962.

Price, Charles, and George C. Rogers Jr. *The Carolina Lowcountry, Birthplace of American Golf, 1786*. Hilton Head Island: Sea Pines Company, 1980.

Pulver, P.C., ed. *The American Annual Golf Guide and Year Book, 1921*. New York: Golf Guide Publishing Company, 1921.

Roberts, Henry, ed. *The Green Book of Golf*. San Francisco: 1914.

Robertson, James K. *St. Andrews, Home of Golf*. St. Andrews: Citizen Office, 1967.

Salmond, Dr. J.B. *The Story of the R & A*. London: Macmillan, 1956.

Servos, Launcelot Cressy. *Practical Instruction in Golf*. Launcelot Cressy Servos, 1905; revised edition, Emmaus, Pa.: Rodale Press, 1938.

Smith, Charles. *The Aberdeen Golfers: Records and Reminiscences*. Fascimile edition. London: Ellesborough Press, 1982.

Smith, Shirlee H. *The Tacoma Golf and Country Club*. Tacoma: The Tacoma Golf and Country Club, 1980.

Steel, Donald, and Peter Ryde, eds. *The Encyclopedia of Golf*. New York: The Viking Press, 1975.

van Hengel, Steven J. H. *Early Golf*. Bentveld, Netherlands: Steven van Hengel, 1982.

Vardon, Harry. *My Golfing Life*. London: Hutchinson, 1933.

Wethered, H.N., and T. Simpson. *The Architectural Side of Golf*. London: Longmans, Green, 1929.

Wind, Herbert Warren. *The Story of American Golf*. New York: Farrar, Strauss, 1948. Third edition, New York: Alfred A. Knopf, 1975.

General

Balfour, Arthur James, First Earl of. *Retrospect, An Unfinished Autobiography*. Toronto: McClelland & Stewart, n.d.

Blakeley, Phyllis R. *Glimpses of Halifax, 1867–1900*. Halifax: Public Archives of Nova Scotia, 1949.

The Book of Sport. Vols. I and II. By many authors. New York: J.F. Taylor, 1904.

Campbell, Marjorie Wilkins. *The North West Company*. Toronto: The Macmillan Company of Canada Limited, 1957.

Chambers, Captain Ernest J. *The Royal North-West Mounted Police: A Corps History*. The Mortimer Press, 1906.

Collard, Edgar Andrew. *Call Back Yesterdays*. Toronto: Longmans Canada Limited, 1965.

Denison, Merrill. *Canada's First Bank: A History of the Bank of Montreal*. Vols. I and II. Toronto: McClelland & Stewart.

Ferguson, Bob. *Who's Who in Canadian Sport*. Toronto: Summerhill Press Ltd., 1985.

Field, John L. *Niagara-on-the-Lake Guide Book*. Niagara-on-the-Lake: John L. Field, 1984.

Forgan, James B. *Recollections of a Busy Life*. The Bankers Publishing Co., 1924.

Fort Macleod – Our Colourful Past. Various authors. Fort Macleod: Fort Macleod History Book Committee, 1977.

Greene, B.M., ed., and others. *Who's Who and Why*. Toronto: International Press, many editions from the 1919–20 edition, under this title or *Who's Who in Canada*.

Guillet, Edwin C. *Pioneer Banking in Canada: The Bank of Upper Canada, 1822–1826.* Reprinted from *The Canadian Banker*, 1948.

Hall, John E., and R. O. McCulloch. *Sixty Years of Canadian Cricket.* Toronto: Bryant Printing and Publishing Company Limited, 1895.

Howell, Nancy, and Maxwell L. Howell. *Sports and Games in Canadian Life: 1700 to the Present.* Toronto: Macmillan of Canada, 1969.

Jackman, S.W. *Vancouver Island.* Toronto: Griffin House, 1972.

Kluckner, Michael. *Vancouver: The Way It Was.* North Vancouver: Whitecap Books Ltd., 1984.

Kluckner, Michael. *Victoria: The Way It Was.* North Vancouver: Whitecap Books Ltd., 1986.

LeMoine, J. M. *Picturesque Quebec.* Montreal: Dawson Brothers, 1882.

MacGregor, James G. *History of Alberta.* Edmonton: Hurtig Publishers, 1972.

March, James H., ed. *The Canadian Encyclopedia.* Second Edition. Edmonton: Hurtig Publishers, 1988.

Mather, Barry, and Margaret McDonald. *New Westminster, The Royal City.* J. M. Dent & Sons (Canada) Ltd., 1958.

Morgan, Henry J., ed. *The Canadian Men and Women of the Time.* Toronto: William Briggs, 1898.

Newman, Peter C. *Company of Adventurers, Vol. II: Caesars of the Wilderness.* Markham: Penguin Books, 1988.

O'Neill, Paul. *The Oldest City: The Story of St. John's, Newfoundland.* Erin, Ont.: Press Porcepic, 1975.

Ormsby, Margaret A. *British Columbia, a History.* Toronto: Macmillan of Canada, 1958.

Rogers, George C. Jr. *Charleston in the Age of the Pinckneys.* Revised edition. Columbia: University of South Carolina Press, 1980.

Ross, Victor. *A History of the Canadian Bank of Commerce. Vol. II.* Toronto: Oxford University Press, 1922.

Roxburgh, Henry. *Great Days in Canadian Sport.* Toronto: Ryerson Press, 1957.

Roxburgh, Henry. *One Hundred – Not Out.* Toronto: Ryerson Press, 1966.

Schull, Joseph, and J. Douglas Gibson. *The Scotiabank Story: A History of the Bank of Nova Scotia, 1832–1982.* Toronto: Macmillan of Canada, n.d.

Shortt, Edward, ed. *Perth Remembered.* Perth, Ont.: Mortimer Ltd., 1967.

Stevens, Dorid, and Claud Stevens. *The Haultain Story.* Fort Macleod: Fort Macleod Historical Association, n.d.

Thompson, Austin Seaton. *Spadina: A Story of Old Toronto.* Toronto: Pagurian Press, 1975.

In addition, the author has consulted the following periodicals:

American Golfer (U.S.), *Athletic Life, B.C. Golf, Canadian Golfer, Canadian Illustrated News, Canadian Annual Golf Review, Canadian Golf Review,* CLGA *Year Book, Canadian Magazine, Canadian Sport Monthly,* CPGA *Bulletin,* CPGA *Yearbook, Golf* (British), *Golf* (U.S.), *Golf and Club News, Golf and Social Sports, Golf and Sports Illustrated, Golf Canada, Golf Illustrated* (British), *Golf Illustrated* (U.S.), *Golf Monthly* (British), *Golfers Magazine* (U.S.), *Greenmaster, On the Green, Outdoors-South* (U.S.), *Journal of Canadian Bankers' Association, Outing* (U.S.), *Score,* RCGA *Annual Report,* USGA *Golf Journal* (U.S.), *The Week, World of Golf* (British).

The author has also consulted microfilm records of a variety of North American newspapers, 1826–1990, as identified throughout the text.

(1977), 564; (1981), 566; (1982), 558-59; (1988), 559; winners, 603-4

Canadian Golf Course Superintendents Association, 372

Canadian Golf Foundation, 391-92, 572

Canadian Golf Hall of Fame, 180, 206, 248, 281, 290, 434, 439, 509, 529, 576, 602

Canadian Golfer, 206-9, *207*, 211-12, 434

Canadian Junior Championship, 385; (1955), 511

Canadian Junior Girls' Championship, 533, 545

Canadian Ladies' Amateur Close Championship, 101, 176-87, 239-42, 247; controversy over, 262-63; discontinuation of, 545; location and timing, 241; (1901), 177, 178, 179, 188; (1903), 177; (1907), 176-77; (1908), 177-178, 179; (1909), 178; (1910), 184; (1911), 184; (1912), 184-85; (1926), 245; (1933), 245; (1935), 186, 258; (1937), 255-56, 259; (1956), 520; (1963), 527, 529; (1964), 529; (1965), 529; (1966), 529; (1968), 527; winners, 605-6

Canadian Ladies' Amateur Open Championship, 177, 185, 240-48, 525; timing and location, 241; (1913), 177, 185-86, 246, 256; (1923), 242, 257; (1924), 257; (1925), 243, 245; (1926), 245; (1927), 257-58; (1933), 245; (1936), 525; (1937), 255; (1938), 259-60; (1948), 516; (1950), 517, 518; (1951), 517; (1953), 523; (1954), 523; (1956), 520; (1957), 523; (1958), 524; (1959), 524; (1960), 526; (1961), 526; (1962), 524-25, 526; (1963), 527; (1965), 537, 538-39; (1967), 529; (1968), 527, 529, 539; (1969), 527, 529; (1970), 527, 528, 529; (1971), 539; (1972), 527; (1973), 527, 529; (1977), 569; (1978), 569; (1983), 571; winners 605-6

Canadian Ladies' Golf Association (CLGA), 187-88, 542-50; annual meeting, 545; course rating, 543-44; funding, 543; and international matches, 546-50; and interprovincial team matches, 544-45; junior development, 544; reorganization, 542-43. *See also* Canadian Ladies' Golf Union

Canadian Ladies' Golf Union (CLGU), 62, 101, 102, 179, 187-88, 189-90, 207, 239-42, 246, 542; Canadian Team Fund Committee, 263; championships, entrance requirements,

240; divisions established, 190; interprovincial team matches, 262, 263; and junior golf, 516; membership fees, 261-62; National Pars Committee, 190; provincial branches, 217, 261; and provincial championships, 261; Toronto base of, 260; and World War I, 204-6; and World War II, 386. *See also* Canadian Ladies' Golf Association

Canadian Ladies' Professional Golf Association (CLPGA), 537

Canadian Ladies' Senior Golf Championship, 461

Canadian Open Championship, 94, 100, 101, 132-47, 218, 303, 304, 305, 306, 321, 435-36, 441, 499, 502, 504, 573; Canadian professionals in, 144-46; commercial sponsorship, 322; at Glen Abbey, 452, 578-80, 581-82, 583-91; host clubs, 470-72; income from, 440; number of entrants, 322; organizational problems, 467-68; and PGA Tour, 327, 328, 329, 462, 465; popularity as spectacle, 323; prize money, 132-33, 321-22, 323, 324, 325, 328, 394, 446-47, 468, 486; scoring, 133; sponsorship of, 394, 445-49, 447-48, 490; television coverage of, 393; U.S. professionals in, 322-26, 331; and World War II, 385-86; (1904), 132-33; (1905), 133, 159; (1911), 146; (1914), 200, 322; (1919), 322, 323, 329; (1920), 323, 329-30; (1921), 323, 330, 335-36; (1922), 323, 347; (1923), 322, 322-23, 323-24, 347; (1924), 322, 324, 331; (1925), 324, 327, 331-32; (1926), 324, 347; (1927), 324, 335, 336; (1928), 324, 332; (1929), 324-25, 332-34, *333*; (1930), 325, 334-35; (1931), 325, 337; (1932), 325, 344; (1933), 325; (1934), 325, 336, 347; (1935), 321, 325-26; (1936), 234, 289, 323, 325, 346-47, 469; (1937), 234, 323, 325, 344, 347; (1938), 325, 338-40; (1939), 325, 340, 344-46; (1940), 325, 340-41, 342; (1941), 325, 342-43; (1942), 325, 343, 386; (1946), 500; (1947), *410*, 469-70, *470*; (1948), 403; (1949), 475-76, 484; (1950), 472, 497; (1951), 472-73; (1953), 478; (1954), 405, 462-65; (1955), 465-67, 478; (1956), 452, 478; (1957), 479-80; (1958), 476, 480, 499; (1959), 476, 480; (1960), 476, 499; (1962), 413, 480; (1963), 413, 478; (1964), *471*, 591; (1965), 473-75, *474*; (1966), *471*; (1967),

480-81; (1968), 476-77, *477*, 510; (1969), 468-69; (1970), 418; (1971), 584-85; (1972), 573-74; (1973), 481-82; (1974), 475; (1975), 482; (1977), 564, 579, 583-84; (1978), 586-88; (1979), 565, 586; (1980), 579; (1982), 566, 587-88; (1983), 590-91; (1984), 565, 588-89; (1985), 589; (1986), 591; (1987), 590; (1988), 560, 562, 565; winners 603-4

Canadian Professional Golfers' Association (CPGA), 146, 386, 483-92; administration of, 489-90; Championship, 218, 303-4, 305-6, 309, 311, 313, 314, 448; 496-98; (1912), 146; (1913), 146; (1914), 200; (1926), 308; (1930), 493; (1940), 493-94; (1941), 495; (1945), 484; (1946), 484; (1948), 496; (1949), 484; (1950), 497; (1951), 497; (1955), 501; (1956), 502; (1959), 497; (1961), 498; (1962), 486; (1963), 502-3; (1966), 503, 504; (1967), 490; (1972), 506; (1973), 506; (1974), 503, 504-5; (1985), 560; (1988), 562; and commercial sponsors, 486; Royal Oak Golf Club, 491-92; Tour, 491, 553, 560, 561, 562, 563, 567; Tournament Players Division, 491, 606; winners, 603-4

Canadian Seniors' Golf Association, 66, 111, 126, 208, 455-58

Canadian Women's Senior Golf Association, 460-61

La Canadienne tournament (1973), 537-38

Cape Breton Highlands Golf Club, 365

Capilano Golf Club (Vancouver), 365, *369*, 370

Cardy, Vernon G., 442, *443*, 444

Caribbean Tour, 447, 488-89

Carling World Open, 448, 449

Carmichael, Sam, 508

Carner, JoAnne Gunderson. *See* Gunderson, JoAnne

Carnochan, Janet, 37

Carrick, Donald, 112, 217, *272*, *272*, 273-74, 281, 282, 286, 287, 404

Carruthers, John Bell, 38

Carruthers, Mrs. John Bell, 38

Carter, G. W. F., 48, 108

Cartier, Jacques, 21, 89

Carts, 168, *169*

Cascade Golf and Tennis Club, 113, 114

Casper, Billy, 465, 468, 476, 480, 481, 499

Cassels, R. C. H. (Bertie), 44, 48, 64, 110, *110*, 115, 116, *235*, 236, 237-38, 241, 270

Cassels, Richard, 44

Cassels, Robert, 44

Cassels, Walter G., 31, 32, 34, 37, 44